Portland Community College Libraries

The World Today Series®

Stryker-Post Publications, Harpers Ferry, WV

The Middle East and South Asia 2002

Malcolm B. Russell

36th Edition

Next Edition, August 2003

Malcolm B. Russell . . .

Professor of Economics and History, Andrews University, Berrien Springs, Michigan. Columbia Union College (B.A., History); School of Advanced International Studies, the Johns Hopkins University (M.A.; Ph.D.), with emphases in Middle East Studies and International Economics. A Fulbright Fellowship allowed him research opportunities in Egypt, Syria, Jordan and Lebanon, and resulted in *The First Modern Arab State: Syria under Faysal, 1918–1920* (Minneapolis, MN: Biblioteca Islamica, 1985), as well as papers at a number of professional societies. Born in Beirut, after a childhood spent there and in Egypt, he attended high school in India and later traveled widely in the Middle East. He is fluent in Arabic and French.

Adapted, rewritten and revised annually
from a book entitled *The Middle East and South Asia 1967*, published in 1967 and succeeding years by

Stryker-Post Publications
P.O. Drawer 1200
Harpers Ferry, WV 25425
Telephones: 1–800–995–1400 (U.S.A. and Canada)
    Other: 1-304-535-2593
    Fax: 1–304–535–6513
    www.Strykerpost.com
    VISA–MASTERCARD

Photographs used to illustrate *The World Today Series* come from many sources, a great number from friends who travel worldwide. If you have taken any which you believe would enhance the visual impact and attractiveness of our books, do let us hear from you.

Copyright © 2002 by Stryker–Post Publications

All rights reserved. This publication, or parts thereof, may not be reproduced without permission in writing from the publisher.

International Standard Book Number: 1-887985-43-3

International Standard Serial Number: 0084–2311

Library of Congress Catalog Number 67–11539

Cover design by MidAtlantic Books and Journals

Chief Bibliographer: Edward Jones

Cartographer: William L. Nelson

Typography by Clarinda Company
Linthicum, MD 21090

Printed in the United States of America by
United Book Press, Inc.
Baltimore, MD 21207

CONTENTS

**Door to the Ka'aba, the sacred shrine of the Great Mosque
in Mecca**

The Middle East and South Asia Today

The slice of humanity captured by this volume is large, and the Middle East and South Asia forms a most interesting and strategically important region. Beginning where the peaks and rainforests separate Southern from East Asia, it includes the Indian sixth of humanity, and Muslim countries such as Iran and Turkey that for centuries bordered Russia and blocked its access to warm–water ports. At least four straits in the region (the Bosporus, Tiran, Bab al–Mandab and Hormuz) play pivotal roles in world commerce. Threats over each of them and the Suez Canal raised tensions or even precipitated wars in this century. Underneath the waters of the Gulf (variously titled as Arab or Persian) and the surrounding sands lie roughly two–thirds of the world's oil deposits. Far beyond its size or wealth, the region bears strategic value and importance to trade routes. It was more than a coincidence that the term "Middle East" was popularized by a geostrategist, Alfred Mahan.

Readers bored with conflict or economics should find much else that is of interest. The three major monotheist religions developed in the west. In the east, India provided both the birthplace of the Buddha and the intricacies of Hinduism. Modern ideas and modern heroes exist as well, from the idealism of Israel's pioneers, to the founders of non–alignment in the Cold War, and beyond that to the hopes and pacifism of Mohandas Gandhi, who earned the epithet Mahatma, "the noble hearted." Aspirations of a tougher, more brutal sort also exist, whether the chauvinism of Jewish settlers seeking to evict Arabs from their ancestral homes, or Arabs and Iranians seized by religion or nationalism to kill innocents. An Islamic revival proclaims that material possessions do not suffice as the measure of value, allowing Westerners a glimpse of the spiritual fervor that motivated their ancestors.

The consistent goal of this series of books is an appreciation of the peoples and governments largely from their own perspectives but moderated by the viewpoints of the author. In the many conflicts, I hope to show the claims and charges of each side to help the general reader understand the reasons for attitudes and actions of people and governments.

Doing this risks accusations of partiality, but I firmly hope that readers will share my respect for these peoples and lands, and an understanding of, if not always sympathy for, their states and political actions.

The region is also a study of contrasts. Despite recent discoveries of natural gas, for the foreseeable future, Bangladesh will rank as one of the most hopelessly and perpetually poor nations, while parts of the United Arab Emirates stand at the top of world per capita income. Economic systems vary equally as income, with

advocates of free trade and autarchy, free enterprise and state socialism. While sharp operators abound, the hospitality of most peoples represented here is famous. The geography stretches, very simply, from the highest (Mt. Everest) to the lowest (the Dead Sea), and from the wettest (Assam in northeastern India) to regions of Arabia so dry it has not rained for years. Aesthetically impoverished cities and flat, featureless farmland contrast dramatically with the desert beauty of *Wadi Rum* in Jordan and the water and greenery of the Bosphorus or Vale of Kashmir.

Sympathy, however, ought not excuse, even in a Western society that tolerates so much. The pages that follow draw attention to the plight of children, bonded into labor for the parents' debts, to girls deprived of school by the Taliban in

Afghanistan, and to women who apparently disappear before census–takers arrive. Female circumcision—really several forms of genital mutilation—sometimes kills young girls in parts of Africa, including Egypt. Moreover, though crime rates in most countries of this volume are relatively low, the treatment of suspects and political rivals can descend from public humiliation to horrifying depths of brutality. Aside from the few democracies represented in this volume, most governments can expect only the worst from their political opponents. Beyond individuals and ideologies, the rivalries of communities over relatively small parcels of land involve passions that Westerners, accustomed to moving from suburb to suburb, cannot fathom.

Technicalities: A few technical comments may help the serious reader. In response to requests from readers, this edition includes estimates of Gross Domestic Product per capita. Especially for the smaller countries, where figures for population may vary significantly (in one case, by more than 100%), any estimates of GDP must be treated as rough. Unless otherwise indicated, I have calculated them using local currency measures supplied in the *International Financial Statistics* of the IMF for the previous year, adjusted for actual exchange rates rather than purchasing power parity.

Another issue requires a brief comment. Exchange rates may fluctuate dramatically; these date from April 2001. English speakers transliterate Arabic words by a variety of systems, and multiple spellings are common. The Egyptian leader of the 1950s was Gamal Abdul Nasser to the press, but Jamal 'Abd al–Nasir to some scholars. In general, this volume retains the common English spellings for well–known personalities but adopts specialized spellings without diacritical markings elsewhere. Thus, the late King Hussein rules Jordan; his great–grandfather was Sharif Husayn. Outside the Arab world, the national transliteration of Muslim names applies, the founder of Bangladesh being Mujibur Rahman, not Mujib al–Rahman.

M.B.R.
Berrien Springs, MI

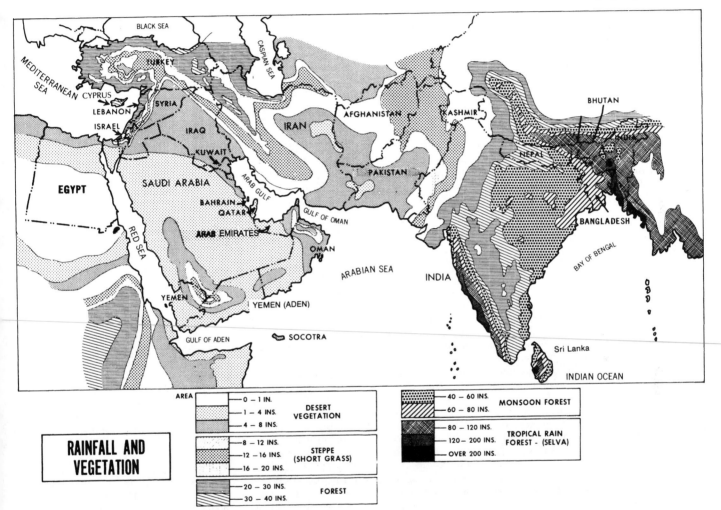

Map by Ray L. Cleveland

RAINFALL AND
VEGETATION

AREA		
0 — 1 IN.		
1 — 4 INS.	DESERT VEGETATION	
4 — 8 INS.		
8 — 12 INS.		
12 — 16 INS.	STEPPE (SHORT GRASS)	
16 — 20 INS.		
20 — 30 INS.	FOREST	
30 — 40 INS.		
40 — 60 INS.	MONSOON FOREST	
60 — 80 INS.		
80 — 120 INS.		
120 — 200 INS.	TROPICAL RAIN FOREST - (SELVA)	
OVER 200 INS.		

WHEN WILL THE TAPS GO DRY?

Water, like bread, comes from God
Arab Proverb

From North Africa to Pakistan and western India, the lands of the Middle East and South Asia receive little rainfall, in many areas far less annually than the 16–20 inches essential for cultivation. With few cloudy days and the sun blazing directly overhead for most of the year, hot temperatures quickly dry out the landscape even when rain has fallen, and keep it dry. From the early days of human settlement, water was always scarce, and now the people of the Middle East face a worsening crisis as individual countries attempt to claim insufficient common resources. By contrast, in the Indian subcontinent, seasonal floods take hundreds of lives annually and rivers inundate productive fields, carrying their valuable silt into the sea.

For thousands of years people living in the region adapted to desert and near-desert conditions. They farmed fertile lands beside rivers, some irrigating with water from mountains hundreds or even thousands of miles away, benefiting from seasonal floods that soaked the soil and deposited nourishing silt. Other less moistened lands were used for livestock raising, particularly camels, goats and sheep.

Desert societies established water rights over the scarce flow of oasis wells and springs, to irrigate crops and water livestock that grazed on the sparse vegetation. For transport, travelers and nomads depend on the camel, with its legendary adaptation to dryness. Their days surrounded by barren desert, nomads dreamed of rivers and greenery, even seeing them in the form of occasional mirages. Each of the religions with a single God portrayed heaven as filled with trees and water.

In sharp contrast, the modern era marked a change. The technology and energy of the 20th century brought the appearance of abundant water to many places. Homes enjoyed taps and sewer connections, carefully irrigated trees lined boulevards in desert cities and industries developed. Urban water use increased rapidly, for example, doubling in arid Saudi Arabia between 1980 and 1985. But most of all, agriculture based on irrigation fed desert nations and even provided for exports of tomatoes, oranges, wheat and other irrigated crops. The desert truly seemed to bloom.

In the Middle East, by the 1990s many countries began to run out of water. Rapidly growing populations, some increasing by 3% per year, rising standards of living, and increased agricultural production now leave Israel, Jordan, and

Egypt facing difficult choices between conservation and development. States of the Arabian Peninsula already depend on non–renewable ground water and desalinization. As the 21st century approaches, water scarcity threatens to cause bitter conflicts within and between the region's nations. Cooperation, by contrast, offers the chance to postpone water shortages, hopefully promoting peace in a region too troubled by war and conflict.

Water as a Threat to Peace

The Jordan River: *neither wide nor deep.*

The Biblical account of Joshua's tribes crossing the dry bed of the Jordan River to attack Jericho created in western Christian society an image celebrated in song as the mighty Jordan, deep and wide. Reality was always different, with the Jordan's flow of 320 million cubic meters hardly more than the size of a large creek. In summer months particularly, the Jordan is now little more than a narrow, salty stream. Consequently, Israel, Jordan and Syria, plus the possibly independent Palestinian West Bank, increasingly face questions of water use so difficult that they may be forced to settle issues by force.

The first attempts to negotiate water rights took place in the 1950s when U.S. President Eisenhower sent Eric Johnston as a special ambassador to negotiate agreements among the countries of the Jordan basin. At the technical level, his findings established shares for the various countries, but politically his mission failed. No international agreement yet apportions the waters of the river.

With dreams of making the desert bloom, Israel in the 1960s constructed the National Water Carrier, a pipeline almost 10 feet in diameter, to bring water from the Sea of Galilee to the coastal plain and the Negev desert. The water was vital: Arab attempts to divert the Jordan's headwaters flowing into Israel from Lebanon and Syria played a major role in the crisis before the 1967 Arab–Israeli war. With Israel's conquest of the Golan Heights and the West Bank, it ensured its use of the Jordan River.

Almost immediately, water from the Jordan proved to be insufficient for Israel's purposes. Along the coast and in the desert, Israeli farmers used two–thirds of the nation's water for farming. To supply their fields as well as thirsty homes and factories, Israel had long pumped the coastal aquifer of the eastern Mediterranean, an underground large mass of rocky, porous nature which is voluminous, containing a mass of water slowly seeping toward the sea.

When the volume of water pumped out began to exceed the rainwater trickling

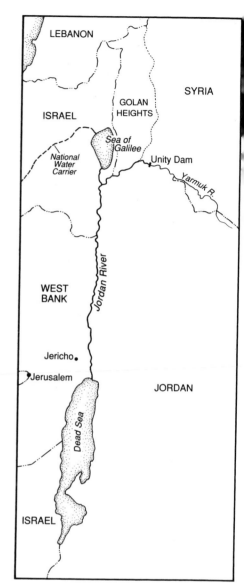

down into the aquifer, water levels and pressures began to fall. Salty sea water started to seep into the aquifer, reducing water quality. By 1990 about 10% of the water from this resource exceeded the national limit for chloride salt. In addition, pollution increased as nitrates from fertilizers leached into the aquifer, no longer carried to the sea by surface water. During the winter, the water authority now pumps surplus Jordan River water into coastal wells, hoping to replenish the aquifer.

Israel's thirst also drains the separate Yarkon/Tannim aquifer. Known as the "mountain aquifer," it collects rain falling on the hilly West Bank. A few points of the aquifer extend into the 1967 boundaries, and Israel currently pumps about 20% of its water from this source. This vastly exceeds the pumping permitted the West Bank Palestinians, whose land supplies the rainfall that annually renews this resource. In addition, the roughly 100,000 Israeli settlers in the West Bank consume about as much water as the nearly 1 million Arabs, whose drilling is restricted in several ways.

The creation of a Palestinian state threatens Israel's total control of the mountain aquifer. Fears of future water shortages may influence political opinion against granting concessions. The figures themselves show few alternatives: some estimates place average rainfall at 1.7 billion cubic meters, but current water use is around 1.9 billion cubic meters. Israelis consume five times as much per capita as residents of neighboring Arab nations. Because of this, the shallow wells of dozens of Palestinian West Bank villages no longer reach the water levels formerly typical of the area. In the Gaza Strip, the contamination of water supplies has reached critical proportions.

Only one tributary of the Jordan remains underused—the Yarmuk River between Syria and Jordan that joins the Jordan River just below the Sea of Galilee. With water resources far smaller than Israel's or Syria's, Jordan proposed building a "Unity Dam" on the Yarmuk at Maqarin to trap winter flood waters for summer use by farms, homes and industry.

For years, Israel threatened to destroy any such dam; it benefitted by capturing some of the flow in the Sea of Galilee. Now, the peace treaty with Jordan commits it to supply 55 million cubic meters of water annually. However, most of the rainfall of the Yarmuk basin falls in Syria, and that country favors smaller, upstream projects within its boundaries. Eventually such projects will capture most of the run-off; already in years of low rainfall like 1999, the Israelis, Palestinians, Jordanians and Syrians all find themselves critically short of water, a deficit that is projected to approach about 600 million cubic meters annually even with average rainfall.

Diverting the Euphrates

To the north and east, dams on another river also threaten violence. The Euphrates River springs forth in the high mountains of Turkey, whose rains contribute 80% of its volume but whose terrain meant little was used. It flows into Syria and then across Iraq to join the Tigris at the Shatt al–Arab just before emptying into the Persian (Arabian) Gulf. Far larger than the Jordan, the flow of the Euphrates averages 31 billion cubic meters per year. Ambitious development plans in the three countries probably exceed the river's capacity. As long ago as 1975 Iraq actually threatened war with Syria over the scanty flow below the Tabaqa Dam.

Upstream diversion of the water to fill dams and supply irrigation essentially caused the crisis. In Turkey, the Keban and Ataturk dams of the vast Southeast Anatolia Project (see Turkey, economy) reduced the river's flow as the lakes behind them rose and irrigation commenced and increased. Similarly, the Tabaqa Dam and agricultural development project in Syria diverted the river flow. Alternative resources do exist for Iraq, since there is excess flow in the Tigris to the east, but development projects to use it require time and funding.

Even worse, the Euphrates, like the Tigris, carries a naturally high level of dissolved salts that may accumulate in the surrounding soils and reduce fertility. Intensive irrigation in turn usually raises the water level in the soil, dissolving even more salts, agricultural chemicals and fertilizers. Unless drainage ditches are constructed to carry away salty and polluted waters, the land eventually becomes useless. Thus Iraq faces not only water shortages, but the danger of water quality in the Euphrates falling to a level unfit for humans, and harmful for agriculture.

For its part, Iraq constructed a massive channel, the "Third River," to carry salty and useless water directly to the Gulf. The goals for the man–made river are to free the Tigris and Euphrates rivers from local drainage wastewater, and to serve navigation as well.

In the Jordan valley, neighboring states have warred frequently since World War II. By contrast, the three nations of the Euphrates basin have not yet fought along their borders, although Syria and Turkey joined the anti–Iraq Coalition in the 1990–1991 Gulf War. In the absence of a settlement of water rights, the potential for violence exists, and diplomatic relations remain poor. Fighting did rage across the lower reaches of the Tigris and Euphrates over Shatt al–Arab during the Iran–Iraq War of 1980–1988, though the dispute over the area had virtually nothing to do with irrigation. Iranian demands for control of the river to mid-stream, as opposed to traditional Iraqi domain to the Iranian shore, led to the crisis that produced the war. Control and navigation rights in the Shatt al–Arab remain disputed.

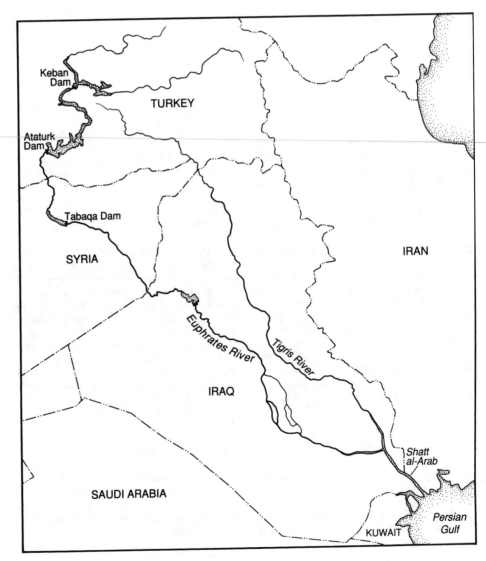

The Nile

Fortunately the potential for conflict over the Nile River seems very low. The world's longest river drains mountainous central Africa and the Ethiopian highlands of about 84 billion cubic meters each year, making Egypt "The Gift of the Nile." For that country and northern Sudan, no other renewable water supply exists. Survival simply depends on the Nile.

In ancient times, Egyptian farmers practiced "basin agriculture." Crops flourished in fields saturated with moisture from the annual summer flood and nourished with silt the *Blue Nile* had carried out of Ethiopia. Egyptian concern about the flow was reflected in the construction of barrages and small dams from the 19th century onwards. Negotiations to establish water rights followed; the first Nile Waters Agreement was signed with Sudan in 1929. Renegotiated in the 1950s before construction of the Aswan High Dam (see Egypt, economy), the agreement presently provides Egypt 55 billion cubic meters yearly, three times the amount allowed Sudan.

By the 1980s, severe water shortages began to appear when years of drought in Ethiopia reduced the flow of the Blue Nile. Some climatologists associate the eastern and southern African drought (as well as that of California) and other unusual world weather patterns with the global effect of the warming of the Pacific Ocean causing wind changes *(el Niño)*. Behind the High Dam, Lake Nasser (Nasir) dwindled. Irrigation required conservation; this reduced the release of water for hydroelectric power and some years cut drastically the almost 40% of national electricity produced at the dam.

Though rains later restored the Nile's flow, at least immediately, the crisis highlighted the inevitable future shortage of water in Egypt. Accurate figures are difficult to obtain, but one study suggested that the nation possibly uses 70 billion cubic meters now. With the population growing by one million mouths annually, and accompanying efforts to provide additional cultivated areas, water demand is naturally increasing. But Egypt's present use is only possible because Sudan fails to consume all of its allotment.

Despite these dire threats, millions are not yet dying of thirst. Agriculture claims more than 80% of available water and opportunities exist for conservation. The *fellah* (farmer) typically obtains his water from unlined canals, and channels it to soak his fields. Cheap water makes sense for these poor people, whose yearly income is only a few hundred dollars. Efficient, water–saving drip irrigation systems remain beyond their purchasing power. Thus, conservation will not be painless, and will impose costs, if not on very poor people, upon an impoverished

government. It may also mean abandoning some lands to the insistent demands of the desert.

Fortunately, international disputes over the Nile water are unlikely to end in violence. Decades of negotiation established rights and precedents. Egypt's determination to receive its historic and vital flow is firmly advertised and well–recognized by Sudan and smaller, weaker nations upstream. Moreover, countries on the upper reaches of the Nile seem unlikely to alter its flow significantly. Tropical countries like Uganda have little incentive to divert a river carrying runoff waters of excessive rain. Eventually, Ethiopia may attempt to construct a dam along the Blue Nile, but this would pose immense financial, engineering and distribution difficulties.

International Cooperation in the Indus Basin

In South Asia, two nations born in hostility faced the challenge of sharing water from the Indus River and its tributaries. By approving a technical solution, India and Pakistan brought prosperity and greater food production to the Punjab, the fertile region divided by their borders.

Simply put, the Indus is a mighty river, fed by monsoon rains and snows in the Himalayan mountains of India and Tibet. Carrying more water than the Nile, its annual discharge reaches 97 billion cubic meters, much of it carried across the plains by five important tributaries. During British rule a system of irrigation canals was dug. After partition, India possessed the strategic advantage of controlling the headwaters, but lacked economic benefit; the water was remote and difficult to use. Pakistan, in contrast, found itself farming with water from India, but strategically disadvantaged in the event India chose to divert or otherwise interfere with the flow.

A mission from the International Bank for Reconstruction and Development (the World Bank) proposed in 1951 a rational solution: consider the issue a technical, not a political, problem. In effect, the key was to base water usage on irrigation potential, not nationality. Compensation for one district's use of another country's water could be made elsewhere. In practice, despite two wars, the system has worked. Dams built with World Bank funds, plus a complex system of canals, enables the two countries to irrigate the Punjab, breadbasket of the sub–continent.

The Peace Pipeline

In the Punjab, the perception of shared water needs led to a peaceful solution of a crisis. In the 1980s the Turkish government revived older ideas and proposed two "Peace Pipelines" to carry water to desert countries. They would carry the

unused flow of the Seyhan and Ceyhan rivers in southern Turkey to thirsty cities and industrial areas of Arab lands.

The plan envisages two pipelines. The western, requiring more pumping to reach the higher elevations of Damascus and Amman, would carry some 3.5 million cubic meters of water nearly 1,700 miles (2,700 kilometers) across Syria and Jordan to the Saudi Arabian cities of Mecca and Medina. The longer eastern pipeline would cross Syria and Iraq, ultimately supplying Kuwait and the Gulf states of the peninsula in addition to coastal Saudi Arabia.

Two drawbacks pose almost insurmountable obstacles to the proposal. The first is cost, initially estimated at $21 billion for construction, plus pumping and other operating expenses. Unless heavily subsidized by governments, the water will cost roughly the same as desalinated ocean water, far too much for agriculture. The second difficulty is security. Oil pipelines across the Middle East have frequently been cut by government directive or politically–related sabotage. Would the water pipelines prove any more immune to interruption?

The Opposite Extreme

Bangladesh and neighboring parts of India struggle with entirely different

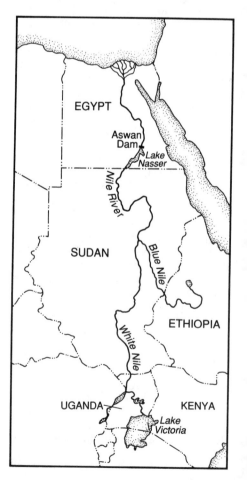

water difficulties. For centuries, Bengalis reconciled their ways of life with the periodic flooding of the Ganges and Brahmaputra rivers, whose water and silt deposits nourished the soil and produced three crops per year. (see Bangladesh). With few possessions and minimal homes, farmers lived knowing floods could strike and recognized that river channels might be altered by hundreds of yards overnight. Nevertheless, they could hope to escape with their lives and a few possessions to begin farming anew.

Such a fate hardly attracted foreign investors, or even modernized city dwellers living in permanent homes. In 1989 the government embarked on the Flood Action Plan to build embankments to protect cities and to confine rivers to channels. Unfortunately, confining the rivers creates the danger that silt will raise the level of the river bottoms, causing them to eventually flow *above* ground level. If this happened, one of the poorest countries in the world would have to construct and maintain a vast system of dikes for the rivers at an enormous cost, if indeed, it could be done, considering frequent devastating hurricanes and monsoons.

Consequences of Dams and Large–Scale Irrigation

Humans first diverted flowing water in the misty years of early history. However, the large dams that tower hundreds of feet above a valley or stretch miles across a lower river basin represent a triumph, however momentary, of the twentieth century. First constructed in the United States and Soviet Union in the 1920s and 1930s the dams proved to be valuable for flood control, hydroelectric power, recreational use and irrigation. After World War II, building dams became a worldwide fad, and 95% of all large dams date from this period.

For all their virtues, dams in the hot climates of the Middle East and South Asia involve a variety of drawbacks. An obvious one is evaporation, largely because the sun's rays strike directly and the desert air carries little of the humidity that would slow evaporation. The loss from Lake Nasser to the air is an estimated 10 billion cubic meters a year, exceeding Egypt's portion of the Nile's flow resulting from construction of the dam. Serious proposals exist to cover the entire surface of Lake Nasser with small floating plastic bubbles to reduce the water's exposure to the air, a tremendous undertaking on a surface of thousands of square miles.

On many rivers, a much more serious problem is the buildup of silt in the reservoirs and lakes back of the large dams. Engineers only recently recognized how great this problem is in warmer climates. The Ganges–Brahmaputra and Indus each

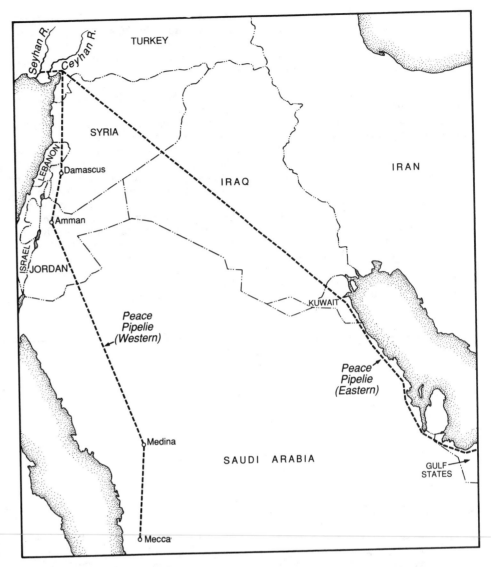

carry roughly 1,700 gallons of silt in each million gallons of water. Quietly, but much faster than predicted, rivers drop this sediment in the slow waters of the reservoirs.

At the Tarbela Dam in Pakistan, for example, some 2% of the reservoir fills with soil annually, and hundreds of tons of dirt settle above the Mangla Dam. Because of the silt, the Tarbela Dam may prove useful for only 40 years, a poor investment in view of its life expectancy of 100 years when built. In Sudan, the Roseires Dam on the Blue Nile ceased effective operation when deposits formed an island above the water intakes for the hydroelectric turbines.

Rapid silting not only spreads a dam's huge construction costs over fewer years, it also renders the location permanently useless as a dam. Unfortunately, projects conceived to reduce soil loss, such as planting trees, often proved less effective than projected.

As environmentalists and others have long pointed out, silt often plays important roles in nourishing fields and supporting the coastal ecosystem. Deprived of sediments, Egyptian and other farmers spread tons of chemical fertilizers on their soil, polluting the earth and rendering drainage water unfit for many uses. Coastlines deprived of silt may succumb to the sea, as has happened in Egypt and elsewhere.

Another possibility which has been explored with little success is the concept of "flushing" a dam by opening wide the gates. This poses several problems. Unless done at least annually, the silt congeals into a solid mass that will not pass through the gates presently in use. If done every year, there would be annual destructive flooding of lowlands below the structure. It is impossible to predict the ultimate effect of the silt sent charging out of control downstream.

Silting risks partly forced the scaling–back of the Narmada Valley Development Project in central and western India. Probably the largest single project in the world, its plans initially included 30 major dams,

5

dozens of smaller ones and thousands of minor ones, constructed over a period of 50 years. The dams would supply irrigation water for millions of acres in the states of Gujarat, Rajasthan and Madhya Pradesh, and generate vast amounts of electricity for homes and industry. However, the new reservoirs will also flood large expanses of tropical forest and require moving hundreds of thousands of people from their homes. A series of court actions in 2000 finally lowered the maximum permitted height of the major dam and, over the objections of environmentalists, permitted construction to resume.

Alternatives

To supply thirsty homes and farms, nations in the Middle East have turned to new sources. Far below the level of traditional wells, deep reservoirs of water remain from moister climatic ages. With government subsidies and assistance, farmers pump this "fossil water," notably in Saudi Arabia, to produce grains for export (see Saudi Arabia, economy). Infra-red satellite pictures suggest that "fracture zones" stretching for hundreds of miles may hold billions of cubic meters of water. Unfortunately, however, fossil water is never replaced. In a few decades these aquifers will run dry.

In contrast, desalinization transforms the free and limitless water of the seas and oceans into the sweet water necessary for human life and agriculture. Despite the higher salt content of the Red Sea and the Gulf, the oil exporting nations of the Gulf lead the world in commercial desalinization. Saudi Arabia alone accounts for almost one-third of the world capacity, over one billion cubic meters annually. Kuwait and the United Arab Emirates provide another fifth. While the ancients used solar power to distill water, efficient, large-scale desalinization plants today employ multi-stage processes for capturing steam and condensing it into water. Costs are lowest for so-called dual-purpose plants that use relatively low-temperature waste heat from power plants. In Saudi Arabia the Ministry of Agriculture, which runs desalinization plants, started generating more electricity than the Ministry of Electricity and Industry.

Despite the availability of bright, hot sunshine, it requires far higher fuel prices—or technological breakthroughs—for solar power to become economical. The most promising method uses saline solar ponds to collect the sun's energy and use it to convert salt water into usable liquid.

Desalinization remains a hope for coastal agricultural regions, but presently the

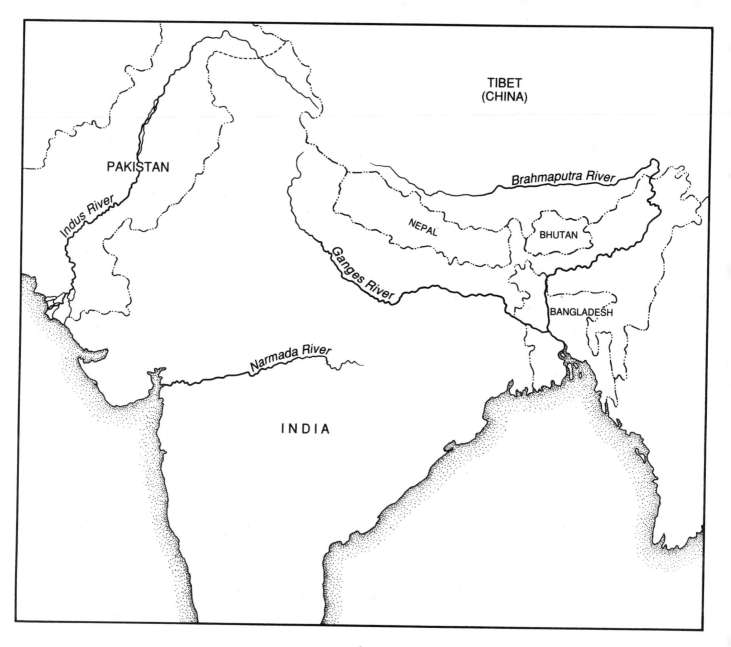

6

A boat bridge across the upper Indus

process is far too expensive for irrigating crops. However, at $4–$7 per 1,000 gallons, its price is affordable for household uses in countries with high per capita incomes. Other difficulties can hardly be solved by money, however. The 1990–1991 Gulf War showed how greatly greatly Saudi Arabia and the smaller oil–producing states depend on desalinization, when a massive oil slick threatened to pollute drinking water and clog equipment. To be efficient, desalinization plants must be large, but large plants mean little reserve capacity and pose tempting targets for attack and sabotage.

Experiments continue in several countries on agriculture using brackish water and seawater. The goal is to discover productive plants that need little or no fresh water and then to determine profitable techniques for growing and processing them. If successful, salt water farming could revolutionize present water use patterns.

For example, in Israel, advocates of brackish water propose a pipeline to carry brackish, undrinkable water *from* desert aquifers *to* farms for irrigating certain crops. Results also appear promising for growing certain oil seed crops using seawater, with the added benefit of using the plants as fodder for animals, Unfortunately the application of the discoveries will be limited and will require close monitoring: salt–water irrigation contaminates any fresh ground water in an aquifer below.

The recycling of sewage and other waste–water has apparently reached the greatest extent in Israel, where some 30% of it is reused in agriculture. The potential

to recycle exists in other countries as well, but the process requires well–trained personnel and careful monitoring of pollutants. Like the use of drip irrigation, the technology exists, and higher water prices will enable its greater use.

Many novel proposals exist to meet the looming shortage. Among several examples, off the coasts of Lebanon and Syria, fresh water springs flow directly into the sea. They might be tapped. Polar ice contains about two thirds of the world's fresh water, so giant icebergs from the Antarctic could be towed to the Middle East and melted to quench the region's thirst. More conventionally, tankers might bring drinking water from European nations with excess supplies such as France and Britain. High prices might also provide the incentive to reduce agriculture in the Nile and Indus valleys, with the water thus saved piped under the sea to cities in Arabia.

Most Americans think that water simply comes from the faucet when it is turned on. By contrast, in many parts of the Middle East and South Asia there are no taps, and the assumption that sufficient water will be there in a decade or two increasingly looks risky. The area's limited water resources are already being developed and used to the maximum. However, for most countries this does not imply that water shortages now threaten living standards or war. But peaceful solutions require major changes and, above all, time.

Even with the best conservation methods, farming remains a thirsty occupation. Nations in the region value agriculture for its employment, the security of food

supplies and realizing national aspirations. But the governments of many developed nations subsidize their farmers and export crops at much lower prices than their citizens pay. Rather than risk war over insufficient water supplies, Middle Eastern nations logically should develop other uses of their lands and workforces.

Unfortunately, logic seems missing almost everywhere in matters of water management and agriculture. In the summer of 1990, the relatively moderate King Hussein of Jordan suggested that water was the only issue that would take him to war with Israel. Given this region's record, trouble lies ahead. In the words of Joyce Starr, founder of Global Water Summit Initiative, Middle East population growth is a "human explosion certain to ignite the issue of water."

BLACK GOLD: THE IMPACT OF OIL

Drilling

Exploration

One quarter of the world's population calls them home, but the countries of the Middle East and South Asia offer few natural riches. Their famous shortage of water is only one among many barriers to productive farming. The soil itself is often poor, low in vital trace elements as well as organic matter. Beneath the surface, the impoverishment continues. Although India and Turkey contain coal and iron, and Iran, copper, most of the mineral deposits famed in antiquity have been exhausted for centuries.

The great exception is petroleum. Over half the world's proven and probable oil deposits lie in the sedimentary basin between central Arabia and the mountains of Iran. Quantity alone does not do justice to the reserves' value. From northern Iraq to the Strait of Hormuz, crude oil often occurs in large fields relatively near the surface. Cheap to extract, without the costs of drilling in deep waters or Arctic tundra, the oil is piped short distances to coastal terminals, loaded onto tankers, and shipped to refineries worldwide.

So abundant is the oil, and so efficient its production, refining and transportation, that the Gulf's gasoline *before taxes*

costs just pennies per gallon, far below the prices of any alternative energy source, whether coal, electricity from solar cells or nuclear power plants, or even oil from Alaska. Of course, outside the producing countries themselves, consumers never paid so little. Companies and governments managed to extract enough profits and taxes to boost prices as high as other energy sources. For example, in mid-2000 Saudi oil probably costs less than U.S. $0.20 per gallon to pump, refine and transport, but it sells for the equivalent of $4.00 per gallon in Europe and $1.60 in the United States.

The Search for Oil in the Middle East

The ancient world knew something about oil. Asphalt seeped to the surface in Mesopotamia, and mysterious fires burned indefinitely, without consuming any known fuel. Early civilizations used tar to calk seams, to mortar bricks and to protect walls. Tar also paved the streets of Babylon.

Although some medieval Arab scientists studied it, and the "Greek fire" of naval battles perhaps derived from it, petroleum's role remained unchanged before the arrival of the industrial revolution. By the nineteenth century, the new

factories in Europe and the United States required great quantities of oil, to give light and to lubricate. Tallow and lard from domesticated animals proved far short of demand, and the slaughter of whales reduced that source of high-quality oil. By mid-century, inventors and entrepreneurs in Europe and North America began to drill wells to obtain petroleum, their first products being grease for machines and kerosene for light.

An integrated industry developed rapidly. Companies drilled wells for crude, transported it by rail or pipeline to refineries and then transformed it into products for market. The system developed first in the United States, but the search for petroleum quickly became world-wide. One major source was the field at Baku, on the Caspian Sea. It enabled Russia to surpass American production in the 1890s and briefly become the world's leading producer. (After World War II the Soviet Union regained that rank, but declining Russian production cost it the premier position to Saudi Arabia.)

The popularity of gasoline-powered automobiles after 1900 spurred demand for oil tremendously, and the search for it spread to the Middle East, where prospecting began first in Iraq and Iran (then known as Persia). After an earlier concession had expired, William D'Arcy, an English entrepreneur who had made his wealth in Australian gold mines, negotiated a concession from the Shah of Persia in 1901. After five years of disappointments, in 1908 his drillers struck the first commercial well in the Middle East, at Masjid-i Suleiman in the southwest.

D'Arcy moved rapidly to exploit the find. He organized the Anglo-Persian Oil Company the next year, which laid a pipeline to the coast and gained permission from a local chief to construct a refinery on Abadan Island at the head of the Gulf. On the eve of World War I, with the Royal Navy switching from coal to oil for fuel, Winston Churchill arranged for the British government to purchase a majority share in the company, known today as British Petroleum (BP-Amoco).

Across the border, Iraq then formed part of the Ottoman Empire. In 1914 the Ottoman Sultan granted a concession for the Anglo-German Turkish Petroleum Company to exploit the rumored oil deposits of Mosul, in northern Iraq. However, commercial production was delayed a decade, first by war, then by a difficult peace settlement that finally awarded Mosul and the rest of Iraq to Britain. After French and American firms became major shareholders in the late 1920s, the company was renamed the Iraq Petroleum Company (IPC), and it negotiated concessions covering the entire country.

Relations between the IPC and the government in Baghdad were uneasy from the first. The problem was not poor finds: the massive Kirkuk field included an amazing well that flowed at 95,000 barrels per day, worth 10% of the nation's exports. However, this find, and most of the other wells, lay hundreds of miles from any deep-water terminal. Finally, Iraqi pressure on the IPC led to the construction of pipelines to Mediterranean ports in Syria and Palestine. In an example of monopolistic behavior, the wealthy companies forming IPC (including Exxon, Mobil, Shell and BP) agreed in the "Red Line Agreement" to avoid any oil activities throughout the former Ottoman Empire except by mutual agreement.

Despite the Red Line Agreement, in the 1920s and 1930s geologists discovered vast oil fields elsewhere in the Middle East. Bahrain first joined the list of oil exporters. Although its deposits were relatively small, they stimulated the search for oil in adjacent Saudi Arabia. At Dammam in 1935, an American company, the predecessor to Aramco, sank its first well in 1935. The seventh attempt produced commercial quantities in 1938, and geologists eventually recognized that separate oil strikes really tapped parts of one vast field, the Ghawar. Some 160 miles long, it ranks as

the largest in the world, even surpassing Kuwait's Burgan field. Oil production in Qatar, the United Arab Emirates, and Oman became significant only in the 1950s and 1960s.

In contrast to plantation agriculture, modern industry or most mining, oil production requires a large local labor force briefly, then depends on machinery. Initially, oil companies explore, drill wells, and construct everything from pipelines and storage facilities to loading terminals and perhaps a refinery. These are often highly technical operations, and even at the peak of such activities in 1952, the industry in Saudi Arabia employed only some 24,000. With maturity, the numbers declined to just 10,000 in 1970. Most Arabs and Iranians hired in the early stages were unskilled laborers; expatriates usually filled technical and managerial positions.

Even though they employed expensive equipment but fairly few workers, the oil companies greatly impacted local society. They established training programs and even schools. Roads, towns, shops, medical facilities and models of new lifestyles often resulted for a relatively small segment of the population. The major impact, instead, was financial. Royalties, taxes, and profit-sharing flowed to the regime, and exports supplied foreign exchange, normally scarce in developing countries.

Countries and Companies Clash over Profits

In contrast to the United States, where mineral rights usually belong to individual landowners, in the Middle East land ownership of untilled areas traditionally belonged to the government. Thus, instead of purchasing oil rights from private citizens, oil companies negotiated agreements, or concessions, from governments. These stipulated the territorial limits of company operations and specified payments to the ruler.

During the initial negotiations, companies bargained from strength, and the rulers from weakness, for the rulers needed money and neither side knew what oil wealth existed. Even where petroleum seeped to the surface, it might not flow in profitable quantities, and many other obstacles might destroy profits. Since the oil industry was dominated by a small number of companies—sometimes titled the "Seven Sisters"—who kept prices relatively high and maintained large reserve capacities, the concessions also reflected these corporate strengths.

In contrast, governments that badly needed money sought attractive initial payments but conceded low royalties on output. Thus, in 1931 Iraq agreed to royalties of only four gold shillings per ton, equivalent to about twelve cents per barrel. Saudi Arabia accepted the same figure two years later. Such rates enabled oil companies to

earn remarkable profits on their productive investments. Of course, some investments proved complete losses, with no oil strikes despite years of searching.

Middle East governments soon recognized that their original concessions provided too generously for the companies and failed to reflect the changed circumstances after oil was discovered. Being sovereign, they could, and generally did, demand revisions in what the companies considered legally binding contracts. The first important changes came with Shah Reza's Iran in 1933. Thereafter, governments repeatedly pressed for greater revenues and the stability of minimum annual payments. By 1950 agreements usually fixed payments as a proportion—often 50%—of gross income less production expenses. Eventually, both sides accepted artificial "posted prices" to calculate the profits to be divided.

In their struggle for greater benefits from oil, the countries faced limits that were highlighted by Iran's attempt to gain control of its oil in 1951. Thinking that Iranians could operate their own industry, and that post-war recovery in Europe provided ample market for Iranian oil, Prime Minister Mohammad Mosaddeq refused to compromise with the Anglo-Iranian Oil Company and nationalized it. In response, the company closed the Abadan refinery, increased output in Kuwait, and diverted its tankers to other sources. Anglo-Iranian halted payments to the government, and its lawyers prevented sales of Iranian oil in Western Europe.

Unable to sell its oil, Iran fell into deep recession and political instability. No solution appeared likely until a coup d'etat backed by the American CIA removed Mosaddeq and reinstated the exiled Shah. Then the two sides agreed on compensation for the nationalization of Anglo-Iranian's assets, and a consortium of companies agreed to operate the oil fields for the National Iranian Oil Company. The lesson seemed clear: a single country lacked the power to force a major oil company to accept its terms, for the companies maintained sufficient excess capacity to meet its customers' oil needs without the exports of any one nation. Governments, by contrast, depended for their very survival on the tax revenues from oil.

In 1959, with world supplies of oil plentiful and market prices soft, the major oil companies announced—rather than negotiated—a lower posted price for crude oil. This lower posted price in turn reduced the profits that could be calculated and divided with the governments. Recognizing that single countries could not respond effectively, representatives of Iran, Iraq, Kuwait, Saudi Arabia and Venezuela met in Baghdad and established the Organization of Oil Exporting Countries (OPEC, 1960). From its inception, OPEC's goals concerned export

Concrete pipeline being completed into the Arab Gulf

prices, royalties, and the taxation of profits, but its members also desired that the companies train and hire their citizens. For a decade OPEC apparently accomplished little besides adding new members.

Major changes in the world's demand and supply of oil prepared the way for major changes in the 1970s. During the era after World War II, demand for energy grew faster than ever. Moreover, cheaper and cleaner oil substituted for coal in many uses, and the rapid growth of automobile and truck transport meant that demand for petroleum grew even faster than energy needs, exceeding a compound annual rate of 7.5% after 1950.

Despite doomsday prophecies, oil reserves—the estimate of future production from known deposits—grew at a matching rate. Thanks to improved technology and vigorous exploration by the companies, no global oil shortage occurred. However, the European and American oil companies increasingly found their new reserves in OPEC countries, while they pumped out at rapid rates the non-renewable deposits in the United States and elsewhere.

Until the late 1950s international oil companies treated Middle Eastern supplies as supplemental, and set prices based on the U.S. market. Around 1970, however, American production peaked and soon began to decline, while U.S., European, and Japanese demand grew rapidly. The increase could only be met from the Middle East. Its oil, hitherto excluded from the United States on grounds of "national security", became increasingly necessary for the world's largest economy.

Against this background, specific events gained disproportionate importance in the early 1970s. A nick in the Saudi pipeline to the Mediterranean, on the Israeli-occupied Golan Heights of Syria, shut the pipeline down, and Syria delayed its repair. When Libya simultaneously acted against some small oil companies for violating training clauses of their concessions, the opportunity existed for OPEC to press for higher revenues. The Tehran Agreement between OPEC nations and the companies in 1971 increased posted prices immediately (to less than $2 for a barrel of 42 gallons), and set them at $5 per barrel by the late 1970s. The countries also gained a higher proportion of oil profits and separately took steps to nationalize their industries.

Hailed at the time as a major victory for the oil exporters, the Tehran Agreement lasted only two years. Both economic and political aspects played essential roles in enabling the countries to obtain far higher prices.

First, in the short run, oil exporting nations do not behave like the typical producer simplified in economic textbooks. The oil, after all, is non-renewable, so unless a technological miracle takes place, or global warming requires cuts in energy use, or automobiles convert to another fuel, future oil prices—when the wells start to run dry—must exceed present ones. Furthermore, the expense of storing it in the ground is close to nothing. Therefore, oil producers face different rules than wheat farmers or cotton growers. Especially when oil prices are rising rapidly, it makes sense for owners of oil fields to cut production, expecting still higher prices later. Logic also predicts that when prices are expected to fall, producers will seek to sell as much as possible immediately.

However, governments have bills to pay and nations often need to import nearly everything, whether essentials or luxuries. As a result, some OPEC nations operate their oil industries primarily to obtain current income rather than to obtain maximum value. They, too, are more likely to produce less oil as prices rise (because the prices generate more revenue than they need). They also export more oil when prices fall, to make up the shortfall in the budget.

The Tehran Agreement, by raising revenues to the countries by 25%, enabled these nations to cut production and still pay their bills. This strength enabled them to reduce world oil supplies and force further price increases on the companies and consumers world-wide.

Politics provided the convenient opportunity for change. In October 1973 Egypt and Syria attacked Israeli forces to regain territory they lost in 1967. Initial Arab victories gave way to defeats, however, when Israel counterattacked, using U.S. weapons and intelligence. Hostility to the U.S. rose in the Arab world, and King Faisal of Saudi Arabia won wide approval when he embargoed oil exports to the United States. To make the policy effective (and keep companies from simply switching oil cargoes), he also decreed a 10% reduction in all exports.

Sensing their power, the Gulf oil exporters took the crucial decision to set export prices without consulting the companies. This broke the previous pattern of negotiated prices. As fears of shortages seized consumers world-wide, prices on the spot market [for immediate delivery] rose to well over $15 per barrel. Gas lines appeared across the U.S., service stations closed on Sundays, and President Nixon

reduced the speed limit to 55 miles per hour. Recognizing the opportunity, OPEC met in December 1973 and raised the price countries would receive to $11.65 per barrel.

Great transfers of wealth followed the 1973 price increase. Prices doubled again during shortages created by the Iranian Revolution in 1979–80, bringing inconceivable riches. OPEC nations produced over 30 million barrels of oil per day, and sold them at $32 per barrel. Iran's revenues, for instance, rose almost seven-fold between 1973–74 and 1977–78. In 1981, Saudi Arabia received roughly $120 billion for its oil, over $12,000 per inhabitant. Massive purchases of foreign goods clogged ports throughout the Middle East, and freighters waited weeks to dock.

Some OPEC nations could not spend all their income, and deposited it in Western banks for "recycling" to borrowers in the industrialized world or in the less developed countries. Foreign aid increased massively, especially from Saudi Arabia, Kuwait and the United Arab Emirates. Some of the money returned to the oil industry as OPEC nations bought out foreign companies that produced their oil. They also invested in the "downstream" activities of refining and marketing in the industrialized countries.

Despite prices that softened in the early 1980s, OPEC's success seemed to suggest that unlike other cartels (associations of producers that limit production and raise prices), it could defy the laws of economics. Normally, if a cartel raises prices, the higher prices lead customers to conserve and reduce purchases. Then cartel members face lost sales at prices far above the costs of production. Secret deals will follow, as cartel members quietly reduce prices to lure customers. Competitors outside the cartel, enjoying the opportunity to sell at prices well above the cost of production, likewise flood the market.

In an attempt to stave off defeat, theory explains, the cartel will impose some sort of quotas on its members. Eventually, though, overproduction, cheating and outright defections will destroy the cartel.

True to theory, oil use in the industrialized world fell by almost 20% in the early 1980s as consumers bought more efficient cars, lowered thermostats and otherwise conserved energy. Producers outside OPEC greatly increased exploration, drilling, and output. However, the cartel did not collapse immediately. OPEC members with high incomes per person initially could not spend their revenues, and consequently cut production almost painlessly to accommodate member countries with larger needs. This greatly slowed the decline of the cartel.

When voluntary cuts proved insufficient to prop up prices, the OPEC nations agreed to cut production by an average of 40%. Again, the large producers with

relatively small populations played a major "swing" role, for Saudi Arabia, Kuwait and the United Arab Emirates accepted reductions in output of 50% or more, while Iran, Venezuela, Indonesia and Algeria, all with lower oil exports per person, escaped with far smaller cuts.

By 1985, however, the market for OPEC crude had tumbled to 15.4 million barrels per day, and many members cheated on quotas and provided secret discounts. Dropping its famous oil minister, Zaki Yamani, Saudi Arabia abandoned its role as a "swing producer" and determined to defend its market share. Crude flooded the world's markets, and prices tumbled briefly to below $9 a barrel in 1986. (After adjustment for U.S. inflation, this figure still represented a 40% increase of 1972 prices.) Greater OPEC discipline restored prices to about $18 per barrel in 1987, and thereafter they fluctuated in the $15–22 range.

The unstable prices reflected serious disputes within OPEC over quotas and prices. Its members could set world prices, by producing just enough, when combined with supplies from non-members, to equal what consumers would buy at a particular target price. By the late 1980s, however, the cartel could not enforce such discipline. Kuwait and the United Arab Emirates over-produced, arguing that fairness should link the size of the quota to oil export capacity, rather than to population or poverty. Consumers benefitted world-wide from the lower prices, but revenues plummeted. Iraq, for reasons including financial desperation when prices plunged to $14 per barrel, invaded Kuwait in 1990 (see Iraq: history).

After seizing Kuwait, Iraq controlled perhaps one-quarter of world reserves, and 20% of OPEC's exports. Thus, U.N. sanctions on Iraqi and occupied Kuwait created fears of oil shortages, and crude prices rapidly doubled. Industrial nations headed for recession, and OPEC soon divided into two camps. Some wished to force higher prices, but Venezuela and Saudi Arabia in particular desired to replace Iraqi and Kuwaiti crude with their own. Despite Iraqi threats, OPEC approved extra output, and with help from oil in storage, a world-wide shortfall was averted. The risk of shortages seemed greatest in refined products, because Kuwaiti and Iraqi refineries lay under sanctions, and the vast Saudi Arabian complexes—just a few Scud missiles away from destruction—were devoted to the military needs of the U.S.-led coalition that would liberate Kuwait in 1991. Retreating Iraqi troops torched much of the industry.

The reconstruction of Kuwait's productive capacity raised the perpetual issue of whether OPEC should permit higher output, or seek higher prices through production quotas, as favored by Iran, Libya, and Algeria. At its 1992 meeting, Saudi Arabia played an unusually passive role, signaling its approval of moderately higher prices. It did not achieve them, as they tumbled in 1993 and 1994. The economy of nearly every OPEC nation stagnated.

In 1996, the market outlook changed, and prices rose. Global use of oil had expanded, particularly in East Asia, while supplies from non-OPEC producers grew slowly during a decade of lower prices. As prices rose well above $20, OPEC nations found that *they could cheat at their quotas and enjoy higher prices at the same time* (see table).

Such good fortune runs rare in human affairs. At the end of 1997, Saudi Arabia persuaded the cartel's members to increase the total OPEC quota from 23.833 million barrels per day (m b/d) to 26.185 m b/d (excluding Iraq). However, the higher quotas coincided with the East Asian economic recession, and market participants realized that some nations, particularly Venezuela, Nigeria and Qatar, exceeded even the larger quotas. Prices dropped immediately and rapidly, and continued to drop through much of 1998 and early 1999, to levels last seen in 1973. Some experts proclaimed the death of OPEC, and argued that the rational policy for Gulf producers was to earn money from volume production, even if prices reached $5 per barrel. In the process, they would render oil from Alaska and the North Sea too expensive to be profitable.

Faced with its members loss of billions of dollars worth of exports and government revenues, OPEC cut quotas in 1998, with little effect on prices partly because the UN

OPEC Quotas and Output[1] (1995–1999)

	1995	1997	Output '98	1999 Quota	Capacity
Algeria	750	909	816	730	930
Indonesia	1,330	1,456	1,390	1,187	1,420
Iran	3,600	3,942	3,600	3,356	3,700
Iraq*	1,200	1,314	2,151	2,250	2,250
Kuwait	2,000	2,190	2,088	1,836	2,650
Libya	1,390	1,522	1,378	1,227	1,500
Nigeria	1,865	2,042	2,370	1,885	2,320
Qatar	378	414	660	593	710
Saudi Arabia	8,000	8,761	8,393	7,438	10,800
United Arab Emirates	2,161	2,366	2,273	2,000	2,650
Venezuela	2,359	2,583	3,500	2,720	3,500
Total:	25,033	27,499	28,619	25,222	32,430

[1]Compiled from various sources; figures in thousands of barrels per day.
*Iraq is not a functioning member of OPEC; the 1997 and 1999 quotas are production.

Oil for Food program for Iraq permitted it to export more oil as prices fell. Finally, in March 1999 Saudi Arabia and other Arab Gulf producers won OPEC consent for further cuts, taking the total without Iraq below the 1995 quota limits. Moreover, sympathetic nations outside OPEC, including Mexico, Norway, Russia and Oman also agreed to cut exports.

Though the cuts took several months to persuade the markets, every American driver witnessed the result. As oil prices soared, gasoline prices climbed, and by March 2000, regular gasoline often sold for more than $2 per gallon in California's Bay Area. So often proclaimed dead, OPEC had again revived. As long as the world remains addicted to cheap energy, the cartel should retain some ability to influence price.

After years of successful conservation and then recession, European and American oil consumption is increasing by 2–3% annually. With Asia's economic recovery, the Less Developed Countries and the Newly Industrialized Countries may boost their use by 4% or more. These figures raise total world consumption up to levels where OPEC can operate more effectively. Moreover, both U.S. and Russian oil output has fallen in recent years.

In the long run, technology and conservation might so reduce demand that world supplies would remain abundant indefinitely. However, even if they do, the Middle Eastern suppliers will enjoy low costs of production. Their huge oilfields, high outputs per well, and easy access to shipping make them the most efficient sources.

Beyond the price of oil, consumers care about the security of fuel supplies. Relations between producing and consuming countries stabilized greatly during the 1990s. Saudi Arabia and Kuwait now own large refinery and retailing companies—"downstream" in the jargon—and thus earn profits at every stage to the neighborhood gasoline pump in Europe and the U.S. This provides consumers with greater security, a feeling reinforced by new pipelines to the Red Sea and the Mediterranean. Finally, the dominant OPEC states seem to prefer stable, gradually rising prices to the dramatic swings of the past evidenced by quota increases in April 2000.

The Future: Whether as crude or gasoline, petroleum would cost more if those who produce it were not so eager to sell. For now prices seem likely to vary about $20. *But very small changes in supply and demand can create great swings in prices.*

The relatively low prices between 1986 and 1995 discouraged conservation and deterred alternative energy sources. The result, predicted in earlier editions of this work, was higher prices as world demand for OPEC oil reached 26 million barrels per day. Given the supply capacities both within the cartel and around the world, consider that figure to represent the point where OPEC's members will really set world prices.

Pipeline section lowered into a sandy trench

Riding High after delivering crude to Western customers, a giant oil tanker returns to the Gulf.

HISTORICAL BACKGROUND

The Emergence of Civilization

In the earliest stage of human history people depended for food upon hunting wild animals and gathering the edible parts of plants. For warmth they clothed themselves in animal skins, and they found protection from the weather in caves or temporary shelters. Archaeologists have found evidence for this kind of life on six continents and many islands.

Climatic changes probably played an important role in the next stage of human history, known as the Neolithic or New Stone Age. As the earth warmed after the last Ice Age, rainy weather retreated northward and to the tropics. A permanent zone of high atmospheric pressure began to dominate Southern Europe and North Africa from the Atlantic to the Middle East, and Southern Asia up to monsoon–blessed India. Under the impact of successive dry, sunny days, deserts formed where previously fishermen lived, and the hunters and gatherers were forced into confined areas, particularly along river valleys, watered by rainfall trapped by mountains and highlands often hundreds of miles distant.

Beside such rivers and streams in Southwest Asia women (more likely than men) first deliberately planted seed—barley and a variety of wheat—and cultivated land, events dated by most historians to around 8,000 B.C. About the same time, people domesticated animals; cultivation

and domestication together formed the Agricultural Revolution. Initially hardly more productive than hunting and gathering, soon farmers were capable of producing a surplus over the minimum requirements of food, clothing and shelter. Such development occurred in other areas of the world, but in later periods. Once mankind had learned how to plant grain crops and raise captive animals, a much more secure supply of food was available. It was no longer necessary for small groups of people to keep constantly on the move in search of food. They planted their fields near sources of water, their numbers increased and village life developed. The sites of the oldest villages so far discovered lie in zone stretching from southeastern Europe across Asia Minor as far eastward as the region of the middle Tigris River.

The level of technology, combined with the tasks of obtaining food, clothing, and continuing generations of the group must have shaped daily activities and society during prehistory. Life was short, even for survivors of infancy and childhood. Food supplies limited the maximum size of the group, for hunters and gatherers had to move further to procure food as the group rose in size. However, high mortality for children and adults—let alone infants— decreed the importance of having many women all either pregnant or about to be-

come so. Only thus could the existence of a next generation be expected. Lacking documentary evidence, historians can only surmise that such societies regarded highly the mighty hunter and a particularly sharp stone axe. One suspects also that they stressed communal rights and obligations in contrast to individual ones, but tempered this with the recognition that adults who could not work would not survive.

Larger communities and more efficient food production allowed—and required— increased specialization of activity; farm lands and permanent buildings required greater property rights. Rulers, warriors, administrators and priests acted to protect from invaders, settle disputes, and establish moral codes. By authority, force, and religion, these new, specialized professions appropriated much of the harvest, leaving the farmers who worked the land little beyond the minimum subsistence necessary for life. Not for the last time, therefore, improvements in mankind's ability to control nature enriched the few who took advantage of the new circumstances, but left most of society little better off than before. Nevertheless, the agricultural surplus made possible a larger population, growing slowly and settling more densely. This, in turn, made possible the early steps of civilization: cities, trade, writing, metallurgy, and the opportunity to seek beauty and truth through art, philosophy, and the early sciences.

The discovery of metals, so important for the future of humanity that historians named epochs for the predominant metal, began perhaps by accident, when rocks containing copper melted around some cooking fire. Far easier to shape than stone, copper nevertheless suffered grave defects of softness and brittleness that hampered its use in tools and weapons. With the invention of bronze around 3,000 B.C., metal became more than an ornament. So important was bronze that its era lasted until approximately 1200 B.C. in Southwestern Asia.

With the new agricultural wealth concentrated in relatively few hands, trade and the production of luxuries increased. New crafts developed and old ones expanded. Artists improved their skills, notably in sculptures and reliefs, sometimes with impressive use of gold leaf. Jewelry of gold, silver and semi–precious stones like lapis lazuli and carnelian showed great concern for personal adornment among the wealthy. For the poor, seashells, colored stone, and beads of painted pottery sufficed. With even greater visual drama, towns developed, and architects experimented with new techniques for larger and more imposing buildings. Frequently the temple of the city god became the focus of town life, and its structure was often designed as much to impress the beholder as to provide shelter for priests and rituals. Not surprisingly, temples provide some of the earliest examples of monumental architecture.

Other discoveries of the Bronze Age included improved and specialized tools

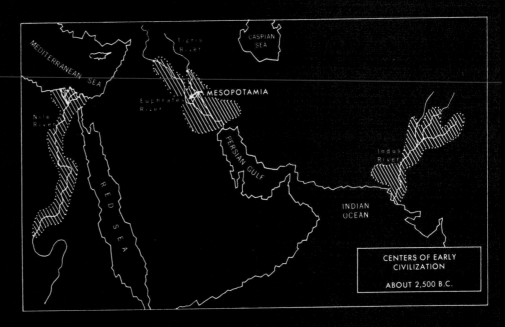

CENTERS OF EARLY
CIVILIZATION

ABOUT 2,500 B.C.

the wheel (or, more accurately, the fixed axle), and eventually the domestication of the horse. Together the last two made possible the chariot, the greatest weapon of the age. Early horses were too small to be ridden in battle, and without stirrups proved most unstable fighting platforms, but a chariot could overwhelm infantry-

men. As technology armed the defenders of the river valleys with weapons superior to those of invaders from the hills, steppes, and mountains, the opportunity arose for the three great river valley civilizations to develop. Already the greatest of their achievements must have been the discovery of writing.

The Spread of Civilization

The development and spread of writing systems during the Bronze Age meant that information about business transactions, deeds of kings, and knowledge about the world could be recorded and preserved, to be read in other places and later times. Around 3,000 B.C., the first true writing appeared, among the Sumerians of the Tigris–Euphrates Plain. Their wedge-shaped characters, impressed with a reed pen on wet clay tablets, produced a script now called cuneiform. Its pictographic origins pre-dated the Sumerians, and it developed from the needs of book-keeping and business contracts in the growing cities. Cuneiform was a cumbersome and

Hieroglyphics

It is not surprising that a third system of writing, the alphabet, replaced both cuneiform and hieroglyphics. Around the 12th century B.C., Canaanites living along the eastern shores of the Mediterranean assigned each symbol to represent a sound, rather than a picture, syllable, or idea. Easily applied to Semitic languages, whose words generally were characterized by three root sounds and simple vowels, the new script vastly shortened the task of learning to read and write. The alphabet thus broke the power akin to monopoly the scribes had previously enjoyed over writing. While the common man remained illiterate, merchants and officials adopted the idea of the alphabet to keep accounts and records, whatever their language.

Propelled by trade, the alphabet spread both east and west from Canaan and Phoenicia. By the tenth century B.C. it began to replace cuneiform in Babylonia,

in the cursive Aramaic script whose descendants include modern Arabic and Hebrew. A century later the alphabet spread to Greece. The Greeks, in turn, used it in their far–flung trading colonies across Southern Europe, preserving in the process the name of the Phoenician city–state of Byblos, whose trade with Egypt provided Greeks with papyrus. The name remains in the English prefix *biblio* for book, and "The Book": *Bible*.

Using the Canaanite alphabet

Only after the conquest of Egypt by Alexander the Great in 332 B.C., and the rise thereafter of a great center of Hellenistic civilization at Alexandria, did the use of hieroglyphics decline. A modified Greek alphabet was devised for writing the native language, Coptic. Its use continued despite foreign rule by Greeks, Romans and Byzantines. Although after the Arab conquest, Coptic gradually fell into disuse in daily speech, it remains today in the liturgy of the Egyptian rite of Christianity, the Coptic Church.

Cuneiform

inefficient writing system, for each symbol could represent any one of several ideas or syllables, and later even sounds.

Consequently, long years of training were required to become a scribe, capable of distinguishing alternate meanings. Nevertheless, cuneiform spread widely, as illustrated by one of the most dramatic recent archeological discoveries, at Ebla in northern Syria, and hundreds of miles from Sumer. Some 16,000 clay tablets, in Sumerian and Eblian, date from about 2,400 B.C. and provided both new knowledge about the Canaanites of Abraham's time and also proof of the extent of Sumer's influence. Indeed, the writing system lingered long after Sumerian died out as a spoken language soon after 2,000 B.C., for cuneiform continued to be used for the Babylonian, Assyrian, Hittite and other languages, only dying out by the time of Christ.

Evidence suggests that writing began rather suddenly in the Nile Valley shortly after 3,000 B.C. Possibly the idea of writing, but not the system, was borrowed from Sumer. Drawings of gods, people, animals, birds and inanimate objects represented words, ideas and sounds. These so-called hieroglyphics were not a very efficient method of writing, but they were capable of recording information.

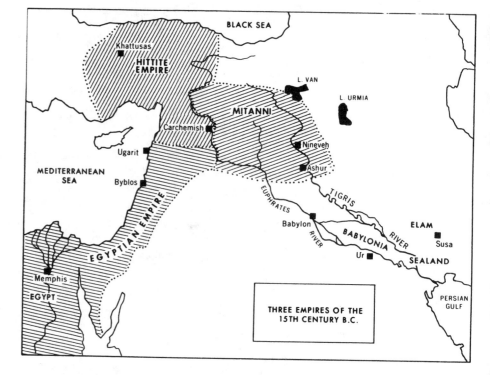

THREE EMPIRES OF THE
15TH CENTURY B.C.

The Rise and Fall of Empires

The sport of an Assyrian king

During the many centuries of civilization's uneven advance, life for ordinary people often proved harsh. Only in the most fortunate times did the countryside and towns enjoy peace. Instead, farmers, merchants and craftsmen alike suffered interruption of work and safety because civilization provided the incentive and means for increasingly well–organized warfare.

Sometimes there were disputes over territory between neighboring communities. This led to a new dimension in fighting when one city set out to dominate others and when one little state began to subjugate others. In modern times, mechanized industrial production has permitted populations of entire nations to enjoy lives of relative comfort and convenience. In ancient times, however, production depended on human and animal energy for power and thus luxuries and comforts could be enjoyed only by small, privileged groups—and only through taking wealth from others, both slaves within society, and increasingly by conquest. Thus, the new inventions of civilization encouraged aggressive people, at first individually, then as groups and finally as nations, to reap personal benefit from the labor of others.

In the Nile Valley, where rival cities and regions had struggled for supremacy, there arose around 2850 B.C. a leader capable of unifying the distinctly separate regions of Upper and Lower Egypt (the Nile Delta). Hardly distinct from associated myths, Menes founded the first of thirty dynasties to rule Egypt. Claiming divine descent, his successors as kings or Pharaohs exerted enormous power over society. By the 26th century B.C., the pyramid age, rulers constructed enormous stone monuments as their tombs. Amazing in size and accuracy as feats of engineering, (e.g., the Great Pyramid contains 2,300,000 blocks and varies only 9 1/2 inches on a side) they also bear dramatic witness to the organization of society and the Pharaohs' ability to extract labor and resources from the populace. However, one of the Pharaohs' greatest weaknesses was organizational: as local governors passed office to their sons, central authority weakened and the dynasty might collapse.

Although Egypt possessed then, as now, relatively secure borders against foreign attack in the form of deserts to the South, East, and West, strong Pharaohs frequently sought conquests abroad. During the Middle Kingdom (2100–1800 B.C.) and the New Kingdom (1550–1085 B.C.), Egyptian armies defeated the Nubians up the Nile and struggled for the wealth and control of Syria against both its inhabitants and powerful kingdoms in Mesopotamia. In the fifteenth century, Thutmose III fought seventeen campaigns and crossed the Euphrates; hieroglyphics at the Temple of Karnak in Egypt portrayed his conquests and booty.

The growth of powerful states in Mesopotamia illustrated many features common to Egypt, including the divine origin of rulers. However, geography decreed greater difficulties for those desiring to unify the land. The broader river valleys allowed city states to develop, and peoples to retain separate ethnic identities and languages. Moreover, invaders repeatedly pierced the natural barriers of desert and mountains and established new kingdoms. Thus, for most of the 3rd millen-nium B.C. the dominant political organization was the city–states of Sumer. In the mid–24th century B.C., however, Sargon (or Sharrukin), ruler of Akkad to the north conquered Sumer and proclaimed himself king of Sumer and Akkad. The next centuries, marked by rivalry between the Akkadians and Sumerians as well as invading Amorites, nevertheless witnessed another great achievement of civilization: the promulgation of codes of law.

The first recorded law–giver, Ur–Nammu, was followed by the much more famous, though significantly harsher, Code of Hammurabi.

In the struggle for territory and the wealth of civilization, empires and dynasties rose and fell. Warfare took a new turn when horses were introduced into the civilized area from the northeast about 1,600 B.C. Horse–drawn chariots could crash through a line of foot soldiers. The infantry, poorer soldiers who could not afford horses and chariots, lost status in the new military organizations.

The rise of iron–smelting in Asia Minor around 1200 B.C. apparently provided an important strength for the next dominant power of Mesopotamia, the warlike and often cruel Assyrians, with their capital at Ashur. Armed with iron weapons and heavy chariots, Assyrian troops proved invincible. They raided as far as the Black Sea and ruled to the Mediterranean, marching into captivity (and often extinction) skilled workmen and sometimes entire populations.

Enriched by conquests and the labor of subject peoples, the kings of Assyria adorned palaces and decorated impressive buildings with monuments and stone reliefs of colossal winged animals. The last powerful king of Assyria, Ashurbanipal (668–627 B.C.), personally directed an effort to collect the literature and learning of Mesopotamian civilizations. His royal library at Nineveh, excavated in the 19th century, acquired thousands of cuneiform tablets, including the Epic of Gilgamesh and the Babylonian Creation Epic. This single most important collection of cuneiform tablets provides modern historians with much of their knowledge of the culture and history of the Tigris–Euphrates Plain.

After the collapse of the Assyrian Empire, the center of power and wealth on the Tigris–Euphrates Plain shifted again to the city of Babylon. The Neo–Babylonian (or Chaldean) Empire, which extended from the head of the Persian Gulf to the Mediterranean Sea, gathered wealth to give Babylon a final burst of glory before it gradually faded away.

The next great empire had its base in the mountains east of the Tigris River. The first Iranian–speaking group to establish an empire were the Medes. They dominated a large territory to the east and north of Babylonia. About the middle of the 6th century B.C. the empire of the Medes was taken over by their fellow Iranians and former subjects, the Persians. Under the leadership of Cyrus the Great and his successors, most of the civilized world except for East Asia and the defiant city–states of Greece, fell under the sway of the Persian Empire.

Like the Assyrians before them, the Persians did not hesitate to use force if the assigned taxes, or "gifts," were not sent by subject communities when due. On the other hand, many of the Persian rulers tried to gain voluntary submission of their

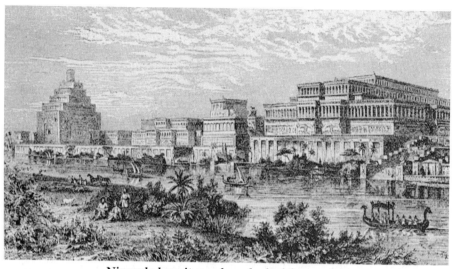
Ninevah: how it may have looked from ruins

subjects by showing toleration for local culture.

The vast Persian Empire was united by improved roads, a postal system for official use, uniform laws and employment of a single language for administrative purposes. The language of administration was not Persian, but Aramaic, which several centuries earlier had become dominant in business in the region between the Euphrates River and the Mediterranean Coast. The empire was divided into provinces, each with a governor (satrap) responsible to the Great King. Eventually the personal ambitions of these satraps contributed to the weakening of the empire. Another destructive force within the empire consisted of civil wars led by rival claimants to the throne. Each

faction sought to gain power, receive honor and control the wealth produced by civilization.

The extension of Persian control over the Indus Valley had significant cultural effects. Interchange of religious and philosophical ideas was one. Another was the spread of the idea of an alphabet into South Asia, apparently in the 5th century B.C. The earliest alphabet used in the Indus–Ganges civilization preserved forms of the Aramaic alphabet used in the Persian Empire. During the period of Persian domination to the west of it, the Ganges Basin was under the control of rival minor kings. The largest of the kingdoms was that of Magadha near the mouth of the Ganges River. Meanwhile, civilization was also developing in the southern part of the Indian Peninsula.

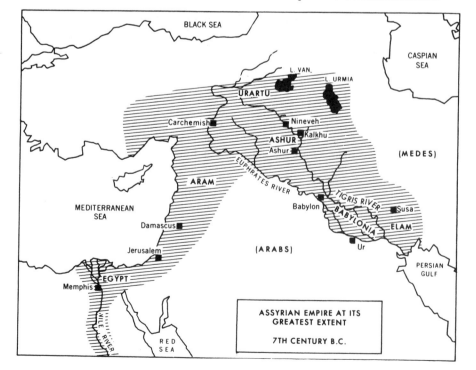

Hebrews and Judaeans

In contrast to the material splendor displayed by the great empires of the river valleys, the Hebrew tribes of the plains and highlands of Canaan gave to the world an idea, monotheism. In sharp contrast to the many gods worshiped by surrounding societies, the Hebrew prophets and scriptures proclaimed that one God, Yahweh (or Jehovah), created all; His legal code stipulated ethical and moral behavior far superior to the times. Preserved by Judaism and expanded by Christianity, the unique religion of the Hebrews has influenced European civilization more than any other cultural achievement of the ancient world.

Historical research in the twentieth century lends credence to the accounts given in the Jewish scriptures, which also form the Old Testament of the Bible. The first patriarch, Abraham, claimed as ancestor by both Jewish and Arab societies, roamed Canaan with his herds, erecting in the midst of polytheism altars to Yahweh. His grandson, Jacob, also known as Israel, is generally regarded as the first Hebrew: from his sons descended the tribes of *B'nai Yisra'el*, the Children of Israel. After settling in Egypt for generations, under Moses the Hebrews escaped from captivity, to be led into Canaan by Joshua, perhaps around 1400 B.C.

Tempted by religions with visual gods—idols physically present that could be worshiped—the ancient Hebrews sometimes seem hardly distinguishable from other Canaanite tribes. They rarely ruled the entire land, and for several centuries lacked political unity even in the central highlands where their population was concentrated, running from north to south between the Mediterranean and the

Jordan River. Their first king, Saul, faced invasions from the Philistines of the coastal plain and nomadic tribes to the south and east. However, after David succeeded to the throne around 1000 B.C., the little kingdom expanded in size and military prowess, reaching its zenith in peace and prosperity under David's son Solomon (961–922 B.C.), who built the first temple dedicated to Yahweh in Jerusalem, the capital.

At Solomon's death the state fractured, with the northern tribes establishing a Kingdom of Israel in Samaria. Lacking the great religious center of Jerusalem, and prey both to Canaanite religions and invasion by foreign armies, the Kingdom of Israel lasted until destroyed by the Assyrians in 722 B.C. Under the somewhat more capable kings of the House of David, the southern Kingdom of Judah survived until finally captured by the great neo–Babylonian ruler Nebuchadnezzar in 586 B.C. His troops carried off to exile in Babylon the royal family of Judah, together with many of the upper classes and skilled workers.

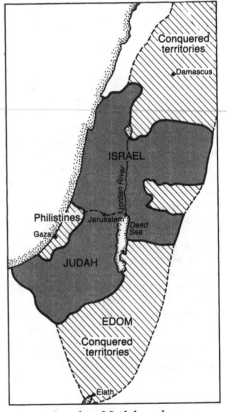

Israel and Judah under King David, c. 1000 B.C.

After Cyrus the Great captured Babylon in 539 B.C. (and in the process ended over two thousand years of Mesopotamian empires), the liberal religious policies of

19

the new Persian Empire allowed some worshippers of Yahweh to return to the land of their forebears, while others remained in Persia and Mesopotamia, developing a large and often prosperous center of Judaism. Despite local opposition, those who returned rebuilt the walls of Jerusalem, then the Temple itself, under tolerant Persian rule.

Far greater threats to Judaism followed the next conquerors, the Hellenistic armies of Alexander the Great in 332 B.C. Greek ideas soon came to dominate the Jewish upper classes as they discovered Greek athletics, music, and art as well as the Greek language itself. Rational religious concepts, especially about resurrection and angels, deeply impressed the wealthy, and separated them from most Jews, with their more traditional and pious values.

Direct attacks on Jewish religion and customs aroused greater resistance. When the Seleucid rulers of Syria, having captured Palestine, ordered pigs sacrificed to Zeus at the Temple, rebellion broke out. After bitter fighting, Jewish independence briefly flared anew under the Hasmoneans, also known as the Maccabees (129–63 B.C.). Split by political rivalry, divided by religious factions and resented by non–Jewish inhabitants, the Jewish territories were easily annexed to Rome by Pompey in 63 B.C. Julius Caesar later appointed a governor named Antipater, an Idumaean from the coastal region previously conquered by the Hasmoneans and himself possibly a descendant of the Israelites' ancient enemies, the Philistines. Converted to Judaism but opposed by the Hasmoneans, Antipater and his sons struggled to control Judea. Finally, declared King of Judea by the Roman Senate, and aided by Roman troops, his son Herod succeeded in capturing Jerusalem (37 B.C.).

All accounts portray Herod as hated by his subjects, for many causes: a foreigner himself, a collaborator dependent on Roman rule, and a tyrant capable of killing his own sons as well as ordering the massacre of the infants of Bethlehem reported in the Gospels. Nevertheless, Herod built cities and established peace; for the non–Jews he provided festivals and Greek arts. For the Jews, he rebuilt the Temple, on a grander scale than ever before. His heirs proved less capable, and Caesar Augustus extended direct Roman rule over the area.

Increasing Jewish opposition to Rome broke into open rebellion in A.D. 66, after increasingly intolerant policies of the Emperors Caligula and Nero. Aided by rivalries for the throne in Rome, Judea became independent again, but four years later Titus defeated the Jewish armies and sacked Jerusalem after a lengthy seige. The temple, so recently rebuilt by Herod, was destroyed, and Jewish zealots holding the

Solomon's temple was made from timber brought from Tyre

fortress of Masada overlooking the Dead Sea finally committed suicide rather than surrender. Again the Jewish population faced persecution and forced exile (called the Diaspora). After a second failed rebellion in 135 A.D. Rome made Judea a pagan colony, prohibiting Jews from living there, although believers survived in neighboring Galilee and elsewhere throughout the Roman Empire, as well as flourishing on occasion in Babylonia.

A rabbi reads from the *Torah* in a synagogue

The Hellenistic Age, Roman Rule and Christianity

ALEXANDER

When the sudden and furious conquests of Alexander the Great shattered the dominance of Persian emperors in Asia, a new language and a new civilization began their lengthy domination of Southwest Asia. For centuries the city-states of Greece had learned from the older civilizations to the East. In the decades after 500 B.C. they fought off Persian invasions with difficulty, in heroic battles such as Marathon, Thermopylae, and Salamis. However, in eleven short years after 334 B.C., Alexander the Great, king of Macedonia though Greek in culture and education, captured the known world as far as India and established the greatest empire then known. This laid the political conditions for a new era of civilization called *Hellenistic*, meaning "Greek–like," in contrast to the previous Greek, or Hellenic.

Although Alexander's empire broke up after his death at the young age of 33, rival kingdoms succeeded him in Egypt (the Ptolemies) and Southwest Asia (the Seleucids). In both kingdoms Greeks and Macedonians who formed the urban upper class of rulers, soldiers, merchants and artisans mixed with the local population, in the process creating Hellenistic civilization. Trade flourished, from India and even China in the east to Italy and North Africa in the west. The growing wealth made possible great libraries at Alexandria and Pergamum as well as new cities and art. Science and learning advanced dramatically: among other achievements, scholars calculated the earth's circumference, founded geometry, and interpreted literature.

After 200 B.C., however, the Hellenistic world began to decline. Never solidly established east of Mesopotamia, the Seleucids retreated from the Iranian plateau and later from Mesopotamia in the face of Parthian invasions. Moreover, within the remaining territories, native populations increasingly rejected Greek beliefs, values, and language. With relative ease, then, the Roman general Pompey captured the remaining Seleucid territories (64 B.C.) and Egypt finally fell to Octavian (30 B.C.). However, the Romans failed to conquer either Mesopotamia or Persia from the Parthians. Moreover, within those Asian territories it did conquer, Greek rather than Latin remained the language of trade and learning. Significantly, the struggle between Hellenistic and local beliefs and culture continued, most importantly in Judea.

Into this world was born Jesus of Nazareth. Educated by his mother, rather than by either Jewish scribes or Hellenistic scholars, in adulthood he preached a message of love and obedience, of humility and enjoyment of the good. As reports of his apparent miracles spread, he rapidly gained a following of Jews and others who hoped for deliverance—divinely aided deliverance—from Rome. Nevertheless, his popularity and message threatened both the Hellenized Sadducees and the carefully traditional Pharisees. Charged by the Jewish leadership with claiming to be the Son of God, he seemed to Pontius Pilate, the Roman prefect, another agitator and resistance leader. Deserted by almost all his disciples and those who desired political revolution, he was crucified as King of the Jews. Dying at about the same age as Alexander, Jesus conquered no territories, founded no cities, and overthrew no empires.

To his followers, however, Jesus conquered much more than the world. According to the New Testament, this "Only Begotten Son" of God defeated death itself. His crucifixion made possible the redemption of mankind from sin. His apparent resurrection three days later, and subsequent return to heaven, brought the assurance of a final Judgment followed by a New Earth ruled by God. Passages from the Jewish scriptures—to Christians now the Old Testament—were interpreted to show him as the fulfillment of many prophecies of the Messiah (Greek, *Christ*). Within weeks of his death an active and growing church sprang up in Jerusalem.

Christianity first spread most rapidly among Jewish communities scattered about the Roman Empire. Within a generation, however, the preaching and writings of St. Paul rendered Christianity a world religion that promised salvation to all who believed, whether Jewish or not. Both hindered and helped by occasional persecution, Christianity spread rapidly, especially among the lower classes. By the middle of the 2nd century, the major rules of the faith had been established, the Canon of Biblical books had been largely selected, and the church had been organized into a hierarchy. When persecution by the Emperor Diocletian failed to destroy the church (303–311), the church triumphed, for his successor Constantine granted toleration and equality for Christianity while eliminating cults of the state.

In matters beyond religion, Constantine changed the face of the Roman Empire as well. In 330 A.D. he moved the capital from "heathen Rome" to Byzantium on the shores of the Bosphorus. During the two centuries that followed, the eastern and western halves of the empire drifted apart, each facing invasion and struggling to maintain order and civilization in the midst of economic decay. Gradually there emerged in the east the Byzantine Empire, ruling over Greece as well as Asia Minor, geographical Syria, and Egypt. Greek in language, and Hellenistic in much of its culture, though still calling itself Rome, the Byzantine Empire mixed Christianity with the grandeur of Oriental potentates. The emperor ruled absolutely, as God's representative on earth, standing as head of the military, government, and church.

For almost a thousand years, the Byzantine empire survived, an enormous accomplishment that contrasts with the total collapse of Roman rule in the West. During those centuries it witnessed great achievements in law, and it preserved Greek and Roman learning largely lost elsewhere. In art and architecture the stunning beauty created by Byzantine craftsmen remains at St. Marks in Venice and Hagia Sophia in Istanbul. As defenders of the faith, the Byzantine military stopped numerous invasions by infidels, and passed along to Russia and much of eastern Europe, Orthodox Christianity and Greek–based alphabets. Nevertheless, bloodshed stains many pages of Byzantine history, and tolerance brightens few. When conflicts in theology and religion followed the same dividing lines as differences in language and culture between Greek rulers and native inhabitants of Egypt and Syria, the consequence was restlessness in those lands and weakened loyalties to the empire. When new armies appeared out of Arabia in the middle of the seventh century, Syrian, Egyptian, and North African possessions were quickly lost.

Zoroastrian, Buddhist and Hindu Cultures

When the Roman legions attempted to press eastward from Syria in the 1st century B.C., they were stopped by another military power, the Parthian Empire. This state had its origins in the 3rd century B.C. when warriors from Parthia, an area in the northeast part of the Iranian Plateau, gained local independence from Hellenistic rulers. Regarding themselves as the heirs of the first Persian Empire, the Parthians eventually expanded their control both east and west, building an empire that stretched from the Tigris–Euphrates Plain to the Indus River.

Hellenistic culture declined, but was not totally eradicated, within the territory under Parthian rule. Native ideas, architecture, art and literature developed along independent lines. Although religious activity in Parthian domains is not well known, it seems that Zoroastrianism made great advances. This faith revered the teachings of Zarathushtra, who lived during the 7th century B.C. In its developed form, Zoroastrianism stressed the struggle between two principal supernatural beings representing good and evil. The leading position was held by Ahura Mazda, the god of light and goodness.

About 225 A.D. the weakened leadership of the Parthians was replaced by a Persian dynasty descended from a little–known figure named Sasan. Occupying the Parthian capital of Ctesiphon on the Tigris as their own, these Sasanians presented themselves as the restorers of the purity of the first Persian Empire. Zoroastrianism took on its most highly developed form as the established religion of the government. The Sasanians increased the level of civilization in their territories by encouraging the development of cities.

The Sasanians also possessed a strong expansionist urge; this kept them in conflict with their neighbors, such as the Late Roman (Byzantine) Empire to the west, which had similar impulses. For a time in the 6th century and the first decades of the next, the Sasanian Empire was the world's leading power. In a final burst of militancy it captured Damascus and Jerusalem from Byzantium in 614, but lost them a decade and a half later. The Sasanian Empire, exhausted by the wars, succumbed to the attacks of the Muslim Arabs beginning with the fall of Ctesiphon in 637.

The golden age of Buddhism in the Indian Peninsula occurred in the state ruled by the Maurya family. At its height in the 3rd century B.C. the Mauryan Empire controlled the Ganges Basin, the Indus Valley and large regions to the south and northwest. The most illustrious ruler was Asoka (or Ashoka); during his long reign (273–232 B.C.) he turned from bloody wars of expansion to the peaceful teaching of Buddhism.

Gautama Buddha had lived several centuries earlier and it was Asoka's patronage of the Buddha's teachings which contributed greatly to the spread of Buddhism as a world religion.

Many inscribed pillars set up on Asoka's orders have been found in all parts of modern India, in Pakistan and in southern Afghanistan. These provide scholars with a picture of that early period, including Mauryan knowledge of the Hellenistic world to the west. After the death of Asoka the Great, the empire of the Maurya declined and finally ended in 185 B.C. It was replaced by many small states about which little information is available.

For nearly five centuries during which there was a notable development of trade with the outside world, attempts to build a new empire in the Indian Peninsula failed. Then in the early fourth century A.D., a territory nearly as extensive as that ruled by the Maurya was brought under the control of the Gupta dynasty. The Gupta period from the early fourth to the early sixth century is often described as the golden age of Hindu culture in the Ganges Basin, though the central and southern parts of the peninsula were to achieve their zenith of classical Hindu culture later.

The Gupta Empire, the capital of which was Ayodhya on the Ganges River, was at its height during the reign of Chandra Gupta II (A.D. 385 to 413). Later, particularly from about A.D. 480 to 490, Hindu civilization was badly mauled by invading Huns, who raided from bases north of the Hindu Kush Mountains. The menace of the Huns and the disturbances caused by various other peoples entering the Indian Peninsula from Central Asia did not subside until near the end of the sixth century. By then the region was again divided into a number of warring local kingdoms.

Little is known about events until the early seventh century, when a youth of only 16 years became king of a small state and attempted to build an empire. This king, Harsha, ruled well for 41 years. Not only was he a patron of art and literature, but was himself a poet and playwright. Three of his plays in Sanskrit have survived, including one called "The Pearl Necklace." With Harsha's death the last great Hindu kingdom in the Ganges–Indus region ended. Then a pattern of rival little kingdoms was a prelude to later foreign invasion.

Life-size sculpture of Buddha
Courtesy: Government of India

Muhammad and the Rise of Islam

A prayer in Tehran (late 19th century drawing)

In the rugged desert landscape of western Arabia, far from civilization's major centers, some six centuries after Christ the third great monotheistic religion arose with the preaching of Muhammad. This solemn and meditative man warned the citizens of the city of Mecca of a coming great cataclysm to end the earth, followed by a final judgment over all deeds that would grant to the righteous heaven, and to the evil, the fires of hell. From his initial messages of repentance and care of one's fellows, Muhammad's teachings expanded to fill almost all aspects of society. This religious protest first attracted a few followers, and later an entire city. Within a generation the entire Middle East

lay conquered by a newly united people, and a new civilization, the Islamic, began its often brilliant rise.

Born about 572, probably after his father's death, Muhammad was orphaned as a child when his mother died. Few details of his early life are certain, but he grew up in a society undergoing dramatic social changes.

Prolonged conflict between the Sasanian Persian and Byzantine empires disrupted the traditional Mesopotamian trade route between India and the Mediterranean. One alternative route ran along the mountainous western coast of Arabia. Several Arabian tribes remained neutral in the great clash

between Byzantium and Persia that stretched as far south as Yemen, and this encouraged trade. So did the religious customs that brought an annual truce to desert warfare and a pilgrimage to Mecca. Some Arab tribes, particularly Muhammad's own Quraysh, seized the opportunities, and exchanged herds for trade caravans. In the process Arab society itself changed significantly. For wealthy merchants, houses replaced tents, and the family structure strengthened as fathers viewed sons as assistants and successors. However, the increasing wealth meant greater disparities of wealth, and also a decline in loyalty to the clan and tribe. As the family strengthened, other social bonds weakened, and the poor increasingly found charity less common.

Raised by relatives and trained as a merchant, Muhammad had the good fortune to marry Khadija, a rather older widow of substantial wealth. Nevertheless, despite his financial success, he suffered inner distress over social wrongs, and meditated extensively. At the age of forty he is alleged to have become conscious of a message from the angel Gabriel to praise the one God, Allah, as the Creator, and to care for the unfortunate.

Though living in a pagan culture, and often using the rhymed prose of common soothsayers, from his travels as a merchant, Muhammad had become familiar with the Jewish and Christian customs and beliefs. He now identified Allah as the God of their scriptures, recognized many of their prophets and considered himself the final Messenger, who recited the words sent from heaven.

Like many religious leaders, Muhammad at first appealed to relatives and friends, as well as the unfortunate. However, he aroused the hostility and anger of the leading merchants and politicians of Mecca by his vision of a dreadful judgment, by his strident demands for greater charity, and even more by his condemnation of pagan idol worship. This struck at the financial foundation of Meccan society, for pilgrimages to Mecca, with its famous black stone *Kaaba* provided great opportunity for trade, and religion sanctioned an annual truce from raids, valuable to merchants and pilgrims alike.

Strongly conflicting with Muslim beliefs, Western scholars suggested that at one point Muhammad appeared to defuse the situation by confirming publicly that three female deities, al–Lat, al–Uzza and al–Monat, were the daughters of Allah; as such they could intercede with their Father. However, Muhammad's faithful soon recoiled at the implication of more than one god, and denounced the goddesses as mere inventions; the verses acknowledging them became the "Satanic Verses."

As pressure became economic embargo and persecution, some followers fled to Ethiopia; by 622 Muhammad himself forsook Mecca for Yathrib, soon renamed Medina, "The City" of the Prophet. Celebrated as the *Hijra,* and marking the beginning of the Muslim era, the event nevertheless supports a variety of interpretations. Did Muhammad flee from persecution, or emigrate by choice? Did he fear the Meccans because of religious opposition, or Meccan opposition to his becoming the leader of a rival community strategically situated to strangle their trade route north?

Once in Medina, Muhammad became far more than a religious leader. He had come, by agreement, as the leader of the "Ummah" or community: he was the primary secular authority. His Meccan followers abandoned the protection of the tribes of their birth by following him to Medina. Now they formed in effect a new tribe, and Muhammad became particularly responsible for their welfare, and that of the converts in Medina. Certainly, too, the visions continued, and included with the calls to repentance much practical material for the lawgiver of a new society.

The ten years Muhammad lived in Medina established the religion of "Islam" (pronounced like "this lamb"), or submission to God. Despite military defeats and political resistance from Jews and other non-believers resident in Medina, the Muslim ("One who submits") community grew and adopted the distinctive beliefs and practices that continue to the present. The individual Believer had five obligations. He must believe, confessing that "There is no God but Allah, and Muhammad is his Messenger", and bow in ritual prayer five times daily, prompted by the call from the minaret of the mosque. Annually, during the Islamic month of Ramadan, he must abstain from food, drink, and sex during the day. If possible, once during his lifetime he should undertake a pilgrimage (haj) to Mecca. Finally, he must contribute annually a portion of his wealth as a charity or tax. Beyond these duties, the Muslim must accept the Quran ("Recitation") as the infallible word of God, interpreted by the consensus of the Islamic community as well as the traditions (or "sayings") of Muhammad carefully handed down over the generations.

Scholarly summaries of Islam, much like the paragraph above, rarely do justice to the combination of religious observances and custom in Islamic societies. The religion deliberately appeals to people of all languages and nations, and promises equality among the believers, who in forming the Ummah attempt to have religious boundaries the same as political. For centuries the Umayyad and Abbasid caliphates achieved this in practice, as they fused subjects of varied languages and religions into a Muslim society ruled more or less within the framework of Islamic law. Despite Muhammad's condemnation of the practices of wealthy Meccans, private property is allowed, and numerous traditions report God's favor towards merchants. The payment of interest is forbidden, paralleling original Jewish and Christian views of usury.

In social aspects, Islam reinforced the position of the husband, allowing up to four wives and divorce on (his) demand, though he was urged to limit himself to one wife if he felt incapable of treating her fairly. Nevertheless, a woman retained the right to property she brought into a marriage, a privilege enjoyed centuries before Western nations granted similar property rights to women. On balance, scholars agree that Muhammad raised the status and condition of women, in part by rigidly punishing adultery as well as condemning the practice of female infanticide.

A Muslim's worship contrasts substantially with certain aspects of Jewish and Christian traditions, yet there are many similarities: sermons, ritual prayers, and reading (or recitation from memory) of the scriptures. However, singing and other music are remarkable for their absence, as are drawings, paintings, or sculptures of living things. Friday, the day of worship, is not a day of rest, and the believers commonly gather in the mosque in the afternoon, entering without shoes after washing hands and feet. Generally in Islam there is no equivalent of a priesthood: any believer may address the congregation, who stand in rows before the pulpit, with the women meeting separately. The dead await physical resurrection and the judgment, and are mourned extensively at the funeral and 40 days thereafter.

Thanks to the media, Westerners are much more familiar with more superficial regulations of Muslim society, such as amputation for certain crimes. The Quran strictly forbids wine, and by extension alcoholic drinks of any kind. Pork, carrion, and blood are forbidden, but in great contrast to the many unclean foods of Mosaic law, Allah is thanked for the abundance of animals created to be eaten. In dress, the veil, often the trademark of a Muslim woman, in fact reflects pre-existing Persian practice rather than explicit commands in the Quran or traditions of Muhammad. Instead, recognizing the power of temptation in sexual matters, Muslims must dress modestly, an injunction interpreted in some circles as requiring a woman's upper arms and shoulders to be covered. Despite the climate, men's legs are always covered.

Perhaps the Islamic doctrine most perplexing to modern, secular societies is the concept of *Jihad,* occasionally listed as a sixth individual duty. In everyday speech the term admits many meanings such as task or burden, or even one's struggle. In the context of religion, it often, though not exclusively, implied an armed struggle for the faith, to extend the boundaries of Islam or defend them from invasion by the infidel. Scholars a generation ago frequently stressed that many kinds of work for the benefit of the Ummah could be considered Jihad. However, recent events, especially the rise of groups such as Islamic Jihad in Lebanon, leave little doubt that to a significant portion of the Muslim world, the struggle continues between Dar al-Salaam, the House of Peace (i.e., Islam) and the Dar al-Harb, the House of War (i.e., the unbelievers), fourteen hundred (Islamic) years after Muhammad's Hijra.

Then did Islam spread largely by conquest and forced conversions? Outside the Hijaz, only rarely: during the early conquests, Arab Muslims regarded with some suspicion those who wished to adopt the faith of their conquerors. In many places, it may have taken a century or two before the majority of the population accepted Islam. The converts' motives were mixed. To some, accepting the new religion removed discriminatory taxes. To others, a new community might bring different laws and personal advantages. Where missionary activity led to spiritual conviction, it often was the work of Islamic brotherhoods. Organized around a master, who initiated disciples in the ritual and beliefs of the particular brotherhood, these *Sufi* (from "one garbed in wool"; a holy man) orders reached beyond formal Islam into mysticism. They frequently incorporated ideas of existing religions, and this, like the missionary fervor of the members, advanced Islam as a spiritual force. On occasion, linked to Muslim rulers, Sufi brotherhoods also aided Islam as a conquering political force.

Islamic Expansion and Society: The Arab Caliphate

A new Mosque near Hofuf, Saudi Arabia combines traditional architecture with modern materials

For eight often–precarious years after the Hijra, Muhammad struggled to maintain the Muslim community in the face of Meccan opposition. After 624, there were raids on Meccan caravans and battles as the Meccans counterattacked, as well as expulsions and massacres of the Jewish tribes of Medina and alliances struck with Bedouin tribes. Finally, in 630, Mecca capitulated, and the entire population converted. Almost all Arabia acknowledged Muhammad as politically supreme, though many tribes hardly accepted Islam. Two years later, however, at the height of his political power, Muhammad died. Although about sixty years of age, and too ill to worship in his last days, he left no messages about the future of Islamic society or its government.

As news spread that the Messenger of God lay dead, Muhammad's closest advisors met hurriedly to select a new leader of the community and thus avoid its disintegration under rival leaders. They settled on Abu Bakr, one of the earliest converts, and the next day the community publicly pledged allegiance to him. His position was imprecise, for Muhammad had been prophet, chief judge, supreme military commander, and sole legislator. Abu Bakr gained the vague title *Khalifat Rasul Allah:* "Successor to the Messenger of God," generally known in English as the Caliph. No prophet himself, but Commander of the Faithful, Abu Bakr led the Muslim community as Muhammad's secular successor and the sovereign in whose name the Friday prayers were offered.

Though only ruling for two years, Abu Bakr decided many of the crucial issues for the new Islamic state. When tribes admitting only political allegiance to Muhammad himself, and denying Islamic authority, attempted to secede, Abu Bakr sent armies under Khalid ibn al–Walid and other generals to conquer all Arabia. Quickly victorious, the Muslim armies established the central control of the Caliph, altering greatly the pre–existing Arab patterns of temporary alliances and confederations. Of additional importance, the apostate tribes soon were permitted to join the Muslim armies almost wholesale, thus turning energies long spent in violence between Arabs into a remarkable weapon directed by the Caliph.

The weapon quickly proved useful. Under Muhammad, Muslim raiders reached the fringes of the Byzantine Empire. Under Abu Bakr, out of the desert Arab columns appeared almost simultaneously, attacking Byzantine cities in Palestine and Persian troops in Iraq. The great mobility of their camel transport enabled them to strike far from the defending forces. At one crucial period Khalid ibn al–Walid's troops rapidly crossed the desert from Iraq to defeat the Byzantine army, leaving Palestine open to Muslim conquest.

Proclaimed caliph at Abu Bakr's passing, Umar (ruled 634–644) continued the policy of conquest. In 637 Arab armies defeated the Byzantine emperor at the Battle of Yarmuk, thus adding Syria to Arab conquests. The homeland of Christianity was lost to Christian rule, Jerusalem surrendering in 638. Meanwhile, at Kadisiya in Iraq, the Persian army was routed and Sasanian rule effectively destroyed. Soon afterwards, raiding forces unleashed by Umar on Egypt proved unexpectedly successful, and in 641 its last Byzantine city, Alexandria, surrendered. For the next century the Muslim expansion continued, to the east across the Iranian plateau into Central Asia, to the west across North Africa and into Spain and France.

To the European Christian imagination the Muslim conquests were a matter of religious crusades. Muhammad appeared as the anti–Christ of scripture; his conquering hordes offered captives the choice of conversion or the sword. Reality was somewhat more complicated, and explanations abound. Some causes lay within Arabia: possibly it was overpopulated, and now unified, its people sought living space outside it. Certainly religion played a great role in motivating individual soldiers, for death in battle to extend the boundaries of Islam brought God's mercy at the judgment and the promise of greater physical comforts and pleasures in heaven than on earth.

Other reasons for the dramatic rise lay outside the Muslim community. For the previous century in particular, the Byzantine and Sasanian empires had fought long and hard over Syria. Now both empires lay exhausted, separated by buffer states of Arab tribes unlikely to halt armies from Arabia. Under Byzantine rule, the Christian farmers of Syria and Egypt had long suffered heavy taxes, an alien language, and religious persecution over their theological interpretation of Christ. When Arab armies arrived, the vast majority of inhabitants did not resist: the Arabs offered not apostasy or death, but rather lower taxes and greater religious freedom. Likewise, in Iraq the native inhabitants had never become Persian; they too welcomed the Muslims. Only in Asia Minor, with its Hellenic population, were the Arab invasions repulsed. In Iran, the collapse of the Sasanian dynasty enabled a rapid Muslim conquest, but it would become complicated in differing interpretations of Islam.

Administration of the new empire from Medina proved a difficult task. The caliph's share of the booty from the conquest provided great riches, but numerous problems arose. One was membership in the Muslim community, now a lucrative benefit, as the caliph's income from the captured territories was distributed among all Muslims, whose taxes in any case were minimal. Conversion, therefore, brought administrative difficulties: taxpayers became welfare recipients. To discourage them, converts had to be attached to Arab tribes. Despite Muhammad's message to all, regardless of tongue or nation, in some cases converts were not freed of their taxes on becoming Muslims. Later the contrast between religious appeal and fiscal expediency would fester and encourage the violent overthrow of one dynasty of caliphs.

Land ownership was another problem. Had Muslim soldiers received lands upon their conquest, their self–interest would have reduced the drive for further conquests. The issue was resolved in theory at least by keeping agricultural land as public land, the property of the caliph, with taxes on the harvest. Muslim troops were established in barracks cities on the fringes of cultivation, the better to keep them accustomed to a hard life and to separate ruling from ruled.

Where the local populations surrendered willingly, and possessed scriptures, they became *dhimmis*—"protected subjects." The exact rights depended on the local surrender terms, but in general, each recognized sect received religious toleration and maintained its own laws of personal status under its chief religious leader, typically a bishop or patriarch. For example, divorce, freely available to Muslim men, remained prohibited in most circumstances in the Christian communities. (A Christian desiring an additional wife, or divorce from his existing one, could usually convert to Islam.) Laws of marriage and inheritance likewise varied by religion.

Islamic toleration, though far greater than the practices in Europe of the period, did not mean freedom or equality, but limited rights mixed with discrimination. Non–Muslim testimony against a Muslim was suspect in the courts. New churches generally could not be built, nor church bells rung often, and any Muslim who adopted Christianity (unlikely though that was) risked the death penalty for apostasy. Members of the protected sects did avoid military obligations, but paid discriminatory taxes and observed separate codes of dress and behavior.

A devout man, Umar also led his community in religious matters as well as political. Many Muslims had memorized lengthy passages of Muhammad's messages, others had been written on palm–leaves, stones, and other available materials. However, renderings could differ. Therefore Umar began the collection of an authoritative book of Muhammad's recitations: the Quran. Completed and authorized by Umar's successor as Caliph, Uthman (644–656), the original *Quran* used the *Kufic* script lacking the dots that distinguish so many Arabic letters from each other. The result, not surprisingly, was variant readings, sometimes on matters of importance between Islamic groups.

The death of Uthman at the hands of assassins revealed deep rivalries within the Muslim world, rivalries of ideology and power. His rule of a dozen years illustrated the strength of the Quraysh, Muhammad's tribe from Mecca who had nevertheless been his most aggressive adversaries. Uthman appointed many Quraysh to high office, some of them close relatives newly acquainted with Islam. Their rule created consternation among political opponents, who saw the actions

Pilgrims visiting the Ka'aba, sacred shrine of the Great Mosque in Mecca

26

undermining Muhammad's goal of a *universal Muslim community*. Their sentiments found much satisfaction in the selection of Ali as the fourth, and final, Orthodox Caliph.

Muhammad's cousin and son-in-law, Ali nevertheless entered office surrounded by suspicions that he was an accomplice to the assassination of his predecessor, Uthman. After moving his capital from Medina to Iraq, and outmaneuvered by his opponents and facing rebellion within his own supporters over his policies, Ali was murdered in 661. His major opponent, Uthman's cousin Muawiya, became Caliph in Damascus, purchasing the acquiesence of Ali's oldest son, Hasan, and established the Umayyad dynasty of caliphs.

From their capital at Damascus, the Umayyads ruled the entire Muslim world. Attacks on the Byzantine Empire were renewed; Constantinople itself came under seige in 717. In some respects Arab, rather than Muslim, in their approach to administration, the Umayyads first used the existing Coptic, Greek and Persian administrations, ranging from coinage to provincial officials. Where necessary, as in Iraq, the Umayyads ruthlessly repressed disorder and established calm, for the first time in years. Religiously, however, by opposing Ali, and especially by defeating and killing his younger son Husayn at the battle of Karbala, the Umayyads split the Muslim world into two factions. Moreover, when they sought to rule by family descent, they introduced a fatal flaw. Those who had opposed in battle Muhammad's son-in-law and shed the blood of his grandson stirred resentments that in ninety years would overwhelm their descendants.

To the strife between Ali and the Umayyads is commonly traced the origins of the major sectarian divisions in the Muslim world. In particular, as the supporters of Ali broke away to form the *Shi'a* ("Partisans" of Ali), those accepting Umayyad rule became the *Sunni*, whose name implied orthodoxy. A number of aspects set Shi'a Islam firmly apart from Sunni practice. Its followers claim that Ali's family had been marked to lead the community from the start. Therefore even the pious caliphs Abu Bakr and Umar should be cursed; the Umayyads were clearly illegitimate. More commonly, however, the Shi'a termed those God appointed over them as Imams, or leaders, who possessed special knowledge needed to guide the Muslim community. Shi'ism commonly traces a succession of Imams, beginning with Ali. To the Imams was given authoritative understanding of the Quran; only traditions used by them are considered genuine.

Beginning as a political and social protest movement among Arabs, and

Arab tribesmen water their horses

quickly spreading to the converts, Shi'ism soon included many different groups with rival interpretations and leaders. According to most Shi'a, however, the twelfth Imam disappeared in 878. While the Imam remains hidden, the law and creed would be interpreted by religious scholars as his agents. Consequently, although Shi'a Islam originally began with stress on the rulership of the family of Ali, it has evolved to allow a greater role in political affairs for the religious establishment than does Sunni Islam. In addition, it awaits the hidden Imam, the Mahdi, who will return to save humanity.

Unsympathetic Western commentators typically note two distinct beliefs of Shi'a Islam, temporary marriage and dissimulation. Despite its obvious meaning, temporary marriage need not prove brief, though it may. Instead, it established a marriage for a period contracted in advance, frequently as long as 99 years in the case of a Shi'a man who marries a Christian woman who does not convert. Dissimulation, a practice foreign to western ethics, allows, or even enjoins a Shi'a to renounce his own religion when facing persecution or difficulty.

Beyond technical differences with Sunni Islam, the Shi'a bring to religion an emotional fervency often lacking in the more rational Sunni variety. The agony and death of Husayn at the battle of Karbala are portrayed annually at the anniversary with marches and flagellation. As their own blood streams from self-inflicted wounds, the marchers feel a unity with one who suffered over one thousand three hundred years ago. For this and other reasons, to many Shi'a life on the earth is a brief interlude, and death fighting for Allah brings rapidly the joys of heaven.

The Shi'a played an important, but not exclusive, role in the overthrow of the Umayyad caliphate. After an extensive propaganda campaign concentrated among converts, in 746 rebellion broke out in the name of Abu al-Abbas, and drew support from many discontented groups in the empire. First Iran, then Iraq fell to the rebels with their standards of black, and in 750 they defeated and later almost annihilated the Umayyads. The new ruling dynasty, the Abbasid, claimed descent from Muhammad's uncle and the support of Ali's family. It ushered in a religious empire for all Muslims, in sharp contrast to the Arab kingdom of the Umayyads. Symbolizing the change, Abu al-Abbas moved the capital from Damascus to Iraq; his successor al-Mansur established the new empire along Persian rather than Arab lines, and constructed for it the magnificent capital of Baghdad. Amidst the pomp and titles, the Caliph exchanged the openness of an Arab tribal *shaykh* for an Oriental despot's glory and seclusion, complete with court executioner.

Trade and agricultural prosperity brought enormous wealth to Baghdad and its caliphs, who ruled an area larger than Alexander the Great. Products from the Indus valley reached the Atlantic coast of Morocco, all without leaving the empire, and banks developed a widespread system of checks and letters of credit. Irrigation and drainage canals in the Tigris–Euphrates valley brought prosperity to the heart of the empire, and new foods, products and technologies spread across the vast area unified by administration, religion, and increasingly, the use of Arabic. Paper making came from China, sugar from India, and the textile centers like Damascus and Musil enriched European languages as city names became synonymous with particular qualities of cloth (damask; muslin).

Under Harun al–Rashid, perhaps the most famous Abbasid caliph, Baghdad became the wealthiest city on earth. It hosted one of civilization's great intellectual flowerings. Scholars from a variety of ethnic backgrounds studied Greek and Hindu authors, advanced the sciences, especially optics and astronomy, adopted "Arabic" numerals from India, and invented algebra. Historians, geographers, and essayists wrote at length. In religion, Muslim scholars collected traditions attributed to Muhammad, and developed schools of law. Meanwhile, theologians disputed at length the role of logic in religion and the appropriate methods of interpreting the Quran.

From the moment they seized the caliphate, the Abbasids faced revolts and challenges to their rule, from disenchanted supporters, Shi'a splinter groups, and opportunists. In such a vast empire, control from the center often weakened along the fringes, where independent Muslim states arose. In Baghdad itself, power fell increasingly into the hands of the vizir, or chief minister, who eventually attempted to make the office hereditary. Generals intervened between rival caliphs to decide succession to the throne, and what little power remained eventually fell in the hands of the Turkish bodyguard. Although caliphs did remain, by the end of the tenth century they ceased to rule even nominally territory outside Iraq. Two hundred years after the Abbasids seized power, the reinvigorated Iranians and Turks, new to both Islam and the Middle East, came to dominate the Asian lands of Islam.

An artist's concept of the palace of the Umayyads in Damascus

The Barbarian Invasions

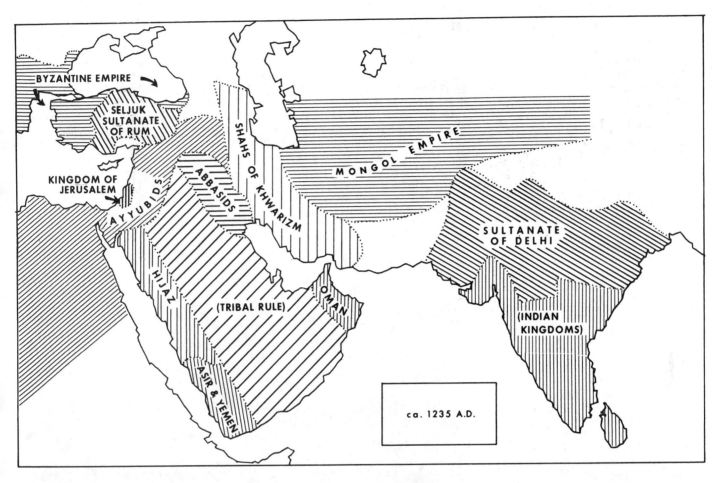

ca. 1235 A.D.

During the Middle Islamic Period (the 10th to 15th centuries A.D.; 4th to 9th centuries by the Muslim calendar) waves of invaders assaulted civilization in Southwest Asia. There was an enormous loss of human life in these invasions, as well as extensive damage to the economy. The Turkish and European inroads in this period were relatively temperate preludes to the far more destructive incursions of the Mongols and their allies.

Adventuring bands of Turks from Central Asia began arriving in Southwest Asia in the tenth century. Soon they started establishing themselves as a kind of military aristocracy, and by the 12th century various regions from Asia Minor to the Ganges River had overlords of Turkish origin. While introducing a new military fierceness into society, the Turkish rulers patronized writers, poets and learned men, especially Persians. They readily adopted Islam with their own modifications.

The rapid influx of Turks into the Tigris–Euphrates area in the 11th century led to the establishment of a vast empire stretching from Central Asia to the Syrian coast. This was ruled by Toghril, of the Seljuk (Saljuq) clan, who made himself Sultan in Baghdad in 1055 while reducing

the Abbasid Caliph to the status of a spiritual figurehead without power. A decade and a half later, one of Toghril's nephews, Alp Arslan, defeated the Byzantine army and made the emperor a prisoner. This victory opened Asia Minor to Turkish immigration; in 1078 these newcomers established the Seljuk Sultanate of Rum. (*Rum*, pronounced like "room" in English, was the Asian name for the Byzantine Empire, which was still called Rome).

Seljuk attacks on the Byzantine Empire and interference with European pilgrims to Jerusalem helped inspire the Pope in 1095 to proclaim a Holy War to recapture the Holy Land. The soldiers of the First Crusade had to fight their way through the Seljuk Sultanate of Rum in order to reach Jerusalem and wrest it from the garrison placed there by a Muslim government based in Egypt. These Europeans joined in the turmoil and warfare of the Eastern Mediterranean, inflicting and receiving great loss of life. On capturing Jerusalem in 1099, the Crusaders set about an indiscriminate massacre of Muslims and Jews, but in general they were neither more nor less cruel than their foes.

The Latin Kingdom of Jerusalem was established to govern the Holy Land. It lost Jerusalem to the Muslims under the

leadership of Salah ad–Din (Saladin) in 1187, but regained it again after his death. The Crusader kingdom finally lost the Holy City in 1244, but held coastal enclaves until near the end of the century. At times, the Crusaders had Muslim allies against other Muslim armies, so confused were the times and intense the political rivalries.

Seljuk power was not permanent, and rival Turkish leaders displaced them. In Iran, a line of rulers known as the Shahs of Khwarezm (Khwarizm) became prominent in the 12th century, but their power was too fragile to protect the region against new invaders.

Turks also established kingdoms in Buddhist and Hindu lands. Although there had been earlier Muslim raids into the Indus Valley, the main Muslim conquerors in the northern Indian Peninsula were Turks. The rival Hindu *Rajputs* (princes) were unable to provide a unified defense against the Turkish warriors.

In the second half of the 12th century, Turkish warriors led by the Sultan of Ghur wrought great destruction on Indian civilization. Their mounted archers swept down the Ganges Valley. Hindu temples were made into mosques and attempts were made to force people to convert to

29

Islam. Buddhism in its stronghold in Bihar had its monks massacred, its books burned and its temples destroyed. Buddhism was virtually extinguished and Hindu rule was ended in northern India. From that time onward, Muslim ruler and Hindu subject were always aware of belonging to different orders.

Muslim rule in India, established following the conquests by the armies from Ghur, took the form of the Sultanate of Delhi. In 1206 a Turkish general (and legally a slave) seized the opportunity created by the murder of the Sultan of Ghur and proclaimed himself Sultan of Delhi. Although hampered by frequent struggles over the succession, the Sultanate expanded, and reached its greatest extent in the early 14th century, when it ruled nearly all of the Indian Peninsula. In some ways, the Sultanate flourished, for despite severe taxation of the largely Hindu peasantry, great prosperity developed in trade and the production of textiles in Bengal, Lahore, and Kashmir. Nevertheless, decay set in rapidly, and during the later 14th century the Sultanate of Delhi ruled only Northern India.

Southwest Asia began to feel the full force of the Mongol Empire in 1219 when an army of some 100,000 led by Chingis Khan (Genghis Khan), invaded Iran. Seeking vengeance against the Shahs of Khwarezm for their early cruelty against Mongol subjects, the invading Mongols looted, destroyed and massacred as they advanced. Tens of thousands of people were slaughtered, while only the craftsmen were spared for use as slaves in Mongolia.

Part of Chingis Khan's hordes turned south to ravage the Indus Valley and Punjab. Delhi became a refuge for Muslims escaping from Mongol terror. Suddenly, for no apparent reason, the Mongol hordes turned back for the long journey home, laden with the wealth of the devastated lands through which they had passed.

Again in 1227 the Mongols and their allied hordes returned to plunder. For ten years they could not be withstood by any force in Iran or in the Tigris–Euphrates Valley. Of all the great Muslim centers of civilization, only Cairo escaped entirely unscathed and the Mamluk rulers of Egypt gained much prestige for defeating a Mongol force in Palestine. By the middle of the 13th century, much of Southwest Asia was either ruled by Mongols or paying tribute to them. However, the next generation of Mongol rulers adopted Islam. Soon the empire began to break up into small states and the way was open for another empire builder.

Claiming to be a descendant of Chingis Khan, Timur Lang (Tamerlane) looms prominently in the Mongol tradition. He rose to power in the second half of the 14th century, using a dubious devotion to Islam for his political purposes. On the one hand, he may be pictured as a fierce warrior on horseback, wielding a bloody sword as he leads his hordes of Mongols and Turks over civilized areas which have no power to resist. On the other hand, he may also quite accurately be visualized seated in a splendid palace, surrounded by poets and admiring rare works of art, in his capital at Samarkand.

Before his death in 1405, Timur conquered all of Iran and the Tigris–Euphrates Plain. He raided the leading cities of his time, including Damascus, Moscow and Delhi. Upon the last–mentioned, he poured such destruction that a century was required for it to recover. In the very last years of his life, he defeated the rising Ottoman Empire in battle, took its Sultan prisoner and seized control of Asia Minor. Using the wealth of his vast domains, Timur made Samarkand a center of civilization.

Timur's successors ruled a smaller territory until near the end of the 15th century. They presided over a mixed Turkish–Mongol–Iranian culture which created many masterpieces of art and literature. With the end of the invasions of Central Asia hordes, a new order could take shape.

Gustave Doré's drawing of the Crusaders storming the walls of Antioch in 1098 on their way to liberate Jerusalem from the Muslims

The Safavid, Ottoman and Mogul Empires

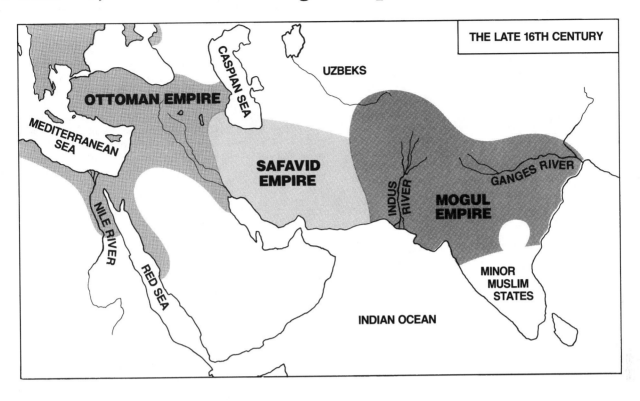

In many ways, Islamic civilization reached its height in the 16th century. Vigorous and ambitious, its religion and rulers dominated southern and western Asia, southeastern Europe, and all North Africa. It also swept south across the Sahara and through the savanna as far as the fringes of the rainforest. The caliphate, by now only an empty title in Cairo, failed to unite the Muslim world, and numerous independent Muslim states existed along the fringes. Nevertheless, the heart of the Muslim world divided into three major Islamic empires, each centers of an important culture.

In the middle, centered on the Iranian Plateau, the Safavid Empire split the Muslim world, for its strongly Shi'a Islam contrasted with the Sunni views both in the Mogul Empire in India and the Safavid's bitter rival to the west, the Ottoman Empire.

The provinces of Iran had witnessed numerous struggles for power after the rapid collapse of Timur's empire, especially among the Turkmen tribes of the north and west. In 1503, Ismail Safavi, a youth merely sixteen years old but hereditary leader of a Shi'a religious order, proclaimed himself Shah and Shi'ism the sole religion. Offering all the choice between conversion to Shi'ism or death, Ismail rapidly united the Iranian peasantry, urban classes and Turkish warriors into a new society and state. In time, Iranian civilians replaced warriors in the administration and central authority replaced

mystical adoration of Shah Ismail as the basis of government.

From its very beginning, the Safavid state struggled with the Ottoman Empire to the West, for it appealed to Turkish tribesmen with Shi'a leanings. Nevertheless, in battle the swords, arrows, and light firearms of Shah Ismail's warriors proved no match against Ottoman muskets and artillery. After losing much of Asia Minor, and then Iraq, the Safavids in the seventeenth century accepted a border between Iran and Iraq that largely remained until this century.

In retrospect, Shah Ismail attacked the Ottoman Empire during the zenith of its 600–year–long history. It began inconspicuously around 1299, when a Turkish warrior named Osman (Arabic *Uthman;* to Europeans, *Ottoman*) proclaimed himself sultan in northwestern Asia Minor. Welcoming all who would fight Byzantium, he allied his dynasty with *Sufi* brotherhoods and merchant guilds, and adopted Byzantine administrative techniques. Steadily the Ottoman forces advanced against Christian Byzantium. By the middle of the 14th century, permanent forces had replaced mere raiding groups across the Bosphorus, isolating Constantinople. The capital itself lingered for nearly a century, spared by Timur's crushing defeat of the Ottomans in Anatolia (Asia Minor). Finally, in 1453, Sultan Mehmet II massed his armies against the Byzantine capital and captured it, ending a millennium this "Rome" had ruled Eastern Christendom.

Under its Turkish name, Istanbul, the city flourished as the Ottoman capital. Sultans and leading officials adorned the city with palaces and mosques, changing the skyline. Meanwhile, the conquests continued; a century later, the Balkans conquered, Ottoman troops unsuccessfully attacked Vienna.

The Ottoman Empire drew its strengths from many sources. To the uncommon valor and wisdom of the first ten sultans must be added the willingness to adopt new skills and technology. The *devshirme,* in effect a tax on Christians paid in young boys who were enslaved and educated into Islam, provided both soldiers for a standing army and administrators single-minded in devotion to the Sultan and lacking family loyalty. Financially, conquests in Europe produced great loot and tribute; in turn they enabled further aggression against Christian states. Only after two hundred years did the sultans attempt significant conquest of Muslim territories. Then, under Selim I (1512–1520) dramatic conquests brought under Ottoman rule much of Anatolia and Iraq, as well as Syria, Palestine and Egypt. Under Suleyman I ("Suleiman the Magnificent"), known to his subjects as "The Lawgiver", the empire reached the height of its power and grandeur.

In contrast, by the 17th century the Ottoman Empire illustrated many signs of decay. At first Austria, then Poland and Russia pushed back the Sultan's armies in the Balkans, recapturing Hungary and

31

"The Golden Horn"—Constantinople in yesteryear

parts of Yugoslavia. In the Mediterranean, the Ottoman navy had suffered decisive defeat. Within the empire, anarchy spread as local administrators attempted to maintain their positions, and the sale of offices became a regular practice. The *devshirme* collapsed, and troops garrisoned in many cities rebelled. Although the capable Korprulu family *vizirs* restored administration, the Ottomans increasingly lagged behind Europe in scientific pursuits and modern learning, with unsurprising consequences for military technology. As the center of world trade shifted to the Atlantic following the discovery of the New World and sailing routes to India, the Ottoman Empire increasingly stag-nated economically as well. If diplomacy and European rivalries slowed the loss of territory, the descent nevertheless seemed certain to most observers.

A Muslim Empire in India

The Mogul Empire did not rise immediately out of the ruins of the Sultanate of Delhi which had ended with a period of peace, prosperity and construction of public works, such as new irrigation canals and dams. The last important ruler let authority slip into the hands of local officials. This meant that there was no unified resistance to the hordes led by Timur Lang into the Indus–Ganges basin in 1398. Some 90,000 horsemen killed and looted without restraint, and it is said that when Timur's army returned to Samarkand, there was not a man who

did not take at least twenty Indians home as slaves.

So complete was Timur's destruction of the Sultanate of Delhi that another great state did not arise in the area until the Mogul Empire was founded in about 1525. In the interim, a number of kingdoms with Muslim rulers flourished. These sultans, mainly of Turkish origin, were in general more tolerant of the culture of their Hindu subjects than the sultans of Delhi had been. Learning and the arts developed a distinctive style in this period of Islamic history in the Indian Peninsula.

The only Hindu state during the period was Vijayanagar, a name meaning "City of Victory," located on the southern tip of the Peninsula. For some two centuries after its establishment just before the middle of the 14th century, Vijayanagar defended itself against Muslim encroachment from the north and carried on Hindu cultural and artistic traditions. The combined forces of three Muslim states in the central plateau of the Peninsula finally defeated Vijayanagar in 1565 after its aged ruler was unexpectedly captured in battle and beheaded. The city of Vijayanagar was sacked by Muslim forces while many Hindus and their temples were destroyed. The fall of this state marked the end of Hindu political power.

Just after 1500, a new Islamic state was founded in Afghanistan by Babur, an adventurer from Turkistan far to the north. Barely twenty years old, and a man of taste and letters as well as the power to

unite his soldiers, he claimed descent from Timur and thus the right to rule as king. Mongol by proclamation, but Turkish in race, his dynasty nevertheless became known as the Mogul or Mughal. Invited to the plains between the Indus and the Ganges by disaffected local chiefs willing to replace their own king with another, beginning in 1524 Babur invaded northern India. His army, small in size but compact and united, possessed two great advantages: unequalled cavalry, and superior cannon from Turkey. In 1526, in a single great battle outside Delhi, he destroyed the enemy military, comprised mostly of Turkish and Afghan foreigners like himself. No national movement resisted his advance, and he found himself master of a personal domain across the plains of northern India as far east as the borders of Bengal.

Plunged into disorder on the early death of Babur, the Mogul Empire finally took shape under his grandson, Akbar. Only thirteen when he came to the throne, Akbar proved a superb general, moving armies rapidly and conquering all but the southern quarter of India. Much more than a soldier, however, Akbar established stable government that would last a century. He reached beyond mere military power to become the accepted ruler of most of India, most importantly by incorporating the Rajput chiefs, though Hindu, as governors and military commanders. Indeed, he even married a Rajput princess. As a result, the Hindu community largely accepted Akbar's empire as their own. Open-minded in religious matters, he welcomed Zoroastrians and Jesuits to his court as well as Hindus and Muslims; there was also an attempt to develop an eclectic cult centered on himself.

His successors lacked both his power and his wisdom; the empire inevitably declined. The decay came gradually, and the Moguls sponsored learning through libraries and schools, and in art perfected a distinctive fusion of Persian and Hindu styles in the Taj Mahal. However, the sixth Mogul ruler, Aurangzab (1658–1707) proved a zealous Muslim whose limited toleration of non–Muslims increased Hindu dissatisfaction and contrasted sharply with the policies of Akbar. A man of battle for much of his long reign, Aurangzab attempted to unite all India, fighting Muslim states as well as Hindu ones in the south. By the time of his death, the merchant vanguard of the next wave of foreign invaders of India had appeared, not in the traditional invasion route in the northwest, but in important ports along the coasts. After decades of disorder, British rule would replace Mogul, though the dynasty nominally ruled in Delhi until abolished by the British in 1857.

European Expansion into the Indian Ocean

Until the end of the 15th century, the direct routes from Europe to the East and its lucrative trade were blocked by the Ottoman Empire and Egypt. Europeans finally overcame the obstacle by outflanking the Muslims entirely, sailing boldly around the southern tip of Africa. When the Portuguese navigator Vasco da Gama reached the Indian Ocean by this route, his tiny fleet opened up a new era. First, only patterns of trade were altered, but in later centuries the total political organization of Southwest Asia was affected. Aggressive Europeans, possessing increasingly superior weapons and better–trained soldiers, gradually made themselves masters of the vast region.

When the first Portuguese reached the Indian Ocean in 1498, they sought only to monopolize sea trade, not to rule a land empire. By 1509 they had put an end to Arab seapower. Portugal then began building a maritime empire. Alfonso Albuquerque, who had become governor of the Portuguese settlements in India in 1509, carried forward the program of building forts at strategic locations on the coasts of India, Persia, Arabia and Africa. His fleet also continued to prevent native ships from carrying items so profitable in European markets. His nation thus gained almost a monopoly on trade in these goods, and required their transport in Portuguese ships, in keeping with the economic theory of mercantilism. Albuquerque on occasion treated with extreme cruelty rebellious subjects or Asian merchants attempting to compete with the Portuguese monopoly.

For over a century the Portuguese remained the chief traders across the Indian Ocean. By concentrating their activities on the sea and a few ports in regions without strong governments, they did not affect significantly the history of the nations of Asia, though colonies in East Africa eventually spread inland. By the end of the 16th century, however, other Europeans, eager for a share of the trade, began forcing their way into the Indian Ocean. Later, in 1650, the Portuguese position further declined after evacuation of the Arabian port of Masqat (Muscat) with accompanying loss of control of the Persian Gulf.

The 17th century belonged predominantly to Dutch merchants and sea power. They left less of a mark on Southwest Asia than had the Portuguese traders, for the Dutch preoccupation was with the spice lands farther east. The 18th century was characterized by rivalry between French and British interests seeking control of India and the approaches to it. In the end, Britain dislodged France from all but a few small enclaves, similar to those retained by Portugal.

The governments of the Netherlands, France and Britain played only secondary roles in this commercial expansion. Companies chartered by the respective kings were the leading agents. The Dutch East India Company, chartered in 1602, achieved remarkable success. With fortified trading depots at two places in Sri Lanka (Ceylon) and a number on the coasts of southern India and Southeast Asia, the company flourished during the 17th century. With aid from the strong Dutch fleet, it captured the spice trade from Portugal, despite British and French competition. When the demand for Asian spices fell, it encouraged the production of coffee, tea, and cocoa. Over two hundred years, its annual dividends reportedly averaged 18%.

The British East India Company, chartered in 1600, became even more important, both as one of the first permanent joint–stock companies and in the English company allowed in the region, it received authority to administer government where it operated. Concentrating on India, while the Dutch withdrew to the Spice Islands (Indonesia), the British East India Company established itself first at Surat on the west coast of India, with the Mogul permission. Surat rapidly developed into the most prosperous trading center in the country. Later posts followed at Bombay, Madras, and Calcutta, each to become a center of British influence. The East India Company traded especially in indigo, saltpeter, textiles and spices, often purchasing goods of greater value from India than it could sell there, and supplying silver to make up the difference.

During the 18th century the French Company of the East Indies (founded 1664) slowly emerged as the chief European rival to the British East India Company in both commerce and political influence. When the two nations fought in Europe, competition between the two companies became military in India. The British East India Company won the struggle and limited French influence to several small ports, which only rejoined India after independence.

The Creation of the British Raj

George III (1738–1820)

A consistent theme in the history of the Middle East and South Asia from the late 18th century until 1947 was the expansion and strengthening of British colonial rule, often described by the Hindi and Urdu word "Raj", meaning "sway" or "rule." Beginning in Bengal, in eastern India around 1750, its encroachment elsewhere often followed the desire to protect existing possessions and trade routes.

By the mid–18th century, India lay ripe for foreign intervention. In the north, the Mogul Empire had reached a state of advanced decay, both in quality of rule and defeats by Indian and foreign enemies. Particularly threatening were the Marathas, a Hindu people adept at warfare and distinguished by their own language. They lived along the western coast and in central India, but spread across the sub–continent. In a series of wars with the Mogul Empire they exhausted its resources, but in the process the Maratha kingdom itself broke up into a loose confederation of states. While they dominated central India, they failed to establish firm central government. Henceforth the Marathas became raiders known for their rapacity and ruthlessness, plundering widely and feared by Hindus as much as by Muslims.

Then, in 1739, the Persian ruler Nadir Shah captured Delhi, plundering the treasury and Peacock Throne, and massacring the city's inhabitants. In a little more than a decade, it was the Afghan army's turn. Finally, in 1761, the Maratha army attempted to stop a renewed Afghan invasion in a battle near Delhi. The decisive defeat of the Marathas and the deaths of many of their leaders appeared to place India within the Afghan king's grasp. At this crucial moment, his troops mutinied. Thus India broke up into many smaller states, divided and lacking in direction just when Europeans sought control.

Learning from its French rival, by the 1740s the British East India company began to strike alliances with Indian rulers. Its weapons included interfering with the succession of Indian princes and bribery. Granting military aid to favorites often proved very effective, for European weapons and techniques increasingly outpaced local ones. With the Company's victory at Plassey in 1757, it effectively conquered Bengal, and British territorial rule began in India.

Circumstances encouraged the British domain to expand. Native attacks on Indian allies led to the retaliation and conquest. War with France in Europe led to conquest in India. Reports of great wealth in the hands of native rulers encouraged Company officials to conquer. That they succeeded so easily also was the result of the caliber of a number of Company officials who possessed the vision of conquest along with exceptional talents and freedom to operate. However, their harsh treatment of the Indian populations led to interference by Parliament in London, culminating in the India Act of 1784. This placed British rule in India under a governor–general, appointed not by the Company, but by the British government. Ironically, it was Lord Cornwallis, loser of Britain's American colonies at the Battle of Yorktown, who preserved those in India as the new governor–general.

Imperial Rule: The British Raj at Its Height—and Fall

Warfare against Napoleon, in Egypt and in Europe, combined with circumstances in India to encourage the last great expansion of British rule. The British conquests were swift. In hardly more than twenty years after 1795, large territories fell: Mysore and Hyderabad in the south, the Marathas in the center, and finally the remaining Rajput states in the west. British India more than doubled in size, and unity of the peninsula within its natural boundaries became an appealing goal. Unity would end foreign intrigue and permit British commercial expansion at minimal defense costs. Moreover, ending the virtual state of anarchy in parts of India would bring peace to the inhabitants. The East India Company had traded with Indians for a century and a half before warring with them; for almost another century and a half the British would rule India.

The British Raj brought many advantages, including peace after the ravages of lengthy wars. Physically the country changed with the construction of harbors, railroads, and irrigation projects. Colleges and universities educated an Indian elite in science and medicine, and the administration became more regular and less arbitrary. *Suttee*, the practice of burning widows on the funeral pyres of their husbands, was banned. In general, though, the British granted religious toleration in areas they ruled directly, and in the many princely states allowed traditional dynasties to continue, whether Muslim or Hindu.

On the other hand, much was not well. Indian handicrafts suffered from cheap cloth manufactured in England. Each improvement in transportation rendered the competition worse, while British policies retarded the development of Indian industry. High taxes rendered the peasants impoverished tenants, and few schools served the masses. Moreover, in Indian eyes British rule involved westernization to an unsettling degree, and in 1857 the introduction of rifle cartridges greased with animal fat offended Muslim troops (over lard) as well as Hindu (over cows' grease). The Indian Mutiny of 1857–58, at times savage and repressed sternly, brought the attention of London and reforms. The East India Company, long stripped of its trade monopoly, was dissolved. The British Raj now meant authority lay with Parliament and monarch in England.

Possession of India encouraged further British imperial expansion, for both strategic and commercial purposes. After the defeat of Napoleon in 1815, Britain's great European rival became Tsarist Russia, whose expansion towards both India and the Middle East seemed threatening. Recognizing that the traditional invaders' route to India came from the northwest, British officials extended their rule in that direction, adding the Punjab and Kashmir, then later Baluchistan (bordering Iran), and finally the North–west Frontier Province (1901). By then, only a thin, very mountainous portion of Afghanistan separated Russia from India, but in three different wars the Afghans proved far easier to influence than to conquer. Afghanistan became, in effect, a buffer state for India, as did Bhutan, Sikkim and (much earlier) Nepal (1816). Another direction of British expansion from India lay to the east, and Burma became a province of India in 1886.

Commercial conquests took place in the west. A naval force from India in 1820 forced Bahrain and rulers in Trucial Oman (now the United Arab Emirates) to recognize British authority. In the latter case, the British strongly desired to end trade in slaves and raids on shipping. At the other end of the Arabian Peninsula, British forces seized the port of Aden in 1839. Administered by the Government of India, it became an important coaling station for British ships.

Far greater British attention turned to the Middle East as a consequence of developments in Egypt. The Nile Valley produced fine cotton needed by the mills of Britain and in Egypt cotton provided government revenues. The ambition and determination of Muhammad Ali (1811–1847) so threatened the Ottoman Empire that it required careful European

Victoria (1819–1901)
First Empress of India

diplomacy, and on occasion Great Power military action to maintain the Ottoman Sultans. Under Muhammad Ali's successors, Egypt also provided an opportunity for European loans, to the ruler as well as to ordinary farmers. Finally, as overlord of the Sudan, Egypt inevitably played an active role in attempts to eliminate the slave trade from Africa.

Each of these reasons for British involvement, however, seems inconsequential beside the construction of the Suez Canal on French initiative. Already British passengers to India had reduced the long journey around Africa by using overland transportation across Egypt to the Red Sea. The canal, by enabling vessels and heavy freight to use the route, quickly became "the lifeline to India". British strategic policy in the region focused on the canal, and the Egyptian shares in the Suez Canal Company were purchased. When Egypt nevertheless went bankrupt and both anti–European riots and a nationalist uprising broke out, British troops landed in 1882 and restored order, defeating nationalist troops. Lightly disguised by diplomatic formalities and the almost total withdrawal of British troops, Egypt became a sphere of British influence though nominally part of the Ottoman Empire.

Its conquests during World War I brought the British Raj to its greatest extent in the Middle East and South Asia. When the Ottoman Empire entered the war as a German ally, Britain quickly annexed Egypt and Cyprus. Shortly thereafter, troops from India landed in southern Iraq, and despite setbacks began the slow conquest of that land. After repulsing Ottoman Turkish attacks on the Suez Canal, British, Australian, and Indian

troops moved forward from Egypt into Palestine, capturing Jerusalem in 1917. When Ottoman Turkey appealed for peace in October 1918, these forces and their Arab allies had captured all of Syria as well. From the Nile to the Ganges, and between the Mediterranean and China, no European power rivaled British influence. British goals dominated the postwar assignment of mandates of Syria and Lebanon to France and Palestine and Iraq to Britain.

Nevertheless, as the Raj reached its greatest extent, the forces of its future downfall became evident. In Egypt the 1919 Nationalist Revolution led to the creation of an autonomous kingdom three years later. Arab nationalism, the ideology of only a handful of people in the Ottoman provinces of 1912, spread rapidly with the imposition of European mandates by force of arms in Syria and Iraq, as well as Zionist immigration into Palestine. In Iran, popular opposition blocked an attempt to establish a veiled British protectorate, and Afghanistan undertook its "War of Independence." In India, nationalism had showed itself a potent force, and its repression at Amritsar produced one thousand dead and wounded. Under the leadership of Mohandas Gandhi, the struggle for self-determination was becoming effective.

Thus from west to east the British Raj tottered seriously in 1919–1920. Twenty-five years later the Second World War left Britain, though armed with weapons of greater sophistication than ever before, too enfeebled to maintain the empire. In 1947 the Raj formally ended for India, though ironically continuing for another generation on the fringes of Arabia, where formal British intervention always had been smaller.

George VI (1895–1952)
Last Emperor of India

The Kingdom of Bahrain

The Kingdom of Bahrain

Area: 231 square miles (598 sq. km.).

Population: 660,000, including 150,000 expatriates.

Capital City: Manama (Pop. 340,000, estimated).

Climate: Extremely hot and humid except for a short, moderate winter. There is very little rainfall.

Neighboring Countries: Saudi Arabia (West); Qatar (Southeast).

Time Zone: GMT +3.

Official Language: Arabic.

Other Principal Tongues: English and Persian.

Ethnic Background: About 75% Bahraini and other Arab, with Indians, Iranians, and Pakistanis forming the largest groups of foreign workers.

Principal Religion: Islam, about 60% *Shi'a* and 40% *Sunni.*

Chief Commercial Products: Petroleum products, aluminum, ship repairs, liquid natural gas, financial services and transportation services.

Major Trading Partners: Saudi Arabia, United Arab Emirates, Japan, U.K., U.S. and Singapore.

Currency: Bahrain Dinar (1 BD = $2.65).

Former Colonial Status: British Protectorate (1861–1971).

Independence Date: August 15, 1971.

Chief of State: Hamad bin Isa Al–Khalifa, King.

Head of Government: Sheikh Khalifa bin Salman Al-Khalifa, Prime Minister.

National Flag: A serration divides a white band at the pole from the remaining field of solid red. Since Bahrain became a kingdom in 2002, its flag has a gold crown.

Gross Domestic Product (GDP): $5.4 billion.

GDP per capita: between $8,900 (IMF) and $13,000.

The land of two seas, as its name implies in Arabic, Bahrain consists of a group of islands located off the coast of Arabia between the Gulf of Bahrain and the Persian (Arab) Gulf. The main island, some 30 miles long and ten miles wide, is largely desert, but springs fed by sources originating on the mainland water some gardens and groves near the northern coast. By decision of the International Court of Justice, the island of Hawar near the Qatar coast also forms part of the country.

History: Bahrain's long history stretches back as far as Dilmun, a prosperous trading center that flourished some 4,000 years ago. Well placed to trade between Iraq and India, Bahrain played a role in Arab trade during the Middle Ages, and the inhabitants became Muslims. The Portuguese conquest of the 1500s led in turn to Persian rule, but in 1783 the Arabian Al–Khalifa family, which had earlier established itself at Zubara on the Qatar

coast, conquered Bahrain mainly to gain control of its valuable pearl fishing industry. In a series of treaties beginning in 1820, rulers of this family allied themselves more closely with Bahrain, on occasion seeking British aid against local threats. In 1861 it became a protectorate of Britain, and by 1913 that imperial power had gained control of Bahrain's defense, foreign relations and natural resources. In return, Britain promised protection to the rulers.

During and after World War II, Bahrain provided Britain's main naval and military bases in the Gulf, and the headquarters of the British Political Resident in the Persian Gulf was moved there in 1946. From 1926 until 1957 Sir Charles Belgrave, as personal advisor to the ruler, directed the modernization of the state's administration and economy. During that period Bahrain led the Gulf states in development, but the inability of the citizens to participate in government created unrest. The most serious demonstrations occurred in 1956 and were suppressed with the aid of British troops. Bahrain became independent in 1971 when Britain withdrew its forces from all the Gulf states, and Bahrain decided not to join the United Arab Emirates.

In 1981 security forces discovered a plot by the *Islamic Front for the Liberation of Bahrain* to overthrow the government. The *Front* represented a renewal of Iran's long-standing interest in influencing Bahrain, this time inspired by Islamic Revolutionaries who wished to export their ideas. Success would have been particularly gratifying because the deposed Shah had abandoned Iran's claims to the island after an internationally monitored plebiscite. Because a majority of the indigenous population is Shi'a, the police and intelligence services—themselves often employing foreigners—remained on the alert for subversive activity. In the late 1980s members of the outlawed *Bahraini National Liberation Front* were sentenced to prison, and police foiled a plot directed at oil installations. By the 1990s, Iranian sympathy with opposition movements was largely lim-ited to refuge, funds and propaganda.

A dispute with Qatar long simmered over Hawar Island and several adjacent reefs and sandbanks valued for fishing rights as well as potential oil riches. Bahrain also claimed Zubara, on the Qatari peninsula, on the grounds it had been the ancestral home of the ruling Khalifa family. The dispute threatened hostilities when Qatari troops arrested workmen building a Bahraini coast guard station on a disputed reef. Saudi mediation defused the crisis by gaining the release of the men, at the cost to Bahrain of demolishing the construction. The rival claims also led the two emirates to acquire similar military hardware, although the few thousand troops on either side were incapable of launching a concerted attack on the other.

In 1995, Qatar successfully appealed to the International Court of Justice to rule on the rival claims. Its ruling in 2001 granted Bahrain Hawar Island, but rejected the claim to Zubara. Both countries agreed to accept the decision.

When Iraq seized Kuwait in 1990, Bahrain's government joined with other GCC states in condemning the invasion and supporting the multinational force. During the Gulf War that followed, Bahrain provided airbases and ports for US and British forces. An Iraqi missile apparently aimed at Bahrain fell short, and landed harmlessly in the sea. Far greater damage was inflicted by the massive oil spill released by Iraq during the fighting. It directly threatened water intakes for drinking water and industrial use, and if unchecked threatened long–term devastation of the local fishing industry.

Resentment over the lack of personal rights and political freedoms led 14 prominent Sunni and Shi'a Bahrainis to petition in 1994 for the reinstatement of the 1975 constitution (see politics). The government responded firmly, arresting a Shi'a cleric, Sheikh Ali Salman, for distributing pro–democracy leaflets and later deporting him and other clerics who preached democracy. Several hundreds were arrested, including women. Demonstrations

His Majesty Hamad bin Isa Al-Khalifa

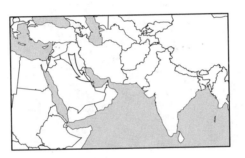

alternated with repression, and in 1996 a wave of protests left thirty dead, including police.

Ominously, the discontent became strongest among the Shi'a majority, whose resentment was fueled by their perceptions of poverty, unemployment, lower-class standing and discrimination. Behind the Shi'a demands, Prime Minister Khalifa bin Sulman particularly discerned "outside meddling" (code for Iran). Despite a minor cabinet reshuffle, riots and sabotage continued, along with hundreds of arrests. The regime chose not to concede reforms that might divide moderate democrats from radical Islamists.

When Sheikh Hamad ascended to power in 1999 on the death of his father, Sheikh Isa, hopes rose that calm might be restored. The new ruler released Sheikh Abdul Amir al-Jamri, a major opposition figure, and acted to increase employment. The following year he appointed several women and a Jew to the *Majlis al-Shura* (Consultative Council). Under the slogan "Building a New Bahrain," he proposed a referendum on a "National Charter," a proposal to bring democracy and constitutional monarchy to the island.

Sheikh Hamad's proposals initially aroused suspicions. The exiled Bahrain Freedom Movement considered the proposed parliament weak and opposed any

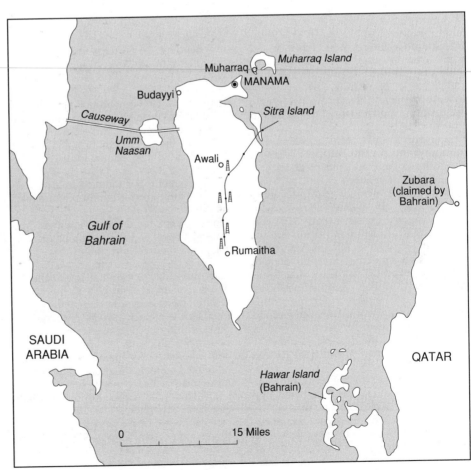

King Fahd Causeway leading to ...

The lower house has the power to dismiss ministers and approve laws, though not to form cabinets from its members; the appointed executive will remain strong, American style. Nevertheless, its parliament will symbolize Bahrain's transition from traditional family rule to the most democratic Arab state on the Gulf.

Culture: The country's first written constitution, made public in 1973, proclaims Bahrain to be an Islamic state. A majority of Bahrainis are *Shi'a* Muslims (see Iran: Culture for details). The remaining 40% of the people, including the ruling family, are *Sunni*. Bahrain's culture is not generally distinct from that found in other Arab states bordering on the Gulf.

Bahrain has a relatively high literacy rate with universal education for all children. In addition to teacher–training colleges and various institutes, the Gulf University was established in Bahrain, sponsored by the smaller states of the Gulf. With facilities larger than its enrollment, it became a refuge for faculty and students from Kuwait who fled the Iraqi occupation.

Some of the largest prehistoric burial grounds have been discovered on the main island, with some 80,000 mounds covering as much as 5% of the island. The country hopes to interest tourists in these remains, as well as the National Museum, opened in 1989, the Gold Souq (market), portrayals of Arab nomadic lifestyle, and water sports along the coast.

Economy: As in the case of most other states bordering the Gulf, petroleum played a major role in the development of modern Bahrain. Its deposits of oil, developed earlier than those of its neighbors, enabled it to begin exports in 1934. However, the country's reserves of oil remain small, and now mostly meet domestic needs. In 1996 Saudi Arabia allocated its revenues from a shared off–shore field. Oil thus remains vitally important directly, as well for revenues from the important oil refinery.

Recognizing its limited petroleum reserves, Bahrain has attempted to diversify its economy away from dependence on crude oil. Government policies encourage companies to invest, including low–interest loans, duty–free imports of raw materials and machinery, and personal and corporate tax waivers. The results are an economy much less dependent on oil than most Arab states of the Gulf. Government plans call for the expansion of small and medium-sized industries, in part to absorb a workforce growing rapidly as young Bahrainis born in the prosperity of the 1980s seek jobs. Fishing employs only small numbers, and agriculture faces an uncertain future because water from the aquifer used for irrigation is turning brackish.

Oldest among its major industries, Bahrain's large oil refinery processes Saudi

referendum as long as hundreds men and some women remained imprisoned or exiled for political offenses. It therefore called for an opposition boycott. However, for reasons subject to considerable speculation, Sheikh Hamad responded to the criticism by promising real power for parliament. *Even before the referendum* he pardoned about 1,000 political prisoners, including some convicted of arson and other crimes of violence.

In an atmosphere of euphoria, most Bahraini men and women chose to vote on the National Charter in early 2001 and granted it overwhelming (98%) support. Subsequently, Sheikh Khalifa, the prime minister and reputed opponent of democracy, suspended the notorious State Security Laws, which had permitted detention without trial. The pace of reforms continues, with elections for regional councils in May 2002, when women were allowed as candidates, and the date for parliamentary elections moved ahead from 2004 to October 2002.

Another reform during the same year promoted Sheikh Hamad from hereditary prince to king. Any domestic reasons for the change seemed somewhat obscure because the ruling family gained neither wealth nor power. But the Kingdom of Bahrain thus set itself apart from the emirates around the Gulf, not all of them

independent. So perhaps more mattered than being titled "Your Majesty" instead of "Your Highness".

Politics: The 1973 constitution provided for a National Assembly composed of an appointed cabinet and 30 elected members. However, the first assembly was dissolved in 1975 after the prime minister complained that it interfered with the workings of government. For the next quarter century, the Emir and his family held the reins of power and ruled somewhat benevolently, except for the imprisonment and alleged torture of political opponents during political unrest and rioting.

Sheikh Isa bin Salman appointed 30 "elite and loyal men" to form a new council, the *Majlis al-Shura*, in early 1993. Composed of wealthy merchants or leaders of important families, the council initially provided the Emir with advice. Soon after he came to power, Sheikh Hamad enlarged the *Majlis* and broadened its membership. By appointing a woman, he changed its character from an exclusive men's club.

The National Charter approved in 2001 envisages a two-house legislature, with an elected lower house and an appointed upper house, the *Majlis al-Shura*. True to culture, women may line up to vote separately from men, but they are enfranchised and may also run for parliament.

Arabian crude as well as local production for export. Abundant natural gas deposits provide energy for the region's largest aluminum smelter, Aluminium Bahrain, which opened in 1972. Later expansion projects increased capacity to 500,000 tons in 1997, the largest plant outside Russia. Other firms process some of the output locally.

The smelter processes imported bauxite, and supplies East Asia and the Middle East, but exports to the European Union face special tariffs. Recent discoveries of bauxite in Saudi Arabia and Sudan raise the possibility of using supplies from the Arab world.

After years of modest operations, the Arab Shipbuilding and Repair drydock began to flourish after the end of the Iran–Iraq war in 1988, with increases of 50% in the number of ships repaired annually. Formerly shipping companies and their insurers had sought to remove damaged tankers as quickly as possible from the zone of conflict.

The cease–fire and general economic recovery in the Gulf also helped to halt the decline in offshore banking operations (those dealing with the accounts of people living elsewhere) that had dropped from 92 units to 57. Financial services also seemed set to play a more important role in the local and regional economy, with the opening of a stock exchange in 1989 that initially listed 30 companies, mostly in banking and insurance. However, in 1990 the Iraqi invasion of Kuwait again threatened the stability of the region, and prosperity for financial institutions again receded as cautious depositors moved funds out of the Middle East.

The construction of a 17–mile (27 km.) causeway connecting Bahrain with Saudi Arabia offered other opportunities for development. Over one million people used the causeway in the first year after its opening in late 1986, most of them weekend tourists from Saudi Arabia, coming as families and interested in shopping and amusement parks. They doubled hotel occupancy rates, although many of the service jobs thus created seem undignified to the island's citizens.

Prospects of encouraging tourism from Japan, Europe, and North America improved with the cease–fire in the Iran–Iraq war in 1988 and expansion of the airport. However, although Bahrain permits the (highly taxed) importation of liquor, tourists could easily upset conservative Muslims, and strengthen the influence of Western lifestyles and entertainment. From a practical standpoint, too, non–Arab tourism requires simple and rapid immigration procedures and inexpensive air fares, both now lacking. Most of all, of course, tourism requires political stability in the region—something far beyond the control of Bahrain.

With prospects of limited oil and water supplies, and a young population rapidly joining the labor force, unemployment is expected to rise significantly during coming years among Bahrain's youth. Although about 60% of the existing workforce is foreign, many of the jobs they perform will hardly attract Bahrain's ambitious and generally well–educated youth.

The Future: Bahrain's long-term economic success depends on peace with its neighbors, further diversification, and competitive firms in its traditional industries of refining and ship repair. Prosperity also demands Bahrainis becoming willing to accept employment in areas

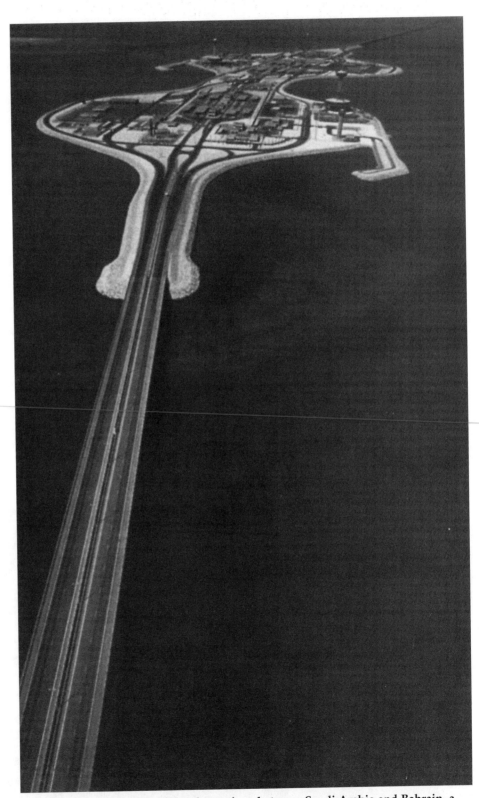

. . . Immigration Island with border stations between Saudi Arabia and Bahrain, a bank, restaurant and mosque.

Courtesy: CALTEX Petroleum Corporation

traditionally considered beneath their dignity and left for foreigners.

Greater economic development requires an educated workforce, and educated populations eventually desire civil rights and freedoms. Relatively young and a military man, Sheikh Hamad has already made very difficult choices toward achieving democracy. Despite antagonism from suspicious extremists who demand more concessions and from traditionalists opposing those already granted, Sheikh Hamad has initiated far-reaching changes in his first two years as ruler, and the pace continues. The Arab march to democracy is increasing its speed where younger rulers have recently come to power. For the moment at least, Bahrain enjoys a rare period of optimism and unity: is it establishing a possible pattern for its traditional ally, Saudi Arabia?

Sultan of Oman Qaboos Bin Said (Rt) and Hamad Al-Khalifah of Bahrain

Courtesy: Embassy of Saudi Arabia

Bahrain

Courtesy: Embassy of Saudi Arabia

The Republic of Cyprus

Marketwoman in Nicosia: "Try these luscious grapes!"

Photo by George Tsappas

Area: 3,572 square miles (9,251 sq. km.), the third largest island in the Mediterranean.

Population: 670,000 Greeks; roughly 200,000 Turks.

Capital City: Lefkosia (Pop. 160,000, estimated).

Climate: Rainfall is usually moderate, but periodic droughts may be severe. Summers are usually hot, humid on the coasts, dry inland; winters are mild, except in the mountains.

Neighboring Countries: The island lies 40 miles from the southern coast of Turkey and 65 miles west of the Syrian coast.

Time Zone: GMT +2.

Official Languages: Greek and Turkish. English is widely used.

Ethnic Background: The people are divided by language and tradition into Greeks (about 78%); Turks (about 18%); Armenian and other (about 4%).

Principal Religions: Most Greek Cypriots profess Greek Orthodox Christianity; most Turkish Cypriots profess *Sunni* Islam, but tiny religious minorities also are found.

Chief Commercial Products: Grapes, citrus fruits, potatoes, carob beans, and grain. Copper and iron are no longer significant exports, but light manufacturing has expanded rapidly, including textiles, shoes, and food products.

Major Trading Partners: U.K., Italy, Greece, Japan, Germany, Lebanon, France, U.S. and Saudi Arabia.

Currency: (£ Cyp. = $1.69)

Former Dependent Status: British Colony (1925–1960).

Independence Date: August 16, 1960.

National Day October 1; November 15 (Turkish Republic)

Chief of State: Glafcos Clerides, President. Rauf Denktash is president of the Turkish republic.

National Flag: White field with outline map of the island in rich gold above two sprigs of green leaves. The Turkish Cypriot flag has two horizontal red bars, and between them a red crescent, on a white field.

GDP per capita: $11,900 (IMF); $13,600 (government). Estimates of $4,500 for Turkish Cypriots may be generous.

Gross Domestic Product: $9.1 billion (official estimate, 2000).

Cyprus is generally a pleasant island in the northeast part of the Mediterranean Sea. Along the entire scenic sweep of the northern coast are the Kyrenia Mountains, often snow–capped in the winter. The higher Troödos range in the west central region, covered with forests and vineyards, is crowned by a peak reaching 6,401 feet above sea level. This lofty mountain is called Chionistra by Greek-speaking Cypriots, but in English it is often known as Mt. Olympus in imitation of the more famous mountain in northern Greece. Between the two mountain ranges lies the central plain of Mesaoria, a rich agricultural region surrounding the capital, Lefkosia (renamed in English from Nicosia in 1995). Thanks to the normally adequate rainfall that favors it, more than half the island's total area is cultivated.

History: As early as 6,000 B.C. this island was inhabited by people who built curious round houses, herded sheep and goats, raised a few crops and wove textiles. The first mention of the island in written records occurred in the Nile Valley, whose ancient inhabitants traded with it, as did the Phoenicians and Greeks at a later time. Christianity began to spread on the island in the first century A.D., when it was part of the Roman Empire. By the fifth century, a Cypriot Church with its own Archbishop was recognized.

Cyprus remained part of the Byzantine Empire (see Historical Background) until 1191, when Richard the Lion Hearted of England conquered the island on his way to the Holy Land as part of the Crusades. The following year King Richard sold Cyprus to Guy de Lusignan, a former Crusader king of Jerusalem. From the Lusignan period, which lasted until 1489, come numerous examples of Gothic architecture in the form of castles and fortifications.

The merchant states of Genoa and Venice in turn sought control of Cyprus as a link in their trade with the Orient. Genoa held the port of Famagusta from 1373 to 1464, but it was Venice which finally wrested control from the Lusignan rulers. Fearing competitors and the growing Ottoman Turkish Empire, the Venetians built massive fortifications at the main ports. They taxed the Cypriots heavily, required free labor from them and attempted to impose Latin Christianity on them, as the Lusignan rulers before them had also done.

Because of the unpopularity of the European rulers, the Cypriots were not unhappy to see them driven out by the Ottomans (1570–71). As Ottoman subjects the Cypriots were permitted civil autonomy within their religious community and with the re–establishment of the office of Archbishop for the Cypriot Orthodox Church, he became their link with the Ottoman government. The important role of the religious community and its head has persisted up to the present in varying forms. Poor administration and heavy taxation later in the Ottoman period led to much dissatisfaction.

The Ottoman government agreed in 1878 to let Britain take over the administration of Cyprus, but not legal sovereignty; the Ottomans were to receive part of the revenues and in case of need British aid in warding off Russian encroachment on Turkey's northern borders. Following Turkey's entry into World War I on the side of Germany, Britain annexed Cyprus in 1914 and in 1925 gave it the status of a Crown Colony. Continuing to regard it mainly as a military base to defend the Suez Canal, Britain did not give much attention to the internal affairs until they became critical after World War II.

The grievances of the Greek Cypriots, aggravated by the economic depression in Cyprus in the wake of World War II, found political form in the idea of union (enosis) with Greece. Long before, some Greek Cypriots had felt themselves a part of the Greek nationalist movement which resulted in the independence of Greece from the Ottoman Empire in the early 19th century. As it gathered force during the British period, Enosis basically represented independence in a broader context than a separate independence for the island. As it gained support among Greek Cypriots, the opposition to it among the Turkish Cypriot minority grew apace.

When the determined and energetic Makarios was elected Archbishop and Ethnarch of the Cypriot Orthodox Church in 1950, the Enosis movement gained more political impact. British plans for alleviating economic conditions came too late; rioting became a characteristic of life on Cyprus. Murder and intimidation were added to the breaches of the peace after the formation in 1955 of the EOKA, a militant Greek Cypriot underground organization.

Negotiators from Britain, Greece, and Turkey met with representatives of both Cypriot communities and finally reached agreement in Zurich in 1959. Rejecting both union with Greece and partition of the island, the Zurich agreement granted Cyprus its independence under a constitution containing collective safeguards for the Turkish minority. Britain, Turkey and Greece also received the right to intervene either jointly or singly to uphold the terms of the constitution. Furthermore, Britain retained sovereignty over about 99 square miles of territory for two military bases.

Accordingly, Cyprus became an independent nation. As specified in the constitution, the President was a Greek Cypriot, Archbishop Makarios, and the Vice President was a Turkish Cypriot, Dr. Fazil Küchük. However, independence did not dispel the old attitudes and suspicions. The representatives of the Turkish minority used their constitutional veto to prevent President Makarios and the majority

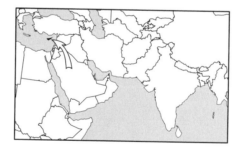

Archbishop Makarios

from enacting laws or carrying out development programs allegedly favorable to the Greeks.

As a result of the use of the veto, major government functions halted. Tempers flared and finally in late 1963 fighting broke out between the two communities. The constitution had failed to solve the conflict between the Greek Cypriot goal of majority rule throughout the island, and the Turkish Cypriot goal of its partition.

A United Nations force in Cyprus (UNFICYP) reduced violence by arranging cease–fire agreements between the two sides and by patrolling areas of possible renewed fighting. Established in 1964, this international force was originally authorized for only six months, but its functions were repeatedly extended.

For a decade starting in 1964 general peace was maintained, but there was little

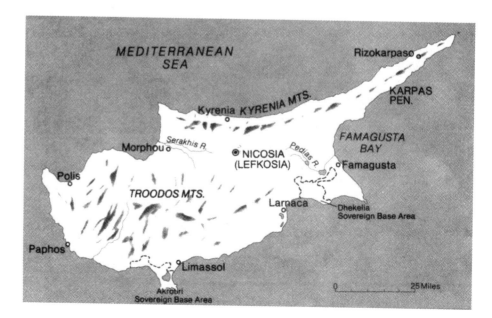

cooperation between the two communities. For instance, the House of Representatives met with only the 35 Greek members present; the 15 Turkish members met separately and denounced the measures taken by the Greeks. Though representatives of the two government factions met periodically from 1968 to 1971, they found no formula for resolving the constitutional issues, even though the popularity of union with Greece declined. The Greek majority could not impose its will because of the constant threat of invasion by Turkey on behalf of the minority's interests.

The year 1974 proved a critical one. In January the head of *EOKA* died and sentiment for *Enosis* began fading more rapidly. Moreover, in sharp contrast to the multiparty democracy and neutral foreign policy enjoyed by Greek Cypriots, Greece suffered a military dictatorship linked to NATO. In these circumstances, determined supporters of *Enosis* saw the chances for union with Greece slipping away, and in a desperate effort engineered a coup in which the National Guard overthrew the Makarios government; the Archbishop himself barely escaped into exile.

During the resulting disorders, the Turkish government seized the opportunity to invade Cyprus, and its forces attacked in July, rapidly seizing Greek-inhabited villages and towns in the north as well as Turkish ones. Successful in military terms, and arguably legal by the Zurich agreement, the assault captured nearly 40% of the island, ostensibly to protect the rights of less than 20% of the population.

The invasion displaced nearly 200,000 Greeks from their homes; a tenth as many Turkish Cypriots fled in the opposite direction. Some regions, like the resort town of Famagusta, lost their entire population. Smaller villages disappeared. Other serious human rights violations included the disappearance of prisoners. Greek Cypriots also allege that during and after the invasion, unique works of art and other antiquities were stolen from churches in the Turkish-occupied zone, a crime rendered easier by alleged neglect or even the connivance of officials and the military.

The invasion had an enormous political and economic effect on the Greek Cypriot community. Glafcos Clerides, Speaker of the House, became Acting President after the leaders of the National Guard coup were discredited. An expanded UNFICYP monitored an uneasy peace between the Turkish army and the Greek Cypriots along the "Attila Line" dividing the two zones. Makarios returned to Cyprus in late 1974, but with reduced prestige. Some 500,000 Greek Cypriots, two-fifths of them refugees from the Turkish zone, found themselves confined to the less productive southern zone. They still regarded Cyprus as one sovereign country, with Makarios as the President.

When Makarios died in 1977, Spyros Kyprianou succeeded him, then won his own term. A hardliner, Kyprianou demanded that Turkish Cypriot leaders recognize that the territorial division should be proportionate to the population of the two zones. In addition, there should be a strong federal government.

Equally unwilling to compromise, the Turkish Cypriots demanded almost all territory north of the Attila Line (keeping about 38% of the island for their 18% of the preinvasion population) and virtual independence for their Turkish Federated State.

In the absence of an agreement, the Turkish-Cypriot Legislative Assembly proclaimed an independent "Turkish Republic of Northern Cyprus" in 1983. Only Turkey recognized this new state, while the Security Council of the UN asked that the independence move be withdrawn.

In the 1988 presidential elections, President Kyprianou and several other major candidates failed to advance to the run-off election. George Vassiliou, a newcomer to politics whose popularity surprised observers, narrowly won the final contest with support from both the newly-founded *Liberal Party* and *AKEL*.

Despite nearly full employment and relatively rapid growth in the economy, in 1993 Vassiliou lost his reelection attempt to the man whom he defeated in 1988, Glafcos Clerides. A veteran politician who attacked rising inflation and sluggish exports during the presidential campaign, Clerides had led the *Democratic Rally*. He narrowly won re-election in 1998.

With international encouragement, representatives of the two communities periodically held talks on a settlement of their differences, but little progress could be discerned. In 1981 Turkish Cypriot leaders finally agreed to a commission to investigate the cases of over 1,600 Greeks who had disappeared during the invasion, to little avail. Finally, in 1996, besides noting that hundreds of Turks were missing as well, Denktash publicly admitted the obvious: prisoners turned over to the Turkish-Cypriot militia had been executed.

In some technical cases the communities appear to work together. Water from the Turkish-held town of Morphou, purified by a Greek processing plant, returns. Similarly, the Greek sector supplies all the electric generating capacity for Turkish Lefkosia, while the sewage passes from the Greek to the Turkish side for treatment. Nevertheless, Lefkosia airport remains closed, and the Varosha resort near Famagusta is shuttered. The continuing division of Cyprus is illustrated by the fact that in the Greek sector a person can dial directly most countries in the world, but until 1998 one could not dial anyone in the Turkish-controlled part of the island.

The Turkish Zone

After the invasion, and protected by the Turkish army, Turkish Cypriots set about implementing a separate state for themselves, one perhaps eventually linked with the rest of the island. In 1975 they approved the constitution for a "Turkish Federated State of Cyprus." Rauf Denktash, who had been elected in 1973 as vice president of the Republic of Cyprus, then became president. In the absence of an agreement, the northern Legislative Assembly proclaimed an independent "Turkish Republic of Northern Cyprus" in 1983. Only Turkey recognized this new state, while the UN Security Council asked that

Turkish soldier guards Greek-Cypriot prisoners, July 1974

Masthead text:

ΙΔΡΥΤΗΣ: ΝΙΚΟΣ ΧΡ. ΠΑΤΤΙΧΗΣ

Ο ΦΙΛΕΛΕΥΘΕΡΟΣ

20 ΣΕΛΙΔΕΣ

ΓΡΑΦΕΙΑ: ΛΕΩΦ. ΒΥΡΩΝΟΣ αρ. 36, 3ος ΟΡΟΦΟΣ
και 34Β – 34° ΙΣΟΓΕΙΟ, ΜΕΓΑΡΟ «ΝΙΚΟΣΙΑ ΤΑΟΥΕΡ
ΣΕΝΤΕΡ». ΤΗΛΕΦ. 463922 (12 ΓΡΑΜΜΕΣ) Τ.Κ. 1094.
ΤΕΛΕΞ: 4999 PHILNEWS. ΤΕΛΕΦΑΞ: ΣΥΝΤΑΞΗ
366121, ΛΟΓΙΣΤΗΡΙΟ 366122. ΤΙΜΗ 25 ΣΕΝΤ.

ΗΜΕΡΗΣΙΑ ΕΦΗΜΕΡΙΣ ΕΙΣ ΤΗΝ ΥΠΗΡΕΣΙΑΝ ΤΟΥ ΚΥΠΡΙΑΚΟΥ ΛΑΟΥ

ΤΡΙΤΗ
3 Απριλίου 1990

ΛΕΥΚΩΣΙΑ, ΚΥΠΡΟΣ ΕΤΟΣ 35° ΑΡ. 1
ΤΗΛΕΓΡΑΦΗΜΑΤΑ: PHILELEFTHE
ΤΥΠΟΙΣ: «Ο ΦΙΛΕΛΕΥΘΕΡΟΣ: Λ

ΛΕΥΚΩΣΙΑ ΕΝΩ ΕΤΟΙΜΑΖΟΝΤΑΙ ΟΙ ΕΝΑΛΛΑΚΤΙΚΕΣ ΕΙΣΗΓΗΣΕΙΣ

ΠΡΟΣ ΠΑΓΚΟΜΜΑΤΙΚΗ
ΤΩΡΑ ΣΤΗΝ ΑΘΗΝΑ

Αμέσως μετά τις εκλογές

ΔΙΑΦΩΝΕΙ Ο Γ.Γ. ΤΟΥ ΑΚΕΛ

Γράφει Α. Λυκαύγης

Λένε ότι ο Νικολάου πλήρωσε το «πρόστιμο» στο Λονδίνο

Το ψευδοκράτος Ντενκτάς ισχυρίστηκε χθες ότι ο σπουδαστής Νίκος Νικολάου στον οποίο είχε επιβληθεί από ψευδοδικαστήριο πρόστιμο για δήθεν ζημιές που προκάλεσε σε αυτοκίνητο Τουρκοκυπρίου «το πλήρωσε (604 δολλάρια) στον αντιπρόσωπο της ΤΔΒΚ στο Λονδίνο μέσω ενός συγγενικού του...

Η ΣΥΓΚΡΟΤΗΣΗ ευρείας σύσκεψης στην Αθήνα, με συμμετοχή των Κυπριακών κομμάτων και της νέας Κυβέρνησης που θα προέλθει από τις κάλπες της ερχόμενης Κυριακής, διαλαμβάνεται στις υπό μελέτη παραπέρα ενέργειες της Λευκωσίας σε σχέση με το Κυπριακό, με στόχο, όπως γίνεται αντιληπτό κι' όπως τεκμαίρεται από συναφείς...

ΛΕΜΕΣΟΣ

Τάφηκαν χωρίς νεκρώσιμη ακολουθία τα τέσσερα «θύματα μαγείας»

ΧΩΡΙΣ τη νενομισμένη νεκρώσιμη ακολουθία και χωρίς παρουσία οποιωνδήποτε στενών ή μακρινών συγγενών τους, τάφηκαν χθες στη Λεμεσό οι τέσσερις αυτόχειρες που πρωτοφανώς κεραυνόν στο διαμέρισμα του θανάτου στη Λεμεσό. Κι' αυτό, αφού προηγήθηκε νεκροψία στα σε αποσύνθεση πτώματα τους, ενώ η Αστυνομία επεκτείνει τις έρευνες και προσπαθεί ν' αξιολογήσει κάποια στοιχεία και τεκμήρια, για να βγάλει άκρη στην υπόθεση που «σόκαρε»...

ΣΤΙΣ 14 ΑΠΡΙΛΙΟΥ

Θάτσερ και Μπους συζητού το Κυπριακό και αντιδρ έντονα η Αγκυρα

Το Κυπριακό έχει τοποθετηθεί στην ημερή διάταξη, των συνομιλιών ανωτάτου επιπέ που θα έχουν στις Βερμούδες, ο Αμερικανός πρ εδρος Τζωρτζ Μπους και η Βρεττανίδα πρω πουργός Μ. Θάτσερ στις 14 Απριλίου. Και όπ γράφει η Τουρκική εφημερίδα «Χουριέτ»:

• Η ΑΓΚΥΡΑ αντέδρασε ήδη έντονα, χαρακτηρίζοντας την εξέλιξη αυτή, ως «αντίθετη προς τις καλές υπηρεσίες του Πέρεζ ντε Κουεγιάρ».

Παρόλο, προσθέτει η εφημερίδα, ότι μέχρι στιγμής δεν υπάρχει τίποτα επίσημο, εντυ...

Μπήκε στα κατεχόμενα συνελήφθη κι αφέθηκε

Lefkosia's *O Phileleftheros* headlines the Third Interparliamentary Union Congress held in Cyprus in April 1990

---

the independence move be withdrawn. Despite surviving for a generation, the Turkish sector remains an international illegality, recognized only by Turkey. Travelers can only fly to northern Cyprus from Turkey, greatly hindering business and tourism. Its products lack convenient access to foreign markets; expanding agricultural exports declined after the European Union banned imports of its perishable food in 1997. In response, international copyright laws are not honored, producing local bargains in counterfeit sports clothing and videos. While some development has occured—Turkish Lefkosia initially possessed no cinema or commercial art gallery and only 5 public telephones for its 40,000 people—the zone imposes great sacrifices on its inhabitants in return for their freedom from Greek control.

Per capita incomes now average only one-third the Greek level ($4,500 to over $13,000), and foreign investment appears negligible. Even this meager existence depends on mainland Turkey, for it provides almost half the zone's government budget and funds all major public works. However, this requires use of the Turkish Lira, one of the least valued currencies anywhere. It thus condemns the island's Turks to inflation sometimes reaching 100%. Moreover, immigration from the Turkish mainland means that by the late 1990s Turkish Cypriots may be a minority in their own territory. Evidence is sketchy, but most students at the six small English-speaking universities apparently come from the mainland.

Despite an economic crisis caused by a loss of export markets and declining tourism, Rauf Denktash won re-election as president in 1995, though for the first time a challenger forced him into the second round. Even more the symbol of Turkish Cypriots in 2000, Denktash again won re-election after his challenger conceded before the second round. The communities do cooperate in some technical cases. Water from the Turkish– held town of Morphou, purified by a Greek processing plant, returns. Similarly, the Greek sector supplies all the electric generating capacity for Turkish Lefkosia, while the sewage passes from the Greek to the Turkish side for treatment. Nevertheless, Lefkosia airport remains closed, and the Varosha resort near Famagusta is shuttered. The continuing division of Cyprus is illustrated by the fact that in the Greek sector a person can dial directly most countries in the world, but until 1998 one could not dial anyone in the Turkish-controlled part of the island.

The Search for a Settlement

Initial attempts to bring peace to the island during the 1970s and 1980s failed even in the humanitarian task of discovering the fate of the 1,600 Greeks and 800 Turks listed as missing persons. The failure resulted partly because President Kyprianou demanded a strong federal government and set terms for negotiations that ensured they would not take place. His successors, however, were more willing to talk without preconditions.

In 1992, the UN Secretary General proposed a "bi–zonal and bi–communal" settlement that required concessions from each side. "Bi-zonal" implied that the Greeks must abandon demands for one strong government for the whole island. Instead, a weak central administration, perhaps under an alternating presidency, would be limited mostly to customs, the post office, the central bank, and the diplomatic corps. The two ethnic zones would remain and administer themselves with great autonomy. This required the Turkish community to accept the withdrawal of most Turkish military forces and a reduction in the size of the zone from 38% to 28%. This would allow one–third of the 1974 refugees to return to their homes while the other Greek and Turkish refugees would receive compensation.

However, the two sides failed to compromise. Rauf Denktash rejected the plan's territorial provisions, and Turkish Cypriots generally feared that the removal of Turkish troops might deprive them of their autonomy. Nevertheless, the plan remained the basis for any settlement. By 1998, differences had narrowed chiefly to the electoral system and how large the Turkish zone should become, with rival concepts between 25% and 30%. Hopes for a settlement may have enabled

President Glafcos Clerides

44

Glafcos Clerides to win re–election as president in 1998 against a more extreme nationalist.

However, after two decades of discussing the bi-zonal, bi-community proposal, in 2000 Denktash broke off negotiations. He demanded a new framework: a confederation of two independent states. While the practical difference may be nil between a federation of autonomous regions and a confederation of independent states, Greek Cypriots feared the Turkish terms amounted to creeping recognition for the northern republic.

Hopes on both sides of the buffer zone cautiously rose for a settlement after Clerides and Denktash met in late 2001 and announced further meetings plus social visits to each other. No Greek Cypriot president had ever crossed into the Turkish zone, but Clerides visited his old acquaintance of the 1950s. Breaking months of isolation, the two leaders agreed to meet three times weekly and set the goal of a settlement by mid-2002. Taking a humanitarian approach to the missing persons, they sought to find mass graves and identify the dead, rather than concentrate on details of their capture.

Clearly there are two major sources for this sudden progress towards solving the island's problems. One is personal: Denktash is in his late 70s, and Clerides in his 80s. Unlike younger politicians, they grew up in a united island, made acquaintances of members of the other community, and actually argued legal cases against each other. The negotiations reflect the desires of two elderly men to settle matters before the end of their days.

The second major impetus is "accession," the planned expansion of the European Union to include Cyprus and a number of Central European nations. Though insignificant in population compared to other applicants like Poland, Cyprus is scheduled to join the EU in 2004, partly because it meets the economic criteria for membership and partly because Greece strongly advocates its admission. Greece has threatened to veto all other new members if Cyprus is not admitted in the first group of countries.

Significantly, the EU recognized the Cypriot government's ability to negotiate for the entire island and also pledged to admit (Greek) Cyprus even without a settlement over the Turkish zone. While this approach resulted in Turkish threats to annex northern Cyprus the moment the south joined the EU, more productively the accession process created a deadline for any attempted settlement.

Potential membership in the EU encourages a negotiated settlement for several reasons. The personal safety and community rights of Turkish Cypriots would be respected far better by a Cyprus subject to EU courts and laws, while Greek Cypriots would have little fear of a Turkish invasion. The economic benefits of admis-

**Leader of the Turkish–Cypriots
Rauf Denktash**

sion would be particularly powerful for the Turkish zone because it would remove the economic isolation in place since 1974. In 2001 some political groups in the Turkish community demonstrated for greater compromise, a political stand previously considered close to treason.

Nevertheless, grave difficulties potentially block a settlement. The terms being negotiated would not provide for all refugees to return to their homes, and the territory to be transferred to Greek control will be too small for many Greeks, and too great for many Turks. Some politicians on either side of the buffer zone will argue that any agreement falls short of what is necessary, and the fate of Turkish troops and Turkish immigrants could prove particularly thorny. Nevertheless, peace looks closer in early 2002 than for decades.

Politics: A notable characteristic of the Constitution of 1960 is that Cypriots were not recognized as individual citizens, but as members of either the Greek or the Turkish community, as determined by

language, culture, or (not *and*) religion. Since the specified religious identities were either Greek Orthodox or Muslim, Armenian Christians would have to find membership in the Greek Community on another basis. In all elections, according to the document, the Greek community was to vote only for officials designated as Greek, such as the president and 70% of the members of the House of Representatives, while the Turkish community was to vote only for officials designated as Turkish, such as the vice president and the other 30% of the House members.

Another feature of the constitution was that the executive and legislative branches of government are separate and elected at different times.

Despite the small population, political opinion in the Greek community is widely divided. The House of Representatives, enlarged in 1985 to 56 seats, includes four parties. They range across the spectrum from the conservative Democratic Rally and the moderate Democratic Party to the socialist EDEK and Communist AKEL, which gained seats in 1991, despite the demise of Communism elsewhere.

In the 1988 presidential elections, President Kyprianou and several other major candidates failed to advance to the run–off election. George Vassiliou, the newcomer to politics whose popularity surprised observers, narrowly won the final contest with support from both the newly-founded *Liberal Party* and *AKEL*. He claimed to appoint ministers "based on merit, not party loyalties."

Despite nearly full employment and relatively rapid growth in the economy, in 1993 Vassiliou lost his reelection attempt to the man whom he defeated in 1988, Glafcos Clerides. A veteran politician who attacked rising inflation and sluggish exports during the presidential campaign, Clerides had led the *Democratic Rally* until he became president. He narrowly won re–election in 1998.

A Greek Orthodox priest at his easel

Courtesy: Embassy of Cyprus

ANGUISH: Clutching large photographs of missing loved ones, mothers and wives plead for information about men who have not been heard from since the Turkish invasion of July 1974, a full generation ago.

Courtesy: Embassy of Cyprus

A new constitution for the "Turkish Republic of Northern Cyprus," similar to one in effect for a decade, was approved in a 1985 referendum. It provides for a president, prime minister, and legislature of 50 seats. The *National Union Party* won 23 seats in the 1998 elections; its leader, Dervis Eroglu, serves as prime minister in alliance with the *Communal Liberation Party*, the third-largest party with seven seats. The *Democratic Party* forms the largest opposition group. President Rauf Denktash, who stands above parties as the symbol of the Turkish community, vigorously defends the Turkish perspective, despite heart trouble and his age (mid-70s).

Although the constitution provides an independent judiciary, individual freedoms are limited. Military forces from mainland Turkey control the local police, and journalists questioning such links have been arrested on dubious charges.

Culture: Cypriots, whether Greek or Turkish, Christian or Muslim, share a number of basic cultural traits. One is that a very large proportion of each group traditionally engaged in agriculture, though the proportion is now much smaller among Greeks than Turks. In both groups the rural population is generally poorer than the city dwellers. Also, for instance, women of both groups traditionally led rather restricted lives and with very few exceptions did not participate in public life nor enter the professions. However, Greek Cypriot women increasingly enter the professions and exercise rights similar to those in Western Europe.

Unfortunately, it has not been the similarities, but the differences that have been emphasized by the two communities. The remark that there are no Cypriots living on Cyprus, only Greeks and Turks, reflects this tragedy. In the cities, members of the two communities cannot often be distinguished by appearance, in the countryside the style of clothing worn is frequently distinctive. They celebrate different holidays. The Greeks celebrate Easter in the spring, while the Turks celebrate their Islamic *Bairam* (at the time of pilgrimage to Mecca) at different times in each year according to a lunar calendar. Then the national holidays of Greece are observed by one community, while those of Turkey by the other.

In any country, people engaged in commerce and industry tend to have more wealth than farmers and laborers. As Greek Cypriots traditionally dominated trade and industry, this gave the feeling to Turks that they were economically oppressed, although Turks relative to their numbers traditionally owned more farmland. Education has tended to follow the systems used in Greece and Turkey in the respective communities and was largely separate even before 1974. Those countries are also the sources of the books and periodicals read by the two communities.

For decades, Cypriot students wishing to study most disciplines at the university level were forced to go abroad, and a high proportion did so. However, the University of Cyprus opened in 1992, incorporating the existing teacher–training institute.

The two communities were already socially separate before the geographical separation of 1974. This social avoidance resulted from reciprocal suspicions and hostility rooted more in tradition and emotion than in culture.

Economy: The agricultural contribution to the economy varies, owing to occasional severe droughts such as the region has suffered in the past few years. Water from the small rivers is used for irrigation, but this is insufficient during an extended period of below-average rainfall. So great has been the shortage of water that running water was not always available. However, when two more desalination plants are completed by 2002, joining two already in service, water for households, industry and some irrigation should be available in Greek areas. Tankers may transport water from Turkey to the northern zone; one proposal calls for airships to be used.

The largest share of arable land is sown in cereal crops, but there is not enough grain produced to meet domestic needs. Production of olives, an important part of the diet, likewise falls short of domestic requirements. The agricultural exports are mainly citrus fruits, potatoes, raisins, carob beans and wine. The Orthodox Church is the largest landowner, a fact that lends it secular influence in the countryside.

Although previously copper was the chief Cypriot export—indeed, the island's name comes from the mineral—mining currently plays only a minor role in the economy. Light industry expanded substantially in recent years, and the British bases provide both jobs and foreign exchange. Nevertheless, the island still imports a far greater value of goods than it exports.

The 1974 Turkish invasion necessitated a drastic reorganization of the economy. For instance, all of the tobacco farms and more than half of the citrus groves and grain lands fell under Turkish occupation, though mostly owned by Greek Cypriots exiled to the South. Turkish Cypriots, though not as experienced in this work, took over these agricultural resources; citrus fruit now comprises half of the exports from the Turkish zone. Turkish unemployment rose rapidly in 1991 after the major foreign investor, the British firm Polly Peck, led by a Turkish Cypriot, declared bankruptcy.

Though more than half of the tourist facilities are in the 40% of the island occupied by Turkey, few tourists go there. On the other hand, Greek Cypriots who were cut off from the hotels and restaurants they owned at Famagusta, Kyrenia and elsewhere, have built anew, mainly along the southern coast. So well managed is their tourist business that the number of visitors both from Europe and Arab countries has grown by leaps and bounds. Government statistics show that often the number of tourists entering the country exceeds its population, and their desires for hotels and apartments boosted the construction industry.

Violence and difficulties elsewhere in the Middle East presented Cyprus with the opportunity to become a center for banking, insurance, and shipping activities. Simple regulations and a skilled population also encouraged companies to locate regional headquarters on the island, and it has received U.S. approval in its efforts to fight money–laundering and the drug trade. In the Greek sector services now employ twice the labor force as agriculture, and Cyprus enjoys one of the highest incomes of any country in this book, oil exporters excepted.

The Future: Over a quarter century after its founding, the United Nations Force still maintains the Green Line between the two sides in Lefkosia. Repeated international efforts failed to persuade the two sides to compromise, partly because mutual distrust and even hatred plays a greater importance than the 170 square miles of land now in contention. Several countries, including Canada and Denmark, have begun withdrawing their units from the peacekeeping force, but despite the UN Security Council's censure of the Turkish position, the two sides continue to remain far apart. How long will the outside world continue to care?

Meanwhile, the Greeks prosper, while the Turkish Cypriots stagnate.

Ancient theater at Curium (Limassol)

The Arab Republic of Egypt

Area: 386,873 square miles (1,002,000 sq. km.), of which only about 3.5% is arable—that in the Nile Valley, the Delta and a few oases.

Population: 67 million; UN estimates around 62 million.

Capital City: Cairo (Pop. 15 million, including suburbs, estimated).

Climate: The Northern belt (including Cairo) has hot, dry summers, cool winters with rare rain. The coast, where Alexandria is located, is normally humid. The central and southern zones, virtually rainless, have extremely hot summers, comfortable winters. Occasional strong winds intensify the winter chill and the summer heat.

Neighboring Countries: Libya (West); Sudan (South); Saudi Arabia (East, across the Red Sea); Israel (Northeast).

Time Zone: GMT + 2 (+3 in summer). At noon in New York it is 7:00 P.M. in Cairo.

Official Language: Arabic.

Other Principal Tongues: English and French as school and business languages.

Ethnic Background: As in the U.S. there is variation in physical appearance, but nearly all think of themselves as Arab and Egyptian.

Principal Religion: *Sunni* Islam (90% or more) and Coptic Christianity.

Major Trading Partners: U.S., France, Greece, Japan, Germany, Netherlands, Italy and Saudi Arabia.

Chief Commercial Products: Tourism, Suez Canal usage, petroleum and refined products, military equipment, cotton and textiles, light manufactures.

Main Agricultural Products: Cotton, sugar, rice and other grains, tomatoes, watermelons, onions, vegetables, dates, animals and flowers.

Currency: Egyptian Pound, commonly called a ghinnayh from the former British coin, the Guinea.

Former Colonial Status: British control, though still part of the Ottoman Empire (1882–1914), then a "protectorate" of Britain (1914–1923). Britain exercised political influence until a military *coup* on July 22, 1952.

National Day: July 23.

Chief of State: Mohammad Hosni Mubarak, President.

Head of Government: Atef Obeid, Prime Minister.

National Flag: Three horizontal stripes of (top to bottom) red, white and black. The eagle of Saladin in gold is centered on the white stripe.

←**The Sacred Lake at the Temple of Karnak, Upper Egypt**
Photo by Jeanne Conte

Gross Domestic Product: $89 billion
GDP per capita: $1300 (IMF); other estimates $800 to $2400.

Strategically located at the junction between Africa and Asia, Egypt holds the rank of the most populous Arab state and the center of Arab culture and entertainment. Most of its territory is in Africa, constituting the northeast corner of the great Sahara Desert. The stark desolation of gravel, sand and rock is interrupted by the Nile River, which flows from south to north for 750 miles in a valley cut through the desert. Yet for most of its length the valley floor, where agriculture is possible, varies in width from a mere few hundred yards to a maximum of fourteen miles.

About 100 miles before reaching the Mediterranean Sea, the Nile divides up into branches which spread out over a broad alluvial plain reaching a width of 150 miles along the sea coast. Because in shape this triangle of fertility resembles the form of the (capital) letter *delta* in the Greek alphabet, since ancient times it has been called the Delta. The metropolis of Cairo lies at the southern tip of this Delta. At the northwest point is the port city of Alexandria, named after Alexander the Great who founded it following his

conquest of the country in 332 B.C. About a quarter of the people of Egypt live in these two cities. They work as shopkeepers, government employees, in manufacturing, or at the many other jobs associated with urban areas.

Most of the remaining three–quarters of the population live in some 4,000 villages and towns scattered in the Delta and up the length of the Nile Valley. Most of them are directly or indirectly connected with agricultural production. A very small fraction of the people live in a half dozen remote oasis centers in the desert west of the Nile Valley, while an insignificant and dwindling number are nomads who wander with flocks of goats and camels in the desert regions comprising about 96% of the country. There are no grasslands or forests. Even the highest point in Egypt, towering (8,652 feet) Jabal Katrina (Mt. Catherine) in the Sinai Peninsula, the area of Egypt that is part of Asia, is barren rock. There is total contrast between the barrenness of the desert (called "the Red Land" by the ancient inhabitants) and the tropical growth of the valley floor and Delta ("the Black Land" of the ancients).

The English name *Egypt* is derived from the ancient Greek name Aiguptos, an approximation of Hikuptah, one of the

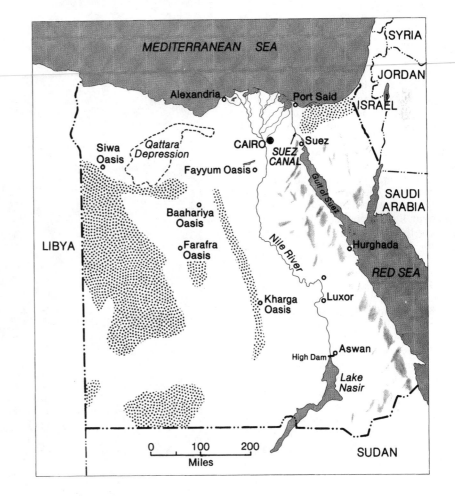

49

names of the ancient capital of Memphis (the site of which is near modern Cairo). The Arabic name of the country, *Misr*, introduced with the Arabic conquest of the 7th century, originated in an ancient name used in Semitic languages. In the hieroglyphics of antiquity, the country was sometimes called "the Two Lands," referring to Lower Egypt (the Delta) and Upper Egypt (the narrow valley south of Cairo, known as *Sa'id* in Arabic).

History: The shadows of an extremely long early history—of the mighty pharaohs claiming to be gods, of Hellenistic civilization that flourished at Alexandria and especially of the brilliant Islamic civilization centered on Cairo—lie across the modern land of Egypt. Yet the modern state of Egypt cannot be traced back beyond the early 19th century. Then it began to take shape under the dynamic rule of an ambitious former Ottoman soldier named Muhammad (Mehmet) Ali, who was neither Egyptian in origin nor a proponent of (not–yet–existent) Egyptian nationalism.

Pre–Christian civilization in the Nile Valley made enormous contributions to the development of human skills and knowledge. In fact, that civilization is best considered as the heritage of all humanity, not only modern Egypt. Later ages also influenced the world. Roman Egypt was one of the first fertile grounds for the spread of Christianity, and its thinkers and leaders played important roles in the history of the Christian Church. The Christians of Egypt adopted a modified version of the Greek alphabet to write their language, the latest form of the old Egyptian language earlier recorded in hieroglyphics. That written form of their language, as well as their church, is called Coptic. The Coptic Church still plays an important role in contemporary Egyptian society.

As the later Roman, or Byzantine, Empire waned in the early 7th century, Muslim armies from Arabia spread their rule to Egypt, little opposed by the Coptic subjects of the Byzantine Empire (639–642). During the following four or five centuries, both the Arabic language of the new rulers and their Islamic faith were adopted by most Egyptians. The land became fully a part of the Muslim world. As the Abbasid caliphate in Baghdad lost control of distant provinces, Egypt fell under the rule of local governors and then Turkish dynasties, including the Tulunids, whose mosque remains impressive today.

Further elegant buildings, and achievements in the arts and learning followed under the Fatimid Caliphs (969–1171), including the founding of the University of al–Azhar, one of the oldest in the world. Claiming descent from Fatima, the Prophet Muhammad's daughter, these caliphs espoused Shi'a Islam but maintained contact with the rest of the Muslim world. Sometimes they ruled much of it, but weak rulers and dependence on foreign slave–warriors called Mamluks eased Egypt's capture by Salah al–Din al–Ayyubi, known to the European Crusaders as Saladin. His Sunni descendants in turn lost authority to the Mamluks (pronounced Mam–*luke)*, warrior slaves often of Turkish or Circassian origins, by the middle of the 13th century.

The most important Mamluk sultan, Baybars, checked the expansion of the destructive Mongol armies in Syria (Ayn Jalut, 1260), and defeated the remaining Crusaders as well. But despite their glories on the battlefield, and their lavish spending on works of art, the Mamluks brought few advantages to the native Egyptians. Generally foreign born, the Mamluks oppressed the Egyptians harshly, and by their intrigues and rivalries brought disorder rather than peace. When the Ottoman Sultan Selim I defeated the Mamluks in Syria and conquered Egypt in 1517, the country entered a new era. However, the Ottoman period witnessed frequent struggles between the government in Istanbul and the remaining Mamluks, who dominated Egyptian society.

A vital turning point in the creation of modern Egypt came with its conquest by Napoleon and the French occupation from 1798 to 1801. Scores of scholars accompanied the French troops, and their accounts greatly increased European knowledge of, and interest in, Egypt. Furthermore, the ending of French rule permitted Muhammad Ali, an officer in the Ottoman army sent to evict the French, to seize power for himself while paying lip service to Ottoman rule.

Although born in Europe, and neither Egyptian nor Arab, by skillfully playing

Napoleon's soldiers pass an ancient temple at Thebes

off his rivals Muhammad Ali emerged as the real power in the country, and in 1806 the Ottoman Sultan appointed him Pasha of Egypt. Challenged by the successes of the French army, as well as by a barren treasury and Mamluk remnants, he set about building a modern state. After drastically reorganizing the land taxes and taking control of foreign trade, he slaughtered the remaining Mamluks in 1811. Military expeditions followed abroad, in Sudan, Arabia, and Greece. The resulting need for soldiers required imposing conscription on Egyptians for the first time. In 1833, under the capable command of his son, Ibrahim, the Egyptian army captured Palestine and Syria from Ottoman armies, but European intervention cut short Muhammad Ali's rule outside Egypt in 1841.

Modernization also attracted Muhammad Ali's attention during the four decades he and his son Ibrahim dominated Egypt. He developed a cabinet system of government, established schools, founded a government press, and attempted to industrialize Egypt with imported equipment, all without borrowing funds abroad. His attempt to monopolize trade failed, but did not deter later rulers from similar schemes. He encouraged agricultural improvements and transferred vast domains to the state from delinquent taxpayers. Though unsuccessful in creating an empire, he separated Egypt clearly as a self–governing region of the Ottoman Empire, and to some historians deserves the title "The Founder of Modern Egypt."

His successors provided no rival for the title. His son Sa'id, however, in 1856 signed a concession giving a Frenchman, Ferdinand de Lesseps, the right to build a sea–level canal from the Mediterranean to the Gulf of Suez, a branch of the Red Sea. By this act, Sa'id Pasha greatly altered Egypt's status in international affairs, as the Suez Canal was regarded by Britain as its "lifeline to India," because it reduced the length of the sea voyage from Britain to the Indian Ocean enormously, compared to the trip around the southern tip of Africa.

The Canal was completed in 1869, after Sa'id's nephew Ismail succeeded him. The new ruler took the ambiguous Ottoman title Khedive, meaning something like "prince", and thus elevated himself above the pashas in other Ottoman provinces, while still remaining in the Empire. Indeed, he offered the Sultan tribute.

Khedive Ismail went far more deeply into debt to European bankers than his predecessor had. He did this to finance his high living and elaborate, often unsound, schemes aimed at developing Egypt to be like a European country. Very quickly he bankrupted the state. In 1875 he was forced to sell Egypt's share in the Suez Canal to the British government. His

Smoking a *hookah*—which has a long flexible tube whereby the smoke is cooled by passing through water.
Courtesy: Susan L. Thompson

profligate spending resulted in European supervision of Egyptian finances, and opened the way for Britain to seize control of the country in 1882 to "safeguard" European investments. Three years earlier, Ismail had been forced to abdicate in favor of a son, Tewfiq, and sail away on his yacht into exile in the Europe he admired so much, just as his grandson, King Faruq (Farouk) would do 83 years later.

The British Occupation

After rioters in Alexandria killed Europeans and people associated with the foreign–supervised government so disliked by most Egyptians, Britain reacted to events by landing troops (1882). The wealthy, landowning elite, many of them Turkish–speaking, failed to unite and oppose the British. However, most Egyptians rallied to support Colonel Ahmad Urabi (Arabi), a nationalist.

At the battle of Tall al-Kabir, the British troops demonstrated an overwhelming supremacy, killing some 10,000 Egyptians while losing fewer than 80 men. Urabi soon surrendered, and although Tewfiq retained the title Khedive, he became a British puppet. Still formally part of the

Ottoman Empire, Egypt did not become a British colony, but the British Consul General, Lord Cromer, became a virtual dictator for over twenty years (1883–1907). After Tewfiq died in 1892, his son Abbas II succeeded him.

The indirect form of British rule changed in late 1914 when the Ottoman government entered World War I against Britain and its allies. Britain responded by proclaiming Egypt a protectorate and replacing Khedive Abbas II, thought to have Turkish sympathies, with his elderly uncle, Husayn Kamil, who was allowed the title Sultan. An Ottoman attempt early in the war to seize the Suez Canal and invade Egypt from across Sinai was repelled by troops from the British Empire. Using Egypt as a base, this force of Indians, Australians, and others slowly pushed the Turkish army into Palestine. When Sultan Husayn Kamil died, his youngest brother, Fu'ad, was installed as the new head of state.

A victorious Britain showed every sign of continuing its domination of Egypt, contrary to the rising nationalist sentiment in favor of independence. This tide found a spokesman in Sa'd Zaghlul, who had long worked against foreign rule. He

The heart of Cairo. Liberation Square can be seen with its raised walkway at left center. In front of it is the headquarters of the Arab League.

and his colleagues sought to form a delegation ("wafd" in Arabic) to present their case to the Paris peace conference in 1919, but they were brusquely dismissed by British officials. When the Egyptian prime minister resigned, the British military arrested Zaghlul and deported him to Malta.

Within days, insurrection spread to all parts of Egypt, forcing the government in London to address the problem. Although Britain offered independence, it proposed to restrict Egypt in many ways and retain British troops in Egypt. When Zaghlul and his *Wafd Party* ensured that no Egyptian would sign such a treaty, Britain ended the protectorate without agreement and declared Egypt independent. Sultan Fu'ad was retitled king, but proved inept in political matters (having grown up in Italy, he was scarcely able to speak Arabic). A parliament was established, but it was generally ineffective until terminated in 1952.

The years between 1923 and 1952 when the monarchy was overthrown did not see many positive developments. Politically the country was rent by continuing rivalry among the weak monarch, the waning influence of British officials and the increasingly corrupt and self-interested Wafd Party and smaller nationalistic groups. The politicians tried to manipulate the poor for their own ends, but did little to improve their lot. King Faruq, whose reign began in 1937, became a symbol of a system which failed to meet the rising aspirations of ordinary Egyptians. Opposition to the monarchy mounted

after the Egyptian army's loss to Israel in 1949, and the fundamentalist Muslim Brotherhood became increasingly active.

Military Rule and Republic

After months of sometimes violent popular protest against conditions, on July 23, 1952, a reformist group in the Army, calling themselves "Free Officers," seized control of the country. King Farouk was sent into exile, and his infant son officially deposed later. The Free Officers sought not merely to change the ruler; they wished to revolutionize the way the country was organized and operated. They believed that an independent, honest and sincere government could reduce poverty, increase education, strengthen the armed forces and bring dignity to the average Egyptian. In keeping with these aims, they set up the *Revolutionary Command Council* to handle affairs of state.

A respected older general, Muhammad Naguib, was named President, but the real leader in the *RCC* was a younger man, Colonel Gamal Abdul Nasser (or Jamal Abd al–Nasir), a tall, imposing orator with an interest in ideas. In 1954 he became President in name as well as fact.

Nasser made an enormous impact upon Egyptians, other Arabs, and people throughout the colonies and newly independent nations of the developing world. Aside from the wealthy and ethnic minorities, Egyptians loved him. When army officers plotted to overthrow monarchies in Iraq, Yemen and Libya, they modeled revolutionary councils after the one in Cairo. On the world stage, Nasser became

a prominent spokesman at conferences of Third World nations, notably in 1955 at Bandung in Indonesia when he, Prime Minister Nehru of India, and Prime Minister Chou Enlai of China established the Nonaligned Movement of countries neutral in the struggle between the Soviet Union and the West.

In 1952, however, these achievements remained in the future. When the idealistic young men of the *RCC* seized power, they lacked experience in government and found few advisors who commanded their confidence. For domestic policy, gradually they formulated principles for building a new society, defined as "Arab Socialism." They aimed to bring progress and greater opportunity for the majority, through education, public health, and other welfare programs. They also desired land reform, to redistribute to the *fellahin* (farmers) the large estates of the rich. As moderate socialists, but not communists, they favored government control of industry, banks, and international trade. In foreign affairs, Nasser proclaimed the ideas of Pan–Arab nationalism popular in Syria and elsewhere. Arab weakness, the philosophy explained, resulted from imperialism and dynasties that divided what should have been one Arab nation.

In the 1950s, Egypt dominated the Arab world. Its population far exceeded those of other Arab states; it boasted the largest (if not toughest) military, and its achievements in the arts and culture ranged from universities to movies. Thus, inevitably, once the Revolutionary Command Council espoused a Pan–Arab policy, it began to champion the interests of the Palestine Arabs and to oppose Israel.

Access to arms supplies proved a crucial issue in Egyptian policy. In 1953 the Western allies, the dominant weapons suppliers in the region, agreed to limit combined Arab armaments to the level possessed by Israel. From an Arab perspective, the decision meant indefinite Israeli military superiority over any Arab state or likely alliance. In a decisive stroke, in 1955 Egypt arranged to purchase arms from Czechoslovakia, thus escaping from Western limitations while increasing Soviet influence in the Middle East.

The arms purchases sharply illustrated the contrast between the dominant Western goal in the region—defense against Soviet expansion—and the Arab goal of victory over Israel or Arab rivals. When the United States reacted to the arms sale by withholding aid for the proposed Aswan High Dam in southern Egypt, Nasser obtained Soviet assistance for the dam as well.

To pay for the arms, and to finance long–overdue development projects, in 1956 Nasser announced that Egypt was seizing ownership of the Suez Canal Company, but paying French and British shareholders the current value of their shares. Amid great international furor, Israel, Britain and France secretly plotted an invasion. The Israeli leadership hoped to defeat Egypt before the new Soviet arms rendered it strong, and then to force it to sign a peace treaty. The other two nations hoped to compel the downfall of Nasser in favor of a more tractable administration.

Israeli forces quickly occupied the Sinai Peninsula. Britain and France then used the fighting as a pretext for a joint expeditionary force to take control of the Canal Zone. This reversion to power politics, entailing great loss of civilian property and life, was overwhelmingly opposed by the international community. At the U.N., a withdrawal resolution introduced by Canada, won support from the U.S., the U.S.S.R., and nearly all other member countries in demanding unconditional withdrawal. Nasser emerged from this episode as a hero in the eyes of Africans and Asians who had been or still were under European rule. In 1958, at Syria's request, Egypt merged with it to form the United Arab Republic. Nasser became President, and very possibly his influence reached its highest level, until an Iraqi revolution created a rival anti–colonialist regime.

After Syria's withdrawal from the United Arab Republic in 1961, the Egyptian president continued his policy of socialism at home, neutrality between the superpowers and support of the Palestinian cause against Israel. For all these reasons, he strongly condemned the more conservative Arab states.

The attempts to spread Arab socialism to other Arab countries through radio and other means of propaganda aroused the stiff opposition of the endangered regimes, as well as the U.S., Britain and France, who saw their interests best served by the status quo. Among the examples, France gave an exaggerated importance to Egypt's support for the Algerian Muslims struggling for independence from that country. Egypt's military support for a republican government in Yemen following a 1962 coup might threaten vital US interests in neighboring Saudi Arabia. Britain resented Cairo's calls for liberating the Gulf States which it still supervised.

The Six–Day War

In the spring of 1967, despite his army's continuing struggle in Yemen, Nasser permitted himself to ally publicly with Syria, and later Jordan, against Israel. When radicals criticized Egypt for sheltering behind borders pacified by the U.N. observers, Nasser ordered out the observers, who left quickly. He then announced a blockade of the Straits of Tiran, and hence the Gulf of Aqaba, to Israeli commerce. With the Suez Canal already denied to Israeli cargoes, closing the straits threatened to deprive Israel of all trade with East Africa, Southern Asia and the Far East. Israel publicly considered the action cause for war, and reorganized the cabinet. Nasser moved troops into the Sinai and delivered bellicose speeches. But Egypt otherwise failed to prepare for war, perhaps miscalculating Israeli strength, or presuming the United States would restrain Israel from invasion.

Sudden attacks on Egyptian, and later Syrian, air bases marked the beginning of the Six–Day War. In a few hours, the Arab air forces practically ceased to exist, and Israeli control of the skies ensured victory on land.

Nasser's miscalculation cost his army devastating losses in men and equipment. He accepted responsibility for the defeat, and resigned, but emotional demonstrations in Cairo led him to return to power. Other consequences of the defeat proved

A Cairo chef

Courtesy: Susan L. Thompson

53

longer–lasting. Egypt lost all Sinai, with its recently–discovered oil fields and revenues from the Suez Canal, because it could not be reopened without unacceptable political and, probably, territorial concessions. The Israeli occupation affected politics for the next decade. It impoverished the economy and soon led to a War of Attrition, a period of intense shelling and air raids along the Canal.

From Attrition to Peace

When the Gamal Abdul Nasser died of a heart attack in 1970, numerous economic and social reforms had been achieved within the country. Egyptian grief was immeasurable. However, in spite of the great impression he made on the contemporary world, his goals in international affairs had been largely frustrated because the opposition he faced was determined, and Egypt lacked either economic or military strength to achieve his aims.

To replace Nasser, Egypt's leaders turned to former Vice President Anwar Sadat, one of the few former Free Officers to remain in public life. His presidency (1970–1981) marked a distinct change of economic philosophy from the state ownership of the previous decade. Hoping to lure American and other foreign investment to the country because Soviet aid and socialism led to stagnation, Sadat's government lifted many, but by no means all, restrictions imposed when Arab socialism held sway. Much touted as liberalization, the reforms largely failed in their purposes: Egypt was not particularly attractive to foreign investors anyway. The reforms also contributed to influence peddling and profiteering by politicians, military officers and their relatives. The perennial problems of unemployment, lagging industrialization and overpopulation worsened, and the resulting dissatisfaction found both political and religious expression.

Initially the Sadat administration adhered to Nasser's foreign policy, including support for Palestinian interests and the unconditional withdrawal of Israel from the Sinai and other lands captured in 1967. The War of Attrition continued along the Suez Canal. Despite frequent warlike rhetoric, however, in 1973 Egypt dismissed the many Soviet military advisors and other personnel.

Suddenly, in October, the Syrian and Egyptian armies attacked Israeli forces occupying their territory. Egyptian troops successfully crossed the Canal and advanced into the Sinai. There, protected by anti–aircraft missiles from Israeli bombing, they fought monumental tank battles with the Israelis.

Within days, however, the tide of battle shifted. Massively resupplied by US airlift with sophisticated weapons, the Israel Defense Forces also crossed the

Canal—into Africa, threatening Cairo and encircling large Egyptian armies. Given the risks of warfare, and its enormous human and material costs, Sadat and his advisors concluded that further confrontation with Israel was not only harmful to Egypt but also futile.

In the months that followed the war, Sadat's policies moved dramatically away from those of his predecessor. He restored diplomatic relations with the United States, and shuttle negotiations by Henry Kissinger, the U.S. Secretary of State, produced an Israeli withdrawal that returned both the Suez Canal and Sinai oil wells to Egypt. Domestically, Sadat promised economic freedom and political liberty, and he invoked Egyptian, rather than Pan–Arab, nationalism. Nevertheless, while oil exports and Suez Canal tolls provided foreign exchange, and trade increased, prosperity hardly trickled down to the masses. Likewise, peace remained only a hope.

Just as a new crisis over affairs in Lebanon was beginning in 1977, Sadat, aware that his country could not afford another war, took the drastic step of offering peace with Israel. In a dramatic gesture he flew to Jerusalem and addressed the Knesset in November 1977, offering to accept the legitimacy of Israel in exchange for its withdrawal from territory seized in 1967 from Egypt, Jordan and Syria. When diplomacy seemed to falter in 1978, President Jimmy Carter invited both Anwar Sadat and Israeli Prime Minister Menachem Begin to Camp David, the U.S. presidential retreat in Maryland. There, isolated from the press and their domestic political pressures, the two leaders reached terms of a peace settlement.

The Camp David Accords, signed in 1979, fell far short of Sadat's initial goals for the Arab nations. Israel retained full control of territory captured from Jordan and Syria, and the Palestinians received only the promise of a distant and vague autonomy. Egypt, however, regained all the Sinai, including Israeli settlements.

President Mubarak

Although diplomatic relations were established in 1980, and Israeli troops withdrew by 1982, it was only in 1989, after an international tribunal verified Egyptian claims, that the Egyptian flag finally returned to the beach resort of Taba, near Eilat.

The Camp David agreements aroused widespread anger in other Arab states, for they removed Egypt from the struggle with Israel, leaving it far improved militarily, while the basic problems resulting from the creation of Israel remained unsettled. Arab nations broke diplomatic relations with Egypt, and financial aid from oil exporters dwindled. Not surprisingly, many Egyptians also viewed the accords with misgivings, and disliked having diplomatic relations with Israel, especially during violence between Israelis and Palestinians. Nevertheless, given Egypt's poverty and military weakness, the accords seemed necessary.

When Anwar Sadat was assassinated by religious zealots in 1981, there was little spontaneous outpouring of grief as when Gamal Abdul Nasser had died. He never had succeeded in persuading the mass of Egyptians that he was working for them, particularly when they saw spiraling inflation rather than the prosperity he had promised.

With the death of Sadat, Vice President Mohammad Hosni (Muhammad Husni) Mubarak was sworn in as the new head of state. He saw his task as pursuing the policies embarked upon by his predecessor, at least until he established himself firmly in office. During his first years as president, major attention was directed toward organizing the economy productively and reconciling the highly divergent opinions in the country. Every effort was made to present an image of stability and moderation. Mubarak also released from prison many (though not all) political opponents and Islamic fundamentalists.

Persistent Islamic Opposition

Throughout the 1980s, the real opposition to President Mubarak remained the same broad movement whose militants had assassinated Anwar Sadat. The revival of Islamic values stretches from peaceful calls of professional groups to adopt Islamic law, the *Sharia* (see Historical Background), through the *Muslim Brotherhood*, to extremist and violent groups such as the paramilitary *Salvation from Hell*. In the mid–1990s, *al–Gama'a al–Islamiyya* (the Islamic Group) became the largest radical group.

Until the 1987 elections, the government effectively banned the Islamist opposition from contesting elections and entering parliament. Partly as a result of this suppression of opinion, opposition activities took—and now take—the form of demonstrations and protests, as well as destruction and murder. Feeding on popular dissatisfaction with inflation, food shortages, unemployment and Israeli actions in Palestinian territories, the militants came to pose a shadowy yet significant threat to the regime. For example, in 1992 alone, some 70 people perished in religious violence, among them the prominent columnist Faraj Fuda, shot despite police protection. Coptic Christians in Upper Egypt, government officials, and the police themselves suffered fatal assaults. By early 1995 terrorist attacks on buses, boats and trains had left several tourists dead, and nearly three dozen injured; more than 600 Egyptians died. As travelers avoided Egypt or stayed fewer days, the industry's earnings fell to half the 1992 record of $3 billion.

The conviction of Egyptian suspects in the New York World Trade Center bombing illustrates the international links of the Islamic opposition. Bonds forged by volunteers assisting the Afghan *mujahidin* apparently provide shadowy ties among Arabs from many different states.

Some critics fear the government response to militant Islamic groups may heighten their appeal. Allegations that Iran and Sudan trained and armed the militant *Islamic Group* lacked direct evidence. Repressive measures by the police and military include widespread arrests and rough treatment of suspects, allegedly involving torture. Suspicions rose in 1994, for example, when a defense lawyer for the militants died after his arrest, allegedly of lung failure but with skull damage. In late 1992 the government attempted to take control of all mosques in the country, a task as impossible as it was undemocratic.

To some critics, these desperate measures reflect the government's inability to strike at the poverty, corruption and social distress that foster religious extremism. Moreover, the revival of Islamic sentiment reaches far beyond the unemployed. Candidates supported by the *Muslim Brotherhood* captured the leadership of the Bar Association, while Islamic charities won recognition for responding effectively to the Cairo earthquake that killed hundreds and left tens of thousands homeless, in contrast to alleged government incompetence and corruption. In 1995 the government struck repeatedly at the nonviolent *Muslim Brotherhood*. It changed the voting rules so a small minority of activists could not seize control of professional associations like those of the physicians and lawyers. Police detained hundreds of activists. Scores of leaders were sentenced to hard labor for belonging to a banned organization. In fact, though technically banned, the *Brotherhood* had been tolerated for years, while it constructed a network of charities and businesses.

The arrests in the years after 1995 went beyond simple intimidation before

Television in an ancient courtyard   Courtesy: Wayne C. Thompson

upcoming elections. Instead, they symbolized Mubarak's determination to crush all Islamist opposition, with little distinction between non–violent critics and those who attempted to assassinate Mubarak himself.

Extremists such as *al–Gama'a al–Islamiyya* and its offshoots undoubtedly invite repression. Their behavior includes actions such as the murder of 17 elderly Greek tourists and the massive attack in 1997 on tourists at the Temple of Queen Hatshepsut near Luxor that killed 62. However, whereas the government interprets these actions as the end result of moderate Islamic criticism, human rights advocates suggest that the repression of moderates strengthens the militants. By 1998 the militant organizations apparently lay shattered, *al–Gama'a al–Islamiyya* had called for a ceasefire, and violence was mostly confined to Upper Egypt. The next year hundreds of imprisoned Islamists were released, and leaders publicly urged a non-violent struggle for their aims.

Regaining International Prestige

In foreign affairs, in the late 1980s Egypt emerged from its isolation within the Arab world that had followed its signing the Camp David Agreements. Symbolically, it returned to the Arab League in 1989, and a high–ranking Egyptian official was elected its Secretary–General in 1991. The greater prominence often resulted from Egypt's backing for Iraq against Iran, as well as President Mubarak's support for Yasir Arafat and the *Palestine Liberation Organization*. Ironically, Egypt's international role was enhanced when it joined the anti–Iraqi coalition and President Mubarak condemned both Saddam Hussein of Iraq and Yasir Arafat who sympathized with his policy.

Friendship with Iraq had threatened to disintegrate for several years. Egyptian workers fleeing from Iraq in 1989 brought tales of discrimination and brutality.

Others, less fortunate, returned only in caskets. Commentators saw deeper issues at work: a historical pattern of rivalry between Baghdad and Cairo dating to the Caliphs.

When Iraq invaded and subsequently annexed Kuwait in August 1990, Egypt condemned the move, and worked through diplomacy and the Arab League for a peaceful settlement. When these failed, however, Egypt dispatched 35,000 troops to defend Saudi Arabia, the third largest foreign force. President Mubarak came to play a crucial role for the Western–led alliance as an Arab leader who supported the integrity of Kuwait. This tended to weaken Iraqi attempts to portray events as a struggle between nationalist and Muslim Arabs on the one side, and foreigners and their puppet monarchs on the other. Egyptian troops did not invade Iraq, but played a major role in ground combat in freeing Kuwait.

The Gulf Crisis immediately harmed Egypt's economy. More than 500,000 Egyptians working in Kuwait and Iraq fled, often returning unemployed, with little to show for years of labor. War fears virtually eliminated the tourist trade, and shipping through the Suez Canal declined. Only petroleum exports did well, as world prices rose.

By 1991, for most Egyptians optimism had replaced pessimism. The ceasefire ended student and anti–war protests, and left perplexed and discredited those Islamic fundamentalists who had predicted Allah's bestowing an Iraqi victory. Allies grateful for President Mubarak's actions reduced Egypt's debt by $14 billion, or one–third its total. They also released previously–blocked funds, and promised further generosity. Arab Gulf states placed billions of dollars with the Egyptian Central Bank, removing a threatened balance of payments crisis.

The private sector benefitted as well. The wartime alliance gave Egyptian firms greater opportunities to win contracts for reconstruction in Kuwait. Egyptian workers found opportunities in several Gulf countries to replace non–Arabs and Arabs from pro–Iraqi countries. To one commentator, the changes amounted to a "Ten Year Extension on Life," but by 1993 observers had become much more pessimistic about Egypt's ability to overcome poverty and extremism, partly because the layers of government restrictions discourage investment. Egypt's red tape is proverbial.

Under cover of war, the government adopted radical measures, removing controls over the currency and interest rates, raising some prices to world levels, and imposing an unpopular sales tax. These bitterly opposed—but probably necessary—measures had often been postponed, out of fears of protests by the poor who depended on subsidized food, fuel, and medicine. Such measures also widen the disparity between wealth and poverty. In 1997 the government even abolished rent controls on farmland, despite occasionally violent protests by some of the one million tenant farmers hurt by the change. As many as one–third of all Egyptian households probably fell below the poverty line by the end of the decade, a plight worsened because parents found themselves paying much more for their children's education.

For the fortunate there was remarkable progress: a growing private sector, increasing exports, the privatization of some government firms, and firmer control of government spending. These enabled the economy to grow relatively rapidly, and Egypt became a showcase for the success of reforms demanded by the IMF. However, even faster economic growth (e.g., 8% annually) is necessary to absorb the half million additional workers each year.

The Gulf War also left Egypt with a greatly enhanced international role. Egyptian diplomacy, long concerned with solving Arab–Israeli issues and reducing tensions in the area, encouraged Syria to enter negotiations for a regional peace agreement, and the United States to support conditions necessary for the Arab states. Despite the demise of plans for an Egyptian role in the defense of the Gulf states, Egypt increasingly played an independent role in the Middle East, often supporting causes unpopular in the Western nations but important to Arab popular opinion. One example was Mubarak's appeal to lift the economic sanctions against Iraq for humanitarian reasons.

When the Nuclear Non–Proliferation Treaty (NPT) approached its expiration in early 1995, Egypt strongly objected to signing a renewal. Israel, armed with perhaps 100 nuclear weapons, refused to sign either the original treaty or the proposed extension. Egyptian diplomats argued that nuclear weapons in the hands of one country of the region would lead to their spread,

Country barber shop

Courtesy: Wayne C. Thompson

and thus Israel should sign the treaty or propose a plan to do so later. For this and other reasons, Egypt's relations with Israel are diplomatically correct, but frosty.

Following the September 11 terrorist attacks on the United States, President Mubarak moved skillfully on the international scene. He joined the American coalition against Osama bin Ladin and his organization, al-Qa'ida, but only after consultations with other Arab and Muslim leaders, and opposed extending the war to Iraq. By attempting to mediate between the Israel and the Palestinian Authority, Mubarak subtly increased the pressure on Prime Minister Sharon, who wished to avoid direct meetings with Arafat.

Within Egypt, however, the regime seemed to have lost its sense of purpose. Its privatization program faltered, leaving suspicions that favoritism had lined the pockets of some investors in profitable companies, while the many money-losing government firms continued to require subsidies. The exchange rate was controlled, then devalued, leading wary investors to flee from Egypt. The stock market and economic growth slumped, even before the disastrous impact of the September 11 attacks on Western tourism. Unemployment climbed over 20%; for a variety of reasons the economy had failed to grow and produce the necessary jobs for the 800,000 new workers annually.

In difficult times, the government turned to repression, targeting homosexuals, alleged (but unlikely) spies, and a well-known Egyptian-American professor for investigating the treatment of Coptic Christians and electoral fraud.

Politics: The constitution of 1971, introduced by Anwar Sadat and amended several times under his successor, declares that Egypt is a "democratic, socialist" state. It provides for a strong president, who in fact is able to dominate the Advisory Council and People's Assembly both directly and through influencing the electoral process. Furthermore, the president is not elected as in more democratic countries from among several candidates, but is first nominated by at least one-third of the People's Assembly (which is dominated by the government party), then approved by two–thirds of that body and finally "elected" for a six–year term by popular referendum. Thus, President Mubarak's was the only name to appear on the ballot in 1987. To no surprise, he won a second term then, and a third in 1993.

Following another overwhelming victory as a single candidate in 1999, Mubarak reshuffled the cabinet, and the new prime minister, Atef Obeid, brought in a reputation for getting things done, and the economy minister, Yusef Boutros-Ghali, appeared to gain more authority. A Coptic Christian, he reflects the importance of family in Egyptian politics, for his great-grandfather served as prime minister during the British occupation, and his father became the U.N. secretary-general after lengthy service in the Egyptian foreign ministry.

For decades, political realities tainted elections to the People's Assembly, despite the democratic claims of Egypt's constitution. Once known as the *Arab Socialist Union* but now titled the *National Democratic Party*, the president's party always won impressive victories. Official pressures, ranging from publicity and use of influence through police intervention and sometimes outright rigging, ensured a majority so large the legislature rarely served as more than a rubber stamp.

The electoral system also helped to produce the victories. It reserved 400 of the 448 elected seats in the People's Assembly for party members. Thus in the multi–member districts, the second–ranking independent candidate might receive more votes than a party, but still fail to win while the party gained a seat. Furthermore, the large, multi–member constituencies have a vote threshold of 8%. This means that votes for parties receiving less than 8% of the district's votes are applied to the winner's total. Not surprisingly, despite some electioneering, city dwellers rarely voted, but in rural districts elections might be taken seriously and even violently.

Elections in 1984 and 1987 produced the predictable results for President Mubarak's centrist and moderate *National Democratic Party*. Despite the obstacles, a variety of opposition parties manage to exist. The conservative *New Wafd Party* traces its origins to Zaghlul and the 1919 Wafd. The *Muslim Brotherhood*, much more than a party, runs candidates on occasion. In 1987 it allied with the socialist *Labor Party* and under its label won more seats than any other opposition party. Besides the small centrist *Liberal Party*, several left–wing parties reflect varying viewpoints.

Despite their many differences, the major opposition groups formed a Joint Political Platform, demanding an end to the state of emergency, a halt to torture, and a new constitution. However, they often seem more suited to permanent opposition than to governing. For example, in 1990 Egypt's Supreme Court ruled the election laws unfair to independent candidates and forced new elections to the People's Assembly. Never had the opposition's chances seemed greater, with popular discontent over growing sectarian rivalries, Islamic resentment of Egypt's alliance with the United States against Arab Iraq, rising unemployment, and steep increases in the prices of subsidized food and fuel. Nevertheless, the major opposition parties, except the *Progressive Unionists*, boycotted Egypt's fairest elections for decades. The *National Democratic Party* again won a resounding victory.

A host of irregularities marred the 1995 parliamentary elections. Members of the *Muslim Brotherhood* were prevented from running on another party's ticket and harassed when they campaigned as independents. Allegedly the ballot boxes were stuffed with the votes of the young and the dead, giving the ruling party 400 seats. However, the manipulation of voting had gone too far: in 2000 the Supreme Constitutional Court ruled that the 1995 elections had been illegal because they had been supervised by the executive rather than the courts.

Strengthened by hopes for greater fairness, opposition parties approached the 2000 parliamentary elections with some enthusiasm. Despite crackdowns on the *Muslim Brotherhood* and a ban on the (Islamic) *Labor Party* for its role in student riots, the Brotherhood backed individual candidates, and in the first round of elections, several *NDP* candidates suffered defeat. However, in later stages of the elections, citizens likely to sympathize with opposition candidates (easily predicted by dress) often found police and gangs of toughs blocking them from polling stations. Thus, although judges helped protect against ballot stuffing, and the *Muslim Brotherhood* became the leading opposition party, *NDP* party members and affiliated independents command 80% of the seats.

Culture: Perhaps no other country in the world is so overshadowed in the popular mind by the monuments, buildings, ruins and tombs of an ancient civilization as is Egypt. Archaeological remains from five millennia of civilization abound everywhere in the Nile Valley and the Delta. There are royal tombs from as early as 3,000 B.C., the giant pyramids from the 26th century B.C., the magnificent tombs of kings and queens of the 15th and 14th centuries B.C. (including that of Tutankhamun), sculpture and painting from every period and innumerable elaborate inscriptions on stone in a continuous succession attesting to the cultural development of the country at a very early time.

Only a few miles separate the incredible traffic jams and skyscrapers of modern Cairo from the great pyramids at Giza on the edge of the desert. Yet the modern

Temple of Dandara, Upper Egypt

culture of the country has little to do with ancient civilization. New religions, crops, and ways of living largely obliterated the customs of ancient times. Even the agricultural cycle for the Egyptian farmer—known as the *fellah*—has weakened, for the Aswan High Dam prevents the Nile from flooding his lands and depositing nourishing silt for the next year's crops.

In the 7th century Islam began to mold life in the land, and the dozens of impressive mosques, some many centuries old, attest to the significance of this faith. Yet the neon lights in the cities and cotton mills in the country towns, coupled with jet aircraft and satellite TV dishes all bear witness to recent influences of the modern, industrialized world. These new influences do not merely affect the physical appearance of Egypt; they also modify ideas and social patterns. It is an ancient land in the midst of continuing social change that is felt unevenly.

Islamic traditions run deep in Egypt, particularly among the impoverished masses, but increasingly among students and even some professionals. In contrast, some of the upper classes, whether Muslim or Coptic Christian, often attempt to follow Western styles, though most remain more faithful to religious customs. The broader culture, however, finds some kinds of behavior and appearances offensive, while the West ignores them. Thus in 1997 the police arrested a number of students and other heavy metal fans on charges of Satanism. Possession of CDs or T–shirts with the wrong symbols—let alone long hair on men—provoked trouble. Another example: in 1999 an unmarried couple caught kissing passionately in public were sentenced to one year in jail!

Probably the most delicate difficulty that tradition presents Egypt's government and society is female circumcision. The term actually applies to several different procedures, often involving removal of the clitoris, and the practice has been defended as an Islamic solution to avoid female immorality. In fact, the custom seems largely African, rather than Islamic, and Coptic Christians continue it. Given its intimate nature, little is known about its effects on women (for example, does it render a woman uninterested in sex or increase the search for satisfaction?). On the other hand, it kills girls every year and leaves women maimed. Nevertheless, most Egyptian mothers apparently desire to have their daughters circumcised, despite a (poorly enforced) government ban on it in 1996.

Though relatively poor, Egypt in many respects remains the cultural center of the Arab World, known for its novelists, short story writers, dramatists and poets. Indeed, in 1988 Naguib Mahfouz, known best in the English–speaking world for *Midhaq Alley* and *The Beginning and the End*, won the Nobel Prize for Literature. The first Arab writer to receive the honor, Mahfouz borrowed liberally from the traditions of European literature in his realistic novels of life in Cairo, because Arabic lacked a literary tradition in fiction. However, international recognition brought Mahfouz more than adulation from the literary world. It revived criticism of his work as blasphemous for portraying irreligious individuals questioning Islam. Mahfouz bravely condemned Ayatollah Khomeini's death sentence on Salman Rushdie. Then, in his 80s, he barely survived an assassination attempt, but after recovering resumed walking the streets and alleys of his beloved Cairo.

On a more popular level, Egyptian musicians dominate popular music and videos from Oman to North Africa. In particular, the "golden voice" of Umm Kalthoum captivated hearts across the Arab world during a career of six decades, and her recordings continue to sell well.

Cairo's constant flow of new films and television dramas makes it the Hollywood of the region, many filmed in a billion–dollar production center that opened in 1997. Plots frequently revolve around marriage and family problems against a background of conflict between traditions and modern individuality, as well as the persistent issue of class consciousness. The all–too–often hackneyed stories dramatize the sufferings of life. Difficulties sometimes arise with Islamic conservatives. In one example, a film about Joseph (*Al–Mohager*, "The Emigrant") was banned for showing a prophet on the screen.

Films, television dramas and music have made the distinctive accent of Cairene Arabic familiar, and sometimes mocked, throughout the Arabic–speaking countries. Television programming originating in other Arab countries is markedly reducing Egypt's lead in this field. Its first place in journalism is also being challenged by countries such as Saudi Arabia, as they stride forward with money and education.

Founded in 988, the mosque school of al–Azhar in Cairo is one of the oldest universities in the world. Traditionally its professors sat at the base of one of the mosque's pillars, lecturing to students who came from many lands. There were no official examinations, but when the faculty considered a student proficient in a subject, they issued him a license to teach. Modern changes include formal diplomas, branches in medicine and other non–theological disciplines, and a women's program. The Grand Imam of al–Azhar remains an important spokesman for Sunni Islam, and offers guidance to believers on many theological issues.

In recent years Egypt lost its lead among Arab states in education, largely because of financial limitations. As in most professions, teachers in Egypt receive pitifully small salaries, so many of the best qualified have been lured to more prosperous countries to work at much higher remuneration. The quality of education at the University of Cairo and the half dozen other universities in Egypt is generally good, though in common with other Less Developed Countries, Egypt turns out too many liberal arts graduates, who fill (often needless) government positions or seek work abroad. In contrast, the country needs scientists, and especially skilled manual workers and technicians.

For decades education for all remained a dream rather than reality. However, the government built thousands of new schools in the 1990s, for the 90% of young boys and 80% of girls who enroll. Adult literacy climbed from 40% in the 1970s to 60% by the end of the century. However, with their salaries as low at $35 per month, teachers have encouraged the practice of guiding the best learning in private tutoring sessions, and classroom study often decays into rote memorization. Not surprisingly, many children drop out: the law requiring nine years of school cannot be enforced. After just three or four years inside a classroom, many children begin working, even in agriculture and building construction, because of family poverty.

Health services vary greatly according to family income and education. Although the universities train doctors to the best world standards, poverty prevents adequate medical services for many. Sanitation is often deplorable. In Cairo, some 2 million people live in areas without sewers. Preliminary construction of a new sewer system for the city was begun in early 1985. Years will be required to complete this project which is an urgent matter of public health.

Two new cultural events promise to enrich the country during the coming years. In Alexandria, home in ancient times of a famous library, funding from UNESCO, the government, and other sources will provide a $200 million library and conference center. The international competition to design the library drew over 500 entries, and the winning entry symbolizes Egypt's ancient heritage. It envisions a disc–shaped building slanted with one side in the earth, the other raised, recalling the ancient Egyptian sun–god.

The second cultural landmark, in Cairo, recalls the Islamic heritage in its dome, geometric windows, and marble colonnades. The New Opera House on the island of Gezira replaces the 19th century landmark gutted by fire in 1971. Built with Japanese assistance as an educational and cultural center, it offers the potential of becoming much more than a mere stage for musical and other art forms in Western languages.

Economy: Although systematic efforts to modernize began earlier than in other Arab lands, and recent growth rates have been commendable, personal incomes remain low. A rapidly growing population, misfortune in war, misguided government economic policies and a tradition of government regulation all reduced opportunities in the past fifty years. In addition, natural resources are few. There is no timber, no coal, and outside the Nile Valley, almost no water. Mineral deposits provide little wealth for a population so large, and are limited to modest oil deposits, natural gas, salt and manganese.

Visual evidence of the mixture of poverty and progress strikes even the casual tourist, in the form of barefoot children, simple farming methods, and the ever-present unemployed. Less obviously, the gap between the poor and the rich is enormous, the latter receiving incomes some 5000% of the former. Cairo's taxi drivers include some of the best educated in the world—university professors who must somehow supplement modest salaries of about $300 per month. Similarly, the average Egyptian's diet includes little variation: bread, well-flavored broad (fava) beans, greens, and occasionally meat. The latter frequently comes from camels, and

may be noted hanging in the butcher shops, distinguished by its size and yellowish hue. The press of millions of poor makes Cairo one of the world's most crowded and noisy cities. Indeed, a survey reported that 60% of Cairenes used sedatives at least once against the noise and stress.

Unrelated to Cairo's noise, the population growth rate fell from more than 3% in 1985 to 2% ten years later, a welcome decline that still provided one million additional mouths needing food every year. Almost all live in the 4% of the country's territory comprising the Nile Valley and Delta. Egypt's population is roughly seven times that of New Jersey, but lives in only twice as much territory. Moreover, because one-third of the population is rural, average farms measure only a few acres. This overwhelms the ability of the fertile soil and warm climate to provide either sufficient food or a good standard of living.

Traditionally, agriculture formed the basis of the Egyptian economy. Famous for its desirable long-staple cotton, Egypt also produced and sometimes exported grains such as wheat and rice, as well as sugar. Vegetable crops included broad beans, a major protein source for the

middle and lower classes, and the variety of fruits extended from oranges and other citrus along the coast to dates and tropical mangoes and guavas.

Before the 1952 Revolution, much of the land belonged to absentee landowners whose domains included entire villages. Under Gamal Abdul Nasser, the government attempted significant agricultural changes. Land reform, instituted in part to break the political power of conservative landlords, limited ownership to a maximum 50 acres in traditional farming areas. Irrigation schemes brought large tracts of desert under cultivation, and the Aswan High Dam (see below) provided more areas with successive crops per a year. Public health and education improved in the villages.

Unfortunately, government regulations offset much of the progress. Investment in agriculture came low on the list of government priorities, while the new landowners lacked credit ratings to borrow. They often lacked formal education and technical training as well, both required to benefit from scientific advances in agriculture.

Often government policies hampered the farmer further. To benefit politically-active urban consumers, controls kept prices far below world levels, and prohibited farmers from selling abroad. Bread, for example, remained at 2 *piasters* per kilo (about 1 U.S. cent per pound) until 1989, and farmers on occasion fed animals bread rather than more expensive feedgrains. Required to grow crops important to the government, such as cotton and wheat, farmers only survived because of subsidized fertilizers and other supplies. In turn, the subsidies distorted prices and production. Meanwhile, hundreds of thousands of acres returned to desert, and Egypt turned to imports for half its food.

Recent reforms show the potential for substantial improvements in farm production and income. When wheat was deregulated, its price rose, and output increased by 100%. Besides rewarding farmers, this reduced somewhat the 6 million (of 8 million consumed) tons of wheat and flour imported yearly. Likewise, when the government permitted the private export of oranges, quantities rose by one third, at the cost of higher prices at home. New policies towards reclaiming the desert stress the importance of high-research, low technology solutions, including the use of genetics to obtain salt-tolerant plants.

Above all else, Egypt under Nasser trusted the Aswan High Dam to solve poverty and raise farm output. The dam promised to store the summer floods in the largest man-made reservoir in the world (Lake Nasser) and then provide year-round irrigation for many areas and water for thousands of acres of desert. A great technical achievement as well as a foreign-policy success, the dam at its

A Cairo street scene

Goat market in Cairo

completion in 1971 met these goals, and its massive turbines generate much of Egypt's electricity.

For all its benefits, however, the High Dam also brought problems. After dropping their silt in Lake Nasser, the Nile waters flow swiftly, and now scour its banks. Some Delta lands began to subside, deprived of the fertile soil previously deposited during the annual flood. Several species of fish—especially sardines—disappeared from the coastal Mediterranean waters now denied the Nile's nutrients. Across Egypt, the underground water table rose, threatening historical sites, and year–round irrigation spread bilharzia and other parasitic diseases, as well as obnoxious water hyacinths.

Two predicted difficulties, rising soil salinity and the loss of silt that enriched the soil, require expensive drainage systems and chemical fertilizers. Thus the benefits of the High Dam—including protection for Egypt from years of drought in East Africa—carry several costly side effects. Furthermore, the experts are deeply divided about how much water the dam will collect. Some claim that even without major diversions upstream, early in the next century water shortages will appear, in part because of seepage and evaporation from Lake Nasser. Any major diversion upstream in Ethiopia or Sudan would magnify the shortfall. Complicating matters, two massive schemes under construction are planned to irrigate two million additional acres, by bringing Nile water to the "New Valley," a series of oases in the Western Desert, and to the north-east and Sinai. Skeptics doubt the Nile's flow will prove sufficient.

World environmental issues pose other, less certain, risks to Egyptian agriculture. The low–lying Delta and coastal cities face inundation from the sea if the more alarming predictions of Global Warming prove true. Air pollution around Cairo poses a threat to plants and animals as well as

humans. However, solutions to environmental problems sometimes benefit society. Alexandria's sewage, now flowing out to sea with harmful results, may be treated on land less expensively than a new treatment plant for sea disposal. As a bonus, the nutrient–rich waste water will irrigate desert areas.

Industry: Industrial production began modestly in Egypt, partly because foreign and local entrepreneurs first sought profits from government contracts. After World War I some factories began to process food and cotton textiles, logical early industries given the few raw materials. The officers that led the 1952 Revolution desired to industrialize the country, motivated by socialist ideas that encouraged national self–sufficiency in many areas and equated modernity with heavy industry. However, the same ideas abhorred foreign investment and discouraged the domestic private sector. The state nationalized firms in a number of areas, eventually controlling 85% of manufacturing assets, while those that remained suffered paralyzing regulations. Egyptian red tape became famous, hampering almost all trade and commerce.

Attempts to produce many types of manufactured goods within the country, from appliances to cars, often provided expensive products of poor quality that required high tariff protection to compete against imports. (In contrast, the rapidly growing countries of East Asia follow the opposite policies, encouraging exports and foreign trade.) Anwar Sadat modified the plan with a program of economic liberalization, but many regulations remain. Automobile production, for example, took the form of assembling about 25,000 cars yearly from kits supplied by FIAT of Italy and related countries in Eastern Europe. The economics were hopeless: the state–owned El-Nasr Company spent more foreign exchange per car kit than the price of the complete vehicle; Egyptian costs were additional.

Similarly, the General Motors plant operated well below capacity.

Even well–intended regulations often harmed private companies. For example, to encourage investment in factories and equipment, laws decreed low interest rates on loans to industry. Perversely, this made such loans so unattractive to banks that they avoided making them.

Trade policy from the Revolution to 1991 involved maintaining artificially high values for the Egyptian pound. Earnings from certain exports provided foreign exchange that the government used to purchase essential imports. Bought with overvalued pounds, the favored imports—from food and medicines through weaponry—cost relatively little. However, such an overvalued pound prohibited many potential exports, so multiple exchange rates were created, at one time at least a dozen of them. The system proved both inefficient and corrupting, and in 1991 Egypt adopted a single rate, one step to winning approval and aid from the International Monetary Fund.

Egypt's leadership in the Arab world also slowed economic growth. Opposing Israel militarily meant five wars (including the War of Attrition) in 25 years between 1948 and 1973. Besides the personnel costs of a large military force and several generations of weapons largely destroyed on the battlefield, the damage included Israeli attacks on economic targets and the devastation of cities along the Suez Canal. In addition to untold sums owed the Soviet Union for arms, the country purchased military hardware on credit from the United States, ironically during a period of peace with Israel. Paying the high–interest loans became a crushing burden on the Egyptian economy before the U.S. cancelled the debt of $7 billion.

In contrast to past military expenses and losses, Egypt today has become a substantial and presumably profitable producer of weapons. By early 1988 military exports ranked (with cotton) for fifth place among exports, earning some $500 million. Although still dependent on imports for aircraft, electronics, and other sophisticated items, reports indicated Egypt had become self–sufficient in light anti–aircraft guns, armored trucks, rockets, bombs, and towed artillery.

Four Uncommon Assets

For its present growth and future prosperity, Egypt depends on four uncommon assets: a work force employed in wealthier Arab countries, oil, tourism and the Suez Canal. Each of these benefits provides foreign exchange, vitally important for a country whose foreign debt reached $50 billion before reductions in 1991. Oil and the canal also provide alternatives to tax revenues.

In years of high prices, the export of crude oil provided the largest source of foreign exchange, and so enabled Egypt to import food, equipment, and consumer goods. Although not a member of the Organization of Petroleum Exporting Countries (OPEC), it exports around 450,000 barrels of oil and gas equivalent per day. Oil revenues are crucially important, and falling international prices (from the $30s to below $10 per barrel in the mid–1980s) severely disrupted the economy. Egypt's oil reserves appear to be limited, and domestic demand for oil is growing. Without large new discoveries, oil exports will continue to decline, though partly replaced by natural gas.

For two thousand years travelers have marveled at the Pyramids. A century ago, the wealth and beauty of Tutankhamun's tomb rendered a minor Pharaoh a household word. For the present era of mass tourism, Egypt possesses some of the world's most spectacular archaeological treasures and monuments. Other attractions exist as well, often inexpensive and rarely spoiled by rain. They range from sandy beaches along the Mediterranean to relatively unspoiled fishing and diving in the Red Sea. They include Mt. Sinai, where Jews and Christians traditionally believe God gave Moses the Ten Commandments. Arabs from oil states often seek culture and entertainment in Cairo, while visitors from West and East seek bargains in the city's *souks* (or suqs, pronounced like "duke") or

enjoy luxury cruises on the Nile. Despite attacks by Muslim militants, the industry earns $3 billion during prosperous years, and its employees support some one million people.

Several improvements could easily improve tourists' impressions of Egypt and encourage more visits. Cairo airport, often crowded and confused, can present an unattractive first impression. More direct flights from Europe to other destinations in the country could relieve congestion and encourage more travelers. While street hawkers may be inevitable in a land of poverty and unemployment, discourteous government employees are unnecessary obstacles. Museums offer little information for the more serious visitor, and frequently fail to do justice to their magnificent collections. While Western and Asian visitors flock to antiquities famous from their school textbooks, they often lack an understanding of Islam. Thus, an opportunity exists to use Cairo's Muslim heritage for both tourism and education.

One unique Egyptian economic benefit comes from the country's location connecting Asia and Africa. Cut through the Isthmus at a cost of 100,000 lives, the Suez Canal reduces greatly the distance ships must travel between Europe and Arabia or the Indian Ocean. Tolls from ships passing through the canal provide a very

important source of foreign exchange, amounting to about $2 billion in recent years, less than oil or tourism. Dues are not cheap for the 15-hour journey, with the largest of loaded tankers reportedly levied a fee of $450,000 in 1999. Dredging to widen, deepen, and straighten the Canal continued in the late 1990s, aaaawith the goal of permitting passage by any vessel.

No longer the most important source of foreign currency, remittances sent home by the two million Egyptians working outside the country still play a very important role. Before the Gulf War, nearly four million Egyptians—almost all male, mostly young, and often educated—worked abroad, primarily in the Gulf. Many were unskilled laborers, but others were teachers, doctors, and other professionals. They sought foreign jobs, some of them dangerous, difficult or dirty, because remaining at home meant unemployment or low wages, and they often planned to return in a few years, with funds saved for marriage and the purchase of a little land, a house, or perhaps a business. With pay abroad often 10 times the Egyptian rate, four years hard work could equal the gain of 20 years at home. Repatriated earnings, in the outstanding year of 1989/90, reached $8 billion.

The Gulf War and the 1990s recession in the oil states threw hundreds of thousands out of work. As foreigners lacking

Early morning rush hour in Cairo

61

unemployment benefits, some could neither find work nor afford the return airfare. A decade later, the number of workers and their earnings had fallen by half.

The combination of religion and economics brought another difficulty. Because Islam (like the Old Testament) forbids interest, many Egyptians avoided placing their savings in banks. In recent years a number of Islamic Investment Companies formed, to provide savers with a share of profits instead of becoming depositors who received (forbidden) interest. Initially the "Islamic banks" grew rapidly, paying annual dividends at double the interest rate paid by banks. But the companies operated outside the law, and one of the largest failed to make payments. Its officers were convicted in criminal court, and the government responded with strict legal conditions for other Islamic Investment Companies.

Though often seeming piecemeal and half–hearted, the economic reforms of the 1990s created an environment for sustained economic growth. Difficulties like the budget deficit, inflation, and the balance of payments deficit that had plagued the country for decades dwindled to insignificance when the government, hesitantly and slowly cut subsidies and controlled its spending.

The subsidies had distorted prices badly—kerosene, for example, had cost only $.20 per gallon, and legends exist of farmers feeding bread to their animals,

since it was cheaper than grains. Removing the subsidies encouraged more efficient use of resources, but in addition, Egypt's poor and middle classes found significant holes in their economic safety–nets. Afraid of popular backlash—in 1977 rioters had chanted at President Sadat, "Hero of the Crossing (of the Suez Canal), Where is our Breakfast?"—the cuts were scheduled gradually, and as subtlely as possible. Rather than raise the price of bread, for example, the government cut the size of the pita–style loaf.

Cutting the government's large payroll and privatizing the companies it owned proved a more difficult task. In 1990, nearly one-third of all employed Egyptians worked for the government and its companies, far more than needed. A major purpose of the privatization drive was to provide jobs for the roughly 800,000 new job-seekers annually, but many legal, political and practical complications slowed the sale of government firms to private owners. Fortunately, new private companies flourished as the government removed regulations, and by 1999 only about 20% of output came from government firms, and the government's share of the workforce had fallen to 25%. However, crowds protested against an emergency plan to hire recent graduates in 2001, for many earlier high school and university graduates remained unemployed, anxious for the $50 monthly salary and lifetime security of a government job.

The Future: The spirit of the ancient pharaohs accustoms Egyptians to stable, if sometimes dull, central government. Only three men have ruled Egypt in the 47 years since Nasser became president in 1954. President Mubarak intends to lengthen that period, and he has not appointed a vice president as a prospective successor.

During recent years Egypt faced one challenge after another: violent extremists, frightened tourists, low oil prices, stagnant world trade, popular passions aroused by the Palestinian struggle for independence, dramatic building collapses and train fires resulting from inadequate safety supervision. Most economies would have floundered under the impact, but Egypt's grew fairly rapidly before stagnating in 2000. At last, and very unevenly, Egyptians sense growing economic opportunity, but they also desire the safety of subsidies and controls. So many are becoming rich that corrupt businessmen are the new stock villains in the movies and TV soap operas.

For years, a mixture of manipulation, control and fraud has prevented a democratic opposition from emerging. However, despite the legendary patience of Egyptians, the newly rich often seek to influence politics, and the impoverished stubbornly demand a voice in decisions. At some point desires for democracy and political development could overflow the present narrow limits.

The Pyramids attract all nationalities

Courtesy: Juliet Bunch

The Islamic Republic of Iran

Supporters of the new Iranian President Muhammad Khatami celebrate his victory on May 25, 1997.   AP/Wide World Photo

Area: 636,000 square miles (1,647,240 sq. km.).

Population: Perhaps 62 million. Official estimates revised from 68 million to 60.7 million in 1997.

Capital City: Tehran (Pop. 6 million, plus surrounding area total more than 10 million).

Climate: Most of Iran is arid, but the northwestern part receives moderate to heavy rainfall. Temperature range is extreme, from cold winters of the central plateau and northern mountains to the intense heat of the humid southern coastal districts.

Neighboring Countries: Armenia, Azerbaijan, Turkmenistan (North); Afghanistan (East); Pakistan (Southeast); Iraq (West); Turkey (Northwest).

Time Zone: GMT +3 hrs. and 30 min.

Official Language: Persian, called *Farsi* in Iran.

Other Principal Tongues: Kurdish, Baluchi, Luri, Armenian, Turkish, Shushtari, Azeri and Arabic.

Ethnic Background: People are identified mainly according to language (about 80% Persian or Iranian), but also according to tribal group or religion.

Principal Religion: Shi'a Islam (93%), Sunni Islam (5%), Baha'i (1%).

Chief Commercial Product: Petroleum.

Agricultural Produce and Livestock: Wheat, barley, pistachios, rice, sugar beets, sugar cane, potatoes, sheep, goats, cattle and chickens.

Major Trading Partners: Japan, Germany, Spain, U.K., Italy and France.

Currency: Rial (R 3,000 = $1 U.S. officially; black market rates reportedly exceed R 8,000 per dollar in early 1999.)

Former Colonial Status: Under influence of Russia and Britain (1907–1923); occupied by Soviet and British troops (1941–1945).

National Day: February 1.

Chief Executive: Muhammad Khatami, President.

"Head of the Revolution": Ayatollah Seyyid Ali Khamenei. Khamenei received the title as successor to Ayatollah Ruhollah Khomeini, along with the title "Supreme Leader."

National Flag: Three equal horizontal stripes of (top to bottom) green, white and red. Along the edges of the green and red stripes, in narrow lines next to the white, are 22 repetitions of the words *Allah–o–Akbar,* "God is Great." In the center of the white stripe is the emblem of the Islamic Republic of Iran in red, an emblem designed to symbolize in modern–appearing, simple lines the main ideas of the Islamic Revolution.

Gross Domestic Product: $100–$133 billion.

GDP per capita: $1,900 (IMF); other estimates: $1,100–$4,700.

Geographically, much of Iran (pronounced like "ee rahn") is neither picturesque nor fertile. The center, occupying more than half the territory, is a bleak, windswept combination of desert and salt–flats—scorching hot by day in summer and freezing cold during winter nights. Nevertheless, nearly 70 million people consider Iran their homeland, since the outlying mountains, watered plains and other regions support large populations.

The least typical region is the southern coast of the Caspian Sea, which like many inland seas lies below the level of the oceans. This garden of Iran, created by abundant rainfall and warm weather, is

63

the most densely populated area of the country. Several million people also live in the extreme northwest province of Azerbaijan, a land of green mountains, valleys and good rainfall. Tabriz, Iran's second largest city, is the center of this province. Other important populations of farmers and herders live in the mountainous regions along the border with Iraq on the west, and east of the Caspian Sea near Turkmenistan.

The rest of the country is largely uninhabited except for nomads who make great seasonal wanderings from north to south. The elevation of the central plateau (3,000 to 6,000 feet) produces great extremes of temperature; 110° or 115° during the day in the summer contrasts with sub–freezing temperatures of the winter nights. The southern coast and neighboring areas are the hottest regions of Iran; frost is unknown there. Light rainfall provides sparse pasture for livestock.

Tehran has grown in two centuries from a village to a huge city and the seat of a highly centralized government. Railroads, roads and trade center on it; industry is concentrated there. The other major cities are Tabriz and Isfahan, both of which are commercial and handicraft centers with long histories.

History: Civilization stretches back thousands of years in Iran, whose name means "Land of the Aryans," and its Indo–European peoples formed several of the notable kingdoms of ancient history (see Historical Background). Later invaders added Arab Islam and Turkish warriors to Iranian society.

So ancient is the history of Iran—or Persia, as it was traditionally known—that the modern period began hundreds of years ago, with the Safavid dynasty in the 16th century and the widespread adoption of Shi'a Islam (see Historical Background). The Safavid Empire reached its greatest power and extent under Shah Abbas (1587–1629), after whose death it declined. By the early 18th century, Persia was threatened by Turkey on the west, Russia on the north and the Afghans on the east.

After an Afghan invasion ended the Safavid dynasty, Nadir Shah (1736–1747) restored much of the country's unity and conquered additional territory. Famous for his military exploits and adventures, he returned from invading India with incredible wealth and the famous Peacock Throne, but failed to found a dynasty. The peaceful reign of Karim Khan Zand (1750–1779) was followed by the establishment of the Qajar line of rulers. Though often beset with tribal revolts and bloodshed over the succession, the sometimes–brutal Qajars maintained power until 1925. Shah Agha Mohammed Khan made Tehran his capital in 1788.

Under Qajar rule, Persia fought unsuccessful wars with Russia, the Ottoman Turks and the Afghans, and lost territory to each. The most noted of the Qajar rulers was Nasir ud–Din, who began ruling in 1848 as a boy of only sixteen and continued in power until his assassination in 1896. In the first years of his reign he depended on a capable and honest minister who achieved important financial and military reforms; for this the minister's reward was execution in 1852 at the instigation of corrupt officials. The latter part of Nasir ud–Din's rule was stable from an administrative point of view, but it did not bring many changes in a country that was not advancing with the times.

Rivalry between the Russian Empire and the British Empire tended to concentrate on Persia. Russia sought to expand to the warm water ports of the Persian Gulf, while Britain was concerned primarily for the security of India. Russia enjoyed more influence in Persia, though the British worked to gain favor through agents in Tehran. Finally, in 1907 Russia and Britain arrived at an agreement—without any consideration of Persian desires in the matter—providing Russia a "sphere of influence" in the north, and Britain the south. A strip of less important territory in the middle was left as a neutral zone.

Dissatisfaction with foreign influence in the country and the ineffectiveness of the monarchy in resisting it grew stronger in the late 19th century, symbolized by disapproval of granting British companies a tobacco monopoly in 1890. It produced protests and a ban from the clergy on using tobacco.

Partly influenced by Western ideas of political freedom, in 1906 groups of merchants, religious leaders and reformers compelled the Shah to grant a Constitution and allow a parliament *(Majlis)*. Known as the Constitutional Revolution (1905–1911), these changes began an era of numerous struggles between the monarchy and the *Majlis* over control of the government.

After a decade and a half of struggle, marked by several closings and reconvenings, the Majlis and the political reformers had no more success to show at strengthening the country and reducing foreign influence than the monarchy.

64

A map of Persia from a 1560 atlas

and won approval from the *Majlis* in 1949. The plan's expenses required about $58 million a year beyond local taxes. With little foreign aid available, Iranian politicians sought what they considered a fairer share of income from oil exports. When Anglo–Iranian refused higher payments, in an atmosphere of emotional nationalism the *Majlis* nationalized the entire petroleum industry in 1951. An elderly politician who had championed the bill, Mohammed Mossadeq, became Prime Minister. His government found itself unable to produce and market oil in the face of an international boycott organized by Britain, and during the next two years the country became poorer and political disturbances more serious. However, Mossadeq firmly refused any compromise agreement short of full national

The late Shah of Iran

Indeed, during World War I central authority collapsed almost entirely, as Ottoman, Russian, and British forces and puppets occupied parts of the country. This set the stage for the rise of a dictator. In 1921 Reza Khan, second ranking officer in the Cossack Brigade, joined a *coup d'etat* that forced the Shah to change the prime minister. After creating the national army to replace various foreign–influenced units, in 1923 Reza compelled the Shah to appoint him Prime Minister. The Shah then left the country, and in 1925 Reza Khan had the *Majlis* depose the Qajar dynasty. Later that same year he proclaimed himself Reza Shah Pahlavi, taking the ancient name Pahlavi from Persian history because he needed a dynastic name.

A man of action rather than theories, Reza Shah improved and enlarged the army—then used it to establish law and order in every corner of the country. He worked to gain the nation full independence, make himself its master and make it as much like modern Europe as possible. He commanded the construction of roads, and a railroad from the Caspian Sea to the Persian Gulf. He introduced new secular laws and moved away from Islamic religious law. He encouraged modern technical education, forced people to dress more like Europeans and started factories—by 1942 they employed half a million workers. Reza Shah even changed the name of the country from Persia to Iran to impress the world that things had changed. A moderate but steady source of income to finance the new projects came

from oil exports produced by the Anglo–Iranian Oil Company.

After the German invasion of the Soviet Union in 1941, Soviet and British troops occupied Iran to prevent Reza Shah from allying with Nazi Germany and to secure the country's oil and transportation routes for Allied use. Reza abdicated and went into exile, where he died; his son succeeded him as Mohammed Reza. Troops from the United States eventually joined the occupation.

When the Allied troops began to withdraw from Iran after the end of the war, young Mohammed Reza faced wide opposition to his rule. Rival factions, all previously repressed by his determined father, vied to control the government. Great landowners, though paying nearly no taxes, attempted to dominate politics, and nomadic chieftans sought to free themselves and their tribes of Reza Shah's central authority. Shi'a religious leaders denounced secular government, and elderly politicians schemed for office. In the streets, the Communist-leaning *Tudeh Party* held sway, and foreign powers courted ethnic minorities.

In these circumstances, the Soviet Union attempted to form an autonomous Communist regime in Azerbaijan, the Turkish-speaking northwestern province. However, the United States and Britain stood by the Shah, and Soviet troops withdrew in 1946. The Iranian army dealt severely with the separatist leaders.

In response to the dire economic conditions, a Seven–Year Plan was drawn up

economic independence, meaning Iranian control of its oil.

The Shah dismissed Mossadeq in mid–1953, but the Prime Minister refused to leave office. Lacking authority and fearing mobs and riots in Tehran, the Shah and his Queen fled the country. Iran tottered, near financial collapse and anarchy as Mossadeq attempted to seize more power. However, urged and financed by the U.S. CIA, forces loyal to the monarchy took to the streets, and the army arrested Mossadeq and restored order. The Shah returned, and the United States provided an emergency grant of $45 million to begin the country's recovery. Large–scale military and technical assistance was promised, and in 1954 a compromise agreement on the oil industry permitted exports to flow and provided fees and royalties. Thus, linked to America, the Shah began to dominate the political scene in alliance with the army.

Facing continued opposition from such groups as wealthy landholders, extreme religious elements, politically active students and politicians of various outlooks, the Shah developed several methods of maintaining his authoritarian rule. The National Security and Intelligence Organization (SAVAK) was created in 1957 to control political activity and the press. Possessing almost unlimited power, SAVAK grew in importance over the years. Through arbitrary arrests and torturing of prisoners, it made many enemies for the Shah's government. While effective for a decade at suppressing Islamic fundamentalists, SAVAK also divided the modernized middle class and left it suspicious of the Shah.

To win the support of peasants and moderate reformers, and decrease the appeal of leftist revolutionaries, the Shah proclaimed a "White Revolution" in 1963. Two aspects of it, land distribution and greater rights for women, aroused the fierce opposition of the Shi'a clergy. They considered that the changes in the role of women threatened family morality, and the distribution of land to the peasants from vast religious foundations endangered substantial revenues they received as administrators. While a national referendum overwhelmingly approved the reforms, they turned Shi'a leaders such as Grand Ayatollah (the highest religious rank in Iran) Ruhollah Khomeini into irreconcilable enemies.

To support his government, the Shah rewarded the upper ranks in the civil service and army with good incomes. Thus, he gained support among a small elite, but almost ubiquitous bribery and other forms of dishonesty among officials contributed to the hostility of others. Increasingly the Shah proposed grand projects, and emphasized his imperial title, notably in 1971 when he spent millions of dollars celebrating the 2,500th anniversary of the founding of the ancient Persian Empire.

To prevent opposition in the Majlis and yet maintain a form of representative government, the Shah sponsored his own political party. This was formed in 1963 as the *Iran Novin* ("New Iran") Party and then in 1975 enlarged and renamed the *Rastakhiz* ("Resurgence") *Party* while other parties were outlawed.

Though failing, perhaps unavoidably, to meet the needs and desires of most citizens, the Shah attempted to assert Iran's role as a responsible regional power with large and well–equipped military forces. This power influenced neighbors. After decades of tension, in 1975 Iran and Iraq agreed to move their border from the Iranian shore of the Shatt al-Arab to mid-channel. Because the river connects the oil center of Abadan with the Gulf, Iran gained long-sought benefits. In return, the Shah halted supplies for Iraq's rebellious Kurds.

Vast increases in oil revenues during the 1970s enabled the government to rush development at home while purchasing the latest U.S. weapons such as the F-15 fighter. The guns-and-butter approach created wealth for many Iranians, but the lower classes gained little prosperity, suffered high inflation, and resented the corruption and westernized lifestyles of the rich. In between, the middle class found few legal political opportunities. With the parliamentary opposition stifled, illegal left-wing parties and Islamic groups widened the appeal of extremists.

Riots in the religious city of Qom and in Tabriz in early 1978 showed serious popular dissatisfaction, and the army fired on the mobs, killing many. These deaths triggered further riots, and despite official bans, demonstrations spread to Tehran and elsewhere. Massacres by the Shah's troops ended all pretense of popular support, and the bloodshed united the rival opposition groups in the single goal of ousting the monarch. Ayatollah Khomeini, for 14 years a harsh critic from exile in Iraq and France, assumed leadership of the movement despite his age of 76.

After months of strikes and confusion, with oil production and exports halted and the economy in chaos, the Shah finally left the country in early 1979. As a concession, he placed the government under a long–time critic. However, the concessions came too late. Khomeini quickly returned to a triumphant welcome, and appointed Mehdi Bazargan prime minister. Despite the lavish attention the Shah had paid it, the army abandoned its struggle against the revolutionaries. Voters overwhelmingly approved the creation of the Islamic Republic of Iran; it became official on April 1, 1980.

The Islamic Republic immediately faced major problems. Restive ethnic minorities, many of them Sunni rather than Shi'a, threatened rebellion. The economy required emergency measures, but was largely ignored. Rival groups and individuals who had united against the Shah now

Ayatollah Ruhollah Khomeini

Iran's Imperial Family in exile, Panama (1980).

struggled violently for power. To maintain power, self-appointed "revolutionary courts" began imposing long prison terms or death sentences on former officials, accused wrongdoers or "sinners". By mid-1979 some 200 executions had been carried out—often within hours of arrest. Opposing groups has also begun political assassination, and Khomeini had ordered the establishment of a special militia for his *Islamic Revolutionary Council*.

When militants seized the U.S. embassy in Tehran in late 1979 and took 63 hostages, they won wide approval in the streets. Many political leaders approved the illegal action, but the Bazargan cabinet resigned almost immediately because it had no effective authority. Khomeini then directed the *Islamic Revolutionary Council* to take control, and international pressures on Iran to release the hostages proved useless. An American attempt to rescue the hostages in 1980 ended unsuccessfully in the Iranian desert, but after the deposed Shah died in Egypt, the hostages finally were released in 1981, an inauguration present for Ronald Reagan.

Against this chaotic background, a plebiscite overwhelmingly approved a new Constitution. Besides the typical democratic institutions of the elected *Majlis* (parliament) and president, the Constitution established two novel centers of power. The first, the Council of Guardians, is an appointed committee of clergy charged with ensuring that proposed laws conformed with Islam. The second source of authority, known in English as the Supreme Leader (or faqih), is the chief theologian, who interprets religious law and acts on behalf of the Hidden Imam who disappeared in 878. Thus, Islamic law as interpreted by religious scholars is supreme, rather than the sovereign nation. For the first decade of revolutionary Iran, Ayatollah Khomeini held the position of Supreme Leader.

The relatively moderate Bani Sadr won the 1980 presidential election, but by 1981, facing impeachment over military defeats, he fled the country. The clergy's *Islamic Republican Party* then completely dominated government, but faced an uprising by the secular and socialist *Mujahedin-e Khalq*. The regime suppressed the uprising with great brutality and torture, executing tens of thousands of alleged *Mujahedin*, who turned to bombings and assassinations, and decimated the party leadership in one blast.

The War with Iraq, 1980–1988

Just when Iran had weakened from a deteriorating economy, political tensions and international isolation, Iraq launched a full-scale invasion of southwestern Iran in 1980. Capitalizing on the Iranian military's disorganization and shortages of supplies for its U.S.-supplied weapons, the Iraqi forces captured border cities and drove miles into Iran. Within months, however, Iranian troops and Revolutionary Guards counterattacked, largely regaining the border by 1982. Expediently,

the government purchased military equipment and supplies from Israel, though publicly condemning it, and sold oil to the "Great Satan," the United States.

In the mid-1980s, major Iranian offensives failed to cross the marshy terrain into Iraq, despite enormous loss of life. To compensate for Iraq's superior weapons, Iran began human wave attacks with poorly-trained teenagers. Nevertheless, Iraqi tanks, aircraft, helicopter gunships and even poison gas effectively stalled the human wave and conventional attacks.

Despite the casualties and growing war–weariness, Khomeini rejected any peace that kept the Iraqi president, Saddam Hussein, in office. Desperately seeking weapons and intelligence, the government secretly worked to release American hostages seized by pro–Iranian groups in Lebanon in exchange for arms and intelligence. Thus equipped, in 1986 troops and the Revolutionary Guards crossed the Shatt al–Arab waterway below Basra and occupied the Faw peninsula, Iran's most successful offensive during eight years of war.

Although Iraq seemed on the verge of collapse, Iranian dominance rapidly faded. Rivalries between the Revolutionary Guards and the military ended their effective cooperation, and the U.S. cut supplies of anti-tank weapons, other vital equipment and spare parts for aircraft after the Iran-Contra scandal broke. Iran never again mounted a successful offensive.

Iraq responded to its loss of Faw by widening the conflict. It bombed oil export centers at Khark Island and tankers hauling Iranian crude oil. When the Iranian forces responded by attacking tankers carrying crude from Iraq's Arab allies, the United States and other Western nations became involved and destroyed most of the Iranian navy.

In late 1987, defeats began to follow disasters. Tehran and other major cities came under missile attacks and bombing raids. Iraq quickly recaptured the Faw peninsula and advanced elsewhere. The Iranian *Mujahedin-Khalq*, aided by Iraqi troops, attempted to "liberate" Iranian territory. Meanwhile, the obvious Iranian role in the hijacking of a Kuwaiti airliner isolated Tehran in world affairs, so that when a U.S. cruiser mistakenly shot down an Iranian airliner, Iran failed to gain a U.N. condemnation.

At last the leadership in Tehran recognized that the war threatened the Islamic Revolution itself, and quickly accepted a ceasefire (August 1988). The ceasefire did not ensure peace, however. Disputes remaining over the Shatt al-Arab, and the repatriation of POWs soon halted.

Domestic Concerns During the War and After Khomeini

The war had lasted almost eight years—and the Islamic Revolution had not yet celebrated its tenth birthday. When the war began, the Islamic Revolution faced violent insurrection, and in response, the *Islamic Republican Party* ruled by repression, appeal to religion, and torture. Members of the pro-Moscow *Tudeh Party* joined the *Mujahedin* as victims after its membership list was purchased from a Soviet KGB spy.

The 1984 elections to the *Majlis*, however, brought significant changes, although the only legal opposition party boycotted the vote as undemocratic. Newcomers, some of them professional men rather than clergy, formed about half the membership. The new *Majlis* approved several economic reforms, only to find them blocked by the *Council of Guardians*, which deemed them contrary to Islamic principles.

The Council of Guardians also gained a major role in elections through its power to disqualify candidates. Thus, in his successful campaign for re-election in 1985, President Ali Khamenei faced only two candidates, both of them insignificant. Some 50 other candidates, including Mehdi Bazargan, never appeared on the ballot. Such manipulation of public expression proved only partly successful. Street protests in 1985 and 1986 showed how strongly many people felt about what they saw as a useless and costly war. Some opposition groups, to protest the strife and the economic suffering planted bombs in public places, especially in Tehran. By 1987 growing disagreement over the war surfaced increasingly in public, and one of the five Shi'a Grand Ayatollahs decreed the continuation of the war a sin.

After the guns fell silent, debates raged within Iran over the future of the Islamic Revolution. Hundreds, even thousands of supporters of opposition political parties, were executed, apparently the savage response by a divided government to opposition viewpoints and the *Mujahedin-e Khalq's* invasion.

Bitter struggles deepened within the leadership. Foreign policy provided abundant room for controversy. "Hardliners," those determined to spread the Islamic Revolution, supported the overthrow of unsympathetic Arab regimes, and waged a vitriolic struggle against Israel and the United States. By contrast, "Moderates," (a fateful label in Tehran) wished to use world-wide horror at Iraqi's use of chemical weapons to gain closer ties with Western Europe and even the United States and thus hasten reconstruction.

The scope for rebuilding was vast: beyond perhaps 300,000 dead, thousands were maimed for life. Important cities and industries lay devastated, including one of the largest oil refineries in the world. Contemporary estimates placed the probable cost of reconstruction at $200 billion.

Disputes continued to rage over the role of privately owned companies and farmland and the degree of individual freedom. Some leaders advocated greater

political toleration; others warned against relaxing social regulation: "There are neither seaside beaches nor evening parties … Those un-Islamic things no longer exist … The old ways will never return to Iran." In one case, Ayatollah Khomeini disagreed publicly with President Khamenei and asserted that the government "can stop any religious law if it feels it is correct to do so," including the monthly fast and daily prayers. This extraordinary claim for a Muslim apparently supported those favoring socialism and land reform during the 1988 *Majlis* elections.

Events abroad provided an emotional issue for the hardliners when the novel *The Satanic Verses* appeared. For a variety of reasons, Muslims found the book offensive. Its author, Salman Rushdie, lightheartedly portrays compromise, not a mistaken vision, as the cause of Muhammad's depicture of three idol goddesses and the daughters of Allah (see: Historical Background). In addition, Muhammad appears unable to recognize changes his secretary makes to the wording of the angelic message—but the Qur'an to Orthodox Muslims is the Word of God, dictated word-by-word.

When Ayatollah Khomeini sentenced Rushdie to death—a response perhaps considered appropriate 1,000 years ago—Iran's hardliners won popular support at home. However, this isolated Iran internationally: any Western sympathy with the anguish of devout Muslims rapidly disappeared in the face of death threats against an author.

In 1989, Ayatollah Ruhollah Khomeini died, just weeks after he disowned his heir apparent. Nevertheless, the succession flowed smoothly. The Assembly of Experts appointed President Ali Khamenei, of modest clerical rank, Supreme Leader, and for good measure, ayatollah. This appointment preserved the unity of mosque and state, at the cost of appointing a low-ranking clergyman successful in politics to the highest theological position.

Weeks later, with 80 candidates removed from monination, the Speaker of the *Majlis*, Ali Akbar Hashemi Rafsanjani, handily won the presidency against token opposition. The voters also approved constitutional reforms giving the president control over the Cabinet, budget, and military, and dropping the position of prime minister.

A shrewd politician and an eloquent speaker, Rafsanjani drew power into his own hands. He removed several powerful hardliners from the cabinet, despite opposition from the *Majlis*, including the interior minister who had controlled local government and probably plotted with the Lebanese Hizbullah to seize Western hostages. Rafsanjani's priority was reconstruction, and he recognized that this required normal international behavior. He visited the Soviet Union, and brought

back promises of Soviet factories and electric generating stations in return for natural gas. To the United States he hoped for the release of the hostages in Lebanon, and he announced that Iran would not export its revolution. Nevertheless, he remained an Islamic Revolutionary with limited control over radicals.

In domestic politics, the ruling Islamic Republican party divided into factions initially labeled (revolutionary) radicals, (religious) conservatives, and pragmatists. By nature inclined to compromise, President Rafsanjani attempted to reduce the role of the radicals gradually, rather than dramatically. Moreover, the regime often balanced friendly gestures towards traditional opponents like the United States with fiery denunciations of the "Great Satan," and crackdowns on opponents.

The decline of the radicals continued in two competitive though manipulated elections. In 1990, the conservative *Council of Guardians* disapproved a number of candidates for the Assembly of Experts, and also required other candidates—some of them prominent radical leaders of the Islamic Revolution—to prove their religious competence by examination. Several well-known militants, including former government ministers and the speaker of the *Majlis*, failed the test. Similar tactics helped President Rafsanjani's allies in the 1992 elections. The *Council of Guardians* disapproved nearly one-third of the candidates, including many prominent radicals. The voters then tended to select pragmatists, strengthening the practical politics of the president.

Despite the electoral success, several signs portrayed a discontented public. Protests in 1991 became full-scale riots in 1992, when thousands took to the streets and destroyed government buildings in Meshed, Arak and smaller towns. Typically the troubles began with attempts to clear squatters who had settled on the outskirts of cities, but the strife suggested deeper disenchantment with the revolution as well as distress over economic issues, including inflation, unemployment, corruption, and falling real incomes. Pov-erty and joblessness contributed to massive drug addiction (see Culture). Other signs of unrest included clashes between Revolutionary Guards and students or bazaar merchants, whose level of satisfaction provides a barometer of popular well-being.

The unrest reflected difficult economic conditions. A shortage of foreign exchange, partly caused by arms purchases, cut imports, slashed the rial's value and raised the inflation far higher than the official figures. Faced with widespread corruption, parliament probed the Central Bank and many government-owned companies. U.S. attempts to isolate the regime delayed major projects that depended on foreign financing. However, the American economic offensive probably strengthened the regime politically. After all, it provided a convenient scapegoat to blame for shortcomings that in fact long preceded the actions.

Reelected in 1993, President Rafsanjani accomplished little during his second term, which was marked by faced conflict with former allies, including Ayatollah Ali Khamenei and a *Majlis* whose radicals increasingly blocked economic liberalization. Meanwhile, the conservatives, linked to the bazaar merchants, favored Rafsanjani's freer trading links with the West, but opposed specific economic policies, greater freedom of expression, and social liberalization, pariculary for women.

Foreign Relations in the 1990s

Iraq's invasion of Kuwait presented Iran with a dilemma. It benefitted from the world's condemnation of Saddam Hussein, the bitter enemy. However, Iran also opposed the presence of any foreign troops in the region, and the crisis brought hundreds of thousands of them to Saudi Arabia and foreign naval vessels to the Gulf. Consequently, Iran accepted Iraq's gestures of peace, and repatriated most prisoners from the Iran–Iraq war. Iran also adopted—and enforced—U.N. sanctions against Iraq and seized the Iraqi military planes flown to its airfields. Following the war, when more than one million Iraqi Kurds and Shi'a fled to Iran, the government undertook strong relief efforts that won international respect.

Until the late 1990s, Iran presented itself as the scourge of Western influence. It condemned the Middle East Peace Conference, and sympathized with suicide attacks on Israeli civilians. Egypt accused Iran of training fundamentalist terrorists, and Iran clumsily completed the Shah's 1971 seizure of three Persian Gulf islands from the United Arab Emirates. When

President Rafsanjani modestly improved relations with Arab and Western countries, the Supreme Leader, Ali Khamenei, often condemned the West. Consequently, Iran remained isolated, cut off from friendly relations with most nations. There were notable exceptions among the former Soviet republics to the north, where cultural and trade links increased, especially after completion of a rail connection to Central Asia.

Fearing Iran's role in the region, some Western analysts worried about its rearmament and atomic research. In the early 1990s Iran sought to rebuild its military. Weapons came cheaply from North Korea and the former Soviet bloc; they included aircraft, SCUD missiles, and submarines. While the arms hardly equaled purchases by Saudi Arabia, they created concern that Iran sought to dominate the Gulf.

Beyond conventional weapons, the official statement that "because the enemy has nuclear facilities the Muslim state too should be equipped with the same capacity" fed fears of Iran's nuclear ambitions. After Russia agreed to complete a nuclear power plant begun under the Shah, in 1995 the United States hardened its opposition to the Islamic Republic. It blocked the foreign subsidiary of a U.S. oil company from developing Iran's oil industry, embargoed commercial contacts, and set up a fund for covert actions. The U.S. unsuccessfully pressured Russia to halt work on the power plant, though the deal satisfied international law, and all fuel will be reprocessed in Russia.

As the decade ended, the international isolation decreased greatly, as Iran abandoned much of its hostility. An Iranian warship docked in Saudi Arabia, and pilgrims joined the Hajj, despite the deaths of Iranian pilgrims in the 1980s. Overcoming or ignoring U.S. sanctions, foreign companies including Total of France

signed deals to develop the giant South Pars gas field underneath the Gulf. The President of Iran flew to Italy and visited with the Pope. Relations with Western nations generally improved when the foreign ministry promised to take no action to implement the *fatwa* condemning Salman Rushdie to death.

Khatami and the Dawn of Reform

Despite its dramatic impact on foreign relations and the position of women, by the late 1990s, two decades after it began, the Revolution remained incomplete. Income inequality had probably widened, with the poorest 40% of the population sharing only 2.9% of national income, and the top 1% receiving 22% of it. Partly offsetting these figures, roads and electricity reached many more villages; the higher rural standard of living was an important success story.

Socially and politically, the country seemed stagnant. Despite holding elections, the regime limited freedom. It punished journalists and artists whose views become too independent, and manipulated information about its opponents. When a professor, Abdol Karim Soroush, analyzed the role of religion in society and suggested that the cleargy's involvement in politics might harm religion, he was forced into exile in 1996. Thousands of the alleged drug offenders probably faced trumped-up charges, or confessed after torture. Executions continued, and a Bahai who converted to Islam but then reverted to his former faith was sentenced to death. Capital punishments often became secret, to complicate information-gathering by human rights groups. Five authors and politicians were murdered in Tehran within a few weeks. "The work of foreign powers," claimed Supreme Leader Ayatollah Khamenei, but evidence insinuated agents from the Intelligence Ministry.

Thus the 1997 presidential election proved a shock to political patterns of politics. Conservatives of the *Combatant Clergy Association* had dominated the 1996 *Majlis* elections, and the *Council of Guardians* disqualified all but four of 238 prospective presidential candidates in 1997. Most observers expected an easy if inconsequential win for the leading conservative, the speaker of the *Majlis*. However, Mohammad Khatami, the relatively tolerant Minister of Islamic Guidance in the 1980s, upset the analysts' calculations.

Even outwardly, Khatami symbolized the changes in society, for he often appeared wearing both fine European-style clothes and the black turban that designated a descendant of the Prophet Muhammad. No secularist, his book *Fear of the Wave* proclaimed Islam superior to the West. However, from his study of philosophy Khatami came to appreciate the role of freedom, the benefits of justice, and

Presidents Rafsanjani and Gorbachev in Moscow, June 1989   AP/Wide World Photo

the importance of civic responsibility. He campaigned on these themes, and attracted a variety of supporters: the middle classes, the young who resented personal restrictions, women, and advocates of greater economic freedom. Even leftists who desired state control of the economy united with his cause, hoping to prevent the presidency from falling to a conservative.

When the ballots were counted, the results were astonishing, particularly from the countryside, because some rural clergy had openly forbidden their followers to vote for Khatami. He won there as well as the cities, and captured 20 million of nearly 30 million votes, a decisive victory in a very heavy turnout.

Though losing by a landslide, the conservatives did not fall from political leadership. The speaker and the conservative Supreme Leader retained two of the country's three most powerful positions, and combined to block the reformist president. Their followers allied with fundamentalists (who desired Islamic law to guide the country) to block change. One group raised the bounty on Rushdie's head, and a majority of deputies in the *Majlis* signed a petition supporting the *fatwa*. Within the government, they blocked reformers from the Assembly of Experts, and on the streets, fundamentalist toughs attacked moderate political rallies, and assaulted a group of U.S. tourists. Several student demonstrators were sentenced to death, without any evidence of a trial.

Perhaps the most decisive battleground took place in the press. Brash reformist newspapers sprang up and attracted wide attention for their attacks on individual officials and narrow-minded policies. For example, *Neshat* questioned the role and authority of the Supreme Leader, Ayatollah Khamenei. *Zan* published an announcement by the last Shah's widow, officially a "non-person." Another paper reacted to the reappointment of the conservative director of the national TV network by publishing a cartoon showing a TV set as a toilet.

Conservatives, who still controlled the courts, parliament and the police, reacted to the explosion of criticism by arresting editors and closing papers. Some sentences were severe: the leading reformer, Abdollah Nouri, was fined, sentenced to 74 lashes with a braided leather whip, imprisoned for five years, and barred from writing or publishing for the same period. However, the conservative courts often discredited themselves by their methods and the harshness of their sentences. In Nouri's case, his public defense won widespread public admiration.

The most serious public crisis for the Islamic Revolution came in 1999, after students protested yet another newspaper banning. The police responded with a violent raid on a dormitory at Tehran

The tomb of Darius I, who reigned 521–486 B.C. The ancient kings of Persia had their tombs carved into cliffs so high that they could only be reached by ropes and, thus, could not be burst into to plunder.

University, killing one student and injuring many. As news of the death and injuries spread, students demonstrated in Tehran and Tabriz. When suppressed by the police and fundamentalist gangs, they turned to rioting for six days. Though the students had strongly supported President Khatami's reform policies, he could not condone violence, and condemned the rioters. Nevertheless, the episode perhaps shook the confidence of the Supreme Leader, Ayatollah Khamenei, who during the crisis backed the president when he might have attacked him.

With the approach of the *Majlis* elections early in 2000, political activity exploded among supporters of reform and change. For the first time, identifiable political parties appeared, rather than factions of the clergy. For reasons not made public, the *Council of Guardians* permitted

hundreds of reformists among the 6,000 candidates. The reformist electoral alliance included 18 parties, the most prominent of them the Islamic Iran Participation Front (IIPF) headed by the president's brother. In contrast to the lively reformist election rallies, the conservative parties held few public meetings.

A rout of the conservatives followed. Before the runoffs they gained only 45 of 270 seats, to the 175 of the reformist alliance. Within that alliance, Tehran's voters had carefully selected candidates closest to the president. In particular, they punished Rafsanjani and those close to him. The former two-term president and speaker came dead last among the thirty victorious candidates, despite (or because of) the fact that he had agreed to run as a conservative candidate as well. Instead of cautious change under Rafsanjani's leadership, the Iranian public expected dynamic new laws under President Khatemi and his allies. However, the reformist victory aroused conservative officials in the police, courts, and elsewhere. With the backing of Ayatollah Khamenei, they closed every reform newspaper, arrested many journalists, and generally halted the progress of reform. They also used a number of occasions to isolate Iran from the West.

When the 2001 presidential elections approached, speculation arose over whether Muhammad Khatemi would run for another term. His administration had not achieved its goals, and its many popular expectations remained unmet. Apparently the president himself shared these perspectives. When he ended the speculation by filing for re-election, a weeping Khatemi told reporters he wished he were elsewhere, and analysts suggested that disappointment with his regime could lead to a reduced share of the vote.

Instead, Khatemi demolished the conservative candidates and won 77% of the vote, better than previously. However, the president's new cabinet retained many unpromising ministers from the previous cabinet, largely because of opposition from the Supreme Leader, Ayatollah Khamenei, and other conservatives.

Losing elections apparently strengthened the conservatives' determination to enforce strict Islamic rule. Police and paramilitary volunteers attacked crowds in Tehran celebrating the elections, and in the months that followed secret trials convicted journalists, old-time nationalists, and even three members of parliament for opposition to the Islamic Republic. Hardliners attacked peaceful reformist rallies and infiltrated student organizations. Reporters *sans Frontiéres*, an organization dedicated to press freedom, labeled the country "the largest prison for journalists in the world." Judges increasingly sentenced young men to public whippings for drinking alcohol or making social advances on women. They were determined to maintain purity, but heedless of the danger of alienating public opinion.

Hardliners probably deserve credit also for worsening relations with the United States. After the September 11 terrorist attacks, Iran and the U.S. seemed to move closer together. They were mutual enemies of the Taliban rulers of Afghanistan and supporters of factions of the Northern Alliance. Even Ayatollah Khamenei condemned terrorism, and Iran permitted U.S. relief supplies for Afghan refugees to cross its territory. However, a shipload of arms to some Palestinian group, intercepted by the Israeli military, came from Iran, and Revolutionary Guard units may have permitted al-Qa'ida and Taliban fighters to escape into Iran. Combined with longstanding U.S. suspicions of Iranian interest in chemical, biological, and nuclear weapons, these events placed Iran in President George W. Bush's "Axis of Evil," alongside Iraq and North Korea.

Culture: More than half the people of Iran live in the 25 largest cities. The men are mostly merchants, craftsmen or casual laborers, but an increasing number work in industry. Some women also find employment. Life in the towns and cities is generally crowded and the cost of living very high compared with wages.

Most of the rural population lives in small communities, whether peasants who farm in the Elburz and Zagros Mountains, or nomads who live in goat–hair tents which can be carried from place to place as they wander in search of pasture for their flocks. These people are as hardy as their life is hard, generally as hospitable as their environment is inhospitable.

Except the Kurds of the Zagros Mountains, nearly all Iranians follow the *Shi'a* sect of Islam, which Ismail Shah imposed in the 16th century. *Shi'a* Muslims have a traditional animosity toward the Orthodox, or *Sunni*, Muslims who form the great majority in the Islamic world. The relations between Iran and Afghanistan, for instance, are tempered by the fact that most Afghans are *Sunni* Muslims.

Although *Shi'a* Muslims make pilgrimages to Mecca as do other Muslims (see Saudi Arabia: Culture), they also have important shrines in Iran, particularly at Meshed, where their eighth Imam, Ali Reza, was buried. Politics permitting, many also journey to Najaf and Karbala in Iraq, places sacred by virtue of the association with Ali, the fourth Caliph and first Imam, and his two sons. The division of Islam between *Shi'a* and *Sunni* goes back to a dispute over whether Ali and his sons, or the Umayyad clan (see Historical Background) were the rightful successors to Muhammad as rulers of the Muslim community.

A variety of religious officials exist in *Shi'a* Islam. Simple teachers and the preachers at Friday prayers in rural villages form the bottom rank. Above them are judges of religious law, then Mujtahids who interpret the law, Ayatollahs, and Grand Ayatollahs. At the top, the Shi'a Imam has remained hidden for a thousand years, although Ayatollah Khomeini's followers applied the term to him.

Iran is a country famous for its architectural monuments, some in ruin, as those of the Achaemenid Empire, but some still standing, such as the mosques of Isfahan. Museums have also been established to display the antiquities which represent every period of the country's history.

During the last years of the Shah, the rapid expansion of colleges and universities accompanied a decline in the quality of education. Partly a byproduct of new institutions that need time to develop traditions, and students valuing degrees for job placement rather than learning, Iranian education suffered widely from a unique defect. Students who demanded high grades threatened professors by hinting at connections with *SAVAK*, the Shah's dreaded secret police.

Feeroozah bazaar in downtown Tabriz, especially noted for the sale of handwoven rugs.
Courtesy: Faranak A. Benz

71

After Khomeini came to power, although *SAVAK* was demolished, the decline in education gathered speed. The Revolution shut some schools, closed the universities, and banned women from many teaching positions (and from much of public life in general). The practice of sending students abroad to gain a modern education was stemmed and the lower curriculum reduced to reading, writing, arithmetic and religion. Many teachers with good training fled the country; some who stayed were executed. In 1982 the medical schools in Tehran and Shiraz were reopened for practical reasons, and the universities followed, but there are still few signs of a policy to rebuild the general education system. This crisis threatens to become acute at the turn of the century, when the large generation born after the revolution seeks university education. Given present patterns, it will need double the present number of professors.

During the Shah's era, many middle- and upper-class Iranians rapidly adopted aspects of Western culture, from stylish clothing to skiing, plus parties and rock music. Religious conservatives and the traditional poor opposed and resented these changes; with the Islamic Revolution, they ended. Most obviously, new laws forced women to wear *hejab* attire, notably the *chador,* or headscarf. Officials and Revolutionary Guards suppressed Western magazines and music; only in 1988 did Khomeini approve instrumental music. Thus symphonic music may now be enjoyed, but rock music or female vocals remain sinfully enticing and prohibited. Other regulations prohibit unmarried men and women from walking or dining together in public. While two girls may hitch rides from passing automobiles, unmarried couples ought not ride alone in a car, especially after dark.

Not surprisingly, after more than a decade of revolutionary fervor, by the war's end private behavior began to show signs of restlessness. Despite heavy penalties if caught by revolutionary committees, some young adults apparently enjoy parties and dancing with members of the opposite sex, and in small groups a few women appear "uncovered" (bare-head-ed). Pale lipstick worn by coeds in university classes, colored headscarves, and brightly colored track shoes likewise suggest widening desires for a relaxation of social regulation. There were risks: in one month an estimated 1,000 women were arrested for offenses like failing to cover their ankles or wearing too much makeup.

Advancing technology presents those who interpret Islam narrowly with additional targets. Parliament debated video-recorders, as a prelude to banning them, until it became obvious that leading politicians and clergy found them useful. When a western company began broadcasting TV programs to Iran by satellite,

however, the government hastened to condemn that means of Western cultural influence. To back up its condemnation, in 1995 it eventually banned satellite dishes, thus placing would-be TV addicts at the mercy of inspectors from the local revolutionary committees.

Drug Addiction and Youthful Rebellion

A severe and growing social difficulty is the swelling population of drug addicts, which climbed during the 1990s from one million to six million users by 2001, approximately 15% of all adults and teenagers. Given its lengthy and desolate borders, Iran had a drug problem before the Revolution. In the 1980s the problems worsened, with heroin largely replacing opium, and the number of addicts growing. As addicts lost the label "miserable persons" and became "enemy infiltrators in society," officials predictably blamed the problem on the American Central Intelligence Agency and the Mafia. Possession of more than 30 grams of heroin became a capital offense; hundreds were executed. All addicts were required to register, with many being sent to labor camps in distant desert regions to break the habit. Drug-related convictions account for seventy percent of Iranian prisoners.

Despite these harsh measures, the state welfare organization estimates an additional 600,000 users each year, *three-fourths of them women.* Such large-scale use of narcotics points to more than cheap supplies. Like the riots that followed world cup soccer games, it is an indicator of a society that lacks faith in the future, a remarkable phenomena for a religious republic.

In the traditional realm of marriage, two hardships illustrate the reality of social conditions under the revolution. First, with so many men absent for military service, families faced difficulties arranging marriages for their daughters. Second, once the husband was obtained, inflation and unemployment frequently limited the family's ability to provide the traditional dowry, furniture for the new household.

If such difficulties hampered the marriage rate, the birth rate approached world record levels and population grew at 4% annually. This reflected a combination of cultural values and the regime's initial desire for more children to boost Iran's greatness. However, after planners convinced leaders of the enormous economic and social pressures such growth would create, Ayatollah Khomeini approved family planning, and in 1989 Ayatollah Khamenei declared that birth control was not against Islam. By the mid 1990s all forms for contraception (but not abortion) were available—and free, and family benefits were ended with the third child. As a result, the rate of population growth fell to less than 2%.

Economy: With a growing population as large as Egypt's, but far better endowed with mineral deposits, fertile lands, and larger irrigable areas, Iran is one of the Middle Eastern countries most able to develop a large variety of industries. Beyond all these other advantages, Iran possesses large oil resources and natural gas deposits so vast they rank second only to Russia's. The earliest oil exporter in the region, in recent years it ranked the second largest oil exporter in the Middle East, after Saudi Arabia, and in addition supplied the Soviet Union with natural gas by pipeline. Not surprisingly, economic policy in the country revolves around two issues: first, the policy over petroleum, the greatest producer of foreign exchange, and second, agriculture.

Agriculture always played an impressive role in Iranian history. The farms vary greatly, from the well-watered lands near the Caspian Sea to plots in the mountains and plateau that depend for irrigation on systems of underground channels. Large-scale commercial agriculture also began in the Shah's era, especially near the border with Iraq.

Generally life for farmers meant working another's land; until the Shah's land reform program started in 1963, some 10,000 of the country's villages had belonged to landlords owning five or more villages. Indeed, a few families and religious endowments dominated the lives of farmers across the country. While unsuccessful in satisfying the hopes of the peasants, the Shah's land reform broke the power of the large farming families. It encouraged the replacement of subsistence farming with cash crops and began improvements in the supply of credit, seeds and agricultural techniques.

Dams permitted the irrigation of additional lands, and new roads reduced transportation costs. However, all land reform proposals in Iran face a difficult choice, between equality and economic growth. Because only 10% of Iran can be farmed, attempts to redistribute the land to all existing peasants will result in farms too small to be efficient or market oriented. But without redistribution, the great differences in wealth cause political stress, and industry and the services are not growing enough to absorb the thousands who leave farms every year.

For years after the Islamic Revolution, attempts at agrarian reform—essentially, the seizure of larger landholdings—were blocked by the Council of Guardians, whose conservative clergy believed that the Qur'an upheld private property. Although demands for land reform played a major role in the revolution, only 3% of the nation's farmland was distributed during the republic's first decade. However, feeling threatened by calls to seize their lands, the owners of large farms cautiously stopped investing in irrigation and

72

equipment, or even repairing the vital irrigation channels.

Predictably, farm output fell. At the same time, the population rose by 3%–4% per year, one of the highest rates in the world, and flocked to the cities. Thus a country that until 1970 exported surplus food found itself spending over one–third of its oil earnings during the last years of the war to *import* food. Millions of refugees from Afghanistan and Iraq added to the shortages.

Iran has some 50 million acres of forests. These were all taken over by the government in 1963 and are now cared for as a national resource by a forestry service. Fishing is a large industry; the larger volume of fish is taken from the Persian Gulf, but the best known is from the Caspian Sea, the source of sturgeon whose eggs, caviar, earned the epithet "black gold". Pollution in the closed sea, combined with legal and illegal over-fishing, threaten the long-term future of this delicacy.

The mineral resources of Iran other than oil have not yet been surveyed thoroughly. At present, lead, chrome and turquoise are exported, while coal and iron are mined for domestic use, along with some sulphur and salt.

Besides oil, a number of other industries exist. Textiles are the second industry in importance, but a distant second to oil in cash returns. Cotton is grown in several parts of the country, especially in the vicinity of Isfahan, which developed a significant textile industry. The coast of the Caspian Sea has long been famous for its production of Persian silk.

Much pride was taken in the steel mill constructed in Isfahan with technical assistance and a large loan from the Soviet Union. By the mid–1990s the country actually exported significant quantities of iron and steel. The large northern neighbor also imported natural gas from Iran by pipeline before the Revolution. Since then, deliveries have been erratic, depending on the political atmosphere in Tehran, but recently Iranian leaders spoke of hopes to export natural gas to Western Europe. Despite U.S. objections, in 1996 Turkey signed a massive, multi–year contract for Iranian natural gas.

Although handicrafts are losing importance, Isfahan, Tabriz and other cities remain famous for their metalwork, carpets, ceramics and textiles. The best carpets come from the Safavid period, but those of recent manufacture deserve fame—and next to oil are the most important export. Curiously, by 1985 large numbers of Persian carpets began appearing in shops in Syria at quite reasonable prices, contrasting with the very high prices an older one will fetch in fashionable international markets. The explanation: Syria is one of the very few choices for Iranians wishing to vacation outside the country. Smaller carpets are frequently taken as part of the family baggage and then sold to help pay vacation expenses.

Under the Shah's rule, Iran followed a policy of rapid economic expansion and industrialization. It exported vast quantities of oil to pay for large development projects as well as consumer goods and sophisticated weapons. Using its oil revenues on a massive scale, Iran contracted for entire factories to be built and put in operation by foreign companies. A number of different cars and trucks were assembled in the country, and dozens of other industries were founded. By 1978, the number of industrial employees reached two million.

The policy achieved one of the world's highest rates of economic growth, and the middle class prospered. Other results included inflation and resentment by the unskilled urban poor and landless peasants, who migrated to the cities in search of work.

Economic Policy After the Revolution

In its first and second decades, the Islamic Revolution provided little economic progress, though it greatly changed business conditions. The government quickly nationalized the oil industry completely, thirty years after Mossadeq's failed attempt. It also took over many large manufacturing firms, and the entire banking and insurance industries, partly because many owners had fled. Divided among themselves about the appropriate role of private property, especially in agriculture, the clergy who ruled Iran failed to establish the economic rules of the game. While relatively few firms were confiscated in later years, leftist clergy advocated socialism, and blamed inflation and shortages on hoarding by private businessmen. Lacking consensus, the government simply intervened to suit the needs of the moment. Wealthier investors reacted by avoiding long–term projects, and favoring trade, where seizure seemed less likely. The result was devastating: output fell to only 40% of capacity.

Oil policy likewise changed dramatically. In the new view, imports implied dependence on Western nations and Japan, and encouraged imitation of their lifestyles. Furthermore, the inflationary rush to development had created some very rich merchants and industrialists, but left most peasants and many unskilled workers in poverty. In response, Iran adopted a policy of economic self–sufficiency, exporting only enough oil to cover vital imports.

At first the policy met with success: the second major OPEC price rise accompanied the Revolution, and the country could export half as much oil for almost the same earnings. By 1986, however, oil prices had fallen to one–third their previous level, and Iran suffered great shortages of foreign exchange and revenue as it attempted to import arms and necessities during the war with Iraq.

Beyond the costs in human lives, Iraq's aggression against Iran inflicted widespread destruction on the oil–rich southwest and bombing damage on cities, the oil industry, and other economic targets. Iranian estimates of the costs of reconstruction eventually exceeded $1 *trillion*, far exceeding typical oil revenues of $12–20 billion annually. As a result, reconstruction of oil facilities such as oil platforms and the Khark Island loading terminal became a priority, and production increased to nearly 4 million barrels per day.

During the first half of the 1990s, military rearmament plus demands for consumer goods overwhelmed the foreign exchange earned by oil. Imports soared, doubling in three years. Although the Islamic Revolution rejected both foreign assistance and foreign loans, Iran often financed imports through short–term suppliers' credits. Despite barter deals such as the $15 billion swap of natural gas for Soviet factories, short–term debt mounted. By mid–decade, Iran was rescheduling its debts, and difficulties with financing imports of raw materials and machinery had put economic development at risk.

Beset by economic crises and shortages, from its early days the regime responded with price controls. Though perhaps momentarily successful, they illustrated the absence of coherent policy and the resort to expediency. Moreover, controls failed to halt inflation, which tended to range from 20%–60% per year. Unevenly but certainly, Iran's prices diverged from shortage of electrical capacity, which often led to daily blackouts until greater output in the mid-1990s. For example, gasoline sold for the equivalent of *seven US cents per gallon*! The Rial became vastly overvalued, exceeding the free market rate by 2,000%. Not surprisingly, it became more profitable to seek access to foreign exchange at the official rate than to manufacture in Iran. Technically, Iran rewarded rent–seeking over production; consequently the service sector, especially trade, expanded while agriculture and industry stagnated. Less abstractly, profits were greater and more predictable from importing at the official rate of 70 Rials to the dollar when the market rate was 1,500.

Price controls on domestic products create another set of difficulties. To maintain prices of bread, gasoline and other essential items, the government subsidized them, often at astounding levels. For example, bread prices fell by 90% compared with other consumer products, because subsidies fixed its price. This provided cheap bread for low income groups, but ironically may have aided wealthy farmers more, by providing bread at a lower price than feedgrains. Eventually such extensive subsidies became unbearable

Scene of central Tabriz, the second largest city in Iran.

Courtesy: Faranak A. Benz

even for an oil exporting nation, but reducing them in 1995–96 ignited higher inflation and aroused social discontent.

While food subsidies undoubtedly harmed the national budget, ordinary inhabitants often suffered deeply from inflation, because wages failed to rise with prices. A typical civil servant who earned 70,000 Rials per month in 1980, received little more in 1990, but his buying power of foreign goods dropped from $1,000 to $35. Domestic goods were cheaper, but even official figures imply that per capita income fell in half during the 1980s. Black market activities continued to thrive, because supplies of subsidized food and other essentials often ran short. One particularly annoying difficulty was the shortage of electrical capacity, which often led to daily blackouts.

Major purchases of weapons, food, electric generating equipment and other machinery *on short-term credit* in the early 1990s rapidly built up large foreign debts. By 1994, the Central Bank's international funds nearly disappeared, and repaying

the debts on schedule became impossible. During the rest of the decade, Iran faithfully exported greater value than imports, and used the difference to repay the debts, until 1999. Then oil prices fell to less than $10 per barrel, caused further postponements, and the rial depreciated to $1 = IR 10,000. However, the very high oil prices of 2000 ($25–$35 per barrel) greatly benefitted the budget and the economy.

The Future: Reactionaries still control many of Iran's revolutionary courts where they fight a desperate rear-guard retreat, and justice remains far from blind. In 1999, student demonstrators swiftly received death penalites in secret courts, but allegedly murderous police and intelligence agents managed to postpone their trials. However, *a new Iran is emerging*; conservatives and religious radicals no longer lead public opinion.

The recent past discourages hopes for rapid political change and economic reform. President Khatemi wears the

reformist mantle, but he is a religious scholar and supports the basic philosophy of the Islamic Revolution. He says fine things about a civil society and personal liberty, but he has not moved effectively to defend even those liberties found in the constitution.

Little-noticed by the Western press, greater social freedoms in the late 1990s made Iranians happier. But with economic failure and the conservatives' success in halting reform, the country's educated are losing faith and emigrating whenever possible. Football riots and drug abuse proclaim the domestic failure of the Islamic Revolution, but like the valve on a pressure cooker, they let off steam that might otherwise lead to an explosion. So Iran stumbles along internally, while its disunited foreign policy (nice guy-president vs. evil guys in the Revolutionary Guards) contributes to its international isolation. Each domain affects the other, and labels like "Axis of Evil" weaken those who favor social reform and peace. Expect more muddling through.

The Republic of Iraq

In April 1995, Iraqis protested the proposed UN Oil for Food Program. The next year, they celebrated it. AP/Wide World Photo

Area: 169,235 square miles (438,317 sq. km.)

Population: 22 million, (estimated; may not fully adjust for the deaths of 1–1.5 million Iraqis who died from economic sanctions).

Capital City: Baghdad (Pop. 4.5 million, estimated).

Climate: Extremely hot in summer, moderately cold in winter; rain is usually deficient, falling in winter. The northern mountains are cooler, with snow in winter.

Neighboring Countries: Iran (East); Kuwait (Southeast); Saudi Arabia (South); Jordan (West); Syria (Northwest); Turkey (North).

Time Zone: GMT +3.

Official Language: Arabic (and in appropriate northern districts, Kurdish).

Other Principal Tongues: Persian, Armenian, and (as language of education) English.

Ethnic Background: The mixed population is generally identified as Arab (80%), except for a Kurdish–speaking minority (about 17%) and a few Persian–speaking communities.

Principal Religions: *Shi'a* Islam (55%), *Sunni* Islam (40%) and Christianity (3%; Chaldeans, Assyrians and Armenians). There remain a few Yazidis, somewhat inaccurately characterized as Devil Worshippers.

Chief Commercial Products: Petroleum, natural gas, petrochemicals, textiles and cement.

Main Agricultural Produce and Livestock: Wheat, barley, rice, tomatoes, watermelons, grapes, dates, rice, cotton, sheep, goats, cattle and chickens.

Major Trading Partners: (pre–war) Japan, Germany, Italy, Great Britain, France, U.S., Brazil, Turkey and India.

Currency: Dinar. $1.00 = 2,000 Dinars, but fluctuates. Inflation renders the highest note, 250 dinars, almost worthless.

Former Colonial Status: British occupation and Mandate (1918–1932).

Independence Date: October 3, 1932.

National Days: July 14, establishment of the Republic (1958); July 17, anniversary of the Revolution of 1968.

Chief of State: Saddam Hussein (Husayn), known as al-Takriti from his birthplace of Takrit.

Head of Government: Saddam Hussein, Prime Minister (May 1994).

National Flag: Three equal horizontal stripes of (top to bottom) red, white and black, with three green five–pointed stars on the white stripe.

Gross Domestic Product: Unknown.

GDP per capita: Unknown. Pay for government officials and teachers runs about $2–3 per month; people survive on second jobs and cheap but insufficient food rations.

Iraq (pronounced approximately *Ee–rock*) is about two–thirds the size of Texas. Modern Iraq stretches across the birthplace of human civilization. Ancient Mesopotamia, the land "between the rivers," flourished because the Tigris and the Euphrates provided water. Without the rivers, nearly the entire country would be desert. About 18% of the land is under cultivation.

The southwestern third of the country is a flat desert of gravel and rock, rising very gradually in elevation between Kuwait and Syria. Along the northern and eastern borders are the Zagros Mountains. The two rivers flow southeast across the alluvial plain between the mountains and desert. Except on the slopes of the mountains there is little annual rainfall, ranging from 6" in the South to 15" in the northern plains. Most of the water in the rivers comes from melting snow or rain in the mountains of northern Iraq and southern Turkey.

The people differ as much as the land. Declining numbers of Arab nomads (*badu*) still roam the deserts. In the southern marshes upstream from Basra are the *Ma'dan;* these Arabic–speaking people live in reed huts, raise water buffalo and travel by boat. In most of central Iraq farmers live along the rivers, their tributaries and canals, while Kurdish mountain villages dot the heights and valleys in the north.

In recent decades people from all parts of the nation have migrated to Baghdad in search of work in that rapidly expanding city. They represent all the linguistic, religious and social variety of the country. It is this nationwide diversity which makes political agreement so difficult in Iraq.

History: This is the land where some of the first cities evolved and where writing was first invented, the land of the Caliphs of Islam and the *Arabian Nights* (see Historical Background). Yet the present shape of Iraq has little to do with ancient history. After serving as the capital of a vast empire, Iraq suffered invasions, the worst of all by the Mongols. In 1258 Baghdad was devastated, and much of the remaining population killed or forced into exile. Untended irrigation canals silted up; equally seriously drainage canals to remove salt deposits from the fields disappeared. Today vast areas, over two–thirds of the irrigable land, lie idle, sparkling in the sunshine but barren because of the high salt content of the soil.

For nearly four centuries the Ottoman Empire ruled Iraq. After decades of intermittent warfare, it established the border with Iran. It administered Iraq as the three provinces of Mosul (or Musil), Baghdad, and Basra that the Iraqi flag symbolizes today. Beyond controlling the main towns, the governors attempted to maintain order among the often unruly tribes, who enjoyed practical autonomy. As European nations seized control of trade in the Indian Ocean and the Far East, commerce through Iraq stagnated, and little development took place. Modern schools, hospitals, and newspapers only appeared in the late 19th century. Located on the remote southeast fringe of the empire, the provinces generally received few improvements, though Germany began to build a railroad to Baghdad from Istanbul.

When the Ottoman Empire entered World War I as a German ally, British Indian troops landed in Basra and slowly moved inland. They found the population generally unsympathetic or even

King Faisal I (1885–1933)

hostile. However, Iraq as a nation did not exist: the politically conscious population commonly supported the Ottoman empire or desired greater autonomy within it. Only a few, most of them army officers, promoted the newly–conceived idea of an independent Arab nation encompassing at least the Ottoman–ruled areas from Iraq through Syria to the Mediterranean.

By the end of the war in 1918, British troops occupied most of the country, and shortly afterwards added the province of Mosul, valuing it and the region around Kirkuk because of their oil deposits. In the secret Sykes–Picot Agreement, in exchange for control over Syria, France had pledged to support British rule over Iraq in any peace settlement. However, Britain also had promised to recognize the independence of Arab lands, with reservations about the Syrian coast and Basra.

In the months following the armistice, most inhabitants came to recognize that Britain meant to occupy and rule under the guise of a mandate from the League of Nations. A nationalist uprising then spread rapidly. However, to quell the rebellion, Britain sought a political solution as well as military victory, and gained popular approval for Prince (Emir) Faisal, son of Sharif Husayn and commander of the Arab forces who had fought in Syria, to become king.

The new nation adopted the Arabic name al–'Iraq, originally referring to the southern part of the country, for the entire nation. The state's inhabitants, however, were not all Arab. In the North, where Britain desired influence because of oil deposits, lived Kurdish tribesmen.

As a Hashemite, King Faisal traced his descent from the Prophet Muhammad

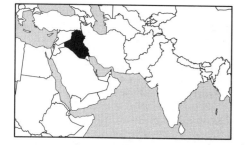

through Hasan, son of Ali, the fourth Caliph (and first *Shi'a* Imam). He therefore brought a semblance of unity to the Arab population with its *Shi'a* majority but *Sunni* ruling class. Having lost his throne in Syria in battle with the French, Faisal worked in Iraq to gain independence by compromise with Britain. In 1922 a treaty promised independence after a training period of ten years. Accordingly, on October 3, 1932, Iraq received its formal independence and became a member of the League of Nations.

The Kurdish Problem

Even before it received formal independence, Iraq faced rebellion from the Kurds. Hardy and brave, but isolated from commerce and education, Kurdish tribes for centuries had maintained dialects of their Indo–European language. After they adopted *Sunni* Islam, Islamic or Arab names became common. Lacking sea access or rail transport, and little influenced by democracy and nationalism, Kurds populated the eastern lands of the Ottoman Empire as well as western Iran. In effect, the Kurds had the misfortune to inhabit the region where three great civilizations (Arab, Persian, and Turkish) came together; their own identity and achievements mattered less by contrast. Ruled lightly from distant capitals through tribal leaders who often challenged each other, the Kurds received little attention. They were simply Muslim tribesmen in Muslim Empires.

After World War I, the victorious Allies forced a peace treaty on Ottoman Turkey that provided for "Kurdistan," a Kurdish homeland, and an independent Armenia. However, Turkish nationalists rejected the treaty and won their struggle for independence. This led to the 1923 Treaty of Lausanne that included much of Armenia and Kurdistan in Turkey. Having fought for the Ottoman Empire as loyal subjects and Muslims, the Kurds carried little weight in Allied deliberations. Christian Armenians, however, fared no better.

Given Britain's desire to control the oil–possessing regions of Kirkuk and Mosul, these areas were joined to Iraq despite their Kurdish majority. Although Turkey and Iran each contained more Kurds than did Iraq, its smaller total population centered on the plains meant that more than elsewhere, the Kurds formed a large and distinct community.

In every country where they form a significant group, the Kurds revolted. They first took up arms in Turkey in 1925; they were brutally suppressed and their leaders were executed. The first Kurdish uprising in Iraq lasted from 1930 to 1933, when it was put down and its leaders confined to non–Kurdish parts of the country or fled to the Soviet Union. During World War II, a second rebellion was briefly successful. After the war, its leader,

Mustafa Barzani, continued the struggle for Kurdish independence by creating, with Soviet sympathy, a republic around the city of Mahabad in Iranian Kurdistan. After years of exile in the Soviet Union, Barzani led later revolts against Iraqi regimes and died in exile supported by the U.S.

Foreign governments often sympathized with Iraq's efforts to transform its Kurdish population into orderly civilians. Granting Kurdish demands also threatened oil revenues, and growing nationalism blocked any government in Baghdad from ceding its territory. On the other hand, Iraq generally lacked the military force to control a fierce and individualistic people living in rugged mountains with few roads. Years of calm and order, therefore, proved the exception.

An Independent State

For over a generation after the formalities of 1932, many Iraqis recognized that they were not really independent. British military bases remained, British and French companies controlled the Iraq Petroleum Company, and British advisors played very influential roles among government officials. Restrictions placed on free elections always seemed to favor those Iraqi politicians closely tied to Britain. On the other hand there was the

beginning of a modern school system. Iraqis also gained experience in the affairs of state, both in politics and administration, as well as in modern military practices. A modern economy began to develop beside the traditional crafts and agriculture, aided significantly by the production and export of oil after 1934.

After the unexpected death in 1933 of Iraq's first king, Faisal I, renewed dissatisfaction and political unrest grew in the country. The last of seven attempts by army officers to seize power between 1936 and 1941 was led by Rashid Ali Gailani, who in extreme bitterness toward British policies allied with the Axis powers in World War II. With the help of the Arab Legion from Transjordan, the British quelled the revolt and reinstated friendly officials. The new government declared war on the Axis in 1943 and thereby qualified to become a charter member of the United Nations when it was formed in 1945.

National feeling developed even more during the post–war years with the spread of education and modern ideas. King Ghazi had died in an accident in 1939 and was succeeded by his son, Faisal II, who was only a boy unable to take the throne as an adult until 1953. In the interim, an uncle, Abd al–llah, served as Regent. This man became the focal point of nationalist

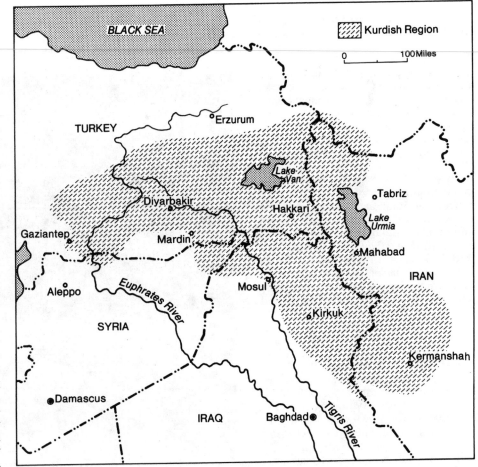

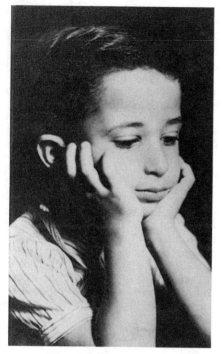

King Faisal II (1935–58)
The six-year-old monarch, 1941

attacks because of his close cooperation with the British and because of his elegant manner of life and great wealth in a country where most people were extremely poor.

In this postwar period, Nuri Said, a very capable politician, controlled parliamentary affairs on behalf of the Throne—and in the opinion of many Iraqis, on behalf of the British. Iraq joined with Britain, Turkey and Iran to form the Baghdad Pact, a military alliance, but Nuri appeared increasingly isolated by the rising popularity of Egypt's President Gamal Abdul Nasser and Arab nationalism. Domestically, the monarchy invested oil revenues in long–term projects that favored wealthy landowners, and banned all political parties.

On July 14, 1958, a day regarded by many Iraqis as their real day of independence, the Iraqi army overthrew the monarchy, the government and foreign influence in a lightning but bloody revolution. The King, the former Regent, Nuri Said, and dozens of other hated officials were killed by mobs. The new Republic of Iraq turned sharply toward a neutralist position in international affairs and renounced treaties with Britain.

The leader of the military revolt, General Abd al–Karim Qasim, emerged as dictator and proclaimed Iraq democratic and united with the Arab world. A political amnesty allowed exiles to return, including the Kurdish leader Mustafa Barzani. Land reform began. Within weeks, however, Qasim clashed with his fellow revolutionaries, especially Colonel Abd al–Salam Arif, who desired rapid unity with Syria and Egypt under Gamal Abdul

Nasser, at the time wildly popular with most Arabs. Thus, instead of uniting Iraq with other Arab states, the revolution created new rivalries between it and Egypt.

Faced with assassination attempts, an army mutiny, and opponents urging a merger with Syria and Egypt, Qasim turned for help to the Soviet Union and the *Communist Party of Iraq.* However, public opinion recoiled when the communists massacred their opponents in Mosul, and Qasim grew isolated, though popular among the poor for his spending on housing.

Other initiatives proved less successful. When Kuwait received its independence in 1961, Qasim claimed it as part of Iraq, but British and then Arab troops protected its independence. That same year Mustafa Barzani, disillusioned by the lack of progress towards Kurdish autonomy, again led the Kurds to revolt.

In 1963 military officers favoring the *Ba'th* (pronounced "Ba–ath") *Party* seized power, and to prove their victory executed Qasim and displayed his body on television. Nevertheless, his legacy to republican Iraq remained: military rule, government control of the economy, Kurdish rebellion, and claims to Kuwait.

Pledged to Arab unity and social equality, once in power the *Ba'th Party* stumbled over relations with Egypt, for President Nasser remained the popular leader of Arab nationalism. Formally named the *Arab Ba'th* ("Renaissance") *Socialist Party,* its doctrine espoused collective, rather than individual leadership, and relations

with Egypt were complicated because *Ba'thist* officers ruling Syria—the birthplace of the party—opposed and feared Nasser.

In late 1963 Iraq witnessed a second coup, led by Colonel Abd al–Salam Arif, who formed a non–party Arab nationalist government. Relative political moderation became the rule, national morale improved, promises of autonomy ended the Kurdish revolt, and relations with other Arab countries were mended. Iraq also formally recognized Kuwait. Killed in a helicopter crash in 1966, Arif was replaced by his brother.

Iraq Under the Ba'th

In 1968, one year following the dramatic Israeli military victory that discredited many Arab armies and governments, a nearly bloodless military coup under General Hasan al–Bakr restored the *Ba'th Party* to rule in Iraq. Members of the party gained total control over the *Revolutionary Command Council (RCC),* the group who formed the chief governing institution. Generally composed of officers, the *RCC* included a significant young civilian, Saddam Hussein. Related by marriage to al–Bakr and a former plotter against Qasim, he directed internal security for the party and now country.

Though socialist and Arab nationalist rather than communist in its philosophy, the *Ba'thist* government strongly opposed the United States over its support of Israel. It also regarded Iran warily as a prospective enemy because Iran claimed the eastern half of the Shatt al–Arab

The Mustansiriyah University

waterway. It also allied with the U.S. against Iraq's patron, the U.S.S.R., and ambitiously aimed to become the regional superpower. Consequently, Iranians in Iraq, many of them for years or decades residents of the holy cities of Najaf and Karbala, faced sudden deportation. At the same time, dissidents opposed to the Shah received refuge, prominently including Ayatollah Khomeini. Foreign relations likewise remained strained with many Arab states and the Western world.

The new government dealt harshly with individuals and groups remotely capable of becoming rivals to the regime, often attempting to discredit them as agents of foreign countries. Accusations of espionage flowed freely; among those first executed publicly were leading members of the remaining Jewish population. Islamic fundamentalists and others met similar fates. Twenty–one communists were hanged while the Soviet Union was warned not to interfere in Arab countries; nevertheless, Iraq remained linked to the U.S.S.R. in international affairs.

When Saddam Hussein, for years the real center of power, became simultaneously President, Chairman of the Revolutionary Command Council, and Secretary–General of the *Ba'th Party* in 1979, rivals within the party were purged (and often murdered), while the public suffered kidnapping and assassinations. To the regime, the only trustworthy group were members of Saddam's clan from Takrit. Some held high office; others played key roles in the country's several secret police and intelligence services.

If the development of democracy lagged, oil revenues meant economic progress. After decades of dispute with foreign oil companies, often at the cost of lost production, Iraq gained total control of its oil production in 1973. Later that year OPEC raised the price of crude oil four–fold (see Black Gold: The Impact of Oil). Iraq's revenues financed both economic prosperity and military equipment. Living standards rose, education expanded, and new industries and housing multiplied. Young, rural Iraqis flocked to cities for jobs in industry and government offices.

After the *Ba'th* consolidated power, Iraq's isolation became selective when foreign affairs could be manipulated, though hostility remained towards the United States and Israel. Fierce disputes between *Ba'thists* ruling Syria and those in Iraq increased the natural rivalry of the two countries. Nevertheless, in 1973 Iraqi tank units joined Syrian troops fighting Israel on the Golan Heights.

In 1975, Saddam Hussein compromised with Iran, granting the Shah's demand to move the boundary to the center of the Shatt al–Arab, the normal international custom, but contrary to longstanding treaties between the Ottoman Empire and Iran. They had placed it instead on the eastern shore. In return, Iran ceased supplying the Iraqi Kurds, who once again had risen in revolt under Mustafa Barzani, because the self–government and other advantages agreed in 1970 had not been carried out. The rebellion rapidly collapsed amid deportations and executions, and again promises of autonomy failed to be implemented.

Saddam Hussein al-Takriti

A second difficulty with the mosaic of Iraqi's ethnic groups arose with the *Shi'a* population, concentrated in the south. Though Arab, and in fact a majority of citizens, they identified strongly with the religious values of Iran (see Iran: Culture). The Iraqi *Shi'a* had never played a political role appropriate to their numbers, even before independence. Thereafter, *Sunni* officers dominated the army, the focus of political power during both monarchy and republic. As a Hashimite, King Faisal I could claim a special relationship based on the family. However, with the overthrow of Faisal II in 1958, military officers of modern ideologies came to dominate Baghdad's government.

The *Ba'th Party*, with its secular and strongly pan–Arab ideology, particularly evoked little following among the *Shi'a*. *Ba'th* governments, largely military and *Sunni*, traditionally spurned issues cherished by the *Shi'a*, and the absence of democratic government meant that the largest community in the country influenced national policy in only limited ways.

Rivalry with Iran brought particular tension for the *Shi'a*. To oppose the modernizing Shah, the *Ba'thists* accorded refuge to his dedicated enemy, Ayatollah Khomeini. However the support was only tactical, as the Iraqi regime allowed less religious interference with government than did Iran, and dissatisfaction arose among Iraq's *Shi'a* as well as Iran's. In 1977, demonstrations and riots broke out in the holy cities of Najaf and Karbala. When civil disturbances in Iran threatened an Islamic revolution against the Shah, Saddam Hussein expelled Ayatollah Khomeini.

After their Islamic Revolution, Iranian religious leaders, now under the charismatic Khomeini, called on the Muslims of Iraq to revolt. Disturbances spread in Baghdad and elsewhere, followed by repression. Ayatollah Muhammad Bakr Sadr, a prominent *Shi'a* leader, was executed in Baghdad for

Downtown Baghdad

subversion. Amid such turmoil, controlled elections to the powerless National Assembly meant little.

War with Iran

Angered by Iranian calls for an Islamic revolution in Iraq and anxious to gain additional territory, Saddam Hussein sensed an opportunity to force concessions from a divided and internationally isolated Iran. He therefore terminated the 1975 treaty over the Shatt al-Arab, and invaded Iran in 1980. Iraqi troops captured Khorramshahr and pushed into oil-rich regions beyond.

Despite early victories, the president and his generals miscalculated. By advancing broadly, they failed to deliver a fatal blow. Politically, the war united Iranians against an ancient and often despised foe; by 1981, Iraq had lost the initiative and began to retreat. The nation now faced the onslaught of religiously–inspired and often fanatical Iranians determined to obliterate the *Ba'th* regime in Baghdad. By 1984 probably 80,000 Iraqi troops had died, and more soldiers had surrendered. To defend the country, almost all able-bodied men were drafted. Iranian naval and air attacks destroyed tanker facilities on the Gulf near Faw, and as oil exports fell, government revenues plummeted. Aided by Iran, Kurdish groups rebelled in the north.

In the crisis, aid from other Arab governments sustained Iraq. Jordan, Saudi Arabia, Kuwait and the smaller Arab Gulf states feared that a victorious Iran would export its Islamic Revolution. Consequently, although formally neutral, they favored Iraq morally and materially. Arab oil states "lent" an estimated $35 billion, and large numbers of Arab laborers filled civilian jobs. Egypt alone supplied over one million workers, roughly equivalent to one-fifth the number of Iraqi men. Alone among Arab nations, *Ba'thist* Syria supported Iran. It halted the flow of Iraqi crude oil through Syrian ports, almost completely ending Iraqi exports of crude.

In 1984 and 1985 Iran launched massive attacks against Iraq's second largest city, Basra. Fighting on their own soil, Iraqi soldiers discovered the will to resist, aided by chemical weapons despite international prohibitions. The destruction of life and property in Basra, a largely *Shi'a* city, signified the failure of the Iranian Revolution to inspire Iraq's *Shi'a*. However, a surprise Iranian assault gained the Faw peninsula west of the Shatt al-Arab in 1986. Despite heavy losses the Iraqi army stopped the advance and repulsed another attack on Basra. Nevertheless, national defeat had seemed distinctly possible.

Stalemated on the ground, the war took other forms. Having lost its ports, Iraq bombed Iran's oil export terminals, and a "Tanker War" developed when Iran retaliated against vessels carrying oil from Kuwait and Saudi Arabia. Eventually the U.S. and other powers sent naval units to escort shipping and clear the Gulf of mines. A "War of the Cities" in 1987 involved missile and bomb attacks on Tehran, Baghdad, and lesser cities. While of limited destructive power, the attacks caused civilian casualties and created fear.

Iraqi forces finally gained the initiative in 1988. They recaptured the Faw Peninsula, damaged Iran's oil export installations, and attacked across the border. Isolated and lacking heavy weapons for defense, Iranian morale collapsed and Tehran finally sued for peace (see Iran: history).

On the verge of military victory, Iraq engineered a public relations defeat. Attacks on rebellious Kurdish areas sent more than 50,000 people, many of them women and children, fleeing to refugee camps in Turkey to escape bombing raids and poison gas like those that killed 5,000 civilians in the town of Halabja.

After the ceasefire, wildly celebrated in Baghdad, President Saddam Hussein encouraged symbols of openness, promising a free press and multi-party democracy. However, hopes of reform and freedom quickly proved false. Demobilization proceeded very slowly; military industrialization remained a priority. Popular generals and other officers were arrested or disappeared. Iraq defiantly executed a foreign reporter, and secrecy cloaked information considered public elsewhere, such as budget, trade, and social characteristics. Torture extended to executions of children, to persuade their parents to confess.

Why? Beyond doubts about the judgment and personality of Saddam Hussein, other explanations focus on the problems of governing. Dependent on his own intuition and advice from a narrow circle of officials, the president sought to release tensions from eight years of war: hence talk of democracy and reform. However, intelligence services reported *Shi'a* and Kurdish assassination attempts; some military officers and party members plotted coup d'etats. Moreover, with the treasury exhausted, few jobs existed for any demobilized soldiers, who demanded far higher wages than the Egyptians. Thus Iraq maintained its military at one million men, and in 1990 threatened a small neighboring country in a desperate gamble for money that might not have led to war had Kuwait paid on demand.

Another theory takes support from massive programs to develop chemical, biological and nuclear weapons, and the "supergun," a cannon with a 1,000-mile range. Still believing the *Ba'thist* slogan "One Arab nation with an eternal mission," Saddam Hussein saw himself the liberator of that nation from its regional rulers. He considered the U.S. too traumatized by Vietnam to fight, and had learned, bitterly from the Iran-Contra Arms deal, that Western leaders sometimes lied. Protecting terrorist Palestinians or gassing Kurds had led to few difficulties: American sales of subsidized rice and wheat continued. If Arab unity involved conquest, the collapsing Soviet Union meant it must come quickly. Luckily, the closest target ranked among the richest.

Kuwait and the Second Gulf War

On August 1, 1990, negotiations between Iraq and Kuwait collapsed. Besides border concessions near its naval

The interior courtyard of a traditional Iraqi home

base, Iraq had demanded money: billions of dollars to pay for Iraqi oil allegedly pumped by Kuwaiti wells; billions more to compensate for Kuwait's production beyond its quota, causing low world prices. Hours later Iraqi troops swiftly conquered all Kuwait.

As the Emir and government fled to Saudi Arabia, the UN Security Council demanded an immediate withdrawal. Western nations froze—i.e., rendered unusable—Iraqi bank accounts and financial assets, and the Soviet Union sus-pended military shipments. Soon the Security Council imposed an almost complete economic boycott on Iraq and Kuwait. Both Turkey and Saudi Arabia halted Iraqi oil exports across their territory.

In contrast, Arab reactions varied. Some leaders sought compromise: a withdrawal in return for concessions. The Arab League demanded an immediate withdrawal, but the resolution split the League. Fearing that Iraq might invade Saudi Arabia, the Gulf Cooperation Council–composed of the nations most menaced—decided that UN actions were not foreign intervention. Thus Saudi Arabia— protector of Islam's greatest Holy Places—accepted U.S. troops for a defensive international force. Egypt and Syria later pledged troops, and smaller Gulf states provided bases and token units.

In Kuwait itself, Iraqi rule appeared brutal; those previously opposed to the ruling family refused to cooperate with Iraq. Many fled or hid. Devoid of local support, Saddam Hussein revived old claims and annexed Kuwait. His officials and troops set about systematic looting. Museums, libraries, warehouses, hospitals and offices in Kuwait provided plunder for Iraqi hospitals, university libraries and government offices. The Central Bank yielded foreign exchange and gold worth billions. Soon Baghdad's civilians could purchase, cheaply, consumer goods long denied them. Sharing in the booty made accomplices of thousands of otherwise honorable civilians.

Iraq soon prevented Westerners who had worked in Kuwait from departing and placed many as hostages near likely military targets; non-Westerners became pawns for food supplies. In contrast, a single-minded President Bush orchestrated UN resolutions and American policy. Thanks to Soviet cooperation, the U.S. and its Coalition partners gained UN author-ity to enforce an economic block-ade. Momentously, the Security Council imposed a withdrawal deadline of January 15, 1991: the military build-up could not be maintained in the hot summer.

Apparently Saddam Hussein reasoned that if the U.S. attacked, widespread Muslim protests plus anti-war emotions in the U.S. would limit the battle. He refused to back down, and last-minute peace attempts failed. One day later, Coalition aircraft and missiles began massive attacks on military and economic targets. Precision weapons struck through doors or ventilation shafts to destroy buildings without causing high civilian casualties. Electronic countermeasures foiled many air defenses, and Stealth aircraft penetrated the remainder easily. Much of the Iraqi air force fled to Iran, where the jets were impounded.

For 38 days and nights the aerial campaign pounded weapons depots, communication links, bridges and highways, water and sewage treatment plants, refineries and factories, and the national electric power grid. Military units, especially the better-equipped Republican Guard divisions, suffered intensive bombing by B-52s and other aircraft, but to avoid arousing Muslim and anti-war sentiments, the Coalition kept secret the casualty estimates.

Television pictures of the destruction of one bomb shelter with the deaths of many civilians nearly upset the public relations policy. However, the Holy War declared by Baghdad and some Islamic militants elsewhere never took place.

In defense, Iraq attempted to conserve its military and widen the war to a broad Arab–Israeli dispute. Hoping to draw Israel into war and thus split the Coalition, it fired Scud missiles at Tel Aviv and other Israeli targets (see Israel: history). Other Scuds landed in Saudi Arabia and the Gulf, but U.S. Patriot missiles soon gained a reputation for disrupting though not necessarily destroying them. None of the warheads carried chemical warheads, but Iraq stunned the world by pumping millions of barrels of crude oil into the Gulf to create one of history's largest oil slicks. It destroyed wildlife and threatened the water desalinization plants in Saudi Arabia and Bahrain.

As the ground battle approached, Iraqi Foreign Minister Tariq Aziz and the Soviet Union proposed peace based upon Iraq's withdrawal. By refusing to accept all UN resolutions, however, Iraq offered too little, and left its troops defending territory it already proposed to surrender.

Striking swiftly, Coalition ground forces punctured the dreaded Iraqi defenses with surprisingly few casualties. By threatening a Marine landing on the coast, the strategy drew Iraqi forces in Kuwait eastward. Then, tanks and airborne units, mostly American but also British and French, swept around Iraqi defenses from the west. Some moved north across the stony desert to the Euphrates, cutting off an Iraqi retreat, while others struck at Republican Guard divisions north of the Iraqi–Kuwait border (see map). Simultaneously, Egyptian, Saudi and other Arab troops joined U.S. Marines to push northwards to Kuwait City. After three days of fighting, Saddam Hussein ordered a withdrawal. The next evening, President Bush announced a cease–fire; the ground fighting had lasted just 100 hours.

Against some 200 Coalition deaths, the war cost Iraq an estimated 10,000–30,000 dead and some 3,700 tanks destroyed. Its military no longer threatened neighboring countries with conventional weapons. The physical destruction cost scores of billions of dollars.

Peace did not return to Iraq with the cease–fire. In several cities, despondent

The canals of old Basra

81

troops and Shi'a militants attempted to seize power from officials and the Ba'th party. Unrest broke out in Basra, and the revolt became a bitter civil war throughout Shi'a–populated southern Iraq. Soon Kurdish *pesh merga* guerrillas also revolted in the north. Iraq appeared to be disintegrating, and years of systematic oppression of political parties left only ethnic and religious loyalties as the basis of popular expression.

To face the crisis, Saddam Hussein reshuffled the cabinet, installing as the interior minister Hasan al–Majid, who had earlier "pacified" the Kurds. He dispatched loyal military forces methodically against rebel areas, pounding relentlessly any districts offering resistance. Mosques were not spared, nor the families of those resisting. In fact, both sides retaliated brutally against even civilian opponents.

Though fighting bravely and bitterly, the rebels lacked communications and an over–all command, so the military picked them off, city after city. Soon the Islamic revolutionaries lost Basra, the Shi'a holy cities of Najaf and Karbala, and many smaller towns. Perhaps 30,000 died in the fighting; tens of thousands of refugees flooded into U.S. occupied territory or Iran.

Meanwhile, Kurdish forces liberated Kirkuk, other northern cities and the mountains beyond. During the war with Iran, some Kurds had allied with Iran and seized Iraqi territory. In response, the Iraqi military gassed villages, brutally evicted thousands of mountain villagers, demolished their homes, and moved those who survived to the hot deserts, where many were buried alive. Perhaps 180,000 had died; to no surprise, the largely non–Arab populations of northern Iraq threw off Baghdad's rule in a spirit of euphoria.

After crushing the Shi'a rebellion in the south, Iraqi forces moved north against the Kurds. Just one month after the end of the Second Gulf War, their overwhelming superiority in armor and helicopter gunships captured Kirkuk and its oilfields. Nearly two million civilians, mostly women and children, abandoned their homes and fled for sanctuary in neighboring Iran and Turkey. Stranded during freezing weather in the mountains, some never made it. Those who did found desperate camps and a nightly death toll estimated at 1,000.

Their agony televised around the world, the Kurdish refugees presented Coalition leaders with a dilemma. For the West to do nothing aroused a sense of moral injustice: in public opinion, two million Kurds seemed as worthy of intervention as 600,000 Kuwaitis. However, sanctuary outside Iraq meant Turkey, and thus the physical, economic and political challenges of two million refugees living indefinitely in the remote regions where Turkey, fearing nationalism among its

One of thousands of leaflets dropped on Iraqi troops during the Second Gulf War

82

The Highway of Death—The scorched remains of both civilian and military vehicles litter the main highway leading from Kuwait City to Basra and Baghdad. The vehicles were destroyed in allied bombing raids against the retreating Iraqi army.

own Kurdish population, would allow them to live.

The alternative, sending back the refugees to Iraqi, required the removal of Saddam Hussein's authority over them. However, any military assistance for the Kurds violated Iraqi sovereignty. Though this was only a legal technicality, the very existence of an independent Kurdish state would probably threaten to destabilize Turkey and Iran. Consequently, with UN cooperation, Coalition forces forced Iraqi troops to withdraw, then erected refugee camps inside Iraq protected by UN police. When the UN forces withdrew, a Kurdish alliance took control of northern Iraq, about 10% of the country, and formed an autonomous administration to govern it.

Post–War Difficulties in Arab Iraq

In central Iraq, Saddam Hussein and the *Ba'th* party retained power, despite reported military conspiracies and popular dissatisfaction. Cabinet shifts preserved hard–line control of the military and police, while the more–moderate Prime Minister was replaced. Promises of democracy proved a fiction. To combat the lingering violence in Shi'a regions, military governors fortified most cities and aircraft flew raids until the Western coalition allies created a southern "No Fly Zone" like the one over Kurdish territory.

Across Iraq, UN economic sanctions took bitter effect, pending the certified destruction of its biological, chemical and nuclear weapons programs, as well as the missiles to deliver them. Most critically, the sanctions banned oil exports, and limited imports to humanitarian goods like food

and medicine. However, without oil exports, Iraq could not generate foreign exchange to pay for them: food for civilians was not the government's priority. So effective were the sanctions that shortages of spare parts and raw materials reduced industrial production to one–tenth of capacity, and dire shortages of insecticides, herbicides and seeds depressed farm output.

To shift the blame for inflation, Iraq claimed that the U.S. had counterfeited the currency. In addition, it arrested dozens of merchants, accused them of profiteering, then executed them. Public works projects such as the "Third River" (designed to drain salty run–off and other pollutants) helped lower unemployment, but popular frustrations rose as family savings disappeared and heirlooms were pawned. Monthly salaries that had once provided middle–class living standards fell to $40 in 1991; by 1999 a public school teacher earned only $2.

Any open expression of discontent, however, risked severe punishment. Few places on earth exhibited official brutality at the Iraqi level. For example, penalties initially included amputating the limbs of profiteers or farmers who hoarded their harvest, and removing an ear or tattooing the forehead of military deserters.

During the first two years after the war, Iraq harassed UN inspectors and attempted to hide weapons facilities. Nevertheless, evidence mounted of a vast operation involving over a dozen factories to produce an atomic bomb, possibly by 1993. Fueled by widespread Western concern about the weapons, the Security Council again demanded the destruction of the weaponry. Amid fears that some facilities

remained hidden, the demolition of factories and material increased.

By forcing disputes with UN inspectors, President Saddam Hussein attempted to portray the United Nations as a U.S. puppet. However, in 1993 cooperation replaced confrontation and the UN established a vast monitoring system involving planes, helicopters, ground inspectors, tagged equipment, sensors and video cameras. By late 1994, though new evidence sometimes surfaced, it had become obvious that Iraq could no longer produce the prohibited weapons, and suggestions surfaced for a trial period of oil exports.

Charging that over 500,000 men, women and children had died from shortages during the sanctions, Iraq launched diplomatic efforts to remove them. It claimed that it met the Security Council demands to destroy its missiles, chemical and biological weapons, and the atomic bomb project (Resolutions 687, 707, and 715). Iraq also promised to recognize Kuwait.

However, because the Third River project dried up the southern marshes and chemical weapons were used against Shi'a rebels, Iraq clearly violated another resolution (688). This resolution demanded humane treatment of the population, but it authorized neither force nor sanctions. Moreover, just before the Security Council met to review sanctions, the Iraqi army massed near the Kuwaiti border, and international support for removing sanctions declined.

In 1995, biological experts from UNSCOM, the special commission of inspectors, discovered that Iraq had imported vast quantities of growth media for toxic bacteria, far more than necessary to culture and identify hospital germs.

Evidence mounted that despite Iraqi denials, a vast germ warfare program had existed, producing anthrax, botulinum toxin and aflatoxin.

Very possibly, the inspectors' discovery of the project caused the man ultimately responsible for it, Saddam Hussein's son-in-law, Hussein Kamal, to flee to Jordan with his wife, children, and documents. Upstaging any evidence he might give, Baghdad released further evidence of the construction of biological missile warheads and spray containers for pilotless aircraft. However, Iraqi officials claimed that these had been destroyed (contrary to agreements) soon after the Gulf War. For his part, Hussein Kamal returned to Baghdad, where he was shot days later.

Despite the inspectors' suspicions of hidden weapons, the Iraqi people's desperation won public sympathy in many countries. Rather than lift the sanctions, the UN Security Council approved a strict "Oil for Food" program. It allowed $2 billion (later raised to $5.2 billion) in oil exports every six months, to pay for food, medicine, and vital equipment, plus contributions for war victims, weapons inspectors and the Kurds.

The Iraqi capture of Arbil from pro-Iranian Kurds led to an immediate suspension of the plans, but in late 1996 Iraqis celebrated in the streets as the oil began to flow. However, the funds failed to remove the great social distress. Instead, the food and medical imports stabilized the population, at a death rate of some 6,000 children per month. These "silent" deaths, largely unreported by the world's media, occur largely because of poor public health: untreated or impure water supplies, open sewage, past malnutrition and poorly functioning medical facilities.

From 1997 to 1999 Baghdad often refused UN attempts to inspect presidential palaces and government ministries. In response, Secretary-General Kofi Annan flew to Baghdad and reached a compromise: diplomats would accompany inspections of palaces. However, the arrangement only postponed the violence: in early 1999 Britain and the U.S. used a UN report criticizing Iraq as a pretext to bomb military targets again, after UNSCOM departed.

Perhaps Saddam Hussein created such crises because he feared the inspectors could find biological and chemical weapons, or the missiles and bombs to carry them. Perhaps also he overestimated the splits in the Security Council, and hoped that China, Russia and France would attempt to ease the inspections and economic sanctions. He also apparently misinterpreted popular Arab sympathy for the suffering Iraqi people as sufficient to lead their governments to ban U.S. use airspace for bombing. In any case, the air raids exceeded the number of missions

flown over Kosovo, and gradually destroyed much of the air defense system and damaged possible weapons factories, while his bitter personal attacks on Arab leaders reduced the chances of later diplomatic support.

However, Saddam Hussein used the bombing to prevent the UN inspectors from returning. Soon afterwards, press reports confirmed what Iraq had charged: the inspectors had worked with the CIA, which used the inspections to bug Iraqi communications. In addition, information from inspections was used later to select bombing targets. These revelations ensured that any future inspection system must be far different in personnel and method of operation.

Throughout 1999, diplomats at the UN sought for agreement on a new inspection system, because if Iraq is a rogue state bent on destroying enemies with weapons of mass destruction, the bombing campaign and withdrawal of UNSCOM left it closer to its goals. A vaguely-worded plan won Security Council approval in December; it offered the suspension of sanctions in return for full cooperation with the inspections. Although Baghdad did not reject the plan outright, by appointing a former head of UNSCOM to direct the new inspection agency the UN hardly signified a helpful start.

Sullen resentment among the *Shi'a* majority in southern Iraq exploded into riots following the assassination of their most prominent leader, Grand Ayatollah Muhammad Sadr in 1999. The regime blamed the murder of the third ayatollah within a year on *Shi'a* agents acting for foreigners. However, all the victims had expressed some criticism of the regime before their deaths.

Amid the popular suffering, the country's fortunate few seem to live well. New presidential palaces appeared frequently after 1990, often symbolically linking the current president to past rulers. Statues of Saddam Hussein litter the country. A new luxury resort opened at an artificial lake near Baghdad in 1999, with nearly every brick carrying his initials.

Meanwhile, imports of food, medical supplies and other essentials were handled inefficiently. More interested in rewarding friends with contracts than seeking the best supplies, on occasion Iraq ended up paying for inferior goods. Others rotted before they could be distributed.

In early 2001, President George W. Bush appointed several cabinet members who had held vital positions under his father during the Gulf War. These men had participated in the decisions that reasonably, but unpopularly, left Saddam Hussein free in Baghdad after Kuwait was liberated. They included Colin Powell, the general who became secretary of state, and Vice President Dick Cheney, who a decade earlier had served as secretary of defense.

Given other appointments and the memory of an Iraqi assassination attempt on the elder George Bush in Kuwait, it was no surprise that the U.S. abandoned the policy of containing Saddam Hussein. Instead, the goal became replacing him.

The sanctions regime was visibly crumbling. Syria reopened the long-idle oil pipeline and began to import oil, violating sanctions semi-officially. Jordan reduced inspections of Iraqi-bound merchandise, and its airline joined others in flights to the reopened Saddam International Airport in Baghdad. Egypt and other states improved diplomatic ties and discussed free trade. Though its own citizens died due to poor medical facilities, the Iraqi government found the money to donate to Palestinians killed in their Intifada against Israel. Iraq even demanded a commission on every barrel of Oil For Food, paid into its own accounts rather than to the UN.

Besides bombing raids on improved air defenses, the first U.S. initiative was "smart sanctions." As noted in the boxed material on sanctions, by victimizing innocent Iraqi civilians, sanctions had given the Iraqi government a public relations victory. Meanwhile, the regime smuggled in the goods it desired. Smart sanctions were designed to retain UN control of Iraq's oil export earnings, but to limit only imports of items useful for military purposes.

Desiring an end to all sanctions and to control all its oil revenues, the Iraqi regime naturally opposed smart sanctions. Nevertheless, the UN Security Council approved them, to take effect in 2002, despite suspicions that smart sanctions would not work. Given the many dual-purpose goods that would be prohibited from entering Iraq anyway, "smart sanctions" may make no difference from the existing "dumb sanctions." By early 2002, various nations had blocked over $5 billion worth of orders, sales of Iraqi oil had dropped precipitously under a system that established its price several weeks after the sale, and "Oil for Food" seemed ready to collapse.

The September 11 terrorist attacks on the U.S. both reinforced the U.S. determination to oust Saddam Hussein and strengthened U.S. world leadership. However, weaknesses existed in the U.S. position, particularly the lack of a "smoking gun." With al-Qaeda and Iraq united by little except hostility to the U.S., attempts to tie Baghdad to the attacks proved groundless. Despite President Bush's condemnation of Iraq as part of an "axis of evil," many NATO allies (except Britain) publicly rejected the use of force against Iraq.

A variety of proposals to oust Saddam Hussein now circulate in Washington, and the U.S. replenishes its hi-tech weaponry. Most involve using U.S. aircraft and the smart weapons that proved successful in destroying Taliban rule in Afghanistan to back up an attack by ground forces. Among the most popular suggestions:

➢ a Kurdish attack from the north,
➢ a Shi'a attack from the south,
➢ invasion by an Iraqi opposition army, and
➢ a military *coup d'etat*.

Each of these possible policies faces significant problems. Recognizing that they cannot become masters of Iraq, the Kurdish leadership fears losing their autonomy. They would presumably need guarantees of the region's near-independence that would be consider treason by Iraqi Arabs. By contrast, given the size of their community, many Shi'a probably desire to lead Iraq. However, the only significant Shi'a opposition groups are linked to Iran, and a Shi'a dominated Iraq would likely become a close ally of Iran and a disturbing influence over Arab Shi'a minorities in the Gulf.

For its part, the secular Iraqi opposition has no army and by early 2002 not even enough accountants to keep its books well. Although the U.S. restored its subsidy, the opposition apparently lacks deep roots in the country, and no neighboring country is likely to grant it a base.

While the threat of a military *coup d'etat* or an assassination attempt can never be ruled out completely, Saddam Hussein operates vast intelligence services designed to minimize the odds of success. Furthermore, the open knowledge that torture and death await even distant relatives of unsuccessful plotters must deter many potential rebels. For example, one military officer who fled the country reported receiving a videotape of a female relative being brutally raped because of his defection. Conscious of world opinion, the Iraqi military is also likely to place own citizens near military targets, as hostages, thus making a bombing campaign much bloodier in civilian lives than that in Afghanistan in 2001.

It is clear that surrounding Arab nations (except Kuwait) perceive Israel-Palestinian fighting a greater threat to regional peace than Saddam Hussein. They are likely to limit U.S. use of bases. U.S. doctrine that "who is not with us is against us" may not sell well.

Kurdish Autonomy in the North

Protected in large part by the U.S. no-fly zone over Northern Iraq, in 1991 the three million Kurds nevertheless found themselves short of fuel, food and the supplies needed to reconstruct hundreds of entire villages destroyed by the Iraqi army. Menacing Iraqi troop movements often suggested an attack and created new waves of refugees. To establish a government framework, Kurdish leaders sought autonomy from Saddam Hussein. They failed over issues such as the division of revenue and whether to include oil–rich Kirkuk in the Kurdish zone. With no alternative, they formed their own administration, eventually known as the Kurdistan Regional Government (KRG).

Sanctions, Suffering and Responsibility

In the years after losing the Gulf War, food shortages threatened one million Iraqis with starvation. As a result, children died at astounding rates, some 6,000 per month according to UN estimates because their bodies never received sufficient nourishment and medical care to resist childhood diseases and those spread by unclean water.

For their parents, survival came at enormous cost. Government rations of essentials—flour, cooking oil, rice, sugar and tea—cost almost nothing. However, the rations meet only half the daily needs, and non–rationed food cost prohibitively. In early 1995, for example, flour sold in the open market for 400 dinars per kilo, and a box of 30 eggs for 1,650 dinars. By contrast, civil servant salaries average only 3,500 dinars per month. Only by selling everything, including its heirlooms, could a family survive.

Normally world opinion responds to such suffering with humanitarian aid. For the unfortunate Iraqis, however, the suffering resulted not from natural disaster, but from sanctions imposed by the UN Security Council. The critical decisions about their fate were taken, and their moral consequences often evaded, by the American and Iraqi presidents. Each exhibited some degree of cynicism. The U.S. linked sanctions on oil exports to concerns never voted by the Security Council, possibly to avoid repeating President Bush's mistake of "letting Saddam get away." Thus the U.S. argued—against the evidence of many executed plotters—that worsening conditions will eventually lead the Iraqis to overthrow Saddam Hussein.

For his part, Saddam Hussein's belligerent behavior reinforced American arguments that he could not be trusted. For years he also refused to accept the UN offer of limited oil sales to finance food and medicine, arguing that the conditions violated Iraqi sovereignty. Did a country criss–crossed by no–fly zones, weapons inspectors and a rebel area enjoy pristine independence?

In fact, the real basis for his rejection was the plight of Iraqis. Improve the lot of starving children, and sanctions became far less objectionable to consciences in the West. Finally, in 1996, conditions became so bad that both the U.S. and Saddam Hussein relented—but they still disputed details of limited sales long enough for thousands more children to die.

International difficulties pressed heavily on the Kurdish zone. Legally part of Iraq, it suffered UN sanctions aimed at Saddam's regime. As rebels against that regime, it endured sabotage and terrorist explosions by Iraqi agents, as well as the UN trade embargo. Factories closed for lack of supplies and customers, trade languished, and the aftereffects of Iraq's depopulation policies hampered agriculture. Initially, the Kurdish zone survived largely on handouts of aid. Later taxes on Turkish tanker trucks breaking UN sanctions by purchasing cheap diesel fuel in Iraq became the sole significant revenue.

The independence struggle led by the *Kurdistan Workers Party (PKK)* against Turkey (see Turkey: History) complicated matters greatly. By threatening to attack the tanker trucks, vital as the sole source of taxes, the *PKK* gained freedom of action in Iraqi Kurdistan. However, Turkey remained Kurdistan's vital link to the world, and it demanded the freedom to raid *PKK* bases in the Kurdish zone. Major invasions in 1992 and 1995 proved of doubtful value against small *PKK* units in mountainous terrain, and the Turkish incursions inevitably destroyed homes and villages. To compensate, Turkey offered humanitarian aid and electricity to a few border areas and allied with the zone's administration and political parties to limit *PKK* activities.

The two major political parties faced each other in the heated 1992 election campaign for the assembly of the KRG. Divided by geography, dialect, tribal affiliation, and personal ambitions, the Kurds had formed two major groups in the 1960s. Mas'ud Barzani's *Kurdistan Democratic Party (KDP)*, strongest in northern and western Kurdistan, reflected the spirit of his late father, Mustafa, the legendary hero of the independence struggle. The *KDP* cooperated with the Islamic Republic of Iran, much as Mustafa had received support from the Shah's government in the 1960s and early 1970s. Initially more sympathetic to Baghdad, Jalal Talabani founded the *Patriotic Union of Kurdistan (PUK)*. Drawing its strength in southeastern Kurdistan, the *PUK* later reversed its alliances and fought for independence as an ally of Iran.

When the 1992 elections gave each party an equal number of seats, despite their past rivalries Barzani and Talabani agreed to share executive power, rather than hold a run-off election. Eventually they even agreed to merge their guerrilla forces to form an army of 30,000. In practice, however, unity proved impossible. Disputes over taxes, property ownership and other matters set one party against another.

Widespread fighting broke out in the summer of 1994, when fighters of the *PUK* evicted Barzani's followers from Arbil (Erbil), the Kurdish capital. Strife continued, despite truces, and in 1996 at the invitation of the *KDP* Iraqi troops captured Arbil from the *PUK* (and in the process destroyed the CIA's major Iraq operations). As the *KDP* advanced, aid from Iran enabled the *PUK* to regain some lost territory. U.S. and Turkish pressure eventually led to a formal ceasefire.

Lacking any international recognition, and soon forgotten by the world's social conscience, Iraqi Kurdistan thus proved to be neither a nation nor a well–administered refugee haven, but rather a limited form of anarchy in a tightly limited area. Kurdish rivalries, no doubt encouraged by foreign powers, facilitated a result that most conveniently served the interests of surrounding nations.

In 1998, in Washington, the two rival parties signed an agreement to divide the Kurdistan Regional Government between themselves, forming two administrations, each headed by a prime minister. The *DPK* dominates a region of about two million inhabitants, including the capital, Arbil, and the vital road between Iraq and Turkey through Dahuk. With control of the road comes the ability to tax trucks carrying cheap Iraqi oil to Turkey. This widely-ignored violation of UN sanctions provides over 80% of tax revenue for the zone. To the east, the *PUK* capital is Sulaymaniyah, a large and vibrant city despite its location outside the U.S.-imposed no fly zone.

Often deprived of education and culture in their own language, and still lacking regular postal service, the Kurdish territories emphasize electronic communications. Both regions sponsor satellite TV broadcasts in their local dialects and permit the satellite dishes needed to receive the broadcasts. Kurdistan's freedom to watch TV and to use the internet is unmatched by any neighboring state. For the moment, at least, freedom also extends to printed communications, with dozens of newspapers and magazines appearing in the small region, some sharply critical of the ruling party.

A decade after its liberation from Iraqi rule Kurdistan maintains the legal fiction of forming part of Iraq while gradually creating institutions common to independent nations. Politicians rotate through coalition cabinets, and the fifteen government ministries address the same problems as government bureaucracies elsewhere. Though the ministry of foreign affairs is missing, the KRG has representatives abroad, and the Ministry of Pesh Merga Affairs clearly handles defense.

Despite the poverty and anarchy of the 1990s, new roads cross the land, and new apartments house refugees previously living in tents. Two new universities (at Dohuk and Sulaymaniyah) share with Salahaddin University in Arbil the mission of concentrating research on Kurdistan's people and resources. In 2001, a central bank was created to provide currency for a region that legally had used only Iraqi dinars dating from before the invasion of Kuwait in 1990.

Charges & Counter-charges about Oil for Food

Approved in 1996 to relieve the worst civilian suffering inflicted by sanctions, the Oil for Food program initially permitted oil exports worth $2 billion (later $5.6 billion and more) every six months to buy food and needed supplies. U.S. spokesmen claim the program can succeed and that Iraq diverts supplies and fails to place human needs first. They also contrast lower death rates for Kurdish children in the north.

Simple arithmetic, however, shows the program's woeful insufficiency. Iraq receives only two-thirds of the earnings; the rest pays program costs and compensates Kuwaitis and other victims of Iraqi's invasion. At first, Oil for Food earned Iraq about *$0.30 per person per day*, inadequate for even bulk purchases of the cheapest foods. By 1999 the total reached $0.85 per day, still a modest amount. UN Secretary-General Kofi Annan then announced delivery of 12 million tons of supplies, but this *averaged only one pound per Iraqi per day*, hardly sufficient for medicine, food and reconstruction of essential services. In 2000/2001 average caloric intake finally approached pre-war levels.

More food alone will not restore life expectancy. The gravest dangers come from the war-damaged sanitation system and the collapse of health facilities (hospitals often lack sheets and disinfectants). However, the U.S. blocked $2.5 billion of "dual purpose" (civilian and military) goods, including power turbines, heart and lung machines, pesticides, erasers, water purification chemicals, Pentium II chips and pencils. Pencil graphite might serve as a lubricant; more realistically, the chlorine commonly used to treat water is well known as a poison gas.

The UN Humanitarian Coordinator for Iraq resigned in 2000, saying he had lost hope. Despair among UN officials seems widespread: his two predecessors quit for similar reasons, and the Food for Peace director resigned days later. Even in the U.S. Congress, a letter signed by 70 representatives condemned "infanticide masquerading as policy."

Many factors improve the health of Kurdish children. Besides better administration, they benefit from cleaner water supplies in the mountains, less destruction from bombing during the Kuwait war (and since), better access to smuggled materials, and fewer concerns about "dual purpose" equipment.

The UN's Oil for Food program deserves much credit for the stability and progress. Its funding for reconstruction and other projects is only available if the KRG maintains order and stability. Whereas in the mid-1990s the *KDP* and *PUK* fought each other bitterly, a variety of political parties is now active in each area, and the *KDP* governs its territory in coalition.

One significant domestic threat comes from Islamic fundamentalism, possibly fanned by non-Kurds, which threatens the relatively free and democratic society. Operating along the Iranian border, at least two fundamentalist groups, the *Islamic Unity Movement of Kurdistan* and the *Jund al-Islam* have clashed with the PUK, and the *Jund al-Islam* allegedly massacred a number of villagers.

For the moment, Kurdish Islam appears moderate, and the fundamentalists remain confined to the eastern border. Far more worrisome to the Kurdish leadership are Western analysts and politicians who propose Kurdish fighters as the means to accomplish Washington's desired overthrow of Saddam Hussein. Without adequate American protection, such an attack could invite terrible Iraqi reprisals, including civilian executions of Kurds living in areas controlled by Iraq. On the other hand, a refusal to serve as Iraq's equivalent of the "Northern Alliance" might mean the end of the West's vital protection of the no-fly zone.

Of course, for most Iraqi Kurds the total defeat of Saddam Hussein remains a potential disaster. For various reasons, all countries in the region (except perhaps Israel) oppose dismembering Iraq and the appearance of an independent Kurdish state. The creation of a legitimate and peaceful government in Baghdad would raise all kinds of awkward questions about the practical independence of the KRG. The present justification for the existence of the Kurdish Region is the horrors Saddam Hussein's forces would inflict on the Kurds. To remove Saddam's rule over Baghdad

Pre–war Baghdad: A high–fashion model shows off a gown

thus threatens to remove "government by the Kurds and for the Kurds" in Arbil and Sulaymaniyah.

Culture: As Muslim Arabs, Iraqis share major cultural features with other peoples of the Middle East, ranging from the father's authority to food to religious holidays. The family remains the basic social unit, with parents, children, and grandchildren often forming a single household. Though their education may postpone it, girls usually marry young, by arrangement between her family and the groom's, and soon bear the first of many children. Large families have been encouraged by both traditional values and government policies. Consequently, the population has grown rapidly, and about half the population is less than 15 years of age.

Before the 1958 Revolution, most Iraqis lived in rural areas, typically in small, mud–brick houses except in the north, where the climate required stone. Agriculture occupied perhaps three–quarters of the population; their living conditions were simple or even harsh, with diets restricted to bread, rice, lentils, beans, onions and dates. As oil revenues provided prosperity in the cities, they attracted a great migration, until by 1990 some two–thirds of the nation lived in urban areas, usually in neighborhoods of people from the same district. Agriculture, often neglected though still important, proved unable to feed the nation during the UN embargo.

Of course, two decades of war and sanctions mean these are not ordinary times. Poverty and inadequate food discourage having large numbers of children. Though the family remains the basic social unit, marriage has become far more difficult, and reportedly there are now at least one million single women aged over thirty-five. Few men can afford the traditional dowry or furnish a home, while many educated women seeking a successful career prefer to remain single.

Sixty years ago, large Bedouin tribes like the Shammar roamed the deserts. However, the number of nomads has dwindled to insignificance due to motor transport, resettlement programs, education, and easier sedentary life.

Modernization most visibly affected the large cities of Iraq, as the government constructed roads, shopping centers, and large buildings. The well–to–do now live in modern homes and apartment houses in new suburbs that contrast with the narrow streets and homes above the stores of old sections of the cities. Poor migrants, on the other hand, find temporary shelter, often of reed matting and mud on the outskirts. Many urban men and some women select Western styles of clothing, though the traditional gowns for men and the voluminous black *abayas* for women remain widely used, and dominate rural areas. Rural Kurds wear distinctive clothing, the men in baggy pants and women in long gowns over pants.

For centuries, the Marsh Arabs, known also as the Madan, formed a sharp contrast to the traditional image of Arabs as herders of sheep and goats in a desert landscape. Inaccessible except by canoe, the Marsh Arabs lived in a world of water, surrounded by vegetation and living in reed houses with high, arched ceilings. Some homes were even built on artificial islands constructed of reeds. All this was made possible by the flat terrain between the lower Tigris and Euphrates rivers, where the annual flow and flooding of the rivers created an area of permanent and seasonal marshes, lakes, and waterways that stretched across 10,000 square miles. Invaluable for fish and migrating birds, the marshes also provided an environment for rare species of otter, lizards, wild boar and other animals.

Shi'a by religion, the Marsh Arabs' major occupations included fishing, herding water buffalo, and weaving reed mats. They several unique customs and except for limited trade, they mixed little with outsiders, rarely marrying them. During the two Gulf Wars, military deserters sought sanctuary amidst the isolation of the marshes.

In response, the Iraqi government determined to control the region. Because irrigation and dams upstream diminished the flow of the rivers and ended the seasonal floods, some areas became accessible by roads. Then the "Third River" (see Economy, below) diverted water to regions below the marshes. By the mid-1990s, the marshes effectively ceased to exist, and most of the Marsh Arab population had fled to refugee camps in Iran.

Formal culture in Iraq, like most other Arab countries, stresses achievements in poetry and learning, while sculpture, painting, music and drama received less interest. The great recent exception is statues of Saddam Hussein, whose visage and hands feature prominently on war monuments and other public decorations.

Few of the older generation of Iraqis formally entered school, but in recent decades the government vastly extended the educational system. Primary education is compulsory, and schools now dot villages and cities alike. Their modern curriculum replaces the Quranic emphasis of the kuttabs, or mosque schools. Beyond secondary education, universities in the major cities offer instruction in most disciplines. Although the role of women remains less public, all schools and universities are coeducational, in contrast to some conservative Gulf states. Despite the higher levels of literacy, newspaper readership remains low, a function no doubt of the state– and party–controlled press.

Economy: Until the invasion of Kuwait, oil exports provided the major source of revenue for development and 95% of foreign exchange earnings. Iraq's proven reserves are vast: over 100 billion barrels, or about 10% of the world's total. Only Saudi Arabia contains more. Its efficient production methods keep the average well producing many times the level of U.S. oil wells. Nevertheless, reaching overseas markets with the oil from an almost land–locked country proved difficult from the start. The pipeline constructed to Palestine before World War II proved useless with Israeli independence. Another line to ports in Syria and Lebanon depended on the goodwill and security of those nations, and this interrupted exports. Given the lack of a natural harbor along the Gulf shoreline, offshore loading terminals provided for the export of crude oil from the southern fields. But that route depended on freedom to navigate the Gulf and the Strait of Hormuz, and the facilities also lay uncomfortably close to Iran.

Seeking other export routes, in 1977 a new pipeline was completed to carry oil through Turkey to that country's port of Yumurtalik. In 1983 a Turkish company won a contract to increase the capacity of this pipeline, Iraq's only access to the Mediterranean after Syria closed the old pipeline across its territory. Iraq also arranged construction of a vast new pipeline across Saudi Arabia to the Red Sea, capable of raising the export capacity above the country's OPEC quota.

Economic sanctions imposed after Iraq invaded Kuwait distorted Iraq's development in almost every regard. However, the ambitious reconstruction plans promised after the earlier war with Iran provide a possible guide to the future. They stressed new industry and the rebuilding of homes and commercial areas. Devastated Basra rapidly received funds to restore roads, replace housing, and beautify the canals of the "Venice of the East" into a showcase. It now again lies in shambles. The port of Faw, so obliterated by nearly seven million artillery shells that nothing remained, likewise received new housing, government buildings in the modern Islamic style and entertainment areas.

Plans call for a large petrochemical complex at Basra, chemical fertilizer plants and processing plants for imported metal ores. Cement production is being increased to meet domestic demand. Present industrial production includes leather, shoes, cotton textiles, beer and household articles, such as matches. Small shop or home manufacturing is still important, especially for homespun woolens, rugs and reed mats.

Iraq once grew 70% of the world's dates. Smuggled through the blockade they remain an important export, far more valuable per ton than oil. However, because the date groves are infested with insects, and pesticides can not be imported because of sanctions, harvests are a small fraction of levels in the 1980s.

Wheat and barley are the main winter crops, while rice and cotton are grown in irrigated areas in the south. Sheep, goats, cattle and water buffalo are raised for meat, milk and hides; wool was a significant export. Agriculture improved markedly before the Gulf War as a result of irrigation schemes and the introduction of scientific methods, but several problems hampered it: an emphasis on industrialization, land distribution policies, weak management, and the reluctance of educated Iraqis to use their hands. Furthermore, the living standards among urban workers rose more rapidly, thus encouraging ambitious and talented young men to leave rural life. In the years following the war, irrigation pumps often failed to work, and sanctions on pesticides, equipment, and fertilizers combined to reduce output by at least 30%.

After the 1958 Revolution, industry and large–scale business in Iraq came under government control. For reasons of quality, pragmatism, or a revision in ideology, by the late 1980s the emphasis had shifted to private initiative in many sectors, including agriculture, tourism, and light industry.

Reduced controls over foreign exchange and prices also provided greater incentives for private investment. While the changes did apparently boost productivity, they also spurred inflation, privately estimated at 25% in early 1990. After the Gulf War, inflation became essentially incalculable.

One noteworthy project inaugurated after the war was the Third (or Leader's) River in the south, a 350–mile ditch some 300 feet wide and over 100 feet deep, ostensibly to drain the salty and polluted irrigation water that "leaches" into some 3 million acres of soil, rendering farming impossible. By draining much of the region's marshlands, the project carried other consequences as well. It deprived Shi'a rebels and army deserters of their refuge, and destroyed Marsh Arab soci-ety, a unique culture for hundreds of ears. It also destroyed the habitats of many species, some of them rare or threatened.

The Future: The odds of an indefinite rule over Iraq worsened perceptibly for Saddam Hussein after President George W. Bush took office. They worsened to a much greater degree when the U.S. became the direct target of terrorists on September 11. Though Washington may never possess evidence of direct Iraqi involvement in

the September attacks, the administration is convinced that as long as he rules Iraq, Saddam Hussein represents a potential terrorist threat to Americans everywhere.

Certainly publicly and probably privately, Arab governments except Kuwait's fail to share these American perceptions. Some of the very countries that in 1990 sought U.S. forces to protect them from Iraqi aggression now refuse to let U.S. forces use bases on their territories for an invasion of Iraq or a bombing campaign against it. Moreover, nearly all nations in the region fear that a change of regime in Baghdad could mean dismembering the country and raise many issues better left ignored.

Thus Saddam Hussein continues to rule, aided by the fears of his local enemies about Iraq's future without him. For his part, he (and his ghostwriter) apparently had the time to pen a second novel, *The Fortified Castle*. Its 713 pages relate the story of a servant who betrayed his master, stole his possessions, and plotted his death. In the end, the master took revenge and killed the servant. This symbolic story apparently displays Saddam Hussein's vision of the future. Fear of his grim revenge postpones his demise in ways that both Westerners and Middle Easterners find abhorrent but successful.

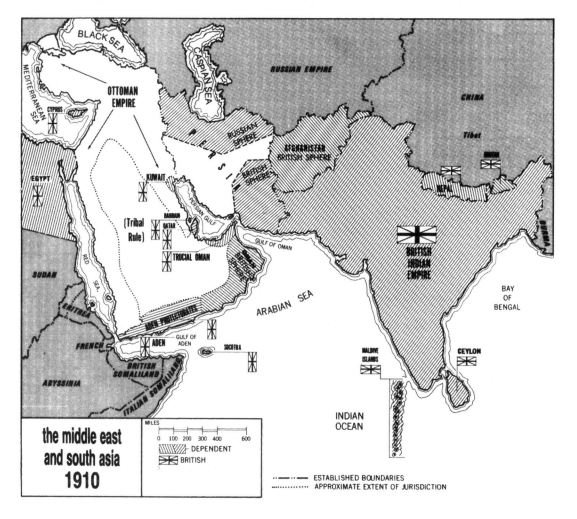

The State of Israel   מדינת ישראל

Introduction: Whether for its heroism during the War of Independence (1948–49) or later conflicts, its farming that "made the desert bloom", its democracy, the achievements of its citizens in music, science, or its military prowess, no other nation of the region captured the imagination of the Western world like Israel. Its immigrants from around the globe provide a more diverse culture than any other nation, and it remains a special focus even of Jews who live elsewhere by choice.

——————— • ———————

Area: 8,017 sq. mi. (20,700 sq. km.) within the Armistice Demarcation lines effective 1949–1967. In addition, since 1967, the West Bank (of the Jordan River), the Gaza Strip and part of Syria have been under Israeli military occupation and subject to Israeli civilian settlement.

Population: Nearly 6 million (1999), including 4.8 million Jews and 1 million Arabs.

Capital City: Jerusalem (Pop. about 600,000), more than two–thirds Jewish. The United States and nearly all other nations do not recognize Israeli sovereignty over East Jerusalem (captured in 1967) and maintain their embassies in Tel Aviv (with suburbs, Pop. 1.8 million, estimated).

Climate: Summers are hot and dry, winters mild with moderate rainfall, except in the arid south part of the country.

Neighboring Countries: Egypt (Southwest); Jordan (East); Syria (Northeast); Lebanon (North).

Time Zone: GMT +2 (+3 in summer).

Official Languages: (Modern) Hebrew and Arabic.

Other Principal Tongues: English, Yiddish, Ladino, Polish, Russian, Persian, German, French, Hungarian, Bulgarian and Romanian.

Ethnic Background: European, North African and Asian.

Principal Religion: Judaism (83%), Islam and Christianity.

Chief Commercial Products: Computer software and high–tech applications, armaments, aircraft and aircraft servicing, military electronics equipment, cut and polished diamonds, copper, machinery, food processing, precision instruments, plastics and potash.

Main Agricultural Produce and Livestock: Oranges and other fruit, vegetables, wheat, potatoes, poultry, sheep and cattle.

Major Trading Partners: U.S., Japan, Germany, U.K. Switzerland, France, Italy, Hong Kong and Belgium.

Currency: New Shaqalim (New Shekel).

Former Colonial Status: Britain conquered the territory now controlled by the State of Israel from the Ottoman

Theodor Herzl

89

Empire during 1916–1918 and held it until 1948.

Independence Date: May 14, 1948. As all holidays, Independence Day is celebrated according to the Jewish calendar and falls on varying dates in the latter part of April.

Chief of State: Moshe Katzav, President (a largely ceremonial office, 2000).

Head of Government: Ariel Sharon, Prime Minister (2001).

National Flag: White field with a broad blue horizontal stripe near both the top and bottom; centered between the stripes is a large blue "Shield of David," that is a cut–out six–pointed star.

Gross Domestic Product: $93 billion.

GDP per capita: $16,000

Lying on the coast of the Mediterranean Sea with the Arabian Desert at its back door, Israel has considerable variety in climate and geography. The northern part enjoys good rainfall, sometimes as much as 40 inches in a winter, but the southern part is arid desert of gravel and rock. Summers can be unpleasantly warm throughout the land, but winters are not severe, though chilly at higher elevations.

The Mediterranean seaboard is bordered by a coastal plain averaging about ten miles in width and broken only by a ridge extending northwest from the West Bank to a promontory just south of Haifa. Much of this plain is under cultivation, as it has been for many centuries. A central ridge then runs south from the border with Lebanon through northern Israel and the West Bank, then fans out in Israel's southern desert. The rainfall caught on the western slopes of these central hills allows a variety of fruit trees to flourish, as well as small fields of grain and vegetables. The Hula Plain north of the Sea of Galilee has been partly reclaimed from marshes. A fertile plain lying to the southeast of Haifa has been a source of grains and other foods since ancient times.

Flowing from sources on the slopes of Mt. Hermon and the Golan Heights, the Jordan River provides the major source of fresh water in the region. South of the Sea of Galilee the Jordan Valley lies entirely below sea level, and at the Dead Sea it reaches the lowest point on earth (about 1300 ft. below sea level, and falling). South of the Dead Sea, the deep valley rises gently to the Gulf of Aqaba and Israel's southern port, Eilat.

History: Proclaimed independent on May 14, 1948, Israel represents the triumph of modern Zionist dreams for a Jewish state. Its origins reach back, however, for centuries. After the Romans crushed Jewish revolts in Palestine during the first and second centuries A.D., Jews overwhelmingly lived scattered outside their Promised Land, forbidden for centuries to reside in Jerusalem by pagan Rome and then

ZIONISM: For centuries Zionism reflected the yearning of Jews to return to Zion, meaning the citadel at Jerusalem, and even the entire Holy Land. After increasing nationalism in Europe, Theodor Herzl and others transformed cultural and religious Zionism into a political ideology. It holds that Jews everywhere form *one people,* whose protection requires a Jewish state.

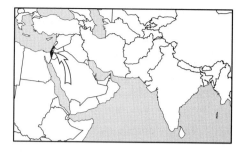

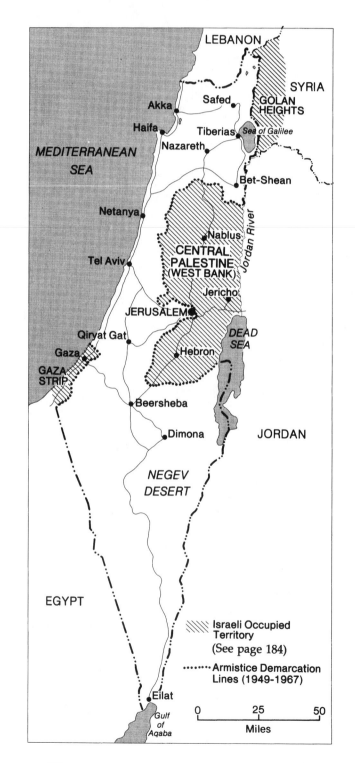

Christian Byzantium. The small Jewish minority in Palestine welcomed Arab rule (635–8), and Jews began to return to Jerusalem after the Muslim conquest. The restoration of Christian rule, in the form of the Crusades, meant the massacre of almost all Muslims and Jews in Jerusalem (1099).

The restoration of Muslim rule after the defeat of the Crusaders improved Jewish fortunes in Palestine, and a trickle of immigration began, in part by refugees from persecutions and expulsions in Western Europe. Despite ravages of the Black Plague, famines, and rival rulers, the Jewish communities survived, then strengthened after 1492 with a rapid influx of Spanish Jews expelled from their homeland. Ottoman rule (1517) decayed relatively quickly in Palestine, however, and amidst insecurities and disorders the Jews suffered alongside Christians and Muslims. By 1800 the Jewish presence in Palestine had dwindled to the lowest level for centuries, and nations like the United States and France had removed all legal disabilities of Jews. Events took the unexpected turn, however: a century later, Zionism had infused the Jewish world with the idea not merely of Jewish settlements in the Promised Land, but of a *Jewish state* there.

The Birth of Political Zionism

The origins of Zionism lay far from the traditional and pious Jewish settlements in Palestine. Persecutions (pogroms) in Eastern Europe, especially in Czarist Russia and Poland, led Leo Pinsker to demand a home for oppressed Jews in 1882; a colonization society sprang up. By the end of the century thousands of Jews fleeing the anti–Semitism of Eastern Europe entered the Holy Land to pioneer new settlements with the goal of developing a self-supporting economy based on agriculture. By 1900, the number of Jews in the land had thus increased to an estimated 45,000.

Against the backdrop of this often religious migration, the concept of political Zionism arose, the belief that the Jews scattered across the world constituted a single nation, that their right to liberty and independence—perhaps even their survival—included a return to the Promised Land and the establishment there of the State of Israel. The best known person in the early development of the Zionist movement was Theodor Herzl, who published *The Jewish State* in 1896 and established the movement with the first Zionist World Congress of 1897 in Basel, Switzerland. Under the influence of European anti–Jewish persecution and discrimination, he envisioned "the establishment for the Jewish people of a home in Palestine."

Only accepted by a handful at first, this application of 19th century European territorial nationalism to Jewish existence began to grow steadily. Eventually the main ideas of political Zionism came to

include (1) the concept of "a Jewish People," not merely various communities following the religion of Judaism; (2) the inevitable recurrence of anti–Jewish persecution; (3) the impossibility of Jews living full and complete lives outside a distinctive and territorial state; (4) the historic right of "the Jewish People" to *Eretz Yisrael*, the Land of Israel (see Historical Background) and (5) the duty of all Jews everywhere to support the national cause. These ideas formed the basic ideology in building the State of Israel and in its history to the present.

Until Britain conquered Palestine in 1916–1918, it was part of the Ottoman Empire. Most Ottoman authorities did not favor the Zionist immigration and land procurement because of local Arab opposition, but were only partly able to resist external European support for Jewish immigration, as well as internal subterfuges and bribes that provided land to Jewish settlers, if expensively.

The vigor and ideals of a new generation of Zionist immigrants, known as the Second Aliyah, influenced deeply the founding of modern social institutions by 1914: they established newspapers, trade unions, and political parties. Hebrew became the language for Jewish schools, the first secondary school started, and land was purchased for a university. Moreover, the character of Zionist settlement had been formed. The native Jewish settlements were primarily urban, and other Jewish immigrants lacked a clear philosophy of purpose, some producing wines for export using French experts, Arab labor, and Baron Edmond de Rothschild's subsidies. In contrast, socialists within the Zionist organization sought to build a society of collectives where Jews worked together at even the most menial tasks and refused to employ (cheap) Arab labor. By the beginning of World War I, about 100,000 Jews lived in Palestine, compared to roughly 550,000 Muslims and 70,000 Christians.

World War I proved a major turning point for Zionist hopes. Having agreed secretly with France to internationalize Palestine, Britain also implied in correspondence with Sharif Husayn, leader of the Arab Revolt then in progress, that Palestine would form part of an independent Arab state. However, the persuasive influence of a prominent scientist, Dr. Chaim Weizmann, led on November 2, 1917, to the Balfour Declaration. It promised British favor for the establishment of a "national home for the Jewish people" in Palestine, although it expressed support for the civil and religious rights of the non–Jewish populations.

Significantly, it did not promise Palestine as the Jewish National Home, and the British explained to Arabs that the Jewish settlements would not compromise "the political and economic freedom of the Arab population." Most Palestinians opposed

the declaration, and testified their opposition to the American King–Crane Commission during the peace talks. Nevertheless, incorporated into the 1920 San Remo Agreement that divided the Middle East between France and Britain, the Balfour Declaration also formed part of Britain's Mandate for Palestine in 1923. Unlike mandates for other Arab areas, this mandate did not prescribe a constitution and eventual independence for the inhabitants.

Jewish Achievements during the Mandate

With the end of war and a sympathetic nation in control, Jewish immigration rapidly expanded, with predictable Arab reactions. sIn 1920 serious rioting broke out, as it did frequently during the Mandate. Complicating matters further, administration of the territory and its peoples fell to four distinct organizations. First, the British authorities under Sir Herbert Samuel established normal government departments, while the Jewish national council (*Vaad Leumi*) represented the Jewish population and governed their personal law and religious matters. Third, the Zionist Organization, though headquartered in London, intervened in Palestine over matters such as education, industry, immigration, and public works in the Jewish communities. Finally, the Arab executive under Musa Kazim al–Husayni attempted to represent the interests and development of the Muslim and Christian Arab–speaking inhabitants.

Jewish immigration rose sharply after Hitler gained power in Germany. By 1939, despite Arab riots and consequent British reductions in permitted immigration, nearly one–third of the population was Jewish. The relative prosperity of Palestine also attracted Arab immigrants, though the numbers are poorly documented. In any case, Zionist leaders could plan for the day when Jews formed a majority of the total population. Until then, Jewish organizations bought land, settled it, and established industry.

The development of Jewish industry caused relatively little strife within the Arab community, and its products occasionally found their way to neighboring countries. However, land purchases provided a major source of Arab resentment. Fertile, watered farmland rarely lay vacant, and frequently cost far more than similar land in the United States. Nevertheless, many acres remained idle, their cultivation handicapped among other things by qualities the twentieth century would change: the low level of agricultural technology and education, the absence of engine–powered pumps, incursions by Bedouins, expensive transportation by animals, and blocked foreign markets.

Against this background, the Jewish National Fund purchased farmland, often at high prices, from Arab landlords. The land had rarely been owned by those who farmed it, however. For example, significant purchases came from absentee landlords residing in Syria and Lebanon. With the change of ownership the Arab tenant farmers became dispossessed, for whether a communally–run *kibbutz* or a *moshav* with private ownership, a Jewish settlement stressed the dignity of Jewish labor. Moreover, once purchased, the land became the inalienable property of the Jewish community. Superior in education, technical knowledge, machinery and

incentives to the Arab tenant farmers they replaced, the Jewish settlers often succeeded in bringing the desert to bloom. Indeed their example influenced the remaining Arab farmers, whose production increased substantially. Jaffa's oranges won fame as Jewish exports, but Arabs had cultivated them for centuries and accounted for about half of all orange exports in the 1930s.

The social development of the Jewish community continued apace before World War II. The Hebrew University was founded in 1918, and universal elementary education was achieved in the 1930s. The Jewish Agency was established in 1929 to assist in fostering the immediate goals of immigration and the acquisition of land, as well as the promotion of religion and the use of Hebrew. The Jewish Self–Defense Force, the *Haganah,* developed in secret, coming to possess a strong organization and significant weapons. However, the entire Jewish community was not united. One minority, firmly orthodox, feared that the nationalism of Zionism destroyed the religious basis of Judaism. At another extreme, the Revisionists led by Vladimir Jabotinsky demanded the immediate fulfillment of the Jewish national home, on *both sides* of the Jordan River, thus including the East Bank or Trans–Jordan.

Arab Palestinians failed to achieve similar progress under the Mandate. By 1936 their frustration reached the point of a general strike, violence, and rebellion. Again the British government investigated, and again promised, this time in the 1939 White Paper, to limit Zionist immigration and implied future self–government for Palestine. World War II and the death camps of Hitler's Germany, however, placed Zionism deep in the imagination of most Western peoples. Moreover, particularly in the United States, a restored Israel seemed to fulfill Biblical prophecies.

The War for Independence, 1948-1949

In this climate, skillful Zionist leaders in America, cooperating with David Ben–Gurion, managed simultaneously to uphold U.S. limitations on Jewish immigration, and to encourage President Truman to urge it publicly for Palestine. No longer a great power, and no longer valuing the Suez Canal as a route to India, Britain found the difficulties of ruling Palestine too

Entrance to the Dome of the Rock, a sanctuary erected in the 7th century by Muslims on the site of the Temple of Solomon and the Second Temple, then in ruins. This is one of the most sacred of all Islamic shrines. Photo by Linda Cook

great and turned the problem over to the new United Nations. There the Zionists won a major legal and psychological victory in late 1947 when the General Assembly voted by a narrow margin to recommend the political partition of Palestine. It assigned about 60% of the territory to a "Jewish State" although the Jewish settlers comprised only a bare one–third of the population. The Security Council did not endorse this recommendation nor did it provide any enforcement. As Britain had announced its plan to withdraw from Palestine by May 15, 1948, the issue was left open to settlement by force.

Within Palestine, force pitted the Arab majority against the Jewish minority. The latter were organized militarily into three groups. Representing the mainstream Zionist movement, the *Haganah* counted some 60,000 fighters, armed even with a few tanks and backed by a supply system that smuggled arms from Europe. In contrast, the Revisionists of the 1920s influenced the two right–wing and smaller groups, the *Irgun* of Menachem Begin, and the *Stern Gang.* Sabotage of British military and transport installations already showed their capabilities. The *Irgun* and *Stern Gang* in particular adopted methods which

1947 UN Recommendation

Prime Minister David Ben-Gurion signs the independence declaration, May 14, 1948
AP/Wide World Photo

today are considered terrorist. In one of the most daring examples, in reprisal for British arrests of Jewish leaders, the Irgun blew up the British headquarters at the King David Hotel, killing 91.

The Palestinians, by contrast, organized no comparable military force, but counted on help from the surrounding states. As the British forces withdrew, Syrian volunteers and army officers entered Galilee (January 1948), and an Arab Liberation Army formed, financed and supplied in part by Egypt and Iraq. By April 1948 full–scale war broke out on many fronts, as both sides fought for as much land as they could obtain, regardless of the UN partition plan. Jewish forces quickly gained the Galilee region and Haifa, according to the partition part of the Jewish state. In addition, they captured Jaffa and Akka (Acre), allocated to the Arab state.

In contrast to European wars mostly between soldiers, this fighting involved entire communities, and descended quickly to brutality. In particular, the Irgun attacked the Arab village of Dair Yasin, near the vital road to Jerusalem, and massacred some 250 people, many of them women and children. In response, Arabs attacked a convoy headed for the Hebrew University and Hadassah Hospital outside Jerusalem; 77 professors, students, and medical personnel perished. In fear, to escape the fighting, or pressured by Jews, Arabs fled from exposed villages and cities captured by the Zionists. The Jews had nowhere to flee and fought rather better.

As the Mandate officially drew to a close, on May 14, 1948, in Tel Aviv David Ben–Gurion proclaimed the establishment of the State of Israel, and won immediate recognition from the United States. The next day, backed by resolutions of the Arab League, armies of Egypt, Iraq, Trans–Jordan, Syria and Lebanon entered the war. The first war between Israel and the Arab states began, with the Israelis fighting for their independence and very existence as a separate state. The Israeli army outnumbered the Arab forces in Palestine and soon gained the offensive, striking at enemy targets in turn. Poorly coordinated on separate fronts, their equipment often obsolete or defective, the Arab armies also failed to evade a United Nations arms embargo successfully. Like the four major wars that followed, this ended in Israeli victories almost everywhere, though one Jew of every 100 in Israel died.

Building the State of Israel

The boundaries of the various armistices of 1949 found Israel much enlarged from those of the partition plan, with about 70% of the mandate's territory. The highlands of the West Bank remained largely Arab and controlled by the Arab Legion of Trans–Jordan, except for a Jewish sector including part of Jerusalem. The only remaining portion of Palestine not under Israeli rule was the Gaza Strip in the southwest, inhabited mostly by wretched refugees and administered by Egypt. Equally important for the future, 700,000 Arab refugees fled what was to become the State of Israel.

For Israelis, independence meant a national government. Chaim Weizmann was elected to the largely honorary position of president in 1948, while the next year elections were held to the *Knesset,* the national parliament, whose majority leader is the Prime Minister. Israel's electoral system is one of the fairest in the world at translating preferences for political parties into seats in the legislature. With only one electoral district (the entire country), and proportional representation, each party's number of seats in the 120–member *Knesset* reflects very closely its percentage of the national vote.

Many parties seized the electoral system's opportunities in 1949, and have ever since. David Ben–Gurion headed the largest, *Mapai,* (the core today of the *Israeli Labor Party*), but it never won a majority in the *Knesset* although it dominated every cabinet until 1977. Consequently, Israeli governments have always been coalitions, in the early years largely between *Mapai* and the *National Religious Party*. The need to form a parliamentary majority often gives small parties disproportionate weight in forming a coalition.

The first government faced an immediate economic crisis. War had disrupted trade and production, and an Arab trade embargo blocked logical industrial development by cutting the oil pipeline to Haifa from Iraq and destroying dreams that saw Jewish capital and knowledge uniting with Arab labor. To help in the crisis, aid flowed in from private sources, especially the United Jewish Appeal in the United States, as well as from the American government. Well into the 1960s a major source of funds came from West Germany in the form of reparations for the Holocaust. Nevertheless, in a poor parcel of Asia, Israelis enjoyed living like Europeans, and the balance of payments often reflected a sharp deficit.

Besides the burden of defense, the government budget faced enormous costs of absorbing Jewish immigration. One of the first enactments of Israel, the Law of the Return, granted citizenship to all Jews who landed in Israel. In the first four years of independence, some 700,000 responded, many relatively poor and less–educated from Arab countries such as Morocco, Yemen, and Iraq. In contrast to the Eastern European *Askenazi* Jews who had dominated the Zionist movement and Israeli society, the new immigrants were overwhelmingly *Sephardic* Jews, with differences significant for Israeli politics and society (see Culture). Another important project was the Israel National Water Carrier, a system of canals and pipelines bringing water from the Jordan River to the coastal plain and then the Negev desert for irrigation.

For the Arabs who remained, Israeli rule brought the second-class citizenship of a discontented and distrusted minority.

The symbols of state reminded them that they had lost: the Star of David on an alien flag and an official language they could not speak. Israeli development often removed all traces of previous Arab habitation, even buildings and cemeteries, so Arabs witnessed the destruction of the memories of their past. The annual commemoration of Land Day (March 31) protests the confiscation of Arab land.

Less educated and relatively impoverished, with a high birthrate, Arab towns often failed to develop municipal services in a country where welfare came from charitable organizations more than from the state. Except for members of the Druze community (see Lebanon, culture), Arabs are relieved of military service and thus of veterans benefits. Nevertheless, their economic progress generally exceeded that of most of the Arab world. Israeli Arabs also enjoyed the right to vote in genuine multi-party elections, in contrast to most Arabs' lives under dictatorships and authoritarian rulers.

After living on the margins of national life for decades, many Israeli Arabs joined the protests that initiated the "al-Aqsa Intifada" in 2000 (see below). For this they suffered pillage and vandalism by Jewish mobs. The police shot Arab demonstrators, but put their weapons away when facing Jewish mobs. In fact, after decades of resignation, in the late 1990s the Arab community became more assertive, electing Arab members of the Knesset rather than voting for *Labor*.

Although armistice agreements formally took effect with neighboring states, peace along the demarcation lines was frequently disturbed despite the efforts of the UN Truce Supervision Organization. The longest armistice demarcation line was with Jordan. Although that government sought to prevent crossings into Israel, displaced Palestinians, armed and eventually organized, were able to cross from time to time and inflict damage or injury, sometimes killing civilians. Perhaps partly to satisfy public opinion that something was being done, partly to intimidate Jordan or discredit its army, Israel undertook, beginning in 1953, a policy of "retaliatory" military raids. These resulted in the destruction of property and death of many civilians on the Jordanian side of the demarcation line. Roughly ten times as many Arab civilians died as Israeli civilians through violations of the armistice lines.

The Suez Crisis and War, 1956

After serious tensions on the demarcation lines with Egypt had been mounting for more than a year, at the end of October 1956, Israel launched a massive surprise attack on Egypt. Within ten days Israeli forces occupied almost all the Sinai Peninsula, including Sharm al-Shaykh, which controlled the Straits of Tiran at the entrance to the Gulf of Aqaba and thereby

Israel's maritime route to the Orient. The Israeli attack formed part of a secret arrangement with France and Great Britain, both of them hostile toward Egypt over the recent nationalization of the Suez Canal (see Egypt). France and Britain participated in the aggression against Egypt, invading the Suez Canal Zone and bombing Egyptian airfields. However, under the leadership of the United States and the Soviet Union, the U.N. halted the fighting and supervised the withdrawal of foreign troops. A U.N. Emergency Force took up positions on the Egyptian side of the frontier to prevent incidents, and the Straits of Tiran remained open for Israeli shipping.

Domestically, the years after 1956 in Israel resembled the earlier ones, with Ben-Gurion dominating the government until his resignation in 1963 and replacement by Levi Eshkol as leader of *Mapai* and Prime Minister. The termination of German reparations in 1965 precipitated

an economic recession; more serious difficulties arose in foreign affairs. In 1964 the Arab states voted to strengthen their armed forces and divert their major tributaries of the Jordan River, thus threatening Israel's major source of fresh water.

Victory and Conquest: June 1967

Equally troublesome, Palestinian guerrilla raids increased in 1965 and 1966, leading to Israeli retaliation against the Jordanian-ruled West Bank and air battles over Syria. Against this background, in the spring of 1967, Egypt moved troops into the Sinai, ordered out the UN Emergency Force posted along the borders, and announced the closure of the Straits of Tiran. As world diplomacy sought to relax the tensions, Israel demanded that the Straits remain open, and Jordan and Syria formed a united front with Egypt.

On June 5, 1967, Israel launched a new war in full force. Caught by surprise,

---

SPECIAL DOCUMENT

UN Security Council Resolution 242

On November 22, 1967, the Security Council of the United Nations unanimously approved—and has subsequently reaffirmed—a resolution outlining the basis for peace between the State of Israel and the Arab countries with which it is in conflict. The United States, Israel and Egypt, in the Camp David accords of September 1978, specifically endorsed the implementation of this resolution "in all its parts." The following is the text of that resolution:

The Security Council,

Expressing its continuing concern with the grave situation in the Middle East,

Emphasizing the inadmissibility of the acquisition of territory by war and the need to work for a just and lasting peace in which every state in the area can live in security,

Emphasizing further that all member states in their acceptance of the Charter of the United Nations have undertaken a commitment to act in accordance with Article 2 of the Charter,

1. **Affirms** that the fulfillment of Charter principles requires the establishment of a just and lasting peace in the Middle East which should include the application of both of the following principles: (a) Withdrawal of Israel armed forces from territories occupied in the recent conflict; (b) Termination of all claims or states of belligerency and respect for and acknowledgment of the sovereignty, territorial integrity and political independence of every state in the area and their right to live in peace within secure and recognized boundaries free from threats.

2. **Affirms further** the necessity: (a) For guaranteeing freedom of navigation through international waterways in the area; (b) For achieving a just settlement of the refugee problem; (c) For guaranteeing the territorial inviolability and political independence of every state in the area, through measures including the establishment of demilitarized zones.

3. **Requests** the Secretary-General to designate a special representative to proceed to the Middle East to establish and maintain contacts with the states concerned in order to promote agreement and assist efforts to achieve a peaceful and accepted settlement.

4. **Requests** the Secretary-General to report to the Security Council on the progress of the efforts of the special representative as soon as possible.

despite bellicose speeches and talk of "pushing the Jews into the sea," in a matter of hours the air forces of Egypt and Syria were destroyed on the ground while Jordan's airports were bombed to uselessness and the Iraqi air force largely disabled as well. By the time the fighting ended on June 10, Israel had occupied the Sinai Peninsula to the banks of the Suez Canal, the Old City of Jerusalem, the West Bank, and a strip of Syria's Golan (Arabic *Jawlan*) plateau about 20 miles wide.

Diplomatic wrangling in the UN Security Council before, during, and after the war meant that not until November 1967 did it vote formal conditions for peace. Underneath a bland exterior and unanimous approval, however, Resolution 242 masked strong divisions of interpretation. Israelis stressed the need for peace and acknowledgment of their right to sovereignty. Thus, withdrawal "from territories occupied" meant some withdrawal to secure boundaries. To Arabs, however, the phrase meant the evacuation of *all* territories occupied. A "just settlement" of the refugee problem held no common meaning, and the Palestinians resented being classified merely as refugees, not as a nation. Not surprisingly, the United Nations peace mission failed.

From the victory Israel gained much, at a relatively small cost in lives and wounded. Because Arab speeches before the war had threatened Israel's very existence, no American president demanded withdrawal to the 1949 Armistice lines, as happened in 1956. Egypt's defeat largely broke the wide emotional appeal outside Egypt of the most popular Arab leader, Gamal Abdul Nasser. Virtually the entire armaments of the Arab states lay destroyed, and the ceasefire lines, though encompassing three times the territory of 1949, actually stretched fewer miles. Individual reputations benefitted, too: Moshe Dayan, hero of the 1956 Sinai campaign, again had played a dominant role, joining the cabinet as Minister of Defense. His popularity soared.

More importantly, the Jewish *Diaspora* again felt deeply its attachment to Israel. Thousands came to fight or replace men and women called to battle; funds flowed to aid society and government. Discouraged and worried about emigration before the war, Israeli self-confidence returned with victory.

While postponing decisions on the fate of most occupied territory, Israel moved quickly to incorporate East Jerusalem into Israel itself. Within the Old City lies the Wailing Wall, remaining from the Second Temple and the most sacred Jewish shine. Prohibited from worshipping there during Jordanian rule, the Israelis rapidly bulldozed neighboring houses for better access. (Greatly complicating the achievement of peace, the Wailing Wall borders the Haram al–Sharif, one of the holiest Muslim shrines, containing the Dome of the Rock and al–Aqsa Mosque.) Reconstruction of the old Jewish quarter commenced, as did the removal of barbed wire and barricaded roads that marked the armistice lines after 1949. Under Mayor Teddy Kolleck, one of the most remarkable leaders in the Middle East, the municipal administration of Jewish Jerusalem stretched east.

In the years after 1967 Israel continued its rapid economic growth. Industry expanded, an oil pipeline from Eilat on the Gulf of Aqaba to the Mediterranean provided a new transit trade, and personal incomes climbed rapidly. Under the influence of prosperity, the idealistic culture of early Zionism matured increasingly into materialism. Arab labor from the West Bank and Gaza filled menial and low–paid jobs, and the territories provided new markets for Israeli products. Traditional problems existed: military expenses devoured the national budget and charity from abroad failed to cover the trade deficit, so the currency continued to depreciate. However, in the United States Israel found a new arms supplier, one often willing to turn its loans into

grants, thus easing the financial burden of defense. Not surprisingly, the Labor alignment of *Mapai* and its allies won the 1969 elections, and following the death of Levi Eshkol, Golda Meir became prime minister.

In foreign affairs and defense, however, severe difficulties remained. Retaining the territories captured in 1967 brought a degree of diplomatic isolation, even in Europe. Militarily, by 1969, battles along the Suez Canal escalated to become the War of Attrition. Though its aircraft wreaked havoc on Egypt, the cost to Israel in lives and funds was not insignificant. However, victories for conventional Israeli arms lent support to the radical view propounded by Yasir Arafat of *al–Fatah*, as well as many other guerrilla leaders, that only unconventional warfare could regain Palestine. Civilian casualties had been relatively small in 1956 and 1967; now they climbed in both Israel and the Arab lands as terror against civilians, used as a weapon by both sides under the mandate, grew common.

The October 1973 War and Disengagement

On October 6, 1973, while Israel observed *Yom Kippur*, the Day of Atonement, simultaneous attacks by Syria and Egypt opened the next Arab–Israeli War. Technically, the Egyptians and Syrians attacked not Israel, but Israeli forces on their own national territories. Enjoying substantial surprise, and at first protected from Israeli aircraft by Soviet surface–to–air missiles, Egyptian armies crossed the Suez Canal, pierced the Bar Lev Line, and entered the Sinai. Syrian troops also advanced, capturing Israeli positions on the Golan Heights.

Rapidly mobilizing, the Israel Defence Force (IDF) counter-attacked, and the intense tank battles destroyed perhaps 2,000 tanks and 500 aircraft. Both Israel and the Arab armies required replenishment by emergency airlift. Sensing a weakness and benefiting from advanced arms and technical superiority, General Ariel Sharon led his troops across the Suez Canal into Egypt itself, encircling an entire Egyptian army and leaving Cairo almost defenseless. The Syrians likewise retreated, but the enormous cost of the war convinced many on both sides of its futility. Three weeks after it began a ceasefire took effect.

Disengagement agreements mediated by Henry Kissinger, the American Secretary of State, followed the ceasefire. In 1974-75 Israeli troops withdrew into the Sinai, returning parts of both banks of the Suez Canal and oil fields used since 1967. Egypt allowed non-military cargoes for Israel through the newly-reopened Canal. Separately, Israeli troops returne portions of the Golan Heights to Syria, including the devastated town of Qunaytra.

In the elections that followed the war, *Labor* lost seats, but remained in power,

The West ("Wailing") Wall within Jerusalem where Jews pray. Tradition is that the wall was partially built of materials from Solomon's temple.   Photo by Linda Cook

while the *Likud*, an alliance of right-wing parties, gained seats. Internal economic problems worsened, as Israel, like other countries, suffered from OPEC's quadrupling of the world oil price in 1973-4. Double-digit inflation and heavy taxes continued apace, as did devaluation of the currency. In the West Bank and Gaza, Jewish settlements incurred Arab resentment and U.S. condemnation, while raids and terrorist actions by Palestinian guerrillas based outside Israel frequently provoked Israeli retaliation.

As new elections approached in 1977, the *Labor* government virtually disintegrated under charges of mismanagement and corruption. Supported strongly by Oriental Jews, *Likud* triumphed. Menachem Begin, former leader of *Irgun* and a long-time advocate of keeping all occupied territories, formed a coalition with a diverse group of parties. Abandoning socialism, the government raised taxes, devalued the currency, and reduced subsidies, as the labor unions went on strike.

Peace with Egypt and Camp David

The basic tenor of foreign relations suddenly altered in November 1977 when President Sadat of Egypt offered to visit the Knesset in Jerusalem in quest of genuine peace. For the first time, an Arab ruler publicly met with the prime minister of Israel and talked directly to Israelis in their country. Sadat offered full peace; in exchange he asked Israel to agree to the principle of withdrawal from the occupied lands and to the right of Palestine Arabs to determine their own future in the West Bank and the Gaza Strip.

Sadat's dramatic moves posed a difficult political decision for Israel: the choice between territory and peace. After weeks of equivocation, Prime Minister Begin responded that his government could not give up "Judea and Samaria" (to Arabs, the West Bank) because they formed part of the "historic land of Israel." The best his government could do for Palestinians "living in the Land of Israel" would be civil autonomy under Israeli control.

Against a background of terrorist attacks by Palestinians and an Israeli invasion of Southern Lebanon, President Carter invited the Israeli and Egyptian leaders to Camp David, in rural Maryland. Secluded from the press and political pressures, for nearly two weeks Menachem Begin and Anwar Sadat negotiated. Finally, on September 17, 1978, the two leaders signed two agreements before television cameras at the White House. Israel obtained one of its major policy goals: a peace treaty with Egypt, the most powerful Arab state. In return, Israel promised to return the Sinai to Egypt without a commitment to relinquish the West Bank, the Gaza Strip, or Golan Heights. For Palestinians, the Camp David Agreements offered only the prospect of eventual autonomy, later interpreted by

Presidents Sadat, Carter and Prime Minister Begin, September 17, 1978, at the White House
Courtesy: Jimmy Carter Library

Begin to mean little more than city and town councils. Israel, he affirmed, would *never* agree to surrender Jerusalem, Judea, or Samaria.

After a formal peace treaty between Egypt and Israel in 1979, Israeli troops began staged withdrawals from Egyptian territory, including the removal of militant settlers at Yamit. The Begin cabinet promised that no other settlements would ever be removed, words that became *Likud* policy and effectively ruled out peace for other occupied territories. Some 750 yards of beach and their accompanying luxury hotel near Eilat remained a problem for years. Arbitration in 1988 established that the boundary markers had been moved during the Israeli occupation and that the territory, indeed, belonged to Egypt.

War in Lebanon 1982

Against a background of restive Palestinians in the West Bank and Gaza and condemnation, particularly in the UN General Assembly, of its policy of encouraging Jewish settlements there, the Begin government became worried about the growing Palestinian military strength in Lebanon. Under plans drawn up by Defense Minister Ariel Sharon, but not revealed completely to the cabinet, in mid-1982 Israeli forces used a terrorist attack in London as a pretext to began a massive invasion of Lebanon. Rapidly smashing conventional Palestinian forces, the IDF eventually reached as far north as Beirut and linked up with the Maronite Christian enclave there (see Lebanon: History). Many Lebanese offered no resistance. Indeed, *Shi'a* villagers, who for years had suffered from Palestinian indiscipline and Israeli reprisal bombings, often welcomed Israeli troops with salt and bread, the traditional signs of hospitality.

At Beirut, the conquest slowed. The besieged defenders held out for almost two months, and Israeli casualties began to mount, eventually making the invasion of Lebanon Israel's most costly foreign

war, measured in lives. Moreover, Israeli troops permitted Maronite militiamen to enter captured Palestinian camps, where they massacred nearly one thousand men, women, and children. Israeli opinion grew increasingly divided. Many citizens, including some officers, demonstrated for a withdrawal from Lebanon; the *Peace Now* movement reflected such concerns.

As it became clear that the expensive and controversial assault on nearly half of Lebanon brought few clear gains, Prime Minister Begin fell into a state of depression and finally resigned in 1983. Foreign Minister Yitzhak Shamir then moved into the prime minister's office to face the staggering economic problems caused by tremendous overspending and the enormous cost of the military occupation in Lebanon. The policies of the Begin government also led to overwhelming dependence on American financial support with little hope of rectifying the underlying problems.

After parliamentary maneuvering by the *Labor Party*, the 1984 Knesset elections again left all parties far from the 61-seat majority. Neither major party found agreeable coalition partners among the minor parties, so in spite of vast ideological differences, they eventually agreed to a delicately-balanced formula for sharing power and the cabinet. Shimon Peres of *Labor* became prime minister for the first two years, with Yitzhak Shamir replacing him for the final two years of the Knesset.

Soviet Immigrants

Two events from the late 1980s and early 1990s, the immigration of Jews from the Soviet Union and the Palestinian *intifada*, combined to challenge Israel's occupation, politics and society. Aided by changes in Soviet society and blocked from entering the U.S., after 1989 a growing flood of thousands of Jews and spouses of Jews emigrated monthly from Russia to Israel. This massive wave of population touched the very basis of Zionism. Soviet immigrants

THE JERUSALEM POST
INTERNATIONAL EDITION

The perfect gift for
your friends and relations
overseas

FREE COPY

THE JERUSALEM POST

Vol. LII. No. 15711 Sunday, September 16, 1984 ● Elul 19, 5744 ● Zi al-Heja 20, 1404 IS200

DON'T MISS THIS COPY
The Economist
September 15, 1984
★ **COVER STORY:**
EVERYTHING ABOUT ISRAEL
SOLE DISTRIBUTOR
BRONFMAN
INTERNATIONAL
PRESS & BOOKS

The cabinet

Shamir determined | Unity terms | Histadrut 'won't accept' C-o-L reduction

The "government of national unity," September 1984

boosted the productive population, and for decades they will offset the threatened Arab majority. Further immigrants were airlifted to Israel from Ethiopia in 1991.

In the short term, the immigration created difficulties. Given the shortage of housing, rents rose, and new housing fell short of needs. Job openings (90,000) fell behind the number of new workers (120,000), and the unemployment rate climbed above 10%. Positions for so many technical workers and professionals—about half the immigrants—posed a challenge. Settlement costs began to exceed defense costs, the first time in Israel's history that the military did not come first. In time, the immigrants changed Israeli society, with Russian newspapers and even Orthodox churches appearing. Politically, the new immigrants generally opposed withdrawal from the occupied territories, and they elected politicians usually willing to ally with *Likud*.

The First Palestinian Intifada

The combination of strikes, civil disobedience, rock-throwing and other violence that constituted the first Palestinian *intifada* began in December 1987. Coordinated in secret, it took by surprise both the military and the cabinet. The violence of the *intifada* marked a distinct change from the physical threats posed by Arab armies to Israel's very existence in the wars of 1948, 1967, and 1973. It stood in similar sharp contrast to violence during the mandate and by Palestinians guerrillas during the 1970s and 1980s, because the *intifada*, stressed defiance, not attacks on Israelis. Indeed, only 15 Israelis died

in its first year, compared to more than 360 Palestinians.

For Israel to crush the uprising meant a military solution to a political problem, thus using one of the world's most highly rated war machines against teenagers throwing stones and Molotov cocktails. Annual reserve duty was extended beyond the normal 30 days, and troops adopted increasingly lethal tactics. Nevertheless, force did not crush the uprising: rather, the *intifada* focused world attention on the Palestinians. The U.S. secretary of state attempted a peace shuttle between Jerusalem and Arab capitals, and his department officially accused Israel of violating human rights and inflicting "many avoidable deaths."

Against this background, as the 1988 Knesset elections approached, the fate of the territories captured in 1967 became a major issue between *Likud* and *Labor*. The former declared Israel's sovereignty over Judea, Samaria, and Gaza and promised support for Jewish settlements there. It claimed that the Camp David Agreements, by allowing for Palestinian autonomy, precluded independence. In contrast, *Labor* favored retaining some territory for defense reasons, but advocated a Jordanian-Palestinian state that would remove 1.5 million Palestinians from Israeli rule without their forming an independent state.

The election results clearly showed that voters considered other issues more important than the occupied territories. Both major parties lost seats; the real victors, the ultra-religious parties, gained six. Natural allies of the strongly right-wing *Likud* on many issues, and vowing to keep

all the occupied territory, the ultra-religious parties nevertheless maintained one demand, an amendment to the "Law of Return." This denied the validity of conversions according to Reform, Conservative and Reconstructionist Judaism. Although few such converts immigrated to Israel each year, some 90% of American Jews belonged to these groups, and the proposal reflected badly on their rabbis. Consequently, threatened with major difficulties with Israel's chief financial and political supporters abroad, Prime Minister Shamir again arranged a coalition of "national unity" with *Labor*.

Carefully formed during intense negotiations, Shamir's new cabinet balanced many political groups and became the largest government in Israeli history. *Labor* received two crucial ministries. Shimon Peres became finance minister, and thus responsible for restoring the nation to prosperity and reforming the financially ailing companies owned by the *Histadrut* (Trade Union Confederation). At defense, Yitzhak Rabin retained the burden of crushing the Palestinian uprising. The cabinet maintained Israel's refusal to negotiate with the PLO and rejected any Palestinian state west of the Jordan River.

While politicians struggled to finalize plans for a new government in Israel, Yasir Arafat, Chairman of the PLO, addressed the UN General Assembly and later met terms for official discussions between the United States and the PLO (see Palestinian National Authority). Meanwhile, voting 138-2, the General Assembly favored an international peace conference which would grant Palestinians "official observer" status.

Diplomatic successes for Yasir Arafat meant a painful sting of reversal for Israel. While UN votes meant little, the United States seemed to change sides just as Israeli politicians strove to form a new cabinet. More perplexing, many American sympathizers and major Jewish groups supported Israel-PLO talks under certain conditions. One poll suggested that 54% of Israelis approved negotiations with Arafat if PLO attacks stopped.

Israeli Objections to a Palestinian State

Opposition to a Palestinian state arose for many reasons. Some were, and remain, military and strategic. For example, those expecting another conflict after five major wars in 40 years argue that Israel cannot defend itself better by retreating before the battle begins. The Jordan River provides a far shorter and tactically superior border than any alternative. Similarly, Palestinians also demand essentially all of the 1967 West Bank, whose old borders threaten vital highways and now run close to cities like Tel Aviv. Another strategic argument holds that any Palestinian state would prove incapable of controlling its extremists. Therefore, occupation of the West Bank may be less damaging in terms of Israeli lives and world opinion than Palestinian cross-border raids and Israeli reprisals.

Other reasons to keep the territories lie in ideology. Revisionist Zionists, like Jabotinsky of the 1920s and many ultra-Orthodox Jews today, stress that modern Israel must occupy the whole of the Biblical Promised Land, ignoring the brevity of Jewish rule over some parts of the area. To them, yielding the East Bank (modern Jordan) is compromise enough.

Over Jerusalem the refusal to withdraw becomes almost universal. To Palestinians, Arab Jerusalem is the largest city in the West Bank, but physically it forms part of a city almost all Jews promise never to divide. Moreover, Judaism's most sacred shrine, the Wailing Wall, lies within the largely-Arab Old City.

Political reality presents another major hurdle. Withdrawal runs counter to the strongly held opinions of much of the population. *Likud*, for example, traditionally refused to yield one inch of (greater) Israel for peace. Moreover, the policy of "creating facts" involved the settlement by 1991 of over 100,000 Jews in the West Bank outside Jerusalem and the seizure of possibly more than 50% of its land. Though less than 10% of the electorate, these settlers constitute an enormous political force against withdrawal. Finally, there are economic reasons: after 1967 the West Bank proved a profitable market for many Israeli goods, and its surplus of water provides that vital resource for Israel itself.

In contrast, pressures do exist for compromise. One is the difficulty of occupying indefinitely a land and depriving

its inhabitants of self-determination. Ruling the restive population unavoidably requires military control. This inevitably increases military influence in public and private life, a possibly troubling prospect for the long run. Moral questions arise also, symbolized by predictions that the greater Arab birthrate will eventually create more Arabs than Jews between the sea and the Jordan River. The occupation inevitably complicates foreign relations, both at the United Nations and bilaterally with otherwise sympathetic countries.

Perhaps crucially, though, the *intifada* changed the equations that previously favored retention of Arab-inhabited conquests. It became more expensive in Israeli lives and shekels, it cost far greater goodwill in Western societies, and it increased doubts in many Jewish minds.

To respond to Arafat, and regain the diplomatic initiative, Prime Minister Shamir presented a peace plan in 1989 that provided a five-year transition to local self-rule. Vague on several important issues, the plan ruled out negotiations with the PLO and failed to offer "land for

Binyamin Netanyahu

(See page 184)

Israeli occupied territory

Israeli settlements in the occupied territories

GOLAN HEIGHTS

WEST BANK

Tel Aviv

Jerusalem

Dead Sea

GAZA STRIP

Jordan River

0   25 Miles

peace." Probably, Shamir merely aimed to prolong diplomacy until the military quelled the *intifada*. However, *Labor* accepted the Egyptian-American proposals and resigned from the cabinet (March 1990). Within days, Shamir's National Unity government collapsed. However, *Labor* proved incapable of forming a majority, and Shamir formed a coalition of six right-wing and religious parties that won the allegiance of a bare majority—62 votes—in the Knesset. The most hard-line cabinet in Israeli history, it halted attempts to construct peace. Dismayed, U.S. Secretary of State James Baker publicly challenged Prime Minister Shamir: "When you're serious about peace, call us."

1991 Gulf War

Iraq's seizure of Kuwait in August 1990 seemed a grave threat to Israel's security. An increasingly anti-Israeli Saddam Hussein gained wealth and territory, and he defended his refusal to abide by UN resolutions by pointing to Israeli non-compliance over Palestine. His boasts clearly indicated that Baghdad considered a war over Kuwait actually a war for Israel. The IDF placed its airmen on alert, and the government issued gas masks. However, Hussein failed to split off the Arab members of the multinational coalition formed against Iraq.

Hours after coalition forces attacked Iraq in January 1991, the first of 39 Scud missiles landed in Tel Aviv, destroying and damaging homes in a residential area. Scores of injuries and a few deaths resulted from the attacks. In a remarkable change of policy, Israel did not retaliate, reluctantly depending on others for its defense. Undoubtedly strong American urging led to the decision, for the transformation of the Gulf War into a general Arab-Israeli conflict would have benefited Iraq, and conceivably Israel, but not the United States or its Arab allies. As Patriot

Bitterness and frustration: Palestinian youths defy the Israeli army

missile crews arrived to defend Tel Aviv, coalition aircraft renewed attacks on well-hidden Scud launchers in western Iraq. Israel sought hundreds of millions of dollars in aid to cover missile damage, greater military expenses, and economic losses such as the decline in tourism.

Another clear Israeli gain came when the PLO supported Iraq during the Gulf War. Media reports claimed that Palestinians cheered as Iraqi missiles struck Jewish cities, a reaction at odds with world opinion.

The Gulf War left Israel militarily unrivaled in the Middle East and its most threatening Arab rival in shambles. Military security became completely assured. Moreover, thanks to immigration from the Soviet Union, the Arab demographic time bomb—the threat of an Arab majority in Israel and the territories—began to disintegrate.

From Madrid to Oslo

After its victory in Iraq, the first Bush administration desired to establish a Middle East peace and to that end convene a peace conference. Israel remained reluctant, favoring bilateral negotiations because an international conference might pressure it. But the Arab nations, militarily weak and partially occupied, sought a forum subject to world opinion. In a compromise sponsored by both the U.S. and Soviet Union, in 1991 a conference met in Madrid for formal speeches, then broke up for bilateral talks. In the months that followed, no breakthroughs were reported. However, the very discussion of autonomy for the Occupied Territories led two minor parties to withdraw from the coalition, precipitating elections.

During the campaign, a small but significant number of voters shifted from *Likud* to *Labor*. Disputes between Shamir and David Levy, a leader of the Sephardic community, cost support from that traditionally pro-*Likud* ethnic group. Recent

immigrants favored change because the economy suffered from growing unemployment and rising inflation. Finally, rather than Shimon Peres, *Labor* selected the more popular Yitzhak Rabin as leader. Though a tough general, he favored Palestinian autonomy and peace through concessions over occupied territory.

Labor won a decisive victory, a total of 56 seats with its ally *Meretz* (the merger of three small leftist parties). Rabin achieved a majority by bringing a single religious party, *Shas,* into the cabinet. Acting decisively on several issues, he halted "new settlement" construction in the Occupied Territories (though permitting security settlements to expand). This won American loan guarantees for housing construction within Israel and raised hopes at the peace talks. Rabin's negotiators even conceded a possible withdrawal in the Golan Heights in return for peace with Syria.

The *intifada* continued to prove the most pressing, and increasingly lethal, problem (see Palestinians: **history**). After the deaths of six soldiers in 1992, Rabin expelled 400 alleged activists from *Hamas* and the *Islamic Jihad.* However, those exiled were mainly intellectuals not charged with individual crimes, the expulsion contravened international law, and Lebanon refused to admit the exiles. Camped in a snowy no-man's land, poorly housed and fed, they won world sympathy. After the Security Council demanded their return, Israel immediately admitted 100 of the men, reduced the sentences of the remainder, and allowed several dozen individuals expelled years previously to return.

Despite the expulsions, violence increased. Finally Rabin closed Israel to the 60,000 workers from the Occupied Territories, effectively cutting off most contacts between Israelis and Palestinians. As calm returned, most Israelis

favored making the ban permanent, despite hardship in the industries where the Palestinians worked and some recognition that unemployed and destitute men would probably become more militant. On the deeper level, many also recognized that the practi-cal separation of the Territories made some later withdrawal likely.

The reality of withdrawal suddenly approached far closer when Prime Minister Rabin and PLO Chairman Yasir Arafat publicly shook hands at the White House on September 13, 1993. Secret negotiations in Oslo—outside the stagnated Madrid talks—had produced a Declaration of Principles for an eventual peace agreement. The Declaration stipulated deadlines for a withdrawal from most of the Gaza Strip and Jericho and the creation of a Palestinian Authority to administer them. It also specified later withdrawals from much of the West Bank.

It is important to remember that the Oslo Accords were not a peace settlement. They deliberately left many matters undecided and imposed a deadline of September 2000. Indeed, very difficult issues such as the final borders, the fate of the Palestinian refugees, and the status of East Jerusalem (part of united Jerusalem, but claimed as the Palestinian capital) remained for the "framework" of the final agreement to be discussed after confidence-building measures established greater trust between the two sides. Naturally, leaders on each side have attempted to create stronger bargaining position. However, radical Jewish and Arab opponents of peace sought to destroy the Oslo Accords through violence. Civilians and children on each side often became random victims that would require countermeasures that in turn would incite reprisals that ensured a further cycle of violence. Wary about domestic political opposition, each leader initially sought concessions based on vastly different perceptions.

Some 150 Palestinians and 45 Israelis died by the missed deadline for the 1994 withdrawal. The worst single event was when an Israeli settler massacred some 30 Muslim worshippers at the mosque of the patriarchs in Hebron. However, "Oslo" had established a timetable, and after last-minute bickering and hasty PLO preparations to administer the territory, in May 1994 the Israeli flag was lowered over Gaza and Jericho.

The withdrawal brought neither economic bonanza nor safety to Israel. Suicide attacks by *Hamas* and the *Islamic Jihad,* particularly against buses in Tel Aviv and at the Beit Lid Junction, killed scores of Israelis. In response, the cabinet again sealed the border with Gaza and the West Bank and halted the agreed release of prisoners. Fearing for the safety of isolated zsettlements, the cabinet halted further withdrawals. In turn this postponed the

Palestinian elections scheduled by the peace agreement.

The cabinet also continued to expand existing Jewish settlements, particularly north and east of Jerusalem. Technically, the swift pace of building violated neither the "no new settlements" pledge made to the U.S. in 1992, nor the Oslo Accords. However, moves to confiscate largely Arab-owned land around East Jerusalem, aroused widespread Arab and Muslim condemnation in 1995. It might have imperiled the negotiations had not a most unlikely—some would say unholy—alliance between *Likud* and the few Arab members of the Knesset forced its suspension.

Despite such shortcomings, the Oslo Accords brought welcome progress towards peace with some Arab states. Morocco established diplomatic relations. Much more dramatically, Jordan signed a peace treaty, after settling its demands for water rights and the small occupied territory (145 square miles) along the border. Visionaries predicted broad trade and development links, as well as hydroelectric and desalination schemes at the Dead Sea. More practically, King Hussein could pilot a civilian aircraft across Israeli airspace.

Peace with Syria proved more difficult. It involved, and still involves, the domestically hazardous issue of the Golan Heights. Syria has compromised its sovereignty over the area by accepting its demilitarization, but it demands the entire territory. However, *Labor*-voting Golani settlers demand to remain, and many Israelis fear losing important strategic advantages. To defuse the issue, Rabin proposed a national referendum on any Golan settlement; meanwhile, years of negotiations have accomplished little.

The Assassination of Yitzhak Rabin

Despite vicious attacks by right-wing extremists, including posters depicting Prime Minister Rabin as a Nazi, in 1995 the cabinet approved a further withdrawal from several West Bank cities as a prelude to Palestinian elections. Two months later, on November 4, the usually unsmiling Rabin celebrated at a peace rally in Tel Aviv. When he turned to leave, a fanatical Orthodox law student, Yigal Amir, shot him in the back. As the nation mourned, it learned the assassin had connections to other extremists. He murdered, he said, because Rabin had negotiated away Israel's God-given land and endangered settlers' lives.

As Shimon Peres formed a new cabinet, the policy of peace through negotiation momentarily captured the vast majority of Israelis. However, a series of suicide attacks in early 1996 slaughtered 58 Israelis, avenging the death in Gaza of the *Hamas* suicide mastermind, Yahya Ayyash, and the *Islamic Jihad* leader in

Malta. Once again, extremist violence by one side weakened the advocates of peace on the other. Israelis buried the dead while elections approached, and they noted that "peace" brought higher casualties than occupation. Revulsion at the bombings translated into greater electoral support for the *Likud*. Peres immediately closed off the West Bank and Gaza, sending their economies into depression. He did not withdraw troops from Hebron and ordered shelling and bombing in Lebanon.

Stagnation, not Peace, under Netanyahu

In 1996, for the first time, voters cast two ballots. One indicated the chosen political party, as always. The second ballot offered the novelty of voting for a person, for prime minister. Its purpose was to speed the process of forming a government, and it worked despite very close results. The Knesset proved more divided than ever, with *Labor* winning 34 seats, *Likud* 32, and religious parties 23, while Binyamin "Bibi" Netanyahu defeated Shimon Peres by less than one percent. Netanyahu then overcame enough issues that divided the electorate—ranging from peace and economic policy to non-kosher McDonald's—and took office.

A forceful and complex personality, Netanyahu was relatively young, telegenic, and adept at communicating on television. He cared deeply for the security of the Jewish people and acted to ensure their defense. *Likud* had opposed the whole Oslo process, but in a last-minute gesture that perhaps clinched the election, Netanyahu accepted it and the goal to win a more secure peace.

In reality, stagnation resulted, not peace. From the first, there was violence: the sudden opening of an ancient tunnel along the western edge of Temple Mount outraged Arab opinion and led to the most serious fighting in years, including tank and helicopter fire in the West Bank for the first time since 1967. While lopsided casualties reinforced Israeli military superiority, some 15 Jews died in bloodshed that had been a predicted consequence of opening the tunnel.

Trouble also followed the 1997 decision to construct a Jewish settlement, *Har Homa*, on traditionally Arab land between East Jerusalem and Bethlehem. Symbolically and literally, the project completed the Jewish encirclement of Arab East Jerusalem and cut it off from access to the West Bank. It meant that by the time negotiators finally addressed the issue of Jerusalem, there would be little to discuss. As the bulldozers moved in, Palestinian leaders halted the peace negotiations.

Despite these setbacks, there were achievements. Netanyahu withdrew troops from most of Hebron (retaining occupation of 20% of the city to protect 450 settlers), and Israeli troops left there and

Rabbi Arie Deri, *Shas*

elsewhere on schedule, something never accomplished by *Labor* prime ministers.

Within Israeli society, Netanyahu's actions aggravated the deepening social fragmentation. Russian and Ethiopian immigrants demanded spending to meet their needs, while many Sephardim (descendants of Middle Eastern Jews) sensed the Askenazi (European-descended) elite looked down on them. Students went on strike for lower tuition, and government workers for higher pay. Both groups were angered that funds seemed available for the settlers and religious purposes.

The strikers struck a sensitive nerve: pollsters found the religious/secular divide among Jews a greater issue than peace. So strong are the emotions that they challenged the integrity of government institutions. For example, when the Supreme Court ended the draft exemption for the Orthodox and allowed farms to operate on the Sabbath, a mass rally attacked the court. Similarly, supporters of *Shas* (the ultra-Orthodox *Torah Observing Sephardim Party*) believe their leader,

Former Prime Minister Ehud Barak

Rabbi Arie (Aryeh) Deri, was convicted of corruption because he had been singled out for his ethnic and religious position. Secular Jews objected to the automatic draft deferments for ultra-Orthodox (*Haredim*) students in yeshivas.

Pressured by President Bill Clinton during meetings at the Wye Plantation in Maryland to implement the Oslo Accord's terms for further withdrawals, Netanyahu promised to do so, in return for Palestinian cooperation against terrorist attacks. Very possibly Netanyahu never intended to implement the withdrawal, but the very agreement violated a cardinal *Likud* principle. Burdened as well by personal resentments and political instability (four finance ministers in thirty months), Netanyahu's coalition collapsed.

The 1999 election campaign illustrated a vibrant democracy. Thirty-three parties competed for the Knesset, and five significant candidates ran for prime minister. The latter contest rapidly became a referendum over Netanyahu, and three candidates dramatically withdrew at the last minute, leaving "Bibi" challenged only by Ehud Barak of *Labor* (renamed *One Israel*), who had waged a careful campaign neither too leftist nor sympathetic to the Palestinians.

With four of his former cabinet ministers campaigning against him, Netanyahu turned to desperate measures and attempted to stir up Palestinian passions. However, there were no significant terrorist attacks, and Barak won a resounding triumph.

Barak Rule

An Askenazi and "Israel's most decorated soldier," Barak desired a strong cabinet to represent the nation, rather than merely parties. However, his personal win carried no coattails: *One Israel* lost 8 seats. Natural allies like the leftist *Meretz*, the strongly secular *Shinui*, and a Russian immigrants' party meant a coalition of 55 seats, dangerously dependent on Arab members for a majority. For a wider support, Barak drew in the *National Religious Party* and *Shas*, the latter without Rabbi Deri, its corruption-tainted leader. However, by appointing only two women and no Arabs to the cabinet, Barak disappointed those interest groups.

The cabinet tackled difficult and divisive issues, against the background of increasingly harsh culture wars between secularists and practicing Orthodox and ultra-Orthodox Jews. Barak moved to end the abuse of draft deferments by ultra-Orthodox men, and Yossi Sarid, the minister of education, changed the curriculum significantly, reinterpreting the 1948-49 War of Independence, admitting Israeli mistakes, and adding a Palestinian nationalist's poetry. For this, the leader of *Shas* described Sarid (a cabinet ally) as a "Satan" to be wiped from the face of the earth. Through its brinkmanship over the budget, *Shas* retained large subsidies for its badly-run school system.

For many Israelis, the difficult work of government reform seemed overshadowed by scandals. President Ezer Weizman, accused of receiving illegal payments from a French businessman, fell from office, as did Deputy Prime Minister Yitzhak Mordechai, over allegations of sexual assault. Binyamin Netanyahu was blamed for corruption and misuse of gifts he received as prime minister, though the charges were dropped . Further from politics, financial irregularities in some *yeshivas* vied for publicity with the national soccer team. Its players lost a match after a pre-game visit to a house of ill repute.

In foreign affairs, Barak sought to bring peace to all remaining conflicts. He initiated negotiations with Syria. In contrast to Netanyahu's duplicity, he bluntly accepted an eventual Palestinian state. Overcoming right-wing criticism, he opened a 27-mile route connecting the Gaza Strip with the West Bank. Ten unauthorized Jewish settlements on the West Bank were closed (though more than thirty others remained). Although Barak often proved a tough defender of Israel's interests, his months in office will most likely be remembered for the withdrawal

Prime Minister Sharon

from Lebanon. Unable to negotiate terms for leaving a territory occupied for two decades, the IDF withdrew under pressure in 2000. The collapse of its local ally, the *South Lebanon Army*, brought forth comparisons with Vietnam, even in Hebrew papers.

Conscious of two rapidly approaching deadlines–completion of the Oslo Accords (September 13, 2000) and the end of his term, President Clinton summoned both Prime Minister Barak and Chairman Arafat to Camp David in July. There, removed from the media spotlight, he attempted to settle the outstanding issues: borders, settlements, refugees, and East Jerusalem. Conceding what no Israeli leader had yielded previously, Barak offered Arafat a Palestinian state with a capital in the Jerusalem suburbs, some local control in Arab districts of the city, and the possibility of international sovereignty over the Muslim Holy Places (the Haram al-Sharif). A small number of refugees would be reunited with families in Israel.

With this offer, Barak defied the almost universal Israeli desire for a united Jerusalem. It outraged the settlers, *Likud*, and most religious parties. Vague talk of treason and assassination prompted increased security for the prime minister. But Yasir Arafat rejected the proposal because it failed to meet the minimum Palestinian demand for sovereignty over the Arab parts of the city. In practical terms, this outright rejection was a grave mistake. Despite the deaths of hundreds of Palestinians since, no similar offer seems likely.

Barak returned to Jerusalem to a political crisis. As prime minister, he had combined an unusual mixture of leniency and toughness that alienated many of his party allies. When coalition partners fought fervent ideological battles against each other over education and secularism, Barak's interventions came too late and too highhandedly. The religious parties left the cabinet before Camp David; on his return, the Knesset took steps for new elections.

Recognizing that former prime minister Binyamin Netanyahu had regained much

View of the Sea of Galilee

Photo by Eugenia Elseth

For your shopping convenience
**THE JERUSALEM POST
BOOK DEPT.**
is open Sun. - Thur.,
9:00 a.m. - 3:00 p.m.
Fridays 9:00 a.m.-1:00 p.m.
10 Harav Kook St.
Downtown Jerusalem.
Tel. 02-241282

THE JERUSALEM POST

SECOND
EDITION

Make international
connections.
177-100-2727
AT&T

VOLUME LXIII, NUMBER 19113   SUNDAY, NOVEMBER 5, 1995 ● HESHVAN 12, 5756 ● II JAMAD 12, 1416   NIS 4.20 (EILAT NIS 3.60)

RABIN ASSASSINATED

Peres pays tribute to longtime rival, partner

DAVID MAKOVSKY, BATSHEVA TSUR and agencies

AN empty chair draped in black marked Prime Minister Yitzhak Rabin's place at the cabinet table as the nation's leaders met in emergency session and declared a transition government hours after he was assassinated at a peace rally.

Ministers wept while acting Prime Minister Shimon Peres paid tribute to his long-time political rival and partner in

forging peace with the Palestinians.

"He was a rare leader in Jewish history...in the last three years as Israeli prime minister he effected a revolution in the positive sense in the Middle East," Peres said in televised remarks.

"I asked myself if this happened to me, what would I want to happen later," Peres

(Continued on Page 12)

A black day for the whole Jewish nation

EDITORIAL

THE shock is universal. No Israeli, no Jew, no decent human being anywhere can help being shaken to the core, shattered to the depth of his and her soul by the news of the assassination of Prime Minister

Pronounced dead at 11:15 p.m. after being shot

RAINE MARCUS, SARAH HONIG and ALON PINKAS

PRIME Minister Yitzhak Rabin was assassinated last night by a 27-year-old Herzliya law student, who fired three bullets from a pistol at him at point-blank range. Rabin was felled as he was entering his official car at 9:50 p.m. at the conclusion of a massive pro-peace rally in Tel Aviv's Kikar Malchei Yisrael attended by some 100,000 people.

Rabin was pronounced dead at 11:15 p.m. by doctors at Ichilov Hospital, where he had been brought with wounds to his back, abdomen, and chest. He died on the operating table from massive hemorrhaging and heart failure, without regaining consciousness.

The prime minister was not wearing a bullet-proof vest,

that he "did not regret his deed," which he said was "planned for some time."

A police source said that Amir had twice before attempted to assassinate Rabin, but no more details were available. In the two previous attempts, said the source, Amir tried to get close to the prime minister and was armed both times.

Amir was apprehended immediately after the shooting by police and pressed up against a cement wall, as dozens of policemen surrounded him.

Eyewitnesses reported seeing Rabin collapse. His bodyguards pushed him into the car and whisked him off to Ichilov Hospital, some 500 meters away. One of Rabin's bodyguards was also wounded by bullets.

Health Minister Ephraim Sneh told reporters at midnight that Rabin sustained bullet wounds in

---

popularity, Barak resigned. This forced an election only for prime minister, which Netanyahu could not contest because he was not a member of the Knesset. Instead, *Likud's* nominee was the much less appealing party leader, General Ariel Sharon, whose career symbolized an aggressiveness that had contributed to the deaths of many Arab civilians – particularly Jordanian and Lebanese.

To boost his electoral changes, Barak undertook frenzied negotiations with the U.S. and the Palestinians at Sharm al-Sheikh and in Washington. However, they failed to achieve a breakthrough to peace. Without a settlement, Barak could not turn the election into a referendum on peace; he thus offered little to the voters, many of them highly distressed by the violence and insecurity of the new *intifada*.

The Election of Ariel Sharon

By contrast, General Sharon ran a slick campaign, avoiding debates and serious interviews, but using jingles matching his name with peace (in Hebrew, shalom). After his landslide victory (62%) in February 2001, Sharon formed a government of national unity, including *Labor* leaders in sensitive positions (Shimon Peres, foreign ministry; Binyamin Ben-Eliezer, defense).

Significantly, Sharon himself bore responsibility for torching the renewed violence, for the single act that set ablaze passions already very hot. His widely publicized visit to the Haram al-Sharif in September 2000, designed to assert Israeli

sovereignty, involved a bodyguard of 1,000 police. It was a show of force designed to assert that the Temple Mount was not negotiable. The next day, after angry Palestinians gathered near the al-Aqsa mosque and began stoning Jews at the Western Wall below, the security forces opened fire, killing a number. A wave of protests spread across the Palestinian territories and became known as "*al-Aqsa Intifada*". It entered Israel itself when Israeli Arab demonstrators were shot by police and attacked by Jewish mobs.

Intense violence marked this new *intifada*, with televised images of a twelve-year-old Palestinian boy, Muhammad Dura, shot to death while crouching beside his father, or militants with bloody hands celebrating the lynching of two Israeli soldiers, or Israeli youth maimed and killed by a suicide bomber at a nightclub. That most victims were Palestinians, many of them shot in the head or neck, proved cold comfort to grieving Israelis.

With the *Aqsa intifada*, the Oslo peace process collapsed. Palestinian suicide bombers, adopting tactics successful in Lebanon, killed and maimed Israelis gathered in markets, at receptions, waiting for buses or eating pizza. The (recently resigned) tourism minister, Rehavam Zeevi, became an assassin's target in an East Jerusalem hotel. In response to the attacks, Israeli troops surrounded Palestinian-controlled areas, limiting travel and trade, thus squeezing them economically. A policy of preventive assassination killed dozens of alleged terrorist leaders (and

often innocent bystanders), and Palestinian security forces became frequent targets. Yasir Arafat himself was limited to the city of Ramallah, then to his headquarters.

After a bloody attack on a Passover gathering in the spring of 2002, the cabinet approved more serious action to root out the terrorists. Israeli tanks and infantry invaded the major West Bank cities of Ramallah, Nablus, Bethlehem and Jenin, as well as smaller towns and villages. Troops confined Yasir Arafat to just two rooms of his headquarters. He was unable to attend the Arab summit, or even to bathe. In Bethlehem, retreating Palestinian gunmen took refuge in the Church of the Nativity, knowing that Israeli troops dared not attack one of Christendom's most sacred places.

Particularly bitter fighting occurred in the refugee camp at Jenin. Its maze of interconnected houses and narrow alleyways far to narrow for tanks enabled its defenders to plant booby traps that caused significant casualties. The invading troops captured the camp only after house-to-house combat that often involved entering a house through holes in the walls. Large areas of the camp were destroyed, and U.N. and U.S. officials expressed shock at conditions. When the army prepared to bury Arab dead, the Palestinians claimed that a massacre had taken place.

When even the U.S. supported the creation of a U.N. mission to report on events in Jenin, Israel initially agreed, but later

Caffeine Free
For A Healthy Life

THE JERUSALEM POST

There's no such thing as
hard to reach
177-100-2727
AT&T

VOLUME LXIII. NUMBER 19216   MONDAY, MARCH 4, 1996 ● ADAR 13, 5756 ● SHAWAL 14, 1416   NIS 4.20 (EILAT NIS 3.60)

Hamas suicide bomber kills 18 in Jerusalem

Peres: We are at war with Hamas

BILL HUTMAN

PRIME Minister Shimon Peres declared that Israel is at war with Hamas, following yesterday's deadly suicide bus attack in Jerusalem.

A Hamas suicide bomber blew up a No. 18 Egged bus on Jaffa Road in Jerusalem yesterday morning, killing 18 and seriously wounding seven, exactly a week after another suicide bomber took 25 lives on the same line.

An angry Peres listed new security measures to be enacted, and declared his commitment to "separation" between Israeli and Palestinian peoples. (See story below).

The bomb was similar to the ones used in last week's attacks in Jerusalem and Ashkelon, a senior police source said.

"The evidence points to the same hand being involved in all the attacks," the source said. In all the attacks, 15 kg.-20 kg. of TNT were used and metal scraps, in

Security and medical personnel run for help immediately following yesterday's deadly bus bombing.   (Brian Hendler)

Bodies were flung into the air, and glass flew everywhere," he said.

"The rescue work was finished within minutes," Amit said. "It's sad to have to say that we have become experts in dealing with this type of event."

Light rain began to fall after the injured had already been evacuated, and did not appear to affect the police work.

Several police officers commented that the location of the attack, even if coincidental, near the police station and City Hall, made it that much more enraging.

Prime Minister Shimon Peres came to the scene about two hours after the attack to see the devastation first-hand. There were a few anti-government calls from the crowd during the short briefing Peres received from Amit and Inspector-General Assaf Hefetz.

Amit and Hefetz later met with Peres at the Prime Minister's Office, where they discussed the government's planned security moves, including beefing up police and army presence in the capital.

There were brief pushing and shoving matches between police and the crowd of several hundreds onlookers, including many who openly expressed their outrage by chanting "Death to Arabs," and "Peres go home."

Amit said police were bracing for demonstrations and possible attempts by Jewish extremists to carry out revenge attacks on Arabs. Dozens of protesters chanting "Death to Arabs" rushed toward the Old City in the afternoon, but were halted by police.

Mayor Ehud Olmert called for restraint from the crowd. "I understand that people are angry, but this type of behavior is not helpful at this time. It only makes the work of the security forces

---

blocked the mission on various grounds, contesting both its membership and the possibility of it questioning Israeli soldiers. When evidence showed that no massacre had taken place–apparently fewer than 100 Palestinians had died, including fighters, the U.N. Secretary-General called off the mission. While this spared Israel undesirable probing, it also left the suggestion that war crimes had been committed, such as refusing access to medical care for wounded civilians.

Under pressure from the United States (world opinion mattered little), Israeli troops withdrew from the West Bank, and Yasir Arafat emerged from his headquarters. The European Union mediated a settlement that ended the siege of Bethlehem's Church of the Nativity and took into exile some of the fighters Israel had sought to capture.

Why had Palestinians and Israelis, by the Oslo Agreements partners in a peace process, fought a local but savage war? Certainly Palestinians began the violence, and many Israeli actions constituted self-defense, justified by both international law and common sense after suicide bombings on civilians. However, historians may well conclude that Prime Minister Sharon also bears significant responsibility for the hostilities.

Clearly Ariel Sharon bears a personal grudge against Yasir Arafat, terming him

a terrorist, the Palestinian "bin Ladin," and attempting to end his international role. Israeli policy during 2001-2002 also aroused Palestinian resentment in a variety of ways from the normal (expansion of the settlements, economic blockades of Arab areas, frequent searches) to the violent and illegal under international law (the assassination of those allegedly planning suicide bombings or otherwise on the "wanted" list). As prime minister, Sharon also gave Israeli troops great freedom to attack Palestinian suspects, and many eyewitness accounts suggest the killing of men and boys sleeping or otherwise unarmed.

However, non-Israelis must remember that the prime minister frequently faces harsh criticism from right-wingers whose solutions often include ethnic cleansing. Though militarily strong, Israel is fractured politically. Furthermore, public opinion moved rightward in the face of suicide bombings, blaming the Palestinians completely for the violence. The peace movement shrank, despite opinion polls showing that a majority supported separating Israel from Palestine. The prime minister bravely opposed the *Likud Central Committee's* vote against any Palestinian state, ever, west of the Jordan River, and apparently not simply because it was a public relations disaster after U.S. President Bush had publicly supported such a state.

American, Egyptian, European and other mediators vainly tried to calm the crisis, but found themselves blocked by both Palestinian and Israeli intransigence. Many Palestinians abandoned hope in the Oslo process and supported groups calling for the armed *intifada* to continue until victory. Others considered that only force would lead to a peace settlement. Therefore attacks and bombings became more popular, with or without the Palestinian Authority's alleged involvement.

However, for much of 2001, the crisis worsened because the Israeli cabinet refused to talk peace during violence and therefore demanded seven days of calm before talks could begin or the Mitchell Plan take effect. While superficially plausible, Sharon excluded from the definition of "violence" Israeli assassinations of Palestinian leaders, so that dead Arabs did not count, while acts of revenge did. Very possibly Sharon initially considered that Israel could crush the Palestinians militarily and thus end the violence, but carefully timed suicide bombings (for example, just as Sharon met President Bush) suggested that military force was only a temporary help. Alternatively, the cabinet sought ways to evade implementing the Mitchell Plan.

Proposed by an international group led by former U.S. Senator George Mitchell, the plan called for a ceasefire followed by a complete freeze of settlement activity, thereby eliminating even the "natural" growth of existing settlements. Such a straightforward plan clearly challenged the unity of the Sharon cabinet: its acceptance meant the resignation of right-wing members, while *Labor* threatened to join the opposition if it were rejected. Intended or otherwise, Sharon's demand for a "significant cooling-off period" ended the issue without a cabinet vote. A similar fate met the Saudi peace plan of Crown Prince Abdullah that offered peace and full recognition of Israel by all the Arab states in return for an Israeli withdrawal to the 1967 borders and a Palestinian state.

A conflict so severe and so extended created a recession. Business suffered as tourists stayed away, and the stock market lost billions of dollars of paper profits. Moreover, the conflict coincided with a downturn in international trade, especially in high technology, a key Israeli sector.

Culture: As the Zionist settlers of the pre–independence period were mainly Europeans, their culture has been fixed in a dominant position. An attempt has been made to Europeanize the later waves of immigrants from Persian, Afghani, Kurdish, Yemeni, Iraqi or North African backgrounds. Because these Sephardic Jews now outnumber the European Jews they have begun to assert their own cultural values.

Israel in fact has the greatest cultural diversity found anywhere, because its people have come literally from the four corners of the world. Approximately half of all Israelis were born in some other land and so brought a variety of cultures with them. Though Jews, they neither act alike, think alike nor look alike, though most now wear European style clothes.

About four out of every five people in Israel live in cities. The Sephardic Jews and non–Jewish minorities are better represented in the villages and rural areas than are the Europeans. The non–Jewish minorities are almost entirely Arabic–speaking and are made up of about 250,000 Muslims, 70,000 Christians and 35,000 Druze (see Lebanon: Culture). In general these minorities suffer harsher living conditions than others, and receive less education. One recent study found 48% of Israeli Arab families living below the poverty level, and the high school drop out rate reached 50%. However, there was not much benefit to remaining in school: in one sample, educated Arabs suffered 33% unemployment.

The complex educational system includes both state and private schools, but even the private schools are partly subsidized and controlled by the government. Within the state schools there are three systems: secular schools, religious schools and schools for Arabic–speaking students. Secondary schools receive no direct

public financing, but the government helps pay the fees for qualified students on the basis of need.

Of the seven institutions of higher learning, the oldest and most prestigious is the Hebrew University of Jerusalem. Many faculty members have been educated in Europe or North America, and there is significant interchange with universities on those continents. In terms of its research accomplishments, publications, and student quality, the university outranks all others in the Middle East.

At independence, Orthodox Judaism became the established religion of the state. Today a minority of Israeli Jews adhere to this branch of Judaism. Many Jews consider themselves secular, or worship at Reform synagogues, but the fastest growing congregations are the ultra-Orthodox. Differences between members of these groups have led to intellectual disputes, sometimes labeled culture wars. At one extreme, a secular Jew might regard anyone was a Jew who considers himself or herself such, even though an atheist. In contrast, many Orthodox and ultra-Orthodox hold secular Jews responsible for the loss of Jews to assimilation in other societies. A few consider this a loss to Jewry equivalent in numbers to the Holocaust.

Lifestyle issues also divide society. Sabbath observance by public transportation and industry is one point of conflict. Marriage and immigration laws are others, made more pressing by numbers of Russian immigrants of mixed backgrounds. Tensions between groups have in recent years shown a dramatic escalation, with antagonisms ranging from cultural events to advertising regarded as immoral.

In the first decades of Israeli statehood, reported crimes were relatively few, a feature of citizens bonded together by the

experiences of the Holocaust and winning independence. Zionism unified diverse populations, and the socialist ideology minimized differences of wealth and income among the population. Concern with morality even delayed the introduction of television to Israel.

As Israeli society matured, individualism played a greater role, and distinctions grew between economic classes. Against this background, and in common with many other developed societies, the crime rate began to rise. Reaching on occasion from high government officials to youths from the less prosperous *Sephardic* Jewish and Arab communities, the criminal acts range primarily from fraud and corruption to burglary. In addition, the occupied territories continue to witness high levels of crime, including murder, often between Israeli settlers and Arabs.

Economy: During the first two decades of its existence, Israel enjoyed one of the fastest rates of economic growth of any country, despite serious limitations from the meager natural resources. Following a basically socialist pattern, the government established new towns for immigrants and subsidized worthy essentials like bread and milk. Extensive medical care and other benefits came through the widespread system of labor unions. Some of the highest taxes in the world accompanied these social advantages, with rates as high as 70% on upper middle class income. Not surprisingly, budget deficits, inflation, and trade deficits accompanied the rapid growth.

By the late 1970s it became clear that economic development faced increasing difficulties despite massive US aid amounting to nearly $1,000 per citizen. A 1988 Israeli study termed the economy a "relic" incapable of supporting national

Panoramic view of Tel Aviv

Courtesy: Embassy of Israel

defense or attracting immigrants. Personal income hardly grew after allowing for inflation and population growth. With a trade deficit almost twice as large per person as the United States, a $26 billion foreign debt, historically high unemployment and short–term interest rates exceeding 20% after adjusting for inflation, in the later 1980s Israel suffered net emigration until the influx of Soviet Jews.

A number of causes contributed to the economic difficulties. Besides the heavy defense burden (10% of GNP), economists blamed the marriage between socialism and Zionism that produced a bloated bureaucracy, government regulations, and heavy taxation. To some extent, too, the high unemployment and low growth rates resulted from the successful fight against inflation. After it exceeded 400% annually, Israelis ceased using their own currency for most business activity. Government policies then successfully cut it to about 20%, aided by additional U.S. grants and the drop in world oil prices. However, the bloated bureaucracy remained largely unchanged. The budget deficit continued to be large despite high taxes, and few failing non–profit companies have been forced to close.

The government and labor unions also own major portions of the economy. By 1985 the 192 state–owned firms employed 65,000 workers, and produced a significant portion of the country's total output. The largest industrial conglomerate, Koor Industries, is owned by the labor federation *Histadrut*, and another major source of manufactured goods is the collectively-owned farms (*kibbutzim*). Typically, then, about one–third of business value comes from non–profit sources. As a consequence of the 1983 financial collapse, the government acquired most bank shares. Recent attempts to sell state-owned companies, almost exclusively to foreigners, accomplished little. However, with the upswing in the world economy, in 1995 the government began to privatize *El Al*, the nation's air line, thirteen years after it faced bankruptcy.

International trade in particular means a delicate balancing act. Relatively high inflation means that exporters need a currency depreciation, because higher inflation will overprice Israeli exports. Unfortunately, depreciation in turn leads to higher prices for imported goods and thus higher inflation, higher wages, and higher prices for Israeli exports.

International Trade

In the mid–1990s two international developments offered greater opportunities for the Israeli economy. First, the Arab boycott of companies doing business with Israel, a form of secondary boycott illegal in many countries, shuffled towards final collapse when the Gulf States abandoned the boycott. Second, the Free Trade Agreement between the United States and Israel came into full effect in 1995, and included Israeli agricultural products excluded by the Free Trade Agreement with the European Union.

Separately, relatively poor natural resources also create difficulties. Although good deposits of phosphates are exploited, and potash and several other chemicals are extracted from the Dead Sea, only rather insignificant oil, natural gas, and coal deposits exist. Israel imports the bulk of its energy requirements as well as other raw materials, and it benefited from the decline in world oil prices in 1986. However, the diamond finishing industry, depending on gems from South Africa and suffering from Indian competition at much lower wages, appears headed for long–term decline.

Agricultural output has expanded enormously since 1948. The introduction of new crops, chemical fertilizers and irrigation systems increased production more than 500%. Besides land formerly farmed by the displaced Palestinians, irrigation from the Jordan River and perhaps the most advanced dry–climate agricultural cultivation methods in the world turned sparse grazing lands into farms. Chiefly exporting high–value and out–of–season fruits and vegetables to Europe, Israel imports other foodstuffs, including beef.

For a small country, Israel produces a wide variety of industrial products, from simple furniture to cut diamonds to satellites. Armaments comprise the largest category of exports, valued at perhaps $1.5 billion in 1988. This includes guided missiles, artillery, and fighter aircraft as well as the most famous, the Uzzi submachine gun. Customers range from the United States to Taiwan, South Africa, and a number of Latin American nations. Israel Aircraft Industries had hoped to become a major producer of high-technology fighter aircraft with its *Lavi*. However the withdrawal of American and Israeli government aid to develop the airplane doomed it in 1987, and the aviation industry now concentrates on equipment and service rather than entire aircraft. The industry also suffered in 1991–92 from claims it had violated U.S. law by selling weapons with U.S. parts or U.S. technology without approval, and engaged in spying on American companies. Another dispute with the U.S. arose in 2000, over the possible sale to China of airborne early-warning radar that the U.S. feared could change the strategic balance between China and Taiwan. Despite such complications, Israel ranks as the world's fifth largest arms exporter.

In the 1990s, Israel's talented and highly educated workforce proved particularly adept at high technology, particularly computer software. Hundreds of startup companies worked with U.S. firms and made the country one of the world's centers for innovation in computing.

The second largest industry in terms of foreign exchange earnings has been tourism. Jerusalem contains the holiest shrines for both Jews and Christian pilgrims, and numerous other Biblical and historical sites attract visitors. There are beaches and other attractions both scenic and cultural. Understandably, tourist arrivals in the 1980s proved disappointing, reduced by the 1982 invasion of Lebanon, fears of terrorist attacks, and the *intifada* at the end of the decade. In 1991 news of the Gulf War discouraged tourists whose idea of pleasure did not include gas masks and sealed rooms. Tourism fared better with the peace treaties, however, and there were expectations of perhaps four million Christian visitors in the year 2000. By the following year, many hotel rooms were empty, a byproduct of the renewed *intifada*.

Given its outstanding—and growing—scientific and technical talent, its pioneering research in desert agriculture, and the enterprising nature of its people, Israel retains the promise of prosperity. However, as they have ever since independence, two major difficulties stand in the way. First, government regulations now appear as some of the most bothersome outside the Less Developed Countries. Second, a ceasefire without peace diverts too many resources to military use.

The Future: It is tempting for non-Jews to despair about Israel's prospects. Alarmed by violence in the streets and territories, and unable to place Hebrew rhetoric in perspective, outside observers find it difficult enough to evaluate the Israeli present, let alone construct reasonable estimates of the future.

However, Israel did not become a modern economy, intellectual powerhouse, and the region's dominant military power by depending on outside judgments. Firm instincts and tough positions have served well a people whose neighbors desired to evict them. It is not surprising that Israelis prefer to trust themselves, rather than a United States whose regional interests (e.g., obtaining Arab nations' support for an attack on Iraq) sometimes demand caution by Israel.

Peace for Israel is only possible by agreement with the Palestinians, or by their expulsion. But ethnic cleansing is now a crime against humanity, and for the moment, both the cabinet and public opinion in Israel oppose halting the settlements as a condition for an effective ceasefire. In the short run, then, military force remains the way of life. Expect some reduction in violence from the horrendous levels of spring 2002, but in the long run military repression is no solution to hatred.

The Hashemite Kingdom of Jordan

The Treasury building at Petra comes into view at the end of the Siq, a long narrow gorge through solid rock, the only access to this ancient Nabataean city discovered in 1812—an architectural and archeological wonder.

Area: 34,443 square miles (89,206 sq. km.).
Population: Estimates range between 4.4 and 6.1 million.
Capital City: Amman (Pop. 1.2 million, est.)
Climate: Hot and dry in the summer, but winter can be cold with moderate rain and even snow in the northwest. The Jordan Valley and Aqaba area are warmer. The eastern and southern regions are desert.
Neighboring Countries: Syria (North); Iraq (Northeast); Saudi Arabia (Southeast); Israel and Occupied Territories (West).
Time Zone: GMT +2. When it is noon Pacific Standard Time in the U.S. it is 10:00 P.M. in Jordan.
Official Language: Arabic.
Other Principal Language: English is widely used as a secondary language.
Ethnic Background: Physical appearance is of Mediterranean type; except for small Circassian communities, nearly all are identified as Arab.
Principal Religion: Sunni Islam (about 91%) and Christianity.
Chief Commercial Products: Phosphate, olive oil, tomatoes, wheat, barley, figs, lentils, tobacco, sheepskins, hides, cement, salt and refined petroleum products.

Major Trading Partners: Saudi Arabia, U.S., Germany, Iraq, Japan, U.K., Syria and India.
Currency: Dinar, divided into 1000 fils or 100 piasters
Former Colonial Status: Under British control (1918–1946).
Independence Day: May 25, 1946.
Chief of State: Abdullah II (Abdullah ibn Hussein al-Hashimi), King.
Head of Government: Ali Abul-Ragheb, Prime Minister.
National Flag: Three horizontal stripes of black, white and green and a red triangle at the pole bearing a white seven-pointed star.
Gross Domestic Product: $7.25 billion
GDP per capita: $1300 (IMF); some estimates higher.

The borders of Jordan, like those of many other countries drafted by colonial powers, often fail to reflect either natural features or differences in populations. In the years immediately following World War I, the boundaries were drawn to suit British policy, and they have been modified little since. The country takes its name from the Jordan River, which with its tributary, the Yarmuk, is the only real river in the area, and provides the only natural boundary.

The Jordan River, deprived of most fresh water by diversions, is merely a small stream when it empties into the salty Dead Sea, the lowest body of water on earth. Its surface lies about 1,300 feet below the level of the oceans, and is falling. Because the Jordan's scanty flow falls short of the very rapid evaporation caused by the heat and solar rays in the depression, the Dead Sea is drying up. About 50 miles long from north to south just a generation ago, as shown on the map, it has lost the southern third. However, the sea will not disappear: its maximum depth reaches about 1,300 feet. The salt concentration is almost ten times that of ordinary sea water. This allows bathers to read the newspaper with ease, but they suffer stings from each scratch through the skin.

Immediately east of the Jordan Valley the land rises steeply to the edge of a high plateau. The strip along the edge of the plateau, wider in the north, receives moderate rainfall (about 25 inches annually). As the plateau drops in elevation to the east and south, rainfall diminishes rapidly to nothing. Only the hardiest *badu* nomads wander out into that area in search of a livelihood.

Amman, the capital of the country, lies on the plateau, spread onto the sides of several converging valleys. In 1925 only a small Circassian village built among the ruins of ancient Roman Philadelphia, Amman has grown into a large, modern, and fairly comfortable city.

King Abdullah of Jordan (1882–1951)

History: Although the high plateau was farmed extensively during the Roman and Byzantine periods, and Umayyad caliphs built palaces in the desert, for much of the last thousand years Bedouins dominated the country. During the later Ottoman period, government control increased, as did settlement, and the Hijaz railroad from Damascus to Medina was built through the territory a decade before World War I. During the war, Jordan became a major battlefield for the troops and Bedouin allies of the Arab Revolt against the Ottoman Empire. The port of Aqaba became their first important conquest outside the Hijaz. Under Emir Faisal, and supported by British supplies and advisors such as T.E. Lawrence (Lawrence of Arabia), the Arab forces used their mastery of the desert to outflank the Ottoman forces, tying down large numbers of them in garrison duties.

After the war, Jordan came under Arab rule from Damascus, and thus in 1920 formed part of Faisal's Kingdom of Syria. However, French forces soon marched on Damascus, ousted Faisal, and subjected Syria to the French mandate. Jordan, though the southern portion of Syria, lay in territory that by Anglo–French agreement fell under British rule. Hence France did not occupy it. Several weeks later, Faisal's brother Abdullah arrived in Amman from the Hijaz, hoping to regain all Syria for Arab rule, but only minor raids took place against the French.

Acting on the wishes of Britain and France, the League of Nations had granted Britain control over the area as part of Palestine; the term "Jordan" referred only to the river and valley. However, conditions contrasted greatly between the two banks of the Jordan River. The western territory had cities and towns, settled farmers, and Zionist immigrants. The East Bank resembled much more a frontier society, with raids by tribes of nomads and semi–nomads, no cities but only a

scattering of towns, and only the skeleton of modern government. For the practical reason that Abdullah already ruled the area as Faisal's replacement, and as a reward for his family's alliance with Britain in World War I, Britain formed the Emirate of Transjordan for Abdullah. Claiming descent from the Prophet Muhammad's family, and thus a Hashemite, Abdullah eventually gave his family name to the state.

Aside from settled areas around the towns of al–Karak, al–Salt, Ajlun and Irbid, nomadism remained the dominant way of life in much of Transjordan. Abdullah selected Amman as his capital. An impressive city in ancient times, it was located on the Hijaz Railway, and a few Circassian refugees from Russian expansion in the Caucasus had settled in nearby villages. During the 1920s Emir Abdullah's small government attempted to establish law and order, protect the frontier, settle nomadic tribes, and undertake the beginnings of modern government.

The Arab Legion, composed of Arab soldiers with British officers, became the instrument that brought order to Transjordan and fought for the Allies in Syria and Iraq. As the Emir's government showed more competence, the treaty with Britain was revised in several stages, each one giving his officials more authority. Finally, negotiations in 1946 led to a treaty recognizing the independence of Transjordan,

and on May 25, Abdullah proclaimed himself King of a sovereign nation.

A mutual defense treaty went into effect at independence, permitting British troops to remain in the country. British officers controlled the Arab Legion, though technically under orders from Amman rather than London.

When the United Nations voted in late 1947 to partition Palestine between Jews and Palestinians (see Israel: History), King Abdullah saw the opportunity to realize one step in his cherished dream of ruling a kingdom of "Greater Syria," including Transjordan, Syria, Lebanon and Palestine. When Britain's mandate over Palestine expired on May 15, 1948, he sent the Arab Legion across the Jordan River to fight the newly proclaimed Jewish state of Israel. Other Arab states acted likewise, but in the War of Israeli Independence (1948–49) Arab armies generally suffered defeat, and Israeli forces occupied areas reserved by the United Nations partition

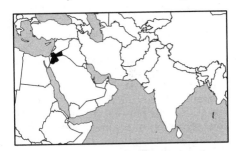

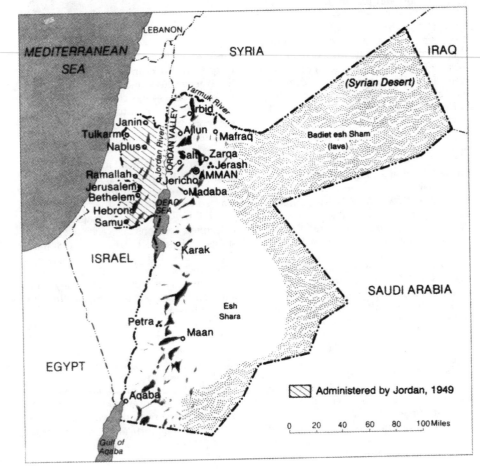

plan for the Arab state. Before the final armistice, the Arab Legion was forced, by Israeli ultimatum, to pull back.

To most Palestinians and many historians, King Abdullah had intervened in Palestine as much for dynastic gain as to repulse the Israelis. As the fighting ended, he established secret contacts with high Israeli officials to assure them of his limited intentions. Later he convened a congress of Pal-estinian notables in Jericho. They proclaimed him King of all Palestine; in 1949 he annexed formally the central portion that his troops controlled. Thus most of Palestine saved from Israel became the West Bank of the Hashemite Kingdom of Jordan, and Abdullah came to rule the holy places in Jerusalem, Bethlehem and Hebron.

However, Jordan also gained a large and restive population, including several hundred thousand refugees on both sides of the river. They widely opposed Abdullah, considering him an agent of Britain and a traitor to the Palestinian cause. Furthermore, because of their greater achievements in education, larger population, and greater sophistication, Palestinians tended to consider Transjordan as backward. Not surprisingly, tensions arose between the Palestinians and those east of the river.

In 1951 a Palestinian conspirator assassinated King Abdullah as he walked in Jerusalem. His popular but nervous son Talal succeeded him, though shortly afterwards he was declared mentally ill by court officials, and placed in a hospital in Istanbul. Talal's son Hussein, who was present when his grandfather was shot, then became king, although guided by a regency council until he turned 18 in 1953.

At first Hussein permitted political activity and allowed parties to organize. Most of them were extremely nationalistic and anti–Western, owing to the roles played by Britain, France and the United States in the creation and support of Israel. Perhaps the most democratic election ever held in Jordan took place in 1956, and translated public feelings into an extremely nationalistic lower house of parliament.

In a showdown in 1957, King Hussein staged a personal appearance at the main army camp at Zarqa; he asserted that cabinet officials were conspiring with Palestinians in the army to overthrow him. The army took control of Amman; the Prime Minister and other members of the cabinet were arrested and parliament was dissolved. Hussein also dismissed Glubb Pasha, the British officer who had led the Arab Legion for more than two decades, and ended the Anglo–Jordanian defense treaty.

These events marked the beginning of a period when the young King exercised personal authority. To replace British aid, he sought financial, military and technical assistance from the United States, which hoped to counter anti–Western trends in the Arab World by demonstrating its support

The late King Hussein of Jordan

for Jordan. Nevertheless, following the Iraqi Revolution in 1958 that overthrew the Hashemite kingdom in Baghdad and murdered Hussein's cousin, Faisal II, British troops returned to Jordan to uphold the monarchy.

Given Israel's military strength, Jordan wished to preserve the 1949 armistice agreement with Israel. However, politically active Palestinians, especially those exiled from homes and property in Israel, wanted Jordan to join other Arab nations in a military confrontation against it (see Palestine). Tensions between several Arab states and Israel led Egypt's Nasser to start actions that promoted a crisis with Israel in May 1967 (see Israel: History). King Hussein was drawn unwillingly into a military treaty with Egypt and then into war with Israel on June 5, 1967.

In four days of fighting, the vastly superior Israeli army and air force crushed all Jordanian units west of the Jordan River. After 17 years, Jordan's rule ended over what had come to be called the West Bank, the richest portion of the kingdom. With nearly half the population lost, and economic benefits from the major tourist locations such as Jerusalem ended, Jordan faced great economic, political, and social difficulties.

Most immediately, nearly 400,000 Palestinians fled to Jordan, creating a new wave of refugees. Large communities of displaced Palestinians remained from 1949 around Amman, at Zarqa and elsewhere. New camps were set up with international aid, to provide food and tent shelter for the flood of persons crossing the river. The burden of the refugees stretched Jordan's finances; their numbers swamped the available jobs.

The camps both old and new became fertile recruiting centers for al–Fatah and other guerrilla groups linked to the *Palestine Liberation Organization (PLO)*. Claiming they would succeed against Israel where the combined Arab armies failed, these groups launched attacks against Israel and Israeli–occupied areas. Massive Israeli reprisal raids turned much of the Jordan valley into a zone of sporadic battles, but at Karameh in 1968 the guerrillas held their positions, consequently gaining fame and support in the Arab world (see Palestine: history).

At first Jordan permitted the guerrillas to operate in its territory, but then, fearing both Israeli retaliation and their growing power as a "second government," it attempted to curtail the armed groups. Finally in "Black" September 1970, King Hussein ordered his army to crush the guerrillas. Perhaps 10,000 people, most of them Palestinians, died in Amman during the fighting; much of the city was heavily damaged. A tank invasion by Syrian–based units of the Palestine Liberation Army met defeat from Jordan's small air force, while troops set free Western passengers hijacked by Palestinian radicals.

After sometimes bitter fighting, by late 1971 guerrilla strength in Jordan was almost entirely destroyed, though the firm suppression of the fashionable guerrillas evoked fierce hostility from Palestinians and many other Arabs. Jordan avoided direct warfare with Israel during the 1973 war, but sent a tank corps to aid Syria in the southern sector of the Jawlan (Golan) front.

The 1978–79 Camp David Agreements (see Israel: history) brought peace between Egypt and Israel, thus removing the strongest Arab threat to the Jewish state. Worse, from the standpoint of most Arabs, the agreements permitted continued Israeli military rule over the Occupied Territories and failed to halt Zionist civilian settlements there. Thus, despite U.S. requests for Jordanian endorsement of them, King Hussein opposed them vigorously, and broke diplomatic relations with Egypt. He continued to insist, however, on Jordan's sincere desire for peace with justice, as envisioned in United Nations resolutions (see Israel: UN Resolution 242).

In the 1980s Jordan developed deep friendship with Saudi Arabia, ironically ruled by the very family that forced King Hussein's great–grandfather out of his kingdom in the Hijaz (see Saudi Arabia:

history). Along with the smaller Arab states of the Gulf, during the early 1980s Saudi Arabia provided money toward Jordan's expenses as a front–line state in the conflict with Israel.

Although Syria holds a strong influence on the political thinking of some Jordanians, relations with that neighbor have varied from very friendly to outright hostility. Sensing the threat to the Arab oil states from Iran and its "Islamic Revolution," King Hussein offered full support to Iraq in its war with Iran. This increased the animosity of Syria, which favored Iran. Technically at war with Israel, threatened politically by Syria and risking subversion from Iran, Jordan entered an informal alliance with Iraq that increasingly brought the two countries together in economic and foreign policy issues.

Throughout the 1980s, Jordan continued to pursue diplomacy of the possible, even when faced with contradictory pressures from various internal and external sources. The native "Jordanians" of the East Bank, nearly half the population, traditionally considered their best interests served by alliances with the Arab Gulf states, the U.S. and Britain. In often sharp contrast, those of Palestinian background favored alliances with anti–Western, anti–capitalist and anti–Israeli states.

The widespread nationalist uprising (*intifada*) in the Israeli–occupied territories that began in December 1987 showed again that the inhabitants of the West Bank considered themselves Palestinians, not Jordanians. The uprising naturally aroused admiration mixed with political concern in Jordan. In 1974, the Arab summit at Rabat in Morocco had proclaimed the PLO to be the only representative of the Palestinian people, thus denying Jordan's claim to the West Bank. In response, King Hussein had dissolved the lower house of parliament, for it contained Palestinian representatives. However, Jordan continued to pay the salaries of some civil servants in Palestine, and in 1986 established a West Bank development scheme as part of the Jordanian five year plan. As the *intifada* gathered strength, however, such links aroused widespread opposition among Palestinians and other Arabs. Consequently, in 1988 King Hussein dramatically recognized the Palestinians' wish to form their own country. Soon thereafter Jordan announced it would cease paying salaries to public employees in the West Bank. Similarly, the lower house of parliament—last elected in 1967—once again was dissolved.

Widespread dissatisfaction with the government's financial austerity measures sparked off rioting in many parts of Jordan in early 1989. Short of foreign exchange, and running a deep budget deficit, partly because subsidies from Saudi Arabia and other oil–rich states expired, the government of Prime Minister Zayd Rifai found itself unable to pay its foreign debts. When it imposed higher gasoline and cigarette prices and increased charges for telephone and other services, riots forced the prime minister to resign. He was replaced by Jordan's dependable manager in crisis, the king's distant cousin and former military commander, Sharif Zayd bin Shaker.

The king moved rapidly to regain the initiative. The protests had broken out not in refugee camps or Amman, recognized centers of opposition, but in the small cities and towns of Jordan, traditionally loyal to the monarchy. Professional associations and businessmen echoed the protesters' demands. Unable to reverse the increased prices, King Hussein reacted by accepting many of the political demands, while showing himself a monarch who ruled. He called the first general elections in 22 years for the lower house of parliament (the Senate is appointed), restored press freedoms to journalists previously banned, and amnestied those arrested during the riots.

Although political parties remained prohibited, especially the *Communists*, *Ba'thists*, and the radical *Democratic Front for the Liberation of Palestine*, they functioned discreetly. In addition, the *Muslim Brotherhood*, though banned as a party, had

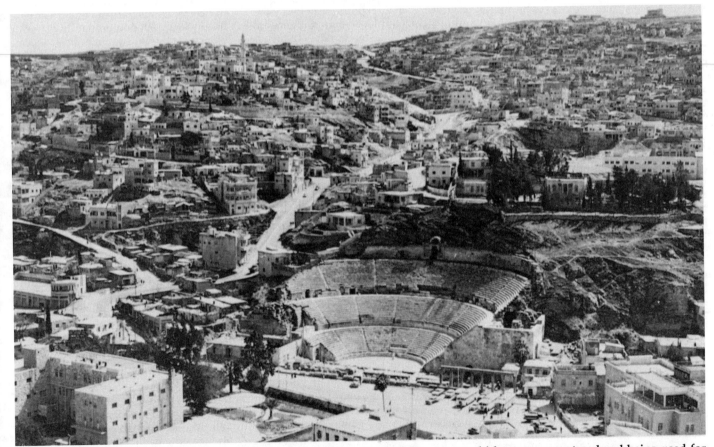

Amman, a city built on seven hills. Against the slope of one is this large Roman amphitheater now restored and being used for performances as it once was almost 2,000 years ago.

A mounted officer of the Desert Camel Corps

operated as a charity; in effect it now ran candidates. Thus both leftist and Muslim fundamentalist candidates enjoyed some organized support, while in the political center loyalists to the monarch operated as individuals. In several respects, the country enjoyed the freest elections the Arab world had witnessed in many years.

The results proved dramatic. Despite the king's aversion to "mixing politics and religion," candidates affiliated with the *Muslim Brotherhood* and other fundamentalists won 32 of 80 seats, and swept the capital, Amman. Had electoral districts been more evenly apportioned, they might have gained a majority. An alliance of leftists and progressives known as the *Democratic Bloc* also took several seats. In contrast, scores of notables lost—court favorites, former cabinet members, retired army officers. Observers generally considered that Jordanians had voted against financial retrenchment as well as the corruption widely alleged in the old government. In addition, the *Muslim Brotherhood* had provided its candidates with organization and support that individual politicians could not match.

Until the Jordanian elections, Arab regimes had generally responded to growing Muslim fundamentalism either by repression (with little success), or by adopting publicly its symbols. By design or chance, Jordan offered a third response to the Islamic reformers: involving them in the legislature, seeking elective office rather than revolution, and perhaps converting them from idealists to practical politicians. Very substantial differences separated the *Muslim Brotherhood's* ideology from the king's. Nevertheless, the new prime minister, Mudar Badran, selected ministers from both leftists and the Islamic right. The *Brotherhood* won an expansion of Islamic

education, restrictions on alcoholic beverages, and a greater role for the *Sharia*.

International issues swept the kingdom when Iraq seized Kuwait in 1990. Depression hit the economy when exports to Iraq, the main destination, collapsed after the United Nations imposed sanctions. Insurance surcharges on shipping wiped out profits from phosphate exports, and for the year, total exports dropped 40%. About 200,000 Jordanian workers returned from Gulf states, reducing the annual remittances sent their families, and raising unemployment to 25%–30%. Affluent tourists stayed away, but tens of thousands of foreign refugees flooded the borders, requiring temporary housing, food and other needs the government could ill afford. Individual incomes fell sharply.

The Jordanian government's political response proved difficult for non–Arabs to understand. While refusing to recognize the conquest, King Hussein proposed border concessions from Kuwait as well as subsidies for Iraq. He flew thousands of miles attempting to bring peace, proposing his "Arab solution." This avoided placing non–Muslim troops on Saudi territory, traditionally considered prohibited to non–believers. A close friend of Saddam Hussein since the 1980s Iran–Iraq war, the king also feared a conflict pitting Arabs armed with chemicals against nuclear–equipped Israel. Furthermore, Jordanians averaged little more than 10% the annual earnings of Kuwaitis, and the king appeared sensitive to the imbalance of wealth in the Arab world. Finally, in Jordan's view, U.N. Resolution 262 calling for an Israeli withdrawal from the Occupied Territories had gone unenforced for 23 years. Consequently, the Palestinian problem called for parallel treatment to Kuwait.

King Hussein's arguments won wide domestic popularity. Islamic fundamentalists appreciated the challenge to the West, and the Palestinians' insistence on ending the occupation of their homeland. Many Jordanians who had worked in Gulf countries resented their second-class status there. Nevertheless, despite popular support for Baghdad, Jordan maintained strict neutrality in the fighting, though it did not emerge unscathed. Long a recipient of funds from Saudi Arabia and other Gulf states, Jordan found itself cut off financially, isolated by its refusal to join the anti–Iraqi coalition.

In the aftermath of the war, King Hussein ended martial law imposed in 1967. Political leaders signed the "National Charter" that re–established multiparty democracy and secured allegiance to the king. Prime ministers followed in rapid succession, including Sharif Zayd.

The Madrid peace negotiations over Palestine affirmed the importance of King Hussein to regional diplomacy and signified friendly relations with the United States. By providing the crucial cover of a "joint" delegation with the Palestinians, Jordan permitted their participation in the peace process.

Surgery to remove a cancerous tumor from King Hussein in 1992 sharply reminded Jordanians that his 40–year rule could end. Nearly one–third of the nation's population lined Amman's streets to welcome his return. His steadying hand soon proved important in domestic affairs. He pardoned two militant Islamic parliamentarians convicted, on widely disbelieved evidence, of treason. The pardon deftly prevented the case from becoming a rallying point for the opposition.

Some 15 political parties, including the *Islamic Action Front* of the Muslim Brotherhood registered for the 1993 National Assembly elections, but the *Communists* and *Ba'th Socialists* were excluded. Despite worries about the PLO–Israel agreement, Jordan held its first multi–party election since 1967. The new and sometimes uneven electoral districts helped independent candidates from traditionally important families to triumph. This weakened parties generally. The *Islamic Action Front* gained 16 seats, and as the largest group, it led the opposition with allies of Arab nationalists and leftists.

Signalling the importance of peace negotiations, King Hussein appointed Abdul Salam al–Majali, Jordan's chief negotiator, as Prime Minister. Quiet and symbolic diplomacy, sometimes in a tent straddling the border, resolved the major disputes, and in 1994 a peace treaty formally ended forty–six years of belligerence with Israel. Jordan regained some small bits of land (totalling 145 square miles) occupied by Israel, and leased some parcels to the *kibbutzim* cultivating them. More importantly, the treaty also restored water rights in the

The 1989 elections in Jordan demonstrated vividly the deeply–held differences between Muslim fundamentalists and women influenced by Western concepts of equality and women's rights.

In her campaign for parliament, the TV personality, Tawjar al–Faisal, raised a number of social issues, including child abuse, polygamy, and wife–beating. For this, she was charged in the Islamic court by two Muslim radicals, one a deputy to the Mufti (legal scholar) of the military, on grounds she had "defamed Islam". As punishment, according to *The Middle East,* her critics demanded the court declare her legally incompetent, dissolve her marriage, remove her children, and grant immunity to anyone who shed her blood.

The Islamic court dismissed the case, possibly at the urging of the royal palace. Neither Tawjar al–Faisal nor any other woman won a seat in the elections, but soon after King Hussein did appoint Layla Sharaf the first woman in the Senate.

Jordan and Yarmuk valleys, and the U.S. promised to waive repayment on loans of nearly $1 billion. Jordan gained a privileged role at Muslim sites in Jerusalem, though it promised to turn them over to Palestinian authorities once Israel withdrew.

Peace required Jordan to amend its anti–Israeli laws and permit trade with Israel. However, popular opposition made this difficult. Some professional associations banned all their members from dealing with Israelis; Islamic, leftist and Pan–Arab parties demanded that the treaty be scrapped. The opposition gained strength because the first visible benefits seemed limited to tourism, mostly in the form of short–term visitors bound for Petra. By contrast, Jordan's factories are unlikely to export to Israel, and hydroelectric projects in the Jordan Valley will require years of planning and construction.

An ill–conceived attack in Amman by agents of Israel's *Mossad* confirmed many Jordanians' suspicions of an unjust peace. Caught after attempting to poison a *Hamas* political leader, the agents' action led King Hussein to demand successfully that Israel release the head of *Hamas* from prison.

Other resentments fueled dissatisfaction before the 1997 parliamentary elections. The government restricted the press, used a biased electoral system that favored rural areas, and cut the subsidy on bread, an economically logical but politically difficult measure. Bread forms the staple of almost every meal, and an attempt the previous year to raise its price led to riots and restored subsidies. The *Islamic Action Front* and smaller opposition parties boycotted the election, and in the low turnout, especially in the cities, independents favoring the government won most seats.

The last months of King Hussein showed again that real power in the country lies not with parliament but with the royal family. Stricken with cancer, Hussein twice left treatment at the Mayo Clinic in the U.S. First, he joined President Clinton in mediating differences between Palestinians and Israelis at the Wye Plantation talks. Second, in early 1999 he flew home to Amman, where he very publicly replaced his heir. His brother, Hassan, had served as crown prince since the 1960s, but apparently for family reasons as well as concern about some of Hassan's administrative changes, Hussein appointed his eldest son, Abdullah, as his heir. Days later, after final medical efforts back at the Mayo Clinic failed, King Hussein returned home to die.

Hussein had ruled Jordan for nearly 47 years, many of them tumultuous, and he cut a much larger figure on the world stage than his country's population and wealth merited. A vast assembly of world leaders gathered for the funeral—the only significant absentee seemed to be Saddam Hussein of Iraq.

The son of Hussein's British second wife, Abdullah had spent almost his entire life in the military, commanding the special security forces for the royal household. Educated in Britain and the U.S., he apparently had accepted that his uncle would become the next king. Nevertheless, commentators commended the initiatives and energy he displayed as a ruler. Within weeks, Abdullah visited most Arab capitals, where he improved relations with political opposites like Syria and Kuwait. During other trips, to Western capitals, he sought economic concessions, particularly debt relief.

In Amman, Abdullah proved adept at symbolic gestures popular with most citizens, appearing in the streets disguised as an ordinary individual. He also appointed a new prime minister, who included in the cabinet both Islamic critics of previous regimes and modernizers. However, the

T. E. Lawrence described Wadi Rum as "vast and echoing and God–like."

Photo by Michael Russell

cabinet failed to move as quickly as the king desired, and he gained a reputation for pushing Parliament to grant greater press freedom and to adopt measures providing economic reforms and reducing corruption.

The regime also suppressed the Jordanian branch of *Hamas*, the militant Islamic Palestinian group, perhaps to support Yasir Arafat's Palestinian Authority, and charged a group allegedly linked to Osama bin Laden, the fugitive Saudi, with planning a series of explosions at tourist sites. Yet another extremist group planned to attack the royal yacht. Military trials convicted a number of alleged plotters, sentencing several to death in absentia.

By contrast, in a deft political counter-move, the government also persuaded the opposition *Islamic Action Front*, the largest party in the country, to reconsider its policy of election boycotts. The king's policy of unity and equality no doubt receives subtle support because Queen Rania is Palestinian.

In the summer of 1998, Jordan faced a prolonged and devastating drought. Initially, piped water in Amman became highly bacterial and foul-smelling, apparently from pollution at the main reservoir. Normal winter rains nearly disappeared from the region in 1999, and Israel announced it could not supply the water agreed in its peace treaty with Jordan. Wheat and other crops that depended on rainfall failed; many herders could find neither water for their flocks to drink nor stubble for them to eat.

Heavier rains and even significant snowfalls during the past winter raised hopes that weather patterns were turning "wetter". Jordanians hope so, but can do little else in the short run about a water shortage they shared with neighboring countries. For the longer term, several

proposals exist to desalinize seawater and create hydroelectric power in the valley south of the Dead Sea, but that source of fresh water will be distant and expensive.

Culture: Antiquities lie strewn profusely across—and beneath—the landscape of Jordan. Perhaps as many as 500,000 identifiable archeological sites exist, and teams of workers from many lands descend annually to discover remains dated from the Paleolithic to the Ottoman periods. In years of good fortune, they unearth seals, broken pottery, and occasional pieces of jewelry. In the popular imagination, however, the foreigners must come for gold. As a result, archeological pillaging constitutes a widespread crime.

Although desert palaces of the Umayyads and the Byzantine mosaics at Madaba constitute a priceless treasure, the most impressive ruins date from the Roman era. Now the scene of a cultural festival, the columns, buildings, streets and amphitheater of Jerash rank as one of the Empire's best preserved cities outside Italy. By contrast, Semitic Nabateans carved residences and tombs in the nearly vertical limestone cliffs of a narrow gorge. The home of enterprising merchants, Petra flourished for about 200 years after 100 BC. Already in decline by the Arab conquest, it became a lost city, rediscovered only in the 19th century. Tourists today endure sand and sunshine to marvel at the intricately carved columns, the splendor of sunlight on rose–colored sandstone, and carved channels that brought water from a distant spring.

The modern culture of Jordan is essentially similar to that found in Syria and parts of Lebanon, although the eastern and southern parts of the country are more like Saudi Arabia. Nevertheless, observers often notice differences in Jordan, including a greater respect for standing in line and obeying traffic regulations. In towns and cities, Western styles and habits are being adopted more often, but there is popular resistance to this in some communities.

Universal, compulsory education through six elementary and three preparatory ("junior high") years has almost been attained, partly due to facilities provided for children by the U.N. Relief and Works Agency for Palestine Refugees. Every town has a secondary school and larger towns and cities may have several. The quality of instruction tends to be good in Arabic language and literature, as well as in mathematics, but qualified teachers in other subjects are not available in the numbers needed, partly because thousands of Jordanians sought teaching jobs in Saudi Arabia, Kuwait and elsewhere.

The University of Jordan opened on the outskirts of Amman in 1963, and remains the most prestigious in the country.

Yarmuk University was established at Irbid in 1976, while the 1980s saw the beginnings of Mu'ta University in the south. Then, in the 1990s, numerous private colleges and universities sprouted across the landscape, often to serve students whose families had lived in the Gulf States.

Soccer is the most popular sport in Jordan. Most high schools have teams and the competition is sometimes quite keen. Television sets dominate living rooms much as in the rest of the world. Jordan TV has two channels, one mainly Arabic, the other for programs in English, French and Hebrew. Its programs, many from Europe and the U.S., are viewed by many Israelis.

Economy: A century ago life in Jordan revolved around nomadic and semi–nomadic herding and farming, with a handful of small towns. Today, where rainfall and irrigation permit, settled farmers cultivate a variety of crops, ranging from grains and other staples to tomatoes, melons and warm–weather vegetables. Agricultural exports account for around one-fifth the total, but many foods must be imported. The climate and soil usually ensure that farmers, many of them tenants paying one–third of the crop to the landlord, achieve only a modest standard of living.

After independence the government undertook a series of irrigation projects and other assistance for agriculture, particularly the East Ghor Project to use water from the Yarmuk River for farms in the Jordan Valley. Other economic development projects included exploiting the phosphate deposits that account for about 25% of the nation's exports. Ambitious plans exist to exploit the Dead Sea for potash. Unlike its Arab neighbors to the northeast and south, Jordan contains no significant oil deposits. The country plays a modest role as a regional trade and commercial center, partly because its drier, cooler climate contrasts favorably with the Gulf, partly because Westerners find their lifestyles less restricted.

The economy has alternately suffered and prospered because of international events. Disputes with Syria often cut access to the Mediterranean. War with Israel in 1967 inflicted 400,000 new refugees, the collapse of tourism, and the loss of the most highly–developed portion of the kingdom, which accounted for 40% of GNP. Civil War with the Palestinians in 1970–1971 caused economic stagnation. One the other hand, financial aid rewarded Jordan's rejection of the Camp David Agreement (1978), and the economy grew at 10% annually. Evidence of prosperity multiplied. While many Jordanians (330,000 in 1988) worked abroad, often as skilled professionals in oil–exporting countries, some 200,000 other Arabs filled low–paying jobs in Jordan.

King Abdullah II

Arab hospitality quickly means hot tea   Photo by Michael Russell

The collapse of world oil prices in 1986 marked the beginning of an era of eco-nomic retrenchment. Aid from Arab oil exporters fell, and job prospects weakened abroad. Interest and repayment on the foreign debt soared, and foreign exchange reserves fell. The dinar fell steeply against the dollar, losing as much as 50% of its value in one year. Thus, by early 1989 several economic difficulties hit simultaneously: lower aid, debt repayment, precari-ous reserves, inflation, rising imports, and a budget deficit surpassing 20% of GNP (the U.S.: 2–3%). Clearly Jordanians had lived beyond their means, and could no longer borrow to do so.

Although the government responded with economically–reasonable measures such as higher indirect taxes and cuts in subsidies, as well as canceling new weapons purchases, popular resistance led to riots and political change (see History). Friendly Arab nations responded with promises of modest aid, and rescheduled debt repayments. The cabinet cut spending for investment projects, and devoted more to debt repayment. In these ways the country survived the immediate crisis, only to suffer lost subsidies and disrupted trade during the Gulf War.

Flooded with hundreds of thousands of new Palestinian refugees, this time from the Gulf, the economy recovered surprisingly rapidly after 1991. Construction boomed, as former workers in the Gulf invested their savings in homes, offices, and apartments. Foreign exchange reserves rose, the economy grew rapidly (over 5% per year), and yet inflation remained modest.

The UN sanctions on Iraq deprived Jordan of its major export market, and the lost transit earnings themselves have reached billions of dollars. Lacking a great economic dividend from peace with Israel, in the late 1990s the country entered a significant recession. Unfortunately, the standard tools of economic policy could not be used to restore output. A rapid increase in the money supply would lead those with financial wealth to send it abroad, before the *dinar* would fall in value. Fiscal policy was also immobilized: massive budget deficits, covered partly by foreign aid, marked good years as well as bad.

The Future: Abdullah II inherited a kingdom whose debts of $8 billion exceed its annual GDP. However, its credits include a great reservoir of sympathy built up by his father in Western nations in particular. Hopefully Abdullah can retain that sympathy, while steering Jordan to friendlier relations with Arab neighbors like Syria, Saudi Arabia and Kuwait.

As the Israeli-Palestinian peace process collapses, so does the Jordanian economy. Since 1996 the population has grown faster than the economy. Unemployment, at 25% of the labor force matches U.S. levels during the depths of the Great Depression. While the newly-signed Free Trade Agreement provides easier access for the few Jordanian goods shipped to the U.S., the country's natural markets are Iraq and the West Bank, where politics preclude prosperity. Many Palestinian and Islamic groups think that peace with Israel was a mistake, but without a wider regional peace the country will continue to suffer.

The Muslim Brotherhood and many less politicized residents initially allowed King Abdullah time to select his policies. However, his allies are often old-guard conservatives slow to make changes. It will be a challenge to conduct the 2002 parliamentary elections in a peaceful atmosphere without boycotts by Islamic and other opposition parties.

Hospitality in a Jordanian family

The State of Kuwait

The Kuwait City

Area: 6880 sq. mi. (17,819 sq. km.; estimates differ).

Population: 1.9 million (estimated, under 40% native Kuwaiti).

Capital City: Estimated 45,000 in Kuwait City itself, pre–war, and over 1.2 million in the metropolitan area.

Climate: Very hot except for a short comfortable winter, which usually brings a few inches of rain.

Neighboring Countries: Saudi Arabia (South) and Iraq (North).

Time Zone: GMT +3.

Official Language: Arabic.

Other Principal Tongues: Persian and English.

Ethnic Background: Overwhelmingly Arab, with communities of Persians, Indians and Pakistanis.

Principal Religion: Islam.

Chief Commercial Products: Crude oil and refined products.

Major Trading Partners: Japan, U.K., U.S., Netherlands, Italy, Germany, South Korea and Singapore.

Currency: Kuwaiti Dinar (KD .30 = $1 U.S.).

Former Colonial Status: British Protectorate (1914–1961).

Independence Day: June 19, 1961.

Chief of State: Sheikh Jaber Ahmed Al–Sabah, *Emir*, or Ruler.

Head of Government: Sheikh Saad Abdullah Al-Sabah, Deputy Ruler and Prime Minister.

National Flag: Three horizontal stripes of green, white and red, with a black trapezoid at the pole.

Gross Domestic Product: $31 billion

GDP per capita: $17,500

Kuwait (pronounced *Kwait*) is a tract of flat desert at the head of the Arab (Persian) Gulf. There are only a few natural oases in the country and no significant supply of fresh water for the city of Kuwait, which gives its name to the state.

Most of the population lives in the modern capital and its suburbs, a vivid change from the old town of mud houses that existed a generation ago. The wealth produced by oil attracted hundreds of thousands of immigrants, who with their descendants amount to over 60% of the population. The Arab world, especially the nations from Egypt to Syria, provided teachers, engineers, doctors, office staff, and skilled workers. Sharing language (but not dialect), culture and usually religion with native Kuwaitis, before 1990 these immigrants formed a majority of the population.

Aside from some Iranians, the other immigrants present a physical contrast. Indians, Pakistanis, and other Asians fill service jobs, and even build *dhows*, the boats that for generations established Kuwait as a trading center and base for pearl diving. The few European and American expatriates work in the oil industry and hold scattered positions in finance and commerce.

History: Although ancient ruins on Failaka island show human settlements thousands of years ago, by the 18th century the inhabitants were overwhelmingly nomadic. Then, in 1756, members of the Anayza tribe from central Arabia, possibly searching for greener pastures during a drought, settled and built a fort where the city of Kuwait now stands. In Arabic, Kuwait means "Little Fort", and the little collection of mud huts, benefitting from a natural harbor, grew into a trading outpost and pearl–diving center. It eventually came to possess a defensive wall.

The ruling family of Kuwait descended from the first ruler, and carries his name, al–Sabah (pronounced es–sabah). Though formally titled Emir (prince), the ruler and other important members commonly use the honorary Arab title of Sheikh. Arab custom and a tradition of consultation limited the sheikh's autocratic powers, and senior men in the extended family selected the most appropriate successor. Because the early Emirs proved to be long–lived, there was less opportunity for interference by the swiftly–growing Ottoman Empire, which claimed the territory as part of the Wilaya ("province") of Basra.

At the end of the 19th century, Emir Mubarak faced a critical decision. Fearing the increased ability of the Ottoman Empire to rule its distant territories, in 1899 he negotiated a secret treaty with Britain that placed Kuwait under its protection. Then, when the Ottoman Empire entered World War I in 1914, Britain easily declared Kuwait a protectorate. The Sabah

The Emir of Kuwait

The Prime Minister of Kuwait

remained the boundary. The 1932 demarcation agreement between (British–protected) Kuwait and (British–influenced) Iraq contained neither map nor detailed descriptions, so that Kuwaiti territory began "south of the southernmost palm tree at Safwan."

With independence Kuwait moved towards democracy. The first elections were held in 1961, selecting twenty men to serve with members of the ruling family in a Constituent Assembly that would draft a constitution.

The 1962 Constitution retained the Emir as the chief executive of government, assisted by a Prime Minister and a cabinet, titled the *Council of Ministers*. An elected *National Assembly* received the power to make recommendations and serve as a forum of discussion. The electorate, however, extended only to males whose family possessed citizenship in 1920. Thus the Constitution excluded from voting all Kuwaiti women as well as non–Kuwaiti Arabs of long residence or even born in Kuwait. Only about 10% of the population thus could vote.

The first elections for the National Assembly took place in 1963. Many of those elected held views similar to the ruling family; others depended directly or indirectly on the state for employment, as

did 70% of working Kuwaitis. Thus, opposition to the Sabah family remained limited. Nevertheless, a dispute arose between the ruling family and the *National Assembly* in 1965 and escalated into a mini–crisis. As a result, the cabinet was strengthened and the powers of the Assembly declined. Members of the Sabah family continued to dominate cabinet posts, and when Emir Abdullah died in 1965, the elders of the family broke this once with tradition and selected not a cousin, but his brother, Sheikh Sabah, as successor, a decision ratified by the National Assembly.

Elections in 1967 brought little change. However, facing a series of difficulties— foreign military tensions, the hijacking

family retained internal authority over the town, which remained an uninviting and lonely little trading center.

On the death of Sheikh Mubarak in 1915, the succession passed to each of his sons Jabir and Salim. This established a pattern of the succession alternating between their two families. Thus a "Crown Prince" is not the son of the current Emir, but rather a cousin who traces his paternal ancestry through a different line.

As geologists searched for oil deposits near the Gulf, British and American companies formed the Kuwait Oil Company and received a concession from the Emir. The company began drilling for oil in 1936, and soon discovered some of the richest deposits in the world. Exports began after World War II, and oil production and revenues soon made a startling impact on the dusty little town as it began the awkward change into a large, modern city.

Sheikh Abdullah al–Sabah became ruler in 1950; the early period of wealth was presided over by that benevolent, constitutional monarch. He initiated the policy of using the fabulous wealth brought by oil for the benefit of all through a program of public works. In spite of this, much of the money was squandered.

British protection ended in 1961, with Kuwait becoming independent in June. However, Britain remained an ally, and its troops returned quickly when President Qasim of Iraq claimed the state, threatened to invade, and blocked Kuwait's membership in the United Nations. Weeks later, Arab League forces replaced the British units. However, after the overthrow of Qasim in 1963, the *Ba'thist* government in Iraq recognized the independence of Kuwait, reportedly in an arrangement involving money. Several treaties followed between the two states. One difficulty

Kuwaiti women weep at the graves of relatives killed by the Iraqi army during the 7-month occupation

AP/Wide World Photo

of Kuwaiti airliners, and terrorist violence—the Emir again suspended the Assembly and imposed press restrictions. This action also ended inconvenient criticisms from its members, and press censorship halted unflattering commentary by journalists. Thus Kuwait reverted to government by decree, in common with the other Arab Gulf states.

During the 1980s, Kuwait viewed the war between Iran and Iraq with extreme nervousness. The conflict pitted two ideological opponents of dynastic and tolerant rule against each other: socialist republican Iraq against Islamic republican Iran. Fearing Islamic revolution more than the traditional threats of its large Arab neighbor, Kuwait loaned more than $10 billion to Iraq at no interest and sold oil on its behalf against promise of repayment. Kuwait also allowed Iraqi military supplies to pass through its territory. At the same time, however, Kuwait planned construction of a city on territory contested by Iraq.

When the combatants resorted to attacks on neutral vessels in the Gulf, Kuwait sought help from the five permanent members of the UN Security Council. The U.S. initially turned down the request, but

when the Soviets offered to charter Kuwaiti tankers, the U.S. provided naval protection.

Besides the attacks on its tankers, Kuwait suffered direct attacks from Iranian missiles in 1987; one damaged the main oil terminal. In response, Kuwait sought increased cooperation within the Gulf Cooperation Council, as well as with Egypt and the United States. To strengthen its military capabilities, Kuwait purchased armored personnel carriers, missiles and aircraft from the Soviet Union, missiles and aircraft from the United States and further weapons elsewhere

Fears also existed in Kuwait that Iranian sympathizers would sabotage oil, power, and water installations. Terrorists had attacked the United States and French embassies in earlier years and attempted unsuccessfully to assassinate the Emir, but only several small bomb attacks occurred before the Gulf War ended.

After the cease-fire, popular protest swelled among native Kuwaitis anxious for democracy, an end to censorship, and the restoration of parliament. However, parliament's members had included the entire political spectrum from Islamic fundamentalists to socialists. Their lively

questioning had extended to foreign affairs and the royal family's role in a stock market crash. Therefore the government balked, and police used unexpected violence on what must have been the wealthiest demonstrators in the world. To weaken demands for reform, in 1990 the Emir ordered elections for a *Shura*, (a consultative council rather than legislature). Members of the former National Assembly boycotted the elections, complaining that *Shura* "lacked teeth," and condemned the arrest of opposition members.

Tensions with Iraq mounted rapidly in July 1990, when President Saddam Hussein fiercely denounced Kuwait, warning that "cutting necks is better than cutting the means of living." The Iraqi complaints involved three major issues. First, Kuwait had exceeded its OPEC quota and thus (possibly) drove down oil prices, costing Iraq $1 billion annually for every $1.00 decline in oil prices. After the long war with Iran, Iraq could not afford the loss.

Second, Iraq demanded money: billions in aid besides writing off the wartime loans, plus compensation for $2.4 billion worth of Iraqi oil allegedly pumped from the Rumaila field that straddles the border. Finally, Iraq demanded long-term leases on the islands of Bubiyan and Warba, to protect Iraq's access to the Gulf and its naval base.

While the Kuwaiti government negotiated with Iraq, foreign leaders attempted to mediate, and Saddam Hussein promised to avoid violence while the diplomats worked. He kept his word: Iraqi forces attacked Kuwait the night after his diplomats left the suspended negotiations.

Caught by surprise, Kuwait's military offered piecemeal resistance. Iraqi troops entered Kuwait City in five hours, and by nightfall had crushed all resistance. The Emir and Crown Prince barely escaped to Saudi Arabia; other members of the ruling family were arrested.

Initially Iraq claimed it had acted to support Kuwaiti revolutionaries. Given the boycotted election for the *Shura*, to some minds this resembled American interventions in Panama and Grenada. However, courageous Kuwaiti opposition leaders refused to join the "Provisional Free Kuwaiti Government." Deprived of any Kuwaiti authenticity, Iraq annexed Kuwait six days after the invasion (see Iraq: History).

In exile, the government reformed. The Kuwait Investment Office and other funds in London provided money to maintain a government and support hundreds of thousands of citizens who fled the fighting or were trapped abroad. The government also lent to Kuwaiti banks, preserving them from default, and promised $5 billion to the coalition forces gathering against Iraq. Further billions were pledged to countries suffering severe hardship from the invasion and economic sanctions against Iraq.

Besides its diplomatic pressure for an Iraqi withdrawal, the government undertook to unite its citizens. The Emir and Crown Prince met with opposition figures, and before hundreds of delegates, the Crown Prince pledged further trust in the people, i.e., the 1962 Constitution and parliament. For its part, the opposition agreed to support the dynasty.

Meanwhile, Iraqi forces plundered Kuwait. From the Central Bank came gold and foreign currency worth billions; from warehouses, stores, and homes, truckloads of consumer goods. Cars were stolen from the streets. The vast booty depressed prices in Baghdad. Government organizations joined the wholesale robbery. Hospital equipment and library books disappeared; even traffic lights were stolen, along with cadavers from the medical school. Iraqi university officials apparently came to Kuwait to divide the academic spoils before shipping them home.

The pillage greatly encouraged resistance by the 200,000 citizens who remained. Government employees stopped work, and people often hid their cars rather than register them for Iraqi plates. At night, defiant women shouted "Allahu Akbar," from rooftops, implying that Allah, not Saddam Hussein, was great. The resistance undertook some military actions, helped subvert Iraqi rules, and aided foreigners sought as hostages by the Iraqis. Equally important, it maintained morale and social order.

In response, the occupying forces deported thousands of Kuwaitis to Iraq. Those that remained risked torture and other atrocities: perhaps thousands died in such conditions. Six hundred of those arrested remained missing a decade after the conflict, a constant reminder after the city was rebuilt.

Some foreign residents felt little loyalty to Kuwait: they had built the state, but never received a fair role in its society. For the Palestinian community of nearly 400,000, the occupation proved a disaster. Its poorer members failed to observe the work boycott, and a few joined the "Popular Army" militia. In contrast, despite Yasir Arafat's support for Saddam Hussein, the Fatah leader in Kuwait opposed the occupation and was assassinated. By the end of the war, over half the community had fled. Those remaining often faced reprisals and legal charges, such as serving as informants for Iraq.

During the battle to liberate Kuwait, Iraqi forces deliberately sabotaged industry and the environment. Vast quantities of crude oil were dumped into the Gulf, creating one of the greatest oil slicks in history. It threatened desalinization plants in Saudi Arabia, coated hundreds of miles of beach, and damaged seriously the food chain of Gulf marine life. Iraqi units set afire 732 of the nation's 950 oil wells. They burned up to 6 million barrels of oil daily, about 10% of all petroleum consumed world-wide. Huge palls of smoke damaged neighboring countries with soot, acid rain, and other pollution. Led by the legendary Red Adair, teams from nine nations extinguished the fires far ahead of schedule. However, escaping oil reduced underground pressure in the oilfields, thus permanently reducing the nation's oil potential.

The euphoria of the 1991 liberation soon yielded to concern. Destroyed water mains and electrical generating plants took time to repair, despite stockpiled equipment and parts. Within days, leaflets condemned the government for the lack of food and utilities, apparently delayed because of bureaucratic fumbling. The Western media noted the tardy return of the Emir, who only entered his capital after a visit by the British prime minister.

As criticism mounted, a "Democratic Forum Movement" called for the early lifting of martial law, a broader-based cabinet, and restoration of the 1962 constitution. In response, Emir Jaber reshuffled the cabinet (though keeping family members in important posts) and promised elections to a restored National Assembly.

Some of the greatest questions surrounded the fate of foreign workers, who with their families made Kuwaiti citizens a minority in their own country. Private reprisals against foreigners left dozens dead, and trials of collaborators violated normal standards of justice. Many Palestinians and others left voluntarily; several thousand were deported. One continuing concern is the fate of the *bidoun*, literally, "those without." Local desert Arabs whose families wandered across national boundaries, the *bidoun* lack citizenship because ancestral residence cannot be proven. Although Kuwait moved to offer them citizenship gradually, at present rates most will have died of old age before receiving their papers.

In its foreign relations, Kuwait's search for greater security surpassed many traditional concerns. The post-war demarcation of the border increased the likelihood of future disputes because it placed several oil wells, a ship channel, and the major Iraqi naval base within Kuwait. Though approved by Saddam Hussein's rubber-stamp parliament in 1994, the new border undoubtedly remains an irritant.

After the Gulf War, Kuwait gained the distinction of spending more on arms per capita than any other country. Defense spending exceeds 20% of the total budget, and long-range plans project $12 billion worth of weapons purchases by 2004. Nevertheless, it will take years for the tanks, aircraft and missile boats to arrive and for troops to master their use.

Seeking allies from outside the Gulf region, Kuwait signed a defense pact with the U.S. in 1991 (renewed in 2001) that covers joint training and military exercises, as well as U.S. stockpiles of equipment. Similar arrangements provide French and British support in time of conflict. The U.S. and Britain met one such challenge in 1994 by airlifting troops and equipment when Iraqi troops massed near the border. In a rare move for an Arab country, during the 1998 crisis over UN inspection in Iraq, Kuwait agreed to let UN forces use its airbases, should Iraq's defiance lead to bombing selected targets.

After the U.S. and Britain launched air attacks on Iraq from Kuwaiti bases in 1999, Saddam Hussein denounced the country's leaders and denied its sovereignty. Increasingly the country depends on U.S. promises of protection, including from biological and chemical attack. For the long run, many U.S. military personnel desire bases in Kuwait so that families could accompany soldiers on extended tours of duty. American spouses and teenagers, however, threaten the culture and society of any Gulf state. They would inevitably create incidents that could easily antagonize Kuwaitis sympathetic to the West, let alone the Islamic conservatives.

Domestic Politics after Liberation

In 1992 elections for parliament proved honest and even festive. Given the few thousand male voters in each two–member district, the numerous candidates met the electorate at *diwaniyas* (see **culture**) to chat about politics and society. Lacking political parties, voters could chose between candidates sympathetic to the Emir or opposition candidates reflecting three broad groupings: the *Democratic Forum* (secular liberals), Islamic viewpoints, and traditional politicians. By winning 35 of the 50 seats, this "Opposition" dominated the National Assembly. When Sheikh Saad al–Abdullah al–Salim al–Sabah formed his new cabinet, he included six "Opposition" members of the Assembly in important positions such as the ministries of oil, justice and Islamic affairs.

In practice, the ministry proved a debating society rather than an effective instrument of action. A new, more cohesive cabinet took office in 1994, again under Sheikh Saad. Nevertheless, after its first year critics felt it largely failed to address long-term issues common to many Gulf states: a severe budget deficit ($5.6 billion in 1994, some 20% of GDP), an over-large bureaucracy, and government-owned companies that would gain efficiency from privatization.

To no one's surprise, the opposition majority in parliament provoked legalistic wrangling. Some even challenged the validity of decrees issued during the National Assembly's suspension, to little effect. Pro-government and Islamist candidates

A Kuwaiti oilfield worker kneels for midday prayers near a burning oil well
AP/Wide World Photo

won an overwhelming majority in the 1997 elections, but Islamist criticism forced Sheikh Saad to form a new cabinet in 1998, after a minister from the ruling family permitted the exhibition of allegedly blasphemous books at a book fair. The next year, the assembly was dismissed by the emir, Sheikh Jaber, when it attempted a motion of no confidence because free copies of the *Qur'an* had been distributed despite a missing verse. (Since Muslims believe the book to be the uncreated word of God, publishing an imperfect version is more significant than, say, translators overlooking a few verses of the New Testament). The Assembly had passed only four laws in two years.

Displaying a flair for getting things done, in the two months from dissolution to elections the government issued 60 decrees for new laws, including one to grant the vote to women. Constitutionally, all the decrees stood unless rejected by the new National Assembly. In possibly the world's hottest election (118° Fahrenheit), liberals gained seats, while strict Islamists lost. Press reports therefore trumpeted the virtual assurance that the new National Assembly would let women's suffrage remain. However, tradition triumphed instead, and the

Assembly narrowly rejected the decree, leaving Kuwaiti women to file suit in court (on International Women's Day) claiming the vote under a constitution that established equality between men and women.

Beyond its legalism and sometimes petty issues, parliament is significant. Instead of driving dissent underground, it allows discussion of Islamic, liberal, Arab nationalist and other perspectives. Nevertheless, throughout the 1990s, it failed as anything more than a debating society—and one so poorly attended that it often lacked a quorum. Blame for the ineffectiveness no doubt falls on the narrow perspectives of some members, and the impractical visions of others. Roughly one-third of the members have been "Service" politicians, unable to act constructively on anything larger than the pork-barrel projects desired by their districts.

While politicians make easy targets, the ruling family also bears responsibility for the failure. Sheikh Jaber, the emir, suffered a brain hemorrhage in 2001. He and his cousin, Prime Minister Sheikh Saad, came to their positions in 1977 and 1978 respectively. Now in their 70s, they are visibly aging, with predictable effects on their leadership. Because Sheikh Saad is

also heir to the throne, little initiative is expected from the family until Sheikh Sabah, the energetic foreign minister and next in line, becomes either prime minister or ruler.

Following a fatal explosion and fire at a Kuwait Oil Company facility in 2002, allegations of corruption and incompetence in the state's key industry forced the oil minister to resign. However, choosing a successor proved very difficult. Men whose qualities made them desirable candidates rejected appointment to an office with great responsibility but little power to reorganize a bloated bureaucracy often selected for political reasons.

Culture: Kuwait shares the basic culture of its neighbors. Until the affluence resulting from oil production, its population of less than 100,000 wandered with flocks, engaged in trading in the town or worked as seamen on the sailing vessels that plied as far as India and East Africa. Its culture was indistinguishable from that of southern Iraq or eastern Saudi Arabia.

Oil wealth following World War II changed the face of the town and the people. The poverty–stricken *badu* virtually disappeared, as did the Kuwaiti sailors, while poor shopkeepers become wealthy businessmen. Mud huts gave way to air conditioned houses, often of palatial proportions. Before the destruction of 1990 Kuwaitis held the world's top ranking in ownership of many consumer items, from cars to boats to electronics.

Non–Kuwaiti professionals and even workers have benefitted from free medical service, educational facilities and other welfare programs. The educational system in Kuwait is the best financed in the world; students are not only provided with free education, including books and other equipment, but are given at least one free meal a day. Secondary school students receive living allowances.

The University of Kuwait, founded in 1966, grew to one of the best in the region, with the pre–war student body numbering over 10,000. About half of the students came from Kuwait, a quarter from other Gulf states and the rest from various Asian and African nations. The faculty was drawn from Egypt, Syria, Iraq and other Arab countries.

For the past twenty years, women have formed a majority of the graduates at the University of Kuwait. This achievement reflects the surprising roles held by women in the country's liberal professions and business community, and provides the educated women who enable that role to continue. Although Kuwaiti women drive, shop, and otherwise play a much more public role than women in other Gulf countries, politics remains restricted.

In a society without alcohol, and some restrictions between men and women, *diwaniyas* traditionally played an important role in Kuwaiti society. Held in the relaxed atmosphere of private homes, with segregation by gender, these evening gatherings bring together the relatively small number of citizens. In recent years they provided forums to discuss political and social issues, and increasingly seem to take the function of political parties, which are banned.

Economy: Fifty years ago Kuwaitis earned their living by pearling, nomadic herding, and trading with sailing vessels. By contrast, by 1990 they became the only country in history whose foreign investments provided the greatest source of foreign earnings. The key to the transformation was petroleum. After reconstruction, it regained its position as the source of almost all (roughly 95%) exports, nearly half (45%) of the GDP, and most government revenue.

Despite its small size—about that of New Jersey—Kuwait sits atop the Burgan field, one of the largest in the world. The country ranks fifth in world oil reserves, about 10% of the total, slightly below Iran and the United Arab Emirates. Given the small population, a very modest share of global oil output provides one of the highest per capita incomes in the world.

Before the occupation, oil revenues allowed Kuwaitis to live in substantial comfort despite the climate, consuming an average of 22,000 gallons of fresh water per capita annually. While some springs have been tapped, five giant desalination plants provided most of the amount. Brackish water from springs served for street cleaning, livestock watering, and when mixed with fresh water, for irrigation. While any agricultural production was surprising, given wealth and climate, the level of government aid is not. Besides an annual stipend, farmers receive interest–free loans, seeds and other supplies at 50% of cost and subsidies for drilling wells.

After immediate development needs were cared for, in 1966 Kuwait established the Reserve Fund for Future Generations. Its income from oil revenues was to be invested but not consumed until the twenty-first century. In 1990 its assets approached $60 billion, or over $100,000 per citizen. Additional government funds brought total assets to roughly $100 billion. So large were the amounts that the Kuwait Investment Office (KIO) found it difficult to invest the money abroad without arousing opposition. For example, in 1988 it purchased nearly 22% of the shares of British Petroleum, but was forced by the Thatcher government to reduce its holding to under 10%.

Wartime expenses, subsidies to Coalition allies, and the costs of reconstruction reduced the value of assets by $40–50 billion. Other billions disappeared in Spain, where the KIO had invested heavily during the 1980s. Its holding company, Grupo Torras, filed for bankruptcy in

1992, the consequences of more than the world recession. Allegations of embezzlement and malpractice suggested large–scale corruption. Kuwait froze the assets of several officials involved.

Despite the abundant assets, during the 1980s the Kuwaiti economy performed poorly. Political insecurity and terrorism, combined with Iranian attacks on tankers and on rare occasions on targets within Kuwait itself, naturally depressed the private economy. The decline in oil prices and output similarly reduced government income.

The collapse of the *Souk al–Manakh* in 1982 also depressed the financial sector. An unofficial stock market played for very high stakes in a parking garage—half the investors placed over $860,000 apiece in the market, much of the money lent with little collateral by banks—its crash left $15 billion in unsecured debt. For years the banking industry struggled to cover its losses, and a final settlement was often postponed. Nevertheless, by 1990 the private sector showed signs of recovery, just before the invasion.

The Iraqi occupation imposed enormous economic devastation on the small country. The entire oil industry, including all three refineries and almost every well suffered deliberate sabotage. Seeping and burning wells destroyed an estimated $20 billion of crude petroleum. However, reconstruction moved rapidly, and both oil exports and refining resumed in 1991. The pace of reconstruction surprised the experts, and the next year oil production rose to its pre–invasion quota. By 1993, Kuwait's higher exports prompted other OPEC nations, who had waived the country's quota, to demand cuts as part of an effort to balance world supply and demand.

Revenue from oil sales helped fund reconstruction costs, estimated at $20 billion rather than the initial $60–$100 billion. By 1994, many major reconstruction projects had been completed. In the oil industry, refinery capacity had climbed to 800,000 barrels per day, and for the first time revenues from oil surpassed the prewar level on exports of nearly two million barrels per day. However, despite its greater OPEC quota, and oil revenues exceeding $10 billion annually, the government had to borrow massively to fund subsidies, the bureaucracy, and military rearmament.

In 1995 the banking crises resulting from the Souk al–Manakh and Gulf Wars finally appeared resolved, when the government completed buying up the bad debts of local banks, some $24 billion involving 7,000 debtors.

When oil prices set new lows in 1998–99, Kuwait received only about U.S. $8 per barrel of crude, and government revenues fell in half. To cover the resulting deficit, the cabinet promised comprehensive economic reforms, including higher prices for subsidized electricity and fuel. Other proposed

reforms included privatizing some 60 companies owned at least partly by the state, and cutting the government bureaucracy. However, until education prepares students for private sector jobs, cutting government workers clashes with the policy of keeping unemployment low by giving jobs to university graduates.

The necessity for such unpopular measures disappeared after OPEC cut production and oil prices recovered in 1999–2000. While much of the economy remained stagnant, with share prices depressed by economic and political concerns, Kuwait again received enough revenue to continue providing a comfortable life for its citizens.

The occupation raised anew the question of the economic future of Kuwait. It cast doubt on its ability to survive as a workplace for foreigners (82% of the workforce). If the government reduces the number of foreigners permitted to work, citizens will then have to survive with fewer employees and servants. Kuwaiti women, who now form only 2% of the workforce, face cultural objections to their working.

The Future: Though located in a tough neighborhood, Kuwait is now safely protected by alliances with the United States and European powers. Until sustained low oil prices force the ruling family and National Assembly to pass major reforms, expect only minor economic and social changes. Even if the courts or the National Assembly grant women the vote, politics will not change much, due to the traditional and conservative inclinations of many women.

Until that day, Kuwait remains like many customers of its petrol: stuck in heavy traffic, getting nowhere, but comfortable in the luxury oil provides and enjoying one of the world's highest rates of cell phone ownership. However, political reforms elsewhere mean the inhabitants of other Gulf states (except Saudi Arabia) enjoy the discovery of life in the passing lane while Kuwaitis accomplish little.

The Republic of Lebanon

The *Souk el Nasr*, one of Beirut's most colorful markets, with beautiful materials, sacks of flour, exquisite handicrafts, and fresh vegetables—side-by-side.

AP/Wide World Photo

Area: 4,015 square miles (10,360 sq. km.).

Population: Estimates vary from 3.0–4.1 million, the latter including about 400,000 Palestinians. Last census: 1929.

Capital City: Beirut (Pop. 900,000, estimated).

Climate: Summers are often hot and humid on the coast, cooler and drier in the mountains; winters are mild on the coast, but colder at higher elevations with snow in the high mountains. Rainfall is plentiful in winter normally, rare in summer.

Neighboring Countries: Syria (North and East); Israel (South).

Time Zone: GMT +2. When it is noon Central Standard Time in the U.S., it is 8:00 P.M. in Lebanon.

Official Language: Arabic.

Other Principal Tongues: French, English and Armenian.

Ethnic Background: About 93% of the people are identified as Arab on the basis of language. The largest cultural minority are the Armenians, who comprise about 6% of the population.

Principal Religion: Islam (somewhat more *Shi'as* than *Sunnis),* Christianity (mainly Maronite and Greek Orthodox) and the Druze faith.

Chief Commercial Products: Citrus fruit, apples, olives, wheat, potatoes, tobacco, leather goods, vegetable oil, cotton textiles, cement and chemicals.

Major Trading Partners: Italy, United States, United Arab Emirates, France, Germany, Syria and Switzerland.

Currency: Lira or pound, once divided into 100 piasters

Former Colonial Status: French Mandate (1920–1943).

Independence Date: November 22, 1943.

Chief of State: Emile Lahoud, President (since November 1998).

Head of Government: Rafiq Hariri, Prime Minister.

National Flag: Three horizontal stripes; a white stripe is twice as wide as red stripes above and below it. A green cedar tree with a brown trunk is centered on the white stripe.

Gross Domestic Product: About $12 billion (No official figures; author's estimate).

GDP per capita: About $3,000?

The smallest mainland nation of southwest Asia, Lebanon historically connected the interior of the *Fertile Crescent* with lands across the Mediterranean Sea. Over the centuries, ideas, (including the alphabet), the military (the Persian fleet against Greece) and a variety of products made the journey in one direction or the other. After World War II, Lebanon became an intellectual and commercial center for the entire Arab world, but disputes among its peoples—disputes that involved how closely it should link with the West or East—plunged the nation into a civil war that nearly destroyed it.

Four zones run the length of the country, and resemble layers of a sandwich. The first, a narrow coastal belt, sometimes disappears in places where the slopes of Mount Lebanon (a range rather than one mountain) rise directly from the sea. The towering peaks that reach 10,000 feet above sea level mark the second zone.

On the inland side of the Lebanon range lies the third zone, the *Biqa'* (or Biqaa) valley, a plain up to fifteen miles wide. Its rich soil and flat fields provide most of the country's grains and vegetables. The Litani, the only significant river entirely in Lebanon, flows southward through most of the plain before turning sharply to the west to empty into the Mediterranean. The Orontes River begins in the northern part of the Biqa' Plain and flows north into Syria.

The last and easternmost division is the Anti–Lebanon Mountains; these form the border with Syria on the east. Near the southern end of this range is Jabal al-Shaykh or Mount Hermon, a snow-capped peak which in clear weather can be seen from the tropical Jordan Valley to the south. Lebanon has no desert.

The winter and early spring constitute the rainy season. Much of the country receives at least 30 inches of precipitation annually, some areas much more. Snowfall is often heavy in the higher mountains, making the area suitable for winter sports.

In general the population is similar to the people of neighboring Syria in physical appearance, culture and linguistic dialects. In both cases the vicissitudes of history have left a variety of traits.

History: Homeland of the ancient Phoenicians, its strategic location made Lebanon a battleground in ancient times. Inscriptions at the Dog River commemorate conquerors ranging from Egyptian pharaohs and Babylonian kings to Roman emperors. The territory fell to the Ottoman Empire in 1516.

Given its rugged terrain Mount Lebanon traditionally provided a haven for persecuted minorities and it often achieved autonomy under the control of local leaders. Besides the *Sunni* Muslims along the coast, three religious communities populated Mount Lebanon. Two of these, the

Maronite Christians in the north and the Druze in the center, were uniquely Lebanese. In the south and east, *Shi'a* Muslim villagers shared religious ideas with fellow Arabs in Iraq and most Iranians.

During the 17th Century the powerful Druze chieftain Fakhr al-Din extended his control beyond Mount Lebanon to parts of Syria and Palestine, but conflict with the Sultan in Istanbul led to his execution. After years of little change, the 19th Century witnessed greater trade and missionary activity, especially schools. A decade of Egyptian occupation brought greater rights for Christians as well as (hated) conscription. After communal violence in 1860, to protect the remaining Maronites from further massacres and mistreatment, France landed troops, and forced the Ottoman Sultan to grant Mount Lebanon a special legal status under a Christian governor.

As European nations sought zones of influence in the Ottoman Empire, France's traditional protection of Roman Catholic Christians naturally led it to expand its contacts in Lebanon.

When Ottoman Turkey allied with Germany in World War I, its officials seized French documents that compromised

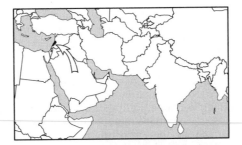

many leading notables, and several were executed. As a further punishment, the Ottomans prohibited the transport of grain into Mount Lebanon, and thousands starved to death, particularly after an attack by locusts.

Secret negotiations during the war (the Sykes-Picot Agreement) assigned the coast and the Syrian interior to France. Thus, soon after British forces liberated the inhabitants from Ottoman troops in 1918, a French detachment landed in Beirut and occupied the coast and Mount Lebanon. However, they did not take control of the Arab-ruled Biqa' valley and Anti–Lebanon mountains until 1920, when a French invasion defeated the nationalist government in Damascus.

While the League of Nations prepared a mandate for the region, in 1920 the French High Commissioner divided Syrian territory into four districts. "Greater Lebanon" included the coast, Mount Lebanon itself, and the entire Biqa' plain. Nearly twice the size of Ottoman Mount Lebanon; its population was evenly divided between Christians and Muslims. In 1926 France proclaimed this the Republic of Lebanon.

Though many Muslim Lebanese opposed the mandate, many Christians favored a separate Lebanese state under French protection. Between 1926 and the start of World War II, occasional outbursts of violence against French rule proved local affairs. The concentration of French military forces in the country discouraged overt resistance. The Lebanese government received internal autonomy subject to veto by the French High Commissioner, while France continued to control international

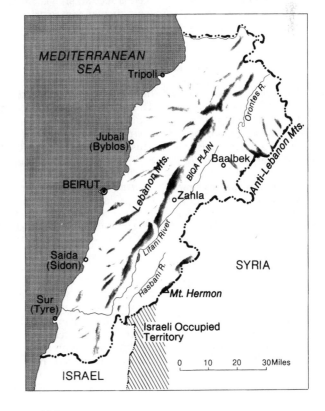

The cedars of Lebanon

relations. Just before World War II, Lebanon negotiated a treaty for greater autonomy, but it failed to be ratified in Paris.

After France surrendered to Nazi Germany in World War II, British and Free French troops invaded Lebanon and Syria in 1941, and the Free French commander afterwards proclaimed the two countries independent. However, in 1943 the French arrested the elected Lebanese president and his cabinet. This united Christian and Muslim politicians in favor of independence, and pressure from Great Britain and the United States forced France to free the officials and grant independence. The final withdrawal of French troops took place on December 31, 1946, since celebrated as Evacuation Day.

Traditional political leaders began maneuvering for the interests of their communities even before the foreigners departed, and formalized the agreement as the National Pact. Broadly revered as the unwritten constitution, this stipulated a Maronite president, a *Sunni* Muslim as prime minister and a *Shi'a* Muslim speaker of the parliament. Citizens of the various smaller religious groups were thus barred from the highest offices (see Politics). Unfortunately, Bishara al-Khuri, the first president after independence, manipulated the political system for corrupt ends and so was forced from office.

During the presidency of his successor, Camille Chamoun (1952–1958), ideas of Arab unity associated with Egypt's President Nasser further stirred the tensions in Lebanese society. The champion of conservative Maronites who insisted that the Lebanese were not "Arabs," Chamoun

saw an opportunity to gain support from the U.S. and monarchial Arab regimes trying to stop Egyptian (Nasser's) radical ideology from spreading.

With foreign money, some reportedly from the CIA, Chamoun organized the election of sympathetic candidates in the 1957 elections, filling the Chamber of Deputies with his men. He then proposed to change the constitution so he could have a second six-year term. This would have allowed him to orient Lebanon to the West, strengthen Maronite supremacy and subdue the opposition.

1958 Disturbances

Dissension caused by the president's actions led to a restrained civil war in 1958. This divided both the country and the capital city into zones controlled by local political bosses and their private armies. Muslims sympathetic with Pan-Arabism and Nasser fought Maronites sympathetic to Chamoun. The national army remained neutral, and used its strength to police danger zones and minimize conflicts.

At Chamoun's request, after a revolution overthrew the pro-Western king of Iraq, U.S. Marines landed near Beirut, ostensibly to support Lebanon's independence from communist threats. Chamoun's attempt to garner further American support for his power play failed, however, and he left office when his term ended.

When the Chamber of Deputies met to select a new president, opinion overwhelmingly favored Fuad Chehab, the army commander. A neutral and less partisan figure, Chehab's term as president was the most successful in the country's

history. The crisis of 1958 settled none of the basic issues facing the country. During the rule of Chehab's successors in the late 1960s and early 1970s, dissatisfactions smoldered, factionalism persisted, the gap between the rich and poor widened and animosities grew. Handicapped by a lack of consensus regarding national goals and the virtual monopoly on power held by a few communal leaders, governments rarely acted positively or decisively.

Necessary steps were not taken. Lebanon was unable to impose fair taxation or finance free public education. Attempts to build a strong, unified army were blocked by leaders fearful that such a force might override their individual communities. In time, solutions might have been found, but regional issues forced their way into Lebanon, and its governments could never formulate a widely-accepted policy toward Palestinian activity within Lebanon.

Neutrality

After playing only a nominal role in the 1948 war with Israel, Lebanon's small military avoided the 1956 and 1967 conflicts. Soon afterward, however, the country became the hapless victim of Israeli reprisal raids against Palestinians who launched guerrilla raids into Israel from Lebanon (see Palestine Authority). Both Palestinians and Israelis resorted to tactics directed at civilian targets, including an Israeli raid on Beirut airport that destroyed many of Lebanon's civilian airliners. Concerned about the reprisals and national sovereignty, but pressured by Arab states and political opinion among the growing Muslim majority, the government proved unable to assert control over the Palestinians.

By 1975 Lebanon displayed many classic signs of society and government breaking down. Assassinations and small-scale violence erupted between rival groups. Journalists were kidnapped. Armed Palestinian units operated freely in parts of the country, scrutinizing—and sometimes seizing—Lebanese travelers at checkpoints along roads and streets. In the atmosphere of lawlessness and disorder, frustration mounted. Slogans of the 1960s, suitably adapted, appeared on the walls, among them, "Lebanon: Love it or Leave it."

Militia and Proxy Warfare

As tensions rose, political rallies increasingly featured armed supporters. Private Maronite militias trained for battle. Most of all, their leaders hoped to regain Maronite supremacy, restore order, and rid the country of all Palestinian fighters. In early 1975 Maronite militiamen attacked a bus loaded with Palestinians. Palestinian forces retaliated, and for 19 months, war engulfed the country and especially its capital region.

Described abroad as a struggle between Christians and Muslims, the fighting was not purely sectarian. Palestinian and leftist groups joined together and though overwhelmingly Muslim, included a few Christians. Nevertheless, many civilians were murdered or maimed simply because of their religious identity.

Foreign involvement added further complexity. Weapons, supplies, finances and advice fueled the conflict. Besides representing a struggle for power in Lebanon, the war was a means of containing the Arab struggle with Israel. To accomplish their national aims, first Syrian, then Israeli (1978) troops invaded parts of Lebanon. In Syria's case initially, the invasion was against the Palestinians as well as other Lebanese. Other foreign troops played a peace–making role, with the United Nations (UNIFIL, in the South) and the Arab League. Neither proved successful. By the early 1980s, however, violence became more infrequent, crossing the previously–deadly Green Line that divided Muslim and Christian Beirut became more common, and some attention focused on reconstruction.

Israel's War in Lebanon (1982)

Chaos returned, however, when Israel again invaded in mid-1982, publicly to gain "peace in Galilee" but secretly aiming, under General Ariel Sharon, to destroy Palestinian military forces and create a zone of influence in Lebanon. The massive assault besieged the capital and occupied the southern half of the country. Saturation bombing ahead of the Israeli advance kept Israeli casualties to a minimum; about 90% of the 20,000 killed were civilians. Material devastation was extensive; nearly a quarter of all the buildings in Beirut were damaged. As the siege of Beirut stalemated, international pressures grew on Israel, and negotiations produced the evacuation of Palestinian forces from the city.

Despite the war and occupation, Lebanon's political system struggled to function. With elections due for a new president, the Chamber of Deputies met, surrounded by Israeli soldiers and Maronite militiamen. Its members elected Bashir Gemayel, head of the right-wing *Phalangist Party* as president. Before he could take office, however, a massive bomb killed him at his headquarters, presumably the work of one of his many enemies, Lebanese or foreign, using a dissident militiaman. Parliament then selected Bashir's brother, Amin, as president, though he lacked Bashir's political and military authority.

In response to Bashir's assassination, Israeli forces extended their control around Beirut. Fatefully, they allowed pro-Israeli militiamen into the Sabra and Chatila Palestinian refugee camps south of the city. There the militiamen sought revenge for their past losses by murdering about 1,000 civilians while the Israeli military ignored the gunfire.

U.S. and European troops were needed to restore order from the chaos. First the troops maintained public order as Israeli units withdrew from Beirut; then they assisted in the reorganization of the Lebanese army. Soon, however, the army became involved in the political and sectarian fighting, and the peacekeepers role became partisan. After a suicide truck bomb killed 241 U.S. Marines in their barracks, the remaining American forces withdrew, and Lebanon returned to its usual war patterns. The president governed the palace. The rest of the country fell under the control of foreign troops or local militias, but some technical departments attempted to function.

The worst violence continued to occur in the south, where Palestinians and just about everyone else fought among themselves and against each other. Central Lebanon, while not free from violence, suffered less. The *Lebanese Forces* collected taxes and imposed some order and administration on East Beirut and the surrounding countryside, in contrast to the near anarchy in West Beirut.

General Aoun Takes Control

When the aging parliamentary deputies failed to select a successor to President Gemayel in 1988, minutes before his term expired, he appointed General Michel Aoun, Commander-in-Chief of the (divided) Lebanese Army, as prime minister. This highly unusual action placed a Christian in the highest office reserved for Sunni Muslims and created a rival regime

Beirut "Paris of the Middle East" before the ravaging civil war

Stylish, bustling Beirut in times before invasion and civil war

Credit: National Council of Tourism in Lebanon

to the existing cabinet because the incumbent prime minister refused to resign.

A straightforward general determined to reunite Lebanon and expel all foreign troops, Aoun first deprived Muslim regions of easy access to flour, fuel, and other imported goods. Then he blockaded smaller ports where militias imported goods and military supplies duty-free and often exported illegal drugs, one of Lebanon's few products to flourish during the fighting. Aoun balanced these measures against Muslim areas by battling the *Lebanese Forces* for control of the Maronite heartland.

Proclaiming liberation, Aoun then turned on Syrian troops around Beirut. Intense battles raged in 1989, with indiscriminate shelling of civilian targets. One million fled; hundreds died, and survivors spent days and nights underground, often without electricity, fuel, or running water. Industry ground to a halt, and most factories were damaged. The Maronite community strongly supported Aoun, and at moments of crisis civilians created a human wall of defense at his headquarters. Aoun hoped for foreign intervention, but although Iraq provided arms, no nation intervened.

Under pressure from Saudi Arabia and other Arab states, in 1989 most of Lebanon's parliamentary deputies met in Taif, Saudi Arabia, and hammered out a new constitutional arrangement (see Politics).

Their first choice to fill the vacant presidency was murdered, but the deputies elected Elias Hrawi, a Maronite, as president. He quickly recognized the Muslim prime minister and gained support from important Maronite elements, including the *Phalange Party* and the *Lebanese Forces* militia.

Civil War Zones, 1983–1990

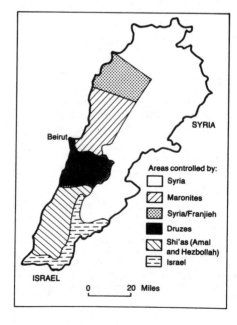

However, General Aoun condemned the entire political settlement because it legalized an indefinite Syrian occupation. In 1990 he attempted to crush the *Lebanese Forces* and control the Maronite enclave in fighting whose brutality reached—or even exceeded—typical Beirut levels. However, protected from Israeli interference by the Kuwait crisis, in late 1990 President Hrawi requested a Syrian attack on Aoun's headquarters. Fierce fighting followed, including Syrian air attacks previously avoided for fear of Israel. Aoun fled, and his followers surrendered, the last major actions of the war that had claimed possibly 170,000 lives.

Joyless Peace Under Hrawi

Seizing the initiative, President Hrawi asserted control over East Beirut and began to destroy the many walls dividing Lebanon. The Green Line defenses came down, and the Christian, *Druze* and *Shi'a* militias started to disarm. The army took over small ports previously valued by the militias for customs revenues and drug exports. Daily life improved, business activity strengthened, funds flowed into the country and schools reopened. The new cabinet included many militia leaders, in an attempt to link them to the success of the new order.

The army moved to regain control of South Lebanon in 1991. Troops entered

124

Sidon and Tyre to public cheers, and they defeated *PLO* units that refused to yield their heavy weapons. However, possibly under Syrian influence, the army did not move against *Hizbullah* units, which continued to attack Israeli troops and the *South Lebanon Army* in the Israeli Security Zone. Israel retaliated. Despite worthy attempts and the release of Western hostages, sovereignty and peace proved elusive. Car bombings occurred even on the American University campus.

The government met little success with its economic policies, but it produced raging inflation. It doubled official salaries despite an empty treasury and printed money to cover the costs. The *Lira* fell drastically against other currencies, so stores and gas stations demanded payment in U.S. dollars. Allegations of corruption forced the prime minister to resign.

Deep controversy arose over elections scheduled for 1992. To proponents, who were often linked with Syria, it was a major step towards peace. A parliament chosen 20 years previously would be replaced. Critics—including even the Maronite patriarch—opposed elections under foreign occupation. Moreover, hundreds of thousands of refugees could not return home to vote safely. Given the electoral system, this meant, for example, that Christian deputies from the Shuf region east of Beirut would be selected without votes of the local Christians because they

had fled years earlier. Finally, opponents feared the results would be manipulated to benefit Syria.

Despite protests, the elections were held as scheduled, although a boycott left the purely Maronite Kisrouan region short of both candidates and voters, so a later poll was held. *Hizbullah's* alliance proved the unexpected "winner," gaining 12 seats of the 128. Despite allegations of rigged results, observers credited these wins to popular support for the party's social welfare programs and attacks on Israel. Because most Maronites had boycotted the election, pro–Syrians elected by Muslims gained most Christian seats. This left the Maronite community isolated, its leaders outside parliament, and consequently the nation badly divided once more.

President Hrawi selected Rafiq Hariri as his new prime minister. Born in Sidon, his business activities in Saudi Arabia had made him a billionaire and brought him close friendship with King Fahd. A naturalized Saudi, Hariri had maintained close ties with Lebanon, supported plans to reconstruct Beirut and provided scholarships to thousands of Lebanese. News of his appointment sent the *Lira* upwards, and as a man expected to give Lebanon far more than he would take, he won support from even traditional Maronites.

Hariri aimed to fight corruption, cut the bloated bureaucracy, and restore government services: schools, hospitals, electri

ity, water and telephone. He enforced discipline on his cabinet, sought foreign aid, and extended army control to the *Hizbullah* suburbs south of Beirut. However, *Hizbullah* retained considerable freedom to strike at Israeli forces and the *South Lebanese Army*.

The prime minister faced three great difficulties: maintaining political support, reviving business confidence, and restoring Lebanese rule despite Syrian and Israeli occupations. Syria, Israel, Iran and other countries continued to manipulate events in Lebanon for their own purposes. Many thousand Syrian troops remained; they indirectly assisted *Hizbullah*, and they provided an excuse for Israel to occupy a "security zone" in the south. The connection with Syria extended beyond military matters. Treaties signed in 1991 linked the two countries politically and diplomatically. By prohibiting media attacks on Syria, the treaties clearly violated the traditional freedom, bordering on license, exercised by the Lebanese press.

The Syrian link alienated most Maronites. Christians saw events such as a church bombing as an example of lawlessness during Syrian occupation, but prosecutors charged the *Lebanese Forces* leader, Samir Geagea, already convicted of murdering a Maronite rival. Many Maronites sensed political discrimination because former militia leaders from other communities benefited from amnesty for wartime acts.

Bleeding Beirut: bomb blast killing 30 people, July 1986

AP/Wide World Photos

The Faraya ski resort—a far cry from the desert heat found in neighboring nations.

The prime minister attempted with little success to mend fences by appointing several important Maronites to the cabinet: the non–political Patriarch condemned a regime that too often ignored human rights, but tolerated corruption and ran huge deficits to pay a bloated bureaucracy hired for patronage and sectarian loyalties.

Attempts to regulate broadcasting stations illustrated the political manipulation. Reform was a technical necessity because of interfering signals from the 38 TV stations and 150 radio stations in such a small country. However, reforms benefited President Hrawi's allies and shut down others, thus symbolizing the misuse of power. Further alienation resulted when parliament decided in 1995 to extend Hrawi's term of office for three years, thus avoiding an election that might raise awkward questions about the Syrian occupying troops.

Lebanon's recovery from the devastation of nearly two decades of war proved uneven and slow. Annual economic growth rates as high as 7%, though impressive as statistics, failed to bring general prosperity. International aid came only in trickles, and by the mid-1990s taxes still reached only 50% of expenditures, and exports only about 10% of imports. Government salaries fell behind those of similar private jobs, and teachers, whose salaries hardly exceed the minimum wage, struck for a pay raise.

In 1996 the labor confederation attempted a general strike to double the minimum wage (to $300 per month), greatly increase public and private wages, and freeze prices. But even a billionaire prime minister lacked the magic to couple such pay

increases with a price freeze. Arguing that such strikes destabilized Lebanon, Hariri used the army to clear everyone from the streets. His compromise solution, higher wages especially for the worst-paid, failed to satisfy labor and angered business.

By contrast, the nation's wealthy anticipated prosperity. Investors, including the prime minister, eagerly bought shares in Solidere, a $1.8 billion company set up to rebuild the heart of Beirut. Funds poured into real estate development, and hundreds of buildings were torn down. As the bulldozers moved in, archaeologists found remarkable ruins from almost every era of history, adding another complication to reconstruction. Rebuilding central Beirut was largely complete by the late 1990s. Prosperity, however, still eluded the country.

Lahoud's Election and the Liberation of the South

As President Hrawi's extended term concluded in 1998, Syria approved the nomination of the Maronite military commander, General Emile Lahoud, as president. Parliament quickly amended the constitution to permit the election of a government employee and later unanimously elected the general. Personality differences led Lahoud to replace the prime minister with a veteran politician. The new president pledged to work within the law, fight corruption (it had obviously worsened despite Hariri's pledge to combat it), and cut the budget deficit. The new cabinet quickly restored the freedom to demonstrate. The most significant developments, however, came in South Lebanon.

When Hizbullah's attacks on Israel's self-proclaimed security zone and northern Israel had sharpened in 1996, Israel responded with large-scale bombardments from land, sea, and air. To force Beirut and Damascus to limit the guerrilla fighters, Israel attacked economic targets, including a water reservoir and an electricity installation in Christian Beirut.

In many ways, Hizbullah emerged the winner. Only a few of its fighters died, and the rocketing continued. But Israeli gunners, deliberately or carelessly, shelled Lebanese civilians sheltered at the UN post at Qana, killing about 100 and drawing international condemnation. Tel Aviv and Washington had initially proposed peace terms that would disarm Hizbullah "terrorists." After the slaughter at Qana, "terrorist" hardly seemed a label for one side alone. Shuttle diplomacy only restored the earlier understanding in written form: no cross-border attacks.

Continuing casualties, sometimes as many as thirty dead per year, led several Israeli politicians to propose withdrawing from Lebanon, and during his successful campaign for prime minister in 1999, Ehud Barak promised to do so. The difficulty, as always, was security: Lebanon and Syria used UN resolutions to demand an unconditional withdrawal, rather than to guarantee the safety of farms and towns in northern Israel. However, Hizbullah attacks continued, and morale declined in both the South Lebanon Army (SLA) and among Israel troops.

Slowly disintegrating, the SLA withdrew from the Christian town of Jezzine in 1999. Meanwhile, the occupation raised Lebanese patriotism through incidents like an illegal land-grab of a different sort. Trucks carried fertile soil from occupied Lebanon to Israel to construct new fields. Another emotional focus was the village of Arnoun, just outside the occupation zone. Israeli forces advanced on the village, but a few days later university students and villagers defied warning shots and stormed the barbed-wire barricades to liberate the village. However, Israeli forces later seized it again.

Abruptly, Israel withdrew from the entire zone in May 2000, months ahead of Barak's deadline, abandoning supplies and equipment in a rapid retreat that saved Israeli lives despite the collapse of the SLA. Hizbullah had forced an Israeli retreat; the war for Lebanon was the only Arab victory in a century-long struggle. The retreat largely ended the violence. Hizbullah had attacked Israel towns and farms across the border. Instead, along the border fence, Israeli Arabs could talk to relatives not seen for over 50 years, and brash adolescents chanted anti-Israeli slogans.

One significant border dispute remained: the Shabaa farms region on the slopes of Mt. Hermon, a few hundred acres that Israel and the UN claim was

Syrian in 1967, though they were claimed by Lebanon historically. Death stalks within Shabaa farms and Hizbullah captured three Israeli soldiers in a sophisticated operation designed to gain counter-hostages for the dozen Lebanese imprisoned in Israel.

Despite predictions of a bloodbath for collaborators, South Lebanon remained calm under Hizbullah control; Lebanese military and administrative control only gradually returned. The SLA collapsed completely. Its members who remained were tried and often sentenced to short prison terms. Others members fled to Israel with their families.

Continued Occupation and Economic Distress

Gerrymandering, manipulation of regulations, and intimidation marked parliamentary elections held after the Israeli withdrawal in 2000. Nevertheless, in a political system where personalities matter more than parties, voters decisively favored candidates linked to former Prime Minister Rafiq Hariri. Despite personal animosity between the two men, President Lahoud reappointed him.

In fact, the campaign rhetoric overshadowed the actual winners. Some candidates openly raised the issue of foreign—meaning Syrian—domination. Even Walid Jumblatt, the Druze leader long close to Damascus, called for a new relationship between the two countries. Clearly, Lebanese across the political spectrum felt that with the Israeli occupation ended, Syrian troops should withdraw and Syrian influence decline.

Responding to such pressures, Syria withdrew its troops from Beirut in 2001, removing an eyesore. However, strong Syrian influence remains, exercised through officials in the Lebanese intelligence services, the manipulation of politics, and the presence of 25,000 troops in the north and east. Perhaps to counter any sense of declining Syrian prestige, the security forces (rather than regular police) arrested hundreds of Maronites on flimsy charges. Although most were soon released, several prominent personalities, including international journalists, were charged with treason for communicating with Israel. Such maneuvering weakens the growing desires for reconciliation and the rule of law.

Probably still a billionaire himself, in his second term Hariri governs a country whose debt of $25 billion exceeds its GDP. Interest and debt repayment exceed tax revenues, so in effect the government runs entirely on new loans, making Lebanon the most indebted country in the world. While appealing to foreign governments for assistance, Hariri took one well-noticed public action: closing the government television station for months and laying off its personnel.

The country's great debt plays a double-edged role in the U.S. war on terrorism. The U.S. placed Hizbullah on its list of terrorist organizations, based on its support for Palestinian groups that murder Israeli civilians and its shadowy links with individuals suspected in hijackings and the 1983 Marine barracks bombing. But in today's Lebanon, Hizbullah runs schools, dispensaries, and public works projects. It provides fertilizers and agricultural advice to thousands of farmers, and clean drinking water in slums. With twelve representatives in parliament, it is a major political force, and across the Arab world it is hailed for liberating South Lebanon. These achievements render Hizbullah too strong for the Lebanese government to challenge.

However, the U.S. clearly desires that the Lebanese government to freeze Hizbullah's financial assets. If it presses the issue and proclaims Lebanon a "sponsor of terrorism," many foreign banks may leave and Beirut's standing as a financial center will be harmed.

Politics: The Lebanese constitution stipulates an indirect election of the president by the single-house Chamber of Deputies (parliament) for a single term of six years. Though not responsible for daily decisions, the president became the most powerful authority, for he could dismiss and select the prime minister, subject to parliamentary approval. The *National Pact* of 1943, in effect an unwritten amendment to the constitution, reserves the presidency to a Maronite (Christian) and the premiership to a Sunni Muslim.

The Chamber of Deputies was enlarged in 1960 to 99 seats, distributed by confession and based on a population census 30 years earlier:

Maronite Christians	30
Sunni Muslims	20
Shi'a Muslims	19
Greek Orthodox Christians	11
Greek Roman Catholics	6
Druze (see Culture)	6
Armenian Christians	4
Other minorities	3

In 1989 the Taif Accord (see below) increased the Chamber to 128 deputies and brought equality between Muslims and Christians. However, it distributed seats for the country's six districts based on political compromise, not the actual number of residents:

Mount Lebanon	35
North Lebanon	28
Greater Beirut	19
South Lebanon	23
Biqa´	23

Within this formally democratic structure, traditional leaders dominated parliamentary politics. Electoral districts followed community divisions, so voters often chose only among candidates of their own faith. This granted electoral success to members of important local families, known as *za'ims*, rather than national political parties based on ideology. Once elected, a *za'im* developed a patron-client relationship, using the political system to obtain benefits for his district and his family, a sometimes foggy distinction. While they clung to privileges for their communities and their class, *za'ims* recognized the benefits of cooperating with leaders from other sects. Alliances might even be formed across the religious divides against rivals of the same faith.

Although opportunism and narrow self-interest marked politicians, and officials often seemed to represent sect as much as nation, for years Lebanon seemed to work. Its politics appeared a reasonable compromise between communities that had within memory fought each other bitterly, and it might have evolved into a more responsive democracy. In the early 1970s several foreign political scientists, favorably impressed, concluded that democracy had struck roots. However, government could be manipulated by a privileged few, most of them Maronite, for their own special interests.

In the mid-1970s, two factors overwhelmed Lebanon's politics. First, remembering distant eras of Muslim domination and persecution, the Maronite community refused to relinquish the presidency and command of the army. At one time the size of the Maronite community justified this, but in later years its wealth and education combined to reduce family size and encourage jobs abroad. Thus the Maronite domination of high office increasingly seemed undemocratic to other sects. Through astute political maneuvering, the Maronites might have

President Emile Lahoud

maintained power for a few more decades, in isolation from the rest of the Arab world. However, intense external pressures removed the opportunity to evolve greater power sharing. These external pressures formed the second factor that destroyed the Lebanese political system.

From its independence, Lebanon exhibited a degree of schizophrenia in foreign affairs. The elite felt linked to Europe by reason of religion and education, but language, commerce and Islam drew others to the Arab world. Nevertheless, despite failures, such as Camille Chamoun's in 1956-1958, compromises were achieved. With the rise of the Palestinian guerrilla

movement against Israel, however, an external force split Lebanon deeply.

Leftists, pan-Arabists, and admirers of Egypt's Gamal Abdul Nasser naturally sympathized with Palestinian aspirations. They supported Palestinian use of Lebanon as a base for raids into Israel. In contrast, the well-to-do feared Israeli retaliation and the impact on domestic politics of any armed Palestinians, even though the Lebanese military could not defend the refugee camps.

In turn, the Palestinian presence brought in other outsiders: Lebanon became the focus of Middle East rivalries. Syrian, Israeli, American and probably

Iranian troops fought one Lebanese group or even several. Other Middle Eastern states armed and funded various militias. In 1974 a satirical magazine suggested that backward and politically unimportant South Lebanon become a "rent-a-battlefield." For the next sixteen years, the entire nation became exactly that.

Despite the civil war, the political system often observed its formalities, though power belonged increasingly to the gunmen. Gradually the politicians who had led the country to independence in the 1940s faded from importance. Their successors, however, proved less accommodating: they often rose through the

Sidon: Temple of Eshmoun. Mosaic of the four seasons.

Courtesy: CNT/Yetenekian

128

ranks of the militias, rather than the compromise of parliamentary politics.

Presidential elections succeeded in 1976 and twice in 1982. In 1988, however, Syria attempted to maneuver the election of a pro-Syrian Maronite. Parliament twice failed to achieve a quorum, as deputies from East Beirut refused to attend or were intimidated from doing so. After September 1988, the country lacked a head of state. Lebanon seemed poised for a de facto partition.

Almost exactly one year later 62 of Lebanon's 73 surviving deputies met in Taif, Saudi Arabia, summoned by the Arab League, to solve the impasse. Christian and Muslim deputies clashed strongly over the role of the president and the Syrian occupation. Under pressure from King Fahd of Saudi Arabia, Arab rulers, and Western governments, the deputies reached a compromise. It retained a Maronite president, but he relinquished important powers in military and national security affairs to the cabinet, equally representing Christians and Muslims but led by a Sunni.

The constitutional compromise divided the Maronite community, now the country's third-largest (see History). Fundamentalist Shi'a groups criticized the accord for enhancing the Sunni prime minister despite the larger Shi'a population. A confessional Lebanese state also conflicted sharply with their vision of an Islamic Republic of Lebanon, ruled by Muslims in accord with the Sharia.

Culture: Though they may be Westernized in dress and style of living, many Lebanese naturally retain their own social values. A more traditional life and dress is found in small towns and villages, especially in those inhabited by Muslims; the culture found there differs very little from that of Syrians and Palestinians.

The Maronite (Arabic *Maruni*) Church is unique to Lebanon. Originated as a distinct group in Syria about the 6th century, the Maronites have preserved many ancient customs in the Lebanon Mountains. Arabic and Syriac are both used in the liturgy; the marriage of priests is permitted, but the Maronite Church has been in communion with the Roman Catholic Church since the First Crusade. In recent centuries, Maronites have been rivals with the *Druze* for control of the Chouf Mountains overlooking Beirut. In 1860, when Maronites were suffering defeats at the hands of their enemies there, French soldiers intervened on behalf of the Christians. Many Maronites, including monks

Front page of a newspaper published in Beirut

129

who own some of the best land, still believe that Western Christians have a duty to help the Maronites gain victory over their non–Christian rivals.

Long before the Israelis adopted the argument, many Maronites presented themselves as isolated defenders of the "values of Western Civilization" among unruly Arabs. However, the continued bloodshed which has been typical between rival Maronite factions indicates a perverse understanding of "western values." In a recent example of such violence, in 1988 presidential bodyguards killed two officers of the Lebanese Forces over some petty dispute. Four days later, two of Gemayel's supporters were murdered in retaliation, following the age–old principle of the vendetta.

The *Druze* (Arabic singular: *Durzi*) are a cohesive community whose origins lie partly in *Shi'a* Islam. Some Christian ideas and practices have also been incorporated into the sect along with unique beliefs. Some of these are secret, and interpretations belong only to the initiated. Besides their stronghold in the Chouf southeast of Beirut, they are also found in Jabal al-Druze in southern Syria.

Lebanese of all religious communities have respected Martyrs' Day, a memorial to the twenty–five nationalists executed by the Ottomans during World War I. In 1995, for the first time, the annual holiday commemorated the sufferings of a much larger group: the estimated 170,000 who died during the 1975–90 Civil War.

The Lebanese value education very highly. Thanks to its mixture of state, private and church-supported schools and universities, the country long enjoyed the distinction of some of the finest education in the Arab world. The American University of Beirut attracted students and faculty from many lands; so did other colleges and universities, helping to maintain Beirut's status as an intellectual center. However, while the government developed a public school system after independence, its teachers or facilities often lack the qualities and advantages of the better private schools.

For many years, the highlight of Lebanese cultural activities was the Baalbeck Festival, held under the stars. Orchestras from Europe and the United States, pop stars, and dramatic groups performed against the imposing backdrop of some of the greatest Roman–era ruins. A wartime casualty, the festival returned to the hearts of Lebanese when Fairouz, one of the Arab world's most famous singers, returned to the stage in 1998. During the civil war, she had refused to perform anywhere in Lebanon, and though a Christian she had remained a national symbol. Thus her return to Baalbeck represented the return of peace.

An even greater cultural challenge is the recovery of antiquities looted from museums or kept privately, contrary to the law.

Officials have seized thousands of works, including mosaics and sarcophagi, but in 1998 Beit Eddin, one of the most famous historical sites in the country, remained controlled by an armed militia.

Economy: In the first decades of independence, many Lebanese prospered from their country's role as a center of international banking and trade. Beirut became the natural location for companies' Middle East regional headquarters. Tourism flourished, transit fees on Iraqi and Saudi Arabian oil helped meet the government's budget, and Lebanon visibly achieved the highest Arab standard of living outside the oil states.

The decades of civil and international war destroyed much of the formal economy. Banks and factories lay gutted, the transit trade collapsed and government revenues plummeted as militias collected customs duties for themselves in the many small ports. Once aspiring to a moderately wealthy standard of living, many Lebanese faced destitution.

The collapse of the Lebanese Lira symbolized the wider economic catastrophe. Worth roughly $0.40 when the wars began, the lira initially maintained its value remarkably well. However, sometimes the government printed money to pay its bills, especially after 1986 and 1992. The resulting inflation drove the exchange rate so low that one lira became worthless. Money, in fact, became cheaper than wallpaper. Similarly, because new stamps in higher denominations were not printed quickly enough, an envelope covered with stamps on both sides might fall short of the required postage. The human effects of inflation have been disastrous. It wiped out the lifetime savings of many people, and because wages failed to rise equally, impoverished most others.

The chaos of civil war provided a little-noticed example of the unacceptable face of unregulated capitalism. An Italian company, Jelly War, shipped thousands of barrels of toxic waste to Lebanon, burying the containers in the mountains or near the sea. Although complaints initially led the Italian government to repossess much of the material, Greenpeace advocates in 1995 claimed that some 10,000 barrels still remained.

The task of reconstruction is enormous. Wartime destruction and neglect proved particularly devastating to the networks of electric and telephone cables, water pipes and sewer lines. Enterprising Lebanese often coped by makeshift arrangements that conveniently avoided payment for the erratic services, but massive rebuilding was required. By the late 1990s government reconstruction funds had reached about $20 billion, and a construction boom brought new housing as well as roads and commercial buildings. Symbolically, by 1996 the capital again enjoyed

electricity a full 24 hours per day, though often through a tangle of wires. However, many of the construction workers were not Lebanese, but Syrians and other Arabs, who formed roughly 20% of the workforce.

In the short–term, poverty and unemployment seem inevitable. Foreign workers receive too little for a Lebanese standard of living, and peace greatly reduced opportunities for smuggling by tough young males previously in the militias subsidized by outsiders. Countries providing foreign aid demand a halt to major marijuana and heroin production, thus limiting opportunities in the drug trade.

Given current exchange rates, Lebanese products should win markets across the region. Unfortunately, Lebanese and foreign investors alike await political stability before risking their money in the country. The stock exchange, reopened in 1995, will help, but thousands remain refugees, often in derelict or abandoned buildings.

Many villagers in the fertile Biqa' Valley in eastern Lebanon discovered that peace brought economic hardship rather than prosperity. Before the war, government policies encouraged sugar beets and other crops. During the fighting, many farmers turned to opium poppies and marijuana, profitable even though smugglers kept the high profits. With peace, the UN and western governments promised financial support to destroy the drugs, and in 1993 the government began to burn fields producing them. However, the promised money never arrived; neither did alternatives such as licenses for vineyards or arrangements for export markets. The barren fields of the Biqa' thus provided a great contrast to the reconstruction of Beirut. Perhaps one–third of the rural population lives in destitution, some even sending their young children to work as maids (as slaves?) rather than to primary school. To no one's surprise, thousands of acres were secretly returned to producing drugs.

The Future: Despite the flashy surroundings of the 2002 Arab summit conference in Beirut, and the Lebanese trait of succeeding against the odds, from many perspectives the future looks gloomy. The Palestinian refugees are not headed home soon, the debt burden on future generations is immense, and corruption rather than patriotism pervades politics.

No wonder emigration proves appealing. The price of land in Lebanon (sometimes $1,000 U.S. per square yard in Beirut's modest suburbs) creates a great divide between those who own land and buildings and those who work for a living and rent housing (e.g., government teachers receiving a few hundred dollars per month). This inequity keeps Lebanese unemployed while poor foreigners (who need not save for a home) do the work for less.

The Sultanate of Oman

Small village in the interior of Oman

Area: About 82,000 square miles (212,380 sq. km.).

Population: 2.4 million, including 400,000 South Asians.

Capital City: Muscat or Masqat (Pop. 870,000, estimated, including suburbs).

Climate: Extremely hot and dry except for the short winter season which is comfortable in most areas, cool in the mountains. Winter normally brings adequate rainfall at higher elevations.

Neighboring Countries: United Arab Emirates (North); Saudi Arabia (West); Yemen (Southwest).

Time Zone: GMT +4.

Official Language: Arabic.

Other Principal Tongues: Baluchi and languages of the Mahri group.

Ethnic Background: Omanis are predominantly Arab, with significant African and Asian intermarriage. Small communities in Dhofar preserve the remnants of older linguistic and ethnic groups.

Principal Religion: Islam.

Chief Commercial Products: Petroleum, dates, dried fish, grain, pomegranates, limes, goats, cattle and camels.

Major Trading Partners: Japan, United Arab Emirates, U.K., U.S., West Germany, The Netherlands.

Currency: Riyal (1 Riyal = $2.60 U.S.).

Former Colonial Status: Independent in the modern period, but under British influence from the middle of the 19th century until recent years.

Chief of State: Qabus bin Said, Sultan.

National Flag: At the pole there is a vertical stripe of bright red bearing the national emblem (crossed swords behind a broad dagger on a belt) at the top; the remainder of the flag consists of three horizontal stripes, white, red and green, top to bottom.

Gross Domestic Product: $15.6 billion

GDP per capita: $6,500 (IMF); $10,000 at purchasing power parity.

One of the hottest and driest countries on earth, Oman lies on the southeast corner of the arid Arabian Peninsula. Facing the Gulf of Oman to the northeast and the Arabian Sea on the south, it extends along 1,000 miles of coast.

Stretching from Sur at the eastern tip on the country toward the northwest, the Hajar Mountains form one of the major geographical features of Oman. The highest part of the range, with peaks rising more than 9,000 feet, is *Jabal Akhdar*, the "Green Mountain." Average annual rainfall on the upper slopes is a modest 20 inches per year, far exceeding the country's typical precipitation of only 3"–4" annually. By contrast, then, the mountains are green.

Between the Hajar Mountains and the sea from just north of Masqat to the border beyond Sohar lies the fertile Batina Plain. It receives some water from streams flowing from the mountains, though inhabitants more often depend on water raised from shallow wells. Nearly all sedentary Omanis live on the Batina Plain, in Masqat or its twin city Matrah, or on the eastern slopes of the mountains.

The remaining three–quarters of the country is arid steppe, with no standing water and scant pasturage for goats and camels. One unusual climatic feature helps a few varieties of wild animals survive in otherwise uninhabitable regions. Sea breezes moving inland bring fog and dew. To survive without streams or drinking holes, animals must lick the moisture off the leaves of plants. In one such area conservationists are attempting to reintroduce the once–extinct Arabian oryx with animals bred in captivity in the United States.

In the southwestern corner of the kingdom lies the smaller coastal plain of Dhofar around the town of Salala. Rising

behind it, the Qara Mountains receive enough moisture during the summer monsoon to support cattle and goats. In ancient times, Dhofar flourished as a supplier of frankincense, the aroma famed in the Biblical story of the Three Wise Men. In the late 1990s, the moist climate of Salala began to attract Arab tourists who found vacationing in clouds and rain cheaper and more congenial there than in Europe.

History: Before the 19th century, the history of Oman was largely a series of tribal wars, interludes of peace under powerful rulers, and foreign invasions, from other parts of Arabia or Persia. Saif bin Sultan, who died about 1711, extended Omani control over ports of East Africa and Zanzibar.

The present line of rulers, who belong to the Al Bu Said family, was established about 1744 with the expulsion of the Persian invaders from Masqat and other coastal towns. In an age when Britain ruled the seas, the reign of Said the Great (1804–1856) saw Oman as the strongest

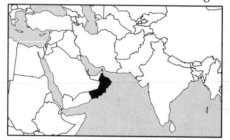

native power in the Indian Ocean. The newly established cloves plantations on Zanzibar and—until curtailed by the British—the slave trade accounted for Said's wealth, along with his active fleet of sailing craft. When he died, his empire was divided between two sons. One took Zanzibar (now a part of Tanzania), where his descendants ruled until the last was deposed in a 1964 revolt by his African subjects. The other Oman, which then played a less important international role. Gradually, Oman came under increasing British influence, though it retained its legal independence.

Sultan Taimur, a great–grandson of Said the Great, abdicated in 1932 in order to retire in India; he left the throne of Oman to his young son, Said, who became the thirteenth member of the Al Bu Said to rule Oman. Unlike his father, Said bin Taimur took to the job readily, though after two decades of uneventful rule, he faced two crises.

The first was a dispute over Buraimi Oasis, which Oman shares with Abu Dhabi (see United Arab Emirates). Saudi Arabian soldiers occupied this collection of villages in 1952, and a Saudi governor took up residence. Eventually, after several years of adverse publicity, Sultan Said reoccupied the villages he claimed with the aid of British–trained and British–led soldiers from Trucial Oman (now the United Arab Emirates).

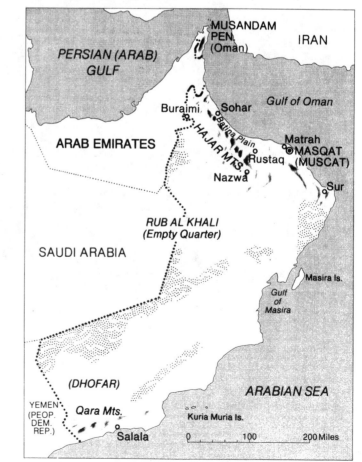

132

A young couple in traditional dress

The second major crisis was an armed rebellion (1957–1959). In addition to the religious title of Imam, Ghalib bin Ali claimed to head an independent state in the interior of Oman, with its capital at Nazwa. Ghalib's followers, led by his brother Talib, received weapons and training in neighboring Saudi Arabia. Returning to Oman, they seized control of Nazwa before the Sultan had time to act. They were joined by a powerful, but disreputable sheikh, Sulaiman bin Himyar, who had ambitions of his own.

The rebellion was suppressed with the aid of British soldiers and aircraft after a few months duration. After hiding on the summit of Jabal Akhdar until early 1959, the three leaders escaped and lived in other Arab nations, accusing Sultan Said of being an agent of British imperialism.

A palace coup deposed Sultan Said in 1970. His only son, Qabus (also spelled Qaboos) swiftly seized power and quickly began modernizing conditions. To symbolize his new policies, he changed the name of the Sultanate from "Muscat and Oman" to simply "Oman."

The scope for domestic social reforms was vast. Committed to preserving the traditional lifestyle, Sultan Said had failed to spend for social good the revenues from oil exports after 1967. The country's sole hospital had 12 beds, and only six miles—10 kilometers—of road had been paved. Fewer than 1,000 students attended primary school; no high school existed. Communications likewise languished, with only 550 telephone subscribers, and infrastructure items such as ports, airfields and public utilities remained primitive. The new Sultan's government attempted to develop all these areas, as funds permitted.

Under Sultan Qabus the country also began to emerge from diplomatic isolation, participating in international organizations and allowing foreigners to enter. Oman was admitted to the League of Arab States and the United Nations in 1971. That same year, diplomatic relations were established with Saudi Arabia, the most important neighbor and a past supporter of rebel movements in Oman.

The first six years of Sultan Qabus' reign fell under the shadow of the Marxist–oriented rebellion in Dhofar, which his father had failed to restrain. Supported by the People's Democratic Republic of Yemen, the leaders of the rebellion had as their ultimate goal the overthrow of all the conservative rulers in Arabia and control of the oil–producing regions. Advised by British officers and aided by Iranian units supplied by the Shah, Omani forces claimed victory in 1976. This freed the government's attention for economic development.

In the 1980s relations between Oman and South Yemen improved, and Oman came to play an important role in the Gulf Cooperation Council. It provided the United States with access to military bases, and during the Second Gulf War fought in the coalition against Iraq.

In 1990, Sultan Qabus called for the creation of a Consultative Council free of official appointees, and thus wider citizen participation in government. Although restricting voting to tribal sheikhs and leaders of religion and commerce, the country held its first elections in 1991. In its initial years, the Council provided a broad–based sounding board for proposals.

Though a member of the Saudi–dominated Gulf Cooperation Council, Oman frequently adopts initiatives in foreign and defense policies. Israeli representatives appeared at an international meeting in Muscat, and in 1994 Prime Minister Yitzhak Rabin flew to Oman for discussions, the first known visit by an Israeli leader to a Gulf state. Radical Palestinian groups and Iran strongly condemned the visit. However, Oman also cooperates with Iran in developing joint oil and gas fields, and sent observers to Iranian military exercises.

Like other oil producers, Oman often suffers a substantial budget deficit because government spending for social improvement and development plans exceeds revenues when oil prices drop. In 1995 it announced plans to cut the deficit to zero by the end of the century, partly through privatizing state-owned companies. However, declining crude oil prices automatically reduced government revenues and made a balanced budget essentially impossible. In 1999 the deficit doubled, and the government responded with several new taxes and cuts in spending. But as oil prices climbed in 2000, so did revenues.

A modernizer of both the economy and government, in 1996 Sultan Qabus proposed a "Basic Law" or constitution that included a supreme court and added an upper house to the legislature, now known as the Council of Oman. However, by the late 1990s the political elite seemed more interested in personal success than the national good. Apparently in response, the sultan reshuffled the cabinet in 1997 to bring in more reformers, and he appointed women to both houses of the Council.

For the 2000 elections to the Consultative Council, the government invited tribal leaders to appoint some 175,000 citizens from the adult population of 600,000 to serve as electors for the 82 seats in the Council. About 30% of the electors were reportedly women, as were several dozen candidates. The previous Council had included two women, a first for a Gulf state.

Conceivably the Sultan, born in 1940, plans to lead the country towards representative government in his lifetime.

His Majesty the Sultan Qabus

However, the succession is not clear: Sultan Qabus never married and never named an heir. The Basic Law stipulates that male members of the ruling family determine the succession within days of his death; if no agreement is reached, Qabus's secret nominee will be designated.

Culture: Oman has one of the highest percentages of nomads of any country in the world. Over half its people spend most or all of the year wandering with their herds. The remainder of the population is divided between farmers and townspeople. In the principal ports of Masqat and Matrah, many Baluchis and Indians work respectively as laborers and merchants.

Most Omanis follow the teachings of the *Ibadhi* sect of Islam. This group may have its origins in the *Khawarij*, a faction that disagreed with Ali, the fourth Caliph of Islam. Many traditions and rituals found in *Sunni* and *Shi'a* Islam are not followed by the *Ibadhis*, who stress the importance of proper belief, righteous conduct and the supreme authority of the Quran.

Through much of *Ibadhi* history, a leader called the *Imam* led the community in both religious and secular domains. He was selected in theory by all believing males, but in practice by tribal leaders. His duty was to rule the true Muslims, i.e., the *Ibadhis*, and force heretics—*Sunni* or *Shi'a*—to follow him. Outside Oman there are only scattered *Ibadhi* communities in North Africa, India and Pakistan.

The Dependency of Dhofar is administered separately from Oman itself, and has communities that are distinct from other Arabians. Most important among them are the *Qara* people, who give their name to the mountains in which they live. Their language is distinct from Arabic, though related to it. They dress differently and have different social habits. They are the only Arabians who depend primarily on cattle rather than on goats and camels for a livelihood. Their cattle are very small, about half the size of usual breeds.

One of the most important recent developments in Oman has been the expansion of educational facilities. In 1970 there were scarcely half a dozen schools. Today hundreds of schools, with thousands of foreign teachers, most of them Egyptian, enroll over 300,000 students, more than half of them girls. Evening classes provide learning for adults. Sultan Qabus University opened in 1986 with a largely Western curriculum, and in 1994 plans were announced for an Islamic university.

In common with many other Arabs, however, Omanis find the study of the humanities, Islamic studies, and the behavioral sciences more appealing than technical skills, engineering and the physical sciences. Around one-half of the university students enroll in the former programs, although the country needs technicians and scientists.

Thanks to the classical music tastes of its sultan, Oman boasts the only professional symphony orchestra of the entire Arabian peninsula. When the Royal Oman Symphony Orchestra was founded by the Sultan's decree in 1986, there were no pianos or violins worth mentioning in the entire country. No Omanis had studied music, and the first high school was only a decade old. British instructors conducted a talent search and identified musically talented children, who today, mostly twenty-something, form the orchestra. Its performances, though considered surprisingly good by Western critics, lie outside the country's culture and tastes, so Omanis generally ignore them.

Economy: Unlike the smaller, oil-rich nations of the Arab Gulf, Omanis acquired a strong agricultural tradition over the centuries. This provides a significant focus for economic development. Even with oil revenues, farming, herding and fishing remain vital parts of the economy; the government, however, no longer depends on taxing produce and livestock to meet its budget.

Oman entered a new economic era in 1967, three years after the discovery of petroleum deposits, when oil exports finally began and revenues flowed to the ruler. After Sultan Qabus seized power, development activities increased rapidly. Agricultural projects improved water supplies and crop varieties for farmers.

The up-to-date shipping facilities at Matrah and an international airport improved transportation links with the rest of the world, while paved roads and airfields eased travel within the country. Electrical generating plants, housing projects, and radio stations increased the enjoyment of life, while modern hospitals and public health programs extended the lifespan.

Given these favorable conditions, private businesses also expanded rapidly, in the retail trade, services, and other areas. In 1989 the Stock Exchange opened, with 71 companies, mostly in services such as insurance and transportation. The pace of economic development attracted foreigners as well.

The highway at Matrah

Like other Gulf states, Oman will face growing difficulties finding suitable jobs for its young. Half the population is 15 years of age or younger, but already some 4,000 youth graduate from high school annually. They often aspire to government jobs that compared with private businesses pay higher salaries, offer greater job security and require shorter hours. However, even by replacing its foreign employees, the government cannot absorb many of the job seekers. In the private economy Pakistanis and Indians accept far lower wages and often fill lower–status jobs. To legislate higher wages for Omanis, or force out foreign workers, means raising the cost of doing business.

Although income from oil constitutes about 80% of government revenues, known reserves are estimated at a modest 5 billion barrels. Peak production has only reached 800,000 barrels per day, and Oman never joined OPEC. However, in the mid 1990s an ambitious program to develop natural gas resources raised confirmed reserves to 25 trillion cubic feet. The government created Oman LNG, a joint venture with oil companies and private firms to build a multi-billion dollar plant to export 6.8 million tons of luquified natural gas annually. Despite financial concerns when a customer in Thailand withdrew from the project, its construction continued, and the first shipments took place in 2000.

Oman also seeks diversification outside the energy sector, and copper is mined, refined and exported. In 1995 Japan promised assistance in searching for further copper and gold deposits. However, though encouraged, industrial output remains small, and large projects to produce aluminum, fertilizers and petrochemicals remain incomplete.

In 1999 the Raysut transhipment terminal was opened not far from Salala. A major deepwater port costing over $250 million, the project was designed to unload the Gulf–bound cargoes of large vessels, then transport them into the Gulf on smaller ships. A direct competitor to Jebal Ali in the UAE, the project will only succeed if it operates efficiently and if major shipping firms prefer to avoid the sometimes troubled waters of the Gulf.

The Future: Political stability seems set to continue, especially because of relaxed relations with united Yemen and the end of the Gulf War. The time bomb of rapid population growth ticks away, and while not critical yet, the problem of creating suitable jobs for the young will assume serious proportions soon.

The Qurum Natural Park in the Heart of Muscat

Courtesy: Embassy of Saudi Arabia, Oman

The Palestine National Authority

CAN THIS FRAGMENTED HOMELAND SUCCEED?

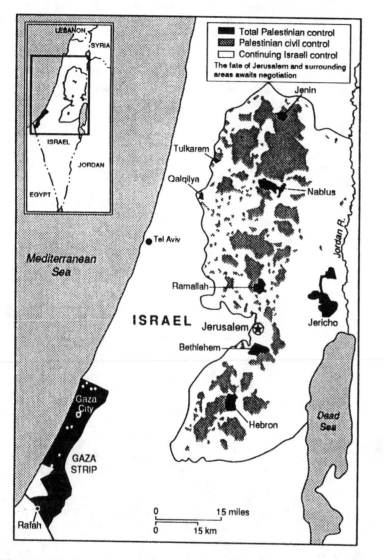

Total Palestinian control
Palestinian civil control
Continuing Israeli control
The fate of Jerusalem and surrounding areas awaits negotiation

Official Language: Arabic.

Other Principal Languages: Hebrew (used by Israeli settlers); English.

Ethnic Background: Arab.

Chief Commercial Products: Citrus, including oranges; olives, grapes, figs, vegetables, flowers, grain, handcrafted items and services.

Major Trading Partners: Israel; Arab states (for oil imports).

Currency: Israeli New Shekel; dollars preferred.

Colonial Status: Still subject to Israeli sovereignty; previously under direct Israeli occupation (1967–1994) as well as rule by Egypt (Gaza) and Jordan after the British mandate ended in 1948.

Official Holiday: November 15, commemorating the National Council's declaration of independence of the West Bank and Gaza, 1988.

Head of Administration: Yasir Arafat, Ra'is (President) of the PNA and Chairman of the *Palestine Liberation Organization* (PLO).

National Flag: Three horizontal stripes of black, white and green and a red triangle at the pole.

2. East Jerusalem and other Israeli–controlled areas

Area: Desired by Palestinians: about 25 square miles annexed to Jerusalem in 1967; other areas near strategic locations or Jewish settlements.

3. Israeli Arabs

Population: 820,000 (1996 census).

4. Refugees and Emigrants Abroad

Population: Perhaps 4 million, 10% living in refugee camps. Major concentration live in Jordan (2,250,000), Saudi Arabia and other Gulf States (450,000), Lebanon (350,000), Syria (300,000) and Egypt (100,000). Such numbers are only estimates, often supplied by those with political or financial interest in the numbers.

Palestinians rule no state, but their National Authority rules many aspects of life for those living in scattered bits of territory not much larger than Rhode Island. Dismissed at one time as stateless refugees who were Arab in culture and nationality, they now claim nationhood.

Arabs historically living between the Mediterranean and the Jordan River, Palestinians unite around a common flag, but divide over most other aspects of a nation–state. Neither sovereign nor the home of most Palestinians, the Palestine National Authority (PNA) nevertheless represents the current aspirations of most Arabs living in the territory. The PNA lacks a capital, and controls no borders, but even the United States recognizes its passports. Former guerrillas incorporated into the police patrol the streets, and limits on the freedom of the Palestinian press come from Yasir Arafat as well as Israeli censors. Such advances toward statehood merit listing the Palestinian National Authority (PNA) among the formally independent states of *The Middle East and South Asia*.

After the many calamitous events they suffered during the twentieth century, the Palestinians now reside under four distinct governments:

1. The Autonomous Territory: Gaza and most Arab areas of the West Bank

Area: Gaza: about 136 square miles, less Jewish settlements. West Bank: Palestinian autonomy in roughly 800 square miles of the 2,140.

Population: Palestinians claim up to 1.7 million on the West Bank and 1.0 million in Gaza. Palestinians consider Arabs in East Jerusalem as West Bankers; Israelis regard the entire city and suburbs as part of Israel.

Capital City: Ramallah (legislative). The desired capital: Jerusalem.

Climate: Mild winters; summers hot (Gaza) to very hot (Jericho).

Neighboring Countries: Israel; eventually Egypt and Jordan.

Time Zone: GMT + 2.

Most who live in the area support minimum demands for a state in the West Bank and Gaza Strip. Two intertwined events or processes since 1988 brought formal recognition to their aspirations.

The first event was the desperate, continuing uprising in the West Bank and Gaza known as the *intifada*. It provided the necessary background for the second process, the sometimes dramatic diplomatic breakthroughs from December 1988, when Yasir Arafat renounced terrorism and accepted Israel's right to exist, and, ultimately, to the Palestine National Authority formed in Gaza and Jericho in 1994.

The likely territory of a Palestinian state lies in two portions of the ancient Biblical holy land. The smaller but more densely populated is Gaza, a narrow strip at the southern end of the coastal plain. The larger region, whose boundaries perplex negotiators, is the West Bank, located on the ridge of hills that rise in the interior between the Mediterranean Sea and the Jordan River. The western slopes of the hills enjoy substantial rainfall that seeps into important aquifers that extend into Israel. By contrast, the eastern slopes and Jordan valley receive little precipitation and appear barren.

History: Civilization extends further back in the land between the Jordan and Mediterranean than almost anywhere else, and human habitation stretches back further into pre–history. Jericho, for example, is one of the oldest continuously–occupied towns in the world. Given the light rainfall, much of the population must have lived outside areas of permanent settlement, herding flocks of sheep and goats. The Biblical narrative in Genesis of Abraham and his descendants, and similar accounts in the Quran, suggest a semi–nomadic life under the authority of a family patriarch.

Some 3,000 years ago two new peoples invaded the lands of the Semitic Canaanites who had inhabited the region. From the desert to the east, the *Bnei Israel*, (Sons of Israel), crossed the Jordan River and seized the central hill region. They spoke a Semitic dialect similar to the Canaanites, and differed from them chiefly in religious matters. From the west, the Philistines, a sea people, landed and occupied the coastal plain. Influenced by the Greeks and others, the Philistines enjoyed a technological (and physical, e.g. Goliath?) superiority over their rivals, but eventually the Israelites managed to subdue them.

Nevertheless, the Philistines contributed their name to the territory for both Greeks and Romans, who successively ruled it. Only briefly was it known as Judea.

Jewish revolts against Roman rule in the century following the death of Jesus of Nazareth led the Romans to disperse religious, politically active Jews from the territory and to forbid that they live there. The handful that remained married into other societies, essentially becoming non–Jews and disappearing into a mixture of many cultures and beliefs. Greek culture and Christianity then united to influence the area in the years after Emperor Constantine, but some of its inhabitants retained Aramaic speech.

The Arab conquest of Palestine (635–38) produced major changes in religion and language. Although the wealthiest Greek families fled Muslim rule, most inhabitants remained, as Christian subjects initially. In the centuries that followed, a majority converted to Islam. With the exception of the Crusades, the chronological record of Palestine differed little from those of neighboring territories (see Historical Background). In 1517 the Ottoman Sultan I conquered the entire region from the Mamluks of Egypt.

The first impacts of modernization appeared during the 19th century, and the first substantial Jewish immigration took place at the end of the period (see Israel: History). Nevertheless, the population remained largely Muslim and overwhelmingly Arab. Only about 10% of the inhabitants were Jewish when forces from the British empire defeated Ottoman armies during World War I and ended Muslim rule.

Arab nationalism grew rapidly during the first decades of the twentieth century, but the Arab Revolt itself took place east and south of the Jordan River. Palestinian Arabs played important roles in the Arab government of Syria. The King–Crane Commission sent in 1919 by U.S. President Wilson reported that both Christian and Muslim Palestinians desired to form part of a united Arab state.

For Palestinians, Muslim and Christian alike, life under the British mandate from the League of Nations in 1923 witnessed little successful development. Hardly touched by nationalism before World War I, many initially espoused a united Syria, independent and Arab. Thwarted by the 1919 Peace Conference's division of Arab lands, and threatened by Zionism, increasingly they perceived themselves distinct from Arabs in Transjordan, Syria or Lebanon. Led, or misled, by Hajj Amin al–Husayni, the Mufti of Jerusalem and president of the Muslim Council, the Palestinians failed to develop pragmatic leaders of the caliber of Chaim Weizmann or David Ben–Gurion. They likewise lacked methods to influence quietly the government in London.

There were other weaknesses. Arab society lacked funds for investment, and because the mandate left many aspects of health and education to the communities, rather than government, Arabs found themselves falling further behind. While material living conditions did improve, dissatisfaction marked all classes. Leading families desired the prestige, authority, and riches reaped from politics by Arab notables in Beirut, Damascus, and Baghdad. The poor resented the domination of an alien government, and all the politically aware opposed a colonial government that promised immigrant Jews a National Home in the midst of Arabs.

Lacking a coherent ideology, the Arab population watched as Hebrew became a legal language of the country. With increasing panic, they noted the loss of Arab land, cultivated and grazing alike, to Jewish settlements. With no difficulty, they realized that if immigration continued they would eventually become minority citizens in a Zionist state (see Israel: History). Often illiterate, and lacking organization, sophisticated spokesmen and united leaders, many Arabs turned to large–scale communal violence in 1929. Although during World War I Britain had promised in the Balfour Declaration that there would be no "prejudice [to the] civil and religious rights of existing non–Jewish communities in Palestine," by 1936, Britain dropped plans for self–government in response to Zionist pressures, and Arab Palestinians turned to a lengthy general strike. When a British commission later favored the partition of Palestine, virtual civil war broke out, with Arabs fighting both the British and Jews. British attempts to restore order included promises in a 1939 "White Paper" to limit Jewish immigration and land purchases, as well as the prospect of eventual self–rule that implied an Arab majority.

From the Palestinian perspective, the British mandate and indeed the entire twentieth century brought unhappy paradoxes. Their identity to many observers was simply Arab, and with nearly two dozen Arab states, a few hundred thousand Arab displaced persons hardly mattered compared with millions in Europe and India. Social changes increased the difficulty. Within Palestine, the Arab population grew fastest in the same urban areas as Zionist settlement: along the coast at Haifa and Jaffa, and at Jerusalem. Thus any partition to create two states confined the Arab state to the relative backwater of towns like Nablus and Jenin, along with the less fertile hill country. Similarly, insecurity, malaria and primitive technology had left only small portions of the soil cultivated. But Ottoman law treated untilled soil as publicly owned, and therefore easily sold by the Mandate Administration to foreigners.

When the mandate ended with partition by the United Nations (1947) and war (see Israel: history), the Palestinians began the flight that divided them into four groups. Historians and politicians continue to dispute, often with bitterness, the reasons why hundreds of thousands of Palestinians fled their homes during the 1948–49 Israeli War for Independence. Interpretations sympathetic to the Palestinians stress Jewish warnings to Arabs to flee, or face outright expulsions. Moreover, on occasion Arab homes were simply demolished.

At one time, Israeli explanations portrayed the flight as a consequence of Arab radio broadcasts warning the inhabitants to move out of the path of advancing Arab troops. However, no credible evidence exists for this claim, and clearly in some locations Israeli troops ordered the inhabitants out. Nevertheless, generalizations are difficult: at least in Haifa, the Jewish mayor urged the Arabs to remain. Often, as the fighting drew near, news rapidly spread of Arabs fleeing, and this must have encouraged families to seek greater safety while they awaited the verdict of battle. After atrocities such as a massacre of Arab civilians at Deir Yasin, and the reprisal murder of Jewish medical personnel, many families must have felt their lives were at stake.

Western nations, including the U.S., maintained a posture of official neutrality during the events of 1948–9. Public opinion, however, displayed an open and growing sympathy for the Zionists. The cause of fellow Jews was widely supported by Jewish congregations in Western nations both financially and politically. Congressmen representing heavily Jewish districts found it best to vote correctly on any issue remotely related to Israel. Moreover, the vast majority of Americans and other Westerners sympathized with the Zionists after the unimaginable horrors inflicted on Jews during World War II.

The Palestinians who fled to refugee camps enjoyed few of civilization's amenities. Despite a kinship of language, historical experience, and usually religion, the governments of neighboring Arab states discouraged the integration of the refugees into their nations. Policies of separation were economically expedient, for the refugees in the camps, usually illiterate peasants, posed a significant welfare burden on countries whose own populations were very poor. Moreover, if integrated into the nation, the refugees by their large numbers often threatened to disturb existing political alignments. Thus, it was convenient for the surrounding states to do little but police the camps, and to proclaim both their existence and distress as evidence of the moral wrongs inflicted by Zionism.

From their own perspective, the refugees themselves rejected assimilation by the Arab states. They argued that they should return home, to Palestine; some, indeed, could see their houses and lands across the armistice lines. Hence any resettlement program, by incorporating them in other Arab countries, would weaken their claim for justice. Although Israel consistently rejected any form of repatriation, for fifty years hundreds of thousands of Palestinian refugees hoped

for their day of return. While waiting, they lived first in tents, then crowded into houses of concrete block and galvanized roofs. Most lacked running water, and the buildings proved cold in the winter and hot in the summer. Often unemployed and always poor, the refugees remained a fertile ground for political agitation. Minimal levels of food and clothing provided by the United Nations Relief and Works Agency (UNRWA) ensured that none starved. Ironically, UNRWA schools, employing Palestinian teachers, made the Palestinians among the best–educated Arabs and instilled in them an intense nationalism.

The West Bank

For those who remained in the West Bank and Gaza, in territory not conquered by the new Jewish state, the promise of an Arab Palestinian state did not materialize. In 1949, after his Arab Legion proved the only force at least partially effective against Israel, King Abdullah proclaimed the Hashemite Kingdom of Jordan, uniting the West Bank with his existing state of Transjordan. In contrast, Egypt administered, but did not annex, the Gaza Strip.

For the West Bankers, the union with Jordan proved difficult. The poverty of their soil remained under Jordanian rule, on occasion complicated by armistice lines that divided homes in Arab territory from fields in Israel. The state's capital, Amman, lay on the East Bank, and although Palestinians widely outnumbered the Jordanians of the East Bank, and in addition displayed higher levels of education and political sophistication, East Bank Jordanians dominated government and the military.

On the chief political issue, Palestinians distrusted Abdullah's relatively moderate policy towards Israel. The majority interpreted his annexation of the West Bank as enriching his dynasty through compromise, while they passionately advocated Arab nationalism and demanded struggle against Israel. However, though Abdullah had tripled his kingdom's population, he enjoyed the reward only briefly, for he was assassinated by a militant Palestinian in 1951. Under King Hussein, his grandson and successor, government moderation and Palestinian suspicion both continued. Most, though not all, investment was concentrated in the East Bank, an astute policy in view of the increasing military superiority of Israel, though naturally unpopular on the West Bank. Progress towards democracy faced frequent reverses, and the Hashemite Kingdom greatly depended on foreign aid (see Jordan: history).

Conditions were materially worse for the Palestinians in Gaza, a strip about 25 miles long and four to five miles wide. The 200,000 refugees overwhelmed the existing population of 70,000, and the dense

population of 2,000 persons per square mile limited agricultural development. With its own underemployed millions, Egypt lacked funds to develop the Strip, and in fact Cairo prohibited Palestinians from the Strip settling in Egypt.

Israel's conquest of the West Bank and Gaza Strip in June 1967 ushered in a new era for their inhabitants. East Jerusalem was annexed, and its inhabitants therefore given the vote, but the rest of the West Bank came under military administration. Though in the absence of a peace agreement officially part of Jordan, which continued some financial aid and salaries, West Bankers grew increasingly separate from it. Their proclaimed identity as Palestinians, however, met Israeli hostility. Flying the Palestinian flag became illegal, along with nationalist activities. Despite Resolution 242 of the Security Council calling for an Israeli withdrawal, it quickly became obvious the Israelis intended to remain.

Moreover they "created facts." This meant establishing settlements on Arab lands, particularly around Jerusalem, at strategic points along the Jordan River, and places where Jewish settlements had existed before 1948. In 20 years the number of settlers exceeded 60,000 outside Jerusalem; their housing, built at substantial cost, dotted the landscape. Israelis came to control about 50% of the West Bank's land, and 34% of that in the crowded Gaza Strip. Jewish settlers also claimed a disproportionate share of water, with the settlers using almost four times as much per person as the Arabs.

The Israeli occupation brought substantial economic changes. In its first decade, the West Bank's annual economic growth rate reached 13%. Commerce and industry expanded, since government positions offered few rewards. Private education expanded, several colleges and universities were founded, and social support organizations flourished to provide mutual aid. Tens of thousands found jobs in Israel, at higher wages. However, by the 1980s, the growth rate fell to just over 3% per year, and given the high birth rate this meant stagnant living standards. Moreover, social infrastructure investment ranging from paved roads to schools and hospital beds failed to grow as rapidly as the population.

Many Palestinians also perceived the occupation as a source of economic hardship despite some improvements. Their agricultural produce entered Israel subject to permits that reportedly protect Israeli farmers from competition. Exports to markets in Europe often proved impossible. However, the Jewish settlements in the occupied territories face no such permits.

Taxes constituted another grievance. Revenues from the territories exceeded aid to them, and the Palestinians purchased far more from Israel than they sold there. Nevertheless, until 1988, the Israeli

Intifada

occupation faced too little resistance to arouse significant negative opinion in Israel, the United States, or generally in the Western world. Third World nations overwhelmingly condemned the occupation, but lacked the means to change it. Thus, deprived of hope in diplomacy to remove Israeli control, or of any fulfillment of self–determination, Palestinians in the occupied territories increasingly turned to direct action.

As the *intifada* continued, the levels of brutality increased on both sides. In the face of shootings and terrorist bombings, Israel adopted a policy of preventative assassination of militants suspected of involvement in violence without justice, often by helicopter-fired missiles. Increasingly, Palestinians turned to suicide bombings, mostly in Jerusalem, but also in Tel Aviv and smaller cities and towns. These events captured media attention across the world; Palestinian deaths often received less attention. They were, after all, much more common.

Economic conditions, never prosperous in the Palestinian authority, became increasingly desperate. Unable to work in Israel, often unable to move from one divided portion of Palestinian control to another, many men and women could not work, and local unemployment rates often exceeded 50%. Families shared what they had, but only UNRWA food

subsidies and aid from abroad (perhaps averaging $500 per person in 2001) enabled many to survive.

In such circumstances, opinion solidified behind the militant opponents of the Oslo peace process. Increasingly popular opinion backed the militants' argument that negotiations had accomplished little, but created a powerless and undemocratic Authority mis-managed by President Arafat. In turn, the National Authority police did Israel's dirty work: the occupied provided security for the occupier. Israel being unwilling to grant Palestinian demands, reasoned the militants, the *intifada* must continue until victory.

For years, many suspected, Yasir Arafat had alternated between his two roles, serving as president and negotiating partner at auspicious moments, but permitting or possibly encouraging violence if that would further Palestinian arguments. Perhaps, in 2001, he attempted to use terrorism to bring concessions from Israel, attempting to keep the territory and power gained by Oslo without delivering the promised security. Certainly Prime Minister Sharon held him personally responsible for the terrorists' bloodshed.

One alternative explanation suggests that whatever the initial relationships, the militants soon escaped official control. Unlike the first *intifada*, this time religious and secular groups committed to the

armed struggle united, forming the *National and Islamic Forces*. Besides *Hamas* and *Islamic Jihad*, this included part of Arafat's own *Fatah* movement, the *al-Aqsa Brigade* of *Tanzim*. Widespread public support for these groups meant that when Palestinian police and security officials attempted to arrest them, demonstrators sometimes blocked the way. In Gaza they even destroyed a police station to free militants caught when Arafat chose to crack down.

Increasingly, the Palestinian security forces found themselves facing impossible demands. Israel and the Bush administration repeatedly demanded that Arafat end terrorism and arrest its perpetrators before significant negotiations could begin. To make those arrests required the police, but the police became particular targets of Israeli fire. Thus Israel effectively destroyed the only Palestinian Authority agency with any possibility of halting the suicide bombers by force.

After an explosion killed 25 elderly Jews gathered for Passover in the spring of 2002, Israeli forces systematically attacked the major West Bank cities in an effort to destroy terrorist cells. Over two hundreds Arabs died, some resisting, others caught in the crossfire, and some the victim of mistake. Tens of thousands suffered hardships ranging from battle wounds to confinement indoors.

Chairman Yasir Arafat of the *Palestine Liberation Organization*

Government offices, police offices and stores particularly suffered vandalism, and estimates later placed the cost of rebuilding at $500 million.

In Ramallah, the Israelis deliberately spared a few rooms of Yasir Arafat's headquarters, but confined him to two rooms, and prevented him from attending the Arab summit that backed a Saudi peace proposal. Thus imprisoned, he regained some of the respect as a leader that his inept administration had destroyed. Another siege took place in Bethlehem, where resistance fighters and suspects on Israel's wanted list retreated to the Church of the Nativity. Weeks later, the European Union helped devise a plan to send the most wanted militants into exile and the Israeli army withdrew.

Fighting at the Janin refugee camp took the lives of 23 Israeli soldiers, many of them in a carefully planned ambush. An unknown number of Arab fighters and civilians, but the numbers were great enough that the military proposed a mass burial for them in the Jordan valley. Moving in with tanks and bulldozers, the Israel Defense Force left destruction so great that eyewitnesses compared the area to an earthquake zone. While allegations of a massacre were not substantiated, accounts verified by Human Rights Watch suggested war crimes did occur, such as the use of civilians as human shields, or the prevention, for five days, of medical assistance to the camp.

Released days later after American pressure, Yasir Arafat later promised reforms, and the first elections to the legislature in six years.

Economic Prospects for a Palestinian State: Beyond the political aspects of Palestinian statehood, several recent studies attempt to predict economic conditions in the first years of an independent state. Given the high birthrate, and the likely return of many refugees, the population of the PNA could surpass

PALESTINE: Partition Plan recommended by the UN General Assembly, November 1947

3 million by the end of the century. Water use for irrigation, industry, and households by such a dense population would

Intifada

place severe pressure on resources, and imply that current Israeli dependence on West Bank supplies must cease.

Estimates of the cost of establishing a Palestinian state run to $10–$14 billion, against $2.4 billion in initial promises, with large amounts taken for housing, investment in business and industry, and expanding the infrastructure. Presumably independence would reduce further the number of jobs available in Israel. Thus it requires greatly enlarged opportunities in the West Bank and Gaza. Likewise, companies linked to the Israeli market would need to shift to other export markets, or find alternative suppliers. Such financial burdens are substantial, and an independent Palestine located between Israel and Jordan can prosper only with large subsidies from other Arab states.

The Future: Put little faith in the latest ceasefire. From the Palestinian perspective, the Oslo peace process is dead. Almost never implemented on time, its provisions led to squabbling over details, while they hid the fundamental principles at stake. Based on international law, these principles include 1) the inadmissability of acquiring land by force, 2) the illegality of settlements built on occupied territory, and 3) the right of refugees to return or be compensated.

Unfortunately for the Palestinians, between 1947 and 1993 demands based on those principles got nowhere, and living conditions actually deteriorated under Palestinian rule, with the frequent Israeli prohibitions on movements.

The kindest and wisest Palestinian leaders recognize the folly of alienating world opinion by blowing to bits innocent Israeli civilians. In contrast, militants argue that honorable death is preferable to living under an occupation that degrades, dehumanizes, and assassinates.

Perhaps it is time for the international community to suggest the outlines of a reasonable settlement. The outside world provides each side the resources to continue the struggle, thus preventing a conclusive victory that would force one side or the other to accept defeat. In the absence of outside proposals and perhaps even police to separate Palestine from Israel, expect continuing bloodshed of 2000-2002 pattern, though the intensity will probably fall. That fighting created heroes and martyrs on both sides, and left to themselves, Israelis and Palestinians would rather increase their honored dead rather than accept a compromise peace.

The State of Qatar

The ultra–modern Doha Sheraton Hotel

Area: About 4,200 sq. mi. (10,900 sq. km.).

Population: Roughly 600,000 - 750,000. About 25% are native Qataris.

Capital City: Doha (Population 250,000, estimated).

Climate: Extremely hot and humid except for more moderate and drier, but brief, winters. There is almost no rain.

Neighboring Countries: Saudi Arabia (South); Bahrain (off Northwest coast); United Arab Emirates (Southeast); Saudi Arabia claims a corridor between Qatar and the UAE.

Time Zone: GMT +3.

Official Language: Arabic.

Ethnic Background: Of the Arab majority, fewer than half are of Qatari origin. The workforce includes large numbers of Iranian and Pakistani workers.

Principal Religion: Islam.

Chief Commercial Products: Petroleum and petrochemicals; iron and steel; natural and liquified petroleum gas. Urea and ammonia fertilizers; some vegetables during the winter.

Major Trading Partners: Japan, U.S., Germany, U.K., France, Thailand.

Currency: Riyal (R 3.64 = $1 U.S.).

Former Colonial Status: British Protectorate, 1916–1971.

Independence Date: September 3, 1971.

Chief of State: Sheikh Hamad bin Khalifa Al–Thani, Emir

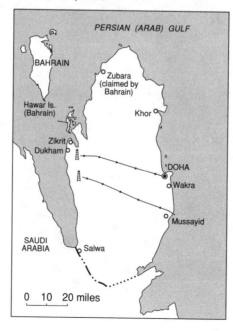

National Flag: An unadorned maroon field with a broad, serrated vertical band of white at the pole.

Gross Domestic Product: $9 billion.

GDP per capita: $16,000.

Qatar, (pronounced *Kah*–tar, stressed on the first syllable) occupies a peninsula jutting northward into the Arab Gulf from the mainland of Arabia. It is little more than 100 miles long and varies from 35 to 50 miles in width. The terrain is almost entirely a barren desert of gravel, rock and sand. Sources of fresh water are extremely scarce. Aside from a few date palms and agricultural experimental stations, little vegetation is found except hardy desert scrub.

History: The earliest settlements in the Stone Age show that humans who lived in Qatar looked to the sea for their livelihoods. Fishermen who traded some goods with the outside world, they shared a common culture with other societies along the coast of Arabia. Early pottery discovered in Qatar bears the design found as far north as the city of Ur in present Iraq. These two fundamentals—the sea for

142

livelihood and a shared culture in the region—influenced life in Qatar for the next 5,000 years.

Given its meager water supplies, Qatar played no significant role in the region's conquests, whether by Alexander the Great's navy, Muslim Arabs nine hundred years later, or Persian rulers in between. However, archaeological evidence suggests that during the Muslim Abbasid era (9th century) the inhabitants used their greater wealth, perhaps from selling pearls, to construct better homes and public buildings. When the Abbasid prosperity declined in Iraq, so did the population of Qatar. By the 13th century an Arab geographer considered it just a village.

After Portugal's brief predominance ended in the Gulf, in the 18th century Safavid Persia claimed the area, and records exist of coastal communities paying royalties for their pearling activities. However, in 1793, the villagers of Qatar provided refuge to those fleeing from *Wahhabi* conquests, and two years later the Saudi forces besieged and captured the important fort of Zubara. In 1809 the Saudis appointed a governor, but within a decade the invasion of Arabia by Muhammad Ali of Egypt destroyed the Saudi state (see Saudi Arabia: history).

Confusion and a lack of order marked much of the 19th century. After raids by Gulf towns on each other and attacks on merchant shipping, in 1820 Britain reached a general treaty with most Gulf ports that established a regional truce. Lacking an established ruler, Qatar did not sign the document, and in the 1860s warfare broke out with its traditional rival, Bahrain, whose forces razed Qatar's largest town, Doha. Following inconclusive fighting in 1868 between Qataris and Bahrain, Britain negotiated a settlement with Muhammad bin Thani, a leading tribal leader, whose authority gradually spread to the entire peninsula.

In the 1870s, Ottoman Turkish troops landed, and appointed Muhammad's son Qasim as the local administrator. However, Qasim later fought with an Ottoman detachment, and the revival of the Saudi state led him and most of the population to embrace *Wahhabism*. Thus by the early 20th century, four states desired to influence the territory: Bahrain, the Saudis, the Ottoman Empire and Great Britain. Despite the rivalries, Qatari pearling activities probably reached their zenith, with hundreds of pearling boats carrying nearly 13,000 crew and divers.

After World War I began, the Ottoman detachment withdrew from Doha in 1915. The next year's Anglo–Qatari treaty ended nearly a century of legal limbo. It established British influence as paramount, gave protection to the pearling fleet, and forbade the slave trade. However, existing slaves were not set free, because fewother work opportunities existed for these household workers. Essentially Qatar was allowed to govern itself under the Al-Thani (this Al translates "family" instead of al-, meaning "the"). Economically, socially, and culturally it remained almost completely undeveloped, with virtually no medical facilities and only one modern grade school.

The 1930s proved devastating for Qataris. World demand for jewelry fell greatly during the Great Depression, while the Japanese discovery of the method of raising cultured pearls meant devastating competition and sharply falling prices. In 1935 another agreement with Britain formalized British protection and granted the (British) Anglo–Persian Oil Company exclusive rights to search for oil. Although Anglo–Persian discovered commercial deposits in 1939, World War II prevented development of the oil fields, and exports only began a decade later.

Oil changed Qatari society. If the ruling family inevitably squandered some of the new wealth from oil, it nevertheless financed roads, schools and hospitals with British advice. A shortage of local labor, unskilled as well as skilled, led to a steady influx of workers and professionals from other Arab and Muslim nations. Soon Qataris found themselves a minority in their country.

With British withdrawal on the horizon, Qatar began in 1968 to discuss federation with Bahrain and the seven sheikhdoms of Trucial Oman (see United Arab Emirates). However, old rivalries stirred distrust, and satisfactory terms could not be reached. Qatar then proclaimed its separate independence and it immediately became a member of the League of Arab States and the United Nations.

As independence neared in 1970, the Emir, Sheikh Ahmad bin Ali, approved a basic law for the state. While no charter of democracy, this included a bill of rights and provided for both a Council of Ministers and an Advisory Council—all appointed by the ruler himself. Soon after independence, a more cautious and hard-working cousin, Sheikh Khalifa bin Hamad, deposed Sheikh Ahmad because he squandered financial resources. The ruling family and most Qataris approved the change.

The new Emir energetically began to use the country's oil income for economic development, including steel and fertilizer projects. He appointed an Advisory Council in order to hear opinions outside the ruling family, and contributed significantly to Palestinian and other Arab causes.

H. H. Sheikh Hamad bin Khalifa Al–Thani of Qatar (left) with Kuwaiti leader Sheik Jaber Bin Salem Al-Sabah
Courtesy: Embassy of Saudi Arabia

An exciting and highly competitive camel race across the desert

Given the then insignificant value of uninhabited coral reefs and expanses of desert, parts of Qatar's boundaries were not clearly demarcated during British rule. In 1986 a dispute with Bahrain heated up over Hawar Island, one such outcropping of reef whose possession includes sovereignty over potential oil deposits (see Bahrain). Failing to obtain a settlement mediated in the Middle East, Qatar applied to the International Court of Justice in The Hague for a ruling on the dispute. In 2001 it ruled that Hawar was indeed Qatari territory, but that the town of Zubara belonged to Qatar. Both sides accepted the ruling.

The territorial dispute with Bahrain led to a minor arms race between the two countries in 1987–88. After Bahrain purchased Stinger surface–to–air missiles from the United States, Qatar also displayed one of the missiles in a military parade. However, Qatar's Stinger missiles had not been obtained from the United States, but apparently from Iranian Revolutionary Guards, who themselves had purchased or seized them from Afghan *mujahidin* armed by the United States. Despite American pressure, Qatar refused to return the missiles to the United States, where a check of the serial numbers would enable them to be traced. The incident carried broader implications for Qatari foreign policy, for in the months following Qatar established diplomatic relations with the Soviet Union, China and Cuba.

A member of the Gulf Cooperation Council, Qatar joined the multinational Coalition to liberate Kuwait. Its forces fought in the first Coalition ground victory of the war, defeating an Iraqi attack on the Saudi city of Khafji. Nevertheless, in 1992 Saudi border guards allegedly attacked a border post, and Qatar revoked a 1965 border agreement. Details of the incident remain murky, for the post may have been caught in fighting between rival Bedouin groups.

The border dispute served to illustrate Qatar's increasingly independent foreign policy. In 1991 Iran agreed to supply it with fresh water from the Karun river, piped through a scheme costing billions of dollars. Of all the GCC states, Qatar also maintained the closest diplomatic contacts with Baghdad and showed its sympathy by donating sugar.

After years as the head of government, in 1995 Sheikh Hamad overthrew his father, Sheikh Khalifa Al–Thani. Much younger than many Gulf rulers, Sheikh Hamad displayed a distinctively independent foreign policy. Though agreeing to base U.S. equipment in the state and host visits by Israeli officials, he expressed sympathy with both Iraq and Iran.

Relations with other GCC states worsened when Sheikh Hamad walked out of a summit meeting to protest an appointment. Later, Qatar hinted that neighboring countries had supported a failed attempt by Sheikh Khalifa to regain power, and broadcast interviews with Bahraini dissidents.

After surviving a counter–coup, Sheikh Hamad took initiatives in both domestic and international politics. He reduced press censorship and encouraged media discussion of serious issues such as the role of women. Qatar's Al–Jazeera satellite TV station broadcast sophisticated critiques and interviews, including some of Saddam Hussein's attacks on Arab rulers. Although several Arab states shut down Al–Jazeera's offices, surveys indicated that audiences enjoyed its fresh approach.

Along with greater freedom of speech, Sheikh Hamad instituted political reforms. Municipal elections proved a success with the voters, and six women ran for office, though they did not win. Current proposals call for a constitution and elected parliament, a level of democracy only enjoyed by Bahrainis and male Kuwaitis on the Arab side of the Gulf. Hamad also emphasized the separation of family and state finance and designated his third son, Sheikh Jassin, as Crown Prince.

In economic affairs, the government extended a number of financial benefits to Qataris working in the private sector, to reduce the advantage of working for the state. Both the government and private companies continued to invest heavily in the petroleum and natural gas industries (see Economy).

Internationally, Sheikh Hamad moved to improve relations with other Arab leaders and the United States while criticizing U.S. policy toward Iraq and Iran. Despite the opposition of many Arab states, he hosted the 1997 Middle East economic summit that brought together Israelis, Arabs, and international business executives.

While the government of Qatar condemned terrorism following the September 11 massacres in the United States, Al-Jazeera's journalistic independence brought it exclusive interviews with Osama bin Ladin. After the U.S. attacked Afghanistan, the *Taliban* expelled all other foreign correspondents. However, such journalistic initiative, combined with extensive coverage of the Palestinian uprising, often represented an Arab viewpoint unappreciated in Western countries. The U.S. officially criticized the station's coverage, arguing that broadcasting the interviews encouraged sympathy with terrorism, and pressured Sheikh Hamad to reduce such coverage. Apparently he refused, politely.

Culture: Traditional ways of living changed drastically in Qatar as people became accustomed to the mechanical conveniences and processed food of the industrialized world. Social values are also in a state of rapid change, particularly with the expansion of free and compulsory education up to the age of 16.

Qatar is the only country besides Saudi Arabia with a sizeable *Wahhabi* community. As most Qataris (but few of the new residents) follow *Wahhabi* practices, strong official ties traditionally linked the state with Saudi Arabia.

Like most Arab countries, Qatar's school system provides six years of elementary school, three preparatory, and three secondary. More than 50,000 children and young people enroll in this twelve–year system. There are also technical schools, a teacher–training school and a religious institute. The University of Qatar, completed in 1985, has an enrollment of about 4,000.

Economy: Though the traditional Arab lifestyle of nomadic herding existed for centuries in Qatar, culturally and economically the most important industry was pearling. In the relatively shallow waters surrounding the peninsula, mollusks grew thickly enough to permit a flourishing trade involving hundreds of boats and at its peak over 13,000 crew and divers. Life aboard the pearling vessels was difficult, for the sailboats would be gone most of the summer. With no underwater supply of air, most divers sought banks of oysters at depths of about 50 feet, descending rapidly and returning to the surface within a minute. The most daring might descend 80 feet, but breathing and other health problems were not uncommon.

The international price of pearls climbed rapidly after the 1870s, and an economic system developed to finance pearling expeditions. However, in the 1930s the Japanese development of cultured pearls undercut the industry in Qatar and elsewhere in the Gulf to devastating effect.

After the discovery of oil in Bahrain and Saudi Arabia, it was not surprising that the Anglo-Persian Oil Company (ancestor of today's British Petroleum) found commercial deposits in Qatar. Thanks to its deep port, Umm Said became the center of petroleum operations and industry, with the result that although Qatar today is relatively industrialized in terms of output, industry is concentrated in a relatively small area. By 1973 annual production of crude oil from offshore fields surpassed that from wells on the peninsula.

In the 1970s the great increases in the price of oil provided Qatar with enormous wealth. Some of those funds enabled the state to buy out the equity of foreign firms and by 1977 all production came under the government-owned Qatar General Petroleum Company (QGPC). The 1980s proved less favorable, with declining oil prices along with lower production quotas from the Organization of Petroleum Exporting Countries. Exports fell by millions of dollars per day.

To compensate, the QGPC invested heavily in exploration and production, and the government invited foreign firms to return. By 1998, output reached about 600,000 barrels per day, far above Qatar's OPEC quota. Thanks to the small population, Gross Domestic Product per capita still remained respectable by international standards, and among the highest in the Arab world. Moreover, when the economy entered recession, Qatar could send home laid–off workers, since roughly 70% of the labor force in private industry came from abroad.

Declining tax revenues from oil naturally required cuts in government expenditures, for spending far exceeded income. The 1988–89 budget, for example, proposed a deficit equaling almost $5,000 per inhabitant—an amount roughly five times the celebrated U.S. budget deficit. However, high oil prices, greater production, and fiscal discipline later reduced the deficit.

By the late 1990s, a policy diversification away from petroleum had been in effect for a decade. Exports of steel, fertilizers and other petrochemicals partly offset the decline in oil revenues. In 1997, Qatar shipped its first exports of Liquified Natural Gas (LNG). The source of the state's future prosperity, natural gas deposits promise to surpass petroleum in importance. The North Shore gas field below the waters of the Gulf is enormous, with reserves estimated at 150,000 billion cubic feet, the equivalent of 30 billion barrels of oil. The largest field in the world, the North Field helps make the country third in proven reserves, behind Russia and Iran.

Both local industry and exports will benefit from the abundant resource. The highly energy-intensive smelting of aluminum provided a logical outlet, as did petrochemical products. Qatar is becoming the Middle East's largest producer of ammonia and urea fertilizers, with export markets in India, China and Japan.

With two LNG plants in operation, both the country and the major corporations acting as its partners have plunged deeply into debt to develop an industry that might cost a total of $25 *billion*, or about

Qatari woman weaving intricately designed heavy rugs

145

$150,000 per Qatari. More distantly, plans exist to export gas through a pipeline to Pakistan and perhaps to India. Revenues from these projects will gradually replace lost income from oil, for at the production levels of the late 1990s, Qatar's oil reserves will collapse in the next decade.

One of the surprises has been in the development of desert agriculture. Although only about 3% of the land is cultivated, Qatar is now self–sufficient in vegetables in the winter rainy season, but still must import about half its needs during the dry summer.

The Future: Careful planning and development made Qatar a very stable state where social unrest is limited and political violence is unknown. Though not yet as democratic as Kuwait, under Sheikh Hamad it continues to develop both politically and economically.

Doha, Quatar

Courtesy: Embassy of Saudi Arabia

The Kingdom of Saudi Arabia

Masmak Fortress Riyadh

Courtesy: Embassy of Saudi Arabia

Saudi Arabia

Area: About 850,000 square miles (2,200,000 sq. km.).

Population: 20.8 million; estimates range from 18.5 to 22 million (2000).

Capital: Riyadh (Pop. 3.5 million, estimated).

Climate: Generally very hot and dry, but humid on coasts; at higher elevations nights are cool. Rain is negligible except in highlands of the southwest part of the country.

Neighboring countries: Jordan (Northwest); Iraq (North); Kuwait (Northeast); Qatar (East); United Arab Emirates (East); Oman (Southeast); Yemen (South).

Time Zone: GMT +3. Solar time, calculated daily from sunset, is used for religious purposes.

Official Language: Arabic.

Other Principal Tongues: English, taught as foreign language in some schools.

Ethnic Background: Generally identified as Arab, including dark–skinned communities found in coastal towns.

Religion: Islam (officially 100%, except for foreign residents).

Chief Commercial Products: Petroleum, dates, salt, gypsum, cement, wool, grain, hides, fish, chemical fertilizers, plastics and steel.

Major Trading Partners: U.S., Japan, France, Italy, Germany, Netherlands.

Currency: Riyal (R 3.75 = $1 U.S.).

Former Political Status: Ottoman rule in the west; British advisors in the east.

National Day: Only religious holidays are officially observed.

Chief of State: Fahd ibn Abd al–Aziz Al–Saud, King and Prime Minister.

Leading Royal Aide: Crown Prince Abdullah ibn Abd al–Aziz Al–Saud, Deputy Prime Minister.

National Flag: The Islamic creed in ornate Arabic script is written in white on a green field; beneath the writing is a horizontal sword, also in white.

Gross Domestic Product: $140 billion

GDP per capita: $7000.

Covering more than two–thirds of the Arabian Peninsula, Saudi (pronounced phonetically *Sah–udi*) Arabia is one of the bleakest desert countries in the world. It has no rivers, no perennial streams and no lakes. Most of its total surface is rock, gravel or sand. Less than 1% of the land has enough natural moisture for agriculture of any kind. There are no real forests at all; only sparse desert plants survive. Nearly one–third of the area is used seasonally as scrub brush grazing land.

From west to east, the country's terrain begins in the Hijaz, with a coastal plain along the Red Sea. From Jordan in the north to Yemen in the south, a chain of mountains then rises steeply. With peaks ranging up to 10,000 feet in the southern

section, the mountains catch some precipitation and allow limited agriculture. Further inland, the land slopes down gradually toward the Persian (Arab) Gulf. The central region, known as *Najd* ("steppe"), receives only two or three inches of rainfall annually, while much of the southern area receives none at all in most years.

Known as the *Rub' al–Khali,* or "Empty Quarter," the south contains virtually no permanent habitation, but the largest stretch of sand in the world. It is a region of giant, endless sand dunes, often several hundred feet high and miles in length; eternally shifting, pushed by the hot desert winds. Finally, along the Gulf coast lies the Eastern Province, Hasa, with a hot, humid climate and abundance of oil.

History: A land of nomadic tribes and scattered oasis settlements, Arabia was

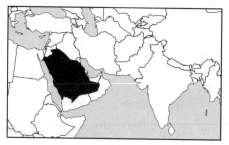

never united until Muhammad proclaimed his prophetic messages and established an Islamic government with its capital at Medina (see Historical Background). However, after Ali, the fourth caliph, moved the capital to Iraq, Arabia lost much of its political importance, though Mecca and Medina played significant religious roles.

When the later caliphs in Damascus and Baghdad lost control of the united Muslim world, most of Arabia returned to tribal rule. Outside influence was greatest in the West, where Ottoman sovereignty was proclaimed in the 1500s.

The origins of the present kingdom lie in the 17th century when Muhammad ibn Saud, leader of a desert tribe in Najd, accepted the teaching of Muhammad ibn Abd al–Wahhab. After study in Damascus and Baghdad, Abd al–Wahhab had become convinced of the need to reform and purify Muslim society, both of the pagan practices remaining among the Bedouin and the philosophical and secular influences in the cities.

Strengthened by the appeal of these teachings, known to Westerners as Wahhabism, Saudi troops and Wahhabi believers conquered and converted large parts of central Arabia and raided north into Syria during the 18th century. While the Ottoman

Abd al–Aziz Al–Saud, King of Saudi Arabia, 1932–53

Empire was preoccupied with problems elsewhere during the Napoleonic wars, the Wahhabis conquered the Hijaz, thus seizing from the Ottoman Sultan the holy places of Mecca and Medina that he claimed to protect. However, the Wahhabis had overextended, and the troops of Muhammad Ali, the ruler of Egypt, ended Wahhabi control over the Hijaz and even destroyed the Saudi capital. Although later Saudi rulers recovered much of central Arabia, in the 1860s civil war divided members of the Saud family. Rival Arab rulers encroached on Saudi lands, and Ottoman troops seized territory along the Gulf.

By 1902 the exiled heir to leadership was a 22–year–old named Abd al–Aziz Al–Saud (*Al* in Arabic means "House," or "Family;" it is written differently from *al–*, meaning "the"). He undertook a daring mission to restore family fortunes. With only a handful of followers, he left Kuwait and seized Riyadh from the rival family of Rashid, based in the town of Hayil to the north.

A tall and powerful man with a natural gift for leadership, Abd al–Aziz increased his following and gradually enlarged the area of his control by warring with rival tribes. In 1913 he conquered the eastern coastal district of Hasa from the Ottoman Turks, not knowing that years later the oil under its sands would make him one of the world's wealthiest men. At the beginning of World War I, Abd al–Aziz promised the British that he would not join the Turks against England in the war; for this he was rewarded with $25,000 a year.

Abd al–Aziz captured Hayil in 1921 from the rival family of Rashid. The dominant leader in central Arabia, he still faced one irritating rival, Sharif Husayn (Hussein), king of the Hijaz, who had won British support by rising against the Turks. However, Husayn by many accounts was a difficult character, and harbored great ambitions for his dynasty. In pursuit of them, he adopted the title "King of the Arabs" and hinted at proclaiming himself caliph, thereby outraging Arabs of many different backgrounds.

Abd al–Aziz's followers, the militant *Ikhwan* ("Brotherhood") who relinquished tribal loyalties for Wahhabism, were eager to cleanse the holy cities of Mecca and Medina from what in their eyes were sacrilegious traditions added by men to the pure faith. At the end of 1924 the *Ikhwan* entered Mecca and within a year took Medina also. In early 1926 Abd al–Aziz was proclaimed "King of Hijaz." By 1932 the various parts of his domain were joined into the Kingdom of Saudi Arabia.

Relatively satisfied with his conquests and limited in the northeast and northwest by Sharif Husayn's sons who ruled Transjordan and Iraq with British support, King Abd al–Aziz turned to consolidating and building the country he ruled. Unhampered by a constitution or democracy, King Abd al–Aziz's autocracy nevertheless faced limits from the Wahhabi religious leaders as well as the ruling family, enlarged by his marriages to daughters of tribal leaders. Moreover, the kingdom was poor: for many years pilgrims visiting the Hijaz were the economic mainstay.

The discovery of oil in Hasa in 1938 marked the beginning of a new era in Saudi Arabia, but the production and export of oil was interrupted during World War II. Pilgrims could not visit the holy cities during the war. Saudi Arabia's government would have been bankrupt and probably would have collapsed except for monetary grants and loans made by Britain and the United States.

After the war, the aging Abd al–Aziz was unable to take care of the kingdom he had created and ruled almost single-handedly. As oil revenues began to pour into the country, his numerous sons and relatives squandered millions of dollars monthly and government descended to such a level that every transaction involved the payment of suitable bribes to officials.

The old king died in 1953 and was succeeded by his eldest son, Saud. Lacking his father's qualities, he failed to grasp the challenges of the modern world. The small signs of progress that did occur were introduced largely because of the criticism and ridicule the country received from more advanced Arab states.

A Council of Ministers was formed, though all important posts went to members of the royal family. Public education was begun, but it was far from democratic and efficient. During a financial crisis in 1958, precipitated by irresponsible overspending, as well as by a political crisis with the United Arab Republic (Egypt–Syria), King Saud was persuaded to permit his brother, Prince Faisal, to take charge of government affairs.

Faisal had gained valuable experience as a representative at the United Nations and through travel abroad; he was supported by those in the country who were clamoring for modernization. Up until that time all government funds were treated as the personal property of the King, so the introduction of a financial system with a government budget and an allowance to members of the royal family was one of the important innovations of Faisal's management of affairs. The waste of money by royal princes was greatly reduced, but not entirely ended.

King Saud reasserted personal control again in 1960. While he did continue the financial regulations introduced by Faisal, he did little else to help the nation progress from the primitive stage in which it still remained. Again in 1962, under strong pressure, Saud permitted Faisal to take complete control of the government; when Saud again tried to assert himself there was a struggle within the royal family from which Faisal emerged victorious. He was proclaimed King on November 2, 1964, and his elder brother departed for Europe. Saud died of a heart attack in 1969.

Reforms under Faisal

Faisal's reign achieved gradual reforms. He greatly increased the budgets for education, medical care and transportation facilities. His government made little effort to promote social change and rejected many aspects of westernization. It refused to allow free political expression or formal public participation in government. The traditional Saudi social system spread responsibility over a large number of relatives, and politically it provided access to the royal family for even the poorest citizen. Rather than replace these features, Faisal worked to render them more honest and efficient.

In international affairs, Faisal firmly opposed the influence of communism in any Arab state. Consequently the civil war in Yemen (see Yemen: history) produced a crisis with Egypt in 1962 after it supplied the Republican revolutionaries with Soviet–made weapons and troops. Saudi Arabia supported the Imam Badr in his attempt to regain power, and the Egyptian air force even bombed Saudi towns. Only after Egypt's defeat in the June 1967 Arab–Israeli War, and its subsequent sharp reduction of ties with the Soviet Union would Faisal cooperate with it. Saudi Arabia also remained a strong supporter of Palestinian Arabs against Israel, paying funds directly to the PLO, to the U.N. to care for the refugees, and to Arab countries partly occupied by Israel in 1967.

The government also showed concern over the future of the small states on the Arabian side of the Gulf. Faisal, anxious as always to maintain the present status, met with the Shah of Iran. He sought to avoid any Saudi–Iranian conflict and to keep "revolutionary" Arab states from spreading their influence into the lands of the Gulf.

Following a clash in 1969 along the undefined border with the Marxist–inspired People's Democratic Republic of Yemen, Saudi Arabia settled most outstanding differences with the Yemen Arab Republic. In the following years, in fact, the two nations cooperated to contain the radicalism from Southern Yemen. An agreement with Abu Dhabi (see United Arab Emirates) in 1974 ended a long–smoldering border dispute with that state, while relations with Oman improved.

During an Arab–Israeli war of October 1973, Saudi Arabia was the only major Arab state to interpret the issues mainly in terms of religion. King Faisal proclaimed an embargo on all oil shipments to the energy–short U.S. "until he was able again to pray in Jerusalem under an Arab flag." However, at the urging of Egypt, he ended the embargo in early 1974 in exchange for vague assurances concerning Israeli withdrawal from Jerusalem.

While the embargo was not fully effective—the United States obtained

The Modern Red Sea port of Jidda

relatively little oil directly from Saudi Arabia, and oil could transfer ownership rapidly on the high seas—the embargo was accompanied by a reported 10% cut in Saudi oil exports. Against the background of tight world oil supplies, these Saudi moves provided the conditions necessary for OPEC to raise the price of oil about 400% (see Introduction: Black Gold). Besides the flood of oil revenues that resulted, Faisal also reaped a great increase in prestige at home and abroad.

King Faisal was shot fatally in 1975 by a nephew at a public reception in honor of the Prophet's birthday. There seemed to be no rational political cause motivating the assassin; he was publicly beheaded the following day. Crown Prince Khalid (pronounced to rhyme with "valid") was immediately proclaimed the new king to succeed his elder brother, and he promised to follow the policies which had been developed under the reign of Faisal. Another brother, Fahd, became Crown Prince and gained a prominent share of authority.

The reign of King Khalid saw serious attempts at close political and economic cooperation with the United States. Saudi Arabia wanted American technological skills and experience, while the United States' balance of payments was greatly helped by Saudi purchases of American goods and services. Both countries shared the common goal of protecting the Arab region from communist encroachment. Saudi Arabia used its own foreign aid to make allies and reduce Soviet influence in several poorer states.

Saudi thinkers interpreted the 1978 Camp David Agreement and later peace treaty between Egypt and Israel as Egypt's withdrawal from the Arab struggles with Israel over Jerusalem and Palestine. King Khalid's government was thus greatly embarrassed when its chief Western backer, the United States, pressured it to approve the peace agreements. Owing to public opinion as well as their own values, the Saudi leaders had little alternative but to join with other Arab governments in denouncing the agreements and opposing Egypt. Saudi Arabia continued to insist that a peaceful settlement with Israel should include that country's withdrawal of its military occupation from *all* territories it seized in 1967.

The government, royal family, and outside world were stunned in 1979 when Islamic extremists seized the Grand Mosque in Mecca and called for revolution. After crushing the rebellion with some loss of life, the Saudis responded with reforms, in particular for the Shi'a inhabitants of the eastern province bordering on the Gulf. The take-over of the mosque served to remind all of the importance of maintaining the royal family's links with the *Ulama'*, or Muslim scholars, and acted as a warning that social change should be restrained.

Military Expansion in the 1980s

When King Khalid died of a heart attack in 1982, he was succeeded by his principal aide, Fahd, while another brother, Abdullah, became the new Crown Prince. Head of the Saudi National Guard, Crown Prince Abdullah continued his planning for increasing the military strength of the country, for as the leading member of the Gulf Cooperation Council (see Regional Organizations) Saudi Arabia plays a pivotal role in the defense of a peninsula containing almost half the world's oil reserves.

By 1985, Saudi Arabia had achieved its quest for the best–equipped military forces in the Gulf region, although the massive armies of Iran and Iraq far outnumbered the kingdom's forces. Spending one–quarter or more of Gross National Product on defense, a ratio surpassed only sometimes by Israel, Saudi Arabia became the world's major importer of advanced weapons and developed elaborate military bases in the northwest, northeast, and east. However, the regular military totaled about 60,000, with another 50,000 in the full–time National Guard.

Given the levels of skills and education of most Saudi adults, many technical tasks required foreign advisors. Drawn from Egypt and Jordan as well as Pakistan and countries in the Far East, thousands of these men worked as trainers, maintenance crew, and sometimes even in combat roles. Skeptics doubted the effectiveness of Saudi military preparations, but the forces performed well in combat in 1991.

The closest military contacts came with the United States. American–built planes guided by American–trained pilots flew from hangers built by U.S. companies while directed from U.S.–supplied Airborne Warning and Control System (AWACS) aircraft. However, although both Democratic and Republican presidents approved Saudi requests for advanced weapons, Congress grew increasingly hesitant, largely out of concern the weapons might threaten Israel in some future conflict. Under the impact of the Iran–Iraq War, Saudi Arabia turned to France, Britain, and even Brazil for weapons ranging from Tornado fighters to minesweepers and light armored vehicles.

Dwarfed in both population and military manpower by Iran and Iraq, Saudi Arabia possibly benefitted from their war distracting both, until Iraq appeared on the verge of defeat in 1986. Then Saudi relations with Iran deteriorated. During the 1987 pilgrimage to Mecca (the "*Hajj*"), Iranian rioting led to some 400 deaths. As the two nations hurled charges at each other, the worsening "Tanker War" threatened the security of Saudi oil installations, and some Iranian–inspired violence occurred.

The next year the Saudis announced limits by nation on the numbers of pilgrims coming on the annual *Hajj*, with the result

King Fahd of Saudi Arabia

that previous Iranian totals of 150,000—the single largest contingent and over 10% of all pilgrims—fell to 45,000. Despite threats from Tehran, and its eventual boycott of the pilgrimage, the government stood firm, and order was maintained.

Following the ceasefire between Iran and Iraq, Saudi Arabia adopted a more neutral attitude towards Iran. With its partners in the Gulf Cooperation Council, it agreed to support moves for peace. Diplomatic relations followed, but in domestic matters, firmness remained, with the death penalty applied to 16 Shi'a pilgrims from Kuwait convicted of murder in connection with a bomb explosion during the *Hajj*.

In contrast to shrill demands and pronouncements of some Arab leaders, Saudi diplomacy traditionally stressed quiet negotiations plus the careful distribution of economic assistance. In the late 1980s, however, King Fahd himself adopted a more public role, particularly as a leading member of the Arab League's committee on Lebanon. Saudi Arabia summoned most Lebanese parliamentarians to its summer resort of Taif, and pressured them to consider reforms that ended their Civil War (see Lebanon: history). Saudi diplomacy also played a prominent role at the Arab summit that readmitted Egypt to the Arab League, and actively sought a solution to the dispute over the Western Sahara.

Invasion and the Gulf War, 1990-91

The 1990 Iraqi invasion of Kuwait placed Saudi Arabia into grave peril. A fellow member of the regional alliance, the Gulf Cooperation Council, lay occupied. The Iraqi forces in Kuwait numbered three times the total Saudi military, and Baghdad threatened attack if its oil exports across Saudi Arabia were halted.

Enormously complicated oil installations—wells, pipelines, tank farms, refineries, ports—lay within range of Iraqi missiles and bombers. Moreover, if he kept Kuwait's oil wealth, Iraq's President Saddam Hussein would control reserves and output rivaling Saudi Arabia's.

The political threat seemed as substantial as the military. Saddam Hussein's invective against the Kuwaiti ruling family obviously applied to all Gulf dynasties, including the Saudi. Demands that Arab oil wealth support all Arabs stirred popular resentment among poor Arabs everywhere. Such claims threatened revolution within Saudi Arabia, and isolation from the Arab world.

By contrast, the United States offered military support and possibly the liberation of Kuwait. However, such an alliance raised objections. To many Muslims, the Protector of the Holy Places must not depend on "infidel" troops. (Baghdad later charged, falsely, that American soldiers were in the Holy Places of Mecca and Medina.) Some Arab nationalists saw a colonialist attack by Israel's allies against Israel's strongest enemy, Iraq. The presence of foreign troops meant foreign journalists, politicians, and unflattering attacks on the lack of Western–style democracy. Domestically an alliance with the US meant quiet scorn about defense by "Jews and women" as well as a display of Western lifestyles ranging from Christmas to women's equality in military affairs.

Despite these risks, King Fahd and his government requested troops from Arab, American and other nations just four days after the invasion of Kuwait. Benefitting from higher oil prices and output, the kingdom pledged money for its military allies as well as countries suffering from the crisis. It also sought approval from the World Muslim League and Arab nations.

As Coalition military strength rose, the United Nations approved the use of force if Iraq did not evacuate Kuwait by January 15, 1991. Hours later, Coalition aircraft, often from Saudi bases, launched the massive aerial destruction of Iraq's military and infrastructure (see Iraq: history).

In response, Iraqi Scud missiles were launched at Riyadh and apparently at oil and military targets in the Eastern Province. Although Patriot missiles intercepted some Scuds, damage did occur, notably to a Muslim religious college in Riyadh, and a barracks housing Americans in Dhahran. An Iraqi tank column also attacked the city of Khafji, but was repulsed largely by Saudi and Qatari troops. In general, the attacks served to increase patriotism among Saudi civilians, including the minority Shi'a of the Eastern Province, rather than undermine the government. Saudi ground forces played an important role in the recapture of Kuwait City, and a Saudi pilot scored the only double kill of the war.

Growing Tensions in the 1990s

If war left the country little changed officially, it did expand popular desires for reform. Partly in response, in 1992 King Fahd proposed a written constitution with a Majlis al-Shura, or council. Keeping Saudi traditions, the appointed council of 90 members wields no executive power. It does advise the king and can question ministers and propose laws. From a balcony, women have been allowed to follow its proceedings. The king remains commander of the armed forces, chief administrator, and sole authority over the royal treasury. Such power influences world oil markets, and prices rose when King Fahd, diabetic and suffering from a stroke, turned control of the government to Crown Prince Abdullah briefly in 1995.

Like Saudis themselves, Western experts remain divided about the impact of the sometimes–conflicting popular desires for democracy and greater Islamic morality. Most Saudis seemed to support the *Majlis al–Shura* appointed in 1993; liberals advocate further modernization. However, Islamist groups grew in strength and political appeal, especially among young, often underemployed, graduates of religious schools. Spreading their messages by fax as well as sermons, such groups idealistically advocate replacing corruption with morality, repression with legitimate Islamic government, and weakness with a strong military.

In response, the regime arrested scores—critics claim hundreds—for allegedly threatening national security, and the Islamic courts declared some activities illegal. One critic, Muhammad al–Masari of the *Committee for the Defense of Legitimate Rights,* fled to London, and there presented carefully bland attacks on the ruling family. Others proved more derogatory and even violent. However, militant Islamists seem concentrated in Najd, and commentators suggest that despite the regime's financial discomforts (see Economy), they probably pose no serious threat in the short run.

In foreign affairs, after the 1991 Gulf War the country adopted a bolder role. Proposals for an alliance with Egypt and Syria failed to be implemented, but the Gulf Command Council decided to strengthen its forces and in 1995 ended the boycott of companies doing business with Israel. Saudi diplomats played a major role in convening the Madrid Peace Conference and supported the peace process, but the country moved more slowly than other Gulf states towards peace with Israel.

Relations with Tehran improved greatly after the election of President Khatemi in 1998. More Iranians undertook the *Hajj*, without incident, and the two countries cooperated in OPEC to raise the price of crude oil. High-level official visits symbolized the spirit of friendship that began to replace the bitter mutual condemnations in the years soon after the Iranian revolution.

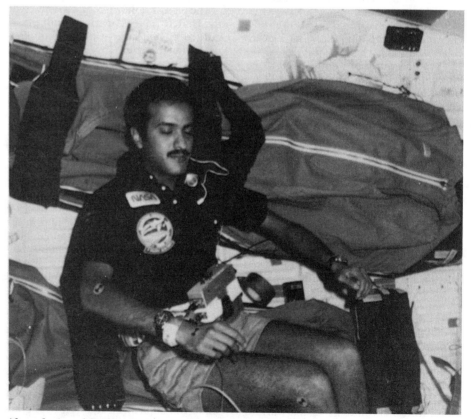

Aboard spaceship *Discovery*: Sultan Salman during an experiment. Courtesy: NASA

Mounted troops of the Saudi Arabian National Guard

Nevertheless, significant tensions remain. Relations with Yemen worsened over that nation's perceived sympathy with Iraq, and Saudi partiality towards the secessionist Southern forces during the 1994 Yemeni civil war. Saudi and Yemeni forces—or perhaps their tribal surrogates—even clashed briefly near the undefined border in 1994, though neither side wished to heighten the dispute over barren but potentially oil–rich territory.

More threatening, a never–contrite Saddam Hussein rules much of Iraq. Defeated but hardly cowed, he demanded compensation from Saudi Arabia for Western flights over Iraq from Saudi bases, and after the increased bombing campaign in 1999, he called on the populace to rise up against the royal family.

Despite such rhetoric, it seems that Iraqi agents were not responsible for the large truck–bomb in 1996 that killed 19 persons in al–Khobar, most of them American military personnel. Initial speculation blamed the little-known *Saudi Hizbullah* and Iran. The sophistication and scale of the act indicated something more than a hasty response to the execution of several men involved in a previous attack on U.S. troops. However, the U.S. and Saudi Arabian governments found it difficult to discover the alleged perpetrators. Saudi Arabia, but not the

U.S., closed the investigation in 1998, and declared that Iran was not involved.

King Fahd's declining health has encouraged speculation in the Western press about the succession. Crown Prince Abdullah is a half-brother to King Fahd and several other important princes, and as the commander of the National Guard he has sometimes seemed more sympathetic to Arab causes and more cautious towards the United States. However, in the late 1990s Abdullah also came to champion reform of the country's bureaucracy and lavish spending. He spoke of the need to reconsider the place of women, and proclaimed that the days of easy living off oil revenues had ended.

Despite the Crown Prince's sympathy, Saudi reforms only inched forward. Some airport services were contracted to private firms, and the government raised the price of first-class tickets on the national airline, Saudia, but these are only small changes. Electric generating capacity has fallen far short of predicted demand, but the government-owned companies that distribute it may not raise prices to gain the revenue needed to buy more equipment. Promising larger roles for private companies in the future, the government invited proposals for investment in the energy sector. In response, international oil firms proposed billions of dollars of projects, but it seemed likely that both oil production and the

petrochemical firm SABIC would remain off-limits to foreign companies.

In contrast to the vast surpluses of the 1970s and 1980s, Saudi Arabia now requires foreign financing for major electric, water, petrochemical and oil projects. The rapidly growing numbers of high school and college graduates—half the population is under 18—strain the ability of the government to employ them, but jobs in the private sector pay only half as well. Until he formally becomes king, Crown Prince Abdullah can make the right noises about possible solutions, but he cannot decree the many changes necessary to avoid stagnation.

Thus most recent Saudi reforms only inched forward. Some airport services were contracted to private firms, and the government raised the price of first-class tickets on the national airline, Saudia. These were only small changes at best significant reforms failed because of traditional Saudi ways.

One enormous change in energy policy appeared in 2001. For decades, Saudi Aramco had held a monopoly on the production of oil and gas, but then the government awarded three vast concessions to consortia of foreign oil companies led by ExxonMobil and Shell. The reason was simple: the price tag of $25 billion to develop the natural gas wells, pipelines, and infrastructure necessary to meet future energy needs with gas and thus spare oil for export. However, both oil production and the petrochemical firm SABIC remain off-limits to foreign companies.

Domestic and Foreign Perils after 9-11

By the summer of 2001, several of the major political pillars of the country showed signs of difficulty. After spiking in 2000, oil prices softened, forcing the government into deficit spending. More seriously, Saudi sympathy with Palestinians engaged in the renewed *intifada* led to widespread accusations that the Bush administration's "hands-off" policy favored Israel. After threatening to review relations with Washington, in early September, the Saudis called off high-level military talks in Washington. However, in the months that followed, shockwaves of the terrorist attacks of September 11 severely shook each pillar of the nation.

News that 15 of the 19 men identified as terrorists came from Saudi Arabia unleashed criticisms by Western politicians and the media. Besides long-standing accusations of human rights violations (e.g., the treatment of women and a harsh system of justice), three new issues surfaced. First, militant Islamic groups had been funded, knowingly or not, by contributions to various charities. Second, Saudi educational and cultural policies, especially since the 1990s, had created a society that encouraged radical fundamentalist religious groups. Third, the kingdom was not much of an ally because it would not allow U.S. aircraft to attack *Taliban* and *al-Qaeda* targets in Afghanistan from Saudi bases.

Within the country, the Saudi-U.S. alliance faced outspoken religious condemnation. An elderly religious scholar ruled that support for unbelievers (i.e., the U.S.) in a struggle against Muslims (the *Taliban* and bin Ladin's followers) removed a person from Islam, in effect, excommunicating the royal family. While mainstream religious leaders did not go so far, many preachers condemned corruption, indebtedness to the West, and the presence of U.S. troops on Saudi soil.

With varying success, Crown Prince Abdullah and others responded to the crisis by stressing to the West that Islam was not the enemy, but rather misguided individuals. Abdullah proposed a peace plan for Palestine that dominated discussion at an Arab League meeting. Despite the public rows, in private he cooperated with the U.S. The royal family continues to value American protection, just as the U.S. values steady supplies of Saudi oil. Nevertheless, September 11 and its repercussions added to the growing social and economic problems felt by the ordinary citizen and tarnished the royal reputation.

Culture: In order to understand the workings of government in Saudi Arabia, one must appreciate some aspects of the structure of its society, such as the unwritten laws relating to kinship. The most important unit is the extended family or clan; accordingly, all the people who are descended from a common ancestor have responsibilities to one another. In the days when there was no strong government to protect people, this system was necessary to protect the group. In determining membership in the clan–family system, only men are considered. A person belongs to the same clan as the brother of his father, but the brother of his mother may belong to a different clan and cannot claim help in the same way; there is even a different word for "uncle" in the two cases. The House of Saud, the ruling family in Saudi Arabia, is just such a clan—these relatives have the duty of looking after their collective interests first, the interests of the rest of the people secondly.

With more wealth, more travel abroad and more education, some Saudis are beginning to break some of the traditionally strong family bonds. Conservative Saudis tend to associate this in their minds with lowered ethical and moral standards and even illegal drugs. Thus, as in other states of the Gulf Cooperation Council, leaders seek ways to maintain the strong sense of family loyalty and discipline which is viewed as part of the Islamic religion.

A group of clans which cooperate for mutual protection and which sometimes believe they have a common ancestor are a tribe. In a tribe there is always one clan with high prestige which is dominant. There are also special responsibilities between the clans within a tribe, but until the establishment of the Kingdom of Saudi Arabia there was no important group larger than the tribe. However the tribes often had temporary alliances—though they were more often warring with each other.

Islamic Beliefs and the Hajj

Hijaz, the western part of Saudi Arabia, is the holy land to all Muslims, who comprise about one–sixth of mankind. At least once in their lifetime, millions perform the pilgrimage to the cities of Mecca and Medina where their Prophet Muhammad lived and was inspired to utter the words of the Quran (Koran), the Islamic scriptures. The Islamic creed, "There is no god but God (Arabic *Allah)* and Muhammad was the Apostle of God" is written on the flag of Saudi Arabia. (Further discussion of Muhammad and Muslim beliefs is found in the Historical Background.)

In the era of inexpensive air travel instead of camel caravans from Cairo or Damascus, nearly two million pilgrims typically perform the *Hajj*. All of them hope to spend the identical five days praying at the Grand Mosque, circling its Ka'aba with its black stone, and joining the final ceremonies on Mount Arafat, where Muhammad preached his last sermon. Transported by 10,000 buses from Jidda to Mecca, most pilgrims sleep in a vast tent city, where they meet fellow-believers from across the globe. They slaughter over half a million animals as sacrifices.

Given the size of the crowds, Saudi officials have attempted to take careful precautions, carefully screening for communicable diseases and providing the services of thousands of medical personnel, guards, food preparers and cleaners. After an inferno killed hundreds in the 1990s, the authorities supplied fireproof tents and carved large water storage tunnels in nearby mountains. They also widened passageways where a crowd might stampede.

The major teachings of Islam rest on the belief in one God, the Creator and Sustainer of the world who will at the final Day of Judgment render justice to both the righteous and the evil. Knowledge of God comes through the prophets, especially Muhammad, whose Quran ("Recitations") is the literal Word of God. Supplemented by the Traditions *(Hadith)* of Muhammad, as well as limited reasoning, the Quran provides the basis for personal behavior, laws for the orderly society of the believers, and a guide to the treatment of non–believers.

Individual Muslims must carry out five major duties. They must testify belief in the Islamic creed (stated above), and pray formally at five prescribed times daily. One must give the poor alms based on one's wealth, adults must fast during the daylight hours of the month of Ramadan, and the physically able ought to make the pilgrimage to Mecca at least once.

There are two principal holy days in Islam. The Day of Sacrifice falls on the tenth day of *Dhu–l–Hija*, the last month in the Islamic calendar and the month of pilgrimage. While celebrated by Muslims everywhere, it relates specifically to the lamb or goat sacrificed by each pilgrim in Mecca. The Festival of Breaking Fast is on the first day of *Shawwal*, the tenth month—it celebrates the ending of the fast during Ramadan, the ninth month.

The impact of a calendar with months rotating through the seasons can best be imagined by remembering that during Ramadan the faithful neither eat nor drink between sunrise and sunset. While in some years Ramadan falls in the winter, with short days and cool weather, when it arrives in the summer the faithful endure a fast of 13 or 14 hours in maximum temperatures often exceeding 110 degrees F.

Time in Saudi Arabia is still largely kept according to the old system whereby a day begins not at midnight, but at sunset. This means that in spring when the days are gradually getting longer, Saudi Arabian time has slightly more than 24 hours in a day; in the fall when the days are

154

getting shorter, there are slightly less. This system of time is not suitable for international airline schedules and business purposes, so Saudi Standard Time (GMT +3) is used more and more.

Although Islam teaches the brotherhood and equality of all believers, class distinctions have developed. In the old days there were tribes that considered themselves more noble than others and would not intermarry with them. There were also clans that had more prestige than others. Modernization reduces class distinctions of these traditional types, wealth and education becoming the tokens of status. But whatever one's social standing, *kabsa* is the main food of all. This Saudi national dish is a large tray of boiled meat and rice, usually covered with a tomato sauce seasoned with mild spices.

Based on Islam and enforced in a traditional fashion, the legal system varies considerably from Western practices. A woman's testimony carries half the weight of a man's, the practice of non-Islamic religions even by foreigners is forbidden, and freedoms of speech and the press are extremely limited. The courts impose one of highest execution rates in the world for drug dealing and rape as well as murder. Lesser crimes may be punished by beating; for example, passengers who persist in using cell phones during an airliner's takeoff have received 70 lashes. However, the severity of Saudi sentences is sometimes offset for the fortunate by royal pardons, or by the substitution of payments to a victim's family.

Foreigners are often surprised by the official and absolute ban on alcoholic beverages in the country in accordance with strict Islamic belief. A non–Saudi businessman found with any quantity of alcohol in his belongings is normally deported on the next available flight. Penalties for possession of narcotics are also strictly imposed, and importers of narcotics risk the death penalty. On the other hand, tobacco is allowed, and an education program warning against the health hazards of smoking is only now becoming significant.

Another increasing social difficulty is tooth decay. With sugar consumption exceeding 110 pounds (50 Kg.) per year, cavities seem to be multiplying. As the supplier of free medical care, the government recently adopted two preventative policies. School children will receive annual inspections, and water supplies will be fluoridated.

One way life in the kingdom is being changed very rapidly is education. In 1953 only ten schools offered public instruction on the junior high school and senior high school levels, with a total enrollment of 1,315. By 1973, however, there were 573 schools at these levels with 105,853 students. During the same 20 years the number of elementary pupils increased from 39,000 to more than half a million. In 1980

Courtesy: Embassy of Saudi Arabia

there were some 800,000 students in school, and nearly double that by the end of the decade. Access to primary education is now virtually universal.

With the decline in oil revenues in the 1980s, national policy for higher education reversed itself somewhat. Beginning in 1986, university admissions were restricted, to avoid producing more highly educated young than the economy could absorb.

There are now six universities in the country. The first was Riyadh University, which is becoming a world leader in solar energy research. One of the newest is the Mecca branch of King Abdul Aziz University, which has its main campus in Jidda.

Modern education carries the burden of separate schools and other facilities for women. In the cause of maintaining sexual purity, Saudi women have been kept apart from men outside the family. Semi–official vice police—known as *Mutawin*—ensure utmost modesty in dress and brevity in contact. Cinemas and theaters are all forbidden, let alone night–clubs, and women do not frequent shopping centers and malls. When several dozen Saudi women broke the tradition against driving and formed a procession of luxury cars in 1990, they were arrested, lost their jobs, and condemned by the vice police as prostitutes. Thereafter, the law was officially changed to prohibit women from taking the wheel.

Economy: Before the discovery of its oil, most inhabitants of the arid lands of Saudi Arabia lived off herding flocks, or raised dates and a few other crops. The yearly pilgrimage, or *Hajj*, to the sacred places of Mecca and Medina employed others, but the trade routes of ancient times could not compete with sea–born transport, especially after the introduction of steam and the construction of the Suez Canal. Today it is difficult to over–estimate the impact of oil on Saudi Arabia. In the early 1990s it funded most of the government budget, directly contributed 25% of GDP, and provided 99% of exports. In addition, rapid industrial development, centered on petrochemicals, depends on oil as a raw material.

Saudi Oil Policy
Prospectors for the American oil companies that later formed the Arabian American Oil Company (Aramco) struck commercial quantities of oil in 1938. However, World War II intervened before significant production took place, despite US approval for steel and other materials to build a refinery at Ras Tanura. Deprived of most pilgrims, and able to export only limited quantities of oil by barge to Bahrain, the country depended on foreign assistance until the post–war era.

Peace brought an explosion of activity. Aramco employment climbed to reach a peak of 24,000 in 1952, half Saudi, half foreign. Post–war oil production increased by nearly 20% a year, and soon Saudi Arabia ranked with Iran and Iraq as a leading Middle East producer. Oil production

155

benefited the country in many ways besides revenues, for Aramco built a hospital, clinics, schools and housing. In addition it provided assistance for agriculture, and lent advice for a variety of projects, including the kingdom's railroad.

A founding member of the Organization of Petroleum Exporting Countries (OPEC), Saudi Arabia usually adopted a firm but moderate stance at its meetings. Given the country's reserves and production, its opinion mattered. In the early 1970s, with its oil sales rising at 25% per year, the country became dominant. Sheikh Ahmad Yamani, the Petroleum Minister, became a leading figure in the cartel, and played a major role in the 1973 oil embargo and later agreements that drove the price of oil from roughly $2.50 in 1970 to $32 in 1980. However, as noted in the introductory section on oil, high prices encouraged production elsewhere and reduced consumption through conservation. In the face of declining demand for OPEC oil, Saudi Arabia endured the greatest cuts in exports, becoming the "swing producer" that cut output when prices softened.

By 1985, Saudi Arabia became weary of serving as the "swing producer" of OPEC, a role worsened by price cutting and over–production by other members of the organization. It therefore adopted a new oil policy and began to increase production rapidly, with predictable results. The "spot" (free market) price for oil fell as low as $9 a barrel in 1986, creating economic havoc for producers such as Mexico and Nigeria, which had borrowed heavily against future production. For consuming nations, the effect was sheer delight. OPEC nations learned the lesson; stricter discipline among producers combined with growing demand in industrialized countries to raise the price

to roughly $20 a barrel during the last few years of the decade.

With extensive pipelines to the Red Sea, and capacity growing to 10 million barrels per day, the now–nationally owned oil company, Saudi Aramco, seems set to benefit from the pivotal role oil will play. During the Gulf Crisis of 1990–91, Saudi Aramco proved able to boost production substantially above its normal quota, and played a major role in meeting world oil needs while exports from Iraq and Kuwait were halted.

As world recession reduced demand for OPEC crude oil during the 1990s, the kingdom attempted to maintain production at 8 million barrels a day, about one–third of total OPEC output while increasing capacity for even higher levels. Policy also shifted towards higher prices, when Saudi Arabia reversed its previous trends in OPEC meetings and supported restraining output to boost prices to about $20 per barrel. However, when supplies still outpaced demand, and prices fell, the kingdom refused to make cuts unless other producers did likewise.

In the longer view, prosperity based on oil seems set to continue. In 1989 and 1990 the newly organized Saudi Aramco announced major discoveries at Dilam and al–Hawtah, south of Riyadh and outside the nation's traditional oil fields. Even more important, the oil should sell at premium prices. Unlike other Saudi crude, it contains little polluting sulphur, and "light" oils are desired for gasoline and other higher–value products. Thus, regardless of future quota increases within OPEC, the country will increase its petroleum earnings by selling a more expensive grade.

After a disastrous slide in oil prices in 1999, Saudi diplomacy and large cuts in

Aramco's output of crude won production cuts from OPEC members like Venezuela and even non-members like Mexico and Norway. Crude oil prices then soared, exceeding $35 per barrel. However, prices over $30 seem unreasonably high because they encourage exploration outside OPEC, reducing Saudi Arabia's share of the world market and thus OPEC's ability to manipulate prices by controlling production.

High prices might also harm Saudi Arabia's longer-term good in another way. When money rolls in, the pain of privatization seems less necessary. Prosperity makes it difficult to build a consensus supporting reasonable but unpopular measures like raising the prices of gasoline or electricity.

In the longer view, steady oil revenue seems set to continue. Major discoveries at Dilam and al–Hawtah, outside the nation's traditional oil fields, provides oil that sells at premium prices.

Growth of the National Economy

In the decades after 1945, the search for oil, its production, and its export revenues completely transformed the Saudi economy. Initially much income was squandered, but from the late 1950s onward economic development became a priority. It created a challenge: even with vast oil revenues, and a few thousand jobs directly in the industry, how could millions of people be transformed from a life of bare–subsistence herding and agriculture to the levels of income and comfort enjoyed by advanced industrial nations?

From the late 1950s to the early 1970s, the government erected public buildings, built roads and highways, and began to provide education and health services for its citizens. Oil revenues provided foreign exchange to purchase cars, food, appliances, cloth, watches, cameras, equipment, and even building materials. Money that found its way into private hands frequently went into large homes, as well as stores and office buildings. Reluctant to have a "Central Bank," with its implications of interest payment, the nation established the Saudi Arabian Monetary Authority (SAMA) to provide modern control over national finances.

Following the 1973 Arab oil embargo and the subsequent spiraling prices for the commodity, the nation's economic development spurted to higher levels of growth. Recognizing that even the country's one–quarter of the world's known oil reserves would eventually run out, the government offered a variety of incentives to attract non–oil industries, from tariffs to tax breaks and subsidies. Factories began to appear, sometimes joint ventures with foreign firms. The early ones typically provided consumer items or construction materials for the building boom, such as the mill outside Jidda for rolling steel rods. With the decline in oil prices in the mid–1980s, government subsidies

The University of Petroleum and Minerals, Dhahran

diminished, but plans existed for a steel industry to use the extensive iron deposits of the northern Hijaz, as well as for an aluminum smelter to process bauxite ores.

In general, Saudi industrial projects suffer from a number of common difficulties. Perhaps the biggest is the shortage of local entrepreneurs, managers, and skilled workers. Lucrative profits in other fields also discourage long–term investment in manufacturing. The lack of developed financial markets makes it more convenient for Saudi capitalists to invest in US Steel (now USX) than industrial projects within the kingdom. Finally, for all its famed wealth, the country represents a relatively small market, with fewer and poorer consumers than Belgium or Illinois.

To date the most impressive industrialization effort is SABIC. Charged with developing a basic petrochemical industry, it rapidly grew to massive size, joining the Kuwait Petroleum Company as the only Arab companies on the international Fortune 500. By 1988 all the major plants had been constructed, and profits soared as the company turned cheap petroleum raw materials into fertilizers, plastics and other products. By 1995, SABIC held 5% of world sales of petrochemicals, with a much larger proportion of specialty products like MTBE (methyl tertiary butyl ether), a gasoline additive that reduces carbon monoxide emissions and replaces lead in enhancing octane. Profits exceeded $1 billion for the first time in 1994, and privatizing the government's 70% share of ownership could provide a windfall to cushion the budget deficit.

Another success is the national airline, *Saudia*. True to national culture, its flights begin with Muhammad's prayer for travelers, and ceiling–mounted compasses indicate to passengers the direction of Mecca for prayer. Attention to religious details did not hamper its rise to the largest regional carrier, offering service between Western Europe and East Asia.

In one of the less predictable turns of fate, Saudi Arabia became a major exporter of grains by the end of the 1980s. After American media suggestions for a food embargo to retaliate for the 1973 oil embargo, the government adopted an extensive program of subsidies for grains. It also covered some costs for wells, fertilizers and other farm supplies. In response, cultivated acreage increased tenfold, and hundreds of giant green circles provided bumper crops of wheat. From a mere 3,000 tons in 1976, output climbed to 3 million tons in 1989, three times consumption.

Besides providing substantial wheat for export, the policy spread national wealth and diminished migration to the cities. About 25% of the population remained in agriculture, and subsidies also raised output of eggs, dairy products, and dates.

Unfortunately the successes came expensively, and as predicted in earlier editions of this book, did not last long. Annual wheat subsidies of $1 billion cost *eight times* the price of imports. During the budget deficit after the Gulf War, payments to farmers fell behind. By 1996 price supports had been cut 25%, and production fell to half the record of 4 million tons.

Nature reinforces trends of financial austerity. As a desert land, about 90% of the country's water supplies come from "fossil" sources, trapped far below the soil during a different climatic age. Currently the nation uses 18 billion cubic meters of this fossil water annually. Given apparently reliable American estimates of only 500 billion cubic meters in the aquifers, water will run out in less than 30 years. Desalinized water, while merely expensive for household use, becomes exorbitant for wheat farming, raising total costs 700%.

Imaginative alternative supplies—from the Nile, Turkey, Iraq, or Antarctic icebergs—likewise appear prohibitively costly and uncertain. Thus despite its policies, Saudi Arabia's future as a food producer seems limited to drought–tolerant crops, plus fish and shrimp from the sea.

Economic and Budget Policies

As a consequence of falling oil prices, Saudi Arabia suffered recession conditions after 1985. Government revenues withered, and the foreign assets of SAMA, the monetary authority, plummeted from $127 billion in 1981 to $59 billion in 1989. To cover its budget deficit, the government attempted to borrow money while obeying the Islamic prohibition of the payment of interest. Thus it issued "development bonds," whose payment depended in theory on the success of the project, though skeptics found the rates paralleled closely U.S. Treasury bonds.

Against this background, the Saudi government has attempted to continue modest spending for social and economic development. Health and education remain priorities, rising in 1989 and 1990 despite an overall budget freeze and cutbacks on new projects. Supplemental taxes are difficult to find, for attempts to impose income taxes on foreign workers created such difficulties that they were withdrawn, and higher tariffs largely breed domestic inflation.

Although defense accounts for 36% of government expenditures, and world rivalries may be decreasing, with neighbors such as Iran, Iraq, Yemen, Sudan and Israel, the kingdom hardly feels more secure. In the aftermath of the Second Gulf War, its purchases of sophisticated weap-

ons from the U.S. and Western Europe exceeded $5 billion per year. However, the pace of spending apparently slowed, as declining oil prices cut revenues and raised the budget deficit. By 1994 the national debt had reached an estimated $55 billion; a year later it hovered around $70 billion, some speculators turned against the riyal, and the government was forced to reduce the planned 1995 deficit to $4 billion.

While the private sector plays an increasingly important role, gyrating oil markets in the late 1990s emphasized the country's great dependence on petroleum. High prices in 1996/97 financed an unexpected surplus and enabled the government to pay some old debts. However, two years later the lowest prices since 1973 savaged profits and revenues and forced the government to borrow billions of dollars from Saudi Aramco and local banks. After OPEC voted to slash production, high prices returned in 2000, making possible a balanced budget proposal for the first time since the early 1980s. More generally, under Crown Prince Abdullah's rising influence, the government attempted to continue its reforms and encouraged investment by foreign companies by allowing them to own property and to operate without finding a local partner to own a majority of shares.

The Future: It's tempting to be optimistic about the country that controls 25% of the world's oil reserves and enjoys the protection of the only superpower. Nevertheless, some sleepless nights should appear in the forecast.

Politically, the U.S. alliance and the presence of American troops arouse continuing popular resentment that will only grow if the U.S. seeks to invade Iraq while not restraining Israel. There are also signs that the country's public desires greater freedom, shown by new-found courage to criticize in print both the religious police and corrupt judges.

Economically, because oil production remains level and prices have slipped, the country earns less from oil now than it did twenty years ago. Then, its oil revenues provided income levels equal to those in the U.S. Now, thanks to both inflation and rapid population growth, those revenues provide per capita income about one-quarter of the U.S. level. Moreover, with 100,000 new graduates every year competing for rare job vacancies, unemployment has soared to perhaps 15% of the Saudi workforce.

Expect significant change soon, even to a degree that threatens some traditions of Saudi economic life. Political and cultural change will take longer.

The Syrian Arab Republic

No one knows who built this castle that overlooks the ruins of Palmyra.

Area: 71,772 sq. mi. (185,935 sq. km.).
Population: 16 million (estimated).
Capital City: Damascus (Pop. 1.7 million, estimated).
Climate: Summers are generally hot and dry; winters are mild in low areas, cooler with increasing elevation. Winter brings adequate rain in the western part of the country, but the remainder is arid.
Neighboring Countries: Turkey (North); Iraq (East); Jordan (South); Lebanon (West); Israel (Southwest).
Time Zone: GMT +2 (+3 in summer).
Official Language: Arabic
Other Principal Tongues: Kurdish, Armenian, Circassian and Turkish.
Ethnic Background: On the basis of language and culture, nearly all Syrians are identified as Arab.
Principal Religion: Islam (about 82%, mainly *Sunni*), Christianity; Druze and Alawi Islamic communities.
Chief Commercial Products: Textiles, wheat, barley, cotton, lentils, grapes, olives, sugar beets, tomatoes, sheep, chickens, petroleum, cement and processed food.
Major Trading Partners: Germany, France, Italy, Netherlands, Greece, Russia, Lebanon.

Currency: Syrian Lira (SL 62.60 = $1 U.S.)
Former Colonial Status: Under French rule (1920–1946).
Independence Date: April 17, 1946.
Chief of State: Bashar al-Asad, President
Head of Government: Muhammad Mustafa Miro
National Flag: The flag consists of three horizontal stripes of (top to bottom) red, white and black; two green, five–pointed stars are aligned on the central white stripe.
Gross Domestic Product $15.5 billion (UN estimate)
GDP per capita: $1,050; purchasing-power figures may be higher.

Lying at the eastern end of the Mediterranean Sea, Syria consists of two main climate zones. The western region includes the coastal mountains, the Orontes River valley, and a range of interior hills or mountains. The zone includes Damascus and Aleppo on its eastern limits, and provides the home for four-fifths of the population.

The eastern zone takes the form of foothills descending from an average elevation of 3,000 feet to the vast, open desert cut by the Euphrates River as it flows across Syria from north to southeast. Its two main tributaries come from the north, and they also support agriculture along their banks. Arabs invading the region called area north of the Euphrates *al–Jazira*, "The Island," a cultivated expanse of green surrounded by desert.

Most of Syria has an average rainfall of less than ten inches a year, but the western zone has more; the seaward slopes of the coastal range may receive as much as 50 inches near the crest, which in some places is 5,000 feet high. Cities such as Damascus and Homs along the eastern base of the inland range are great oases watered by springs and streams fed by the mountain rains.

History: Human civilization extends back as far in time in Syria as anywhere else. Many of antiquity's great empires occupied the country, although no Syrian dynasty arose to conquer the region, a reflection perhaps of its diversity of geography and population. Conquered by many rulers between the Assyrians and the Ottomans, Syria's history is deeply intertwined with the events related in the Historical Background of this book.

In the 7th and 8th centuries, Syria did become host to the world empire of the

Arab Umayyads who ruled from Damascus. Under them it flourished, with the construction of new cities and palaces. However, after the Abbasids overthrew the Umayyads, the capital was moved to Iraq. As the united Muslim empire disintegrated, Syria's important geographical position attracted invasions from every side except the desert: Seljuk Turks, Egyptian caliphs, European Crusaders, Mongols, Mamluks and, finally, the Ottoman Turks.

By the beginning of the twentieth century, most of the territory now included in Syria formed the two major provinces of Aleppo and Damascus. Present international borders did not exist, even as provincial boundaries. Jordan and parts of Israel and Lebanon reported to Damascus, while regions of southern Turkey, particularly Alexandretta/Antakiya west of the city of Aleppo, formed part of that province.

Before the outbreak of World War I, most inhabitants seemed content with Ottoman rule in the name of the Sultan in Istanbul. However, the politically active upper class of landowners, officials and Muslim scholars increasingly demanded a greater degree of local self–government. The *Decentralization Party* reflected this desire, and most Syrian voters sympathized with its reformist goals. However, in the last decades of the nineteenth century greater education and economic development had encouraged the rise of a consciousness of being Arab in language and culture. In the last years before World War I broke out, this cultural identity developed into small, secret societies, *al–Fatat*

and *al–Ahd*, that demanded independence for the Arab lands of the Empire.

After the Ottoman Empire joined the Central Powers in 1914, the Sultan proclaimed a *jihad* against the Allies. Nevertheless, the Arab nationalists plotted with Sharif Husayn of Mecca to gain independence. They provided the details for territorial demands he made from Britain in exchange for an uprising against the Ottoman Empire. After the outbreak of the Arab Revolt in June 1916, Syrian opinion increasingly favored the Allies. By the end of the war, Ottoman troops south of Aleppo faced widespread public resistance.

The great British victory over the Ottoman army in Palestine opened the way to Damascus. British and Arab forces raced for the city—historians still debate who conquered the city—and pressed on to capture Aleppo in the last weeks of the war. Initially the Arab army administered the interior of Syria. French forces were limited to Mt. Lebanon and the coast northward into Turkey, but Britain had pledged to support French rule over all Syria. Hence, as part of the peace settlement, France received the mandates for Syria and Lebanon.

In early 1920 nationalists in Damascus despaired of achieving peacefully their goals of independence and the unity of geographical Syria, including Lebanon, Palestine, and Jordan. In an act that precluded future concessions, they proclaimed Syria independent and united, with Emir Faisal as king. The son of Sharif Husayn, Faisal had led the Arab army into Syria, taken formal responsibility for its

administration and represented the Hijaz at the Paris peace conference. His rule was brief. By defeating Syrian forces at the Battle of Maysalun in July 1920, the French military imposed its rule on Syria and proceeded to occupy it despite local nationalist revolts.

Although the French mandate provided some modernization and technical successes, it failed to convince Syrian public opinion. In the mid–1920s a revolt shook the entire eastern portion of the country. As fighting spread to Damascus itself, French artillery shelled sections of the capital sympathetic to the rebels. During the 1930s, protests and general strikes dominated political life, and when an agreement was reached between the Syrian nationalists and France, a change of government in Paris meant that it was not implemented.

Now free to act without opposition from nationalist diplomacy, the French soon dismembered Syria into small regions that emphasized ethnic minorities, such as *Jabal Druze* and an *Alawi* state based in Latakia. This weakened the overwhelming *Sunni* majority with its nationalist ideas, but proved a great hindrance to any cooperation between the nationalists and French officials. France also transferred to Lebanon the fertile Biqa Valley and the western slopes of the Anti–Lebanon mountains, and in 1939 supervised the transfer of the territory of Antakiya in the far northwest corner to Turkey. Syrians generally opposed these territorial losses, and even today many Syrians argue that without imperialist interference, the territories of Palestine, Jordan, Lebanon and Antakiya would naturally have been a part of Syria.

After British–led troops expelled officials of the pro–Nazi French *Vichy* government from Syria at the start of World War II, Free French forces took control. Their commander announced that French rule would end at the conclusion of the war. However, France bombarded Damascus in May 1945 to intimidate Syrian officials into permitting French troops to remain.

The joint efforts of the United States, the Soviet Union and Britain through the Security Council of the UN finally induced France to withdraw entirely from Syria. The last troops left on April 17, 1946, the day now celebrated as Independence Day.

Syrian independence came to a country uncertain of its destiny. To the generation of nationalists who had opposed the

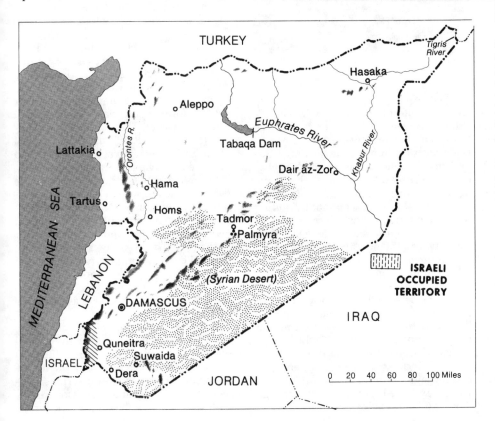

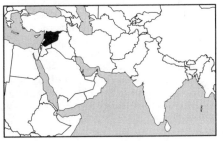

Downtown Damascus

Photo by Ray L. Cleveland

French—and sometimes compromised with them—the opportunity to rule from Damascus was sufficient reward. One such politician was Shukri al–Quwatli, who became the first president.

However, rival ideologies attracted support from students, army officers and even the army at large. Some sought the borders of geographical Syria; others, a merger with Iraq as a counter to Jewish settlement in Palestine. Socialists hoped to weaken the power of the wealthy notable families who comprised the top nationalist leadership in parliament. Increasingly these politicians appeared grasping for power. Corruption proved one cause among several for the Syrian army's conclusive defeat by Israel in 1948–49, when the army entered Palestine to attack the new Jewish state.

Against this background, Husni al–Zaim, the Chief of Staff, carried out Syria's first military *coup d'etat* in March 1949. He arrested leading politicians, arranged a cease–fire agreement with Israel, and

reached a verbal alliance with Iraq. Al–Zaim offered to meet with Israeli Prime Minister Ben–Gurion for peace talks, but was rebuffed—and no Syrian leader ever again made such an offer. After banning political parties, al–Zaim was elected president, but less than five months after seizing power, another military *coup* led to his execution. By ending ineffective though constitutional government, al–Zaim ushered in a long era of instability. For the next twenty–one years, Syrian governments proved most unstable, suffering more than a dozen military *coups*.

There was a resurgence of parliamentary government in 1954 following the exile of a virtual dictator. Elections in that year manifested the appeal which pan–Arab and socialist politicians had for the voters. Reformist groups became engaged in a struggle with the powerful families which exercised great power through their vast land holdings and wealth.

The *Ba'th Party* soon proved more influential than other radical ideologies such as the Syrian Popular Party and the communists. Founded in the early 1940s in Damascus by Michel Aflaq, a Christian, and Salah al–Din al–Bitar, a *Sunni* Muslim, the party took its name from the Arabic word for rebirth or renaissance. Highly committed to a nation uniting all Arabs and thus bringing them self–respect instead of backwardness and defeat, its ideology naturally proved a threat to existing Arab states, many of them created by European agreements rather than a sense of national identity. The party's socialist goals included the creation of a classless state, and by threatening government takeover of industry and trade proved radical as well. With the party's legality sometimes uncertain, it attracted disillusioned military officers in particular, and spread outside Syria as well.

By the mid–1950s, the nationalist and anti–imperialist appeal of Gamal Abdul Nasser of Egypt reinforced the opinions of many Syrians suspicious of Western powers and their clients, Iraq and Jordan. As Syria lurched unsteadily leftward in its domestic politics, and received Soviet equipment for the military, the Syrian government sought a union with Egypt. In early 1958 the two countries officially formed the "United Arab Republic" with Nasser as president and ideological source of all authority. On paper, the merger replaced Syria's political parties with a *National Union* like that being organized in Egypt. The *Ba'th Party* and other progressive groups disagreed with the Egyptian policy, but left public life; conservative elements took control of the *National Union* in Syria.

Economic problems aggravated by drought and friction between Egyptian and Syrian officials gave the conservative groups the opportunity to organize a *coup* which broke up the union in September 1961. Reformist politicians soon regained power, however. Then in 1963 army officers favoring the *Ba'th Party* seized control of the government in yet another *coup* and outlawed all rival political groups.

From 1963–1970 struggles within the *Ba'th Party* led to several attempts to overthrow its government. Nevertheless, it enacted many changes, such as government ownership of petroleum and other major industries. The wealthy and tradition–minded complained in private about the transformation of the economy and society, but they could not successfully oppose the government as long as it had the support of the army.

From the early years of independence, Syria has bordered the militarily–powerful state of Israel. Clashes across the 1949 demilitarized zones proved frequent; occasionally they flared into serious incidents with artillery and aircraft joining the battle. Several clashes followed Syria's

Young Syrians performing a traditional dance at a local festival

attempts to divert for use within its boundaries headwaters of the Jordan River that otherwise flowed to Israel. Public opinion strongly opposed the Zionist state, and sympathized with the displaced Palestinians, whose original refugees in Syria grew to about 140,000 by the mid–1960s.

Tensions along the Syrian border were one of the most immediate causes of a crisis in May 1967 which led to an Israeli attack on June 5 (see Israel: History). After quickly defeating Syria's Egyptian and Jordanian allies, Israeli forces stormed into Syria and up the slopes which rise to the fertile plateau known in Arabic as *Jawlan* or *Jolan* (pronounced *Golan* by Israelis), occupying some 1,250 square miles. Israeli troops forced nearly all the remaining civilians to leave, and they destroyed or damaged public buildings and homes of the regional capital, Quneitra. Rather than permit the Syrian refugees to return to their farms and villages in accord with a U.N. resolution, Israel established its own settlements on the farmlands of the ousted Syrians.

Al–Asad Rises to Power

A new group Ba'thist officers seized power in November 1970. Led by General Hafiz al–Asad, the new regime remained in power longer than all other Syrian governments combined. Al–Asad ("The Lion") was elected president in 1971, as the only candidate on the ballot, and two years later a new constitution provided for an elected legislature, the People's Council. Power remains firmly with the president, who must be a Muslim. He appoints the vice president, prime minister, and cabinet.

Despairing of diplomatic efforts to recover their lost territory, Syria and Egypt began a surprise military offensive in 1973 in a desperate effort to drive out Israeli forces. Three weeks of intensive fighting again demonstrated Israeli military superiority, but with aid from Iraq and Jordan, the Syrian defenses did not break. U.S. mediation efforts led by Henry Kissinger in 1974 returned a small strip of territory to Syria and established a U.N.–patrolled buffer zone between the two armies.

In the fall of 1975, Syrian attention was diverted to the civil war which had erupted in Lebanon. At first acting as an ally of one side, then a mediator, and finally as a military peacekeeper, Syria's basic desire was to maintain—and increase, if possible—its influence in that country. Syria thus attempted to prevent any faction in the country from becoming too powerful, first arming the Palestinians and leftists against the conservative Maronite militias, then later attacking the Palestinians and their allies.

The Syrian military apparently also desired to prevent events in Lebanon from providing pretexts for Israeli intervention. It valued eastern Lebanon for the defense of Damascus and to prevent Israeli tanks moving easily northward through the Biqa Valley, emerging near Homs to cut Damascus from the rest of the country.

Formal international approval for the Syrian occupation followed when the Arab League created the Arab Deterrent Force. Largely Syrian, it sought to restrict operations of both the Maronite militias and the Palestinians. However, Syrian troops never ventured far into southern Lebanon, and failed to oppose the Israeli invasion there in 1978, although they fought bitter artillery battles with Maronite militias.

Most Syrians considered President Sadat of Egypt a traitor for abandoning them and the Palestinian Arabs, for whom they have great sympathy, when he signed peace agreements with Israel in 1978 and early 1979 (see Israel: History). While Israel reluctantly withdrew from Egypt in exchange for peace, it determined to keep the remaining territories it had conquered in 1967. With Egypt neutralized by a peace treaty, Israel found it easier to hold those areas and colonize them.

Syria denounced Iraq in late 1980 for its invasion of Iran, asserting that Israel was the greater threat to the Arab cause.

The late President Hafiz al–Asad (d. June 10, 2000)

Because most Arab states sided with Iraq out of a mixture of nationalism and fear of Iranian threats to export the Islamic Revolution, Syria thus effectively isolated itself in the Middle East. The Israeli government seized the opportunity in 1981 to annex the territory it occupied on the *Jawlan* (Golan) heights. When the few Syrian citizens there, mainly members of the *Druze* community, rejected the use of new Israeli identity cards, the Israeli army used stern methods to force them to do so. Syria lacked any realistic means to protect them.

In its early years al–Asad's government won broad public acceptance for the stability it offered and a reduction of the radicalism common to the previous *Ba'thist* regime. Syria's pragmatism likewise brought increased foreign aid, and the relaxation of socialist regulations encouraged economic growth. While not a democracy in the western sense, Syria held elections to the People's Council (parliament). The *Ba'th Party* regularly won a majority, but some independents and minor leftist parties also held seats.

By the early 1980s, signs began to increase that many Syrians were beginning to desire fresh faces in government and a replacement of military rule. Like many other top military men, Hafiz al–Asad is a member of the Alawi community, an offshoot of Shi'a Islam that incorporates a number of ideas of other religions. Patronized by the French, but ignored in matters of economic development after independence, the Alawis found few opportunities open to them, and thus tended to join the military. As Alawi soldiers moved up the ranks, eventually a military government came to mean an Alawi government, although Sunnis always held important positions. By embracing *Ba'thist* socialism and linking with the *Communist Party*, the

regime presented itself as secular and modernizing.

Given the prohibition on most forms of political activity, opposition to al–Asad's government came largely from the illegal Sunni *Ikhwan al Muslimin* ("Muslim Brotherhood,") which wanted to create an Islamic state. After their supporters undertook several violent acts, including killing nearly 50 *Alawi* military cadets in one incident, revolt broke out in the conservative city of Hama in 1982. Military units crushed the rebellion eventually, but at the cost of hundreds of lives and great damage to an old and picturesque city. The bloodshed ended most dreams of removing the regime by force, but the next year the difficulty of legitimizing the government became obvious when, after Hafiz al–Asad suffered a heart attack, his brother Rifaat and other military leaders started a premature struggle for the succession.

The strong Israeli invasion of Lebanon in 1982 threatened Syria's military and political interests. Israeli aircraft destroyed much of the Syrian air force, and ground losses compelled Syrian troops to retreat, and later to withdraw from Beirut. Influenced by Israeli guns, the Lebanese Parliament elected an anti–Syrian president. Suspicion of U.S. intentions turned to opposition when American units took sides in the civil war and attacked targets in eastern Lebanon, Syria encouraged leftist and Muslim opponents of the Lebanese president and army, including terrorists who blew up a Marine barracks in Beirut.

Throughout 1983 and 1984 Syria adamantly insisted that Lebanon not become subservient to Israel and the United States, and denounced President Gemayel's proposed agreement recognizing

Israel and requiring Syrian troops to evacuate. To Damascus, it appeared that American policy joined with Israel in presenting a threat to Syria through Lebanon. By encouraging anti–Gemayel forces in the civil war, Syria forced the president to turn away from Israel, in search of a settlement.

When Israeli forces withdrew from most of Lebanon in 1985 under pressure from Shi'a militias and other groups, Syrian troops also departed. However, terrorism and anarchy prevailed in much of the country, and when intense fighting broke out in 1987 between the Shi'a *Amal* militia and Druze and allied left–wing groups, Syrian troops again entered Lebanon to restore order. Like al–Asad, *Amal* is Muslim but not Sunni; like the *Ba'th* it envisions a secular state, not an Islamic one. *Amal* became pro–Syrian in its policies, and in turn benefitted from Syrian limits on its rival, *Hizbullah*.

Besides halting the fighting, Syria attempted to shape Lebanese politics. In 1988 it favored a Maronite candidate in the presidential elections. However, the election was not held, and heavy fighting broke out between units of the Lebanese army and Syrian forces they considered foreign occupiers (see Lebanon: history).

By early 1989 Syria seemed diplomatically isolated. Western nations felt disturbed by terrorism allegedly masterminded in Damascus by Abu Nidal's offshoot Palestinian group (since expelled), as well as by one of the Syrian intelligence services. The Soviet Union refused al–Asad's request for high–tech weapons because Syria could not pay for them, nor use them effectively, nor protect their secrets.

A covered 17th century *souk* (shopping area) in the old part of Damascus

Responding to International Isolation

Within the Middle East, the revolutionary socialist *Ba'thist* ideology, combined with its vision of a single Arab state from the Atlantic to the Gulf, naturally prohibited enduring alliances with monarchies. Iraq, a rival strengthened by victory over Iran, posed a physical threat as well, and it armed Christian Lebanese units. Al–Asad's uncompromising stand against the Camp David Agreement precluded friendship with Egypt, and the quarrel with Yasir Arafat isolated Syria when the Palestine National Council and the United Nations favored Arafat's diplomatic approach. Finally, the Arab League proposed a peace for Lebanon, eliminating the need for Syrian troops.

In diplomatic isolation, al–Asad proved his dexterity and craftiness. He skillfully yielded over Egypt, and offered little opposition to the Palestinians. On Lebanon he remained uncompromising, and won: the Arab League failed to demand Syria's withdrawal. Indeed, the agreements reached at Taif, Saudi Arabia, for a revised Lebanese constitution (see Lebanon: Politics) preserved Syria's right to station troops in Lebanon indefinitely. Perhaps not coincidentally, Syria aided in gaining the release of two American hostages from Beirut in early 1990, and generally seemed to seek an end to its isolation.

Further opportunities came when Iraq seized Kuwait in 1990. If successful, the action would have greatly strengthened Syria's long–standing *Ba'thist* rival. Beyond public support for American and other Coalition troops in Saudi Arabia, al–Asad even deployed nearly 20,000 men of his own armed forces there. The Syrian public, however, accepted only reluctantly such behavior by a radical, traditionally anti–American regime. Syrian troops played only a defensive role and did not invade Kuwait or Iraq. Thus, Syria became a member of the Coalition, but on its own terms.

Rewards nevertheless followed. Syria regained international standing. Diplomatic ties resumed with Britain, and the European Community dropped sanctions imposed over an attempted airplane bombing in 1986 blamed on Syrian intelligence. President Bush met with President al–Asad despite the alleged terrorist links. Financial assistance from the Gulf states, Japan and Europe surpassed $2 billion. In Lebanon, Syrian troops crushed the forces of Michel Aoun, thus extending the power of the Syrian–supported president, and the parliament in Beirut approved treaties granting Damascus wide pretexts for intervention.

President al–Asad again surprised observers—and upstaged Israel—when he accepted U.S. Secretary of State James Baker's invitation to a peace conference on the Middle East. The alternative, a

Portrait of a Young Man by noted Syrian artist Fateh Almudarres

military reconquest of the (Syrian) Jawlan was clearly impossible, given the end of Soviet assistance and the destruction of Iraq (often a potential ally against Israel, though daily a bitter *Ba'thist* rival). In addition, when Syria attempted to acquire SCUDs from North Korea, Israel prevented their reaching Latakia, and the U.S., in the cause of arms limitation, attempted to halt their transfer via Iran. To popular opinion, this seemed unfair: the U.S. pays for Israeli missile development.

Syrian negotiations with Israel proved surprisingly hopeful during the *Labor* government of Yitzhak Rabin in the early 1990s. New Israeli negotiators conceded the possibility of withdrawing from the Golan *(Jawlan)*, and Damascus suggested informally that special arrangements

might be made. If Israel acknowledged Syrian sovereignty, demilitarized zones and agreement over water rights might form part of the peace settlement.

However, neither the simplicity of the solution nor the advantages of peace brought rapid agreement. Each side clung to demands the other would obviously reject. Israel insisted on defining peace conditions before conceding its withdrawal, and it proposed retaining observation posts, despite al-Asad's oft-repeated insistence that all territory be returned. This apparently simple phrase lays claim to the 1949 armistice lines rather than the usually identical international boundary. The crucial difference is a section of land in places just over 11 yards wide along the eastern shore of the Sea of Galilee. The

The village of Ma'aloula where the Aramaic language of Christ is still spoken

mandate preserved the entire lake within Palestine (and therefore its successor state, Israel, as shown on the map in this volume), but the 1949-1967 armistice lines recognized a Syrian advance to the water's edge. After the newly-elected Barak cabinet in Israel raised hopes for peace in 1999, negotiations again broke down. It is not clear that Israel is prepared to withdraw to either line in exchange for peace. Major parties like *Likud* oppose a withdrawal.

From the perspective of Damascus, Syria occupies a particularly dangerous portion of Middle Eastern real estate, and problems simmer with most neighboring countries. Because of left-wing solidarity and as a counter-weight to Turkish diversion of the Euphrates River, during most of the 1990s Syria permitted Abdullah Ocalan, the leader of the Marxist Kurdish workers party, the *PKK*, to direct their rebellion against Turkey from Syria or Syrian-occupied Lebanon. When faced with Turkish military threats in 1998, Syria expelled Ocalan, but significant tensions remain with Turkey, particularly over Antakiya, the division of the Euphrates River waters, and its military links with Israel.

Under Hafiz al-Asad, Syria enjoyed official friendship with Lebanon, but relations with other Arab neighbors often seemed chilly. Muslim opposition groups sometimes operated from Jordan, and Iraq remained a bitter and sometimes deadly ideological rival. Not surprisingly, Syria followed an independent and sometimes lonely foreign policy, reflected in the virtual absence of ambassadors abroad.

Domestic Affairs and The Succession

Syrian domestic affairs traditionally received little attention abroad, in part because the public expressed itself little. The controlled press, bland and propagandistic, questioned little. The regime did not remain in power for two decades by fostering a variety of viewpoints, but rather by removing traditional leaders from positions and independent wealth. Moreover, those expressing discontent were frequently arrested and detained indefinitely. After the release of some opponents imprisoned for a decade, in 1992 Syria still held an estimated 5,000 political prisoners; perhaps 1,500 remained in 2000, and others were exiled abroad.

The legislature remained a forum for the non-political discussion of non-partisan matters because opposition parties have been illegal for decades. During the three decades of rule by Hafiz al-Asad, most Syrians accepted the reality of an authoritarian regime and set aside political ideologies. Typically, one-third of those elected to the legislature were formally independent of the *Ba'th* party's *National Progressive Front*, a contrast to the 99.9% "yes" votes for al-Asad in successive elections.

In recent years two overwhelming public concerns have been corruption and a stagnant economy. Following attacks on officials for corruption, al-Asad appointed Mahmud Zubi as prime minister in 1987. He adopted emergency measures aimed to improve Syria's balance of payments, worsened by reductions in aid from Saudi Arabia and other Gulf states. Nevertheless, the population grew faster than the economy, and unemployment proved a severe problem. For the wealthy, however, luxury goods proved abundant, reportedly a result of the Syrian involvement in Lebanon and its drug trade. Increased oil production, plus some reduction in the myriad economic regulations, led to an increase in prosperity for some of the middle and upper classes. However, poverty remains obvious and the infrastructure totters, with

frequent rationing of electricity.

Heavy snows and rain in 1992 promised an end to a severe drought. For several years it had devastated agriculture, reducing the wheat harvest by half. In contrast, good rains by 1994 provided successive record harvests that filled storage facilities to overflowing. Infrastructure difficulties remained: city dwellers still faced water cutoff for half days.

When hydroelectric output resumed at the al-Thawra Dam at Tabaqa, normally the source of 50% of Syria's electricity, it was for reasons unrelated to sparse rainfall. Rather, Turkish engineers had withheld almost the total flow of the Euphrates River to fill the reservoir behind the Ataturk dam upstream. This complicated the country's critical shortage of electricity, and power shortages led the government to compromise its socialism and encourage private investment in generating capacity.

When a car crash in 1994 killed Basil al-Asad, the elder son of Hafiz, it aroused widespread mourning. Basil, an air force officer presented to the public as clean-living and athletic, had seemed a far more acceptable successor than did long-serving cabinet ministers or Rifaat al-Asad, the formerly-exiled brother of the president.

After Basil's passing, his younger brother Bashar slowly emerged from a low-profile, non-political role. He supervised the country's initial computerization, then handled Lebanese affairs. He influenced a major cabinet reshuffle and crackdown on corruption in 2000 and backed Mustafa Miro, an experienced administrator rather than *Ba'th* party leader, as prime minister.

In June 2000 Hafiz al-Asad died; in the month that followed, the legislature nominated Bashar for the presidency. He won overwhelming (and probably genuine) support in the popular vote that followed. In his inauguration speech, Bashar called for openness and reform. Hundreds of political prisoners were released, and the special security courts were abolished. The infamous Mezze prison was closed along with the special security courts, access to the internet was greatly expanded, and new regulations permitted private banks to operate. On the foreign scene, relations improved with Jordan, with Yasir Arafat, and even with Iraq, which began exporting oil to Syria after Syria re-opened the border to trade.

Amid signs of progress towards democracy and individual freedom, Riad Seif, an independent parliamentarian, organized the Friends of Civic Society. Other political discussion groups sprouted, and the first independent newspaper since the 1960s appeared, a satirical paper followed by a business journal. The arts, especially drama, reflected the greater openness, and actors on stage enjoyed the new freedom to express sentiments often felt by people on the street.

What might be called the "Damascus Spring" proved brief. Just one year into

Modern Syria

Bashar's era, Riad Seif and Maamun Homsi, another independent member of parliament, were arrested and charged with the crime of trying to change Syria's constitution by illegal means. More than one hundred other advocates of an open society were arrested but mostly released a few days later. Homsi apparently suffered ill-treatment awaiting trial, and his lawyers resigned in protest at unfairness. Without significant evidence, the court sentenced Homsi to five years imprisonment. It could have been life.

Apparently Homsi's real offense had been an open attack on corruption and the wide activities of the security services. Such charges strike at many members of the old guard, and thus, perhaps, at the very foundations of the regime. Clearly the Bashar administration feels far more comfortable with greater economic freedoms, such as the establishment of private banks, than with free speech.

The worsening international situation strengthens those who repress of normal civil rights, giving them the excuse that "times are too dangerous for liberalization." The U.S. war on terrorism clearly condemns groups such as Lebanon's Hizbullah. President al-Asad ("Dr. Bashar" in Syria) likewise condemns terrorism, but he distinguishes between it and national resistence ("a social, religious, and legal right"). Most Syrians admire Hizbullah for liberating southern Lebanon, and Damascus may encourage it to pressure Israel along the border. With few other means to influence (or punish) Syria, some U.S. legislators are attempting to limit academic links between the two countries.

Culture: Almost half of Syria's population lives in cities or towns of more than 10,000. The others mostly live in villages or farm communities, and a few nomads now form under 1% of the total population. The two principal cities are Damascus and Aleppo (Halab); the latter is slightly smaller than the capital, but both have populations of more than one million. Most industry is concentrated around the two cities and at Homs.

Most Syrians are *Sunni* Muslims. The Arab Christian minority is mainly Greek Orthodox, and the sizable Armenian community of Aleppo is Christian. Several other groups merit mention, including *Druze* (see Lebanon: Culture) in the southeast and *Alawis* along the Mediterranean coast and nearby mountains. Developing their beliefs and ritual secretly in the rugged mountains, the *Alawis* for centuries remained something of a mystery. Modern scholars, little better informed, find major *Shi'a* influences, especially the *Ismaili* variant. The Imam Ali, for example, is revered as the incarnation of God. Other beliefs and the liturgy suggest Christian and other religious influences.

The Jewish community of Damascus is rapidly becoming extinct. After thousands of years of vibrant life and two generations of experience surviving the Arab–Israeli dispute, by 2002 it had dwindled to about 50 members worshipping in one surviving synagogue. The demise did not result from persecution. Rather, legal changes permitted families to emigrate together to the West, and as the community dwindled, the U.S. seemed more appealing to the few who remained.

In spite of the religious differences, there is little intercommunal strife; such ethnic differences are not recognized in the government structure as they are in Lebanon, and political parties have not been built along religious lines. The *Ba'th Party* has no formal religious element to it, and was founded by both Christians and Muslims. Nevertheless, *Alawis* dominate the party as well as the government.

Like Egypt and Iraq, Syria contains numerous archaeological sites of great historical importance. They relate to periods stretching from recent times right back to the earliest village life. The spectacular ruins of the caravan city of Palmyra lie in the middle of the desert beside the modern oasis village of Tadmor. Queen Zenobia once ruled there until defeated by the Romans and carried off to Rome as a royal prisoner. The grandeur of Palmyra's ruins is enhanced by a luxurious French–managed hotel that provides the visitor with modern comforts.

At Aleppo, in the northern part of Syria, a great citadel of bygone days arises on a high mound in the middle of a modern city. Damascus, with its great mosques and fine museums, also has a very long history; the National Museum contains one of the finest displays of Islamic art to be found anywhere. In the center of Damascus, adjacent to the covered market known as the *Suq al–Hamidiya,* the Umayyad Mosque preserves gold leaf from the seventh century. Other museums illustrate the lifestyle of wealthy families during the Ottoman period, while in small villages outside Damascus the inhabitants still speak Aramaic, the language used by Christ.

Economy: Although Syria has a more balanced economy than most nations of Southwest Asia, one–third of the population still depends directly on agriculture, raising cotton in irrigated fields along the Orontes and Euphrates rivers, wheat and other grains on the steppe, or fruits and vegetables in oases like the Ghuta outside Damascus. In years of abundant rainfall, Syrian farmers raise grain for export, but usually the country imports food. There is much room for further development of farming, and experimental programs are

School kids at Citadel

carried on with the United Nations. Given the high cost of importing about one–third of food consumption, agricultural development is vitally important. Increases in the area of irrigated land resulting from the Euphrates dam proved much slower than expected.

The largest single industry is still textiles. Domestic cotton from the Euphrates Valley, the Aleppo Plain and elsewhere supply the mills. Raw cotton is also exported, but in lesser quantities as more and more is woven into textiles in Syria. In view of heavy military expenditures, the country has little money for any large new development projects, so emphasis is being placed on improving production levels in existing projects.

A pipeline to transport oil from the modest deposits in the northeast to a refinery in Homs and the port of Tartus has operated since 1968. Syria's oil exports were a major earner of foreign exchange during the 1970s, but declining exports and lower prices brought a drop in this income. The oil pipeline from Iraq, closed for political reasons by the Syrian government, may have new use. An American oil company discovered promising amounts of oil east of Dair az–Zor. Reaching commercial production in 1989, the fields provided for a rapid increase in exports by 1990 and reached 400,000 barrels per day. The search for oil and its production continued in the 1990s.

In the late 1980s, the economy faced a variety of difficulties. A drought forced the import of large amounts of wheat and other grains, raising costs of livestock and poultry and boosting inflation to rates of 50–100%. When repayments fell behind on loans from Western banks, the World Bank suspended its loans. Soviet military loans that exceeded $11 billion also posed political and economic difficulties. Finally, aid from other countries fell to insignificant levels in 1988. Financial assistance from the anti–Iraqi Coalition clearly arrived at a most useful time.

The Future: Syria seems caught in a race between reform and reaction. The economy requires greater openness and freedom; the public desires it. However, many old-timers in the regime (and those newly retired by it) recognize that if change comes too quickly or too radically, *Ba'thist* rule and their privileges could be swept away.

Reform does not yet mean the possibility of losing power. Expect Bashar to lead cautiously towards greater openness, while the old guard recognizes that seizing control would lead to their downfall. Islamic militants and similar opposition groups will "wait and see" rather than attempt a revolution. Meanwhile, courageous reformers like Riad Seif and Maamun Homsi will suffer for pushing too fast in seeking to change Syria into a more pleasant place to live.

Vender selling nuts

166

The Republic of Turkey

Near the mouth of the Bosporus in Istanbul survive old residences and, looming above them, the Sultan Ahmet I Mosque—the "blue mosque." Photo: Miller B. Spangler

Currency: Lira; $1 buys more than a million.

Former Political Status: Turkey's territory was the heartland of the Ottoman Empire, independent during the period of European colonialism.

National Day: October 23, 1923 (day of establishment of the Republic).

Head of State: Ahmet Necdet Sezer, President.

Head of Government: Bulent Ecevit, Prime Minister.

National Flag: Red field containing a large white crescent with a smaller five–pointed star between its points.

Gross Domestic Product: $200 billion

GDP per capita: $3,000 (but likely to fall).

During the early 1920s, a new nation arose in the ancient peninsula of Asia Minor and the adjacent tip of Europe. In this territory, the Ottoman Empire had ruled a mosaic of Greeks, Armenians, Kurds, and Turks before World War I, but led by Kemal Atatürk, the last of these communities preserved its independence and established a national state. Although the Turkish tribes originated in Central Asia and only 5% of the new country lay in Europe, Atatürk strove to create a modern, secular and European country to replace the religiously–inspired empire.

Geography: Besides the small European portion around the historic city of Istanbul, modern Turkey covers Asia Minor, known as Anatolia, and the mountainous region to its east. Although the nation enjoys a long coastline on the Aegean Sea, almost none of the major islands are Turkish. Instead, though often located only a few miles from Asia Minor, they belong to Greece.

Two long, narrow straits divide European from Asian Turkey. The Dardanelles leads from the Aegean Sea into the small Sea of Marmara. Vessels continuing to the Black Sea then sail up the Bosporus. For centuries, authority over the straits between the Black Sea and the Mediterranean has been important, for whatever power rules the straits influences the commercial and strategic well–being of other Black Sea states.

Apart from its long seacoasts, Turkey is a country of high elevations, and averages more than 3,500 feet above sea level. Asia Minor forms a plateau surrounded, except on the west, by mountain ranges. The highest mountains are in the eastern part of the country. A spectacular mountain on the Iranian border, called *Ağri Daği* in Turkish and Mt. Ararat in English, has a peak towering to 16,945 feet. Many other mountains exceed 10,000 feet, and the plateau itself varies in elevation from 2,500 to 7,000 feet.

Area: 301,380 sq. miles (780,000 sq. km.).
Population: 64 million, officially, 1999
Capital City: Ankara (Pop. 3.2 million, estimated).
Climate: Mostly hot and dry in the summer, except in the coastal regions which are hot and humid; winters generally are wet and mild on the coasts, cooler inland and very cold in the eastern mountains.
Neighboring Countries: Greece (West); Bulgaria (Northwest); Georgia, Armenia (Northeast); Nakhichevan (Azerbaijan) (East); Iran (East); Iraq (Southeast); Syria (South).
Time Zone: GMT +2 (+3 in summer).
Official Language: Turkish.
Other Principal Tongues: Kurdish, Arabic, Greek and Armenian.

Ethnic Background: Most people are identified as Turks on the basis of language and their Islamic culture; there are a variety of physical characteristics and many Turks look much like Europeans.
Principal Religion: Islam (about 98%).
Chief Commercial Products: Cotton and textiles, mohair, tobacco, hazelnuts, raisins, sorghum, millet, barley, wheat, coffee, corn, meat, crude steel, coal, iron ore, chromite, salt, gypsum, petroleum products, diversified manufactured goods, including televisions, refrigerators, automobiles, and textiles.
Major Trading Partners: Germany, U.S., Libya, Russia, Iran, Switzerland and the U.K.

The heart of Turkey to the south of Ankara is a desert because the mountains to the north and south block out rain–bearing clouds. In this region Lake Tuz has one of the highest concentrations of salt and minerals of any lake or sea. To the east, Lake Van also contains high levels of salt, and no visible outlet, although underground channels may connect it to the Tigris or Euphrates. All together, many lakes comprise 3,256 square miles of the total area of the country.

Two traditionally useful rivers are the Kizil Irmak and the Sakarya, both draining into the Black Sea. The Seyhan and Ceyhan empty into the Mediterranean, after running through the fertile plain around Adana on which much of Turkey's cotton is grown. The mighty Tigris and Euphrates both originate in Turkey, but they pass through steep mountain gorges, so their initial usefulness was generating electrical power. Now they serve as the basis for GAP: the Southeast Anatolia Project for agricultural and industrial development.

The western part of the country generally has good winter rains, as does the southern range of mountains known as the Taurus Mountains. The Pontus Mountains along the north coast have moderate rains throughout the year, especially in the spring. Ankara and the central plateau lack adequate rainfall. The eastern highlands have an abundance of precipitation, but the rugged terrain is not suitable for agriculture; at higher elevations snow covers the ground for at least four months of the year. There are forests in the mountains of the east and north, but few trees grow elsewhere.

History: The modern Republic of Turkey rose from the ruins of the Ottoman Empire, which was defeated and dismembered at the close of World War I. Secret agreements made during the war divided many areas with little regard for national feeling, and left only a very small Turkey in northern Asia Minor. At the Paris Peace Conference, the Arab parts of the empire fell as prey to Britain and France, and Turkish–speaking provinces seemed destined for partition among Italy, Greece and Armenia as well.

To enforce their colonial claims, Greek troops occupied Izmir and moved inland, while the French, despite some resistance, sought the region around Adana. Pending a peace treaty, British forces occupied the Sultan's capital, Istanbul, while Armenians and Kurds both appealed to the Peace Conference for their own states. However, in 1920 an energetic and determined army officer, Mustafa Kemal, summoned delegates to Ankara, to save the nation. Calling themselves the Grand National Assembly, the delegates elected Kemal, later to adopt the surname Atatürk, as its president. In the next months, they approved a program to establish an independent Turkish nation with the small railroad town deep in Anatolia as the capital.

To the astonishment of the allied victors, Kemal molded a poor but new following built around the Ottoman Ninth Army into a fervent and disciplined force. It pushed the French back to Aleppo, and retook provinces claimed by Armenia. Kemal persuaded the Italians to withdraw from southwest Asia Minor and began a struggle with Greece and Britain.

Disagreements split the victors into national camps. France recognized the new Turkish regime quickly, hoping to gain national advantage. Peace with Greece only followed a bitter war. When they were forced to retreat, the Greek forces destroyed everything and committed outrages upon

Kemal Atatürk

Turkish villagers. After eliminating Greece from Asia Minor, the Turks turned northward to Istanbul, where a small British force was left alone to defend the city; Britain finally decided on withdrawal. The Treaty of Lausanne, ratified in 1923, gave Turkey full sovereignty over most of the territory it now possesses. On October 29,

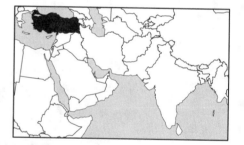

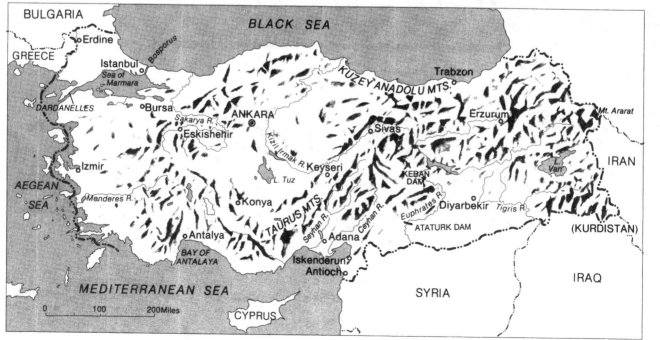

1923, the Grand National Assembly proclaimed Turkey a republic.

Under Kemal's leadership, deep changes shook Turkish society. The office of Caliph was abolished in 1924, along with religious law courts. A constitution, put into effect in 1924, made Ankara the capital, designated the National Assembly as the center of authority and guaranteed freedom of speech, press and travel. While the document provided for a democratic form of government, in fact Mustafa Kemal ruled as a dictator. Opposition, particularly by Kurds in the southeast, was ruthlessly crushed.

The new government adopted many measures to rush Turkey towards modernization. It forbad men to wear (Muslim–style) hats without brims. People were forced to dress like Europeans, and attempts were made to force them to think and act like Europeans. The government replaced the Arabic script with the Latin alphabet, making every book and sign in the country obsolete. In the process it purified Turkish of many Arabic and Persian words. Even names changed, as Mustafa Kemal and the rest of the nation adopted the use of family names; Kemal himself became "Atatürk", Father of the Turks. The first republic in the Muslim world, the state closed religious schools and abolished the dervish orders. The policy of secularization eliminated many other aspects of Ottoman society and culture. The Western calendar replaced the Muslim, polygamy was ended, and women received a new status. Codes of law based on European models replaced Ottoman procedures influenced by the Islamic *Sharia*. The day of rest was moved from Friday to Sunday.

The pace of change moved rapidly in other social and economic spheres. Universal primary education was proclaimed, corruption attacked, and Atatürk committed the military to continuing reform. In subduing the Christian Armenians and Greeks, the Turkish army was ruthless (although most of the 1.5 million Armenians perished during World War I). This caused a flight of almost all of the remaining people of these groups, leaving Turkey short of managerial talent and entrepreneurs, but Atatürk responded with a program of industrialization behind high tariff barriers. When private industry failed to expand sufficiently during the Great Depression of the 1930s, the government created State Economic Enterprises to operate in textiles, metals, banking and other areas. Kemal Atatürk died in 1938, recognized as the hero of his nation in his own lifetime.

The National Assembly elected a close associate of Ataturk, Ismet Inonu, as the second president of the Republic. He soon faced the difficult task of guiding the nation through World War II. Turkey remained neutral, but at the end of the war threats from the Soviet Union forced it to

seek help from the West, particularly from the U.S. Beginning in 1947, Turkey received massive economic and military aid, given to help resist Soviet pressure. Realizing it needed help defending itself against the Soviet Union for many years, Turkey joined the North Atlantic Treaty Organization in 1951.

After becoming a member of the United Nations (1945), Turkey moved cautiously toward democracy at home. Opposition parties contested the 1946 elections, but the ruling *Republican People's Party* achieved an overwhelming victory. In 1950, however, the *Democratic Party* won 408 of the 487 seats in the National Assembly. Celal Bayar became President; Adnan Menderes assumed the office of Prime Minister. The party improved upon its previous victory in 1954 elections.

During the following years, as the *Republican People's Party* made gains in an enlarged legislature, the *Democratic Party* became less democratic; it finally banned all political activity by the opposition. It had its main strength among the old–fashioned and little–educated peasants. Modernized, educated Turks, however, became much opposed to its practices, particularly overspending which was taking the country seriously into debt and producing high inflation. Since military officers consider themselves the heirs of Atatürk's reforms and value modernism, it was not surprising that officers under General Cemal Gursel seized power. All high officials and members of the National Assembly belonging to the *Democratic Party* were arrested.

The military oversaw ratification of a new constitution in 1961 which introduced procedures designed to avoid concentration of power in one office. A Senate was added to the legislative branch and a High Court was created with the authority to rule on the constitutionality of laws. It also included a bill of rights and set "social justice" as the goal of government.

Elections in 1961 gave the *Republican People's Party* almost equal representation in the National Assembly with the new *Justice Party,* which drew some of its members from the outlawed *Democratic Party*. General Gursel was elected President of the Republic for a seven–year term by the Assembly without opposition. Prompting from the army led to a coalition government with the aging Ismet Inonu of the *Republican People's Party* as Prime Minister.

Popular attention focused less on these matters than on the lengthy trials of 592 *Democratic Party* officials for bribery and other illicit personal gain, subversion of the constitution and illegal acts for partisan purposes. Three of the deposed ministers, including Menderes, were sentenced to death and hanged; former President Bayar and eleven others, also condemned to death, had their sentences commuted to life imprisonment. Only 123 of the accused were found innocent of wrongdoing.

Later events showed that the upheavals of 1960 and 1961 did not solve a number of political and economic problems. Indeed, some of the drastic measures created bitterness in a whole generation, while the military intervention set a precedent and established a watchdog role for the military.

Elections of 1965 and 1969 gave the *Justice Party,* led by Suleyman Demirel, control of the Assembly. The administration was faced with demands for more jobs and lower prices along with the sniping of politically dissatisfied groups. The illness of

The Galata Bridge, Istanbul

Stone heads of gods built for King Antiochus I in southwestern Turkey over 2,000 years ago

the president and his replacement by another former military man in 1966 was a reminder that the generals had their eyes on the activities of the civilian government.

Justice Party rule finally foundered in the first half of 1971 and Turkey fell into unrest as serious as that of 1960. Student protests, unemployment and violence by extremist groups along with the threat of a Kurdish uprising in the eastern provinces rendered the government ineffective. The army forced Demirel's resignation and took strong measures to restore law and order, but the political uncertainty remained. The military selected three different prime ministers before the next regularly scheduled elections. Only after 15 ballots could the Assembly finally elect Fahri Koruturk, a retired admiral, as president in 1973.

Although neither major party gained an absolute majority, elections in later 1973 confirmed Bulent Ecevit, a former poet and journalist, as the principal rival to Demirel. As leader of the *Social Democratic Republican People's Party* (its full name resulted from a shift farther to the left in 1966), Ecevit became Prime Minister. Besides the continuing dispute with Greece over the island of Cyprus, tensions flared anew with the 1974 Greek discovery of an oil field in the northern Aegean Sea. Disputes over territorial waters and underwater mineral rights in other parts of the Aegean became important.

When the Ecevit government seized the opportunity for an invasion of Cyprus in 1974 (see Cyprus: History), it gained emotional public support. The premier thereupon resigned, expecting new elections that would return his party with a large majority in the National Assembly, enabling it to govern without a coalition. However, no other party would support the call for immediate elections. A political crisis then lasted for several months until Demirel was able to form a government.

As emotions increased over domestic economic problems and international relations, violence marred the 1977 elections, killing over 200 people and injuring 1,000. No party gained a majority; Demirel formed a shaky coalition that survived briefly and ineffectively. Ecevit became Prime Minister again in early 1978 amid unrest, scattered assassinations and mob violence. The instability resulted partly because the invasion of Cyprus isolated Turkey from Europe and the U.S., and they halted shipments of military equipment. In reaction, Turkey turned, with great uncertainty, toward better relations with Muslim countries and the Soviet Union.

Extremists on both the Marxist left and Islamic right soon reinforced old communal rivalries. By late 1978 unrest erupted into mob fighting in Marash, northeast of Adana. Members of the *Shi'a* and *Alevite* communities, generally poorer than the majority *Sunni* Muslims, suffered more than 100 dead and several hundred injured. Since the *Shi'a* and *Alevite* supported the *Republican People's Party*, and the *Sunnis* backed the conservative *Justice Party*, the conflict was really political, not religious.

Although Prime Minister Ecevit placed many parts of Turkey under martial law, the killing continued; the violence led to an extension of military authority in 1979. By–elections in late 1979 shifted the parliamentary balance and enabled Suleyman Demirel again to take the post of Prime Minister, but in a minority government. Political paralysis continued in 1980 when the President's term of office ended. No candidate received a majority vote in the legislature, and according to the constitution the Senate's speaker became Acting President.

The Council took vigorous steps against terrorism. During the first month more than 10,000 people were arrested and questioned. Other steps were taken to bring discipline to the country, including dismissal of hundreds of mayors across the nation and ordering that taxi drivers shave daily. By the spring of 1981, observers reported that violence had declined and that the country even looked cleaner, while others wondered how many innocent people were suffering in prison.

The Return to Democracy

The military leaders, criticizing the 1961 constitution for its misuse by politicians, formed a 160-member Consultative Council in 1981 to draft a new one. Meanwhile, strict controls were imposed on political discussion in newspapers and by public figures. Former Premier Ecevit, for instance, was jailed more than once for talking to foreign journalists about affairs in Turkey.

The proposed constitution for Turkey went to the voters in 1982. No campaigning against the proposal was permitted, while voters were encouraged by every means to give their approval, and they did so overwhelmingly. The constitution temporarily gave President Evren wide executive powers, but promised an elected Assembly by 1984. It banned about 100 leading politicians, including, Ecevit and Demirel, from political activity for ten years. The previous political parties could not operate, nor members of the previous Assembly accept leadership in new parties until 1987.

Meanwhile, the martial law courts dealt sternly with those accused of violence in the fighting that had left 5,000 dead. By 1983 about 100 alleged terrorists were condemned to death, and over 27,000 sentenced, sometimes for lengthy terms. A decade later, another 10,000 prisoners still awaited trials. Friends and attorneys of the defendants assert that prisoners had been tortured and mistreated in ways common to Turkish prisons, such as being chained during transfers, corporal punishment, solitary confinement in a small, dark cell, or bread-and-water diets.

Despite President Evren's obvious preference for the military-backed *National Democracy Party*, in parliamentary elections in 1983 voters preferred the *Motherland Party*, led by economist Turgot Özal, granting it a majority. Özal became prime minister, but President Evren and the (military) National Security Council retained ultimate control on significant issues. Four years later, the *Motherland Party* won a large majority (292 of 450 seats) in genuinely free elections. The results represented a resounding approval for the austere economic measures Özal had adopted to bring Turkey out of economic chaos.

Though supposedly based on proportional representation, the electoral system actually produced the majority for the *Motherland Party*: it received only 36% of the vote. As the largest party, it benefited from a unique Turkish law, since overturned, that gave to the largest party the popular votes of parties receiving less than 10% of the vote. Moreover, old-style politicians still remained banned from politics. In fact, Demirel's *True Path Party* and Inonu's *Social Democratic Populists* retained many supporters. Only a few percentage points separated the three largest parties.

During his second term as prime minister, the achievements in economic growth and foreign affairs that had marked Özal's previous term began to fade. His party suffered outright defeat in the 1989 municipal elections, and charges of corruption and denunciation of Özal's "family-style" administration filled the press—his brother Yusef was minister of state for the economy, and his son and wife both played important roles.

When President Evren's term expired in late 1989, despite his party's unpopularity, Özal won the presidency, a surprise only to those unaware that parliament elects the president. Though opposition parties condemned the move, the constitutional provisions were met. As a symbol of national unity, the president remains above politics. Özal resigned from the *Motherland Party*; its alliance of free traders, nationalists and devout though moderate Muslims thereafter risked unraveling.

Two issues dominated Turkish political life during the 1990s, challenging both the military and political elite. Throughout the Southeast, a major rebellion by disaffected Kurds led to the deaths of perhaps 30,000 civilians and the evictions of hundreds of thousands of others from their villages. Meanwhile, throughout the country, against a background of political and economic stagnation, the Islamic-influenced *Welfare Party* won local elections and finally came to govern Turkey, before being ousted under military pressure.

The Kurdish Insurrection

For millennia, tough mountain tribesmen have inhabited the heights and valleys of the region stretching from Iraq and Iran into Southeastern and Eastern Turkey. Today the biggest ethnic group lacking independence outside of East and South Asia, Kurds have rebelled against the government of each of five states where they form a local majority.

Today's political problems result from the breakup of the Ottoman Empire at the end of World War I. During that war,

Tanlabas Boulevard in Istanbul. Only the patient and brave (with good lateral vision and quick reflexes!) dare to drive in the city's heart.

Photo: Miller B. Spangler

many Christian Armenians scattered in the Ottoman Empire sympathized with the Allies, and some aided Russian forces. In reprisal, entire communities living in eastern Anatolia were mercilessly exiled and some slaughtered. (One should also acknowledge that many Muslims perished as well). Kurds inhabited many of the same regions in southeastern Anatolia and formed the major population group in the east.

After the war, Armenians, Kurds and Turks all claimed the regions as their national lands. However, the Armenians were defeated, and the Kurds lacked alliances with any of Europe's great powers. The Treaty of Lausanne brushed aside Kurdish desires for independence, dividing them mostly between Turkey, Iran, and Iraq (see Iraq: history).

For decades, Turkey officially classified Kurds as "Mountain Turks," taking advantage of the linguistic differences among them to avoid recognizing a separate linguistic and national group. Kemal Atatürk and his successors rigorously suppressed Kurdish revolts as well as any evidence of Kurdish identity. Regulations prohibited the language from use in registration of personal names, public speeches, and at weddings and similar social occasions. Until the government reversed its policy in 1991, no books, papers, street signs or pamphlets legally appeared in the language. The country still (2001) allows neither TV broadcasts nor education in it. However, the dialects remained alive, even when illegal. Cassettes in Kurdish circulated widely, and in recent years satellite broadcasts enabled programs from Europe to reach viewers.

Traditionally most Kurds lived in mountain villages, divided from those across the mountains by dialect and tribal loyalties. They received little formal education, and that in Turkish, so for many reasons most Kurds tended to ignore politics. However, some, including Ismet Inonu, became successful politicians and advanced to the top of national politics. Those claiming some Kurdish ancestry usually filled one-quarter parliament, but such politicians frequently become assimilated, a threat that television and modernization bring to members of the middle classes. At the other extreme, many Kurds desire their own schools and autonomy, while nationalist organizations exist, illegally.

Beginning in the 1990s, violence spread across the southeast and east, fomented by the *Kurdish Workers Party (PKK)*, a marxist group led by Abdullah "Opo" Ocalan (pronounced O-ja-lan). Financed and supported by Syria and by Kurds working in Europe, *PKK* fighters infiltrated into Turkey. The Turkish military, a largely conscript army, often responded roughly to attacks by the *PKK*. On occasion it used heavy weapons within towns, and its brutal treatment of civilians often alienated the local population. To cut off guerrillas from food and shelter, civilian supplies were often tightly controlled, and by the mid-1990s over 800 villages had been forcibly evacuated.

Despite innovations like winter operations and the claim that a guerrilla's life expectancy averaged just six months, the military proved unable to crush the insurgency. In 1992 and again in 1995, it mounted large-scale attacks on alleged *PKK* bases in Iraqi Kurdistan and reported hundreds killed. In fact, alerted by the massive military buildup, most guerrillas apparently slipped away before the attacks.

Recognizing some popular sympathy for the rebels, some Turkish intellectuals advocated greater freedoms for the Kurds to reduce the appeal of revolution. However, the non-revolutionary *Kurdish People's Labor Party* was barred from contesting the 1991 elections. The prohibition on Kurdish TV programs remained, and a series of unsolved murders began to decimate journalists and leaders possibly sympathetic to Kurdish hopes. One newsboy for a pro-Kurdish daily was shot in front of his mother, possibly the work of a death squad. Human rights also suffered at the hands of the police, who arrested even minor employees and seized files.

For its part, the *PKK* massacred civilians, especially Kurds sympathetic to the government, as often as it attacked police and troops. The annual toll of violence rose from hundreds dead in 1991 to over 2,000 in 1992; the total surpassed 11,000 by the rebellion's tenth anniversary in 1994 and nearly 40,000 five years later. Foreign travelers became targets, even in Istanbul, as the *PKK* threatened the important tourist industry.

Turkey's laws and methods often aroused resentment in Kurds who otherwise found the *PKK* unattractive. Reasoning that terrorism must not be rewarded, military officers and many politicians argued that reforms must follow victory over the rebellion. However, Article 8 of the constitution prohibits separatist propaganda in any form; this applies to ethnic autonomy. Over one hundred journalists, politicians, and labor unionists were jailed on the charge of breaking the constitution. Yasar Kemal, Turkey's greatest living writer and the author of *Memed, My Hawk* (the best-known Turkish work in the West), received a 20-month suspended jail term for condemning the policy toward the Kurds.

The struggle against the *PKK* carried important implications for foreign affairs. Until the 1990s, Turkey and Iraq had cooperated to punish cross-border attacks and deter separatism. However, after the Gulf War hundreds of thousands of Iraqi Kurds sought refuge in Turkey. The government confined them to remote border regions lacking facilities to support them, for it did not wish them to become permanent refugees. Faced a rapidly approaching human disaster, however, Turkey supported European proposals to create a safety zone for Kurds in Iraq and permitted Allied warplanes based at Incirlik (near Adana) to protect them. Opinion polls showed most Turks sympathized with this policy, but in 1992 Iraqi Kurds held elections for a leader and legislature. These moves pointed towards eventual statehood—a result that threatens the very concept of a unitary Turkish state that denies the existence of a Kurdish nationality.

With the war against the *PKK* yielding only modest gains, Turkey strengthened its links with Israel and in 1998 forced Syria to crack down on *PKK* activities and expel its leader, Ocalan. This eventually led to his capture in Kenya by Turkish commandos, a tremendous boost to Turkish pride. Britain also closed down a Kurdish satellite channel, Med-TV. Broadcasting across Europe and the Middle East, it had advocating killing in response to the capture of Ocalan.

Placed on trial for his life, Ocalan called the *PKK* rebellion a "mistake" and ordered his followers to abandon violence and to adopt a peaceful political struggle. Although factions of the *PKK* continued to fight in remote locations, most withdrew to Iraq, even though the Turkish military considered the ceasefire a ploy. In 2000 a party congress formally adopted Ocalan's strategy of becoming a political party seeking to improve the Kurdish community within Turkey. This formally implied the end of the independence struggle.

Two years later, the PKK announced that the party would close. This was presumably a strategic move to avoid the "terrorist" label and resulting international limitations after the September 11 attacks. Possibly the PKK will form a purely political organization; otherwise, Kurdish sympathies will probably be reflected in support for the *People's Democracy Party*, generally known as *Hadep*.

Very likely, the greatest obstacle to peace remains the uncompromising attitude of many Turkish officers and officials. For example, the mayors of three important Kurdish cities were arrested, and leaders of their political party (*Hadep*) imprisoned, for participation in protests sympathetic to the *PKK* after Ocalan's capture. Elsewhere arrests followed a soccer game when a *Hadep*-organized team wore the red, yellow and green stripes of the Kurdish colors. Arbitrary arrest, torture, and bureaucratic heavy-handedness remain the ways of life in the Southeast. For these reasons and others, about 500,000 Kurds migrate to western Turkey annually, some continuing their trek by legal and illegal means to Western Europe.

Economic and Political Stagnation in the 1990s

The second great issue dominating political and cultural life during the 1990s was the economic and political stagnation. As political parties fought petty and corrupt squabbles, they provided the background for an Islamic party to take office, despite the country's tradition of secularism and military misgivings.

Growing unrest among labor unions created a great danger for democracy in the early 1990s. Rampant inflation, a by-product of easy money designed to win elections, eroded workers' wages, and unions demanded pay increases as high as 300%. Militant left-wingers led annual demonstrations on May Day, and strikes spread in government-owned industries. An economist by training, Özal recognized that the workers' pay demands risked even higher inflation. However, a failure to meet their claims and those of farmers and civil servants, combined with agitation by Islamic radicals and Kurdish separatists, risked violence of the sort that provoked military takeovers of previous governments. An opposition party first won office in 1950, but every following decade (1960, 1970/71, 1980) had ended with a military dismissal of the government. With conditions worsening, many expected an intervention.

In a move that may have averted military intervention, the prime minister called elections one year early, in 1991. With inflation high (60-70%) and President Özal accused of autocracy and nepotism, his *Motherland Party* fell to second place and left office. Suleyman Demirel, leader of the winning *True Path Party*, formed a coalition with a smaller party and installed his seventh cabinet.

Despite his previous threats to force President Özal from office, Demirel swallowed the rivalry with his former aide. Indeed, he promised to achieve many of Özal's goals, including privatization of state-owned factories and better human rights. Though threatened by inflation, a large budget deficit, and terrorism from left-wing radicals and the *PKK*, the cabinet initially enjoyed a secure parliamentary majority and broad public support. However, by 1993 the *Motherland Party* and the ruling coalition suffered significant defections when President Özal's unexpected death dramatically shifted Turkish politics and parliament elected Demirel president.

In turn, the *True Path Party* chose an American-educated economist, Tansu Ciller, as prime minister. The first Turkish woman prime minister, Ciller faced formidable difficulties. In 1994, the lira lost 50% of its value against the dollar, and several smaller banks failed. The root of the crisis concerned money: the government could not collect enough taxes to pay its normal expenses, aid inefficient state industries,

Mararias, one of the beautiful summer resorts on the Aegean Sea

and finance the war against the Kurdish *PKK*. So the government met its bills by printing money. Inevitably, inflation rose.

With interest rates of 140% and people fearing an economic collapse, Ciller instituted a temporary "inflation tax," sold bits of state-owned industry, closed unprofitable coal mines and steel plants, and raised prices on goods sold by state monopolies. These measures caused a severe recession, but they also cut inflation in half and stabilized the lira. However, structural difficulties remained. The pension (social security) system tottered near collapse, and state-owned industry still required subsidies.

When the European Parliament approved a customs union with Turkey in 1996, it represented a personal triumph for Ciller, who had even changed the constitution to improve human rights practices. Nevertheless, two weeks later her *True Path Party* finished third in the parliamentary elections, while the Islamic *Welfare (Refah) Party* came first with only 21% of the vote.

Forming a stable ruling majority proved impossible during the three-year life of parliament, as six cabinets took and left office. Initially, civilian and military secularists attempted to keep the *Welfare Party* from office. Over several years they had watched Islamic militancy threaten Atatürk's legacy, as *Welfare* won races for the mayors of Istanbul and Ankara and swept the southeast. On occasion events turned violent, for example in Sivas in 1994 when rioters set fire to a hotel during a congress of leftist intellectuals, killing dozens.

President Ahmet Necdet Sezer

During the elections, Ciller had attacked the *Welfare Party* for "sinking the country into darkness." However, out of office by reason of her party's poor showing and facing parliamentary investigations of corruption, Ciller sought safety by becoming the junior partner of the cabinet, at the price of allying with her ideological enemy. By joining with a party headed by a woman, Necmettin Erbakan thus became the country's first Islamist prime minister.

Erbakan clearly sought to reorient foreign policy away from the West and toward the Islamic world. He visited Iran, where he signed a major gas deal, and visited Libya. The bureaucracy and armed forces limited other initiatives, and extreme proposals like creating an Islamic currency or withdrawing from NATO died quietly.

The generals worried, when some local officials of the *Welfare Party* clearly acted contrary to the secularist tradition. The National Security Council demanded a reduction in the Islamist influence on government, and the military quietly encouraged political maneuvering that led the coalition to collapse in 1997. The Constitutional Court later banned the party because it permitted women to wear headscarves in public buildings, encouraged Islamic schools, and kept (unproven) links with secret societies. The courts convicted Erbakan and several other prominent officials from the party, including the mayor of Istanbul, for making statements deemed too Islamist. The mayor, for example, drew a lifetime ban on political activity for using the Islamic term "jihad" (variously meaning effort, struggle, or battle). Under new leaders, *Welfare* members of parliament quickly reformed as a new group, the *Virtue Party*.

To replace Erbakan, President Demirel favored a coalition led by Mesut Yilmaz of the *Motherland Party*. Lacking a majority in parliament, Yilmaz inevitably found governing difficult and the challenges formidable. Human rights advocates demanded an end to police torture, but the courts dealt out light sentences for the beating death of an imprisoned journalist. Evidence accumulated of links between criminals and the intelligence service, the police, and the military. Inflation continued to rise, and the privatization of government-owned firms moved slowly. In foreign affairs, the European Union excluded Turkey from the list of eventual members

Overwhelmed by these events and by allegations of corruption, Yilmaz was forced to resign, to be replaced after lengthy negotiations by a minority government headed by Bulent Ecevit (pronounced "eh-je-vit"), at 73 years of age well past normal retirement. In the 1999 elections, his left-wing but nationalist *Democratic Left Party* swept to first place, while the West's favorite worry, the Islamic *Virtue Party*, came third. Though Ecevit "won" the election when his party received the most votes and seats, the old bonus for being the largest party no longer applied. After negotiations, Ecevit found support from the right-wing and pan-Turkic *Nationalist Action Party* and the *Motherland Party*.

Though leading an unusual alliance of left, center and right-wing parties, Ecevit provided stable leadership after a decade that had witnessed nine governments in as many years. Personally symbolized by his ascetic lifestyle, Ecevit retained popularity while his interior minister, Sadettin Tantan, waged a war on corruption that landed "big fish" (particularly bankers) as well as petty criminals. When the

Prime Minister Bulent Ecevit (pronounced eh-*jay*-vit)

government clamped down on the Turkish paramilitary group *Hizbullah* (no direct relation to the Lebanese group) it obtained evidence that the group had murdered secular intellectuals and Marxist Kurds. The public was horrified by the discovery of the bodies of more than 100 victims. Economic policies reduced the rate of inflation to under 40%, and a new government agency was created to supervise the financially risky banking system. Internationally, in 1999 the European Union accepted, at last, Turkey as a candidate for membership.

On the other hand, Ecevit and the entire government system faced severe challenges. In 1999 an earthquake devastated parts of seven western provinces—the country's industrial heartland. Both the civil administration and the military initially proved inept at rescue efforts, though better at feeding and sheltering hundreds of thousands left homeless. Despite its location on a major geological fault, Turkey had not developed specialized rescue teams, and it was several days before soldiers joined excavation efforts. Television pictures of a centuries-old mosque and its slender minaret standing intact beside collapsed apartment buildings illustrated an equally serious government failing: for decades, officials had failed to issue and enforce appropriate building codes.

When President Demirel's term of office ended in 2000, Ecevit backed a constitutional amendment to provide another term for a president fondly regarded as "Baba" ("Daddy"). However, Ecevit's coalition failed to deliver the votes. Instead, parliament united behind the nomination of Ahmet Necdet Sezer, chairman of the constitutional court. A legal scholar rather than a politician, Sezer brought to the presidency a strong sense of the importance of the rule of law, and the need to reform the (1980) constitution. Unable to converse in foreign languages, and little known outside Turkey (though quoted in *Middle East and South Asia 1999*), the new president called on parliament to uphold the supremacy of law and enact democratic reforms. Commonly recognized as essential for Turkey to join the European Union, Sezer's proposals are the more powerful because he desires reform not so much to please Europe but to benefit Turks.

Inevitably, the strong personalities of the president and prime minister clashed. President Sezer twice refused to sign Ecevit's decree to permit the dismissal of government employees considered too Islamic, arguing that parliamentary approval was necessary. Another disagreement between the two men cost billions of dollars in 2001, when Ecevit claimed he had been insulted by the president. Stock market investors took flight, and those with money (including, allegedly, the Governor of the Central Bank!) speculated against the Turkish lira,

A combine harvesting wheat in southern Turkey

draining $7 billion from the Central Bank's reserves in hours. Overnight interest rates reached an annual level of 5000%. After September 11, a further crisis hit the country, as exports declined and tourism suffered from Westerners' reluctance to travel.

Only devaluation and massive loans from the IMF calmed the markets, but Turkey plunged into a steep economic recession that cost over 600,000 jobs and created widespread economic misery for the middle class as well as the poor. The GDP fell by 8%, and thousands of businesses collapsed, hit hard by falling sales and interest rates roughly 20% higher than inflation. Nevertheless, prices climbed rapidly, leading to demonstrations by government workers and others whose pay fell far behind. Social distress such as suicide, theft, prostitution and stress-related illnesses rose, and in the media, experts feared a "social explosion." Another symptom of the misery came from the 1.5 million people who canceled their cell phones.

Besides the government budget deficit, the banking system lay at the heart of the trouble. Many banks, including those owned by the government, had lent funds they borrowed abroad for politically important projects with little chance of business success. Saving first the state banks, then private banks, will require billions of dollars, much of it from the IMF, as Turkey became its biggest debtor.

In contrast to the political instability of the 1990s and the dismissal of several ministers for corruption, Ecevit's coalition held together, presumably because the alternative was electoral disaster. Massive popular disapproval of the economic program led opinion polls to show that none of the three coalition parties would win 5% of the vote, the minimum to enter parliament.

Consequently, party leaders resolved disputes that normally would sink a coalition. Moreover, the opposition fractured after the *Virtue Party* was declared illegal, and rivalries among Islamic sympathizers kept a clear successor from appearing.

Empowered by its weakness, the coalition managed to amend the constitution, abolishing the death penalty (except in time of war) and increasing political freedom. An amendment removed the crime of "anti-state comments," though not the poorly-defined anti-state activities. Other changes reduced the period for police to detain suspects without charges from two weeks to four days. In principle they allowed broadcasting in Kurdish (unless considered to threaten national security or public safety). Parliament also granted women legal equality in the home, and wives the right to seek employment without the husband's permission. It ended the practice of high schools testing girls' virginity.

After the collapse of the Soviet Union, many Turks felt sympathy with the newly-independent Turkish-speaking republics from Azerbaijan to Kyrgyzstan. Turkish businesses competed for their contracts, and the government granted assistance from typewriter keyboards to security advice. In 2001 Turkey became the first Muslim state to join the coalition fighting the *Taliban* regime in Afghanistan and later accepted command of the international security force there.

Culture: One cannot think of Turkey without thinking of Istanbul—one of the great

---

The Battle over Head-scarves

At first glance, it seems a clear issue of conscience and human rights. If a devout Muslim girl or woman wishes to enhance her modesty by wearing a scarf over her hair, should government interfere? Certainly government should not interfere with the decision to wear, or not wear, such clothing!

Opponents, some of them practicing Muslims, provide a very different perspective: they consider the head-scarf to be a uniform. The scarf announces a woman's religious persuasion, a view that a woman's attire in the 14th (Muslim) century should be based on customs from the 1st century. By a small extension, the scarf also proclaims a woman's loyalty to Islamist political parties. Political insignia do not belong in public places such as schools and government buildings. Even in the individualistic West, some American schools ban gang-related insignia.

Proponents of head-scarves respond that women in scarves intend no criminal conduct, and may vote for any party they please: it is not a return to the brown-shirts worn by Hitler's followers in Germany. Furthermore, the ban causes unnecessary grief. For example, when the mother of a wounded soldier visits him in a military hospital, she must remove her scarf.

As prime minister, Mesut Yilmaz approved their use in early 1998, only to be overruled later by the courts and military. The election of two scarf-wearing parliamentarians, one from the *Virtue Party*, sharpened the issue. Parliamentary regulations did not explicitly prohibit the scarf, and some reasoned that the elected representatives of the people should be entitled to wear what they deem appropriate. However, traditional secularists regarded parliament as the heart of Atatürk's legacy, and argued it would be difficult to prohibit elsewhere what is acceptable in the legislature.

Although one of the two women chose to approach the rostrum bare-headed, *Virtue's* Merve Kavakci disrupted parliament's opening session in 1999, when she appeared wearing a scarf. Accused of violating the republic's basic secular principles, she refused to remove the offending cloth, or leave the chamber. Parliament was forced to adjourn, and literally as well as symbolically, government came to a halt, even before the president had designated the new prime minister. As critics noted, the legislature did not need this distraction from its most serious business of forming a government. Ms. Kavakci now wears her scarf in peace, in U.S. exile.

historic cities of the world. First an ancient Greek colony named Byzantium, it later became Constantinople, capital of the Eastern Roman Empire. Later it was the capital and center of the Byzantine world in which ancient Hellenistic culture persisted almost into modern times. Finally, after its capture in 1453 the Ottomans renamed it Istanbul and installed their Sultan in the Topkapi Saray, the Great Palace overlooking the Bosporus and Golden Horn.

Although Ankara, located near the nation's center, is the political focus, Istanbul is the modern cultural and economic heart of Turkey. With a population approaching six million it extends for miles along the European side of the Bosporus. Its great variety of people and different ways of living make it one of the world's most interesting cities.

Ankara is a very modern city, but has the unhappy distinction of possessing some of the worst air pollution of any city, anywhere. This is not the result of heavy industry, but of geography—the city lies in a natural bowl, trapping smoke and fumes.

From a country long considered overwhelmingly agricultural and rural, during the 1980s Turkey rapidly changed into a nation of city dwellers. So great is the rush to urban areas that the population of the four largest cities grew by almost 70% in the five years to 1985. Smaller cities and towns felt similar increases. In the past three decades there has also been a movement of young men to Germany and other countries of

Designing a carpet pattern, Istanbul   WORLD BANK Photo

The Keban Dam on the Euphrates River   WORLD BANK Photo

Europe to find factory work and send funds to their families back home.

From the early days of Mustafa Kemal's rule, the government remained aloof or sometimes even hostile to religion. Nevertheless, today Islam lives as a vital part of the beliefs of many Turks, especially in rural areas. The spectacular mosques of Istanbul, built by successive Ottoman sultans, still remain places of deep reverence. Religious classes were allowed back into the schools after the 1980 military coup, as part of the cultural heritage of the country. Instruction about religion was not intended as indoctrination, though sometimes it had that effect. The Özal cabinet reversed the Kemalist ban on words of Arabic origin and Islamic connotation. Terms and phrases used by educated people of the Ottoman Empire are beginning to reappear in writing and on radio and television.

Old ways die hard, and the feeling that women should not attend public events with men is still strong in most villages, though not so much in the larger towns and cities. Women and girls do not attend the *halkevi*, "people's house," which is the center of social life in most villages. In Istanbul and Ankara women work in most positions they hold in Europe or America,

On the Bosporus near the Black Sea   Photo: Miller B. Spangler

but in remote villages the visitor may rarely see a woman's face.

In the cities one hears Western music and can dance in hotels and nightclubs, but the great majority of Turks love their own music. To the accompaniment of three or four instruments, including a ute (bazouki), a native drum and perhaps a kind of violin, one person will sing folk songs telling of love, war, heartbreak or death—often in long, drawn–out and high–pitched quavering tones, using minor toned scales for the most part.

Since the founding of the Republic, educated Turks have deliberately tried to imitate the literature and drama of Europe. There is a state theater performing Western plays or plays following Western forms, but the typical Turk finds this alien. Karagoz, the shadow puppet and his friends and enemies are more to Turkish taste; both fantasy and real–life situations appear in the puppet shows.

Education has been a primary concern of the government for decades. Elementary education is completely free, but the goal of universal availability at this level has not yet been fulfilled, though large sums are budgeted to the expansion of facilities. The "middle schools" are similar to three–year junior high schools, while the lycée corresponds to an academic high school and is primarily intended to prepare students for university study. Only some of the higher–ranked graduates of middle schools are able to enter the lycées.

Turkey now has over twenty universities. The oldest is Istanbul University, which traces its founding to Mehmet the Conqueror in 1453. It now enrolls over 30,000 students; the next largest is Ankara University. Another institution in Ankara, offering instruction in English rather than Turkish, is the Middle East Technical University. Expanded with assistance from the UN Special Fund, the United States, Britain and Holland, it serves other countries of the Middle East as well as Turkey. There are also many specialized colleges and institutions.

Economy: Long famous for carpets, mohair and dried fruits, Turkey long remained a land of relatively poor and traditional farmers who often struggled for a living in remote villages. Industry developed quite slowly, partly because local handicrafts suffered competition from European manufactured goods. The first major thrust of industrialization, by the State Economic Enterprises (SEEs), occurred only in the 1930s, sponsored by the government for political and social reasons as well as economic ones. Protected by high tariffs, regulation and other trade barriers, the SEEs failed to become efficient competitors. As recently as the 1970s agricultural products amounted to half the nation's exports. High inflation and shortages of foreign exchange frequently halted periods of strong economic growth.

Desiring greater links with European economies, in the early 1980s Turgot Özal launched reforms to transform the economy. He extended free markets, reduced tariffs, eliminated exchange controls, and removed the heavy hand of government trade restrictions. This encouraged investment by both Turks and European firms.

The result, export–led growth, transformed the stagnant economy of the late 1970s into one enjoying rates of real GNP growth exceeding 5%. While imports almost doubled, exports rose by 400% between 1980 and 1987. Some businesses collapsed, unable to compete with imports sold closer to world prices, but in general Turkish industry seized the opportunity to expand. However, after initially cutting the inflation rate in half, to about 20%, the Özal administration followed electioneering policies that boosted it to 80% and led to the 1994 crisis. The resulting recession improved the trade balance, but its unemployment and resulting political extremism could weaken Turkey's democracy.

Another Özal initiative, to privatize the often large and inefficient State Economic Enterprises (SEEs), has yet to show significant impact. A marked turnaround from policies dating back to Kemal Atatürk, it offers the theoretical promise of greater efficiencies, as the SEEs shed unnecessary labor. However, many SEE factories serve social purposes. Located far from customers, they provide employment in remote and impoverished areas. Their closure would save money in one budget, but probably lead to expenditures elsewhere.

Seeking both political and economic benefits, successive cabinets sought closer links with the European Community. For several reasons, in 1987 the EC declined to promise membership. In 1995 the European Union (the EC's new designation) approved a customs union designed to reduce trade barriers, provide aid, and symbolically show Turkey as a European nation. However, Islamic groups and the *Welfare Party* find the pursuit of links with Europe less appealing than closer relations with Muslim nations, and (in the short run) the benefits of the customs union may not outweigh its costs.

The success of Özal's free market policies alleviated but failed to eliminate many traditional economic problems. Population growth at 2.5% per year absorbs a major portion of economic growth, so that despite the many Turks working abroad, unemployment hovers around 20%, and incomes reach only a fraction of Western standards—just 34% of the European Union's average. Public education lags greatly, with only four compulsory years of school, and social security is minimal. Yet government services receive a great proportion of the budget. Tax revenues fall far short of

requirements, creating a budget deficit regularly exceeding 10% of GNP, and the foreign debt of about $65 billion requires large payments for interest and principal. Monopolies exist in tobacco, sugar, and alcohol, while regulations elsewhere discourage entrepreneurs.

Nevertheless, several signs point to future prosperity. Profitable opportunities abound in many fields. Tourism climbed rapidly in the late 1980s, hampered only by insufficient infrastructure and sanitary facilities. Given beautiful scenery, a warm climate, some exotic customs, and a wealth of historic locations,

A newspaper from Ankara—*FREEDOM*—featuring former Prime Minister Ciller

178

the nation attracts some seven million visitors annually, and tourism constitutes a multi–billion dollar industry, with foreign exchange earnings second only to textiles.

A world apart from luxury hotels, the Southeast Anatolia Project (GAP) offers the possibility of improving some of the country's most impoverished areas. A complex of over 20 dams and irrigation conduits scheduled for completion in 2005, the project's expected cost will exceed $30 billion. Besides generating large amounts of electricity from the Atatürk Dam, the world's fifth largest, on the Euphrates River, the project is planned to divert enough water to irrigate possibly four million acres.

Several problems threaten completion of the project. The combined plans for water use by Turkey, Syria, and Iraq may drain the Euphrates dry, so armed conflict remains possible (see When Will the Taps Go Dry?, p. 2). Declining economic benefits, combined with rising costs, may cause some curtailment, and concerns over soil salinity and chemical pollution may limit irrigation. Nevertheless, if GAP's electrification, roads and farming services reach the average farmer in the style of America's TVA, even Kurdish strife may lessen.

Ever since 1990, UN sanctions against Iraq have imposed heavy costs on Turkey, depriving it of an export market and legal source of fuel. In addition, until the oil–for–food program began operation in 1996 and restored some Iraqi oil exports, it completely lost revenues from the twin oil pipelines that in peacetime carried 1.2 million barrels per day of crude to the sea.

The Future: In the longer term, Turkey will somehow overcome seemingly insurmountable obstacles. But things look more difficult in the next two years. Prime Minister Ecevit is seventy-seven and frail. His own party holds only five seats more than its coalition partner, the *Nationalist Action Party* (MHP), which would abandon his economic and political reforms. Elections would be equally unsettling because just months after he created the *Ak* (*White*) *Party*, polls show the former Islamist mayor of Istanbul, Recep Erdogan, the most popular politician in the country. He would probably win a landslide in early elections.

Besides Mr. Ecevit's health, the other great imponderable is a possible U.S. attack on Saddam Hussein's Iraq. The Turkish public greatly opposes such a war on a fellow Muslim people. Turkish business and government circles fear that war would bring economic disaster to tourism and trade. Finally, a destabilized Iraq might provide its Kurds the opportunity to declare independence. Expect Turkey's leaders to argue forcefully that while terrorism is wrong, an attack on Baghdad is not the solution.

The United Arab Emirates

The Abu Dhabi business district from a pedestrian crossover

Courtesy: Caltex Petroleum Corp. (Joe Brignolo '95)

Area: 32,000 square miles (82,880 sq. km.).

Population: Estimated at 2.4 - 3.0 million, including about 2 million foreigners.

Capital City: Abu Dhabi (Pop. 360,000, estimated).

Climate: Extremely hot except for moderate winters; apart from reasonable rainfall in the highlands between Ras al–Khayma and Fujayra, there is rarely precipitation.

Neighboring Countries: Oman (Northeast and Southeast); Saudi Arabia (South and West).

Time Zone: GMT +4.

Official Language: Arabic.

Other Principal Tongues: English, Farsi (Persian), Urdu and Hindi.

Ethnic Background: Besides members of the Arabic–speaking tribes, expatriate workers from Pakistan, India and Iran compose a majority of adult males in the cities, particularly Abu Dhabi.

Principal Religion: Islam (92%).

Chief Commercial Products: Petroleum, liquified natural gas (LNG), petrochemicals, including plastic and paint, food processing, dates, machinery, boat repair and aluminum.

Major Trading Partners: Japan, Germany, Netherlands, U.K., U.S.

Currency: Dirham (Dh 3.67 = $1 U.S.).

Former Colonial Status: The seven sheikhdoms in the union placed themselves under British protection and accepted British control of foreign affairs, but enjoyed autonomy in domestic matters (1892–1971).

National Day: December 2, 1971 (Independence Day).

Chief of State: Sheikh Zayed bin Sultan Al–Nahyan (Ruler of Abu Dhabi), President of the Supreme Council of Rulers.

Head of Government: Sheikh Maktoum bin Rashid Al–Maktoum (Ruler of Dubai, 1990), Vice–President and Prime Minister.

National Flag: Three equal bands of green, white and black (top to bottom) are flanked at the pole by a vertical red band of the same width.

Gross Domestic Product: $49 billion

GDP per capita: $19,000

Abu Dhabi and five smaller states along the southern limit of the Arab Gulf, plus one on the Gulf of Oman, comprise the federation known as the United Arab Emirates. Most of the land is desert, and the climate hot and humid. For centuries, the inhabitants farmed or herded sheep and goats in the interior, or sought a living from fishing and pearling. A further career was piracy, especially in the extremely shallow Gulf whose sand–banks and coral reefs protected locals from strangers.

Most of Abu Dhabi (pronounced ah–bu za–bi) is low coastal plain and flat desert. In the south, imperceptibly, they become the Empty Quarter of Saudi Arabia. Their topography contrasts greatly with the rugged slopes of the Hajar mountain range that marks the border between Abu Dhabi and Oman and continues to the tip of the "Horn of Arabia." Scattered rainfall in the mountains provides several oases with water for irrigation; the largest of this is *Al–'Ain* in eastern Abu Dhabi.

While there are no permanent rivers, several dozen dams trap runoff for irrigation or to recharge aquifers.

Each of the seven states bears the name of its capital city, and is headed by an *Emir* ("Prince"), who uses the traditional title of *Sheikh*. The territory of Abu Dhabi, though not its population, is about three times as large as the other six states combined. Each state maintains considerable internal autonomy under its hereditary ruler:

Abu Dhabi (Pop. nearly 1 million, estimated). Sheikh Zayed bin Sultan Al–Nahyan.
Dubai (Pop. 850,000, estimated). Sheikh Maktoum bin Rashid Al–Maktoum
Sharja (Pop. 350,000 estimated) Sheikh Sultan bin Muhammad Al–Qasimi.
Ajman (Pop. 50,000, estimated). Sheikh Humaid bin Rashid Al–Nuaimi.
Umm al–Qaywayn (Pop. 30,000, estimated). Sheikh Rashid bin Ahmad Al–Mualla.
Ras al–Khayma (Pop. 120,000, estimated). Sheikh Saqr bin Muhammad Al–Qasimi.
Fujayra (Pop. 50,000, estimated). Sheikh Hamad bin Muhammad Al–Sharqi.

In a society developing as rapidly as the U.A.E., population figures are very rough estimates at best, and in this country the division of the population is a somewhat delicate issue. From the 180,000 inhabitants at independence in 1971, in twenty–five years the total reached was *12 times* as large. (Had the U.S. population grown that rapidly in the same period, it would total as much as China and India combined.)

Overlapping territorial claims by the various states produced a number of neutral zones, some involving more than two Emirates. They are shown darkly shaded on the accompanying map, the lack of clarity reflecting the actual identity of the territories.

History: Recent archeological discoveries show continuous habitation of the coast for the past 7,000 years, and scattered settlements in the *wadis* for much of the period. One graveyard excavated in Sharja that dated about 200 B.C. included two horses and thirteen camels, apparently sacrificed during burial ceremonies. By 2,000 years ago, ports in the region traded as far away as India and China. Perhaps linked to trade, Christianity spread widely, attested by burials, churches, and even a monastery.

The Islamic conquest apparently brought years of substantial prosperity during the Umayyad and early Abbasid dynasties. Later constructions, however, seem mostly fortifications. After centuries of Muslim Arab settlement and sporadic Iranian incursions, in the 1500s the Portuguese seized the dominant role in the Gulf. They soon lost it to the Dutch and British, who sought freedom of commerce rather than colonies.

At the turn of the 19th century, *Wahhabi* envoys from Central Arabia incited some of the states to attack Western commerce, hence its reputation in Europe as the Pirate Coast. Britain then intervened in local fighting, and beginning in 1820, forced treaties on the states to suppress piracy and prohibit warfare at sea. Thus the terms Trucial States or Trucial Oman came into use, though Arabs generally called it the Oman Coast.

According to treaties signed at mid–century Britain controlled foreign affairs and defense. Internal matters remained under the rulers, and little development took place. Indeed, the major events of world history seemed to have little impact, although competition from cultured pearls drove down profits from pearling and reduced the standard of living. As late as the

1950s disputes over borders or pearling rights led to skirmishes between desperately poor emirates. One continuing dispute in the 1940s and 1950s concerned rival claims by Saudi Arabia, Oman and Abu Dhabi to the Buraimi oasis.

The search for petroleum in the emirates began in the 1930s, and the later president of the U.A.E., Sheikh Zayed bin Sultan, served as a guide to one of the first exploration teams. Twenty years later, in 1958, commercial deposits were discovered, and oil production began in Abu Dhabi in 1962. Four years later the ruling Nahyan family replaced the ruler, Sheikh Shakhbut, with his younger brother, Sheikh Zayed.

Revenues rapidly transformed the economy and society. Dubai also discovered oil, though relatively small amounts, and it became the chief trading center.

Local desires for independence combined with British reluctance to pay the high military costs of maintaining the protectorate. Britain withdrew in 1971, having encouraged six of the seven states to form the United Arab Emirates (U.A.E.). The seventh, Ras al–Khayma, joined the following year.

The federal constitution adopted in 1971 divided responsibility for governance between federal institutions and the individual emirates. The seven sheikhs rule some internal affairs of their own states; they may even possess their own military. However, responsibility for domestic matters such as education, public health and currency belongs to the federation. Given the imposing wealth of Abu Dhabi, other states have tended to cooperate.

At the federal level, authority lies with the Supreme Council of Rulers. It chose as the first president Sheikh Zayed, and re–elected him for five consecutive five–year

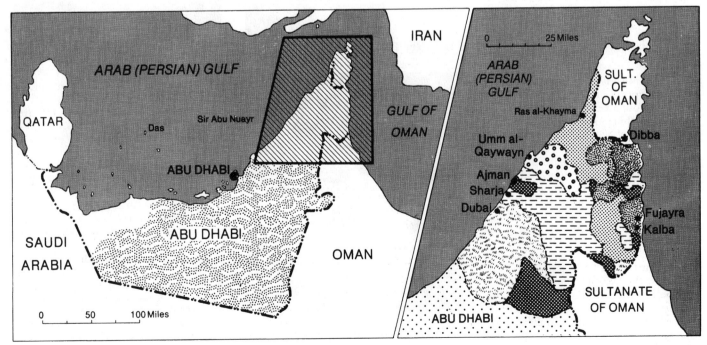

H. H. Sheik Zayed bin Sultan Al-
Nahyan The Ruler of Abu Dhabi and
President of the UAE

H. H. The Ruler of Dubai
and Vice President, UAE

H. H. The Ruler of Sharja

H. H. The Ruler of Ajman

H. H. The Ruler of Umm al–Qaywayn

H. H. The Ruler of Ras Al–Khayma

terms. The president appoints the prime minister, typically the ruler of Dubai. In contrast to other traditional states of the region, something akin to a legislature exists, the Federal National Council, whose 40 members represent individual emirates.

Because Abu Dhabi contains the largest population and contributes the overwhelming portion of the national budget, it finances development in all states and plays the major role in the federation. In 1987 the Supreme Council intervened in Sharja and restored Sheikh Sultan to power after an attempted coup d'etat.

Like many other Gulf nations already injured by the Iran–Iraq War—some off-shore oil platforms were attacked—the U.A.E. suffered recession in the mid-1980s as its oil revenues fell 40%. By 1990, however, construction cranes again sprouted

H. H. The Ruler of Fujayra

across the major cities, signaling a return to economic growth. New tourist hotels, shopping centers, commercial buildings and factories suggested that while oil continued to provide the mainstay of the economy, diversification will play an important role in the future.

To pay for the growth, the U.A.E. allegedly sold more oil than its OPEC quota (see Economy). In 1990 Iraq condemned the Emirates as well as Kuwait, and the U.A.E. quickly joined the coalition to liberate Kuwait in the Gulf War. The conflict emphasized the presence of foreign workers in the Emirates, where a law demanding the replacement of all foreign employees of the federal civil service by 1995 proved impossible to implement.

In 1992 Iran reopened an old dispute with the U.A.E. over three small but strategic islands in the Gulf, Abu Musa and the two Tunbs. Iran had contested their ownership with Sharja after Britain's withdrawal in 1971, but for two decades a working compromise allowed both countries a role. Iran's unilateral action in 1992, perhaps the hasty result of Tehran politics, aroused Arab fears. Prospects for a settlement improved in 1998, as Iran sought to rebuild friendly relations with Arab states of the Gulf. Meanwhile, the U.A.E. remains a major purchaser of modern weaponry.

In the late 1990s, the flourishing trading center of Dubai became the destination for Iraqi oil exports despite UN sanctions against them. Technically illegal (despite official statements that Iraqis had suffered enough), the trade brought profits to merchants. However, its use of old vessels caused serious oil spills and polluted beaches. After several polluting incidents not all linked to Iraqi oil, in 1999 the government proposed the death penalty for deliberate polluters.

As the twentieth century closed, a number of signs suggested that the seven emirates were gradually strengthening their sense of unity. In 1996 a national law replaced emirate rules on traffic offenses, and the next year a federal environmental law took effect. Although probably dwarfed by the (undisclosed) Abu Dhabi budget, the federal budget continued to provide funds for the economic and social development of the poorer emirates, and the rivalries of Dubai and Abu Dhabi remained friendly rather than contentious. The sense of unity seems likely to increase: younger inhabitants reportedly feel a greater loyalty to the UAE than do their parents.

In November 2000, Sheikh Zayed of Abu Dhabi returned home to great celebrations following his surgery and lengthy recuperation in the U.S. The festivities reminded the populace that several emirates face transfers of political power soon. Sheikh Zayed himself was 86 at his return; after five decades of government service, his son Khalifa now carries out many duties of the office.

Culture: The culture of the United Arab Emirates is not essentially different from that found in neighboring countries. The majority of the native Arabs, who are *Sunni*, retain a sense of their tribal backgrounds and traditions.

Women in the U.A.E. play a greater role in society than in many conservative Muslim countries. Not only are girls educated, but the government fosters adult education programs that have reduced their illiteracy rate to around 20%. While some women hold significant positions in the private sector, the government employs large numbers, especially in education and health care. By the 1990s, women comprised 16% of the workforce.

Modern education arrived relatively recently. In 1968, the adult literacy rate was only 21%. At independence, a decade after oil exports began, only 30,000 children attended school. By the mid–1990s, the figure had climbed to 400,000, and enrollments rose even more rapidly in high school. The construction of schools in even the most remote hamlet provides all children with the opportunity to learn; education is compulsory from the age of six.

Long a particular concern of Sheikh Zayed, who grew up when the emirates lacked a single modern school, adult education programs have proved so successful that the literacy rate reached 85% in the mid–1990s. Government policies indicate a concern with the quality of education as well as its extent.

Higher education is represented by two levels of technical colleges and the Emirates University, located in Al–Ain. Founded in 1978, in the early 1990s it graduated its first classes of physicians. Women comprise about two–thirds of the roughly 13,000 students, reflecting the greater likelihood that young men will study abroad.

The Federation's Marriage Fund ranks as one of the most unusual features of a society where the state takes responsibility for the welfare of its citizens between the cradle to the grave. Realizing that

Courtesy: Embassy of Saudi Arabia

marriage to a woman from the country had become prohibitively expensive for many of its young men, in 1994 the Federation created the Marriage Fund. It provides up to $19,000 to couples of limited income who wish to marry and built special "Wedding Halls" where receptions cost far less than at hotels. The government also urged fathers to accept lower dowries, a major expense for many. In its first year the fund gave or lent nearly $100 million to 3,000 couples. By 2000 this had grown to 44,000 couples, and marriages to foreign women had fallen from 64% of total weddings to 26%.

A major purpose for the Marriage Fund is the need to increase the indigenous population. Nationals are outnumbered about three to one by foreign residents who have found work in the country. Native and immigrant Arabs together constitute no more than 40% of the population, with Indians (30%) and Pakistanis (25%) comprising major communities. The federation army has about 40,000 men in it, of whom only some 12% are native Arabs.

In a society with many single men, but few amusements and no (legal) alcoholic beverages, sports attract great attention. Thoroughbreds owned by citizens race both in the Emirates and abroad, aided partly by the longer season for training. Further down the social scale, one finds auto racing and even camel races, held on a special track. The Emirate's powerboat racing team led the world championship in 1995 until an accident killed its most talented driver.

Economy: Despite the relatively late development of its petroleum deposits (exports began in 1962), the oil reserves of the U.A.E. now exceed 90 billion barrels, and rank among the five largest in the world. So vast is this amount that without discovering any new reserves, with present discoveries the U.A.E. can maintain its present level of exports until about the year 2099. Most deposits lie in Abu Dhabi, whose production accounts for roughly 85% of the national total, with the rest mostly from Dubai. Of the smaller emirates, only Sharja produces significant amounts, but oil revenues from Abu Dhabi have transformed much of the country. The U.A.E. also possesses the world's fourth largest reserves of natural gas.

Despite reserves similar to Iran and Iraq, the U.A.E. (like Kuwait) received a much smaller export quota from OPEC (1.1 million barrels per day, 1989). Given its far higher capacity, the country requested a quota of 1.5 million barrels, and generally produced about that amount, disrupting OPEC's attempt to maintain higher oil prices (see Introduction: Oil). This policy carried obvious risks, and perhaps contributed to the Gulf War. The collapse of Iraqi and Kuwaiti exports

provided opportunity for increased exports, and those responsible for oil production in the U.A.E. argued that increasing world demand for oil, plus declining reserves in several OPEC nations, would soon reduce excess supplies and render quotas less important. In fact, a world oil shortage seems some time off. In 1998-99 world prices dropped to the lowest levels since 1973, partly the result of over-production. Only significant quota cuts in 1999 raised prices above $20 once more.

Outside the petroleum industry, the inhabitants find a variety of ways to earn a living. Agriculture remains an important source of employment, with over 20,000 farms, and the government aims at self–sufficiency in food. Currently the Emirates produce roughly half the vegetables the population consumes—and all the dates. In fact, with over 20 million date palms—approximately ten per person, yielding nearly 20 lbs. each—the country is one of the world's most important growers.

The Hajar mountain range provides Ras al–Khayma and Fujayra in particular with greater supplies of water for irrigation. Besides dates and other traditional fruits and vegetables, these areas export strawberries, chrysanthemum, winter tomatoes and other high–value crops to Europe. Agricultural research efforts at a number of locations attempt to adapt plants and animals to the demanding climate conditions, and seek plants that tolerate saline ground–water.

Rain falls infrequently in the Emirates, and several dams store the natural flow of the seasonal *wadis* for agricultural use and to recharge aquifers. By contrast, the population depends on desalinized water, and the al–Taweela plant gives Abu Dhabi the world's largest single unit in the world.

All the Emirates possess long stretches of beach; Fujayra also enjoys a flourishing tourist trade based on trips to the mountains, including picturesque waterfalls. Sharja and other Emirates issue their own stamps, including some of the world's most eye–catching commemorative issues for sale to collectors around the world.

Dubai ranks as the undisputed commercial center of the region as well as of the U.A.E. Until recently, its World Trade Center ranked as the tallest building in the Middle East, and it still claims the world's tallest and most luxurious hotel. Its airport is the Gulf's busiest, and a large dry-dock undertakes more repairs than anywhere else in the Gulf. The Jebel Ali Free Trade zone provides warehousing for transshipping goods through the world's largest man–made port. Over 1,000 companies use the zone, including an aluminum smelter. Its accompanying electric generating plant provides almost half the city's drinking water through desalination.

Other symbols of Dubai's brash confidence abound. In 2001 the government-

owned airline, Emirates, announced it would spend $15 billion on passenger jets, the largest order ever announced. The largest artificial island, also announced in 2001, will take the shape of a palm tree whose fronds, each over a mile long, will triple the emirate's shoreline and provide the setting for luxury homes, each with a view of the beach. Other multi-billion construction projects are also under way.

Together these projects greatly exceed the needs of Dubai's inhabitants. They make sense only because the emirate expects the population to double to around two million by 2010, as wealthy retirees move to a land of perpetual sunshine, and the international business tycoons establish residence where income taxes are negligible and internet service is unsurpassed. Fortunately for Dubai, Abu Dhabi apparently provides enough oil annually to offset Dubai's declining production.

During the years of rapid income growth following the oil price rises of the 1970s, the U.A.E. gained the distinction of providing a greater percentage of national income to foreign aid than any country. Much of the funding comes from the Abu Dhabi Fund for Development. Originally established in 1971 to help poorer Arab states, the Fund by 1995 had aided some 44 countries in Asia and Africa with loans and grants surpassing $3 billion.

The scandals surrounding the fraud and collapse of the Bank of Credit and Commerce International (BCCI) in 1991 touched deeply the ruling family of Abu Dhabi. A minority shareholder until 1990, Sheikh Zayed personally and as ruler owned 77% of the bank when it collapsed, and became its largest victim. In addition, he agreed to donate $1.7 billion to a fund to compensate depositors for some of the $15 billion they may lose. Allegations

Courtesy: Caltex Petroleum Corp. (Joe Brignolo '95)

swirled about BCCI in several countries, including transferring drug money and the secret take–over of First American Bankshares in Washington, D.C. Though details of the links between the bank, the Sheikh, and the state remain murky, twelve former BCCI officials were convicted of fraud and similar charges.

Given its relatively large oil production per capita, the Emirates suffered relatively few vital cutbacks when the region's oil revenues declined in the 1990s. The budget ran a modest deficit in 1994, and the government raised fees for several of its services and utilities to supplement oil revenues. Nevertheless, the country continued to expand its infrastructure with contracts for electrical plants, and its proposed military acquisitions provided a competitive battleground for defense contractors throughout the world, especially for big–ticket items like tanks and jet fighters.

The Future: At its birth, the United Arab Emirates aroused the sense of being just another alliance of traditional rulers the departing colonial officials had hurriedly patched together. Thanks to oil, but probably more important, thanks to the pragmatism and values of Sheikh Zayed in particular, the U.A.E. reached its silver anniversary amid growth and prosperity. In a sign of continuing stability, Sheikh Zayed has designated his son Khalifa as his heir.

The emirate's concentration of oil wealth provides for economic development and social transformation as well as extravagant consumption. With oil prices over $20 and the gradual reduction of effective sanctions on Iraq, expect the U.A.E.'s commercial role to expand further.

A view of Dubai City. The building in the foreground with the ball on top is the headquarters of the Emirates Telecommunications Corporation.

Courtesy: Caltex Petroleum Corporation
Photo by Marina Volochine

The Republic of Yemen

The old part of San'a

Courtesy: Caltex Petroleum Corporation

Area: About 187,000 square miles (484,000 sq. km.). Formerly 112,000 sq. miles (290,000 sq. km.) belonged to the South, and 75,000 sq. miles (194,000 sq. km.) to the North.

Population: 17.5 million.

Capital City: San`a (Pop. 500,000, estiated).

Climate: Extremely hot and humid on the coastal plain, cooler in the mountains, often cold at night. Rainfall is moderate on the western slopes of the mountains and the highest peaks sometimes have snow.

Neighboring Countries: Saudi Arabia (North); Oman (East).

Time Zone: GMT +3.

Official Language: Arabic.

Other Principle Tongues: Mahri; English is used in school and international business.

Ethnic Background: Arab. Physical appearances differ; short and olive-skinned people are found in the mountains; heavy African admixture along the coast.

Principal Religion: Islam, with a few Christians and Hindus in the south. Many followers of the *Zaidi* sect of *Shi'a* Islam live in the northern mountains; most other Yemenis are *Sunnis* of the *Shafi`i* legal school.

Chief Commercial Products: Crude oil, grains (sorghum, millet, wheat, barley), livestock and hides, tobacco, cotton, coffee, qat, vegetables.

Major Trading Partners: U.S., Japan, France, Germany, Saudi Arabia.

Currency: Yemeni Rial (YR153 = $1 US).

Former Colonial Status: Ottoman Rule sporadic after the 16th century; British in the South (1839–1967).

National Day: May 22 (union day).

Chief of State: Ali Abdullah Salih, President.

Head of Government: Abdul Kader Bajammal, Prime Minister.

National Flag: Three horizontal stripes of red, white and black.

Gross Domestic Product: roughly $6 billion.

GDP per capita: Estimated between $280 and $400.

In May 1990, the Yemen Arab Republic (North Yemen) and the People's Democratic Republic of Yemen (South Yemen, or Aden) merged to form the Republic of Yemen. Thus this remote and very poor region witnessed the first union of marxist and non–marxist territories following the collapse of communism in Europe and the Soviet Union. Although the area had never formed a unified state, the population widely felt itself "Yemeni." While the union proved difficult, it continues.

In the southwestern corner of the Arabian Peninsula, Yemen's varied topography contrasts greatly with the flat, stony plains and sand dunes of central and eastern Arabia. In western Yemen, the geography takes the form of zones running from north to south. The first zone, the Tihama plain, lies along the coast of the Red Sea. Level, hot, and arid, the Tihama also inflicts high humidity on its inhabitants.

Some 30 miles inland steeply rising slopes mark a scenic mountain range and plateau that runs from the Saudi border in the north to the Gulf of Aden. Peaks in the range reach 10,000–12,000 feet. By blocking air currents from the sea, they cause summer rains that make the western slopes the wettest region of Arabia, with precipitation averaging 15 inches yearly, and as much as 30 inches in a good year. However, there are

186

no year-round rivers, but rather *wadis*, whose flow disappears in the dry season.

San'a (Sana), the capital, lies in the interior plateau; its elevation of 6,500 feet is one of the highest of any national capital. East of the mountains, the high plateau gradually slopes down to the desert, eventually joining the *Rub al–Khali* or Empty Quarter of Saudi Arabia.

Southern and southeastern Yemen, bordering the Gulf of Aden, endures less fortunate geography. Its lonely, barren landscape of desert plateaus and rocky mountains is broken by two important valleys. In the southwest, the oases around Lahj provide much of the region's limited produce. In the east, the Wadi Hadhramut forms a narrow strip of green. Yemen also rules several islands, including the strategically important Perim Island in the Bab al–Mandab.

History: Ancient and civilized kingdoms existed in what is now Yemen long before the time of Christ. One of the most famous was Saba, or Sheba. Near its capital, Marib, a great stone dam captured the runoff from summer rains. Honored in literature and legend, the dam contributed to the reputation of this region as *Arabia Felix* (Fertile Arabia), famous in Roman times for its trade in frankincense and myrrh. However, during the early Christian centuries rival Jewish and Christian chiefs sought to conquer the region. Foreign armies invaded, the dam failed, and its irrigation system deteriorated. Islam arrived towards the end of Muhammad's lifetime, during the seventh (Christian) century, and spread partly as a reaction against religions linked to foreign powers.

The *Zaidi* sect of Shi'a Islam (see Iran: Culture) became dominant in mountain regions during the ninth century. The Imam, or leader of this religious group, became the traditional ruler. The early years of Islam provided greater security and prosperity. The population of the mountains increased greatly, and many terraces on the steep, rain–fed slopes date from that era.

In the 16th century the Ottoman Sultans lay claim to Yemen, but its remoteness and terrain ensured that it was never completely subjugated. Indeed, the Ottomans withdrew in the 17th century and the British gained influence along the coast, especially at Mukha (Mocha) where they established a station. The interior remained controlled by the dynasty of *Zaidi* Imams.

Invaders from Najd far to the north were driven out by an army representing the Ottomans in 1818, but it in turn left in 1840. British influence inside the country also disappeared by that time. The Ottomans again conquered Yemen in campaigns lasting from 1849 to 1872; from then until 1918, when they were defeated in World War I, the Turks controlled most of the country. As a result of brave resistance to the Ottoman

troops, *Zaidi* Imams were allowed local control in some areas of the plateau.

The strategic port city of Aden was also held by the Ottomans and conquerors from Lahj (Lahej) from the interior, but the remainder of eastern Yemen was controlled by feuding chieftains for untold centuries. The British seized Aden, a port city centered around a bay formed by a long–extinct volcano, in 1839; it was a valuable coaling station for ships plying the Egypt–India route. Britain took minimal interest in the interior, controlled by 23 principalities and sheikhdoms. Between 1882 and 1914, these local leaders signed treaties with Britain that ceded authority over foreign affairs in exchange for protection.

When the Ottoman Empire collapsed at the end of World War I, Imam Yahya tried to expand Yemeni control to the north and south, but was stopped by the British in the south, who defended Aden and its hinterland. Developments were more complicated in Asir, the disputed region lying along the Red Sea coast to the north. Yahya claimed sovereignty over Asir, but its ruler allied with the increasingly powerful Saudi monarch, King Abd al–Aziz. Attempting to halt Saudi encroachments all along his northern frontier, Imam Yahya attacked pro–Saudi tribes. In the war that followed, Saudi forces routed Yahya's poorly equipped forces and captured Hudaida. By the 1934 Taif Agreement, Yahya was forced

to cede Asir, although its eastern border remained unsettled and subject to temporary agreements.

In San'a, Yahya was assassinated in 1948 and was succeeded by his son, Ahmad. His rule followed the pattern of his father: severe and ill–informed. Almost no foreign "infidels" (unbelievers) were even permitted to enter the country; Yemen was as isolated from the world as Tibet, and the inhabitants lived much as their ancestors a thousand years previously.

Ahmad died in 1962 and was succeeded by his son, who lasted eight days until army officers, inspired by the rebellion in Egypt against King Farouk, gained control of San'a after brief fighting. Yemen was declared a republic, headed by Colonel Abdullah Sallal. The Imam made an attempt to return after having fled, but even though he had the support of mountain tribesmen, he was thrown back, and ultimately out of Yemen. The U.S. recognized the new republican government in late 1962 and the UN seated its delegation rather than a rival royalist one.

Civil war followed, with the bitterest fighting in the winter of 1963–4. The Imam was supported by the Saudis, the Republic by the Egyptians. A substantial number of Yemenis wanted modernization and progress under the republic, but they were dissatisfied with Abdullah Sallal and his dependence on Egypt. His position was weakened when Egyptian troops started leaving Yemen during the Arab–Israeli war of 1967. After five years of Egyptian aid and training, the Republicans ousted Sallal in late 1967. A Presidential Council was created with a *Zaidi* religious leader, Abd al–Rahman Iryani, at its head. The Council sought to bring together the different factions in the country while warding off armed royalists who briefly threatened the capital. This danger ebbed by 1969, because Iryani won the

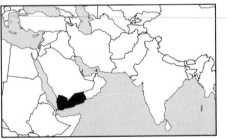

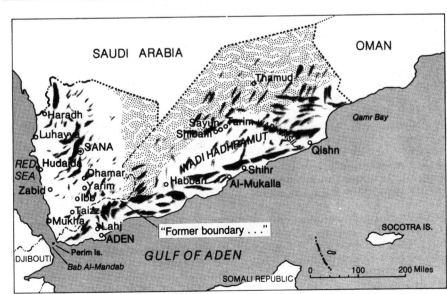

"Former boundary . . ."

respect of royalist tribes by his religious prestige and the moderation of his regime. In addition, Saudi Arabia cut off most of its aid to the Imam.

The civil war ended in 1970 and full attention turned to restoring and developing a country gripped by fighting for almost a decade. In 1971 a Consultative Assembly was established, and Iryani remained in power as president of the Republic Council.

Aden Colony Becomes South Yemen

Events moved separately in the south. In 1937 Britain created a crown colony of the city of Aden, while loosely supervising the local rulers of the interior as long as they refrained from violence. After decades of little political development despite growing Arab nationalism, in 1958 British officials sought to unite the various rulers. By 1966 all had joined the Federation of South Arabia.

Following the rise of political consciousness and the expansion of British bases, unrest and terrorism grew in the 1960s in Aden. Urban nationalists sensed a British desire to govern them through the two dozen tribal rulers of the Federation. Local troops mutinied in 1967, and nationalists seized several of the states. Despite conflict between the Egyptian-influenced *Front for the Liberation of South Yemen* and the marxist *National Liberation Front (NLF)*, the federation collapsed.

In late 1967 Britain ended its control over Aden, permitting the *NLF* to take control of government. Adopting the title People's Republic of South Yemen, the *NLF* divided the country into six states to replace the traditional principalities. For three years the political pot boiled, as alliances shifted almost continuously. President Qahtan al–Sha'bi lost office, and in 1969 a group strongly influenced by commu-nist ideas came to power, under President Salim Rubaya Ali. They soon changed the name of the nation to People's Democratic Republic of Yemen, and promised an elected People's Supreme Council. However, elections never occurred, and the council was filled with members nominated by the marxist leaders.

Because of the country's radical policies and support for the rebellion in Oman by the threateningly–named *People's Front for the Liberation of the Occupied Arabian Gulf*, other Arab governments regarded the regime in Aden with concern and even hostility. During most of 1972 it fought a serious border war with North Yemen, a conflict temporarily resolved with promises to unite the two Yemeni states. Turmoil erupted domestically as well, with the president executed in 1978. Thereafter the *NLF* joined with the communist and *Ba'th* parties to form the *Yemen Socialist Party (YSP)*. In 1986 open civil war broke out in Aden between factions of the *YSP*.

Thousands died before the group considered more influenced by marxism won, and the defeated president fled to North Yemen with thousands of armed followers.

Unnoticed by the outside world, by 1989 considerable social and political change occurred in South Yemen. Despite its marxism, it permitted non–party candidates in local elections and allowed opposition parties to form. The economy in shambles, the Soviet subsidy slashed, and military relations with Moscow reduced,

President Ali Abdullah Salih

it mended links with Arab states and sought closer relations, even unity, with Northern Yemen.

Struggles for power also persisted in San'a. Ultimately a Military Command Council led by Colonel Ibrahim Hamdi took control of North Yemen in 1975. It established a degree of unity between the various factions and maintained firm central control. More important, it developed good relations with Saudi Arabia, which lent financial assistance. But Hamdi and the aide who succeeded him were both assassinated, the latter by a bomb delivered by the communists in Aden. The military continued in control under Colonel Ali Abdullah Salih as president (1978).

In the 1980s Salih established stable government despite two border wars and a major earthquake in 1982 that destroyed 200 villages and left a half–million homeless. The losses were magnified by the fact that most houses, built of stone, lack reinforcing. The first general election for the *Majlis al–Shura* ("Consultative Council") took place in 1988. It was widely contested, and President Salih's *General People's Congress* won the most seats, with the

Muslim Brotherhood and tribal independents also important.

Despite political unrest, assassination attempts, two border wars and a major earthquake that destroyed 200 villages and left a half–million homeless, in the 1980s Salih established stable government. The first general election for the *Majlis al–Shura* ("Consultative Council") took place in 1988. It was widely contested, and President Salih's *General People's Congress* won the most seats. The *Muslim Brotherhood* and tribal independents also acquired significant representation.

Border clashes with Aden flared fiercely in 1979 and 1981, and in Yemeni fashion resulted in attempts at union, including the formation in 1981 of a "Yemen Council" consisting of the two presidents and a secretariat. But this agreement had little practical significance.

In November 1989, the leaders of the two countries again proclaimed plans for union; it seemed merely another ritual. However, as 1990 began, in both North and South Yemen public opinion surged in favor of rapid union. Long divided by conflicting domestic and foreign policies, the two states showed signs of increasing similarity, illustrated by their elections, a rarity for the Arabian Peninsula. Trade increased between them, a consequence of greater freedom for private farmers and businessmen in the South, and its reforms lessened economic differences with the North.

To the surprise of almost everyone, the two states merged ahead of schedule, in May 1990, perhaps to upset domestic and foreign opponents. Approved unanimously in Aden, the merger faced opposition in San'a from members of the *Majlis al–Shura* linked to the *Muslim Brotherhood*. President al–Attas of the South became Prime Minister of united Yemen, and a 302–member Council of Deputies contained a variety of parties.

Merged, but not United

United Yemen faced grave difficulties, starting with a history littered with previous failures at merger. The South's economy lay in tatters; its adjustment to greater competition and imports remained uncertain. The North's relative economic success, combined with a population four times that of the South, created fears it would dominate any union. Socially, perhaps surprising to Americans, the North's modernization lagged significantly behind that of communist-influenced Aden, where women's rights were among the greatest in the Arab world.

The first year of unity provided exceptional challenges. Linked to Iraq by trade and Kuwait by aid, Yemen attempted to maintain neutrality after Iraq invaded Kuwait. However, as the only Arab member of the UN Security Council, its abstentions appeared to indicate passive acceptance of

Iraqi aggression, and its demands for Iraqi withdrawal received less comment than its uncertain position regarding the Kuwaiti ruling family. Greater domestic freedom permitted an outpouring of protest after Western forces arrived in Saudi Arabia.

The consequences threatened economic ruin. Saudi Arabia, already uneasy about the creation of a neighbor equal in population and sharing miles of unsettled frontier, cut all financial aid and expelled roughly one million Yemenis. Returning workers faced unemployment, other nations cut development aid, and inflation climbed. However, a referendum approved unity by a large majority, and oil discoveries announced by 1992 suggested reserves to support greater production.

As parliamentary elections approached in 1992, political and economic difficulties threatened the new nation. A series of murders swept the country, including over 30 members of the *Yemen Socialist Party*, leading Prime Minister Heidar al–Attas to threaten to resign. In response, elections were postponed until 1993. Then food riots broke out in major cities, as inflation surpassed 100% and hundreds of thousands of unemployed faced grim circumstances.

Nevertheless, the country held the first free multi–party elections on the entire Arabian peninsula, with some 5,000 candidates for the Council of Deputies. Despite allegations of vote–buying, and favoritism in television coverage, the elections were considered broadly accurate. General Salih's *General People's Congress* led the Islamic *Islah* in the north. However, the results illustrated strong regional differences, with the *YSP* taking every southern seat but few elsewhere. Nevertheless, the three parties formed a coalition government.

Personal rivalries as well as differences over the budget led to increasing hostility between President Salih and Vice President Ali Salem al–Baidh in late 1993. Al–Baidh left San'a for Aden, paralyzing government. He charged that the president sought a dictatorship, and listed some 18 conditions necessary for his return to government. For his part, President Salih condemned the alleged communist influence in the *YSP*.

As tensions mounted, clashes broke out between military units loyal to Salih and al–Baidh. Arab nations mediated a reconciliation agreement, but it shortly failed. In May 1994 widespread fighting signaled civil war. As Northern troops attempted to capture Aden against determined resistance, Arab nations as diverse as Iraq and Saudi Arabia counseled an end to the fighting. However, aided by water shortages in besieged Aden and tribal resentments against the *YSP*, northern forces crushed the rebellion, whose leaders fled.

The conflict showed that despite their formal unity, the two Yemens had not merged their governments. The two

armies had remained separate. Both currencies had remained in circulation, and disputes within the government paralyzed even the adoption of annual government budgets.

In the months following the war, Salih released southern prisoners of war and proclaimed a general amnesty. He permitted the *YSP* to exist, under new leaders who had opposed the rebellion. He also won re–election as president after parliament approved a new, more Islamic constitution that gave the president greater powers. After clashes in border regions, Salih attempted to improve relations with Saudi Arabia. He reportedly even accepted the 1934 Taif Agreement's borders, something no previous ruler had done.

The war damaged further an already precarious economy. The budget deficit soared, and to meet its bills, the state turned to printing money. Inflation became so great that the government refused to release the figures, though it did devalue the *rial* by a factor of 10. Salaried professionals found their standard of living destroyed, and Yemeni university professors struck because their pay of $140 per month amounted to less than 10% of those of Iraqis and other foreigners. Subsidies for wheat, flour, and oil products became unbearable burdens, but their reductions doubled prices and triggered riots. Unemployment reached 30%. Further cuts in government subsidies occurred according to the IMF–approved plan in 1996. However, some foreign aid was received as a reward.

Fighting broke out in the distant Hanish islands near Red Sea shipping routes in 1995, when Eritrean forces attacked a small Yemeni garrison for reasons outsiders did not understand. Sovereignty over the islands had not been claimed since 1923, and given its lengthy undefined border with Saudi Arabia, Yemen hardly needed another conflict. The two sides accepted arbitration in 1996, but disputes remained over several parts of the border, ranging from the islands to sandy wastes near the Empty Quarter that might contain oil deposits and even territory along the border with Oman. Tensions continued, with unrest and violence allegedly instigated by foreign agents. In 1998, Saudi naval vessels attacked a Yemeni coastguard post on one of the disputed islands.

As expected, the *General People's Congress* swept the 1997 elections for the *Majlis al–Shura*, benefitting from favoritism in the media and the military. The *YSP* boycotted the campaign, and the crucial test matched the *General People's Congress* against *Islah*, the Islamist grouping. Yemen's relatively few but astute feminists entered the campaign to register women as voters, winning support from even *Islah*, though its leaders expected women to vote for the candidate their men chose.

Another step towards democracy came in the 1999 presidential elections. As expected, Salih won a landslide victory over his opponent, and international observers judged the voting was fair and free. However, because parliament had rejected all opposition nominees as candidates, the *YSP* again boycotted the campaign.

The first elections for officials responsible for local development projects and legal issues took place in 2001. The generally festive campaign was marred, however, by a score of deaths in election-related disputes. The country boasts some 60 million firearms, three times its population.

More questionable to Yemen's democratic standing were two constitutional amendments also on the ballot. The first extended the presidential term from five to seven years; the second, the term of the existing parliament from four to six years. Passed with wide support (as referendum proposals often do), the amendments nicely extended the politicians' term in office without their having to face the voters individually. Soon after the elections, President Salih dismissed the long-serving prime minister and formed a new cabinet under Abdul Kader Bajammal, apparently to give greater stress to economic development.

In the 1990s, tribesmen in remote areas discovered a new form of pressure politics: kidnaping foreigners. Tourists, workers in the oil industry, and even diplomats found themselves carefully guarded bargaining chips as the tribesmen demanded schools, roads, water projects and other aid from the government or oil company. To protect the oil and tourist industries, the government typically compromised with the kidnapers, and gained the release of the hostages.

After dozens of such cases, however, the government extended the death penalty to kidnaping. Soon afterwards, a group

Man on the streets of San'a

A potter works his trade near Aden

linked to radical Islamist causes seized a group of tourists in southern Yemen and demanded the release of several sympathizers. When the kidnapers apparently refused to negotiate, and allegedly threatened to kill their hostages, the army attacked. Four tourists died of gunfire; with them perished hopes for the rapid growth of tourism.

Islamic militants struck again in 2000, without warning, when the *U.S.S. Cole* was attacked by one or more suicide bombers who maneuvered a small boat filled with explosives alongside the American destroyer in Aden to refuel. The explosion pierced the side of the vessel and killed nearly two dozen sailors, causing the U.S. Navy to rethink its policies. In the weeks following the attack, Yemeni authorities worked closely with U.S. officials to discover those responsible, though they limited American access to interrogations.

Relatively poor and usually very traditional in their values, many Yemenis regard Western ways with suspicion. However, in the town of Dammaj these feelings extend far beyond the norm. Its Islamic study center, headed by Sheikh Muqbil bin Hadi al-Wadie, trains Muslim students in an atmosphere of fervent anti-American and anti-Israeli feeling. The FBI regards Sheikh Muqbil as an influence on Osama bin Laden, the Islamic militant blamed for embassy bombings in East Africa as well as the attack on the *U.S.S. Cole.*

Rumors that the country could follow Afghanistan as a target of U.S. attacks on al-Qaeda may have prompted the unusually strong (for Yemen) crackdown on Islamic militants after September 11.

Scores of foreign students were expelled, and others arrested. Commanded by the president's son, the military attempted to extend government rule over tribal areas. Nevertheless, popular sympathies lie with those who preach Islam rather than with the West, and thousands of Yemenis cared enough about religion to volunteer for the struggle against the Soviets in Afghanistan. As a result, Western embassies are highly protected, and U.S. diplomats move with extreme caution.

Culture: Today over 70% of the population lives in the traditional style in small towns, villages or isolated clusters of houses. Until recently, most loyalties were local, mainly to the family clan and tribe. National patriotism has been a rather new feeling which spreads slowly. A few people are nomads, mainly in the eastern and southern part of the country, while considerably more live in the growing cities, where the alien architecture of new buildings often clashes with the greater dignity and appeal of traditional designs.

Unfortunately many of the mud–brick skyscrapers are in danger of collapse, threatened particularly by running water and burst pipes. Foreign governments have been funding a UNESCO campaign to restore San'a, paving streets and restoring portions of the *Souk* (market place). However, the walled cities of Hadhramut, east of Aden and for political reasons far from tourist routes despite their beauty, face the danger of buildings 500 years old collapsing.

While virtually all Yemenis are Muslims, they form two major sects. In the

coastal plain and much of the settled south, inhabitants profess *Sunni* Islam and provide a center for the *Shafii* school. In the North, the conservative *Zaidi* sect of *Shi'a* Islam prevails, and for a thousand years until the 1962 revolution, the Imams ruled the country from the mountains.

In a uniquely Yemeni custom, every afternoon, most Yemeni men and many women gather in small social groups to chew leaves of *qat*, a tree cultivated on the terraced mountainsides. Large globs of leaves chewed for hours reportedly produce a mildly narcotic effect that relaxes a person and gives a sense of contentment.

The cultivation and use of *qat* brings undesirable effects to a country seeking development. It consumes vast amounts of time, occupying most of the afternoon (the workday obligingly ends at 2 p.m.) Producing all the *qat* consumed by Yemenis provides employment for hundreds of thousands of farmers, and it is a far more profitable crop than coffee or grains. Much of the nation's limited supply of agricultural water goes to the crop.

Qat consumption often costs a great deal, and some families spend one-fifth their incomes to enjoy it (and escape giving the impression they are too poor to afford it). Though not physically addictive, it may cause serious illness, and it leads to a state of relaxation that discourages hard work. In 1999 President Salih announced that he was giving up the leaves, and he urged the nation to follow his example.

Presumably when Yemeni adults chew the leaves, they find greater enjoyment from them than any other use of their money, but given Yemen's pitiful levels of nutrition, health and education, the habit casts a long shadow over social and economic development.

Throughout Yemen, since the fall of the monarchy and the arrival of freedom from colonialism, education has taken great strides among men, though only 7% of adult women read. There are universities at Sanaa and Aden, and competition to enroll is fierce. The use of English in education is becoming more and more widespread, since one of Yemen's most valuable assets is the workers which it sends abroad, who in turn have sent badly needed money back home.

In their struggle for water, roads, schools and other projects for a better standard of living, Yemenis often formed "development associations," to pool resources for their goals. Relatively rare elsewhere in the Middle East, these community action groups involve both traditional and modern interests, and reflect a Yemeni sense that the poverty requires cooperation rather than simple competition. Unfortunately, the cooperative movement has on several occasions suffered from government attempts to take it over or politicize it.

Busy downtown San'a

Courtesy: Caltex Petroleum Corporation

Economy: Although agriculture is still at the center of the economy, it is fast being overtaken by petroleum. On the coast, one finds date palms and grains suitable to the hot climate. The upper slopes of the mountains, which receive good rainfall, are among the most intensively cultivated in the world. Through the centuries the farmers have built elaborate terraces with stone walls—at some places right up to the crests of the mountains.

Coffee has traditionally been an important crop. Since it used to be shipped by the British from the old port of Mukha, it became renowned as "Mocha coffee." Lower world prices have reduced the price of Yemen's crop and for some time the production of *qat* became more desirable. But since it was exported mainly to Ethiopia, which was virtually bankrupt, it is now mainly used for domestic consumption.

Animal herding plays an important role in the economy. Millions of sheep, goats and humped cattle are raised for milk, meat and hides. Donkeys and mules are still the most common beasts of burden as camels are not suitable in the rugged mountains, though they are far from unknown in Yemen.

It is possible that mineral deposits in commercial quantities exist in the country, but little surveying has been done thus far. Manufacturing remains in the handicraft stage; while it exhibits a high degree of skill and artistic merit, hand-made products cannot supply a comfortable standard of living like machine–factory production.

191

Ever since the 1960s, foreign nations have provided important assistance for development, including roads, health projects and farm programs. Northern Yemen in particular proved adept at soliciting funds from rival nations, including the Soviet Union, China, the United States, West Germany and several Arab oil exporters. By contrast, its communist ties prevented South Yemen from receiving Western and Arab aid.

After oil exports commenced in 1988, the importance of foreign assistance declined somewhat. By 1995 total production reached 400,000 barrels per day, and the country approved a $3 billion project to liquify natural gas for export by the French company, Total. However, only modest quantities of oil have been discovered, and the volume of exports is small. Consequently, Yemen has not joined OPEC, and oil revenues will not lift the standard of living significantly.

The Future: Oil continued to flow from both Northern and Southern fields during the civil war, reflecting a common sense all too rare in other government matters. However, the conflict greatly damaged the business community and shocked hopes for the peaceful unity of north and south. Reconstruction will prove difficult, and unity suspect in the south.

President Ali Abdullah Salih will continue to treat the Zaydi tribes with care, alleged Islamist terrorists with a heavy hand, and the public with further rises in prices. The future looks very much like the present.

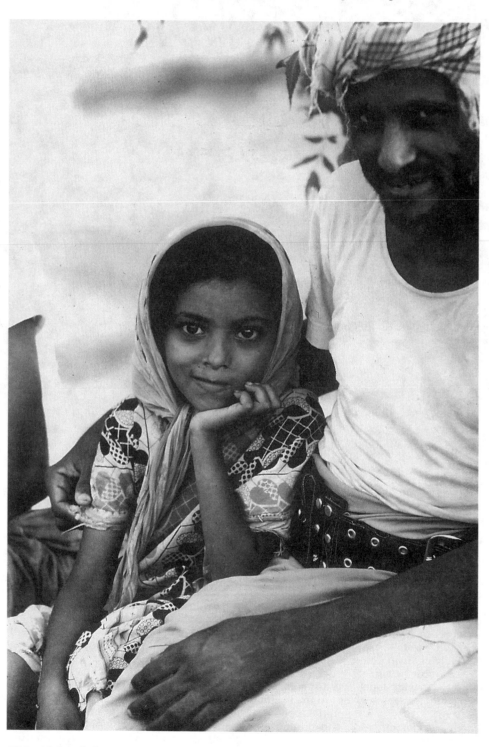

Girl with her father

Courtesy: World Bank Photo by Tomas Sennett

192

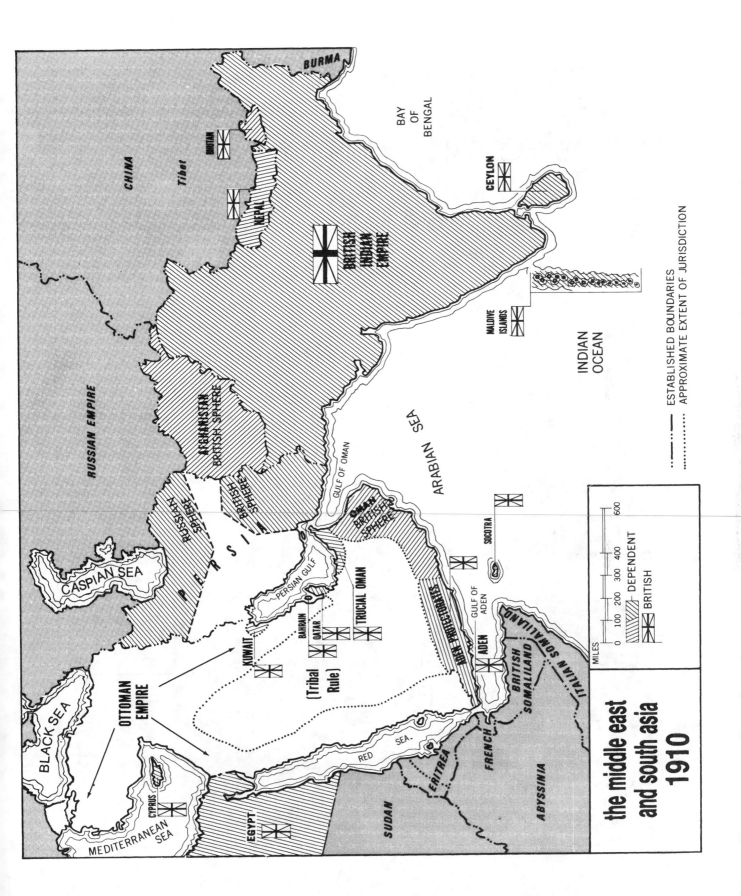

the middle east
and south asia
1910

MILES

0 100 200 300 400 600

DEPENDENT

BRITISH

ESTABLISHED BOUNDARIES

APPROXIMATE EXTENT OF JURISDICTION

BURMA

BAY
OF
BENGAL

CHINA

Tibet

BHUTAN

NEPAL

CEYLON

BRITISH
INDIAN
EMPIRE

RUSSIAN EMPIRE

MALDIVE
ISLANDS

INDIAN
OCEAN

AFGHANISTAN
BRITISH SPHERE

RUSSIAN
SPHERE

BRITISH
SPHERE

ARABIAN
SEA

GULF OF OMAN

CASPIAN SEA

P E R S I A

OMAN
BRITISH
SPHERE

SOCOTRA

PERSIAN GULF

TRUCIAL OMAN

BAHRAIN

QATAR

ADEN PROTECTORATES

GULF OF
ADEN

KUWAIT

[Tribal
Rule]

ADEN

BRITISH
SOMALILAND

ITALIAN SOMALILAND

OTTOMAN
EMPIRE

BLACK SEA

CYPRUS

MEDITERRANEAN
SEA

EGYPT

RED   SEA.

SUDAN

FRENCH

ERITREA

ABYSSINIA

193

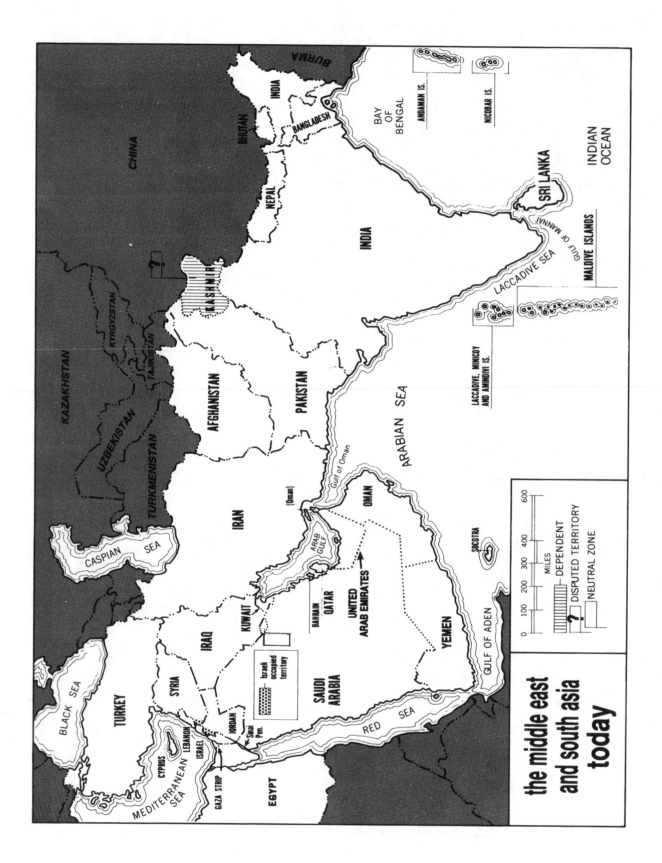

the middle east and south asia today

Afghanistan

Afghan vegetable vendor, Kabul

Photo by Jon Markham Morrow

Area: About 250,000 square miles (647,500 sq. km.).

Population: 27 million (UN estimates), reduced by refugees fleeing drought and warfare, 2000-2001.

Capital City: Kabul (Pop. once roughly 1 million).

Climate: Extremely dry, hot summers (but with cool nights); cold winters with moderate rain and snow in the mountains, scanty rain on the plain. Strong winds and dust storms are common.

Neighboring Countries: Pakistan (South and East); Iran (West); Turkmenistan, Uzbekistan, Tajikistan (formerly USSR; North); China (Northeast).

Time Zone: GMT +4 –1/2. When it is noon Mountain Standard Time in the U.S. it is 11:30 P.M. in Afghanistan.

Official Languages: Pushtu and Dari (the latter is a form of Persian).

Other Principal Tongues: Uzbek, Turkmen, Baluchi and Pashai.

Ethnic Background: The people identify themselves mainly on the basis of language, i.e., as Pushtuns (Afghans), Tajiks (Dari speaking), Uzbeks and Turkmens. The Dari–speaking Hazaras are distinguished from Tajiks by geographic location and traditions.

Principal Religion: Sunni Islam (87%) and Shi'a Islam (12%).

Main Exports: Natural gas; agricultural products (dried fruit, nuts, lambskins, raw cotton, wool, grain), carpets and textiles. Until recently opium production ranked largest in the world, with 75% of total output.

Major Trading Partners: Commonwealth of Independent States, Japan, Pakistan, India, U.K. and Germany.

Currency: $1 = 20,000-40,000 Afghanis in Kabul. A new currency is expected.

Former Political Status: Under British influence (1837–1919).

National Day: August 19 (traditional); May 5 (liberation of Kabul from communist rule).

Chief of State and Head of Government: President Hamid Karzai, elected by the traditional national political assembly, *Loya Jirga*, June 2002, for up to two years.

National Flag: Black, red, and green vertical stripes with a white emblem centered in the red containing Muslim symbols, two flags, and sheaves of wheat (horizontally striped flags are also used).

Gross Domestic Product (GDP): None measured.

GDP per capita: $200 seems a reasonable guess.

Afghanistan means "Land of the Afghans." Afghan in a strict sense means Pushtun or Pathan, that is, a member of any tribe speaking Pushtu, but now Afghan is applied to any citizen of this nation, sometimes described as the Turnstile of Asia."

Except for the spring with its moderate temperatures and the green vegetation after winter rain and snow, Afghanistan has an environment hostile to human comfort and even survival. During the summer, temperatures in the low valley of the Amu Darya (Oxus River to the ancient Greeks) often hover at 110°F. In the winter, blizzards rage in the high mountains, and even in the medium elevation where most people live, as at Kabul, temperatures may drop below zero and snow lie on the ground for a few weeks. Most of the country may be described as a treeless, wind-swept land. It is the low valleys where agriculture is intensively pursued and where native poplar trees abound to provide wood for rough houses.

The most striking geographical feature of the country is the complex series of mountains extending from the eastern tip of Afghanistan for some 600 miles southwest before leveling out in the plateau near the border with Iran. The central Hindu Kush Mountains have majestic peaks towering more than 20,000 feet above sea level. The rugged mountains also make transportation difficult.

Being a landlocked country, Afghanistan must depend on transit through neighboring countries for its external trade. Until fighting in the 1980s increased commercial links with the Soviet Union, the bulk of imports and exports passed through Pakistan, utilizing the railroad between Karachi and Peshawar, but depending on trucks between Peshawar and points inside the country.

History: The mountains of Afghanistan form a natural divide, separating the Indian Subcontinent from Central Asia to the northwest, and Iran to the west. Until modern times, the territory did not form a separate political unit; indeed, its steep mountains and remote valleys usually felt the impact of formal government only lightly. Nevertheless, the land and its people suffered migrations, raids and conquests as a consequence of its position as the "turnstile of Asia's fate." (see Historical Background). Aryan (Iranian) languages were established in the region more than 3,000 years ago, and related languages have been used by the majority of the population since. Islamic religion and culture began spreading there in the seventh century and became dominant by about the tenth century.

The Mongols swept through the area in the 14th century, followed in the next century by the plundering hordes of Timur Lang (Tamerlane). Descendants of Timur ruled Herat and its districts through the 15th century. In the early 16th century, Babur, a Turkish chief who claimed descent from Timur in another line, retreated from enemies north of the Amu Darya and established his capital at Kabul.

Babur's warriors then conquered southward in the Indus and Ganges Valleys, founding the great Mogul Empire. During the same period, the newly–established Safavid Empire in Iran ruled Herat province. Kandahar was sometimes controlled by the Safavids and sometimes by the Moguls. This situation of division and rivalry prevailed for nearly two centuries.

As the Moguls and Safavids weakened, Pushtu–speaking tribes began to exercise more and more local authority, as well as feuding with one another. These tribes referred to themselves as Pushtun (*Pakhtun* was a dialectic variation), but the Persians called them Afghans, a name of unknown origin, and in India they were called Pashtuns.

When Safavid rule proved particularly severe and rapacious at the beginning of the 18th century, the Afghans of Kandahar revolted, defeating the Persian army in 1711 and establishing independence for the region. This marked the beginning of the end of the Safavid dynasty, for under their ruler Mahmud the Afghans marched into Persia and attacked the capital, Isfahan, in 1722. After a bitter siege lasting through the summer, the Safavid Shah surrendered sovereignty to Mahmud, the Afghan leader. Following invasions by both the Russian and the Ottoman Empires, and Mahmud's insanity and death, the Afghans were expelled from Isfahan by Nadir Khan, soon to unite Persia and assume the title Shah. A brilliant military adventurer yet so cruel he erected pyramids of his victims' skulls, Nadir Shah moved against the Afghans in 1738, laying siege to Kandahar for a year. He then advanced through Kabul and the Khyber

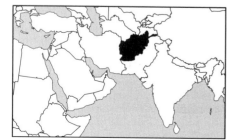

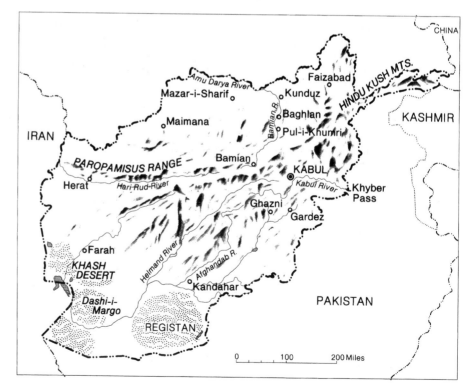

Pass to plunder the plains of northern India. Not surprisingly, after his assassination in 1747 his realm disintegrated, providing the opportunity for the founding of the Afghan nation. Ahmad Khan Durani, an Afghan subordinate of the Persian ruler, proclaimed himself king (shah) in Kandahar as soon as his master was dead. Ahmad Shah then seized control of the whole eastern part of Nadir Shah's empire, including what is now Afghanistan, Pakistan and eastern districts of Iran.

When the firm authority of Ahmad Shah disappeared upon his death in 1773, serious tribal struggles erupted. Intrigues and assassination within the royal family became commonplace; conditions improved only after about 1820 when chiefs of a rival family, the *Mohammedzai*, consolidated their control over principal centers in Afghanistan. The strongest of their number, Dost Mohammed, finally proclaimed himself Amir of Kabul. He ruled as king, though it was decades later before any of his line assumed the title of Shah. He concentrated on controlling a smaller territory rather than over–extending his forces as the previous dynasty had done. His last act before his death in 1863 was to drive Persian forces out of Herat.

From early in his reign and continuing for about a century, the two main themes in Afghan political history were the struggles between rival leaders and the interference of British Indian officials. Direct descendants of Dost Mohammed remained in power until 1978, but only by repeatedly defeating rivals—often brothers and other close relatives. Most rulers died violent deaths; power passed to brothers or cousins as often as to sons.

Between 1839 and 1919, Anglo–Indian troops periodically intervened in Afghanistan, usually in support of a rival claimant to the throne who appeared to be more agreeable to British policy. In the final phase of the First Afghan War in 1841, some 4,500 British and 10,000 Indian troops were massacred by the Afghans in the rugged mountain gorges between Kabul and the Khyber Pass during a British–Indian retreat.

One of the motives for Britain's intervention in Afghanistan was the desire to block Russian influence. After a century of expansion toward the Hindu Kush Mountains, by 1875 the Russian Empire nearly reached the Amu Darya—the later border of the Soviet Union. As Russian expansion continued, a new British invasion of Afghanistan in 1878 began two years of fighting with the Afghan tribes. In the end, the new ruler of Afghanistan, Abdurrahman was required to put foreign relations in the hands of British authorities. Anglo–Russian rivalry in Afghanistan continued until the Tsar's government acknowledged the country to be an area of British influence after Habibullah succeeded his father as Amir in 1901.

Although some leaders wished to use World War I as an opportunity to strike at British positions across the Indian border, the Amir kept his country neutral. However, following Habibullah's assassination in 1919, his son and successor, Amanullah, sought to gain popularity by a half–hearted attack on British India. This war lasted only a month, but ended with Britain recognizing the independence of Afghanistan in foreign as well as internal affairs.

After a celebrated tour of India, Europe, the Soviet Union and Turkey, and his proclamation as king (1926), Amanullah announced in 1928 a program of social and educational modernization. This was a cue for tribal revolt which forced the king to flee Kabul. After months of civil strife, a leader of another branch of the Mohammedzai family was able to establish himself in power, taking the name Mohammed Nadir. Under his rule, some modern organization was gradually introduced into government. A regular army was created and the two halves of the country were physically united by a road blasted through the Hindu Kush Mountains north of Kabul.

When Mohammed Nadir was assassinated in 1933 as a result of a blood feud, his son, Zahir, only 19 at the time, succeeded him. During the first 14 years of Zahir Shah's reign, the country was governed chiefly by his uncle, Sardar Hashin Khan, Prime Minister. Moreover, members of the royal family usually dominated the highest posts in the government throughout the 1940's and 1950's. Domestic modernization proceeded slowly, although the king granted a new constitution in 1964. It prohibited the king's relatives from serving as minister, as Chief Justice or members of the legislature. The constitution also provided that the legal system was not to be based solely on Islamic religious law.

As a concession to an educated minority, the king allowed elections for representatives to a legislative body in 1965 and 1969. Political parties, however, were not allowed, and the king did not permit the elected representatives to assume real law–making power. Wealthy landowners, furthermore, were able to block progressive tax laws in the legislature.

Elections scheduled for 1973 did not take place, because army forces seized power, deposed the king and abolished the constitution. Mohammed Daud Khan, the general who led the coup d'etat, was the king's cousin and brother–in–law, and had served as Prime Minister (1953–1963). He immediately proclaimed the country a republic and named himself both President and Prime Minister. Thus, little changed except the title of the ruling member of the Mohammedzai family

Opposition to the regime of Daud (pronounced *dah*–ood) was unsuccessfully manifested in at least three attempts to

overthrow him; the leaders of the first of these (1973) were executed. There was dissatisfaction with the economy, worsened by drought in 1974, which led to a land reform program adopted in 1975. It limited land holdings and established cooperatives.

Daud was elected for a six–year term as President in February 1977 by the National Assembly (*Loya Jirga*), which was then immediately disbanded. President Daud's dictatorial rule failed to satisfy many people and was finally ended by groups of communists in the army who had studied in the Soviet Union and learned the arts of political subversion besides the art of war. In 1978 a day–long battle in Kabul between communist sympathizers and loyalists ended with the deaths of thousands, including President Daud and some cabinet members.

The victors, who represented more than one communist grouping, set up a Revolutionary Council to rule and appointed elderly Nur Mohammed Taraki, a poet and journalist, as President.

The new regime rapidly moved toward closer ties with the Soviet Union. Domestically, it adopted radical social and economic measures, including a drastic land reform law that limited an individual's maximum holding to 15 acres, the closing of Islamic schools, and changes in family law contrary to traditional Islam. Not surprisingly, opposition surfaced, and perhaps 50,000 to 100,000 people perished during the land reforms. Resistance turned to rebellion, inspired by Islam and its religious teachers. The Taraki government sought Soviet aid to crush the widespread rebellion of the *Mujahidin* (meaning "those who undertake jihad"), but the Soviet presence probably inflamed nationalist and Muslim opposition.

Further complicating matters, the Afghan communists formed the *People's Democratic Party of Afghanistan* (PDPA), but within it they divided into two often hostile factions, *Khalq* ("Masses") and *Parcham* ("Banner"). In September 1979 Taraki, belonging to *Khalq*, was forced out by his subordinate.

To avert a likely defeat of communism, in late 1979 a Soviet invasion force suddenly attacked Kabul, killing the (communist) president before installing Babrak Karmal of *Parcham* as President and Prime Minister. Some 90,000 Soviet troops entered the struggle to defeat the mujahidin, and they successfully occupied most of northern Afghanistan and the major cities of Kabul, Herat, and Kandahar, as well as the roads connecting them. However, the mujahidin, although poorly armed and divided into rival groups, operated across much of the country's rugged terrain, and won many small victories. In response, the Soviets adopted a policy of ruthless air and artillery attacks on towns and villages.

Mujahidin resistance fighters look down on a village after a Soviet aerial attack. At left are terraced crop fields.   AP/World Wide Photos

Far from consolidating communist power, the invasion and its indiscriminate bombing and shelling turned the population into refugees. Nearly five million civilians fled the fighting, some to Iran but most to Pakistan. Their giant refugee camps, funded by Saudi Arabia, other Arab nations, and the United States, became staging bases for the mujahidin.

The Islamic resistance operated most successfully in the mountains near its supply centers in Pakistan. Another stronghold was the Panjsher Valley north of Kabul, not far from the strategic Salang highway linking the capital to northern Afghanistan. There, under the most highly regarded mujahidin commander, Ahmad Shah Masoud, the rebels withstood repeated Soviet attacks. In the west and south, other mujahidin groups fought for Herat and Kandahar, and the fighting destroyed large portions of these two historic cities.

Cruelty and inhumanity accompanied much of the fighting. The UN Human Rights Commission condemned the Soviet forces for bombarding villages and dropping explosives disguised as toys in rebel areas. Amnesty International in 1988 claimed that Soviet and Afghan troops had killed hundreds of civilians in reprisal raids and that captured mujahidin had been tortured and executed. Other international groups decried the massacres and executions of civilians, as well as the deportation of Afghan children to the Soviet Union. On the other hand, some western journalists reported that rebel groups often preferred to take no prisoners and executed government supporters in newly-captured towns.

The years 1985–1986 marked critical changes in the Afghan war. Soviet policies suffered strong condemnation in the world press, even·in many "non–aligned nations" that the USSR had courted carefully for years. Politicians in Moscow began to recognize that the Kabul regime remained entirely dependent on Soviet support, and only a massive occupation force could possibly succeed. As present troop levels, the military situation worsened after the United States finally provided some mujahidin with Stinger anti–aircraft missiles and other modern weapons that threatened to neutralize Soviet air power and render very difficult the supply of remote outposts.

Recognizing that Babrak Karmal had proved ineffective, in 1986 the Soviet Union forced his resignation "for health reasons." Najib Ahmadzai, then head of security in Kabul and a leading figure in *Parcham*, took control of government as the General Secretary of the *PDPA*. In 1987 he was elected president by a *loya jirga* (Grand National Assembly) dominated by the *PDPA* but given a smattering of legitimacy by a few tribal leaders and others.

A more flexible politician than his predecessors, Najib restored the Islamic form of his name, Najibullah, and offered political concessions, including a coalition government. However, he won over only a few inconsequential groups. By 1988, after Afghan casualties surpassed one million dead plus millions more wounded or forced to flee, the Soviet leadership decided to halt their much smaller political and military losses. Mikhail Gorbachev promised to withdraw Soviet troops and let the Afghans decide their future government. An international accord in Geneva formalized the decision.

The last Soviet troops departed in early 1989 against a background of rocket attacks on Kabul and fierce fighting for several provincial cities. In the capital, crowded by over two million inhabitants, siege conditions appeared, for rebel activity often closed the Salang highway to the north and a Soviet airlift of supplies proved insufficient. Food prices rose sharply, so that the price of a large family's monthly flour—the staple food—exceeded two months' average pay. Malnutrition threatened. However, by summer the guerrillas abandoned their use of mass hunger against the regime. Nevertheless, rocket attacks continued from the surrounding mountains and killed hundreds of people, many of them children.

Najibullah

198

A windstorm sweeps down upon an Afghani sheep and camel market

Photo by Jon Markham Morrow

The stalemate at the capital reflected the country at large. The mujahidin fiercely assaulted Jalalabad, between Kabul and the Khyber Pass, but failed despite the highest casualties of the war. Similarly, in Herat, Kandahar and elsewhere the government continued to govern essentially the same cities and territory. Some officials and soldiers defected, but others fought with greater determination, having learned that capture meant death.

Victory eluded the guerrillas largely because they could not unite. Military coordination often proved weak, and separate groups made uncoordinated attacks. Rivalries and traditional blood–feuds often overshadowed the struggle against the communist regime. In particular, the Pashtun *Hizb–i Islami*, dominant along the Pakistani border, hijacked supplies for its northeastern rival, Masoud's largely Tajik *Jamiat–i Islami*. Ambushes and battles broke out between them. In contrast, few mujahidin attacked the departing Soviet troops, and several groups arranged informal cease–fires with Kabul.

Divisions among the mujahidin reflected geography and ethnic rivalries, both within the majority Pashtuns and between them and ethnic minorities. Personal antagonism also played an inevitable part, while other controversies involved religion. Shi'a and Sunni mujahidin differed over their concepts of the state. Moreover the majority Sunni fractured between moderately conservative Muslims and those labeled fundamentalist, who tended to follow Gulbuddin Hikmatyar of the *Hizb–i Islami*.

The disintegration of the Soviet Union in 1991 disrupted food and fuel supplies for Kabul, and the new Russian leaders desired to end an adventure that had cost more than $110 billion. After mujahidin successes against provincial capitals, in early 1992 the Kabul government tottered.

The front lines moved rapidly when General Abdul Rashid Dostam and his tough Uzbek militia at Mazar–i–Sharif in the north switched sides. A local council composed of the military, guerrillas, and the militia took control of the city. This set the pattern for other cities, such as Heart. Dostam also formed an alliance with Ahmad Shah Masoud, the Tajik leader who had captured much of the northeast for the mujahidin.

Moving quickly southwards, General Dostam's militia and Masoud's *Jamiat–i Islami* forces cut the Salang highway and captured the Bagram airbase near Kabul, home of the Afghan airforce. Exiled politicians in Pakistan agreed to form a temporary coalition under Sibghatullah Mojaddidi, with Masoud as defense minister. However, Gulbuddin Hikmatyar of

the *Hizb–i Islami* rejected the prime ministership and sent his forces to infiltrate Kabul. Dostam's militia and Masoud's guerrillas then rushed for the city, some flown by air force helicopters. Najibullah attempted to flee, but was captured, and the communist regime formally transferred power to an Islamic Afghan regime in April 1992.

Deprived of their prize, Hikmatyar's forces rocketed the city, killing and maiming the first of tens of thousands of casualties in the Islamic Republic. However, conditions in the capital did not reflect the country. Many areas enjoyed relative calm under the control of local warlords, and several million refugees returned from Pakistan to their often–destroyed towns and villages.

Kabul changed perceptibly under Islamic rule. Women who previously dressed in jeans and T–shirts now covered their hair and wore long black robes, some perhaps for piety; others for safety from molestation. Alcoholic beverages disappeared from stores, and hotel bars closed. Former officials and agents of Khad, the secret police, disappeared to avoid reprisals; some executions occurred.

Despite the creation of a Leadership Council to guide the country, politics remained confused. The acting president attempted to extend his two–month term,

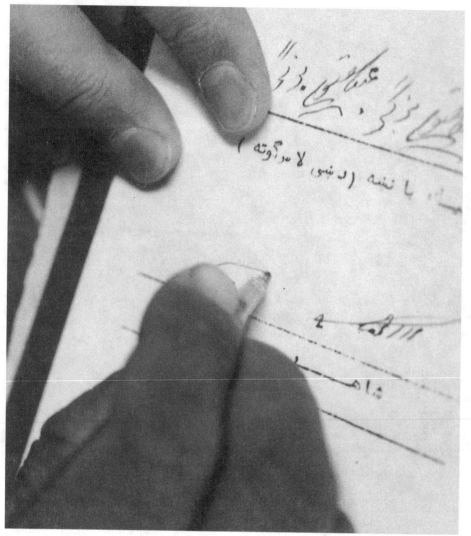

An Afghani farmer signs an application for a tractor   WORLD BANK photo

but finally left office, Afghanistan's first peaceful transfer of power in decades. Amid accusations of bribery and pressure, a large council met in December 1992 and elected Burhanuddin Rabbani of the *Jami-at–i Islam*i as president. However, Rabbani failed to win recognition from Hikmatyar and the *Hizb–i Islami*, and he expelled the party from the Leadership Council. Later attempts to bring Hikmatyar into the government also failed.

Thousands perished during the four-year struggle to rule Kabul. Rival mujahidin leaders made and broke alliances, all apparently to ensure that no one leader became powerful enough to rule the nation. Probably the most ironic alliance was that negotiated between Dostam and Hikmatyar, ideological and ethnic rivals. The latter had condemned Dostam as a Communist, but both resented Rabbani's rule over Kabul. The main market and business areas suffered looting and shelling, and Sikh and Hindu businesses and homes were attacked. Blockades on roads ended most travel, and the airport closed. Hundreds of thousands fled.

The Rise of the *Taliban*

As the nation collapsed into anarchy, a new political force inspired hope in many Afghans. Reputedly a group of religious scholars, the *Taliban* ("Students") emerged in the southern, Pashtun city of Kandahar as a protest movement against the sexual immorality and corruption of local mujahidin. Desiring to end the civil war and establish Islamic government, under the leadership of the reclusive Mullah Omar, *Taliban* fighters ended thievery on the roads and established order.

As their fame spread, so did the students' conquests. Within months, and with little fighting, the *Taliban* conquered much of the Pashtun–speaking south and advanced on the capital. In rapid, almost bloodless victories, it ejected Hikmatyar and the *Hizb–i Islami* from bases outside the capital and entered its Shi'a suburbs. However, Rabbani refused to resign the presidency, and his forces delivered *Taliban* its first defeat. Nevertheless, after their rapid conquest of Herat in 1995, the *Taliban* controlled about half the country. To support renewed assaults on Kabul,

they launched air and missile attacks against residential areas, disproving their claim to avoid civilian targets. However, in late 1996 the capital fell, and Najibullah was quickly executed.

Much of the world recoiled at the social consequences of *Taliban* rule. It banned television and required beards on all men. Female modesty meant total covering of their bodies. To Western and even much Muslim opinion, the treatment of women defied human dignity. Although several hundred thousand war widows struggled to provide for their families, the *Taliban* ordered women not to work outside their homes. Later it relented for necessary tasks like nursing (female patients only), but it demanded extreme measures to keep men from seeing women even at a distance. Even after such precautions were observed, it closed down UN–sponsored bakeries run by women.

The attack on women extended far beyond banning all contact between the sexes to enforce moral purity. After closing universities, the *Taliban* proposed opening them for men only. It apparently desired education for girls to stop at the age of eight, and teachers caught schooling girls in homes were arrested and probably tortured.

Aided by the defection of one of Dostam's officers, the *Taliban* then entered the second largest city, Mazar–i-Sharif, still largely untouched by the entire war. However, the defector then defected again, and Dostam regained the city, his forces apparently murdering perhaps 2,000 enemy fighters, some evidently after being taken prisoner. However, his fractured alliance could not hold the city. In 1998 the *Taliban* successfully attacked Mazar–i-Sharif and conquered much of the north. This isolated the opposition to about 10% of the country, in the Panjsher Valley and the far northeast, a region lacking significant cities, plus Shi'a groups in the central mountains.

To confront their common enemy, Dostam and Masoud formed the *Northern Alliance* and apparently received limited food and military supplies from Iran, India and Russia. This did not prevent battles for local supremacy between Dostam's forces and their formal allies, the Shi'a *Hizb al-Wahadat*. In 2000 the provisional capital of Taloqan fell to a *Taliban* army of 15,000 men, perhaps one-third of them Pakistanis and other foreigners. In the process, Kabul's rule nominally extended to 95% of the country.

Most conquests were relatively bloodless in a land suffering greatly from war fatigue. The *Taliban*'s superior firepower was reinforced by the mobility of their four-wheel drive pickups and the obvious corruption of many mujahidin. However, the 1998 massacre of several Iranian diplomats and thousands of Afghan civilians created international tensions. War fever

President Hamid Karzai

swept Iran, but it was defused with the Afghan release of captured Iranian survivors. However, Russia, India, and several Central Asian republics remained critics, sustaining the *Northern Alliance* and other opposition groups in a bleak existence. Only three countries, most prominently Pakistan and Saudi Arabia, ever extended diplomatic recognition.

Sanctuary for Osama bin Ladin and September 11

Far more serious foreign complications resulted from the sanctuary Kabul offered to the anti–American fanatic Osama bin Laden. One of many sons of an exceptionally successful Saudi construction magnate originally from Yemen, the deeply fanatical Osama had fought the Soviets by joining the Afghan mujahidin. Thereafter, he established a loosely-organized society called *al-Qaeda* ("The Base"), and moved to Sudan. In the early 1990s, he issued increasingly violent diatribes against the U.S., and eventually his Sudanese hosts asked him to leave. Apparently the U.S. considered the remoteness of Afghanistan sufficient to render him relatively harmless, so he returned to the country's rural south.

In 1998, however, truck bombs at two American embassies in Africa killed hundreds. The trail of evidence led to *al-Qaeda*, but Mullah Omar rejected U.S. demands to hand over Osama, arguing both a lack of evidence and the tradition of Afghan hospitality. The continued asylum brought UN sanctions in 1999 that banned most flights to the country and virtually grounded the national airline.

After the infamous September 11 attacks on the twin towers of the New York World Trade Center and the Pentagon, evidence again quickly implicated Osama bin Ladin and *al-Qaeda*. The *Taliban* refused again to hand over Osama, and two events within the country suggest more than traditional Afghan hospitality protected *al-Qaeda*. On September 9, Arab suicide bombers disguised as TV journalists

assassinated Ahmad Shah Masoud. Bin Ladin clearly expected American air strikes after September 11, so was the assassination, a potentially deadly blow to the *Northern Alliance*, an advanced payment to the Taliban for his shelter?

In the second case, the religious police charged two young American women and several other foreign aid workers in Kabul with spreading Christianity. Instead of the normal pattern of expulsion, the Christians faced vague though severe charges. Perhaps the arrest was mere coincidence, but conceivably it was deliberately timed to provide potential hostages against possible U.S. military actions.

Determined to attack both terrorists and those who supported terrorism, the U.S. prepared to attack Afghanistan. Unable to use airbases anywhere in the region, the defense department added to the carrier fleet in the Indian Ocean and obtained permission to overfly Pakistan. Special forces troops secretly infiltrated the country to strengthen the *Northern Alliance* and to mark targets for smart weapons. On October 6, the U.S. aerial offensive began, with the usual attacks on air defenses, command centers, and communications facilities.

Initially the air war went slowly. Mistakes occurred, such as a direct hit on Red Cross warehouse. Civilian casualties inevitably rose. In parts of the world, media pontificators began to proclaim the failure of the air war, and humanitarian organizations became extremely worried that the bombing and fighting would block food supplies for millions of refugees.

At this point, the U.S. bombing shifted to troop concentrations and fortifications. Apparently fearing that the U.S. would assist a *Northern Alliance* attack along the front lines in the north, the *Taliban* had moved much of their army and many Arab and Pakistani volunteers to the northern city of Kunduz before the bombing began. This left the other major cities lightly defended.

Back from exile, General Dostam recognized a key role for Mazar-i Sharif. Its capture would break the *Taliban's* supply line to the north and likewise prevent a retreat by the troops concentrated there. With important assistance from U.S. Navy aircraft, Dostam's forces fought bitterly for the city and won.

Days later, the vital airpower enabled the largely Tajik forces of the *Northern Alliance* to break through the first *Taliban* lines outside Kabul. The capital lay beckoning, but the Pentagon, fearing Pashtun and Pakistani resentment over so prominent a Tajik victory, urged a halt to enable some sort of temporary government to be established. After years of hardship, the *Alliance* forces entered the city, almost unopposed. Despite initial fears that Kabul might again become a battlefield between rival mujahidin, as it had in the early

1990s, the population generally celebrated the *Taliban's* collapse. Widespread approval met the legalization of music, kite flying, and education for girls.

In the south, particularly around Mullah Omar's home town of Kandahar, resistance ended more slowly. Nevertheless, in early December the city fell to local rivals. By that time, the country had a new leader, Hamid Karzai, a Pashtun of notable family. Chosen by representatives of several factions at a council in Germany, Karzai became head of the interim administration pending the *loya jirga* scheduled within six months.

Civilized, thoughtful, and distinguished, Karzai worked effectively to persuade wealthier nations to donate funds for Afghanistan; they quickly promised nearly $5 billion in aid. The funds were critical: civil servants had not been paid in seven months, and the treasury was bare.

In Kabul, Karzai shared power. The interim government clearly recognized the power of the *Northern Alliance*, for its leading officials took responsibility for defense, finance, and foreign affairs. By doing so, they helped ease out Burhanuddin Rabbani, the formal head of the *Northern Alliance*, who in legal fiction remained the country's president.

Besides money, the most important issue was security. Some Afghan forces joined American and allied troops in mopping-up operations that continued for months, particularly in the eastern mountains of Paktia province, south and east of Gardez. Large caves in the mountains had provided refuge for the mujahidin fighting the Soviet occupation. Various groups had stockpiled vast quantities of weapons in the caves, and Osama bin Laden himself had frequented the area. However, he eluded his pursuers unless, of course, he died in a bombing raid or an explosion in one of the caves.

To increase security in the capital, an international force was created, headed first by Britain and later by Turkey. However, the U.S. carefully avoided participating in the force, and Hamid Karzai's strongly-expressed desires to expand the force to Mazar-i Sharif and elsewhere failed. The Bush administration rejected this vital role in nation-building, and too few nations were willing to donate the men and equipment.

The much-anticipated *loya jirga* met in June 2002, after a selection process that, despite some defects, provided hundreds of delegates from all significant population groups and even some (appointed) women. Inevitably, so large a group proved unable to achieve all the high hopes placed in it. After the ex-king removed himself from consideration, the delegates readily elected Hamid Karzai to lead the transitional administration for the proposed two-year period pending elections under a new constitution. However, personal and ethnic rivalries, including Pashtun worries about the power of *Northern Alliance* leaders, delayed forming the cabinet, and the *loya jirga* failed to establish procedures for a parliament.

Politics: The Islamic Republic failed to replace the 1987 constitution ratified by a *Loya Jirga* (National Assembly) selected by Najibullah and boycotted by the *mujahidin*. Ruling all but the northeast by 1998, the *Taliban* restored major constitutional and legal aspects of the regime headed by Mohammed Daud in the 1970s. Until fall 2001 *Taliban* formed the only permitted political grouping in most of the country.

Until 1995, two rival factions dominated politics and the military struggle. The *Jamiat–i Islami* (Islamic League) of President Burhanuddin Rabbani included Ahmad Shah Masoud, the guerrilla leader of the Panjsher Valley. Strong especially among the Tajiks of the northeast, it formed alliances with smaller parties from other ethnic groups.

Its greatest threat came from the Pashtun-dominated *Hizb–i Islami* (Party of Islam) led by Gulbuddin Hikmatyar. His followers supported an uncompromisingly strict interpretation of Islam, opposed education for women, and reportedly threw acid at unveiled faces. Dominant between Kabul and the Pakistani border, the *Hizb–i Islami* for many years received large amounts of anti–Soviet aid channeled through Pakistan and also seized supplies shipped to other groups. After its defeat by *Taliban* in 1995 the *Hizb–i Islami* played a much–diminished role. The largest Shi'a coalition, the pro-Iranian *Hizb–i Wahadat* (Party of Unity), likewise opposed the rule of President Rabbani until the rise of the *Taliban*. Some commentators saw the *Hizb–i Wahadat*'s opposition to Rabbani, then its alliance with him, as an example of a smaller Afghan group opposing any central government.

The rise of the *Taliban* undoubtedly reflected a popular disgust with the factional fighting by *mujahidin* groups. Its successes signaled the end of the era when the wartime *mujahidin* groups dominated Afghan politics.

In the autumn of 2001, the Taliban were driven from power by Northern Alliance and other opposition forces supported by the United States and other western nations. Hamid Karzai was named interim leader. In June 2002, at a traditional national assembly, the *loya jirga*, composed of 1,600 delegates (including women) representing all ethnic groups, he was elected by a landslide as president for up to two years until nation-wide elections can be held. He selected a cabinet for his government, but the assembly was unable to form a legislature after several days of fruitless debate.

Culture: Similar to many nations of the modern world, Afghanistan does not possess a culture which is entirely distinct from that of nearby lands. This is true not only of folkways, but also of religion, art and political organization.

Society traditionally has been mainly pastoral and agricultural, and as in other comparable societies, the ties of blood and tribe are strong. Though tribal organization is beginning to weaken, loyalty to the extended family (clan) remains dominant. It is considered not only a duty, but the normal way of doing things to side with cousins and other relatives or to aid them in time of need, as well as to share in the happy times of weddings, births (especially of sons) and the celebration of holidays. The most firmly implanted of all holidays throughout the country is *No Ruz*, in honor of the first day of spring— March 21st or 22nd.

The great majority of the people in the country are engaged in agricultural work and live in small villages, which typically are located on a slope at the edge of a cultivated valley. Most villages are still fairly isolated, and until the civil war, many people had never traveled any distance from their birthplace. A few nomads move frequently in search of pasturage for their sheep, goats, cattle and (in the case of a few tribes), camels. Another group are townsfolk, engaged in shopkeeping and handicrafts.

Religion is as natural to the people of Afghanistan as the air they breathe. The name of God is invoked on every possible occasion, and political leaders can oppose the dominance of religious practices only at their peril. Though many people speak Dari, a form of Persian, most Afghans feel a general distinctness because they are Sunni Muslims, while most Iranians are Shi'a.

Literary expression has been largely in the form of poetry, ranging from the intricate, elegant poems of professionals to the more direct, forceful and colorful folk poetry which displays the soul of the people. Literature is mainly in either Pushtu or Persian, and shares much in form and content with neighboring Iran and Pakistan.

Education has lagged seriously. It is estimated that only about 12% of the people can read and write, while a high school diploma is almost unknown outside the large cities. Fundamentalist objections and suspicions of Western ideas also limit

A young Afghan farmer

education among refugees to small percentages of boys and very few girls. Indoctrination of the young in government schools formed part of the plan to revolutionize Afghan society along communist lines. Such ideas contrasted sharply with the traditional, religiously–oriented politics and values of the country. Most Afghans, even those rejecting the *Taliban*'s fundamentalism, did not favor the Soviet–enforced attempt to transform their culture, and education suffered with other aspects of society.

Another cultural offensive by the Taliban involved the deliberate mutilation and destruction of statues, particularly of the Buddha, throughout the country despite an international outcry. Officials ransacked collections in the National Museum and also used artillery to demolish the two outdoor statues of the Buddha near Bamian. Carved over 1300 years ago, before the Muslim conquest of Afghanistan, the larger of the two statues measured about 150 feet high and ranked as the tallest standing Buddha in the world.

Economy: The civil war inflicted suffering on some of the world's poorest people and postponed badly–needed reconstruction. Poverty stalks the land, middle class families have lost their wealth, and the child mortality rate exceeds that of every other country. Thousands of orphans struggle to exist on the streets of Kabul and other cities, depending on handouts for food and clothing. Their education virtually non–existent, they face a future nearly as grim as their present.

Survival is uncertain for many adults as well: starvation and poor medical care threaten many Afghans. Homes, irrigation systems, roads and government buildings often lie in ruin. Most of the country lacks electricity, and there is no telephone network. Even major airports lack radar, though foreign aid permitted updating air control systems in 2000. The national airline crashed rather frequently under the *Taliban*; the U.S. bombing obliterated the remaining planes to prevent Osama from fleeing. Finally, millions of land mines still threaten those who wish to rebuild. Over 100,000 Afghans, many of them children, have lost limbs.

The extended drought that struck the region in the late 1990s withered crops and dried up water for animals. Hundreds of thousands, then millions, fled their homes and villages for the chance of food and water in refugee camps, some of them crossing illegally into Pakistan despite that country's attempts to prohibit their entry.

Winter cold killed hundreds in 2001, many of them refugee children living in tents.

Agriculture is the livelihood of the country. Yet, only 20% of the country at most could be cultivated if water were supplied by irrigation projects, and less than half of the potential farm land is actually irrigated and cultivated. In good crop years the country is approximately self–sufficient in cereal grains, but frequent droughts require grain imports even in peacetime. The high price of cotton on world markets has encouraged increased production of this crop.

The northern part of the country has large deposits of natural gas and some oil. Natural gas exports to the Soviet Union, halted when the withdrawing Soviets capped the wells, again may supply neighboring republics of the Commonwealth of Independent States. Mineral resources, such as iron ore and coal in the Hindu Kush Mountains, have not yet been exploited. It is suspected that these, as well as deposits of chrome, tin, sulphur, molybdenum, lead, copper and zinc, had helped make control of Afghanistan desirable to the Soviet Union. An important potential source of energy, which will require costly development, is hydroelectric power.

The skins and wool of the Karakul sheep remain important exports in keeping with long tradition. The United States has been one of the principal purchasers, particularly of the skins of the Karakul lambs. While the wool of the mature sheep is coarse, stringy and brown, that of the newborn lambs is tightly curled and a glossy black, highly prized as a material for fur coats.

In the aftermath of the Soviet withdrawal, perhaps the most surprising fact is that Afghanistan does have an econ-omy—or rather several of them. Local relations between government and some *mujahidin* forces sometimes provided calm, rather than battle. For example, in the northeastern provinces largely captured by Ahmad Shad Masoud, reconstruction began in early 1990. Schools reopened, often under trees rather than within buildings, and the dangerous task began of clearing minefields. Agriculture revived, as did trade with Kabul and other areas.

In the south and west, opium is by far the most profitable commercial crop. The UN Drug Control Program estimated that 1999 production of opium exceeded 460 tons, the world record and 75% of global supply. The literalist thinking of the *Taliban* had quickly imposed Islamic and traditional penalties on alcohol, but found opium poppies a traditional crop and heroin ignored by the *Quran*. As a result,

though formally banned, opium production was often taxed instead of destroyed, until a much more persistent effort to prohibit production, aided by the drought, began to show results during the 2000/2001 growing season. However, the collapse of the *Taliban* encouraged many farmers to plant poppies again.

With the collapse of the communist regime, many of the nearly seven million refugees uprooted during the Soviet occupation desired to return. During the summer of 1992 thousands of families left Peshawar each week, though over one million refugees remained in 1999, some of them women seeking an education prohibited at home. Resettlement began with the removal of explosives—including booby–trapped toys—and rebuilding underground irrigation canals. Agricultural services, housing, health, and education reached the population slowly. Only an extraordinary international aid effort, both financial and technical, can accomplish these tasks.

The Future: Looking up, but expect no miracles. After years of drought, last winter's rain and snow promise decent harvests for farmers, and the more sophisticated inhabitants of the cities enjoy the end of the *Taliban's* culturally sterile rule. Hamid Karzai brings far greater breadth of view to government than the various mujahidin leaders, and his administration includes all significant ethnic groups. Aid organizations are back in action, driving up rents in Kabul to new heights.

However, this is still Afghanistan, and insecurity outside Kabul nourishes the rivalries and feuds of a highly armed population. Extortion on the roads, revenge against Pashtuns in the north, and millions of land mines promise difficulties ahead. Thanks in large part to the American assault, a quarter-century of violence between armies has ended. The struggle now begins for security, reconstruction, and prosperity.

The steady flow of Afghans returning to their homeland suggests that moderate optimism is appropriate. The collapse of the Taliban regime in the fall of 2001 and its replacement by a moderate Pashtun leader, Hamid Karzei, promises a much brighter future for this war-stricken, impoverished multi-ethnic land. The new president promised to lead his ethnically balanced and professionally competent government to improve the lot of his fellow Afghanis until democratic elections can be held in late 2003 or early 2004.

The People's Republic of Bangladesh

Passengers disembark from a ferry boat at Narayanganj, Bangladesh

WORLD BANK Photo

Area: 55,100 square miles (142,500 sq. km.).

Population: 126 million

Capital City: Dhaka (formerly Dacca, Pop. 9 million, est.).

Climate: Tropical and rain soaked; the country is subject to destructive hurricanes.

Neighboring Countries: Surrounded by India on three sides; a short border with Burma lies on the southeast.

Time Zone: GMT +6. When it is noon Pacific Standard Time in the U.S. it is 2:00 the next morning in Bangladesh.

Official Language: Bengali.

Other Principal Tongues: Urdu and (in schools and commerce) English.

Ethnic Background: Over 98% Bengali, with small minorities of tribal groups in the Chittagong hills and Bihari refugees in the cities.

Principal Religion: Islam (87%) and Hinduism (11%).

Chief Commercial Products: Jute, textiles, garments, tea, rice, wheat, sugar, hides and newsprint.

Major Trading Partners: U.S., U.K., Japan, United Arab Emirates, Pakistan, Russia and India.

Currency: $ 1 = 52.80 Taka.

Former Colonial Status: Part of British India (1765–1947) then a province of Pakistan under the name *East Pakistan* (1947–1971).

Independence Date: Proclaimed independent in March 1971; achieved in December.

National Day: December 16.

Chief of State: President Badruddoza Chowdhury

Head of Government: Prime Minister Latifur Rahman (July 2001)

National Flag: A green field with a large red circle in the middle.

Gross Domestic Product: range of $36 billion (IMF) to $44 billion (UN).

GDP per capita: about $250 - $350.

Most of the land of Bangladesh is flat, wet alluvial plain, formed over scores of centuries by three great river systems depositing their silt as they near the Bay of Bengal. Indeed these rivers, the Ganges, the Brahmaputra and the Meghna, lose their identities as their waters become mingled in a maze of waterways and swamps along the southern coast. Much of the country is less than 30 feet above sea level.

Four traditional scourges annually threaten life and property in Bangladesh. The rivers flood during the summer monsoons, while cyclones—tropical storms as strong as hurricanes—sweep in from the Bay of Bengal, strengthened by a funnel effect of the shoreline that creates even higher tides of salt water. Disease and famine, often the result of nature's destruction, complete the traditional list.

In 1989, tornados killed possibly one thousand people, adding more grief and suffering.

Of all the countries in Asia, nature threatens humans most in Bangladesh. Bacteria flourish in the tropical climate, and the frequent floods multiply the consequences of inadequate sanitation. Rapid population growth in a country with little industry forces landless farmers onto silt islands barely above high tide. Then floods, or even shifting river channels, destroy land and crops, threatening famine to those who can not afford to buy food. Beyond individual and local tragedies, the statistics of overpopulation paint a grim picture for the future. Although roughly three–quarters of its people live by farming, and less than 20% in urban areas, the country's population density exceeds 1,800 per square mile— far higher than the Netherlands in Europe where commerce, industry, and services employ most of the population.

The 1998 monsoon floods illustrated the harshness of life. As rivers overflowed their banks, the deluge submerged two–thirds of the country, and destroyed the homes of a fifth of the population. It stranded millions of people on roofs, trees and small areas of high ground where they were threatened by disease and poisonous snakes. Unofficial estimates by relief workers placed the death toll at around 800. The economic impact appeared equally severe: thousands of miles of roads destroyed, bridges swept away and half the season's rice seedlings lost. The depth of the water surpassed even the 1988 flood (the previous "worst in memory"), but better precautions reduced the death toll. Ironically, within a few months the northeast faced drought.

While some foreign nations responded with aid as soon as Dhaka airport reopened, the future appears grim. Ecologists blame the floods on the deforestation of the Himalaya Mountains in India and Nepal, where the great rivers of Bangladesh receive much of their flow. The loss of the trees increases flooding for two reasons. First, the soil retains less water, causing faster runoff. Second, the rapid runoff carries deposits of silt downstream, diverting rivers and raising the level of their beds. Former president Ershad declared the floods a "man–made curse," and proposed regional cooperation to end them, as well as better control of the rivers in Bangladesh. However, geologists suspect the river delta is simply sinking into the ocean.

In 1991 nature struck at Bangladesh with a fury unprecedented in the 20th century. A cyclone bearing winds of 145 m.p.h. lashed the southeastern coast. Cyclonic waves washed across islands, where parents tied their children to trees to prevent them from being swept to sea. The death toll exceeded 130,000, with additional deaths from the cholera epidemic that followed, and the loss of the season's rice crop threatened millions more with starvation. Wildlife perished as well, including perhaps one–third of the estimated 600 Royal Bengal Tigers who had stalked the coastal forests known as the Sundarbans.

Where family farms measure a few acres at best, only rice provides subsistence. Two or even three crops per year, tended with much labor and scarcely any machinery, enable the country in a good year almost to feed itself.

Unfortunately, another consequence of the same deforestation of mountain forests is seasonal drought in the west of the country, worsened until 1996 by the Indian diversion of Ganges water at the Farakka Barrage for the benefit of Calcutta. Essentially, by late winter and spring too little water flows through the southwestern region of the country. Shipping becomes dangerous, and irrigation canals dry up when water is vital for young crops. One solution, the construction of a dam to regulate water flow, will require years of study before construction begins, and its estimated cost exceeds $1 billion.

Geography forces the use of boat and barge for most travel and transportation. There are 3,000 miles of navigable rivers, but only about 6,500 miles of surfaced roads. The marshy ground and many rivers render road building difficult and costly. Many streams of the delta are not bridged, and ferry service causes many delays.

A small region southeast of Chittagong is located beyond the deltas and flood plains of the rivers. Its hills, valleys and forests make this region, known as the Chittagong Hill Tracts, the only one in the nation where virtually all the land is not used for agriculture.

History: The territory of Bangladesh lies in a region which for many centuries bore the native name *Bangla;* this name was taken into English as Bengal. British officials designated Bengal as a presidency, or state, in 1699, and it remained under British rule until 1947. Bangladesh is the eastern part of the former state of Bengal in British India (see India: History). With the partitioning of British India in 1947, the territory then became East Pakistan. Although united by the bond of a common religion, the Bengalis of East Pakistan were not happy with the way they were treated by the Pakistani government dominated by men from West Pakistan.

Dissatisfaction grew rapidly in the late 1960s, with resentment strongest over attempts to promote Urdu, the major language of West Pakistan, as well as policies that devoted foreign aid and development projects disproportionately to West Pakistan. In 1970 the Awami League of Sheikh Mujibur Rahman, pledged to autonomy for East Pakistan, won a majority of seats in elections for the National Assembly of Pakistan. Consequently, Sheikh Mujib should have become Prime Minister. However, General Yahya Khan, the president, prevented the National Assembly from meeting, and hence the Awami League from taking power. Uprisings then broke out in the East.

In March 1971 Bangladesh ("The Bengal Nation") proclaimed its independence. A popular rebellion broke out, but for nine months an occupation army loyal to West Pakistan repressed it, reportedly with three million Bengali deaths (a figure disputed by Pakistan). Millions more sought refuge across the border, and in December 1971 India attacked the Pakistani military in Bangladesh. Two weeks later they surrendered.

During early 1972 the government of the new nation took form. As the Indian army withdrew, and massive international aid reached the country, this administration began the great tasks of providing for the refugees and restoring an economy devastated by war. Several months were required for the nearly 10 million Bengalis who had fled to India in 1971 to return to their homeland—often to find that their homes had been destroyed.

The dominant personality in the political life of Bangladesh during its first years was Sheikh Mujibur Rahman. Although held in a prison in West Pakistan when

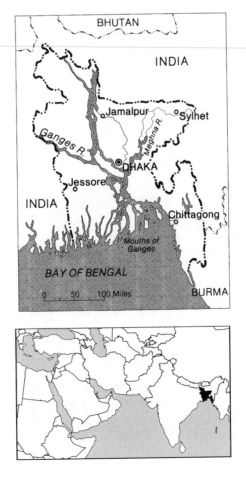

independence was achieved, he was immediately declared President of the new nation. Freed in early January 1972, he received a hero's welcome in Dhaka. His first official acts were to resign as President, arranging the appointment of Abu Sayeed Cowdhury to the position, and to take the office of Prime Minister.

During the first years of independence, the traditional disasters of floods and famines continued, while the increasing population rendered the results calamitous. Furthermore, political power was fully in the hands of Sheikh Mujib and loyal members of his *Awami League*, especially after an election in 1973 which gave the party almost all the 300 seats in the National Assembly.

Those in power frequently abused their positions for personal gain. For instance, much of the international relief sent to alleviate starvation and suffering was used by government officials and army officers to enrich themselves.

Public feeling eventually turned strongly against the authorities and their failure to improve the lot of the poverty-stricken masses. Even Sheikh Mujib's personal popularity melted away amidst the corruption, banditry and violent disorders. Finally, in early 1975, he made himself a virtual dictator, resuming for himself the post of President. Emergency regulations declared late in the preceding year were used to censor the press rigorously and jail critics of the administration without trial.

A military coup overthrew Mujib's government in August 1975. Despite his role in achieving independence for Bangladesh, Mujib was assassinated. The new government ruled only briefly, however, for three months later General Ziaur Rahman seized power. No relation to Mujib, Zia at first placed a retired supreme court justice as President, then assumed the title himself in 1977.

Although initially a military dictatorship, President Zia's government gained

several significant achievements. One was an agreement with India, reached in 1977, for sharing the water of the Ganges River—a problem only in the dry season. In 1978 the government moved toward allowing political activity in the country by organizing its own *Bangladesh National Party (BNP)*. Meanwhile it continued to take care of foes in the army with executions and prison sentences for those convicted of participating in an attempted *coup* in late 1977.

In presidential elections of 1978, Zia received a majority of more than three to one. A movement toward the restoration of democratic government included parliamentary elections in early 1979. Some two–thirds of the 300 seats in the legislative assembly were won by members of the President's *Bangladesh Nationalist Party*. The government began efforts to attain self–sufficiency in food production and also took cautious steps toward slowing population growth.

Zia's assassination during an unsuccessful military coup in 1981 ended an era of relative stability, and severe political difficulties filled an entire decade. Civilian government appeared increasingly ineffective, and in 1982 Lt. General Hussain Mohammad Ershad led a bloodless coup, became Chief Martial Law Administrator and pledged to purge the country of corruption, then return power to civilians. Amid some unrest and violence, in 1983 Ershad proclaimed himself president, and later postponed the promised elections indefinitely.

However, stability eluded his dictatorship. In 1985, Ershad reimposed martial law, banned political activities, arrested more opposition political leaders and closed the universities. Elections that next year, held in an atmosphere of violence and accusations of fraud by the police and government supporters, barely gained Ershad's supporters a majority in Parliament and left politics boiling wildly, with

Sheikh Hasina Wajed

the government ruling by virtue of military control, and the opposition both splintered and extreme in its tactics.

Remarkably for a Muslim country, the two largest parties have been led by women. Sheikh Hasina Wajed, the daughter of Sheikh Mujibur Rahman, inherited his title, a rare occurrence in the Islamic world, and leads the Awami League. The widow of Ziaur Rahman, Khaleda Zia, adopted the Hindu royal title of Begum, and heads the more conservative Bangladesh National Party that her husband founded. Both women cooperated in strikes and protests against President Ershad; their parties successfully boycotted the 1988 elections. In turn, Ershad placed both women under house arrest.

President Ershad sought popular support through other political initiatives. He pledged to establish Islam as the state religion, and the national airline adopted the practice of prayer before takeoff. However, neither reshuffling the government nor greater official use of Islam restored public confidence. Halted by strikes, politics and floods, economic growth eluded Asia's poorest country.

Demonstrations and riots in late 1990 followed the familiar patterns. Universities and schools closed, and Ershad declared a state of emergency. This time, however, opposition groups jointly demanded Ershad's immediate resignation, free elections, and a general strike. Riots followed the reported arrests of opposition leaders, and troops fired on crowds killing dozens. When members of Ershad's own *Jatiya Party* resigned from Parliament and senior army officers refused to take control, Ershad resigned.

The parliamentary election campaign in 1991 seemed an often bitter competition between two dead men. The *Awami League* extolled Mujibur Rahman, while the *Bangladesh National Party* praised Ziaur Rahman. The results brought Khaleda Zia

Fishing for shrimp and rock lobster

Country boats on a Bangladesh river

and the *BNP* an eventual majority in the 300 elected seats of the legislature (30 other seats, indirectly elected, are reserved for women). Despite some violence and criminal charges against ex-president Ershad and a few other candidates, foreign observers pronounced the election fair. A decade after her husband's assassination, Khaleda Zia took office as Prime Minister; the *Awami League*, more socialist and pro-Indian, led the opposition.

By 1994 Khaleda Zia's economic liberalization brought promise of relief for the country's desperate poverty. The annual GDP growth rate reached 5%, industrial output was rising by 10%, and exports grew 20%. In the new, pro-business climate, investment by foreign firms soared. Nearly one million women in over 1,000 clothing factories stitched garments for K-Mart and other U.S. firms, producing about 60% of the country's exports. Appealing for further aid from Japan and Western nations, the government hoped to increase foreign investment, the key to sustained economic growth.

The rare economic prosperity quickly began to recede when opposition by the *Awami League* and *Jatiya Party* became militant and demanded that Begum Khaleda resign and a neutral cabinet supervise new elections. Refusing a compromise offer and Commonwealth mediation, all opposition MPs resigned their seats in late 1994. Mass demonstrations and general strikes became the language of politics.

Roughly 50 million Bangladeshis exist below the poverty line, meaning they often survive on one meal a day. As always, the poorest are usually women and children; these paid a large price as political chaos interrupted work and deterred investment.

Despite the predictable boycott by opposition parties, Begum Khaleda called elections in early 1996 in an attempt to display high public support. Unfortunately her *BNP* won a predictably overwhelming victory through predictably stuffed ballot boxes. Discredited abroad and facing a domestic chaos from the continuous strikes, she resigned in favor of a caretaker cabinet pending elections. In them, the *Awami League* won wide support including a surprising number of retired military officers. Two decades after her father's assassination, Sheikh Hasina formed a government.

During her first year in office, Sheikh Hasina succeeded in negotiating a greater flow of water through the Farakka Barrage during the dry season. India may eventually expect a favor in return: trade with the northeastern states by means of quick and simple truck routes across Bangladesh and from the port of Chittagong. This remains a divisive political issue in Dhaka, because the *BNP* suspects that any concessions to India may be the first step towards eventual Indian rule.

Another contentious issue is justice for the plotters who overthrew and murdered Sheikh Mujib and nearly his entire family. Sheikh Hasina escaped death only because she was abroad; two decades later as prime minister she ordered the arrest of surviving suspects, despite a later promise of immunity from prosecution issued by military rulers. While justice for the actual killers seems popular, complications arise if the list of those guilty should include individuals who later worked with the plotters. Begum Khaleda's husband, Ziaur Rahman apparently did not participate in the plot, but after he took power he sent some of the plotters abroad. Symbolically, Sheikh Hasina's government removed the pontoon bridge to Ziaur Rahman's island grave.

Despite the devastation of serious floods in 1998, the *BNP* intensified a strategy of walkouts and strikes over disputed elections, the same policy that the *Awami League* had used while in opposition. On the popular level, by contributing to a growing atmosphere of violence, the policy probably backfired, and foreign governments warned such tactics could hurt investment. Political meetings, women's groups and secular writers became targets of assassins possibly linked to Islamic extremists.

After criticism from international donors, in 1999 the government attempted to repress violence. The police, themselves suspected of corruption and criminal activities, arrested tens of thousands of bandits, gangsters, and political extremists. Because crime seemed highest in the teeming slums, the government sent bulldozers to demolish the homes of thousands, though creating 50,000 homeless hardly reduced crime or encouraged development. Finally, the government approved a new security law that could be used against both criminals and the opposition.

One major nonpolitical issue facing the government is arsenic poison that

The bicycle–rickshaws of bustling Dhaka.

threatens the water supply of nearly half the population. The arsenic occurs naturally in the soil, and water from deep wells drilled to deliver water with less bacteria frequently carries traces of arsenic. Though not immediately fatal, the arsenic levels often cause scattered tumors and may lead to cancer.

In the months preceding the 2001 general elections, politics turned even uglier than usual. Accusations of corruption flew between Sheikh Hasina and Khaleda Zia. The *BNP* led a parliamentary walkout, and there were frequent general strikes by the opposition. Far more radical were the demands of militant Islamists after the High Court ruled illegal the *"fatwas,"* Islamic judgments sometimes involving public shaming or physical mutilation, rendered by religious scholars. The demonstrations that followed particularly attacked the role of NGOs (Non-Governmental Organizations) in changing the status of women and demanded the expulsion of foreign NGOs.

With broadly similar ideologies, leaders of the *Awami League* and the *BNP* largely campaigned on accusations of corruption and personal insults. The caretaker administration mobilized 50,000 troops to maintain order and jailed 60,000 suspects; nevertheless, violence hovered over the elections, killing 140 and wounding thousands.

After years of economic growth, the voters might have returned Sheikh Hasina and the *League* to power. However, the elections coincided with the buildup of U.S. forces to attack Afghanistan, and posters of Osama bin Laden suggested a backlash against Sheikh Hasina's more secular approach.

The *BNP* won an overwhelming victory at the polls, and with its allies (including the *Jamaat-i Islami*) captured two-thirds of the seats in parliament. The overwhelming majority provides Khaleda Zia the ability to move quickly against the two greatest issues in public opinion: corruption and crime. Ranked the most corrupt nation on earth by Transparency International, Bangladesh proved particularly unable to punish high-level bribe-takers, partly because the anti-corruption bureau operates out of the prime minister's office and has never charged prominent members of the ruling party.

After the elections, popular discontent with crime became so great that in just a few days, mobs lynched nearly a dozen suspected criminals in broad daylight in the capital's streets. Unfortunately, public impatience is unlikely to be rewarded with immediate improvements because the police are considered the most corrupt institution in the country. Crimes with particularly low rates of punishment include throwing acid at women's faces and attacks on the Hindu minority.

As the new prime minister, Khaleda Zia also faced grave economic challenges. The world recession of 2001 struck the clothing industry with particular severity. When U.S. firms cut back sharply on orders for garments, some local factories closed, and others reduced production. Some 100,000 women lost their jobs in a country where the unemployment rate may exceed 30% and half the population lives below the poverty line.

Politics: Four major political groups represent most political aspirations within the country. The *Bangladesh National Party* favors economic liberalization and a conservative Muslim orientation, in contrast to the traditionally socialist and pro–Indian leanings of the *Awami League*. Although it

must be discredited by revelations of corruption during Ershad's years, his *Jatiya Party* retains seats in parliament, more a collection of aspiring politicians than an ideological force, though after his release from prison, Ershad in 1997 hoped to enlarge it at the expense of the *BNP*.

Fundamentalist Muslims form the *Jamaat–e–Islami*, which elected Golam Azam as its leader in 1991. However, in 1971 he had opposed Bangladesh's independence, and for years lived in Dhaka as a Pakistani. His selection as a party leader has led to strikes demanding his trial for treason. Mock trials indicated he should hang.

One particularly unfortunate side effect of the political strife takes place on the university campuses. Well over 100 students have died in political clashes, and dormitories and other facilities burned as the students became players—increasingly pawns—in the struggle to topple one regime or another. The strife worsened in the late 1980s, when Dhaka University canceled classes for 120 of 150 working days. In the late 1990s pitched battles became rare, but women students, frequently harassed and even raped, demonstrated for better security.

Even non-partisan students clashed with police in 1992, after the government approved a law to punish those caught cheating on final exams with five to ten years in prison.

Since independence the structure of government has alternated between presidential and parliamentary styles. Most recently, in 1991 the newly–elected parliament restored its Prime Minister to supremacy and rendered the president a figurehead.

Culture: For the three–quarters of the population directly involved in farming, plus the small–town merchants, craftsmen and officials, life revolves around the agricultural seasons. The typical farmer lives with his large family in a simple hut of thatch and mud. The hut is on a low mound of earth so that the monsoon floods do not reach it. Since the land is extremely fertile, a very small plot can be one man's farm. He sells the produce from his little farm at one of the small towns located on the intersections of waterways. He can afford no modern luxuries; his main entertainment is sitting with his family and friends, talking about the day's events and problems.

Reflecting the poverty of the country, only 40% of the population is literate, with the rate for women half that for men. Fortunately, widespread primary education is increasing the rate for each: roughly 75% of all children receive some formal education.

Besides vocational and professional institutes, there are several universities, the largest of them the University of

Dhaka. Unfortunately, widespread cheating diminishes the respectability of their degrees. Four thousand students were expelled in 2000 for cheating on the English exam required for university graduation.

Despite Bangladesh's staggering population, it has only a handful of large cities. The jute industry is concentrated around the capital, Dhaka, where the urban population has passed the nine million mark. The second largest city is Chittagong, the nation's main port, with more than a million.

The country's 100 million Muslims form the world's fourth largest Muslim community, following those of Indonesia, Pakistan and India. Nevertheless, the Provisional Constitution made the nation a secular state that provided all religions with equal legal standing. Public holidays included not only Muslim holy days, but also Christmas and various Hindu and Buddhist festivals. Islam itself shows a national coloring here, influenced by some Hindu and other ideas.

The rise of fundamentalist Islamic groups coincided in the 1990s with increasing intolerance, and often those who suffered were women. For example, Dhaka University reimposed the "Sunset Law," a 1922 regulation requiring women students to return to their dormitories before darkness. The restriction, said one faculty member, was "a shield to protect the women's chastity."

Other women suffered much worse effects. Village arbitration councils composed of village elders and clerics, designed to settle property disputes, illegally ordered whippings or even stoning for several girls and women charged with sexual immorality. Other women and young girls are victimized into debauchery: police reports suggest that kidnappers annually sell some 10,000 into brothels, some abroad.

In contrast, death by hanging is the sentence commonly demanded by Islamic militants for both Taslima Nasreen and Farida Rahman. The latter, a Member of Parliament, aroused the ire of fundamentalist Muslims when she noted that there would be no harm in allowing women to inherit more than the small Quranic portion. Nasreen, a feminist whose novel of the plight of Hindus in Bangladesh became a bestseller, denied that she had proposed that the Quran be revised to fit the modern world. Arrested for blasphemy but, granted bail, she escaped to Sweden. Returning in 1998 at the time of her mother's death, she overcame her legal problems, but again fled the country, this time because of threats on her life.

The majority of the people speak Bangla as their native language, which is written in a form of the *Nagari* alphabet, widely used for the languages of India. Actually there are two principal dialects of the Bangla language. The older is the literary one. Though much admired, it is not understood by ordinary Bengalis. The other is the modern colloquial, understood and used by both the educated and uneducated.

Since the 14th century there has been an abundance of literature written in Bangla. Until less than two centuries ago it was all in verse, intended to be recited or sung. Bangla prose began in 1800 when a missionary, with the help of native assistants, translated the Bible into that language. During the 19th and 20th centuries a vast literature has been created, including novels and drama. The short stories and poems of Rabindranath Tagore, which received the Nobel prize for literature in 1913, was one of the first awards outside European languages. Besides more modern approaches such as this, there remain the traditional poetry and other aspects of the rich culture of Bengal.

However fertile, the culture of Bengal is not the culture of all inhabitants. During the partition of India in 1947, thousands of Muslims from Bihar and elsewhere moved to East Bengal. Loyal to a Muslim state rather than Bangladesh, they tended to support Pakistan during the conflict in 1971. With Pakistan unable, or perhaps unwilling, to bear the cost of these two–time refugees, about 250,000 of them live destitute in camps in Bangladesh, awaiting some distant solution.

Other non–Bengalis live in the Chittagong Hills, where local tribes practice Buddhism, Christianity or Hinduism. Violence flared in the 1970s after Bengalis moved into the area seeking land. By the mid 1990s, scattered violence for 20 years had caused over 8,000 deaths and thousands more to flee to India and Burma. Following a peace treaty in 1997, some 35,000 refugees returned from India, but slow implementation of the accord leaves some observers fearing renewed violence.

Economy: Even today, most Bangladeshis live on farms. Across most of the country, the climate and soil combine to produce good yields of rice, and in years without catastrophes more than 10 million tons are harvested. However, this is not enough to feed the large population, and output falls after devastating floods or cyclones. The government has made valiant efforts to increase food production—for instance by digging irrigation canals to water an extra crop in the dry season. Much food still must be imported, and paid for partly by foreign aid.

The country's main cash crop and traditional export is jute, the tough plant fiber used to make burlap and rope. About half the jute is exported in its raw state, the remainder in jute manufactures. When industrial nations turned increasingly to synthetic fibers, world demand for jute declined, and the economy of Bangladesh suffered falling profits and cuts in wages and employment. For decades the leading source of jobs and exports, the jute industry now employs only a few hundred thousand workers. Their conditions are pitiful: strikers in 1995 demanded raising the minimum wage of less than $40 per month. However, the privatized mills paid sub-minimum wages and cut their workforces further.

The poverty results partly from misguided economic policies, past and present. Seeking to raise the standard of living by encouraging industry, early in 1972 the new country took over the businesses, banks and industries owned by West Pakistanis. It then nationalized most other foreign trade, banks and basic industry, leaving only British tea and jute interests privately owned. During two decades of mismanagement, few government-owned businesses ever earned a profit. Sectors like telecommunications, electricity and banking still remain inefficient under government ownership.

Privatization and large-scale investment by Japanese and Korean firms seemed the best hope for economic expansion in the early 1990s, but instead, employment grew in an unexpected way. Hundreds of small clothing factories sprang up to employ growing numbers of workers to produce coats, dresses and other garments

Water, water, everywhere . . . river traffic

for export. More than one million women in cities and in towns found jobs in the industry, despite low safety standards and appalling wages of roughly $1 a day, about half that of men. Thanks to the previously insignificant level of exports, Bangladeshi garments are not subject to international quotas, and output often rose at 10%-20% per year. Besides earning important foreign exchange, the industry may improve social conditions by providing vital earnings for women.

One delightful benefit for the nation was the discovery of large reserves of natural gas off the coast. Reportedly one field alone may supply 25% of the nation's demand, and even before the first commercial production began in 1998, the size of possible reserves led to hopes that the nation could become an energy exporter. However, nationalist refusals to export gas to India, the logical market, once again blocked a possible source of

prosperity, and most foreign companies withdrew from the industry.

Other industries, such as an iron plant at Chittagong and a few small chemical factories and oil refineries, have no major economic significance. Minor export products include animal hides and good quality tea which is grown in the hilly areas around Sylhet and Chittagong.

By any standard, Bangladesh remains one of the poorest nations in the world. Per capita income hovers around $ 300 a year, and public health statistics illustrate the poverty. A majority of children are malnourished and stunted. Sixty percent of the population lacks access to even simple health clinics. Nevertheless, there are some success stories. In the mid-1980s, children composed 40% of the workforce, a rate that fell below 10% by the end of the decade. More importantly, most former child laborers attended school.

The Future: Expect the same sort of petty politics out of the *Awami League* in opposition that marked the now-ruling *BJP*, including strikes, accusations of electoral fraud, and parliamentary boycotts. This is normal for Bangladesh; unfortunately it imposes a significant economic toll on Asia's poorest country.

For her part, Mrs. Zia will likely follow the pattern she established previously, including charging the opposition with corruption. Despite the shortage of foreign exchange, she will not likely change the laws and authorize the export of natural gas to India, despite the local surplus.

Nevertheless, Sheikh Hasina managed to govern the country for a full term (no one else had in the previous two decades of independence), with significant economic expansion. If Khaleda Zia can do as well, Bangladeshis should be delighted.

"Two women in Maijpara"

Source: World Bank Photo by Chernush

Taktsang ("The Tiger's Nest") Monastery, situated high in a cliff near Paro in western Bhutan, was destroyed by fire in April 1998. The King has called the incident a national disaster and promised to rebuild it. According to legend, Padma Sambhava—or Guru Rinpoche, as he is also known—flew here on a tiger to meditate when he was introducing Buddhism into Tibet and Bhutan from India in the 8th century A.D. The monastery was built on the site at a later date.

Photo by Edwin Bernbaum

The Kingdom of Bhutan

Area: 18,000 square miles (46,600 sq. km.). 55-1

Population: 760,000 (low official estimate; other suggest more than 1 million).

Capital City: Thimphu (Pop. nearly 40,000, estimated).

Climate: Frigid in the high, snow–covered northern mountains, temperate with good rainfall in the central valley and etremely hot and humid with torrential rains on the southern fringe of the country.

Neighboring Countries: India (South and East); China (North).

Time Zone: GMT +6.

Official Language: Dzongkha, a dialect of Tibetan. English is frequently used by government officials and it appears on street signs.

Other Principal Tongues: Two Tibetan dialects, Bumthapkha and Sarchopkha; Nepalese in the South.

Ethnic Background: Tibetan–speaking Bhutanese (60%), Nepalese in the southwest (25%), Sharchops of Indo–Mongolian origin in the East, and smaller tribal groups and settlers.

Principal Religions: Mahayana Buddhism (about 75%) and Hinduism.

Chief Commercial Products: Hydroelectric power, lumber and wood products, cement, fruit, rice potatoes, coal, woven textiles and other handicrafts. The main livestock breeds are cattle, pigs, poultry, sheep, goats and yaks.

Major Trading Partner: India.

Currency: $1 = 45.80 Ngultrum

International Status: Independent. Foreign relations previously subject to guidance from India under a 1949 treaty.

Date of U.N. Membership: September 21, 1971.

Chief of State: Jigme Singye Wangchuck, King, known as Druk Gyalpo ("Dragon King").

National Flag: A rectangular field of yellow and vermillion, divided diagonally, has a large white serpent–like dragon in the center.

Gross Domestic Product: $400 million.

GDP per capita: possibly as low as $160 or over $500.

Bhutan is a small nation squeezed between two giants. Culturally it is more akin to Chinese–ruled Tibet on its northern border, while its trade and political alignment lie more with India on its southern border.

Geographically, Bhutan resembles Nepal—both are on the southern slopes of the Himalayan Mountains. Bhutan has some half dozen rivers which rise in the Great Himalayas in the North and flow southward through intensively–cultivated valleys—some of the mountainsides have been terraced to provide more fields than are available in the valley bottoms.

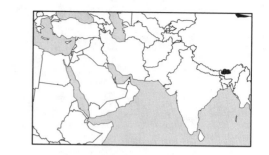

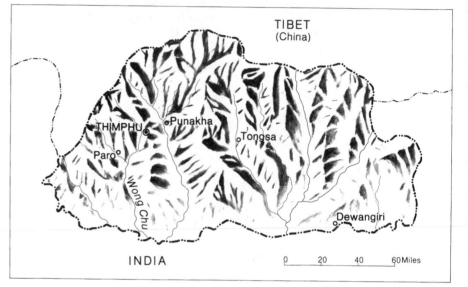

The rivers all flow into India, emptying into the Brahmaputra River.

This is a land of rugged natural beauty. There is striking contrast between the snow clad northern peaks, the lower mountain slopes covered with woods, and the dense, lush undergrowth of the southern foothills, which is the habitat of numerous deer, as well as tigers, elephants and other wildlife.

History: Few documentary sources provide details of the early history of this land, but apparently Hindu princes formed a ruling class in the ninth century when Tibetan– speaking peoples entered it. Followers of Mahayana Buddhism, in the rugged mountain valleys, by the 15th century they structured their society around a fortified monastery known as a *dzong*. Religion and the common ethnic origin provided strong links with Tibet, though Bhutan itself was not united.

During the 17th century a Tibetan lama established himself as the *Dharma Raja*, the political and spiritual leader. His successors to the title appointed a *penlop*, or governor, in each of about four districts. There was also a *Deb Raja*, usually the most powerful *penlop*, who carried the greatest political influence. However, there was no formal government or central ruler. Raiding policies by several *penlops* led to conflict with another expanding power, the British

East India Company, in 1772 when the company began expanding into Bengal and Assam. The Company took control of some territory claimed by Bhutan in 1841 and added it to Assam. Fighting between the two sides finally led to a treaty in 1865 which cost Bhutan further territory, but gained recognition of its autonomy and a British subsidy.

After a series of civil wars, Ugyen Wangchuck, *Penlop* of Tongsa, defeated the supporters of the last *Deb Raja* in 1885 and became the dominant power. He gained British favor in 1904 by joining a campaign into Tibet. Three years later, an assembly of lamas, chiefs and officials elected him the country's first hereditary king. Authority since then has passed from father to son, first to Jigme Wangchuck (1926), then to Jigme Dorji Wangchuck (1952) and finally to Jigme Singye Wangchuck (1972).

Britain recognized Bhutan's sovereignty by the 1910 Treaty of Punakha, although Britain's handling of the isolated state's foreign affairs compromised full independence. The King of Bhutan signed this treaty partly to ward off Chinese designs on his territory based on alleged Chinese control in the 18th century after the conquest of Tibet. The treaty of 1910 remained in effect until Britain withdrew from India in 1947.

India then negotiated a treaty with Bhutan, signed in 1949, which guaranteed

Bhutan's autonomy and provided free trade between the two countries. Bhutan accepted India's advice in foreign affairs, while India increased the annual subsidy to Bhutan and returned 32 square miles of territory around Dewangiri as a gesture of friendship. In 1959, after China claimed parts of the country, defense relations were strengthened with India. As much as any other event, Bhutan's joining the United Nations (1971) marked thenation's full independence.

Until the middle of the 20th century, Bhutan imposed a rigid isolation upon itself so that it remained a nation more closed to the modern world than even Tibet. However, when Jigme Dorji Wangchuck followed his father as *Druk Gyalpo* in 1952, he introduced changes. He freed slaves, ended the custom of making his subjects bow down before him with their faces on the floor or ground, set up schools, restricted land ownership, modernized the system of land taxes and established the *Tsongdu*, or National Assembly.

Political dissatisfactions surfaced in 1964 when the Prime Minister was assassinated and four army officers were convicted in the conspiracy. Soon after, the king began acting as his own prime minister. In 1965 an attempt was made on the king's life, but he escaped uninjured; his assailant was never captured.

A change in the constitution in 1968 denied the king the power to veto acts of the *Tsongdu*. Another amendment in 1969 provided for the king's resignation if demanded by two–thirds of the *Tsongdu* and his replacement by another member of the royal family. In the first vote of confidence, the king received 133 out of a possible 137 votes in his favor. When Jigme Wangchuck died in 1972 from a heart attack, his 17–year–old son, Jigme Singye Wangchuck, ascended the "Dragon Throne." Under the new ruler the country has continued its very slow awakening to the modern world and participation in international affairs.

In late 1988, responding to public worries about the succession, King Jigme Singye Wangchuck married publicly the four sisters he previously had wed privately in 1979. He also named his oldest son Crown Prince and heir. The celebration distinctly echoed the king's desire to preserve Bhutan's society from outside influences: foreign diplomats were not invited, and few tourists would have been present: only a few thousand enter the country each year.

Two changes during the king's 25th anniversary celebrations in 1999 brought images of the modern world to some of the population. First Bhutan inaugurated its internet service, then lifted the ban on the corrupting influence of local television (satellite dishes remain illegal). The single channel will broadcast only a few hours daily, and the government intends to present the arts and culture of the country, rather than rebroadcast Hollywood or

The Dragon King of Bhutan

Indian programs. Though noble purposes underlie such decisions, many prospective viewers may prefer to rent videos.

Ethnic hostility appears to be a growing challenge to the country's traditionally non–political calm. The Nepalese minority in the southern lowlands, boosted by illegal Indian and Nepali migrants across unguarded frontiers, threatens to become a majority. In response, the monarchy vastly reduced the official estimate of population (to 600,000), and as part of educational reforms dropped the required teaching of Nepali in schools.

In 1990 riots and demonstrations broke out in southern Bhutan, apparently organized by the (illegal) *Bhutan People's Party* and other Nepali groups. Police and troops repressed the disturbances; and some 100,000 people took refuge in Nepal. The king took steps to reduce tensions, including reopening schools and reappointing some officials of Nepali origin. Nevertheless, except for Tibet in the north, Bhutan's neighbors are heavily populated, so continuing trouble with immigrants seems highly possible despite an agreement reached with Nepal to determine which refugees had Bhutanese citizenship and therefore the right to return.

Politics: The king is both the symbol of the state and, as chairman of the Council of Ministers, its chief executive officer. Though he rules as well as reigns, the king's powers are limited. A Royal Advisory Council consists of two representatives of the clergy in addition to a majority of members selected by the National Assembly. A 1968 constitutional amendment removed the king's power to veto acts of the National Assembly. In 1998 royal appointments to the cabinet became subject to approval by the assembly.

Known as the *Tsongdu*, the National Assembly, founded in 1953, enacts the country's laws. Its 150 members represent three different groups. Over two–thirds (105) are elected by the populace. A council of Buddhist monks selects ten monastic members, while government ministers, members of the Royal Advisory Council and certain other officials hold the remaining 35 seats. Combined with the judiciary, these institutions provide a carefully balanced system of government in which the king still exercises enormous power.

Culture: The population is comprised mostly of hardy tillers of the soil and herders—who actually go barefoot, even in the snow. They live mainly in small communities scattered in the fertile valleys cut deeply into the rugged mountains of the central and southern part of the country. No one lives permanently in the high mountains of the northern regions, while the people who live in the narrow tropical fringe along the southern border have a way of life not typical to the rest of Bhutan.

No real urban centers exist yet in Bhutan. Communities tend to cluster around a *dzong,* found in every major valley and settled region. A *dzong* was formerly a great fort built on a strategic spot commanding a river; in times of war, the people from the surrounding area sought refuge in this building. Since the warlords have passed from the scene and internal peace prevails, *dzongs* have become administrative centers and monasteries. Many of them have prayer halls with elaborately carved interiors, walls covered with religious paintings, statues of Buddha and quarters for officials, lamas and guilds. More practically, grain is sometimes storied in the *dzongs*.

The new national capital of Thimphu has been constructed beside the great *Tashi Chho Dzong*, once the headquarters of powerful *penlops*. It reflects the country's determination to modernize in its own fashion. The only traffic light has been removed. All buildings must be constructed in the traditional style, and men should wear the approved national dress in public. However, the government provides radio broadcasts, and the newspaper, originally a public relations sheet, appears in Dzongkha, English, and Nepali.

Economy: Modern methods are only now being introduced into Bhutan's economy, which remains essentially one of subsistence farming. The country is not only self–supporting in food, but it is able to export a small amount of citrus and other fruit to India. The mountain slopes provide abundant pasturage for livestock. Cattle are common up to more than 12,000 feet above sea level in summer, and yaks are grazed at even higher elevations.

With the first five–year plan, begun in 1961, the government started to encourage economic development in this land where there are numerous untapped natural resources, including minerals and water power. Economic goals remained similar in the 1970s and 1980s, with the third and fourth plans stressing investment in roads, education, agriculture, health and hydroelectric power. By the late 1990s exports of electricity to India provided increased government revenues and foreign exchange. By the late 1990s government policy shifted to privatizing ownership in several corporations it owned, including the cement and insurance companies. Apparently the goal of privatization was to encourage a modern middle class, rather than selling commercial failures. Unlike government–run corporations in most countries, these were profitable companies with monopoly status.

One of Bhutan's important sources of foreign exchange is unusual—the sale of its colorful postage stamps to foreign collectors. To encourage sales, what were described as the world's first scented stamps went on sale early in 1973, giving off the fragrance of roses!

After building two hotels to provide lodging for foreign dignitaries attending the King's coronation in 1974, Bhutan cautiously permitted a small tourist industry to develop. Added to concern about tourism's sometimes corrosive effects on culture, traditions, and values, environmentalists worried about the side effects such as pollution and erosion. The number of tourists reached a record 5,150 in 1996, sponsored by tour operators. In deference to the sensitivities of local people, temples and other holy places were closed to tourists in 1988, but the *Dzongs* are still accessible. In addition to cultural tours through *Dzongs*, town and villages, there are also organized treks along steep mountain trails to isolated mountain valleys.

Tourists provide a major source of foreign earnings for the country. Like other travelers, they can enter it by one of only two ways: a difficult land route, or by regularly scheduled air service to Paro by Druk Air.

To preserve its natural resources, Bhutan has banned hunting of wildlife, prohibited lumbering and provided a special route for the migration of elephants. However, reports of erosion on barren hillsides and polluted water in some sections of the country suggest that population pressure may degrade Bhutan just as it does India and Nepal. Seasonal flooding in 2000 caused massive landslides and flooding in the south, an indication that the hillsides, denuded of trees, could not withstand monsoon rains.

The Future: If it follows the pattern of other once–isolated countries, Bhutan will likely experience a quickened pace of change in coming years, especially as ethnic disputes deepen, and incomes rise from exports of electricity.

Farm buildings in Bhutan

Photo by Richard Harrington

214

The Taj Mahal at Agra

The Republic of India

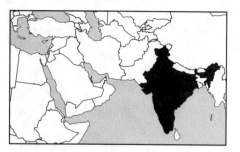

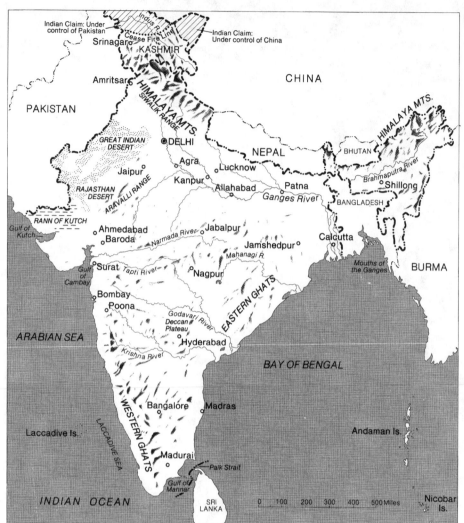

Area: 1,210,700 square miles (3,136,500 sq. km.), including Indian sector of Jammu and Kashmir.

Population: 1,003 billion, initial 2001 census report.

Capital City: New Delhi (Pop. 9.5 million, estimated).

Climate: Mainly tropical except for the mountains on the northern border. The three seasons are the rainy season (June to October), the cool season (November to February) and the hot season (March to May).

Neighboring Countries: Pakistan (Northwest); China, Nepal, Bhutan (North); Burma, Bangladesh (East); Sri Lanka (off southern coast).

Time Zone: GMT + 5 1/2. When it is noon, EST in New York, it is 10:30 P.M. in India.

Official Languages: Hindi and English. Thirteen other languages have regional official status: Assamese, Bengali, Gujarati, Kannada, Kashmiri, Malayalam, Marathi, Oriya, Punjabi, Sanskrit, Tamil, Telugu and Urdu.

Other Principal Tongues: Bhili, Bipari, Dogri, Gondi, Halbi, Kherwari, Kolarian, Konkani, Kurch, Manipuri, Pahari, Rajasthani and Tulu. It is reported that newspapers within India are published in 49 languages.

Ethnic Background: Communities are differentiated primarily on the basis of language and religion; differences in physical characteristics do not generally correspond with these communal distinctions.

Principal Religions: Hindu (84%), Islam (11%), Christian (2%), Sikh (0.7%) Buddhist (0.7%), other.

Chief Commercial Products: Textiles, steel, cement, rubber, coal, motorcycles, automobiles, machinery, processed food, consumer appliances, chemicals and various metals. Recent years witnessed rapid growth in computer software.

Main Agricultural Produce and Livestock: Rice, wheat, barley, potatoes, corn (maize), cassava, bananas, coconuts, beans, mangoes, tea, coffee, tobacco, pepper, sugar cane, cattle, goats, buffalo, sheep, pigs and poultry.

Major Trading Partners: U.S., U.K., Japan, Russia, Germany, Iraq, Iran, Belgium and the Netherlands.

Currency: Rupee (® 42.70 = $1.00 U.S.)

Former Colonial Status: Part of British Indian Empire (1858–1947).

National Day: January 25, Republic Day.

Chief of State: Kocheril Raman Narayanan, President (The first president from a Dalit family, chosen 1997)

Head of Government: Atal Bihari Vajpayee, Prime Minister.

National Flag: A tricolor with equal horizontal bands of deep saffron, white and dark green; centered on the white stripe is the wheel of Asoka in navy blue.

Gross Domestic Product: $427 billion

GDP per capita: $430; higher under purchasing power conversions.

Second only to China in population, India occupies most of the South Asian subcontinent and ranks seventh among the world's nations in area. The size of its population, combined with its historical and cultural heritage developed over thousands of years, often overwhelm the imagination and make comparisons difficult. For example, India's population exceeds that of all Africa south of the Sahara, or more than the population of all the other countries in this volume combined. Indeed, the annual growth in the number of India's citizens exceeds the population of most countries in this volume. A land of stunning contrasts in geography as well as the quality of human life, India represents a major cultural force in the modern world. In areas as diverse as religion, food, and computer software engineering, India's influence greatly exceeds its boundaries.

Three major topographical regions divide the subcontinent. On the northern borderlands tower the Himalayas, the perpetual snow and ice of their summits overlooking lesser peaks and foothills at their base. Rivers and streams from the mountains flow south to the great plain that provides a home for much of the country's population. Centered on the Ganges River, the plain is also watered by the Indus on the west and the Brahmaputra on the east. The third region is the peninsula that juts out into the ocean, a triangle of plateaus, valleys and mountains. The coastal plains around this region are moist and tropical,

Making friends in an Indian Village

particularly in the narrow plain between the Arabian Sea and the Western Ghat Mountains, and densely populated.

Extreme variations in rainfall and temperatures produced great variations in vegetation. On average only a few inches fall annually in the western desert of Rajasthan, but the record in one village of Assam approached *40 feet* of rainfall in a year. The northeast is typically the wettest region; it and the ocean side of the Western Ghats generally receive more than 100 inches of precipitation annually. Most of the rain falls during the summer, brought by the southwest monsoon. The Ganges Plain, the northwest and the coast of Tamil Nadu also receive varying amounts of winter rainfall.

The land and the climate show great contrasts—and so do the people. Religious practices vary greatly within the Hindu majority and there are also followers of a multitude of other religions. Folkways differ considerably in various parts of the country, or even between communities in the same city. Sometime allegiances to language, religion, and ethnic group threaten the unity of India. However, a functioning democracy, the national unity forged in the independence struggle against the British and the economic integration of forty years reinforce the basic sense of allegiance to India.

History: While India possesses a cultural tradition that extends back for several thousand years, the political formation of the present nation began only with the British imperial rule (see Historical Background). By bringing many small states and petty princes under its rule, Britain laid the foundation for both the Republic of India and other nations in the region.

The first British expansion into South Asia in the early 17th century was not effected directly by the government, but rather by the East India Company. Gradually, as British control of the Indian Peninsula spread, governmental regulation of the Company increased. Even so, by the early part of the 19th century, administration still remained largely in the hands of the Company. It continued to scheme to procure influence or even gain control over the remaining areas still nominally independent.

During the first half of the 19th century, India desperately needed reform. It was overtaxed and under–educated, with crime rampant and the arts at a low ebb. Beyond that, British society recoiled at a number of Indian practices, from the (several hundred annual) burnings of widows and other ritual murders, to Indian values expressed by idol worship. Though British opinion divided on which changes deserved priority, in the 1850s a number of westernizing reforms, plus the seizure on various pretexts of Indian states, aroused both Muslim and Hindu opinion, especially in North India. Surprising the British by both its extent and its ferocity, the Indian Mutiny of 1857 (see Historical Background) drew strength from traditional groups outside the army as well as native troops from many backgrounds. Within fourteen months, the British crushed the mutiny; simultaneously Parliament ended the East India Company's rule, replacing it with British colonial government.

The Mutiny produced major changes in the way India was governed. Loyal ethnic groups thereafter played a much greater role in the army, and the close contact between British officers and Indian troops allowed traditions to flourish that remain today. In politics, the policy of seizing territories from princes was abandoned in favor of close contacts with them, for they had generally remained loyal. In general, the attempt to Westernize India weakened, so that land reform was set aside, and the upper classes conciliated.

After the Mutiny, Britain generally abandoned the idea of making Indians Europeans, and turned instead to raising the standards of India. Government initiative turned especially to public works. These changes marked a determination to succeed in governing India, rather than a decline in imperialist fervor in Britain. Indeed, in the spirit of imperial grandeur then in vogue among European nations, in 1877 the government in London proclaimed Queen Victoria Empress of India.

Two trends in India during the height of imperial rule after 1860 deserve mention. First, colonial laws and officials provided an administrative unity for a vast region previously divided by ethnic and religious groups. Second, in time a national consciousness, distinct from religious or social feelings, arose against foreign domination. Factors which contributed to unification were the imposition of a single administrative and judicial system, the building of roads, railways and the establishment of postal and telegraphic communications. Western education, by providing a new professional class with a common language, English, was also of great significance as a unifying factor.

The first outward sign of growing national awareness was the formation in 1885 of the *Indian National Congress*, which aired the grievances of the new professional class. In its early years, the party had little success. It failed to persuade the British rulers to recognize its demands, and proved unable to incite the illiterate masses, especially those in relatively isolated villages, to any kind of action.

Nationalism continued to develop among the tiny minority of Indians educated in English and in touch with European ideas, but it had no visible effect otherwise until the time of World War I. Then a man with rare gifts of leadership appeared on the scene. Mohandas Karamchand Gandhi, later called *Mahatma* ("Great Soul"), was born in the city of Porbandar in western India, trained as an attorney, and became a political activist in South Africa. Unrest and occasional outbursts of violence were already beginning when his public work in India began. His insight and ability to translate nationalist ideas into terms that had meaning for the uneducated masses of Hindus, enabled him to capture the leadership of the *Indian National Congress* by 1920.

Gandhi's method appealed to the religious nature of the Hindus. The weapon he used in the struggle for self–rule for India was passive resistance, which was essentially a program of non–cooperation with the British regime. The first attempt to employ this method failed because it did not remain non–violent, but erupted into riots and bloodshed. He renewed his efforts to impose the necessary discipline, and it became a weapon that the British could not effectively oppose. Concessions from the government were slow, but gradually native Indians were allowed into the Indian civil service and gained limited local self–government. This all served as preparation for national independence.

The *Congress* was—not by Gandhi's intention—mainly a Hindu party. He was not able to bridge the gap between Hindus and Muslims in India, and tensions between the two communities increased. The leading Islamic party was the *All–Muslim League* led by Muhammad Ali Jinnah. Strongly dedicated to the interests of the Muslim community, Jinnah and his party led the move to partition India, although recent scholarship shows the crucial role played in this decision by rebuffs from Jawaharlal Nehru, president of the *Congress Party*, in 1946.

India gained political independence in the summer of 1947. In the first part of that year, British officials arranged a partition plan to give Muslims a separate nation (see Pakistan). The British Parliament passed the Indian Independence Act in July 1947, and on August 14 and 15 two new states declared independence on the territory of British India. The borders remained a British secret, lest the inevitable violence following their announcement spoil the festivities. India initially became a dominion status within the Commonwealth. Lord Mountbatten, related to Britain's royal family, held little power but some influence as Governor General; Jawaharlal Nehru, Gandhi's chief lieutenant in the *Congress Party*, ruled the country as Prime Minister.

Communal strife between Hindus and Muslims characterized the subcontinent's partition into independent states. Boundary problems proved critical, and in the end the British chairman of the boundary commission had to rule on the borders. In many frontier areas the population was mixed, and made it impossible to draw an international boundary that separated Muslims from Hindus and others.

In the Punjab, as soon as the border had been fixed, savage fighting between members of the two religious communities erupted. Fearful of strife and becoming a minority, Hindus on the Pakistani side of the border fled toward India while Muslims on the Indian side fled toward Pakistan. Nearly four million people took part in this two–way flight; many thousands of them were massacred on both sides.

Gandhi was assassinated in Delhi on January 30, 1948, by Hindu extremists who were hostile to his moderation; he had been touring the country preaching peace and cooperation between the two religious groups. This activity before his death is credited with having averted massacres in the eastern sections of the new nation like those in the Punjab.

Less than a year after India gained independence, Lord Mountbatten was replaced as Governor General by Chakravarti Rajagopalacharia, an associate of Gandhi. The tie to Britain through a Governor General ended on January 26, 1950, when a new constitution came into effect, giving India the form of a fully independent republic with its own president. Dr. Rajendra Prasad was elected to the largely ceremonial post—by an electoral college composed of members of the central and state legislatures—and served until 1962.

Government and Politics

Influenced heavily by the British parliamentary system, the Indian legislature is composed of two houses. Political authority lies in the 545–member elected lower house, known as the *Lok Sabha* or "House of the People." In contrast, the relatively powerless members of the upper house (*Rajya Sabha* or "Council of States") reflect the state governments that select them. Though appointed by the President, the Prime Minister governs with the support of Parliament. In recent years, the ability to maintain a majority in the *Lok Sabha* regularly proved difficult, particularly because the rise of regional parties prevented any party from winning a majority.

A major challenge created by independence was the formation of a modern administration. The constitution of 1950 established a federal system of government, dividing the country into states. However, the British had ruled many parts of India indirectly, maintaining the existing rulers' authority as dependents of the British Crown. When granting Indian independence, Britain restored the rights that princes and other rulers had lost generations earlier. Thus the new nation inherited some 562 "princely states" ranging in size from Hyderabad (82,000 square miles, 16 million subjects) to tiny states of a few square miles. To retain the rights of all these rulers meant chaos, and the central government initially took control of defense, foreign affairs and communications. By 1949, through persuasion, threats, and promises of pensions (withdrawn some twenty years later), India had been reorganized into 30 states and territories.

Two cases proved especially difficult. The Muslim ruler of Hyderabad, which had a large Hindu majority, maneuvered toward independence, but unrest and alleged abuse of Hindus provided an opportunity for the central government to send troops to police the state, beginning in September 1948. With his authority thus undermined, the ruler finally ceded Hyderabad to the central government in late 1949. It was then divided between the states of Bombay, Andhra and Mysore. The other case was a dispute with tribesmen and Pakistan over the princely state of Jammu and Kashmir. This remains unresolved after a half century (see Disputed Territories: Kashmir).

Boundaries in British India, often drawn by historical circumstances, frequently separated people speaking the same language. Many members of the *Congress Party* favored the popular idea that, where possible, states should reflect ethnic divisions. Gradually Prime Minister Nehru gave way despite occasional ethnic violence, and changes, especially in 1956, altered the political map of India. While many states disappeared, several new states were created out of the old. For example, Andhra Pradesh, largely Telugu-speaking, emerged from what had been Hyderabad and Madras. Though generally successful, the creation of ethnic states faced difficulties in two parts of the country: first, the northeast and later a continuing dispute in the northwest.

The far northeast of India, near the borders of Tibet and Burma, contains many tribes living in remote areas. Speaking a variety of languages and less influenced by Hindu culture than the rest of India, small ethnic groups there desired their own states in what had been the North East Frontier Agency of Assam. The first, Nagaland, was created in 1961, reducing pressures locally for independence. In the 1970s and 1980s, more states followed, all among India's smallest in population. Political instability has been frequent, whether the consequence of independence movements or an influx of others wishing to settle there.

Arunachal Pradesh faces an unusual difficulty: China claims almost the entire state, based on an interpretation of Tibet's one–time borders. Squeezed between

Mahatma **Gandhi**

british india

legislature; in addition, there is a state governor appointed by the nation's president. When a majority fails to function in the state legislature, or the state government fails to maintain calm, the president may also place the state under presidential rule. This replaces the elected government with an appointed one, usually until order is restored and new elections are held. However, in the 1970s and 1980s presidential rule allegedly served the purpose of discrediting opposition parties or manipulating state government to the benefit of the party ruling in New Delhi. In 1991 this led indirectly to the collapse of the national government when the prime minister proclaimed New Delhi's rule over the state of Tamil Nadu, publicly to limit aid to the *Tamil Tigers*, but allegedly to further the political goals of his own party.

India's numerous political parties represent ideologies, ethnic solidarity and religious beliefs. Some party labels matter, and thus party rebels form factions retaining the party name. Rather confusingly the dominant *Congress Party* split into the Indira (I) and Opposition Branches, while two groups claim the title *Communist Party of India*. Regional parties based on local ethnic groups likewise often split, and the national *Janata Dal Party* divided beyond repair while ruling the country in 1990.

After the collapse of the *Janata*–led government of the 1970s, *Congress* proclaimed itself as the only party able to provide strong government, though it frequently only won 40% of the votes. By the 1990s that claim had failed. Previously considered an outcast for its non-secular philosophy, the *Bharatiya Janata Party (BJP)*, rose to become the largest party by appealing for clean government and Hindu sectarian policies. Besides losing Hindu voters to the *BJP*, the *Congress Party* faced defections of Muslims to the *Janata Dal*, itself striving to win lower–caste Hindu votes by proposing quotas for them.

Indian politics combines the idealism of Mohandas Gandhi, the strengths and abuses of party bosses, and increasing

Nepal and Bhutan, Sikkim gained statehood in 1975, following an Indian protectorate established in 1950 and intervention at the request of the Maharajah in 1974.

In the northwest, besides the dispute over Jammu and Kashmir, tension arose over the state of Punjab. Its southern portion contained a strong Hindu majority, while Sikhs, a separate religious group who favored the use of Punjabi, desired a state where they would form a majority. Complicated by the division of the capital, Chandigarh, the division was completed in 1966, including a new Hindi–speaking state of Hariana (Haryana). Parts of Punjab also joined the mountainous territory of Himachal Pradesh, enlarging it sufficiently for statehood in 1974. By 1989 most major ethnic groups, and many smaller ones, enjoyed statehood. In contrast, the capital city, New Delhi, several remote islands and former French and Portuguese colonies ranked as union territories. As such, they lack the full status and rights of states.

Three distinctive regions within existing states received statehood in 2000, each reflecting distinctive cultures or local resentments of one form or another. Mineral-rich Jharkhand, formed from districts of the eastern state of Bihar, holds major deposits of mica, coal, iron and copper. However, after decades of suffering from the twin evils of Bihar's politics and government-owned mining and steel companies, the region is littered with the remains of dying industries. By contrast, the mostly tribal inhabitants of Chhattisgarh, formed from hilly regions of Madhya Pradesh, had remained traditional

farmers until a severe drought had forced many of them to migrate to cities elsewhere. Both Jharkhand and Chhattisgarh face rebellions and violence from radical groups.

Lying just west of Nepal, Uttaranchal shares with it the Himalayan foothills and mountains. Its population desired statehood to address their particular problems, including land prices forced up when rich city folk purchased vacation homes in the cooler mountains. Strong rivalries within Uttaranchal prevented it from designating its permanent capital by the time it became a state; Dehra Dun became the temporary administrative center.

The state governments follow the broad organizational outlines of the federal government. The executive, the Chief Minister and his council, are responsible to the state

Prime Minister Nehru with Lord Mountbatten   Courtesy: Government of India

levels of violence. The worst abuses occur at the state level, where goons—the word itself comes from Hindi—threaten violence and stuff ballot boxes to ensure victory. Once elected, politicians too frequently changed parties for the benefits of office. Meanwhile, Assam, Kashmir and Punjab face ethnic violence, religious rivalries mount, and *Naxalite Maoists* practically rule through intimidation in a few rural areas.

India Under Nehru

The first elections under the constitution were held in 1951–52. Because the estimated 174 million eligible voters were mostly illiterate but spoke 14 major and dozens of other languages, political parties adopted symbols. Never in the earth's history had that many people voted in a contested election. Moreover, just four years previously, violence during the partition had claimed hundreds of thousands of lives. Thus the election's orderliness was an unparalleled achievement, a worthy tribute to the non–violent principles of Gandhi. The *Indian National Congress*, generally known as the *Congress Party*, continued to hold the dominant position it had before independence in both the national (or central) parliament's lower house, the *Lok Sabha*, and the assemblies of individual states.

Well before Gandhi's death, Jawaharlal Nehru had emerged as a national figure in his own right and Gandhi's successor to lead the *Congress Party*. The idol of young leftists in the party, despite an aristocratic background he appeared the modern, secular socialist needed to lead India into the future. By his patriotism, his integrity, and his sympathy with even the lowest castes— even support for equal rights for women— he also won the hearts of the masses of India. Energetic, and determined, through three general elections he led his party, emerging victorious each time. In the words of one historian, he had a freer hand in molding policy than anyone since the Great Moguls (see Historical Background).

In domestic matters, Nehru focused on economic and social improvements. Impressed by the rapid industrialization of the Soviet Union, but too devoted to democracy to become a communist, he formulated an Indian socialism that reserved for the government heavy industry, transport, and other key sectors, while allowing private enterprise in many other areas. Economic goals and coordination came from planning; the first Five–Year Plan in 1951 stressed agriculture, irrigation, and heavy industry. Much of what India could not finance came from abroad: for example, Britain, West Germany, and the Soviet Union all built steel plants. Largely successful, the first decade of economic planning witnessed a rise in national income of 42%. Although rapid population growth absorbed over half the

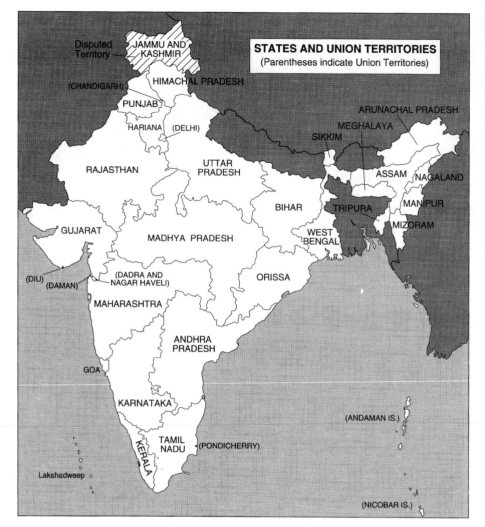

STATES AND UNION TERRITORIES
(Parentheses indicate Union Territories)

increase, Indians still enjoyed an average increase in their personal income of 20%.

Social policy stressed equality. The constitution of the Republic abolished untouchability, and prohibited its practice. Caste distinctions in general were ignored, and the privileged of all types— from the former princes of Indian states to rural tax collectors—came under attack. Landlords, especially powerful in an overpopulated agricultural society, found their lands distributed to the farmers by land reform. Despite opposition from traditionalists, Parliament also passed laws providing women with equal property inheritance and alimony for divorce. Education expanded considerably, but like many other developing countries, it grew too much at the top (university) and too little at the bottom (mass literacy and skills).

If the 1950s meant remarkable progress for India, after 1960 difficulties began to mount. The Third Five–Year Plan failed to meet its ambitious targets, and economic growth slumped. Even the weather proved perverse: monsoons failed, and only large–scale American aid prevented famine and starvation. Evidence mounted that the richest 10% of the country enjoyed most of the benefits of economic growth; they received 40% of personal

income, and enjoyed a standard of living common to Europe. In contrast, most Indians remained desperately poor, some only employed at planting and harvest.

Economic difficulties provoked political dissatisfaction. The *Congress Party*, ruling since 1947, faced challenges on its left from not one but two communist parties. In addition, the *Naxalite Maoists* eventually adopted violent means to achieve their goals. Linguistic minorities increasingly preferred regional parties in local elections. In this climate, many projects stalled when only partially completed, both in industrialization and mass education. At the time, Nehru received much of the blame for the difficulties, and the end of India's peaceful policy toward China dramatically symbolized the failure of his ideology.

Neutrality and the support for independence movements in European colonies initially dominated Nehru's approach to world politics. By the mid–1950s, the non–aligned nations were flourishing, with Nehru as a prominent leader. Always somewhat suspicious of European motives, he criticized the Western allies extensively, and to many outside India he seemed too sympathetic to the Soviet Union. Such sympathy, however, carried a practical value as both Eastern and

Western nations provided economic aid. India's major foreign policy concern, however, remained Pakistan. Although the two countries adopted diplomatic relations after the war over Kashmir, deep suspicions remained, and an arms race began, with Soviet weapons for India countering American jets and tanks to Pakistan.

India initially welcomed the Chinese communist revolution, and Nehru met with Chinese leaders in the early 1950s. This friendly and complacent attitude failed to reflect the strategic implication of the Chinese conquest of Tibet in 1950. This brought together the two most populated nations along a lengthy border through the highest mountains in the world.

Rebellion in Tibet further soured relations with China in 1959. At its failure, the Dalai Lama fled to India to lead a moral struggle for his people, while his supporters sought supplies and weapons for the long–smoldering revolt. Tension increased as China constructed a road across the desolate, but strategic, Aksai Chin Plateau in what India claimed was part of Ladakh in northeastern Kashmir. After sporadic clashes there, Indian troops along the eastern border with China, near Bhutan, advanced beyond even India's claimed boundary in 1962. China responded by attacking Indian troops in the territory it claimed, then by withdrawing. The border dispute soured relations between the two countries for 25 years, because no settlement was reached, and it encouraged China to ally with Pakistan, India's arch–enemy.

Bitterness over Pakistan had preceded independence. Muslim desires for a state based on Islam clashed strongly with Gandhi's dream of a united India where followers of all religions coexisted in brotherhood. The circumstances of independence, including the bitter massacres in the Punjab and warfare over Kashmir (see Disputed Territories: Kashmir), further poisoned relations. Kashmir remained unsolved: the ceasefire, occasionally troubled, brought no peace agreement. Each side denied the other's claim to rule the area.

Following independence, new difficulties arose with Pakistan, especially when Indian irrigation projects threatened to divert water previously flowing into Pakistan and used for farming there. The international community largely solved this problem by a technical solution, for the World Bank provided funds to Pakistan so it could utilize other rivers instead.

After Nehru's death in May 1964, as hundreds of millions mourned, *Congress Party* leaders selected Lal Bahadur Shastri as the new prime minister. Difficulties loomed: many in South India protested violently the proclamation of Hindi as the national language, and the Kashmir problem remained unsolved. Shastri faced opposition within the party, and had yet to consolidate power as the crisis deepened. He would never gain the chance.

Tension flared over Kashmir in the summer of 1965. Pakistan infiltrated irregulars first, then plunged into full–scale war by invading with tank units (see Disputed Territories: Kashmir). The nation rallied behind Shastri, but in early 1966, hours after negotiating an end to the fighting and the withdrawal of armies, Shastri died of a heart attack in Tashkent, Soviet Central Asia.

The Indira Gandhi Years

This time *Congress Party* leaders selected Indira Gandhi as party leader and prime minister. Daughter of Jawaharlal Nehru, long acquainted with political issues, and capable in many ways, she inherited a stumbling economy and a weak party facing elections in 1967. While she retained office, the *Congress Party* fared poorly at the state level and lost eight of the 16 states.

Under Mrs. Gandhi (her husband was not related to Mohandas Gandhi), economic activity revived. Agricultural harvests rose substantially, partly due to favorable monsoon rains, partly to the introduction of the *Green Revolution* with its higher yielding varieties of grains. Natural gas and petroleum production expanded after the discovery of new deposits.

While Mrs. Gandhi showed skill and courage in the face of student unrest and language conflicts, she increasingly adopted socialist policies. When she nationalized the banks in 1969, many party bosses broke with her and split the party. Nevertheless, her popularity with the masses provided a landslide victory in 1971. Her second term in office matched the domestic policies of the first. Nationalizations included insurance, and coal and other industries.

India's hostility to Pakistan was rekindled in 1971 when Bengali leaders in East Pakistan declared independence (see Pakistan and Bangladesh: History). As increasing numbers of Bengali refugees fled to India, it turned border skirmishes into a full-scale invasion of East Pakistan. After a quick victory, India helped establish the new nation of Bangladesh. The damage to Pakistan, India's only rival south of the Himalayas, increased Mrs. Gandhi's popularity to a new high. India's prestige was further increased when in 1974 it became the sixth nation in the world to explode a nuclear device (much to the alarm of Pakistan).

Domestically, Mrs. Gandhi's programs proved less popular. Adverse economic conditions, a compulsory male sterilization program, and higher taxes created unrest. In mid-1975 a state court found

Mrs. Gandhi signs the Visitor's Book at the White House, July 1982

Mrs. Gandhi guilty of election violations in 1971, and opposition party leaders called for her resignation. She responded by declaring a "national emergency" and invoked extraordinary powers to jail several thousand opposition leaders, censor the press, and announce drastic economic reforms.

When over-due elections were finally held in 1977 amid widespread criticism of *Congress*, several opposition parties combined as the *Janata Front*. It won an overwhelming majority, and Moraji Desai, then 81, became Prime Minister, the first from outside the *Congress Party*. However, owing to disagreements among its parties and its failure to fulfill campaign promises, the new government lost popularity and resigned in 1979. As the *Janata Party* splintered, President Reddy called elections for 1980, which returned Indira Gandhi's *Congress Party* with a large majority in the *Lok Sabha*.

The new Gandhi cabinet had to face serious economic problems (especially steep increases in oil prices), sectarian tensions in various parts of the country and violence in the northeast. Mrs. Gandhi also lost her son and probable successor, Sanjay, in a flying accident.

Regional and communal dissatisfactions also proved an unending challenge to the central government. In 1983, the army restored order to the northeastern state of Assam after local militants massacred minorities, including some 2,500 immigrants from Bangladesh. Far greater difficulties erupted in Punjab, India's most prosperous state. Sikh militants, demanding the creation of a separate "Khalistan," turned to violence in 1983, and soon occupied the Golden Temple in Amritsar, the focus of Sikh religious life. Faced with outright insurrection, in 1984 Indira Gandhi ordered the Indian army to assault the temple, a refuge and headquarters for many militants, including their leader. Many Sikhs, not all of them militants, resisted the invasion of their shrine, and heavy casualties resulted. The most fateful consequence of the government's intervention at Amritsar occurred when Mrs. Gandhi was mercilessly gunned down by two of her personal bodyguards, both Sikhs taking revenge.

Later the same day, key cabinet members selected her second son, Rajiv, as Prime Minister. News of the assassination also sent gangs of Hindus rampaging against Sikhs in Delhi and elsewhere; untold thousands of Sikhs were massacred while thousands more lost their businesses and homes.

Yet another disaster soon struck the nation. In the early hours of December 3, 1984 poisonous gas used to make sevin, an agricultural pesticide, leaked into the atmosphere in Bhopal, capital of Madhya Pradesh. More than 6,500 people died; 200,000 suffered immediate injury. Since the poison leaked from a chemical plant owned

Rajiv Gandhi

by the Indian subsidiary of Union Carbide, American lawyers quickly descended on India, searching for clients and demanding steep damages. Legal wrangles in Indian and American courts delayed settlement until 1989, when Union Carbide agreed to an Indian court's settlement of $470 million. Although the government later attempted to reopen litigation, in 1990 it began paying the modest compensation of $12 per month to each of the injured.

Prosperity and Corruption Under Rajiv Gandhi

Heir to the Nehru tradition of leadership, yet in many ways a fresh face, Rajiv's personal popularity was strengthened by sympathy over his mother's death. Seizing the moment, he called fresh elections in late 1984, and *Congress* emerged triumphant, winning the largest margin of victory since independence, more than 50% of the popular vote and 400 of the 542 seats in the *Lok Sabha*.

As prime minister, Rajiv thus enjoyed that rarity in Indian politics, a single-party majority in the *Lok Sabha*. He used the opportunity to begin reducing government regulations and cutting barriers to international trade. He sought improved relations with the United States, and promised to attack corruption.

Rajiv had been Indira's "non–political" son, a pilot, while his brother Sanjay had entered politics. Reportedly bored by the details of governing, Rajiv enjoyed a lavish lifestyle. Moreover, he inherited many personal characteristics from his mother and grandfather, especially high–handedness and opportunism. Not surprisingly, his popularity began to fade, and just thirteen months after his election victory, his cabinet had to reduce announced increases in

oil and food prices because the party threatened revolt and strikes swept the country.

Unhappy results also followed an attempt to bring peace to Sri Lanka, where Tamils whose ancestors came from India rebelled against the native Sinhalese majority (see Sri Lanka: history). Rajiv's intense personal mediation persuaded Sri Lanka to accept a compromise involving a ceasefire, disarming the rebels, and local autonomy. However, the leading rebel force, the *Tamil Tigers,* turned against the Indian troops sent to maintain peace, and killed 1,000 of them in the ensuing fighting. At the same time, the Sinhalese resented the foreign troops, and the new president, Ranasinghe Premadasa, demanded the Indians depart. The last did so in early 1990.

Far greater success accompanied the Indian paratroops rushed to the Maldives to crush an attempted *coup d'etat* there in 1988. They suffered not a single casualty, and provided a favorable example of India's peacekeeping role. Gandhi also improved relations with China, visiting the neighboring Asian giant. He held talks with Prime Minister Benazir Bhutto of Pakistan, raising the prospect of happier relations between the rival states. Unfortunately, the more domineering aspect of Indian foreign policy showed itself in pressures on land–locked Nepal to sign a trade agreement to India's liking.

In domestic politics, Rajiv Gandhi showed himself as heavy-handed as his mother, but he lacked party support that Indira gained by political favors. Political difficulties soon mounted. His Finance Minister, Vishwanath Pratap Singh, possessed a reputation for integrity, and he cracked down heavily on tax evasion by the upper classes, alarming powerful members of the party by unannounced raids on homes. After an outcry, Gandhi transferred Singh to the defense ministry, then dismissed him for investigating kickbacks.

Soon thereafter Swedish investigators discovered payments to secret Swiss bank accounts when the Swedish gun manufacturer, Bofors, sold field guns to India. Gandhi denied any commissions were paid, but his government failed to investigate the charges, and his own relatives and friends met with Bofors negotiators.

As "Bofors" became a by-word for corruption, Singh seized the high moral ground, organized a People's Movement against corruption, and emerged as leader of a six-party alliance of the *Janata Dal* with regional parties such as *Telugu Desam (Telugu Homeland) Party* of Andhra Pradesh and the *Dravida Munnetra Kazhagam* of Tamil Nadu. The alliance also reached separate electoral understandings with the *Communist Party of India (Marxist)* on the left, and on the right with the Hindu revivalist *Bharatiya Janata (Indian Peoples') Party (BJP)*. This diverse group of temporary allies, united by the opportunity to defeat the Prime Minister, papered over differences between the *Janata Dal* and its allies, especially over secularism.

Months before the 1989 elections, the entire opposition resigned from parliament to protest the Bofors scandal. This drew attention away from Gandhi's achievements in liberalizing regulations, expanding education, and generally spurring economic growth. India had prospered at the fastest rate since independence.

The election results portrayed a divided country, without a majority. *Congress* remained the largest party, but found few allies. Despite exceptional gains by the *BJP*, the *Janata Dal* alliance could only form a government under V.P. Singh with support from regional parties.

Divisive Challenges for a Weak Coalition

An honest man handicapped by a fragmented coalition, Singh faced three severe challenges to the very unity of India: ethnic separatism, class- and caste-based disputes, and religious antagonisms intensified by clashes over the fate of one mosque.

Sikh separatism remained acute for a decade after the 1984 raid on the Golden Temple, complicated by divisions within the community, government repression and unfulfilled promises. The killing usually took place in Punjab, but terrorists also blew up an Air India flight from Canada. In 1986, Sikh militants again seized the Golden Temple, and proclaimed the independence of Khalistan. This time the military minimized casualties by starving many extremists to surrender, with the consent of the moderate Sikh *Akali Dal Party* ruling the state. The final assault thus became an anti–climax.

Nevertheless, the killing continued. Commentators placed part of the blame on Rajiv Gandhi's government for attempting to achieve peace primarily by police action rather than political compromise. Initially, political reform reduced tensions. In 1985 his cabinet approved releasing some Sikh prisoners, bringing to justice those who had massacred Sikhs in Delhi, and the transfer of Punjab's capital, Chandigarh, to Punjab. Only 51 died in the violence that year, and the *Akali Dal Party* won state elections by appealing that moderation worked.

When the promises were not fulfilled, however, *Akali Dal* leaders appeared as puppets. Their authority crumbled, and an elected state government was replaced by direct rule from New Delhi to maintain law and order. Repression failed: in 1988 terrorism killed 2,000 and made it "The World's Bloodiest Terrorist War." While some concessions, including the release of prisoners, isolated the extremists, the execution of one Sikh bodyguard for the assassination of Mrs. Gandhi on circumstantial evidence increased resentment.

After taking power, Prime Minister V.P. Singh first appeared to promise reconciliation by visiting the Golden Temple in Amritsar. However, the extremists again massacred innocents—from wedding parties to Hindu religious processions. Singh then postponed state elections, and, like the Gandhis, used force to maintain Indian rule over Punjab, where terrorism claimed 4,000 lives in 1990 and surpassed that grim record the next year with 6,000 dead. Only after the return of civilian rule did violence subside by 1994, with relative calm replacing a conflict that had killed some 20,000.

In its economic policies, the Singh cabinet adopted a moralistic tone. It wrote off loans for poor farmers and craftsmen and raised taxes on consumer goods, from cigarettes to cars. Multinational corporations found opportunities blocked, and India's economic boom slowed. However, the Singh government fell from power in just 11 months—faster than most skeptics had predicted—largely because of religious and social issues.

In 1990, Singh proposed a quota reserving 27% of jobs in government firms and the civil service for those from "Backward" Castes (technically, Shudras). Added to the existing quota of 22.5% for the Dalits ("oppressed"; former untouchables) and tribesmen, this placed half of all jobs outside the reach of the middle and upper classes. Demonstrations and riots followed; a policy inspired by a desire to help the poor divided the nation and reinforced caste conflict.

Though perhaps not astute, Singh's arithmetic was not faulty. The backward castes, Dalits, tribesmen and Muslims to total 80% of the population, and caste-based policies and parties have often proved enticing. In the most populous state, Uttar Pradesh, the *Samajwadi Party* representing lower castes and Muslims took power allied with the *Bahujan Samaj Party* of the Dalits. Their attempts to establish quotas stirred resentment in Himalyan districts.

Worse violence arose over the disputed mosque at Ayodhya. The *Bharatiya Janata Party* and militant Hindu revival groups such as the *Vishwa Hindu Parishad* sought to destroy the mosque and rebuild the temple. The national and state *Janata Dal* governments took extraordinary precautions to prevent violence, arresting the *BJP* leader, Lal Krishan Advani, and some 100,000 others. Hundreds died in demonstrations at Ayodhya and many other places across the country. Nevertheless, protected by the police and military, the mosque remained. In contrast, the Singh government did not: without support from the *BJP*, and weakened by rivalries within, it fell.

Although Chandra Shekhar emerged as the seventh prime minister, his splinter *Janata Dal* (Socialist) party held only 10% of the seats in the *Lok Sabha*, and lost power in four months. To resolve the

political stalemate, President Venkataraman called for elections in 1991.

The country entered the election campaign cynical about politics and stirred by passions of religion and caste. In addition, the economy faltered, suffering from a huge budget deficit, increasing inflation, a shortage of foreign exchange, and rising joblessness. Then, in the southern town of Sriperumbudar, a woman offered Rajiv Gandhi a bouquet of flowers: and triggered the bomb that instantly killed Gandhi and others as well as herself. The work of the *Tamil Tigers* fighting in Sri Lanka, the assassination plunged the country in gloom.

When Sonia Gandhi, Rajiv's widow, refused the party leadership, *Congress* reached beyond the Nehru family that had dominated it for 40 years, and selected P.V. Narasimha Rao as leader. Already 70, in poor health, and lacking a strong regional base, Rao brought years of loyal service to the party—and observers thought him traditional, unlikely to innovate.

When elections resumed, again no party won a majority of the 545 members in the *Lok Sabha*. Strengthened by a small sympathy vote, *Congress* emerged with 233 seats, enough to form a minority government. After defeating rivals within the party, Narasimha Rao became the first prime minister from South India.

Almost immediately the economic crisis demanded far–reaching changes in government policy: with $70 billion in foreign debt, the payment of principal and interest absorbed over 40% of export earnings. India was nearly broke, and neither private banks nor aid agencies would lend until substantial reforms took place.

Under Finance Minister Manmohan Singh, the government began to liberalize the economy and tighten spending (for details, see Economy). Foreign companies responded by proposing to invest, and exports fared well except to former Communist nations. The collapse of the Soviet Union shook the socialist and leftist principles of Indian politics, thus weakening further the traditional *Congress* policies of regulation and control. Public opinion came to favor reform, and market economists supported many of the changes, but the inevitable hardships caused strikes and other difficulties for the minority government.

Destruction of the Ayodhya Mosque

Secularism, another pillar of *Congress Party* ideology and a national tradition, suffered gravely from the activities of the *BJP* and the dispute over the Babri mosque at Ayodhya. Built by the Mogul emperor Babur, it was holy to Muslims, but Hindus regarded it as the sacred birthplace of the god *Ram*. In late 1992, months of political maneuvering gave way to direct action. During ceremonies sup--posedly to construct a Hindu temple, well-organized militants attacked the dome and walls of the mosque. Under orders from the state's *BJP* government not to fire, the police stood by, and in a few hours the mosque lay destroyed, replaced by a makeshift temple.

Within hours, fighting between Muslims and Hindus spread from Ayodhya across India in the worst communal violence since independence. Within days, violence claimed some 1,200 lives and thousands of injured, most of them Muslim, and many the result of police bullets. The violence and curfews halted normal business, and losses amounted to billions of rupees.

Reacting firmly, Prime Minister Rao dismissed the *BJP*–dominated state government of Uttar Pradesh for violating a Supreme Court order to protect the mosque. In the days that followed, the president of the *BJP* and its parliamentary leader, L. K. Advani, were arrested, in addition to thousands of Hindu extremists. The government banned several militant Hindu organizations, including the *Rashtriya Swayam Sevak Sangh* and the *Vishwa Hindu Parishad*, as well as two Muslim groups. Moreover, when the *BJP* governments of three states failed to act on the banning orders—the state leaders belonged to the banned groups—the prime minister placed them, like Uttar Pradesh, under direct rule from New Delhi.

Calm returned only slowly. Further rioting in Bombay, the commercial capital, cost hundreds more lives. Evidence suggests that the March explosions against the city's leading businesses were the work of Muslim terrorists, perhaps linked to Pakistan or Afghanistan.

Violence in Kashmir and Bihar

Sectarian violence flared for different reasons in Kashmir, a perennial dispute with Pakistan since 1948. Given its overwhelming Muslim majority, popular opinion often favors an end to Indian rule, though it appears divided between favoring independence and unity with Pakistan. In the early 1990s protests by Muslims demanded freedom from Indian rule. Armed militants took and occasionally murdered hostages, while the (often non-Kashmiri) police killed dozens of protestors and militants. The leading Muslim activist, Maulvi Mohammad Farooq, was assassinated, and by 1996 the death toll had reached about 20,000.

Only force and undemocratic control from New Delhi retained Kashmir within the country. Its special status continued, with separate laws and land ownership restricted to Kashmiris, but years of political manipulation and election-rigging—most notably in 1987—destroyed any legitimacy of the state government. Economic development languished, and a state with some of the greatest potential for hydroelectric power actually

┌───┐
│   The World's Sixth Nuclear Power   │

Indian interest in atomic power began before independence, when the industrial Tata company set up a research program. In the 1950s, the U.S., Canada and Britain all provided nuclear facilities, hoping to encourage research and generate cheap electricity. However, despite its public stand against nuclear weapons, India never signed the Comprehensive Test Ban Treaty, and its Atomic Energy Commission undertook the design and construction of nuclear reactors free from inspection by the International Atomic Energy Agency.

After China exploded its first atomic bomb in 1965, the scientists at the Atomic Energy Commission secretly began accumulating the enriched uranium from those reactors for possible atomic bombs. In 1974, an explosion in Rajasthan proclaimed that the country was the world's sixth nuclear power, but New Delhi confirmed that its program was peaceful, though it now had the ability to explode weapons.

By the 1990s, politicians desired further nuclear tests, to illustrate the country's ability, and no doubt to enhance their own reputation. Reportedly Prime Minister Rao ordered tests in 1995, but the U.S. discovered the plans, and threatened to publicize them. In response, Rao called off the tests. By contrast, in 1998 Prime Minister Vajpayee publicly promised that India would not test weapons, while secretly authorizing the five explosions that set off the South Asian nuclear arms race with Pakistan.

Even military strategists who accepted the legitimacy of some nuclear weapons frequently condemn India's acquisition of them. Very predictably, the 1974 explosion led Pakistan to create its own bomb. Within both countries, the creation of weapons raced far ahead of designing strategies for their use, and possibly control over them. Thus, far from enhancing India's security, the explosions may actually make South Asia more likely to suffer conventional wars. The resulting arms races for both nuclear and conventional weapons impose unnecessary suffering on populations whose average incomes reach only $300 per year, but no doubt the satisfaction of citizenship in a nation armed with atomic weapons removes the pangs of hunger and stills the sorrows resulting from some of the highest death rates for infants and children.

imported most of its electricity. By late 1996 the population appeared exhausted after years of violence and human rights abuses by both sides, and nearly 50% of the population voted in state elections.

In 1999 several hundred Islamic fighters (*mujahidin*) and Pakistani troops secretly crossed the Line of Control dividing Kashmir and established positions high on peaks overlooking the vital highway to Leh, near the Tibetan border. To attack the invaders, Indian troops advanced up steep slopes with little cover; only after ten weeks of determined battle and significant casualties did they (and world opinion) force Pakistan to withdraw the remaining infiltrators. Two nuclear powers had fought significant land battles without going to war, but many commentators worried that results would not always prove as fortunate.

The high-altitude battles focused attention on military needs: everything from better boots to spy satellites. The defense budget for 2000 boosted spending nearly 30%. After a ceasefire proposed by one rebel group, India seized the diplomatic initiative and attempted to move towards a settlement by offering a unilateral ceasefire.

This policy aimed to reduce the artillery battles across the Line of Control, to win public support in Kashmir for a compromise, and to encourage some rebel groups to accept autonomy within India. However, the Hizbul Mujahideen demanded that Pakistan join the proposed peace talks, while the All-Party Hurriyat Conference (a loose confederation of 23 groups) found it difficult to unite for negotiations. Then India refused passports for some of its delegates to hold discussions in Pakistan. By the spring of 2001 many Indian politicians opposed extending the ceasefire, and militant rebels had responded to it by stepping up attacks and provoking harsh responses. Nevertheless, the policy had reduced the risk of conventional war with Pakistan and won international sympathy.

Violence of a different nature swept portions of rural Bihar during the 1990s. Maoist-influenced Communists known as *Naxalites* had for decades considered Bihar's strong caste divisions and great inequality of wealth a logical place for class warfare, and they organized bands of Dalits (formerly called untouchables), who sometimes used violence against the landowning castes. In return, landowners formed an upper-caste army, the *Ranbir Sena*. Each side apparently indulged in slaughter; extortion, rape and other crimes soared.

Unfortunately, the Bihar state government failed to provide security—or schools, clinics, roads, and electricity. Elected Chief Minister in 1990, Laloo Prasad Yadav, from a cow-herding caste, used state employment and contracts as a source of patronage for his supporters. When corruption charges finally forced

The "cold shower"   WORLD BANK photo by Ray Witlin

him from office in 1997, he appointed his illiterate wife to replace him, and their party won the largest number of seats in the 2000 state elections, though not a majority. In contrast to states where econoic reform and foreign investment have begun to bring prosperity, Bihar's electricity is as uncertain as security in its vilages, and the level of poverty increases yearly.

Corruption Discredits Politicians

Months before the 1996 parliamentary elections, at the Supreme Court's prodding, investigators revealed an immense scandal involving dozens of politicians and officials. A diary kept by a foreign exchange dealer showed illegal payments—presumably for favors—to many prominent politicians. Public uproar forced the resignation of seven *Congress* cabinet members and the *BJP* leader, L. K. Advani. Other news reports discredited politicians and government generally for corruption and even some crimes violent enough for horror movies.

The 1996 electoral campaign marked a decisive change for *Congress*. No longer the natural ruling party, it lacked a champion from the Nehru–Gandhi family and turned for leadership to elderly men suspected of corruption. Social trends weakened its traditional appeal. Among the upper castes, its secular platform was gravely threatened by the *BJP*'s vision of a Hindu nation. Regional loyalties, the defection of many Muslims, and caste–based ideologies likewise cost *Congress* support, as voters selected new groups like the caste–based *Samajwadi* and *Bahujan Samaj* parties or leftist alliances ranging from *Janata Dal* to the *Communist Party-Marxist*.

As expected, the electorate of 590 million gave no party a majority but resoundingly rejected *Congress*. The *BJP* won over 160 seats, and its new, more–moderate leader, Atal Bihari Vajpayee, muted its anti–Muslim slogans as he became prime minister. However, secular parties refused to support him, and lacking a majority, forced him to resign in days.

Because it had suffered its lowest–ever share of the vote, *Congress* clearly could not form a government, but as the second largest party, it supported a cabinet formed by the *United Front*, an alliance of alliance of communists, socialists, free–market sympathizers and regional parties. Overcoming strong party rivalries, the *United Front* selected H.D. Deve Gowda as its leader. The Chief Minister of the southern state of Karnataka, his reputation rested largely on his welcome to foreign investment (including a special alliance with Massachusetts) that helped Bangalore, the capital, become India's "Silicon Valley." However, Deve Gowda's support quickly disintegrated when allegations of corruption were leveled at *Congress Party* leaders and the party withdrew support for his cabinet.

The venality seemed high by any standards. While prime minister, Narasimha Rao had apparently accepted a bribe from a pickle manufacturer, but then bestowed the favor elsewhere—and he failed to return the money. Rao's former allies seemed equally venal. Police seized 10,500 saris and over 60 pounds of gold from Jayalalitha Jayaram, a former movie star from Tamil Nadu. The home of the previous minister of communications yielded over *36 million* rupees *in cash*.

The *United Front's* next prime minister, Inder Kumar Gujral, soon faced allegations of corruption by leading members of his own *Janata Dal* party. Moreover, an official report claimed that one party in the front, the *Dravida Munnetra Kazhagam (DMK)* had aided the *Tamil Tigers*, who were blamed for the assassination of Rajiv Gandhi. Forced by *Congress* to choose between its support and the *DMK*, Gujral called for national elections in early 1998.

Initially the election campaign, like the one just two years earlier, promised substantial gains for the *BJP*. It was changed by the entrance into politics of Sonia Gandhi, Rajiv's Italian–born widow. Though not a candidate herself, she spoke to large crowds and united *Congress* behind her, becoming its leader after the votes were counted. As a result, while the *United Front* lost seats, *Congress* stabilized its share of parliament, and the *BJP* increased its representation only slightly, to 178 of Parliament's 548 seats. Alliances with small parties—a dozen of them—proved enough for A.B. Vajpayee again to form a cabinet.

In office, Vajpayee's platform initially reflected the moderate face of the *BJP*. Its laudable goals included eradicating illiteracy, eliminating child labor, supplying clean drinking water, ending hunger and clearing slums. His coalition

Prime Minister Atal Behari Vajpayee

partners forced him to drop the most extreme planks of his party's platform, such as building a temple at Ayodhya or legislating a unified law of family status that would prohibit Muslims from their practice of polygamy.

Just weeks after the election, the coalition seemed in danger of falling apart, but a series of nuclear explosions in Rajasthan stunned the world and delighted most Indians. The *BJP* had promised vaguely only to "induct" nuclear weapons, but the tests changed India's rank from "nuclear–capable" to "nuclear power."

While the U.S. and Japan immediately halted aid, the European nations did not; pious platitudes proved inconsequential. Vajpayee argued that other countries' improved weapons (apparently Chinese and Pakistani missiles and nuclear abilities) threatened India, so the bomb was needed for its security. The blasts heightened the government's popularity despite Pakistani counter–blasts, and India outlasted U.S. sanctions.

For just over a year Vajpayee played an artful game of foreign policy, to divert attention from the domestic political challenge of keeping united a diverse alliance during a series of crises that ranged from the high price of onions to attacks by *BJP* allies on the small Christian minority. Thus he authorized highly symbolic military actions such the bomb blasts and missile tests that threatened Pakistan and China, but pursued equally publicized acts of friendship. He rode the first bus scheduled between Delhi and Lahore in decades, and despite attacks by militants on Indian cricket facilities, the Pakistani cricket team played a series of matches across the country.

The balancing game ended in 1999 when Vajpayee lost a vote of confidence, deserted by the South Indian actress turned notorious politician, Jayalalitha Jayaram. For the third time in three years, the nation again held general elections, and from the start, the *BJP* seemed likely to win. It claimed Vajpayee as a hero for the bomb, and for the successful defeat of Pakistani infiltrators in Kashmir. Over twenty regional parties joined the *BJP*'s National Democratic Alliance. By contrast, the *Congress Party* fractured over whether the foreign-born Sonia Gandhi should lead the party and nation.

Given these advantages, Vajpayee won a modest victory and a reasonable chance of a working government. The *BJP* alliance captured nearly 300 of 534 constituencies, and *Congress* had its worst parliamentary showing. However, detailed analysis of the election returns showed that Vajpayee's victory was partly good fortune. His party's share of the vote fell, and *Congress* actually out-polled the *BJP*. The vital difference proved to be the success of regional, often caste-based allies, and the collapse of national parties that had belonged to the *United Front*.

With a majority so large that no one ally's defection could destroy the coalition's majority, Prime Minister Vajpayee's cabinet concentrated on economic and defense issues. Given high world oil prices, the government raised prices of diesel fuel and kerosene (used for cooking); the federal budget could ill afford subsidies that kept fuel far cheaper than elsewhere. In the 2001 budget, Finance Minister Yashwant Sinha limited most expenditures and proposed to speed up financial privatization.

Unfortunately, rather than development projects, most additional spending will go for defense. Armed largely with weaponry from the 1960s and 1970s, the fourth largest military in the world now desires an expensive list of weaponry: T-90 tanks, an aircraft carrier and jet fighters from Russia; jet trainers from Britain; perhaps a submarine or two from France; and locally-produced missiles and nuclear weapons. Considering the country's size, India's spending on the military has been modest, but the increases mean it now devotes to defense important resources that would be productive elsewhere. Unfortunately, New Delhi still lacks a coherent defense policy about using its military, despite India's nuclear weapons.

In early 2001 an earthquake of 7.5 magnitude struck the western state of Gujarat. It killed some 30,000 people and rendered about one million homeless. Many of those who died lived in newer districts, and thus the quake emphasized what critics had long claimed: building construction codes were poor, and their enforcement even weaker. Geologically, the quake was unusual because it occurred in the middle of a plate, rather than at its edge. Some geologists predict that a major quake is overdue in its northern regions, where the Indian plate continues to shove against the Eurasian plate. Its past action formed the Himalaya mountain range.

Dealings with Muslims, foreign and domestic, dominated the Indian government in the past year. When Prime Minister Vajpayee held a summit with President Musharraf of Pakistan in 2001, the two men met congenially and nearly achieved a breakthrough. As usual, the critical failure came over Kashmir, which India refuses to regard as an "international problem," considering it instead a domestic issue.

Another semantic difficulty arose when the two leaders agreed to condemn terrorism. The prime minister's aides then desired to use the phrase "cross-border terrorism." However, to any Pakistani, the adjective "cross-border" has always raised two objections. First, it implies Pakistani responsibility for the terrorism, while Pakistan has maintained the fiction of merely moral support for what are only "freedom fighters." Second, "cross-border" implies that the Line of Control, the military armistice line of 1949, now divides not a

battlefield but nations. Thus most of Kashmir would be recognized as part of India.

As a result, the summit failed. Its col-lapse blocked agreements to cooperate in fighting narcotics, for a possible pipeline to bring Iranian gas to India, and for measures to decrease the likelihood of a nuclear attack.

The September 11 attacks on New York and Washington deepened the growing friendship between the U.S. and India. Officially and in popular opinion, India sympathized with another victim of Islamic extremists, and international horror at the massacres in the U.S. suggested a greater understanding of India as a victim in Kashmir. However, because Pakistan shared information with the U.S. and played a vital role in allowing U.S. access to Afghanistan, India did not win conclusive support, and in most countries Kashmir remains a disputed territory.

The dispute between India and Pakistan sharpened following a deadly attack by pro-Kashmiri guerrillas on the Indian Parliament at the end of 2001. Prime Minister Vajpayee responded by demanding that Pakistan ban the two groups allegedly involved, Jaish-e Muhammad and Laskar-e Toiba, then generally clamp down on such extremists. Vajpayee backed his demands with actions: the Indian military moved to the border and obviously prepared for war. Fearful of the first real war between nuclear-armed antagonists, the U.S. and other nations counseled Pakistan to yield, and it did so. However, with the arrival of spring several months later, brutal attacks again took place on the Indian military and non-Muslim civilians of Kashmir.

The domestic crisis with Muslims again began over plans to construct a temple in Ayodhya on the disputed site of the Babri mosque destroyed in 1992. A trainload of Hindu militants, returning home from Ayodhya, was attacked in Gujarat by Muslim extremists, leaving nearly 60 dead. For days thereafter, well-organized Hindu mobs pillaged Muslim quarters of Ahmedabad, the state capital, slaughtering hundreds, vandalizing businesses and homes, and causing thousands to flee.

Significantly, the state of Gujarat is ruled by the *BJP*. Horror at the violence elsewhere in India led to demands within Vajpayee's coalition for the dismissal of Gujarat's chief minister. In particular, some of the *BJP*'s allies in the national government feared losing support in the next national elections. However, none bolted the coalition, even when the *BJP* stood by the minister and recommended early state elections. In part, the *BJP* must consider its own fate at the national elections in 2004 because it had recently lost power in three of four states that held elections in early 2002. In the process, it lost nearly half its seats in Uttar Pradesh, the most populous state.

A stroll through the market

Bombay: The Movie

A Tamil film about love against the background of the Ayodhya riots nearly caused disturbances of its own in 1995. One of India's best known producers, Mani Ratnam, sought to plea for peace by portraying a love story between a Hindu man and Muslim woman. Predictably, the strongest passion he aroused was anger, not love.

For the sake of communal peace, Mr. Ratnam edited portions at the request of Mr. Bal Thackeray, leader of the militant Hindu party *Shiv Sena* that attacked Muslim areas during the riots. The producer also cut portions in sympathy with Muslim sensitivities, and showed newspaper headlines of the attack on the mosque, rather than the attack itself.

Despite passing India's censors, the final version of the film aroused Muslim anger by implying a similar aggressiveness between Muslim and Hindu mobs. Muslim threats of disturbances halted showing for a week in Bombay—it had appeared elsewhere. However, Mr. Thackeray, who boasted of his Remote Control over the newly–elected Chief Minister of Maharashtra, insisted that threats should not prevent its opening. Under tight security, it was released.

Regardless of its portrayal of mobs and politicians, the movie risked Muslim resentment from the start. In Islamic law, on marriage a woman joins her husband's community. When a Muslim man marries a non–Muslim, he thereby adds to the community, an honorable action that provided a Christian wife for more than one caliph. But when a Muslim woman marries outside her faith, she effectively leaves it, an event not dissimilar to apostasy.

Culture: Like most nations, India does not have an official religion; it is a land of many religions. Yet it is a Hindu nation, and that fact is in part responsible for the toleration of other religions. About 80% of the population is Hindu, but even so there are nearly 80 million Muslims and 14 million Christians. There are also many Buddhists in this land where the great Buddha lived in the 6th century B.C. and preached a message which emphasized the sanctity of life in all forms.

Hinduism is not merely part of a culture, it *is* a culture—not simply a religion in the normal Western sense, though with modernization the all–embracing character of Hinduism is retreating to the form of a religion in the narrower sense.

Most noticeable about Hinduism is the rigid social order dominated by the concept of caste. Hundreds of castes exist; all Hindus belong to one of them. Caste membership comes by birth, and remains for life. Marriages rarely cross caste boundaries, and social contacts overwhelmingly occur within the caste. Each caste traditionally involved a particular occupation, and with some exceptions members of the upper castes also represented the upper economic classes. The distinctions are far more than economic, and include dietary restrictions on the higher castes as well as social discrimination against members of lower castes. For example, many Brahmins will not eat food if the shadow of an untouchable" has passed over it.

Traditionally castes fell into four broad groups. At the top, the Brahmins (priest-intellectuals), kshatriyas (warrior–nobles) and vaishyas (businessmen) compose over one–sixth of India's population. The shudras (peasants and laborers), now politically described as the Backward Castes, amount to 44%. Below all of these rank the former Untouchables or "Scheduled Castes." With about 15% of the population, they formerly faced the discrimination their title proclaimed, while

carrying out essential but dirty and dangerous occupations like street sweeping, disposing corpses and human wastes, and slaughtering animals. The Indian constitution removed legal discrimination against these unfortunates, and government programs have provided assistance.

Rituals and ceremonies are prominent also, and these are closely related to the family, for the rites are performed at home. The major rituals relate to birth, marriage and death. The dead are cremated with as much decorum as the family can afford in keeping with its position on the social scale. Other features of Hinduism include the rejection of worldly pleasure, belief in the soul's transmigration after death to another form of life, the sanctity of the cow and the belief in many gods.

One Hindu celebration, the Kumbh Mela, brings together more people than any other single religious event worldwide. The "pitcher fair" is named after drops of the elixir of immortality that fell to earth during a struggle between gods and demons. Every few years, the alignment of the stars makes washing away the sins of the body particularly effective at the city of Allahabad, the confluence of the Ganges, the

Untouchables polishing shoes

Yamuna, and the mythical (but sacred) Sasaswathi. Millions converge on Allahabad, often taking weeks to walk there, carrying everything needed on their heads. About 80 million attended the 2001 ceremony.

Hindi and certain other Indian languages are descended from ancient Sanskrit. Most of the ancient literature of India was written in that language, including the early religious text Rigveda. Slightly later, several dramas appeared in Sanskrit; a playwright named Kalidasa is the most famous. That was the beginning of a long literary history enriched by contributions from Persia and finally Western ideas and forms. Literature flourishes in contemporary India in a number of the native languages, but there are also poems, novels and other works in English.

It is only natural when one thinks of the culture of India to think of the Taj Mahal

From 12th century bronze . . .

at Agra—and this is not an isolated occurrence of architectural opulence in this land. There are rock–cut temples and architectural monuments from as early as the time of the Emperor Asoka in the third century B.C. The most admired buildings come from the era of the Hindu–Islamic synthesis beginning in the eighth century A.D. and continuing up until a few centuries ago. The *Kurb Minar* at Delhi and the *Adina Masjid* at Ahmadabad come from early in this period; the Taj Mahal, Agra Fort and Akbar's Mausoleum, the latter at Sikandra, come from later during the rule of the Moguls (15th–16th centuries). After independence, conscious attempts to create a new national architectural style achieved success in combining elements of the past and present, particularly at Chandigarh.

Painting and sculpture, especially the latter, have an ancient history in India. The stone model for the lion of the State Seal, for instance, dates from the third century B.C. But the new generation of artists is not being limited to any tradition or time; it is boldly experimenting with great freedom.

Dancing, music and drama are three arts that in India belong together. Traditionally, plays are acted in dance to the accompaniment of music. Dancing also exists separately and is a very highly developed art with elaborate symbolism.

Holidays and festivals are associated with cultural community. There are three important Hindu holidays. *Diwali*, the festival of lights, is a happy celebration commemorating the homecoming of the legendary hero Rama after he defeated the demon king Ravana. The family performs special ritual prayers in the home on this occasion. *Dussehra* has varied meanings in different parts of the country and is celebrated in various ways; in some places with great happiness, in others with more

religious ritual, while for some it ends with carefree folk dancing. *Holi* is an occasion in March for noise and fun, and usually folk songs are sung at gatherings around bonfires.

Muslims celebrate the same holidays as in other countries (see Saudi Arabia: Culture) but with local variations. In addition to the religious holidays, three secular festivals are being promoted. Republic Day is celebrated on January 26, Independence Day on August 15, and *Gandhi Jayanti* (Gandhi's birthday) on October 2.

Modern cultural forms play an important role. The movie industry produces more full length films every year (about 700) than does any other country. Because studios in Bombay traditionally dominated the industry, it became known as "Bollywood," but most movies today come from producers in southern India, in languages like Telegu and Tamil. Most Indian movies attract the entire family: they feature little violence, frequent music and dance, and exaggerated emotional attractions. But there is no obvious sexual activity, and the finish is always "happily ever-after." Stars in the industry draw huge followings, and some transfer their talents to the political stage, on occasion becoming a state's chief minister.

Exported for many years across Asia and Africa as an alternative to the culture of Hollywood, the movie industry drew additional strength from the rapid growth of cable TV in India and satellite TV around the world. Because costs of production are relatively low, foreign distribution rights alone can sometimes meet the cost of production. However, until Indian movies are filmed in English, their role in North America will typically be limited to expatriate Indians.

Television, long stagnant under a government monopoly, broke wide open with the growth of (unregulated) cable TV. Now both Indian and Western programs reach the remotest villages, brought by some 30,000-70,000 cable companies to 30 million customers, who pay modestly ($2.50-$4.00 per month) for up to 75 channels.

Independence in 1947 is a dividing line in the history of education in India. Before independence there was no attempt at mass education. Since then the government has tried to provide free and universal education through eight years of "basic school"—not the traditional and unreal book learning, but learning through activities related to the life of the child and his community. These eight elementary years provide instruction in crafts along with reading and writing. After a rapid increase in education during the 1990s, India now has less than half the world's population with no knowledge of reading and writing. Over 80% of children now complete elementary school, and two-thirds enter high school. Nevertheless, nearly half (45%) of the population remains illiterate (and 55% of women). By contrast, in China illiterates number about 15% of the population.

Secondary schools also expanded rapidly in both technical fields and preparation for university study, though India's poverty prohibits universal high school studies. There were 17 universities in 1947; by 1994 nearly 200 universities and some 7,000 colleges enrolled roughly 4.5 million students. Such numbers sometimes overwhelm the economy: India has the largest number of unemployed graduates in the world, as well as the largest number of illiterates. Moreover, higher education is a major government expense, despite budget cuts that

. . . to the most advanced 20th century rocketry

228

threaten higher fees at public schools, placing university education beyond the reach of lower–income families. Quality also remains a continuing problem.

Widespread condemnation of the Miss World contest held in Bangalore in 1996 drew attention to the position of Indian women. Traditionalists condemned beauty contests for degrading women, while feminists pointed out serious problems that women face. These begin at birth, with the killing of unwanted baby girls, and continue through childhood, when more than half of all children are malnourished. Girls typically study for fewer years than boys, and as they mature, the need to provide funds for a dowry sometimes leads to prostitution. Women rarely enjoy a healthy diet: in poor families mothers and sisters often forego food to give husbands and sons more, and 60% of women are anemic. While successful marriage may lead to joy, widowhood on occasion ends in pressures to commit suicide.

Economy: With 650,000 villages and scores of bustling cities, the economy of India is marked by contrasts greater than any other nation. It is home to humanity's greatest collection of the poor—roughly 300 million people, one–third of all those world-wide who are so impoverished that they subsist on less than $25 per month. Nevertheless, the middle class numbers about 200 million, and the number of very wealthy may exceed the number of millionaires in the United States.

The poverty is not inevitable: the land possesses good soil that is easily irrigated. Underground lie large deposits of coal, iron ore, and other minerals.

The conditions that produced modern poverty lay first in human reactions to the natural conditions. Then culture and specific government policies kept poverty in place when economic growth could have alleviated it. Regular rainfall, good soil and tropical warmth encouraged a very

large and dense population in the plains and river valleys. Society then forced the lower strata of society into poverty while some members of the nobility enjoyed vast riches. In the traditional world of religious belief and caste divisions, the mixture of poverty and riches seemed natural and inevitable. Fate, or *karma*, dictated life's difficulties. Accepting it might lead to rebirth in better circumstances.

The British conquest meant some public works and public order, along with free trade with Britain. Factory–made textiles, machinery, and other consumer goods flooded India, causing a balance of payments deficit, undercutting local craftsmen and hindering attempts to industrialize. At the same time, fewer famines and better medical knowledge helped the population grow rapidly. At independence, roughly 200 million people, half the population, lived below the poverty line.

In the first twenty–five years of independence, the number below the poverty line grew to exceed 300 million, and economists applied the term "Hindu Rate of Growth" to the economy's performance. However, the relatively slow growth resulted from conscious government choices, not culture. Impressed by Soviet achievements, Prime Minister Nehru chose to use government planning to select the industries that would grow. Then regulations limited the number of companies that could enter them. Freed from real competition at home, Indian companies lagged in their technology and efficiency, so the high tariffs and quotas were imposed to keep out foreign products. Further regulations kept the rupee far above its market value, and permitted the government to import what it desired relatively cheaply.

To complete the regulation of business, companies were not allowed to close factories or lay off large numbers of workers. For their part, farmers received subsidized fertilizers and electric power for irrigation pumps. In return they had to

deliver much of their output to government agencies at fixed prices.

Public health and other statistics give some sense of the desperate poverty of many inhabitants. Both bubonic and pneumonic plague broke out in 1994, striking initially at slums on the outskirts of cities like Surat and Bombay, where crowded immigrants live without clean water, or sanitation. By official estimates, some 30,000 tons of waste remains uncollected each day, and in rural areas only 10% of homes have a toilet or outhouse.

In the early 1990s, over 300 million people lived in households so poor no one could afford a watch, and utter poverty condemned 30% of the population to fewer than two meals per day. Nevertheless, sales of laundry detergents and cosmetics seem to be rising among those just above the poverty line, and perhaps 5–10% of the population aspires to the material luxuries common in the developed nations.

After drastic food shortages in the 1960s, great efforts were made to increase the country's agricultural production, especially grain. The record 42 million tons of rice produced in 1971 met the country's annual requirement for the first time since independence, and by the late 1970's India had become a net exporter of grain. While the Punjab boasted its best vegetable and grain production in history in 1979–1980, severe drought struck elsewhere, and it was realized that the rapidly increasing population was again straining or exceeding the country's ability to feed itself. Freeing markets in the 1990s led to still greater harvests.

For years, one potential resource remained unexploited around India. Its seas abounded in fish that an efficient industry could exploit, but the lack of processing and storage facilities, as well as poor transportation and organization allowed the fish to swim unmolested in the sea, or if caught, to go to waste. By the late 1980s, however, India had improved the industry, and ranked eighth in the world in annual fishing catch.

A diamond–finishing industry began in India in the 1960s when it was discovered that low wages for hand labor made it profitable to work imported diamonds that were discarded by the South African syndicate. An estimated 350,000 craftsmen in India now work in tiny sweatshops where they are paid by the piece. A socio–religious group, the *Palanpuri Jains* (from the former princely state of Palanpur), have established a worldwide network to market gems cut in India. The industry, based in Bombay, has continued to handle mainly budget diamonds; with lower wages, it can profitably finish stones which competing countries cannot handle. As a result, India has become the leading exporter of cut and polished diamonds, followed by Belgium and Israel.

Shanty town on a Calcutta street

During the 1980s, the economy enjoyed substantial growth, funded partly by borrowing abroad. Exports tripled while imports doubled, reducing the constant anxieties over the trade deficit. As the area irrigated rose 30% and fertilizer use increased even more rapidly, grain production increased by one–third. When officials relaxed the emphasis on heavy industry, and allowed investment in consumer goods, sales of automobiles tripled and companies producing televisions and household appliances flourished. Although slums sprouted outside cities, and inflation cut into higher wages, annual personal income rose by about 25%, the best since independence.

Unfortunately, by 1991 economic problems again loomed seriously. The budget deficit rose rapidly, fueling worries about the national debt. As foreign loans diminished, difficulties devastated trading partners such as the Soviet Union, Kuwait and Iraq. When foreign exchange reserves fell to almost nothing, imports of industrial supplies declined, and economic growth faltered.

The Rao cabinet responded to the crisis with reforms. It reduced regulation, encouraged foreign investors, and ended most industrial licensing that had handicapped Indian industry. After a decade when the country lived beyond its means by international borrowing, in 1992 Finance Minister Manmohan Singh attempted to sell state businesses, simplify taxes, and reduce them for the rich. The opposition charged that the International Monetary Fund wrote the budget, but India seemed poised, somewhat timidly, to follow the East Asian models of export–led economic prosperity.

A billion–dollar financial scam soon shook both reforms and the government. Banks had granted loans for stock market activities in exchange for fraudulent securities; payments had allegedly reached government officials. The scandal sent share prices into a deep dive, closed the Bombay Stock Exchange for a month, embarrassed several international banks, and led to the arrest of a number of important stock brokers and officials.

Despite the scandal, and the economic side effects of the communal rioting, the economy recovered. With lower inflation, higher sales to most countries, and lower tax rates, Indian and foreign companies appeared willing to consider investment. By mid–decade foreign telecommunications giants sought to compete in the newly–liberalized market for basic telephone services, while major investments in electricity and minerals seemed likely as well. As foreign investment gathered strength, a brief outbreak of the plague hurt tourism for a short period.

By 1996 India seemed poised for dramatic economic changes. Newly–permitted foreign companies expanded tele-

The Indian Institute of Science symbolizes Bangalore's long tradition of excellence in science, technology, and the arts. Today, the city's industrial skills have earned it a reputation as the Silicon Valley of India. Photo by Miller B. Spangler

phone links and constructed power plants. Spurred partly by advertising on many new TV channels, consumers sought appliances and household items. Investment by foreign companies soared, freeing Indian funds for other purposes, and exports doubled. As the growth rate of GDP reached 7%, some commentators considered India the next Asian Tiger.

However, by the end of the century it was apparent that the years of relatively rapid economic growth were producing two Indias, the rich and the poor. Surveys showed that economic growth

failed to bring much relief to those living in poverty, especially the rural poor. Over 80% of the population continued to live on less than $2.00 (U.S.) per day, at the same time as the middle and upper classes bought flashy consumer goods and speculated in India's own hi-tech stocks. While to critics this justified halting reforms, those who sought to open up the economy argued that too little reform had occurred to bring prosperity to the lower classes.

In fact, certain states and regions managed to capture most of the economic prosperity, particularly Gujarat (before its earthquake, the richest large state), Maharashtra, and Karnataka in the west and south. By contrast, stretching across the vast Ganges plain, Uttar Pradesh, Bihar and West Bengal witnessed virtually no improvement in personal incomes. Relatively rapid population growth also reduces the growth rate per capita.

Virtually all state governments operate in deficit, and as India seems poised for an economic "take-off", even the best may fail to provide the necessary infrastructure or enable private firms to do so. India lags far behind most other Asian nations in telephone lines (about 3 per 100 inhabitants) and internet use (just 5 users per 100,000 inhabitants). To provide just six telephones per 100 inhabitants will cost $60 billion; to saturate the country with lines for faxes and computers required by the flourishing software industry, far more. Although the necessary funds could come from foreign investment, after a decade of encouraging foreign firms to undertake projects, their annual investment totaled only $2 billion in 1998, far short of government plans for $10 billion, and a stark contrast with China's level of $50 billion.

Much of the investment in the 1990s took the form of large, headline-grabbing projects to meet the tremendous electricity

shortages. However, political interference and red tape deterred many investors from completing their projects. Indians still suffer frequent power cuts and voltage fluctuations that wear out motors, and in 2001 a venture by the American energy firm, Enron, went bankrupt even before the home company did because the Maharastra state government failed to pay the agreed price for electricity. In response to widespread shortages, many software firms and an increasing number of factories generate their own power.

Other problems in the electricity sector typify the challenges facing the country as it moves from socialism to greater free markets. State-owned utilities generally produce and distribute electricity. Their operations are among the least efficient in the world. State electricity boards frequently suffer power "losses" (mostly theft) of 30%; in the capital, New Delhi, losses amount to 55% of production. By contrast, the world standard is just 10%. Other challenges to an effective system include many non-metered users who pay a flat rate (perhaps 60% of all use), and politicians who promise free electricity for farmers and other special-interest groups. When the Chief Minister of Andhra Pradesh, Chandrababu Naidu, attempted to raise rates and cut losses at the state-owned electricity authority (a sum nearly double the state's spending on health and family welfare), violent riots led to deaths.

In electricity and telephones, as in much else except cable TV, government control and ownership lie at the heart of most problems. Privatization has been hesitant, partly because the law prohibits the closure of factories employing more than 100 people, and labor unions protested almost immediately when the government proposed raising the limit to 1,000 in 2001. States like Kerala have such reputations for leftist policies and militant trade unions that neither foreign nor Indian investment was significant. Nor have the heavily-populated states of Uttar Pradesh and Bihar attracted many foreign companies. Subsidies for water, electricity and cheap food consume large portions of state budgets, and reached 10% of GDP in 2000. Moves to slash them meet intense political opposition, but they devour so many resources that little is left for education, public health (800 million people do not have access to clean water), roads, or housing.

The banking sector presents major challenges all its own. The 27 government-owned (51% or more) state banks dominate the industry, thanks to government regulations that kept out private firms until the 1990s, then prohibited foreign banks from owning more than of 20% of a firm, and after liberalization in 2002 permit only a minority (49%) stake. The state banks' profits have been hampered by bad loans to failing government firms and

regulations that allow manufacturing firms to continue to operate without filing for bankruptcy. Political pressures favor, indeed, almost mandate, loans at low interest rates to farmers and other special interests. Poor management, protected by a lack of competition, accepted an enormous and often unneeded labor force concerned mostly about jobs and opposed to technological improvement. At one point, the unions forced banks to agree to computerize only one branch per firm per year. Reform of the financial sector is also a major challenge to the government.

In sharp contrast to such difficulties, the success of Indian-owned firms in the computer software industry, such as Hotmail in the U.S. and Infosys Technologies of India, illustrate the potential of the country's millions of engineers, scientists and other well-trained professionals. Software exports grew at the astounding rate of 40% - 50% *per year* in the late 1990. According to one projection the industry will employ over 2 million people by 2008, who will export products worth $50 billion, more than the country's entire exports in 2000.

For decades after independence, New Delhi's policies favored public transportation over private, with so few cars produced annually that prospective customers had to sign waiting lists years in advance of delivery. Until a joint venture with Suzuki began to produce the Maruti in the 1980s, automobile production was limited to Indian companies that produced copies of outdated European models from the 1950s. By contrast, the railway system usually carried more passengers and possibly more tonnage than any other railway in the world, and buses connect major cities. For many, though, local travel meant walking.

After Asian, European and U.S. firms set up production in the 1990s, car sales often climbed 20-50% per year and reached 500,000 in 1999-2000. The number of cars on the roads doubled in the last half of the 1990s and quickly overwhelmed the streets

and highways. The enormous task of upgrading the highways will cost at least $30 billion, with urban streets costing more. Again, besides success in software, the dominant theme in the Indian economy for the next decade will be "Infrastructure Development."

The Future: After fifty years of increasingly factional democracy, good fortune and a muting of their own political agenda in the 1999 elections brought Vajpayee and the *BJP* leadership of the strongest coalition in a decade. Vajpayee desires a strong, prosperous, and tolerant India, free from discrimination and insecurity, and able to tackle corruption while providing access to clean water, health care, education, roads and housing. He has also shed his party's initial bias against liberalizing the economy and talks of reforms to provide more jobs.

His chances of success will increase if he can control hotheads in Delhi who wish to retaliate aggressively against Pakistan over Kashmir and hotheads in Gujarat who wish to allow Hindu militants into government employment. Leading the most complex democracy in the world has become an almost impossible task, but his odds have been improved by the collapse of rival political parties.

The acceptable face of Hindu nationalism, Prime Minister Vajpayee is looking his age (late 70s), and his health may undermine his effectiveness. His heir-apparent as party leader is Lal Krishna Advani, the home minister responsible among other things for police matters. Then the *BJP* leader, Advani, attended the destruction of the mosque at Ayodhya while Atal Behari Vajpayee opposed the lawless act. Given Advani's militancy, expect the ruling coalition in New Delhi to falter if the current prime minister leaves office.

A diary farmer in Rajasthan   Source: Workd Bank photo by Ray Witlin

The Republic of the Maldives

Typical Maldivian boats known as Dhonis wait for passengers, Malé

Area: 115 sq. mi. (298 sq. km) of land, amid 34,500 sq. mi. (90,000 sq. km.) of water.

Population: 290,000 (estimated)

Capital City: Malé (population is 80,000, officially estimated).

Climate: Warm and humid. The annual rainfall is about 75 inches, mostly from May to October.

Neighboring Countries: India and Sri Lanka are the closest countries, located northeast of The Maldives.

Time Zone: GMT +5.

Official Language: Dhivehi (similar to Sinhala of Sri Lanka).

Other Principal Tongues: Arabic and English.

Ethnic Background: A mixture of Sinhalese, Indo–European, Arab and Negro.

Principal Religion: Islam. All citizens must be Muslim.

Chief Commercial Products: Fish (canned, dried and frozen); garments, boats, handicrafts. The export of many types of live fish and shells is prohibited.

Major Trading Partners: Japan, Sri Lanka, India and U.K.

Currency: Rufia (Rf 11.77 = $1 U.S.).

Former Colonial Status: Controlled by Britain (1796–1965).

Independence Day: July 26, 1965. March 29th is celebrated as Independence Day, marking the complete surrender of rights by the British in 1976.

Chief of State: Maumoon Abdul Gayoom, President.

National Flag: A green rectangle bearing a white crescent is centered on a red field.

Gross Domestic Product: $300 million (UN estimate)

GDP per capita: $1,130.

Long known to Arab seamen as "Islands of the Moon," the Maldives are a string of 26 coral atolls scattered 550 miles along the top of a submarine ridge in the Indian Ocean. These atolls contain altogether almost 2,000 picturesque islets. About 200 of the larger ones are inhabited, but few of them extend even a mile in any direction. Islands rarely reach more than six feet above high tide; neither hills nor rivers exist. However, there are abundant coconut palms, white sandy beaches, and crystal clear lagoons formed by coral reefs. With hundreds of species of tropical fish and many varieties of shells and corals, the islands rank as a diver's paradise.

Located close to the equator, the Maldives experience two monsoons each year, and average about 75 inches of rain annually. Between April and October the southwest monsoon brings rain, but the dry winds of the northeast monsoon of "winter" originate in Asia and bring fair weather from December to March.

History: Straddling the sailing route between the Red Sea and East Asia, the islands were mentioned by voyagers from Rome, Egypt and China, but scholars dispute when the first settlers arrived in the islands. Discoveries by the explorer Thor Heyerdahl suggest that early inhabitants traded with ancient Egypt and Mesopotamia. Nearly nothing is known of those inhabitants, but about 2,500 years ago settlers arrived from Sri Lanka and India. Buddhism came to dominate religious life, and over the centuries sailors from Africa

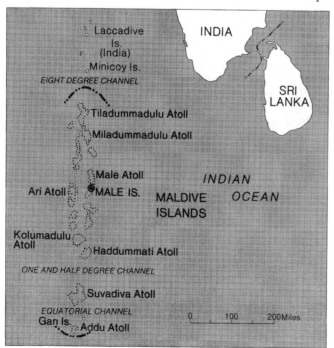

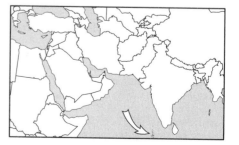

President Maumoon Abdul Gayoom

and Arabia joined the ethnic mix. Besides supplying vessels passing through, the Maldives exported vast quantities of cowrie shells, which became the currency in parts of Africa. From this trade, the islands earned the title "the money islands." In 1153 King Dovemi Kalaminja adopted Islam, a crucial event in the island's culture, and thereafter the kings became known as sultans.

During the following centuries, the islanders developed a unique unwritten constitution. It balanced the powers of monarchs with councils of nobles, and although a dynasty might last more than 150 years, a son rarely followed his father on the throne. One of the most important tasks of most sultans was defense—chroniclers recorded 13 wars against invaders.

Portugal captured the Maldives in 1558. However, fifteen years later Muhammad Thakurufaanu led a revolt against the Portuguese. In the brutal conflict that followed the occupiers were exterminated, and Muhammad Thakurufaanu won recognition as "The Great" for liberating his country, for improving the administration, and for introducing the Thaana script to write Dhivehi. Nevertheless, under most sultans the islands remained relatively weak. Pirates from South India often threatened during the northeast monsoon, and in 1752 one expedition abducted the sultan and ruled the islands briefly.

After Britain gained control of India and then Sri Lanka (1796), the dangers of pirate invasion receded. Britain itself seemed uninterested in the remote, malaria-infested islands whose chief product was dried fish. However, fearing the growing power of Indian merchants, in 1887 the Sultan sought British protection. Aside from control over foreign affairs and defense, Britain left the islanders largely to their own ways, not even posting a

resident in Malé. In 1932 a committee appointed by the sultan drafted the first written constitution. Based on both local and British traditions, it proved the first of fourteen constitutions.

With the proclamation of a republic in 1953, the Maldivians symbolically entered their modern era. Although this First Republic lasted only one year, its president, Muhammad Ameen Didi, won respect for reviving Dhivehi and its literature. He also reformed the system of education, improved the position of women, and opened government stores to undercut foreign merchants. However, Didi also introduced strict Islamic laws. Partly to reduce the drain on foreign exchange, he banned the importation and smoking of cigarettes. Thus the Maldives became the first country in this century to ban tobacco, but popular dislike of such laws, as well as Didi's increasingly autocratic rule, led to his ouster and the collapse of the republic.

In 1965 a treaty with Britain provided full independence for the Sultanate of the Maldives. In return for assistance, Britain kept the use of an airfield and a radio communications station on Gan Island in the southernmost atoll. That same year, the Maldives became the smallest nation then received into full membership of the UN. Britain formally returned Gan Island in 1976.

A constitutional change in 1968 again established a republic. The sultan retired; his prime minister, Amir Ibrahim Nasir, won the presidency. Nasir encouraged modernization and tourism. However, dissatisfaction over rising prices of fuel and other goods encouraged two unsuccessful uprisings, and sensing popular dissatisfaction, Nasir resigned in 1978.

Popular opinion favored Maumoon Abdul Gayoom, a previous cabinet minister, and a referendum approved him as president after the *Majlis* nominated him. The president serves a five-year term, and Gayoom's policies of harbor development, women's rights, and tourism helped him win reelection every five years. In 1998 he won 96% of the vote for his fifth term, again as the only candidate proposed by the *Majlis*.

Tamil mercenaries hired by disaffected Maldivians attempted a military takeover in late 1988, the first invasion in four centuries. The Maldives has no army or navy, but the small National Security Service offered sufficient resistance for President Gayoom to escape his palace and request aid from friendly countries. Within hours, Indian paratroops landed; outgunned, the mercenaries fled by boat. Pursued by the Indian navy, they eventually surrendered. The fighting left more than two dozen dead, some of them hostages, and a nation aware it must consider adopting modern defense measures, from radar and a trained fighting force to patrol vessels.

Looking toward the next century, the Maldives may need defenses against world pollution as well. If the more extreme predictions prove correct regarding a rise in sea levels from the Greenhouse Effect, the nation, whose islands generally rise only 6 feet above high tide, will almost completely disappear. Not surprisingly, the Maldives strongly supports a variety of environmental actions and agreements.

Culture: All Maldivians are Muslims, and often bear Arab names as a result. Their

Tasteful, and not too ostentatious, the home of the president in Malé

No mountains, no traffic, and short distances: no wonder they ride bicycles in Malé.

lives center around fishing, agriculture and a few light handicrafts. To a large extent the islanders follow strict Islamic standards of behavior, and laws prohibit them from drinking alcohol, Western-style dancing, pornography (possession may bring 10 years imprisonment) and extra-marital sex.

Despite geographical remoteness, few resources and relative poverty, the Maldives boast the highest literacy rate for women aged 10–45 in the Muslim world: 98%. This achievement becomes even greater considering that the English–language and modern Maldivian school systems date only to the 1960s and 1970s respectively. Not until 1979 did the government establish primary schools in every atoll, but by the late 1990s it had achieved virtually universal primary education.

For older generations, basic education took place not in a formal school, but in a Kiyavaage, a private home where children studied Dhivehi, a little arithmetic, and the Quran. Thereafter they could enter a Makthab or Madhurasaa, schools adapted from Islamic models. To date there is no institution of higher education in the country, though Islamic, teacher-training, and health institutes exist.

Strengthened by their education, women occupy a distinctive role in Maldivian society. Important even as rulers before Islam, in law and apparently in practice they enjoy equal opportunities in employment, remuneration, and cultural activities. Though respecting the stipulations of Islamic law regarding inheritance, Maldivian practice allows a woman to apply for a divorce even against her husband's desires.

Girls do marry—the minimum age is 15, and most women who do not study abroad marry as teenagers. Negotiations establish the "bride price" the groom must pay, and this is retained by the woman if the marriage breaks up. Nevertheless, the divorce rate of 59% is among the world's highest.

In recent decades, competition from foreign goods and modern factories closed some employment opportunities in traditional women's crafts (mat weaving and rope making, plus agriculture and fish processing). Today, women make important contributions in tourism, business and light industry. They manage companies, and practice law.

Though modernized and expanded both upwards and outwards onto reclaimed land, the capital city of Malé retains a number of unusual features. Its population of about 80,000 has no buses, no dogs, and not a single traffic light. With almost no crime and little entertainment over the single local TV channel, they enjoy socializing outdoors in the evening and weekends at the beach, where the women retain their modesty fully clothed. The relatively few tourists who actually linger enjoy the absence of hassle and a pleasant, laid-back atmosphere with the ocean always a few blocks away.

Economy: Lacking agricultural land, for centuries Maldivians turned to the ocean for fish and commerce. Until very recently, fishing was the principal livelihood for men, and shipments of dried and smoked tuna ("Maldive Fish") accounted for more than 90% of exports. Until the 1970s, fishing craft were small sailing boats, but a government program aided the fleet's conversion to diesel power. Modernization also took place in fish processing, with frozen and canned exports now accounting for over four–fifths of the total.

Many coconut palms and a few species of other fruit trees dot the islands, but agriculture is otherwise very limited by the few areas of fertile soil on the tiny coral islets. The government is eager to encourage light industry, but there are few natural resouces. Saudi Arabia, Japan and China have provided some foreign assistance.

Tourists began arriving in significant numbers in the 1970s, attracted by the natural beauty, easy life and cheap living. However, the islanders gain little economic benefit, and the spread of drugs, nudity and alcohol offended local society.

After President Gayoom took office in 1978, the country radically changed its approach to tourism. The jet airport opened in 1981, bringing tourists on package tours seeking relaxation, sunshine and water sports. Far different from the backpacking crowd of the 1970s, these visitors stayed on "uninhabited islands" at self-contained resorts that were taxed significantly and required to provide increasing levels of luxury. Other regulations reduced pollution, protected reefs and marine animals, and generally preserved the pristine underwater beauty for those willing to pay for it. Foreigners wishing to visit inhabited islands except the capital or a few villages on escorted trips require special permits. Resorts of varying levels of luxury now operate on about 90 islands, and spending by the 300,000 annual visitors from Europe and East Asia provides about one-quarter of GDP and a much larger proportion of government revenue.

One difficulty facing the Maldives is an adequate supply of clean fresh water despite the heavy annual rainfall. The rains do soak to fresh water aquifers underlying most islands, but unfortunately improper sewage facilities often pollute them. The islands' geography offers no convenient reservoirs or storage areas for potable water, and on Malé supplies are now obtained by reverse osmosis from sea water.

The Future: The unique culture of the Maldives, wise leadership, and its unspoiled beauty combined to encourage its commendable achievements in education, opportunities for women, and economic growth. More frequent contact with the outside world will bring socially destructive consequences as well as benefits, but the islanders seem more likely than most to preserve important values.

Beneath this very attractive exterior, a few disturbing signs exist. Some in the business community sense a need for political change. More broadly, frequent contact with the West and East, especially satellite TV, brings influences that threaten to weaken the cultural and religious heritage. The challenges ahead are not so much economic as political and social.

A Maldivian newspaper in Dhiveli

The Kingdom of Nepal

Downtown Kathmandu

Area: 54,362 square miles (141,400 sq. km.).
Population: 23 million
Capital City: Kathmandu (Pop. 1 million, estimated).
Climate: Very hot on the plain along the southern border, cooler in the hills, and frigid in the high mountains on the northern border. The plains and lower slopes have heavy rainfall during the summer monsoon season.
Neighboring Countries: China (North); India (East, South, West).
Time Zone: GMT +5 hours 40 minutes. When it is 1:00 o'clock in India, it is 1:10 o'clock in Nepal.
Official Language: Nepali (also called Gurkhali, Khaskura and Parbatia).
Other Principal Tongues: Gubhajius (Newari), Gurungkura, Hindi, Kiranti, Limbukura (Limbuani), Magarkura and Tibetan.
Ethnic Background: A mixture of peoples who long ago migrated from Central Asia (Mongolia in particular), India and Tibet. They think of themselves as belonging to distinct communities identified by language and traditions.
Principal Religions: Hinduism (about 85%) and Buddhism.
Chief Commercial Products: Woven carpets, textiles, rice, wheat, corn, millet, jute, oilseeds, cane, sugar, timber and hides.
Major Trading Partners: India (more than 50%), Japan, Germany, U.S. and Bangladesh.
Currency: Rupee. (NR 73 = $1 U.S.).
Former Colonial Status: Under limited British control, 1816–1923.
Independence Date: December 21, 1923.

Chief of State: King Gyanendra, crowned June 2001
Head of Government: Sher Bahadur Deuba, Prime Minister
National Flag: This unusual flag consists of two red triangular pennants, one above the other, each bordered in blue. In the field of the upper is a symbolic moon, while the lower bears a symbolic sun.
Gross Domestic Product: $4.9 billion
GDP per capita: $200 (IMF). Some suggest higher incomes.

Because its northern border runs along the crest of the Himalayas and its southern frontier lies on the Ganges Plain, Nepal enjoys as great a geographical diversity as can be found in any small country. From an elevation of about 600 feet in the southeast to majestic Mt. Everest's 29,028 feet is a distance of little more than 100 miles by air. The entire length of Nepal from east to west is about 500 miles; at no point is it wider than 140 miles. The strip of hot, marshy plain, averaging 30 miles wide along the southern border is called the *Tarai.* It is famed for its jungles and wild life, though it has been partly cleared; its population and agriculture reflect those found in adjacent areas of India. While the least typical of Nepal, it is the most productive.

The slopes north of the *Tarai,* known as the *Hills,* are inhabited to an elevation of about 8,000 feet and in summer used for grazing herds to about 13,000 feet. The upper limit of the *Hills* is the high mountain range called the *Snows.* Some parcels of Nepal territory lie on the northern side of the crest of the Himalayas. Tibetans live

there with their yaks and dzos (hybrids of yaks and ordinary cattle).

Another notable characteristic of the land is the pattern of rivers and streams flowing south from the High Himalayas through the *Hills* to the Ganges Plain. These rivers carved out valleys with strips of relatively flat land that can be farmed. Surrounded by high mountains, the capital, Kathmandu, lies in the Valley of Nepal, the intensively cultivated bed of an old lake lying at an elevation of 4,500 feet and occupying about 300 square miles. The Valley of Nepal gives its name to the whole country.

History: Until the 18th century there was no nation of Nepal. Each city and town formed an individual political unit, unless a ruler temporarily extended his control over neighboring areas. Many of the ruling families descended from Hindu aristocrats who had fled from Muslim rule in the Ganges Plain in the 14th Century. They and their retainers subjugated the mainly Mongol–Tibetan population and subsequently mixed with it.

A warrior named Prithwi Narayan arose among the rulers of the town of Gurkha, and gradually expanded the territory it controlled. In 1769 the Gurkhas completed conquest of the Valley of Nepal, including its main towns of Bhadgaon, Patan and Kathmandu previously ruled by a local Newari prince.

Prithwi Narayan and his immediate successors in the Shah Dynasty (which still reigns) then expanded their rule further. After invading Tibet, they were driven back in 1792 by a large Chinese army to approximately the present border and were forced for a time to pay tribute to China every five years. The Gurkha expansion to the south and west was stopped in battle (1815) by the British, who then controlled most of the Ganges Plain. British officials initially regarded the Gurkha Kingdom as merely another Indian state, like many others subject to British influence. A British resident was posted in Kathmandu, and only gradually did Nepal win separate recognition as lying outside India.

After a period of instability and factional strife under weak kings who were unable to rule firmly, a bloody massacre took place in Nepal in 1846. To quell the disturbances, a capable noble named Jang (or Jung) Bahadur seized effective power for himself. He did not depose the king, but kept him as a symbol and virtually ruled in his place. Ten years after seizing power he made his family, the Rana, the hereditary possessors of the office of Prime Minister, the office passing not necessarily to a son, but to a brother or cousin when a previous Prime Minister died. The Rana family held this office until the revolution of 1950–51.

As astute judge of Nepal's needs, Jang Bahadur sought to play China and British India against each other for the benefit of Nepal. He successfully invaded Tibet and forced it to pay tribute. Then, during the Indian Mutiny of 1857 (see Colonial India), he foresaw British victory, and so supplied Gurkha troops to fight those who had revolted. This aroused British interest in the Gurkhas as soldiers, both for their courage and for their loyalty. The tradition of recruiting Gurkhas for the armies of the British Empire began, and Britain henceforth considered Nepal as a friendly ally and favored protected state.

Until well into the twentieth century, little changed in Nepal. Isolated by mountains so great that Kathmandu had an airport before a road to the outside, the country was little touched by modern technology or modern ideas. Rana rule proved fairly uneventful except when rivalry for the office of Prime Minister led to assassination within the Rana family. Though continuing under the stabilizing influence of Britain, the country received formal independence in 1923.

Both the internal and external relationships of Nepal changed when India became independent in 1947. This meant the departure of the British, long allies of the Rana family, which ruled although the kings of the Shah family still sat on the throne. Now, however, the more aware citizens often accepted the new ideas of nationalism and liberalism being spread in India, and they detested the dictatorial methods of the Ranas. Influenced by the Indian party of the same name, activists from a number of leading families formed the *Nepali Congress* to advocate democracy under the king.

After King Tribhuvan, who had an understanding with the *Nepali Congress,* was dismissed by the Rana Prime Minister and fled to India, the *Nepali Congress* launched a revolution and gained control of parts of the country. In early 1951 a compromise agreement urged by the Indian Prime Minister established a cabinet composed of both Rana and Congress members. Under those conditions, King Tribhuvan returned Kathmandu.

By late 1951, the alliance between King and *Congress* had successfully removed the Rana family from the government. The party leader, Matrika Prasad Koirala, became Prime Minister. King Tribhuvan died in early 1955 and his son, Mahendra Bir Bikram, ascended the throne.

In elections held under the constitution issued by King Mahendra in 1959, the *Nepali Congress* won absolute control of the lower house of parliament. Bishweshwar Prasad Koirala then became prime minister in Nepal's first elected government. However, the King quickly moved to rule rather than reign. In 1960 he dismissed Koirala, suspended parliament, and formed a new cabinet under himself.

He had Koirala arrested and charged the *Nepali Congress* cabinet with corruption, inefficiency and actions against national unity. All political activity in Nepal was banned and the King became supreme. When Koirala and other *Nepali Congress* politicians were released from prison, Koirala went to India, then England, where he accused King Mahendra's government of dictatorship.

A new constitution adopted in 1962 provided for a *Rashtriya Panchayat* (National Assembly) of 125 elected and 20 appointed members from whom the King selected the Council of Ministers. Although the constitution provided for a Prime Minister, the ban on political parties remained. The King effectively ruled the country, a role fitting for the historic symbol of the nation, who was regarded by many as the incarnation of the Hindu god Vishnu.

From its first sessions in 1963, the *Rashtriya Panchayat* proved powerless. The King appointed and dismissed ministers at will. The King did assent to a land reform bill introduced in 1964 but it was not very effective, since it failed to limit the vast estates owned by a few wealthy families.

In 1966 Britain announced plans to reduce the number of Gurkhas in the British army from 14,500 to 6,000 by 1972. Nepal then began looking for alternate ways of earning foreign exchange, because the earnings these soldiers sent home was traditionally an important factor in the nation's generally impoverished economy.

The last Rana Prime Minister, Mohun (1950)

Relations with India also became entangled in domestic politics. India's annexation of Sikkim, completed in 1975, brought mass protests in Kathmandu, as many Nepalese became suspicious of India's intentions. Besides a few Chinese goods trucked across Tibet, all of Nepal's trade crosses the Indian frontier. According to the special relationship established in 1950, citizens of the two have common rights of residence and land ownership, and the two military forces will cooperate against any external threat. Not surprisingly, the Nepalese government had reasons to balance its international relations through ties with China.

King Mahendra died in 1972. His son and successor, Birendra Bir Bikram, attempted to exercise strong control and curb the movement for democracy. His firm

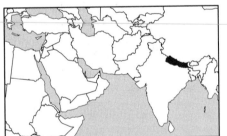

237

methods aroused resentment, however, and in 1979 educational grievances led to student protests that broadened to include political activists who called for more popular participation in government. In response, the King appointed a new prime minister, and called the first direct elections to the *Rashtriya Panchayat* in 1981.

The King still refused to allow political party designations for the candidates, an effective way of reducing the role of political parties. Similar elections were held in 1986 without party participation. Charged with mismanagement of the economy, the prime minister suffered defeat in the *Rashtriya Panchayat* in 1983, but this did not mark the beginning of democracy. Officials friendly to the King continued to fill high offices, but often resigned under suspicion of corruption.

All Nepalese suffered great economic difficulties in 1989, when India blocked most trade across the border. Isolated by geography, urban Nepalese soon found themselves desperately short of gasoline, cooking fuel, medicine and other essentials. Although China attempted to supply some fuel by road from Lhasa, in the winter heavy snows block the route across the highest mountain range in the world, and in the summer monsoon downpours threaten destructive landslides.

India claimed it acted because Nepal refused to block smuggling into India, but the move had wider purposes. In 1987 Nepal had purchased light Chinese weapons for its army, violating a long tradition of arms purchases from India. The economic pressure apparently served to remind Nepal of the importance of India's friendship.

After Indian elections, the new Indian Prime Minister, V. P. Singh, resumed talks with Nepal on new trade treaties, and soon ended the dispute. However, the hardships it inflicted on middle class Nepalese carried profound consequences. Politicians from the Congress Party joined the communist–influenced *United Left Front* in a protest movement in 1990, on the anniversary of the 1950 restoration of the monarchy.

When police repression killed many demonstrators, the shocked nation responded with a series of strikes by almost all groups: newspaper hawkers, health workers and even lawyers. After two months of protests, with the political system unsupported even by the elite, King Birendra dissolved the *Rashtriya Panchayat* and called for elections, a new constitution, and a new cabinet.

The new prime minister, Krishna Prasad Bhattarai, formed a coalition cabinet of his own *Congress Party*, the *United Left Front*, and royal nominees. Though imprisoned for 14 years for his political activities, he nevertheless calmed passions about human rights abuses and corruption by individuals close to the monarchy. Despite last-minute attempts to weaken

Funeral pyre. Women Forbids

its democratic clauses, King Birendra proclaimed the new constitution in 1990. It established multiparty democracy and an independent judiciary. It thus ended absolute rule by the Shah dynasty.

In the subsequent elections, Prime Minister Bhattarai lost his parliamentary seat in Kathmandu. However, its success among rural voters enabled *Congress* to win an absolute majority in the 205–member parliament. It formed a cabinet under Girija Prasad Koirala, a half–brother of the first post–Rana prime minister.

The Koirala cabinet faced many challenges. Sharp price increases for many essential imports stirred violent opposition, and some ministers were charged with corruption. However, the public apparently recognized that austerity was necessary, and the prime minister retained power until brought down by rivals within his own party in 1994. His nepotism made the task easier: his relatives held nearly seventy important positions.

In the election that followed, communists and leftists merged into the *Unified Marxist–Leninist Party (UML)*. Condemning the *Congress* as incompetent and corrupt, they won a plurality of 88 seats. King Birendra invited the *UML* leader, Man Mohan Adhikari, to take office with a minority government. A social democrat rather than communist, his goals included a better deal from India, free elementary schools, more funds to local governments, and tax reform. However, such changes cost much, and taxes covered only two–thirds of spending.

When other parties united to demand a confidence motion in 1995, the *UML* lost power. In the years that followed, coalition cabinets replaced each other in quick succession. Several political parties split, including the largest, the *UML*, making stable government difficult. Under the

circumstances, politics often became the search for the rewards of office rather than an opportunity to serve the public good. Disillusionment with democracy spread widely, and nations that provided foreign aid complained that progress required political stability and low corruption.

Nepal's economic growth stagnated in the 1990s, and the distribution of income became more unequal. For example, the poorest 20% of the population may receive less than 4% of national income, while the top 12% of the population own 70% of the wealth. Of more immediate concern, a stubborn Maoist rebellion broke out in poor western districts in 1996, and soon claimed hundreds of lives.

During campaigning for the 1999 elections, *Congress* stressed the need for a majority party to enable decisive action against the rebellion. Man Mohan Adhikari made similar pleas for the *UML*, even promising to live until Nepal gained a majority government. However, he died within days of the pledge, and the *UML* lost heavily. *Congress* emerged with 113 seats, a clear majority.

Krishna Prasad Bhattarai, who had led the country to democracy in 1990, now formed a cabinet and succeeded in banning the noisy and polluting three-wheeled taxis from Kathmandu, a major achievement. However, the *Congress Party* failed to avoid infighting, and within months it brought down the seventh government in six years. Girija Prasad Koirala, likewise in his 70s, returned to office, and with nearly half his party in revolt, in early 2001 formed a cabinet of 37 ministers, one-third of all the party's MPs.

Unfortunately this game of political musical chairs ignored reality. Conditions in the countryside deteriorated, strengthening the Maoist rebels. Police brutalities further discredited the regime, and the opposition *UML* organized large strikes and demonstrations to demand Koirala's resignation.

Relations with India remained frosty because Kashmiri hijackers had seized an Indian Airlines flight from Kathmandu in 2000. Condemning the poor security, India suspended flights for months, thereby inflicting havoc on the vital tourist industry. India also blocked nearly every Nepali industry that successfully exported to India under the free trade agreement.

Murder in the Royal Family

The nation was stunned to learn, in June 2001, of the murder of King Birendra, his wife, and several relatives during an evening family gathering. Crown Prince Dipendra, surviving in a coma, was declared king, but died within hours. Then Prince Gyanendra, Birendra's brother, assumed the throne, the third king in four days.

To the disbelief of many, who consider the monarch an incarnation of Vishnu and therefore a living god, official accounts blamed a drunken Prince Dipendra for the murders, carried out after a family dispute over his desire to marry an Indian princess. Unable to conceive of such behavior in the royal family, many blamed conspiracies, and riots shook Kathmandu. The nation gradually accepted King Gyanendra, and democracy proved stable. However, Crown Prince Paras Shah, the king's son, is widely disliked and blamed for excessive drinking and the accidental hit-and-run killing of a popular musician.

The first year of King Gyanendra's rule brought little joy to most of the population. Exports fell after recession abroad, and Western travelers hesitated to fly so close to Afghanistan and Kashmir, plunging thousands out of work in the vital tourist industry. *Congress* replaced the aging Prime Minister Koirala with Sher Bahadur Deuba, another veteran politician but one more capable of working with parliament. He initially arranged a ceasefire and prisoner exchange with the Maoists and later opened negotiations with them. Optimism filled the media, with headlines like "Maoists soften stand on royals."

However, the Maoists demanded—and continue to demand—three conditions in any agreement. These are abolishing the monarchy, rewriting the constitution, and establishing an interim government. Failing to achieve this, the Maoist leader, Prachanda (a name meaning "majestically terrible" adopted by Pushpa Kamal Dahal), announced the failure of negotiations. Within hours, rebels launched multiple surprise attacks across the country, killing dozens of police and soldiers, seizing weapons from depots and emptying banks of cash and valuables.

In response, the government ordered the military into the conflict and declared a state of emergency that gravely limited freedom of the press. Initial reports from the military proved enthusiastic: in contrast to the lightly armed and poorly trained police, the soldiers seemed to win clashes even in the rebels' heartland of western Nepal. However, the spread of attacks east of the capital to regions near Mt. Everest on many tourists' itineraries suggests that the rebels move around the country with some ease and that Kathmandu's estimates of rebel casualties are often far off the mark. Indeed, the military seeks supplies and equipment like helicopters from friendly states like India.

As terrorists and Maoists, the rebels hardly seem likely to win public opinion and international support (even China has condemned them). Symbolic actions like bombing the Coca Cola plant in Kathmandu may win grudging support from nationalists concerned about the popularity of expensive foreign drinks, but they discourage foreign investment. However, Prachanda and his supporters stand for more than brutalities and bloodshed. In a country with high illiteracy and 50% of the population below the poverty line, they demand education for all children (girls included) and an end to feudal land holding. Many of the fighters are female, and their women's organization presses for greater rights for women. They also demand a ban on alcohol, which they consider a serious social problem leading to violence within the home.

Behind the battle lines, rampant corruption in nearly every government activity poses another serious challenge for the longer term. It has led the World Bank and some other donors to hesitate on aid projects, reacting to the cynicism that "Governing Nepal is the art of appropriating foreign aid for personal use without getting caught."

Culture: The people of Nepal do not have a unified national spirit, because tribal identification and loyalty is still quite strong. Each group, such as the Magars, Newars or Gurkhalis has its distinctive language and customs; little social contact or intermarriage takes place between them. The Gurkhali have the most prestige; this element forms the military caste and the royal family comes from this community.

Although the predominant physical characteristic is Mongolian, showing that the population came many centuries ago from the North and East, the religion and customs belong to the South and West. Hinduism (see India: Culture) is the religion of most Nepalis; the constitution requires that the King be a Hindu and "Aryan." Hinduism is not always strictly

The late King Birendra, much loved and revered

Nepali school boys meet at Hindu Temple

observed and it has some local variations in Nepal. A few Muslims and rather more Buddhists coexist peacefully.

Dancing and singing are the principal folk entertainment. Men and women usually hold such celebrations separately; it is not uncommon for young men to dress in women's clothing for the performance of certain dances. Except for simple flutes played by herdsmen, Nepalis of noble tribes will not touch musical instruments; the lowly Damais provide musicians for celebrations. Most Nepalis are very superstitious. Beating witches and sorcerers to death is now illegal, but exorcising evil spirits from a person is still practiced. After a person has died, various rites are used to drive his spirit out of the house. Many superstitions relate to animals, such as the belief that keeping three cows is unlucky. If a farmer has four cows and one dies, he must either sell one or obtain another. Nepalis take astrology so seriously that astrologers have been jailed for suggesting that the King's fate was "under bad stars."

Isolated and impoverished by its mountains, Nepal only slowly developed modern health and educational systems. Although most boys and half the girls receive a primary education, only about 40% of adults are literate. The leading center of higher education is Tribhuvan University, established in 1959.

Economy: An agricultural country whose inhabitants live close to the subsistence level, Nepal is one of the 10 poorest countries in the world. Its per capita income ranges around $200 per year, reflecting low levels of agricultural productivity and little industry. Manufacturing concentrates on processing local produce and simple consumer goods. The leading sectors are cotton textiles, pulp and paper, and construction.

The most productive farming region is the low-lying *Tarai*, where farmers raise two successive crops in a year. Rice is grown in the wet monsoon, other grains in the drier seasons. Many valleys, some as high as 5,000 feet above sea level, are also farmed with the help of irrigation, but the uplands are used extensively for grazing livestock.

A series of plans beginning in 1956 aimed to improve farm output, expand public services and generate electricity. India financed projects such as important roads, as did the U.S., the Soviet Union, Britain, and China. The 1992–1997 Plan aimed to boost annual economic growth to 5%, provide 1.4 million new jobs, increase savings, and cut the budget deficit.

Nepal's new highways, sometimes blocked by landslides as they run through the mountainous terrain, have attracted concentrations of population along them. As the main source of energy for cooking and heating is firewood, the mountains have become denuded of trees several

miles on either side of these roads. The result is massive erosion. At the same time the women who carry the firewood in heavy baskets must climb higher and higher on the slopes to obtain their fuel.

Tourism developed at a modest rate in the 1980s but surged in the 1990s, partly because Royal Nepal Airlines now encourages charter flights directly from Europe. The income from tourism exceeds twice the amount earned from the traditional, but declining service of Gurkhas in the British army.

The next order of business is development of Nepal's hydroelectric power potential, optimistically estimated to exceed 83,000 megawatts. Only one quarter of 1% has been exploited, insufficient to supply the present needs of industry and homes. In the mid–1990s the government began to contract with foreign firms for construction of major projects worth probably $15 billion, but funding proved relatively difficult to obtain, not only because of environmental concerns. Neighboring countries sought the electricity, but within India, most state governments widely interfere with electric prices (sometimes providing it free to farmers). That combined with widespread

theft means that many states could not pay for the power they used.

The Future: A decade after the hopeful dawn of democracy in Nepal, its government seems dominated by self-serving politicians. Prosperity remains as distant as ever, while the government, riddled by corruption and factionalism, functions no more effectively than did the royal dictatorship before 1990.

But the Gurkhas and other Nepalese are tough, and the political system survived the turbulent emotional outpourings following the murder of King Birendra. Moreover, Birendra's brother and successor, King Gyanendra, had already managed to become one of the country's leading businessmen, a mark of some ability now at the very top. Finally, the older generation of *Congress* politicians, men like Koirala, Deuba, and Bhattarai, who were "twenty-somethings" when they plotted against the Rana rulers in 1950-51, are now about to pass on top party and government positions to a younger generation.

Expect change. But only after a while: the old partisans have yet to fade away completely.

"Elderly postal delivery man in Kathmandu"   Source: Mary M. Hill Forida

The Islamic Republic of Pakistan

Monumental shrine in Karachi dedicated to Mohammad Ali Jinnah, regarded as the founder of Pakistan   Photo by Ray L. Cleveland

Pakistan

Area: Some 307,000 square miles (796,000 sq. km.), including 32,358 square miles—82,806 sq. km.—of Kashmir.

Population: 134 million (pending release of 1998 census, the first in decades).

Capital City: Islamabad (Pop. 250,000, estimated).

Climate: Generally dry, except for the mountains of the northeast; very hot except for mountainous areas.

Neighboring Countries: India (Southeast), Iran (West); Afghanistan (North); China (Northeast).

Time Zone: GMT +5.

Official Language: Urdu.

Other Principal Tongues: English (as nationwide language of the educated), Sindhi, Panjabi, Lahnda, Pushtu, Baluchi, Jatki, Kashmiri and Shina.

Ethnic Background: Communities are distinguished by language and religion, but these divisions do not correspond to physical features. More than half the people are identified as Punjabis on the basis of language.

Principal Religion: Islam (about 95%), principally *Sunni*.

Chief Commercial Products: Wheat, rice, grain, tobacco, wool, animal hides, cotton products, sugar, limestone, beef, mutton, rubber products, petroleum and natural gas.

Major Trading Partners: Japan, U.S., Germany, Saudi Arabia, Hong Kong, Kuwait, Italy, France and China.

Currency: Pakistani Rupee (PR 51.90 = US $1.00).

Former Colonial Status: Part of British India (1765 to 1947).

Independence Date: August 14, 1947.

National Day: March 23, "Pakistan Day."

Chief of State: Pervez Musharraf, President; elected June 2001.

Head of Government: General Pervez Musharraf, Chief Executive (following military seizure of power in 1999).

National Flag: A large Islamic crescent and a five-pointed star in white lie within a field of green; at the pole there is a broad, vertical white stripe.

Gross Domestic Product: $ 59 billion.

GDP per capita: $400 (IMF); other estimates reach $2000.

Geographically, the heart of Pakistan is the Indus River and its tributaries that traverse a vast plain stretching from the Punjab to the coast near Karachi. Irrigation from the rivers and the system of connecting canals supports intensive farming.

Southeast of the Indus Valley, the Thar Desert extends into India. This arid waste of sand and gravel receives less than 10 inches of rain per year, and supports scattered camel-breeding tribes. West of he Indus Valley desert conditions prevail in Baluchistan, a dry mountainous region with elevations up to 11,000 feet. This

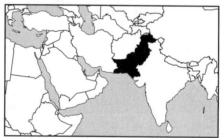

thinly populated area has some irrigation and farming, but most inhabitants are Baluchi nomads who call the region Makran.

History: Before 1947, the territory now comprising Pakistan never formed a distinct political unit. Instead, a variety of states and kingdoms ruled parts of it (see Historical Background and India: History). The Muslim League of India publicly endorsed the goal of establishing a separate state for the subcontinent's Muslims in 1940, after a decade of discussion. Leaders like Muhammad Ali Jinnah dreaded the prospect of becoming a religious minority in an independent India dominated by its Hindu majority. Staunchly opposed to Hindu rule and inclined to exaggerate its potential difficulties, separatist Muslims did not foresee the problems that partition would create.

After deciding to withdraw from the subcontinent, in early 1947 Britain approved its partition: the creation of a two

dominions, a large Hindu nation separating two Muslim areas that would form a single state. However, major problems were inevitable. Many Muslims lived in areas with a Hindu majority, outside any possible Muslim state. British-administered areas like Punjab and Bengal were divided on the basis of population, but the princely states were given the choice of which nation they wished to join. From the partition emerged the new nation of Pakistan, the "Land of the Pure," composed of West Pakistan and East Pakistan—two areas separated physically by India and Nepal (see map of India; Bangladesh was formerly East Pakistan).

With the British withdrawal rapidly nearing, Muslim leaders hastily improvised a government in Karachi, a port city near the mouth of the Indus River. Muslims elected in 1946 to draft the Indian constitution now sat in Karachi as the Constituent Assembly and legislature for Pakistan. Government offices had to be built from practically nothing. Civil servants proved scarce, though soldiers common, for Hindus had dominated the bureaucracy under British rule, just as Muslims had predominated in the army. Unfortunately, the new state soon lost its guiding personalities. Muhammad Ali Jinnah, the *Muslim League* leader who so strongly demanded partition based on religion, became the first Governor General, but died shortly after independence. Liaqat Ali Khan, the first Prime Minister and thus chief executive, was assassinated by a fanatic in 1951. Political crises and instability marked the course of life in Pakistan.

A massive two–way flight of Hindus and Muslims marked the actual partition. Pakistan lost many merchants and clerks while gaining large numbers of poor peasants. Tempers flared with the division of both Punjab and Bengal. While Mohandas Gandhi almost miraculously averted strife in Bengal, in the Punjab militants on each side massacred hundreds of thousands. A dispute over Kashmir led to conventional war (see Disputed Territories: Kashmir), because the Hindu prince of a Muslim–majority state cast its lot with India. About 1.5 million Hindus fled East Pakistan (now Bangladesh) in 1950 for West Bengal in India, while some one million Muslims went in the opposite direction. In all, over 8 million people moved from one country to another.

Many Indian politicians resented the separation of Pakistan, and strained relations between the two nations proved a recurring feature long after partition. A dispute over currency exchange (1949–1951) nearly halted trade between them and caused great economic distress. Conflicts arose over the use of water from three eastern tributaries of the Indus used for irrigation in India. In a rare diplomatic achievement, this dispute was settled by treaty in 1961 (see When Will the Taps Go Dry).

Tension also arose with Afghanistan over the old North West Frontier province (see India: Map of British India). The colonial border had divided the homeland of the Pushtu–speaking Pathans. At first, Pakistan won the favor of the Pathans by providing economic aid and allowing tribal leaders certain privileges. However, in 1954 all the old provinces of West Pakistan were united into a single province. Many Pathans resented the loss of distinct status, and separatists demanded their own land, Pakhtoonistan. Though Pakistan suppressed the movement and arrested its leader, the cause won the sympathy of Pathans in neighboring Afghanistan, where they dominated the government.

Pakistan signed an agreement with the United States for military aid in 1954. While the U.S. sought to recruit and strengthen an ally against world communism, Pakistan valued arms for possible war with nearer neighbors. Pakistan became a member first of the Southeast Asia Treaty Organization and then also of the Baghdad Pact, later reorganized as the Central Treaty Organization.

From independence to the 1990s, constitutional disputes regularly marked politics. The initial Constituent Assembly failed because its members could not determine such practical matters as whether Urdu or Bengali should be the official language. The voting strength of the Bengali—East Pakistani—members of the Assembly countered the Governor General

who was from West Pakistan. After the *Muslim League* lost public support in East Pakistan in 1954, the Governor General dissolved the Assembly for being unrepresentative. The Federal Court ruled that a new constituent assembly must be convened. It was elected indirectly from members of the disbanded provincial legislatures. Simultaneously, economic problems continued to mount, causing widespread dissatisfaction with the government.

A constitution finally took effect in 1956. By establishing the Islamic Republic of Pakistan, it ended the nation's status as a dominion of Britain. Iskander Mirza became the first president of the republic and the Constituent Assembly served as its parliament pending elections. However, the proliferation of political parties and the rapidly changing loyalties of its members prevented parliament from functioning effectively. Elections were never held under that constitution and after just two years, a military coup d'etat ended the flawed attempt at democracy.

The Ayub Khan Years

Although President Mirza officially terminated the constitution, dissolved the central and provincial parliaments and imposed martial law, the army commander, General Ayub Khan, became a virtual dictator. He soon forced the president to resign and go into exile. Ayub Khan then took the title of president.

The decade of Ayub Khan's rule witnessed a feeble attempt at representative government when he initiated a system of "indirect democracy." According to it, the general public voted for electors; in turn they selected legislators. This failed, but a later constitution provided for a strong executive. It also seemed to settle the regional rivalries by basing the federal legislature in East Pakistan, and requiring its speaker to come from a different province than the president. Islamabad would become the permanent executive capital after its construction. Bengali and Urdu were both specified as official languages. The new legislature met in 1962, martial law was lifted and Ayub Khan was sworn in as president.

Border clashes erupted with India in 1965 in the Rann ("salt flats") of Kutch near the Arabian Sea, aroused by speculation about oil deposits. An international commission settled the dispute in 1968, granting Pakistan about one fifth of the territory it claimed. Later in 1965, Pakistan supported Muslim guerrilla fighters who entered Kashmir. To sustain them, it began conventional warfare by an armored thrust aimed at cutting links between Kashmir and India (see Disputed Territories: Kashmir, and India: History). Both the invasion and Indian counterattacks failed to win much territory, and Soviet mediation produced a ceasefire

and withdrawal. However, the Kashmir dispute remained a continuing source of hostility toward India.

In the late 1960s, dissatisfaction led to riots and political unrest directed against Ayub Khan's dictatorial government. By early 1969 mob rule prevailed in many areas, particularly in East Pakistan. Clearly having lost the confidence of the people, Ayub resigned, turning the government over to General Yahya Khan. (*Khan* is a military title used by many families and does not necessarily indicate kinship).

Pakistan Falls Apart

Yahya Khan imposed martial law and restored order within days, but the same political and economic problems festered. In 1970 voters chose yet another Constituent Assembly and gave the *Awami League* of East Pakistan an absolute majority. Leaders in East Pakistan immediately saw the legal means to correct the economic and political discrimination that they believed West Pakistani governments had practiced against them.

President Yahya had not foreseen this election result and felt it threatened his power, so he postponed convening the Assembly and arrested Mujibur Rahman, the *Awami League's* leader. This triggered a predictable outpouring of long–suppressed feeling in East Pakistan and resulted in its declaration of independence in 1971 as Bangladesh.

Yahya Khan's attempt to use the army to hold the two Pakistans together resulted in the destruction of whole villages and the massacre of their inhabitants. After nearly 10 million East Pakistani refugees had fled to India, its army defeated the West Pakistani forces and secured the independence of Bangladesh. After 1971 only the previous province of West Pakistan remained in the country.

Discredited abroad by the brutality of his rule in East Pakistan and domestically by defeat, President Yahya resigned. Zulfikar Ali Bhutto, an experienced politician prominent in the later opposition to Ayub Khan, was sworn in as president.

Alternate Civilian and Military Rule

Inclined towards socialism and generally considered leftist, Bhutto immediately set out to reorganize the country both politically and economically. The pattern of his leadership resembled that of Ayub Khan. His initial popularity gave way to political struggles as economic problems kept many people dissatisfied. Business circles disliked the socialist seizure of companies, and many devout Muslims considered such actions contrary to Islam. Another constitution, in 1973, made the prime minister the chief executive and reduced the presidency to ceremonial status.

As leader of the Sindhi–based *Pakistan People's Party (PPP)*, Bhutto continued to control the country as prime minister. However, an opposition front emerged to challenge the 1977 elections, and after losing to the *PPP*, accused Bhutto's government of fraud in counting votes. Riots and demonstrations against him led to martial law in the cities.

Within weeks, however, the army chief of staff, General Muhammad Zia ul–Haq, led a military coup. He ordered the arrest of Bhutto, members of his cabinet, and some opposition politicians as well. Declaring that his purpose was "to save democracy for the nation," Zia canceled promised elections. Talk of democracy grew even more hollow when political activity was banned in 1978. The military regime ruled firmly, controlling the press tightly and executing Bhutto following a trial.

When the president's term expired in 1978, though a figurehead he refused to continue in the office until a replacement could be selected legally. The solution was simple: Zia declared himself President while continuing as "Chief Martial Law Administrator." His role as an unpopular military dictator was demonstrated again in 1979 when he again canceled elections a month before their scheduled date and banned all political activity.

The Soviet Union's military occupation of neighboring Afghanistan at the end of 1979 posed new problems but rescued Zia's regime from unpopularity at home and distaste internationally. Refugees from the brutal fighting flooded into Pakistan's border areas, burdening local society, disturbing the peace, and arousing resentment. However, the United States and conservative Arab governments thought that with Iran in revolutionary turmoil, only Pakistan remained between Soviet troops and the Indian Ocean. Weapons and economic aid consequently flowed both to the refugees and to Zia's military regime. Moreover, the military's Inter–Service Intelligence coordinated aid to the Afghan rebels, thus allowing Pakistan to foster the more militantly Islamic *mujahidin*.

During the decade of Zia's rule, Pakistan enjoyed high economic growth. Good weather produced bounteous harvests, and industry revived after the strict controls of Bhutto's leftist seizures. Thousands of Pakistanis found jobs in the Arab Gulf states, reducing unemployment and providing foreign earnings. The government benefitted from increased foreign aid.

To foster his regime's domestic legitimacy, in 1984 Zia proposed to add further Islamic features to the constitution and to ban political parties from participating in elections. A classic example of manipulation, the proposal forced Muslims to decide between their religion and political parties. The national referendum endorsed the changes, but in 1985 the voters who cast ballots for the first time in eight

years proved dissatisfied: four cabinet members failed to win Assembly seats. Zia responded by changing the constitution to permit him to override the National Assembly even after the planned end of martial law.

Though capable of manipulating the constitution, Zia was not "home free," by any means. In 1986 Benazir Bhutto, Zulfikar Ali Bhutto's daughter, returned to Pakistan from self–exile. She sought to bring down the Zia government by a campaign uniting

her deceased father's *Pakistan People's Party* and a broad opposition alliance, the *Movement for the Restoration of Democracy*. In defiance of a ban on public rallies, Miss Bhutto (though married, she retained her father's name) spoke to thousands of supporters; for this she was jailed in 1986.

By 1988 Zia faced a restive National Assembly, and he used his constitutional powers to dissolve it. He then evaded requirements for immediate elections. Before non–party elections were held,

Quality control workers inspect carpets when they come off the looms and trim excess wool

Courtesy: Caltex Petroleum Corporation

244

General Muhammad Zia ul-Haq

however, President Zia and several senior officers were killed in a military plane crash. Ghulam Ishaq Khan, a long–time civil servant, assumed the presidency. He permitted the elections to proceed, and the courts ruled that candidates could use party banners.

Amid ruthless ethnic violence, particularly murders and riots between *Sindhis* and *Muhajirs* (descendants of those who fled India for Pakistan in 1947), the *PPP* quickly became recognized as the major national party, and it struck alliances with politicians of other parties. By contrast, the *Islamic Democratic Alliance (IDA)* of the *Muslim League* and its allies appealed to conservatives. Led by Nawaz Sharif, an industrialist, it became the fierce rival of the *PPP*.

The election returns showed a divided nation. The *PPP* carried Sindh, Baluchistan, and the North-west Frontier Province, but it won only a minority of seats in Punjab. The largest party, with 93 of the 205 contested seats, it far outdistanced the *Islamic Democratic Alliance's* 54. However, in provincial elections the *IDA* gained more seats than the *PPP* in every province except Bhutto's own Sindh.

Forming a cabinet with support from local parties and independents, Bhutto lacked a majority, and she courted the military by promising to preserve the defense budget and allow generals to control Afghan policy. She won fame and good relations abroad, resulting in economic and military aid, and Pakistan rejoined the Commonwealth. Relations with India remained surprisingly calm despite the turmoil in the disputed territory of Kashmir.

In domestic politics, however, Bhutto proved ineffective and failed to achieve her goals. Open disputes flared between her and the president, and later with leading generals. With 80% of the budget assigned to the military and debt servicing, she found it impossible to undertake social initiatives that involved significant spending. Both cabinet and the *PPP*

seemed to lack vision. Instead, the struggle to maintain the coalition seemed the purpose of government. The influence of Benazir's mother and her husband's family provoked popular criticism. Relative calm in the Punjab, under control of the *IDA*, contrasted with the *PPP's* base of Sindh, where violence escalated between the native *Sindhis* and the *Muhajirs*. Hundreds died, and Karachi, the provincial capital, became an urban battlezone.

With world attention focused on Kuwait, in 1990 President Ishaq Khan dismissed Prime Minister Bhutto, constitutionally on grounds of corruption and abusing power. He also called general elections and dissolved the National Assembly and provincial legislatures.

The Success and Failure of Nawaz Sharif

Bhutto's alleged corruption and *PPP* incompetence dominated the elections. Despite official intimidation and the party's modest achievements, it won 45 seats in the National Assembly, almost all in Sindh. In contrast, the *IDA* captured 105 seats of the 207. Nawaz Sharif, head of the *Muslim League*, the largest party in the *IDA*, took office. Military rule had been avoided largely because voters chose a prime minister acceptable to the generals.

As the first industrialist and first Punjabi in the office, Prime Minister Sharif broke the tradition that reserved the chief executive's office for wealthy landowners from Sindh. Backed by a large though unsteady coalition, Sharif began to fulfill his promises to establish the Islamic *Sharia* as the highest law of the land and to deregulate the economy. The two goals sometimes proved incompatible, as newly privatized banks discovered when they attempted to charge interest, forbidden by the Quran.

Violence between ethnic and political groups remained disturbingly high, rendered bloodier by firearms diverted from Afghanistan. Under the guise of fighting widespread corruption, the government arrested political opponents, most prominently Benazir Bhutto's husband. Thousands of other *PPP* members were tortured and convicted by special anti-terrorist courts. However, corruption was not one-sided: credit cooperatives that collapsed in the Punjab had made large loans to leading *IDA* politicians.

Internationally, Pakistan increasingly became isolated from the non-Islamic world. The traditional U.S. alliance weakened after Soviet forces withdrew from Afghanistan, when the U.S. Congress responded to Pakistan's semi-secret nuclear arms program by halting all foreign aid and military supplies, including 36 F-16 fighters. Adding insult, American lawmakers continued to aid India and refused (until 1998) to return the $1.4 billion that

Pakistan had paid for the planes. Popular opinion also turned against the West during the struggle to liberate Kuwait, although Pakistani forces did participate in the coalition.

Other political crises shook the country. Violence continued in Sindh, and though reluctant to act as police, the military restored order, moving against violent factions of the *Muhajirs'* political party, the *MQM*, a member in Sharif's alliance. Sensing increasing disenchantment with the prime minister, Bhutto began a campaign of mass demonstrations to force new elections. With the *IDA* coalition weakening, Sharif adopted Islamic themes to retain popular support, such as adding an individual's religion to identity cards and adopting the death penalty for blasphemy against the Prophet Muhammad.

In 1993 Sharif proposed to alter Article 58 of the constitution, which permitted the president to dismiss the prime minister. In response, the president charged Sharif with corruption, dismissed him, and dissolved parliament pending new elections. However, the Supreme Court later ruled the president's actions illegal and reinstated Sharif. Military diplomacy then persuaded both the prime minister and the president to resign pending elections, and Moeen Qureshi, a former vice-president of the World Bank, became prime minister despite having lived abroad for decades.

Appointed chiefly to run honest elections, Qureshi inherited an economic crisis. Sharif had nearly bankrupted the country through schemes such as the "Yellow Taxis" (73,000 imported cars and vans, costing nearly $1 billion, exchanged for a deposit of 10% down). With debt payments equaling 33% of taxes and foreign reserves exhausted, the country faced bankruptcy. Qureshi introduced radical changes. He imposed taxes on agricultural incomes and wealth and ordered property assessments to ensure wealth taxes worked. He ruled that "dishonest" people

General Pervez Musharraf

could not seek election—and defined "dishonest" to include those defaulting on bank loans. Qureshi also began to investigate all sales of government land since 1985, thus threatening another frequent form of corrupt payoffs.

The *PPP* under Bhutto won a clear victory in the 1993 elections. Short of a majority, she allied with other parties to form a working coalition. Her small cabinet won respect, and she managed the election of her candidate, Farooq Leghari, as president. For the first time in the history of democratic Pakistan, the president came from the prime minister's party, thus promising to reduce partisan disputes between them.

Nevertheless, Bhutto's second term in office witnessed more challenges than success. Traditional problems worsened. War sometimes loomed over Kashmir, while violence in Karachi spiraled upward; 800 died in 1994 alone. The security forces failed to contain the violence and were linked to the intimidation and crimes committed by a faction of the splintered *MQM*. The police also acted brutally: according to Amnesty International, more than 100 people died in custody.

Perceptions of worsening corruption discredited officials and politicians generally. Myriad regulations offered great opportunities to extract bribes. Favoritism in contracts and land sales also enriched bureaucrats, but probably the most lucrative source of police and political corruption was the trade in narcotic drugs. A massive industry, its value in the underground economy equaled perhaps 25% of GDP. Initially involved in the transit of Afghan drugs, Pakistan soon became a major producer of opium, with annual output in the mid-1980s exceeding 160 tons. Successive cabinets did little but denounce the trade, and the number of local addicts soared, reaching perhaps three million, half of them heroin users.

As drug gangs added to the violence and Western nations prescribed action, Bhutto issued sweeping anti-narcotics regulations. After years of ignoring the law, some drug barons found their assets frozen or seized, heroin labs demolished, and tons of marijuana destroyed.

Three years in office seem long enough for a Pakistani prime minister to accumulate enough mistakes to justify dismissal. In 1996, after clear warnings, President Leghari dismissed his close friend and mentor, Prime Minister Bhutto, and called fresh elections. While many government failures led to the dismissal, the foremost was corruption at the top. Bhutto's husband, Asif Zardari, served as minister of investments and was widely reputed to pocket bribes. Other shortcomings included Bhutto's defiance of the Supreme Court, attacks on military intelligence—she accused it of murdering her brother—and the breakdown of law and order in Karachi. Once again, a president constitutionally dismissed a democratically elected prime minister.

The *IDA/Muslim League* triumphed in the elections that followed, and Nawaz Sharif again took office. His large majority in parliament removed the need to govern with a coalition. He set about changing the rules of Pakistani politics, beginning with a bill to keep members of parliament from switching political parties. Then parliament unanimously amended the infamous Article 58 of the constitution that allowed the president to dismiss prime ministers.

A fierce political storm followed. The chief justice and the president attempted to force Sharif from office, but his followers invaded the Supreme Court. When the army refused to proclaim martial law, Sharif triumphed and replaced both the president and the chief justice. Dominant in parliament, with a newly sympathetic Supreme Court and a friendly president unable to dismiss him, Sharif held more power than any prime minister in the nation's history.

Pakistan badly needed both political calm and wise decisions. In recession since 1996, it suffered the closing of thousands of factories and worsening unemployment. Tax avoidance intensified the budget deficit. With foreign exchange reserves particularly low, the government

---

Women in Pakistan

After Pakistan elected the first female prime minister in the Muslim world, foreigners might be forgiven for considering Pakistani women far removed from the restrictions traditional in Iran and the Arab world. Little could be farther from the truth. Women play so small a role in public life that some are literally invisible, uncounted even by the national census.

Pakistan's statistics on women portray them confined to very traditional roles. Only 10% of adult women are "economically active" or employed outside the home. Over 80% of adult women are illiterate, and in rural areas the figure exceeds 90%. Male life expectancy (52 years) exceeds that for females. Only three other countries, all in the Indian subcontinent, have shared that distinction. The ratio of women to men, the lowest in the world and dropping, is 91:100. A figure this depressed suggests that the practice of purdah, or seclusion, renders some females non-persons. It also reflects high female death rates, including at childbirth and more sinisterly the estimated 1,000 women murdered annually for allegedly bringing dishonor on their families.

Other evidence reinforces the statistical conclusions. During Zia's rule, television and the media blamed working women for the defilement of society. It became questionable for women to vote, study in classes with men, and even drive. Striking deep roots in the country, such ideas remained during the Benazir Bhutto government. It even proposed requiring women appearing on television to cover their hair.

Despite the 1973 constitutional ban on discrimination against women, later Pakistani legal practices turned strongly against female equality, especially in areas of sexuality. Adultery, defined as intercourse between two persons not married to each other, received the maximum penalty of 100 lashes for the unmarried, and death for an unfaithful spouse. More commonly, prison sentences are imposed, accounting for over three–quarters of the country's female inmates. The pregnancy of an unmarried woman, unsurprisingly, provides sufficient proof of her adultery; her male partner must be tried and charged.

Ironically, one law initiated to enhance sexual purity tends to protect rapists from full punishment. A woman's testimony of rape provides evidence of adultery if the accused is not convicted of rape. Given the risk that both male rapist and female victim may be convicted instead of adultery, unless a single woman becomes pregnant, charges of rape are unlikely. In one case, a nearly–blind servant girl charged her employer with rape. After his acquittal for lack of evidence, she was sentenced to lashes, fines, and imprisonment, but after protests by women's groups was acquitted by the Federal Sharia Court.

Though perhaps a less emotional issue, the 1984 Law of Evidence states that in financial matters, the evidence required of two men may be provided by one man and two women, thus establishing the principle of one man's testimony legally equal to that of two women.

While Westerners may find such conditions unfair, they reflect both Islamic values and the even older customs of the sub–continent. For conservative Muslims, the Quran is the literal word of God, and a country's laws must fit its prescriptions, regardless of secular values or economic harm. Perhaps the greatest challenge to such views comes from education. Here again, Pakistan ranks among the lowest in the world in the percentage of girls in elementary school. Thus the next generation's women, like those of the present, will largely define themselves in the traditional roles of housewife and mother with little freedom outside the house.

In the name of Allah, Most Gracious, Most Merciful

FOUNDED BY QUAID-I-AZAM MOHAMMAD ALI JINNAH

THE PAKISTAN TIMES

National English Daily with the largest circulation — Published simultaneously from Islamabad & Lahore

Regd. No. R-1 Vol. XLVII No. 108 | Islamabad, Thursday, May 27, 1993— Zilhaj 4, 1413 A.H. | Tele: No. 825893, 825766,Reporters 829297; Telex 54672 44811 (Times PK). Fax: 823467. Price Rs. 4.00

Pakistanis abroad hail SC verdict

NEW YORK, May 26: Pakistani immigrants hailed as historic the Supreme Court judgment reinstating the National Assembly and Prime Minister Nawaz Sharif, saying they were proud of the contribution of the country's judiciary to strengthening the democratic process, reports APP's special correspondent.

They said that the Nawaz Sharif government had worked for the betterment of the country and that it had achieved definite progress.

PM lauds role of Press

ISLAMABAD, May 26: Prime Minister Muhammad Nawaz Sharif has lauded Press for its outstanding commitment to democracy from the day of dissolution of the National Assembly till its restoration.

He was addressing a news conference at the Prime Minister Secretariat this evening.

Muhammad Nawaz Sharif thanked the Press for making his (Nawaz) cause its own cause.—PPI.

Supreme Court declares Presidential Order as *ultra vires* in a historic verdict

National Assembly, Nawaz Govt. restored

Court also dismisses review petition

By Muhammad Ilyas

ISLAMABAD, May 26: The Supreme Court of Pakistan, in a historic decision, today restored the National Assembly, the Prime Minister and his Cabinet with immediate effect.

The Court also outrightly dismissed the request on behalf of the President for suspension of the restoration order pending decision on the Review Petition which would be filed against the Court's order on Mr. Nawaz Sharif's constitutional petition.

As soon as the Court's decision became known, the corridors and vaults of the under-construction building of Supreme Court resounded with slogans of "Nawaz Sharif Zindabad" which were chanted by a large number of his supporters thronging the premises.

Mr. Shahbaz Sharif MNA, younger brother of Prime Minister Nawaz Sharif was among those present in the Courtroom when Chief Justice Dr. Nasim Hassan Shah announced the keenly awaited judgement.

(Text of SC verdict)

(See Page 5)

The National Assembly, elected in October 1990, is the 7th Assembly of Pakistan and, thanks to the Supreme Court's verdict, is the first one to be revived. Only two other Assemblies — one elected in 1962 and the other in 1970 — had their culmination under constitutional dispensation. Six Assemblies met with unnatural demise unsung and unredeemed.

In the decision arrived at by the majority of 10 to 1, the Full Bench of Supreme Court comprising 11 judges in its short order said: "... The order of the 18th April, 1993, passed by the President of Pakistan is not within the ambit of the powers conferred on the President under Article 58(2)(b) of the Constitution and other enabling powers available to him in that behalf and has, therefore, been passed without lawful authority and is of no legal effect."

The Court dismissed the Caretaker Cabinet but validated its actions and order "which were required to be done or taken for the ordinary orderly running of the State." The Court is expected to issue its detailed Judgement next week.

The Constitutional Petition of Prime Minister Nawaz Sharif had been filed directly in the Supreme court on April 25 invoking its original jurisdiction under Article 184(3) of the Constitution. The Attorney General had challenged its maintainability under that provision but the Court had deferred a decision on it and gone on to hear the main petition on merits.

In its order today, the Court held, again by majority of 10 to 1, that the petition was maintainable.

Right after Mr. Khalid Anwar, chief counsel of Mr. Nawaz Sharif had completed his reply to the Attorney General's arguments. The advocate on Record (AOR), Mr. Fazle Hussain sought the Court's permission to move what later turned out to be an application for stay of the operation of the

Continued on page 5 col. 2

Prime Minister Muhammad Nawaz Sharif prays at Faisal Masjid Wednesday after the Supreme Court restored the National Assembly as well as his government, five weeks after his sacking by President Ghulam Ishaq Khan.—AFP Photo

Chief Justice Mr. Justice Nasim Hassan Shah at the Supreme Court along with 10 other judges in Islamabad on Wednesday. **(More pictures on Pages 3,5,12)**

NA session today

ISLAMABAD, May 26: The National Assembly has been summoned to meet tomorrow (Thursday) May 27, at 5.30 p.m.

This was disclosed by the Speaker National Assembly, Mr. Gohar Ayub Khan, while talking to newsmen.

He said, "we are ready to hold the session of the assembly at any time but feel it should be held tomorrow (Thursday), at 5.30 p.m."—APP

President to respect SC judgement

ISLAMABAD, May 26: A spokesman for the Aiwan-i-Sadr has said that President Ghulam Ishaq Khan held the country's judiciary in the highest of esteem and would respect the judgement given by the Supreme Court on Wednesday in the constitutional petition of Mian Muhammad Nawaz Sharif in that spirit.

The spokesman emphasised that President Ghulam Ishaq Khan has always tried to the best of his wisdom and belief, to act in accordance with the constitution and the law which were in fact an article of faith with him.

He would continue to do so in future both as a constitutional obligation and a religious duty and in the best interest of the country's integrity, the good of the nation and the future of democracy, the spokesman added.—APP.

Pledge to work within legal framework: Cooperation of political forces sought

Nawaz vows to pursue policies with new vigour

By Maqbool Malik

ISLAMABAD, May 26: Describing the decision of the Supreme Court as historic, Prime Minister Muhammad Nawaz Sharif has vowed to work within the legal and constitutional framework and pursue his programmes with renewed vigour to propel the country out of the setbacks it had suffered in the wake of the dissolution of the National Assembly.

Addressing a crowded press conference at the Prime Minister Secretariat here Wednesday evening after the restoration of the National Assembly and his government by the Supreme Court, he observed that Pakistan suffered heavily in terms of rapid progress, foreign investment and its international image.

He asserted that his government would endeavour to bring about a new political order in the country which would be free of hypocrisy, unscrupulousness and blackmailing.

The Prime Minister urged all the political forces and their leaders including Ms. Benazir Bhutto to cooperate with his government in order to strengthen the democratic institutions, promotion of democratic norms and progress of the country.

He hoped the opposition would respond positively and said "we are beginning with a new spirit and open-mindedness."

He took critical view of the policies of the caretaker government and said it had tried to malign him and his political friends by making out baseless and unfounded charges through electronic media.

The Prime Minister went on to say that the character assassination campaign unleashed against him by the caretaker government died down in the eyes of the public as the caretaker government could not find any valid material against his government. "Had they any valid material against us, why did they not go to the courts to prove it, he questioned.

He asserted that masses did not heed the character assassination campaign launched against "me and my friends, rather they were depressed and unhappy, mourning the dissolution of the National Assembly and dismissal of my gov-

Continued on page 5 col. 2

Gen. Waheed, Admiral Saeed meet Nawaz

ISLAMABAD, May 26: Chief of Army Staff, General Abdul Waheed called on Prime Minister Muhammad Nawaz Sharif at the Prime Minister's Secretariat here today, says a handout.

He remained with the Prime Minister for some time and congratulated him on the restoration of National Assembly and his government.

Matters relating to national security also came under discussion.

Meanwhile, Chief of Naval Staff Admiral Saeed M. Khan called on Prime Minister Nawaz Sharif here at the Prime Minister Secretariat today.—APP

(Picutre on Back Page)

Nawaz offers Nawafil at Faisal Masjid with colleagues

ISLAMABAD, May 26: Prime Minister Muhammad Nawaz Sharif began his engagements by offering thanks-giving "Nawafil" at the Faisal Masjid after restoration of the National Assembly and the Cabinet on Wednesday afternoon.

He drove at the head of a big caravan of motor cars, buses and motor cycles to the imposing Faisal Masjid. Seated on passenger seat of a Pajero, he was accorded rousing ovation on his way to the Masjid.

Speaker National Assembly Mr. Gohar Ayub drove from the Supreme Court to the Parliament House, and then saw Mr. Nawaz

Continued on page 5 col. 1

Restoration of NA is historic—Gohar

ISLAMABAD, May 26: Speaker of the National Assembly, Gohar Ayub Khan Wednesday described the restoration of the National Assembly as an "historic day" and said that sovereignty has returned to where it belonged.

Talking to newsmen at his assembly chamber soon after the announcement of the decision by the Supreme Court, he said it was a tremendous day from where the true democracy will flourish.

"People who usurped the power under false interpretations of the constitution have been defeated", he added.

Responding to a question regarding the imposition of Martial Law, he said, "I don't think so, Martial Law comes only when there is an unpopular government. After all what is army. They are people in uniform. It is not a British army locked into cantonments. It is a national army".

To another question, he ruled out the possibility of declaration of emergency in the country. He said under article 232 emergency can only be enforced when there is a threat of aggression and civil disturbances go beyond the control of the authorities. That situation presently does not exist at all,. he added.

The Speaker, responding to another question said, "I am fully neutral now after the restoration of the dissolved National Assembly.

He said during the last two and a half months the President was

Continued on page 5 col: 8

Mazari thanks all those who trusted him

ISLAMABAD, May 26: Mir Balkh Sher Mazari has said that he had repeatedly declared his intention to accept the Supreme Court's verdict on the dissolution of the National Assembly without reservations and he respects the court's judgment. All those who supported and welcomed the dissolution did so in good faith and our political judgment was and will continue to be based on what we perceive as the national interest, he observed.

Mr. Mazari thanked President Ghulam Ishaq Khan for reposing confidence in him and praised the President for his services to the nation and his commitment to the constitutional democratic process.

Mr. Mazari said he was grateful to all political parties who named him as their consensus candidate for the office of caretaker prime minister. It is unprecedented that all political forces in the country united to oppose misgovernment, corruption and authoritarian tendencies and sought free and fair elections through mutual cooperation, he observed. PPI.

People distribute sweets, fire in the air

Wave of jubilation sweeps the whole country

By Syed Tanwir Hussain

ISLAMABAD, May 26: A wave of jubilation swept the whole country after the decision of Supreme Court restoring National Assembly and Nawaz Sharif government. In Rawalpindi, people came out in the streets in processions expressing their joy by firing in the air.

In Islamabad heat did not prevent people from crowding in market places after Supreme Court decision. Special supplements published by some of the newspapers were sold like hot cakes.

The crowd raised full-throat slogans hailing the decision of the Supreme Court.

"Pakistan is in safe hands and the whole nation has emerged successful from the test it had been put to by a false decision" said the Prime Minister Mohammad Nawaz Sharif while addressing the crowd which had gathered at the residence of Federal Minister for Interior, Ch. Shujat Hussain, to greet Mian Mohammad Nawaz Sharif for the restoration of National Assembly and his government by the Supreme Court on Wednesday.

The crowd was jubilant and in its enthusiasm and was chanting slogans in favour of the Prime Minister and his Government.

They did not seem to be in a speech-listening mood. Mr. Nawaz Sharif asked them to thank God for the favour Almighty Allah had bestowed upon them all.

He had arrived at the place in the evening after whirlwind tour of Islamabad city. He had left the place earlier for Faisal Masjid to offer thanks giving prayers and to visit shrine of Bari Imam. On the way he stopped frequently to exchange greetings with the people.

In the meanwhile at the residence of Ch. Shujat people had swarmed around in large number. Among them were MNAs, Ministers, Senators and other VIPs. They all were hugging one another irrespective of the fact who was Minister and who was not. Everybody seemed to be overwhelmed

Continued on page 5 col. 5

Cabinet meeting held

It is a victory for whole nation: PM

ISLAMABAD, May 26: Prime Minister Muhammad Nawaz Sharif Wednesday said his government policies were so sound that even the caretaker administration failed to find any fault with them.

Addressing a specially convened meeting of his cabinet here he said the interim administration was obliged to state that it will not abandon these policies.

He said everyone knows that we have always endeavoured to run the affairs of the government honestly and with fear of God.

He paid glowing tributes to the dignity of the judiciary. He said the real rule of law in the country has started in fact from today.

He said verdict of the judiciary is no triumph of any single individual. It is the victory of the whole nation. He said we have worked within the framework of the constitution in the past and will do so in future also.

He said he saluted the entire nation which stood like an impregnable wall from Khyber to Karachi and Balochistan.

He said the army has proved that it is a professional force and played a national role.

The Prime Minister was all praise for the national Press for siding with the truth. The Press he said played an historic role in the hour of trial which he said will be written in golden words.

He said we will take along all forces, all those who cooperated with us and those who parted ways due to some reasons. He thanked his cabinet colleagues and asked them to attend their

Continued on page 5 col. 4

We have yet to see the verdict of the people: Benazir

By Aniq Zafar

ISLAMABAD, May 26: Co-Chairperson of Pakistan People's Party (PPP) Benazir Bhutto has said "Wednesday's restoration of the National Assembly and the government is a verdict of the Supreme Court but we have yet to see the verdict of the people".

She was talking to newsmen at the airport after her arrival here on Wednesday Ms. Bhutto said that if the decision of the court is justified then what stopped them from restoring the assemblies in 1988 when Junejo's government was sacked.

Benazir Bhutto further said that decision to attend the National Assembly session on Thursday will be taken by the parliamentary party of PDA.

PPP Co-Chairperson informed that her party was in no hurry to decide about the new political strategy and consultation with party leadership will be sought to finalise the new political plan.

Later, she chaired an informal meeting of the PDA MNA's and ministers of the debunked caretaker cabinet of which PDA was a part. The meeting was participated by Malik Qasim, Maulana Kausar Niazi and Jehangir Badr who are not members of the National Assembly.

Farooq Leghari and Aftab Sherpao informed the meeting about their meeting with the President in the evening. The two PPP leaders had called on the President after the decision of the Supreme Court.

The parliamentary party decided to go ahead with the programme of holding of a public rally at Liaquat Bagh Rawalpindi. The meeting originally was planned as an election campaign rally.

The meeting was also likely to decide about the PDA MNAs' participation in the National Assembly session, although the meeting was continued well late

Continued on page 5 col. 4

PM to address nation on Friday

ISLAMABAD, May 26: Prime Minister Muhammad Nawaz Sharif will address the nation on Friday (May 28) at 7.30 p.m. on radio and television networks, said an official announcement here Wednesday evening.—APP.

A rejoinder to Gen. Gul Hassan

By Maj. Gen. (Retd) A.O. Mitha

(See Editorial Page)

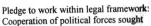

Prime Minister Muhammad Nawaz Sharif presiding over the restored cabinet meeting on Wednesday.—PT Photo by S.M. Akram

pledged to make economic reforms as a condition for loans from the International Monetary Fund. However, it falsified budget records to show that it had carried out the reforms.

Increasingly Sharif used the military where civilian officials had failed. When unpaid use reached 40% of the electricity sent through power lines, 30,000 troops searched for evidence to convict the thieves in special military courts. When Karachi's spiraling political violence claimed 600 lives in 1998, Sharif ordered military courts to render swift justice (three days maximum for trial, another three days for appeal, then execution). The carnage did decline, but civilian courts declared the courts unconstitutional.

After India's nuclear tests in 1998, intense domestic pressure built up to display Pakistan's atomic weaponry. Despite strong foreign warnings and threats of economic sanctions, Sharif ordered tests in response. Their success propelled Pakistan into the small group of nuclear powers, won great public applause, and earned sympathy in some countries for an "Islamic" bomb. However, the blasts also added to the growing discord with India, devastated the stock market, and brought foreign economic punishments. Although the prime ministers of the two countries proved very cordial when a bus route was opened between New Delhi and Lahore in 1999, their sabers also rattled when they tested medium-range missiles.

Probably because Pakistan lacked a clear understanding of the limited role of atomic weapons, Sharif and the military command approved a limited invasion of Kashmir in the late spring of 1999. In the heights far above the snowline, Pakistani troops and irregulars secretly occupied and fortified positions overlooking India's vital road to Leh. Once discovered, the invaders inflicted heavy casualties on the Indian

troops sent to evict them. However, the gamble soon turned to fiasco. Faced with losses on the battlefield and world condemnation, Sharif withdrew the troops without even gaining face-saving gesture of international talks over Kashmir.

In the months that followed the humiliating and unpopular withdrawal, Sharif showed himself incapable of governing. He failed to impose the sales taxes required by the IMF as a condition for a loan. Rampant corruption flourished, and insensitive appointments needlessly antagonized public opinion. A dirty campaign against the press led to the beating and arrest on false charges of a respected journalist. When opposition parties planned a series of rallies, the laws were changed to classify demonstrations as "terrorist acts." Literal terrorism took place in killings by Sunni and Shi'a extremists. It was the third year of his term as prime minister.

When Sharif attempted to dismiss and arrest the chief of staff, General Pervez Musharraf, a bloodless coup d'etat brought the general to power. Proclaiming a state of emergency, but not martial law, Musharraf assumed the position of chief executive. He suspended the constitution and dissolved parliament. He promised an approving nation that he would attack corruption by officials (but ignored the military officers) and make wealthy defaulters repay their loans. However, he did not promise a timetable to return to democracy, though the courts later allowed a period of three years for the military to reform society.

Inevitably, military rule widened in scope. The regime ousted the Chief Justice for refusing allegiance to the new regime and banned outdoor demonstrations. Behind scenes, it encouraged the *Muslim League* to split. However, Musharraf's authority to act also declined. He dropped a proposal to amend the blasphemy law

because Islamic groups opposed it, and he weakened the new sales tax after shopkeepers (who pay no other direct tax) went on strike. The attack on corruption by the National Accountability Bureau snared a few individuals, but moved very slowly and perhaps represents an attempt to control politicians as much as anything. Suspicions mounted that the military intelligence service (the *ISI*) really ran the country despite the formal appointment of civilian ministers and General Musharraf's assumption of the presidency in 2001.

When evidence mounted that the September 11 attacks on New York and Washington were the work of followers of the Islamic extremist Osama bin Ladin, General Musharraf found himself in a dilemma. In many ways a Pakistani creation, the *Taliban* regime in Afghanistan refused to extradite bin Ladin, thereby guaranteeing an American attack. With the only convenient access to Afghanistan across Pakistani airspace, President Bush requested permission for overflights and even use of Pakistani airbases. Thus the dilemma: Pakistan could either provide assistance to the U.S. as it attacked an Islamic ally, or defy those U.S. efforts, in the process losing any remaining international standing.

Risking both himself and his government, President Musharraf chose to support the war on terrorism, initially granting the U.S. overflights and permission to use two Pakistani airfields in emergencies. Later U.S. troops were allowed to enter the country in hot pursuit, and so-called "communications specialists" sought out suspected terrorists in the wild country of the Northwestern Frontier.

After the U.S. bombing began, Muslim extremists in Pakistan led noisy protests. The leaders of two Muslim parties, the *Jaamat-i Islami* and the *Jamiat-ul Ulema Islam* were arrested and charged with sedition for calling the regime illegal. Many foreigners left the country; some others, not so fortunate, died when suspected militants attacked a church during Sunday services.

There were fears of a possible *coup d'etat*, and Musharraf reshuffled the high command, retiring the head of the *ISI* who had sponsored the *Taliban*. The government also ordered the 20,000 Islamic schools in the country to stop any military training and to add the modern and scientific portions of the public schools' curriculum.

In December 2001, a suicide squad attacked the Indian parliament in New Delhi, aiming for high officials and killing a number of police. Again Musharraf faced a dilemma: either go to war, or accept a virtual ultimatum from India and close down militant groups fighting Indian rule over Kashmir. Again Musharraf clamped down on the militants, banning a number of groups and ordering the mass arrest of their supporters.

The war in Afghanistan had mixed effects on the Pakistani economy. Exports

Busy intersection in Karachi

Photo by Ray L. Cleveland

Mangla Dam powerhouse

WORLD BANK Photo by Tomas Sennett

suffered, due to the accompanying world recession and to the reluctance of some American companies to purchase goods from a region perceived as extremist and anti-Western. However, by joining the American coalition, Pakistan reaped significant benefits. The U.S. ended the sanctions imposed after the nuclear explosions, and provided new financial aid. Japan and the IMF did likewise. Both the Karachi stock exchange and the Pakistani rupee surged in value.

President Musharraf's personal reputation also soared. Internationally, his value in the struggle against terrorism led many to a convenient forgetting that he overthrew a democratic government. Internally, the middle classes and more secular-minded citizens saw in the clampdown on extremists an opportunity to restore law and end the sectarian and political violence that had claimed thousands of lives.

Unfortunately, the president tarnished this support by calling a referendum on his presidency, ahead of the October 2002

Baluchistan, a region inhabited mainly by tribes speaking the Buluchi language, is divided between Pakistan, Iran and Afghanistan.

249

deadline for the restoration of democracy. Given a choice to vote "Yes" or "No" on a proposal to extend reform, economic recovery, and much else by granting Musharraf a five-year term as president, some 97.5% of voters agreed. However, despite lavish government propaganda in favor of the proposal, the major political parties boycotted it, and only about half of the eligible voters cast their ballots.

Culture: Pakistan is a land of villages, and traditional landowners dominate society and government. The two cities of Karachi and Lahore best represent urban society. With nearly 12 million inhabitants, Karachi dominates the nation's business as the major port and industrial center. Karachi is hot, noisy, crowded and dusty; the poor are seen everywhere. By contrast, Lahore is a more traditional city of about three million. Like most urban areas, both cities are crowded with picturesque but tiny stores and workshops, where handicrafts are sold directly by the artists. The exception is Islamabad, the newly–constructed capital.

Life in the irrigated valley of the Indus and its tributaries is entirely different from life in the Thar Desert or the mountainous regions to the west. Despite increasing mechanization, especially in Punjab, human muscle still tackles many farm tasks, laboriously digging and repairing the irrigation canals, planting and

harvesting. In the dry areas of Pakistan camel and goat herders move continuously in search of sparse vegetation.

Though the teachings of Islam minimize class distinctions, society in Pakistan is deeply divided between a small class of wealthy landowners and millions of impoverished farm workers, some of them bonded laborers who will never escape their debts until death passes them to their children. Though the laws do not recognize a special status for the landowners, thanks to their political influence the landowners pay almost no taxes, while the urban middle classes are taxed heavily to compensate. Land reforms and the spread of education are very slowly reducing these distinctions.

For those with leisure time, soccer and cricket are popular sports. Another vestige of British rule is seen in the traffic moving on the left side of the road (as also in India and Sri Lanka).

Although it was created as a state for India's Muslims, Pakistan's early leaders avoided direct involvement in religion. However, in the mid 1970s a trend began toward enforcing Islamic practices, possibly to gain political support. Zulfikar Ali Bhutto banned alcohol and replaced Sunday (a tradition brought by Britain) with Friday as a day of rest; Sunday regained its status in 1997. For his part, General Zia announced that criminals would be flogged in public and that convicted

thieves would have their right hands cut off in accordance with Islamic law.

The fates of two boys in the mid–1990s symbolized the difficult status of human rights in the country. Sold by his parents at the age of four to serve as a bonded carpet weaver, Iqbal Masih worked in a factory, often shackled to a loom, until he was ten. His detailed accounts of life as a child slave brought international recognition in Sweden and the United States. Reebok awarded a "Youth in Action" tribute. However, he was shot dead while delivering food to a relative. Although the police reports blamed an alleged sex fiend, Iqbal had received threats. More generally, Pakistan prohibited the employment of children in 1991, but the UN Children's Fund considered the act ineffective, and some eight to ten million children work in carpet factories, small industries, domestic service and agriculture.

The second example is Salamat Masih, a fourteen–year–old Christian who received the death sentence because he allegedly wrote irreverent remarks on paper thrown into a mosque. Convicted under the blasphemy laws, he proved relatively fortunate, for he and his uncle gained asylum in Germany. A third defendant was murdered one day as he left the court, allegedly by the same *Imam* who brought the charge of blasphemy.

However, not all victims of bigotry come from the small Christian minority,

A rural scene in the Sindh area, Pakistan

WORLD BANK Photo

nor are human rights abuses merely a religious issue. *Shi'a* worshippers have been gunned down in mosques, and a mob burned alive a Muslim cleric who accidentally set a copy of the Quran on fire. Women suffer many hardships.

Several factors enhance popular concern over morality and a desire to uphold an Islamic and therefore "just" society. Corruption intensifies the appeal of fundamentalist demands for Islamic purity and justice. The struggle against Indian rule over the Muslims in Kashmir, and a variety of complaints about the U.S. and other Western powers, also strengthen the appeal of political Islam. However, rival Islamic groups also manipulate the sympathies of the population. Iran and Saudi Arabia apparently subsidize *Shi'a* and *Sunni* schools that sometimes become centers for violence within Pakistan as well as across its borders.

Perhaps ignorance strengthens the appeal of groups that preach hatred based on ethnic and religious differences. Only a minority of adults can read even the simplest documents, and given the size of its population, Pakistan spends very little on education. Some 10 million children never attend school; many others make only a brief acquaintance with book learning. Children average only 1.9 years of schooling, compared with 2.4 in India. As always, boys get much more than average; girls, less.

After Zulfikar Ali Bhutto's government seized control of private and missionary schools in 1972, quality dropped perceptibly and foreign language instruction disappeared. In response, a variety of private schools appeared, some expensive, others run cheaply by housewives in their homes. Higher education replicates the pattern, with some private colleges and universities earning excellent reputations. By contrast, the many state institutions face budgetary problems and their graduates lack respect because of widespread cheating scandals.

One novel use of the military illustrates the extent of corruption. In a two week period in early 1998, soldiers visited every reported school in Punjab, the most densely populated province. They discovered that many schools existed only on paper. Everything from teachers to exams, even repairs and sports results, had been faked. Nearly half (40%) of all teachers turned up at work only once per month, to collect their pay, which in any case hardly provided subsistence.

The most important private educational system in the country begins with rural schools and culminates in the Aga Khan University hospital and medical school. The spiritual leader of the millions of *Ismaili* Muslims scattered through some 25 countries of Asia and Africa, the Aga Khan sponsors a variety of charitable works. The *Ismailis* form one *Shi'a* portion of Islam and accept Ismail, an eighth–century descendant of the prophet, as the seventh and last *Imam* (see Iran: culture).

A Pakistani educated at Oxford made world–wide headlines in 1995. Imran Khan, captain of the country's world champion 1992 cricket team, enjoyed high society and luxury, but then he adopted traditional clothes and denounced Western immorality. Though he turned to raising funds for a cancer hospital, many saw the makings of an appealing politician free from corruption. However, his marriage to Jemima Goldsmith, half his age and the daughter of a wealthy Anglo–French financier, shook society in both Pakistan and Britain. Conservative Muslim leaders applauded the Jewish–Catholic Jemima's conversion to Islam, but wondered that none of Pakistan's 30 million single women proved worthy of him.

From 1985 until the police brutally crushed it in 1996, ethnic rivalry produced severe violence and rioting in the Sindhi cities of Karachi and Hyderabad. The antagonists were the native Sindhis and immigrants from Bihar and elsewhere in India, known as *Muhajirs* (Emigrants). Owning little land, and depending largely on their skills and earnings for survival, the *Muhajirs* resent ethnic quotas for university admission and government employment. Because neither a recent census nor elections had been held, they also feel deprived of a fair share of political power.

Economy: Since its creation in 1947, Pakistan has made progress from an exclusively agricultural economy, but agricultural products still account for about 80% of the national income.

Besides the fertile soil of the Indus basin, few natural resources exist. The limited deposits of coal and iron ore are poor quality. Only minor oil reserves have been found, but substantial natural gas fields provide energy. Therefore industrialization tended to develop around local agricultural output, particularly cotton textiles.

In recent decades a large portion of Pakistan's engineers, technicians and skilled labor found employment in the prosperous states of the Arab Gulf. They sent home valuable foreign exchange, but also created severe shortages of qualified personnel in public services. The same factor has slowed the development of industry.

Since 1955 the government has tried to develop the economy through successive five–year plans aimed at increasing both agricultural and industrial production. Farming received the greater stress because of recurring food shortages. Improved methods, more irrigation and better crop planning gradually increased production of both food and export products, but not at the planned rate.

The valley of the Indus and its main tributaries is the largest canal–irrigated area in the world. Further development is being carried forward by the Indus Basin Development Fund Agreement, supported by funds from the World Bank and several western nations. The largest irrigation projects have been the huge Mangla Dam on the Jhelum tributary and the even larger Tarbela Dam, some 200 miles to the northwest. These projects greatly increased the land under irrigation, and supply large amounts of electricity. However, because forests in the watersheds above the dams are being stripped away, the water in the rivers has become very muddy. At the present rate of silting, the Tarbela Dam will be useful for only about 50 years.

Massive floods during the 1992 monsoon season proved too great for the irrigation system to handle. Floodwater swept into the Mangla Dam reservoir too rapidly for the dam to handle. In response, engineers released vast amounts of water with little warning. Cities downstream were saved only by blasting embankments and flooding the vast plains of the Punjab. In the process, more than 2,000 people died, tens of thousands were left homeless, and the cotton crop, the basis of the country's chief exports, was partially destroyed.

Reacting against the dominance of industry by an alleged elite of "22 Families," Zulfikar Ali Bhutto—himself a wealthy landlord—nationalized most large private firms. By 1990 the government owned some 80% of industry. Ironically, when she won power, his daughter, Benazir Bhutto, attempted to privatize government firms rather than seize the remaining private ones. The process proved both difficult and slow. Pakistani businessmen learned the virtue of keeping wealth hidden, and the stock market was too small and erratic to absorb large blocks of shares in enterprises like Pakistan International Airlines and Habib Bank. Sales to foreign investors, while carrying political risks, could provide both foreign exchange and managerial skills. Most of all, though, corruption plagued all privatization attempts.

The Bhuttos owned land. By contrast, as a businessman, Nawaz Sharif naturally favored a flourishing private economy. During his first term as prime minister, the government sold some of its inefficient firms (though far fewer than promised), opened the stock markets to foreign capital, and loosened restrictions on foreign exchange. Despite her earlier threats to re–nationalize firms, in her second term Benazir Bhutto proved no discouragement to private business. Indeed, her cabinet selected 31 state enterprises to privatize in its first few months, though it accomplished little.

In the early 1990s, significant reductions in regulations over new machinery and factories encouraged private companies to invest, and Pakistani workers abroad repatriated more of their earnings. Nevertheless, the country presents many obstacles to firms. The costs of borrowing are very high, and the local market frequently proves far too small for an efficient scale of production. Heavy indirect taxation of industry, to compensate for the almost complete absence of taxes on the farming sector, means high–priced supplies, and the low level of education accounts for much of the low productivity per worker.

Only a few Pakistanis, about 1 million, pay income tax at all, and many well–to–do farmers largely escape taxation. Government revenue therefore comes from high tariffs (70% in the mid–1990s) and heavy taxes on industry. These policies discourage investment in industry by Pakistanis or foreign firms.

According to a study by the World Bank, the next twenty years will pose a great challenge to hopes of continued improvement in personal incomes. By 2010 there will be 50 million more adults of working age than in 1995, suggesting between 25 million and 40 million more job seekers. To provide so many jobs requires steady economic growth. In Pakistan's case, this is threatened by poor educational

achievements, a decrepit infrastructure, growing pollution and an investment climate marred by ethnic violence.

The Future: One shudders to think what might have happened in Pakistan had Nawaz Sharif been prime minister when the crisis over international terrorism struck in September and October 2001. Clearly any optimism about the country rests in part on confidence in a straight-forward ruler.

Nevertheless, President Musharraf remains General Musharraf, disillusioned by his country's politicians' repeated failures in office, and facing the difficult task of using dictatorial powers to create a viable democracy. Pakistan remains a feudal society where most adults can't read and write, and women matter so little that men officially outnumber them. Much of the population lives impoverished on the land, typically at the mercy of wealthy landlords who provide justice and voting instructions along with housing. These workers' jobs, and debts, are designed to trap them indefinitely. With voters like that, not surprisingly, Pakistani

democracy became a kleptocracy, the rule of thieves determined to make their fortunes before being tossed out of office. This political culture of corruption—one of the worst anywhere—threatens all institutions in the country.

The constitutional reforms proposed by Musharraf may represent the country's last chance at coherent and rational reform. Fortunately, he seems a more reasonable man than previous military dictators like General Zia ul-Haq. Expect a parliament, parties and all, and thus the trappings of democracy. However, the people's elected representatives will share political power with a National Security Council where the military will exercise pressure on the politicians.

Expect, too, the tide of Islamic militancy and fundamentalism to recede. For years it was nourished by military assistance (through the *ISI*) and by support for both the *Taliban* and Kashmiri militants. But militant leaders had predicted millions of demonstrators if the U.S. attacked Afghanistan. Events proved such threats hollow, and the government now fears them less.

Farmer inspecting a new tractor   WORLD BANK Photo

The Democratic Socialist Republic of Sri Lanka

The way home from school on a rainy afternoon

WORLD BANK photo

Area: 25,332 square miles (65,500 sq. km.).

Population: 19.8 million.

Capital City: Colombo (Pop. 1 million, estimated). Parliament now meets in Sri Jayawardene, technically a suburb.

Climate: Uniformly warm throughout the year, except for comfortably cool temperatures in the higher mountains. It rains almost continuously from May to August in the Wet Zone of the southwest; elsewhere rainfall varies unpredictably.

Neighboring Countries: At its closest, India lies some 33 miles away across the Palk Strait.

Time Zone: GMT + 6

Official Languages: Sinhala; use of Tamil is recognized by law in northern and eastern provinces.

Other Principal Tongue: English (among the educated).

Ethnic Background: The main communities identified by language and tradition are Sinhalese (73%), Tamil (19%), Moor (7%), Eurasian Burgher, and Malay.

Principal Religions: Buddhism (70%), Hinduism, Christianity, Islam.

Chief Commercial Products: Textiles and clothing, tea, rubber, rice, consumer goods, petroleum products, spices, coconuts, sugarcane, manioc and gemstones.

Major Trading Partners: U.S., U.K., Germany, Japan, India, Iraq—prewar.

Currency: Rupee (SLR 86.88 = $1 U.S.). The rate now floats.

Former Colonial Status: British Crown Colony (1802–1928); self–governing British Colony (1928–1948).

Independence Date: February 4, 1948.

Chief of State: Chandrika Kumaratunga, President.

Head of Government: Ratnasiri Wickremanayake, Prime Minister

National Flag: Centered on a dark crimson field with gold borders is a large gold lion in profile facing the pole and holding a sword in its right paw; at the pole are two vertical stripes, one of green and one of saffron, framed together in a gold border.

Gross Domestic Product: $15.6 billion

GDP per capita: $825; other estimates are higher.

The pear–shaped island of Sri Lanka, or Ceylon as it was generally known in English, lies at the southeastern tip of India. Its climate and people resemble those of the nearby regions of India, but under the influence of Buddhism it developed a distinctive culture. Until weakened by civil war in the past two decades, Sri Lanka offered the possibility of social development—good health and education—despite relatively low incomes.

Most of Sri Lanka is low, flat country, including all the northern half of the island and a coastal belt around the south end. The remaining one–fifth, lies above 2,000 feet in elevation, with mountains rising to peaks above 8,000 feet. These highlands force the humid summer monsoon winds from the southwest to rise, producing heavy rainfall in the southwestern quarter of the island and earning it the title "the wet zone" in recognition of its annual precipitation of 100–200 inches.

The rest of the island forms the dry zone, although its rainfall would be considered sufficient in cooler climates. Rain in the dry zone is unpredictable; it may be quite sudden and heavy, causing damaging floods, while much of the precious water is lost in the ocean. Precipitation in the dry zone also comes from the northeast winter monsoon. Ground water can be raised for irrigation in most of the dry zone, from Jaffne to Batticaloa. Sri Lanka's tropical climate and agriculture revolve around the seasonal pattern of rainfall rather than temperature. Wet and dry replace the familiar summer and winter of temperate climates.

The two major population groups inhabit distinctly different climate zones. The Sinhalese majority is concentrated particularly in the wet zone, while the Sri Lankan Tamils live almost exclusively in the northern and northeastern limits of the dry zone—principally on or near the Jaffne (Jaffna) Peninsula.

History: Sinhalese kings ruled from their capital at Anuradhapura in the third century B.C. when Buddhism reached Sri Lanka and gradually spread over the island. Early Buddhist culture absorbed many existing religious practices and like the Sinhalese kingdom was concentrated in the dry zone. Its advanced society skillfully designed irrigation systems and storage reservoirs to make maximum use of scarce water. By contrast, the wet zone apparently remained dense jungle. Anuradhapura remained the capital until about the 10th century A.D.; its kings repulsed adventurers from India who occasionally tried to seize the island but never succeeded in retaining it.

In the fourteenth century a Dravidian ruler from South India succeeded in establishing a Tamil kingdom at Jaffnapatam on the northern end of the island. Meanwhile, the Sinhalese kings had moved their capital south into the wet zone—when the first Europeans arrived in the early 16th century, the Sinhalese kings ruled from Kotte, near modern Colombo.

The first European sailing vessels came from Portugal and reached Ceylon in 1505 and anchored in the sheltered area of Colombo Harbor. In their search for spices, the Portuguese soon built forts and gradually began to exert authority. By the end of the 16th century the King of Portugal laid claim to all Ceylon, but the highland kingdom of Kandy maintained its independence. The cultural differences between the coastal Sinhalese ruled by Europeans and the Kandyan Sinhalese started during this period.

Merchants of the Dutch East India Company touched on the east coast early in the 17th century, and soon became rivals with the Portuguese for domination of Ceylon's trade. Gradually proving superior in both business and warfare, the Dutch

captured Colombo from its Portuguese defenders in 1656. The Kandyan king innocently hoped that the Dutch would stick to trading and recognize him as ruler of the island. Instead, they controlled Ceylon's trade by holding all the ports, and found no need to rule the interior.

The period of Dutch domination noticeably influenced the different communities of the island. Many settlers arrived from Holland and other European countries, and their descendants are now known as Burghers. From their Indonesian colonies the Dutch brought soldiers and workers. Their descendants remained Muslim—the Malay are still distinct from the earlier Muslim communities who are known as Moors, using the Portuguese term for them. In a few cases the Dutch rulers moved either Tamil or Sinhalese communities to other parts of the island.

When Holland allied with France during the Napoleonic wars in the late 18th century, Britain moved from its position in India to capture Ceylon from its Dutch rulers. A rebellion against British rule led to Ceylon's being declared a Crown Colony in 1802. The last Sinhalese king of Kandy was captured and sent as a prisoner to India in 1815.

It proved a successful colony. Plantations to raise coconuts, cotton, coffee, sugar, indigo and opium flourished by the mid–18th century. Sinhalese and Europeans shared in the coffee boom which began about 1845, though some 35 years later a plant disease ruined the industry and tea began to replace the coffee bean. When

a shortage of plantation workers developed, laborers were imported from southern India, most of them Tamils. Their descendants now form a separate community known as the Indian Tamils, and they made a strong impact on the Kandyan Sinhalese regions where the tea plantations were located.

In the latter half of the 19th century a cultural reaction developed against European ways implanted by foreign merchants and rulers. A revival of Buddhism and Hinduism began then and later strengthened in the twentieth century. Renewed interest also arose in the ancient arts and literature. These movements all encouraged national feeling by restoring attachment to the period before European domination.

British officials very slowly permitted representative government on the island. A Legislative Council established in 1833 still had a British majority after a reform in 1912, despite a campaign among educated Sri Lankans for meaningful representation. The constitution of 1931 made further improvements, including voting rights for all adults, but not for independence. The constitution of 1946, with provisions to protect the interests of Tamils and other minorities, established the legislative system that continued in effect when independence came peacefully in 1948.

Representing the Sinhala elite of the colonial period, the *United National Party (UNP)* dominated the first post–independence government. It fell in 1956 when the

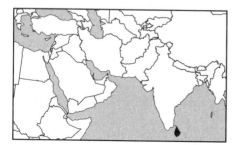

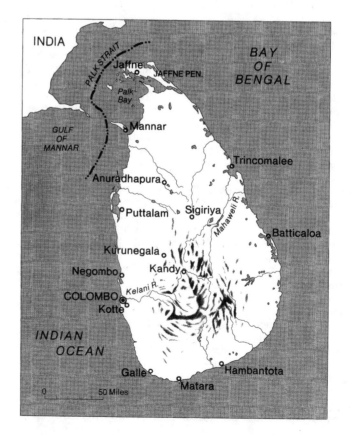

Fishermen at sea with their catamarans

rival *Sri Lanka* (Holy Ceylon) *Freedom Party*, led by Solomon Bandaranaike took power and enacted a number of reforms. However, it blundered by adopting Sinhala as the only official language and stripped English of its official status; Tamil was permitted "reasonable use." Violence immediately broke out in many Tamil areas. The party began to fall apart rapidly after the murder of Mr. Bandaranaike in 1959, but was saved by his widow—she led the party to victory at the polls and became the first woman prime minister in history.

Rivalry between the *UNP* and *Sri Lanka Freedom Party* dominated politics during the 1960s. Besides differing over the appropriate rights for Tamils, the two parties clashed over economic issues, with the *Freedom Party* typically seeking a more socialist solution. Mrs. Bandaranaike again won power in 1970, but soon faced a guerrilla uprising led by the *People's Liberation Front*, known by its Sinhala initials *JVP*. A communist group whose Maoist–influenced doctrines attracted many educated but unemployed young people, the *JVP* capitalized on the lack of economic development. With military equipment supplied by friendly foreign nations, Mrs. Bandaranaike's government was able to suppress what had developed into a violent uprising.

She also undertook several radical changes. Although a member of a high-caste family long dominant in the island's politics, she adopted socialist policies like supplying free rice that led to economic recession and shortages. Symbolically, a 1972 Constitution ended the nation's ties to the British Crown and changed its name to the Socialist Republic of Sri Lanka. The presidency became largely ceremonial,

while Mrs. Bandaranaike continued as Prime Minister.

These decisions, and her style of ruling, provoked opposition. Continued high unemployment and a declining economy, coupled with charges of mismanagement and corruption led to her electoral defeat in 1977. The *United National Party* won an overwhelming majority, and formed a government with Junius Jayewardene as Prime Minister. After parliament restored the president's wide authority, Jayewardene became president, an office he won again in 1982.

Months later, Jayewardene proposed a novel idea: to replace parliamentary elections with a referendum asking the voters' approval to extend the parliamentary term for another six years. A heated campaign followed, conducted partly by symbols. The lamp, symbol of the pro–extension viewpoint, won a modest victory, and the *UNP* maintained its solid majority without risking general elections. The president insisted it was an entirely democratic choice, while opposition parties accused him of acting as a dictator.

Ethnic Strife Rises

The worst communal violence since 1948 swept the country in mid-1983. After *Tamil Tigers* ambushed soldiers near Jaffne, Sinhalese mobs attacked Tamils in Colombo, Kandy and elsewhere. Security forces also sought revenge on Tamils. Altogether nearly 400 people died, mostly Tamils, while arson rendered some 50,000 Tamils homeless, mainly in Colombo. Calm was not restored for more than a week.

Parliament then catered to Sinhalese nationalism by banning any party that advocated separatism. This move was clearly aimed against Tamil moderates seeking autonomy, because pro–independence groups like the *Liberation Tigers of Tamil Eelam* (the *Tamil Tigers*) had already been banned. Parliament dismissed its members from the *Tamil United Liberation Front* because they would not take the new oath foreswearing separation, and so ended any effective Tamil representation in parliament. In effect, Sinhalese leaders adopted a policy of reducing tensions and violence when convenient or possible, but Tamils responded that the rift had become too wide to bridge with minor reforms.

As Tamil guerrilla activity increased, their terrorist acts were matched by massacres by undisciplined units of the army—almost entirely Sinhalese. Some Buddhist leaders abetted Sinhalese extremism. By 1985 the dispute had plunged Sri Lanka into ethnic civil war. Sinhalese leaders intended to reassert the (Sinhalese) government's rule over a united country, while many Tamils demanded their separate cultural identity in an independent Tamil state.

Trained and armed in the South Indian state of Tamil Nadu, Tamil guerrillas attacked the police, army units, and Sinhalese civilians in the north and east. The *Tamil Tigers* soon proved to be the strongest force. Headed by Velupillai Prabakharan, it defeated other Tamil militias and took control of the Jaffne Peninsula. Their ferocity and willingness enabled the *Tamil Tigers* to extend their sway over large areas. In return, the (Sinhala) army and police tended to treat all Tamils as rebels, with the result that moderate political viewpoints were extinguished.

The Indian Prime Minister, Rajiv Gandhi, attempted to make peace in 1987. He pressured President Jayewardene to accept an agreement he had apparently reached with the *Tigers*. It called for a ceasefire, the Sri Lankan army's return to barracks, and a small force of Indian peacekeeping troops to maintain order while disarming the Tamil militias. After peace was achieved, Sri Lanka would unite the northern (undoubtedly Tamil) province with the Eastern province, where Tamils, Muslims, and Sinhalese had lived in approximately equal numbers.

The agreement aroused mass opposition among the Sinhalese, who feared partition and an Indian occupation. Furthermore, the accord ignored the political interests of the non–Tamil majority in the Eastern province. The formerly communist *People's Liberation Front (JVP)* then adopted the cause of militant Sinhalese nationalism, and bloodshed spread to the south. It especially took the form of assassinations of members of Jayewardene's

United National Party. In 1988, more than 3,000 people died on the island, an increasing proportion of them Sinhalese killed by Sinhalese.

Meanwhile, the correct but strained relations between the Indian Peacekeeping Force and the *Tamil Tigers* plunged into open warfare. Acting as if they never intended to keep the agreement, the *Tigers* ceased surrendering heavy weapons and other arms, and presented additional conditions for peace. They attacked other Tamil militias, killing scores of fighters, and massacring hundreds of Sinhalese civilians living in the Eastern province.

Amid Sinhalese charges that Indian troops had failed to defend innocent civilians and enforce the accord, the Indian military mounted a major invasion of Jaffne. Although the Indian force rose to 50,000 soldiers, far outnumbering the entire Sri Lankan army of 32,000, victory proved elusive.

In an amazing feat for a nation drenched in ethnic bloodshed and facing a terrorist campaign by the *JVP* to murder voters, Sri Lanka held provincial, presidential, and parliamentary elections in 1988 and early 1989. At the age of 83, Jayewardene did not run for re–election. The *UNP* nominated the Prime Minister, Ranasinghe Premadasa, who strongly opposed the agreement with India, and Mrs. Bandaranaike again led her *Sri Lanka Freedom Party.* Despite violence by the *JVP*, including the assassination of a cabinet minister, around 55% of the electorate voted, and gave Premadasa just over 50% of the vote.

As president, Premadasa took steps to reduce tension. He ended emergency rule (among other things, it had allowed the military to bury dead civilians without an inquest) and offered to meet with both the *Tamil Tigers* and the *JVP.* He proposed a significant government subsidy to poor families, and led his party to victory in the first parliamentary elections in eleven years, gaining 125 of the 225 seats. Despite political maneuvering, Premadasa's *UNP* handily won local elections in 1991.

Nevertheless, national reconciliation proved elusive, and the generous welfare benefits promised by Premadasa threatened financial stability. With the death rate rising, the president sought an all-party conference, but the *JVP* opposed talks. Soon after this political blunder, several *JVP* leaders were killed, and the Indian troops withdrew. As causes of nationalist extremism declined, Sinhalese regions received a respite from the violence.

The cost of victory had been high. Possibly 20,000 - 50,000 people had died, many at the hands of death squads. Most victims were innocent, secretly denounced by rivals or opponents. In one case, a school principal settled grudges against 31 of his students by fabricating allegations about them to the military.

Their bodies were found years later in a mass grave.

Brutality against civilians marked the fighting in Tamil areas as well. In the north and east, warfare remained the way of life. Despite government concessions, the *Tamil Tigers* launched another offensive in 1990 that forced the army to abandon Jaffne fort and most of the peninsula. The *Tigers* attempted to offset the military's superiority in numbers and equipment with daring attacks, and increasingly depended on teenagers who entered battle with cyanide capsules, ready to prevent capture by committing suicide. In the Sinhalese heartland, the *Tigers* turned to the assassination of military commanders and politicians.

In the midst of the violence, a suicide bomber on a bicycle killed President Premadasa. A complex personality who combined authoritarianism, learning, and an insistence on getting things done, he had crushed the *JVP* and apparently hoped to negotiate with the Tamils. Although the assassination bore trademarks of the *Tigers*, including a broken cyanide capsule, many suspected retaliation for the death of a Sinhalese political rival.

Elections in 1994 confirmed that after 17 years of *UNP* rule, the voters desired a change from its authoritarian style and increasing corruption. After winning the parliamentary elections as head of the left–leaning *People's Alliance* that included the *Freedom Party;* Chandrika Kumaratunga became prime minister. A few months later, she won a smashing victory for the presidency. Mrs. Kumaratunga did not exactly come from nowhere: her mother, the elderly Sirimavo Bandaranaike, regained the office she had held in the 1970s.

During the elections, Mrs. Kumaratunga promised to investigate corruption, negotiate peace, reform the economy and replace the authoritarian presidency with parliamentary rule. As president, she

Village belle with a basket of mangoes

suspended suspicious contracts by the previous government and cut taxes on imports to reduce inflation, but failed to return executive authority to parliament. She established commissions to examine the fates of those missing from the *JVP* rebellion, and achieved an extended cease-fire with the *Tigers*.

During negotiations made possible by the cease-fire, in 1995 Mrs. Kumaratunga refused the *Tigers'* demand that the army evacuate a major military base in the north. Without warning, the *Tigers* suddenly shot down a transport aircraft and sank much of the small navy. As the war resumed, clashes soon revealed that the *Tigers* had used the cease-fire to isolate army bases along the east coast as far south as Batticaloa.

In defeat, the government purchased jets, patrol craft, and artillery from Israel, China and elsewhere, adding to a war that by 2000 rose to $1 billion annually. The better-equipped troops recaptured Jaffne city and much of the peninsula, while the *Tigers* responded with human wave attacks and truck bombs that devastated the Central Bank, the port, and other economic targets in Colombo. Another bomb exploded at the shrine housing the Buddha's tooth in Kandy. It disrupted the celebrations of the island's 50 years of independence but missed the precious relic.

President Kumaratunga simultaneously sought political peace and military victory. She proposed greater autonomy for the northeast, and won initial support from the moderate leadership of the *Tamil United Liberation Front*. They recognized that while the plan did not formally grant federalism, any greater concessions would stir fierce opposition from militant Buddhist priests and Sinhalese nationalists. However, the plan languished in parliament. More importantly, the *Tigers* rejected it.

Within the Sinhala areas, political animosities sharpened during the provincial elections in 1998-99. Opposition parties alleged vote-rigging and intimidation by the ruling party, a continuing complaint in the country's politics. However, the *Sri Lanka Freedom Party* clearly won the presidential contest in 1999, days after a suicide bomber wounded Mrs. Kumaratunga and killed twenty others at an election rally.

Despite her victory at the polls, President Kumaratunga's second term began in difficulty. Her own injuries required treatment abroad, and her aging mother's health started to fail. Sometimes neither president nor prime minister could fulfill the duties of office. Constitutional proposals to permit greater autonomy for the Tamils bogged down in discussions.

Lulled by hopes of Norwegian mediation to end the war, the military proved unready for new assaults by the *Tamil Tigers*. After first extending their control southward, in early 2000 they concentrated on

the army's large base at Elephant Pass. It dominated the southern tip of the Jaffne peninsula and the causeway linking it with the mainland. Using long range artillery, the *Tigers* shelled the camp, then advanced to capture its water supply. When the direct assault came, the garrison vastly outnumbered the attackers, but the fort fell quickly, the greatest defeat in two decades of war.

With secure access to the peninsula, the *Tigers* moved steadily towards Jaffne city and the vital airstrip. Sri Lanka appealed to India, Israel and other nations for immediate military assistance to avert the city's fall and the complete defeat of 35,000 troops. Reinforced and rearmed with advanced weapons, the military halted the *Tigers'* advance just outside Jaffne city. Later in 2000 and 2001 it undertook the slow task of regaining lost territory, against a background of cease-fires proclaimed by the *Tigers*. These probably reflected the *Tigers'* weakness in sustained conventional warfare; once again, they used young teenage draftees.

Parliamentary elections in 2000 brought the usual strident denunciations of rivals and dozens of deaths. Despite significant vote-rigging and a system of proportional representation that provided it a bonus, the *People's Alliance*, including the president's *Sri Lankan Freedom Party*, lost its majority. However, both the

President Chandrika Kumaratunga

Tamil United Liberation Front and the Muslim-dominated *National Unity Alliance* joined President Kumaratunga's coalition.

A dramatic suicide raid on Colombo's international airport and military airbase in July 2001 significantly changed the struggle. The loss of eight military aircraft greatly reduced the government's air power, and the budget could not afford

their rapid replacement. Moreover, the military proved unwilling or unable to reply with a similarly devastating attack on the *Tigers*.

By wiping out half the country's Air Lanka jetliners, the *Tigers* also created international fears about the safety of commercial property. Tourists canceled plans to visit, and some airlines halted flights to the island. Marine insurance companies imposed a war zone surcharge of roughly $500,000 per vessels entering Colombo port. Many companies suffered directly: exporters had to absorb the extra freight costs, while importers had to add the extra freight charges. Inflation rose; many employees lost their jobs at the airline, port, and in the tourist industry. The economy slumped into a severe recession.

Meanwhile, after the loss of her Muslim ally, President Kumaratunga's coalition began to collapse. Desperate for parliamentary allies, her *People's Alliance* sought to ally with the *JVP*, even paying the *JVP's* price of cutting the number of cabinet ministers in half. Predictably, this desperate attempt failed when several dismissed ministers and their supporters deserted the *People's Alliance*. Eventually this forced Kumaratunga to call new parliamentary elections.

After a vicious campaign that left 60 dead and thousands of Tamils deprived of the opportunity to vote, the *UNP* won an unexpectedly decisive victory for its platform of seeking peace and prosperity. After a brief constitutional crisis heightened by Kumaratunga's initial refusal to give up her cabinet posts, the *UNP* and its allies formed a cabinet under Ranil Wickremesinghe, "cohabiting" with a president whose party formed the parliamentary opposition.

Taking the initiative, Wickremesinghe quickly met many *Tiger* demands. After the *Tigers* announced a ceasefire, he restored trade with the north, ending an embargo that had kept even food and medicine out of the area. Norwegian mediation arranged a limited, then a "permanent" ceasefire, a detailed agreement to treat many expected problems. Then the government lifted restrictions on travel by Tamil civilians; such controls had long been used to harass them. The *Tigers* in turn opened highway A9, the route north to Jaffna.

The progress toward peace was only possible because the *Tigers* also showed signs of desiring peace, possibly a public relations gesture after Britain and Canada declared them a terrorist organization. However, talk of self-determination and a Tamil homeland replaced many calls for independence, and Velupillai Prabhakaran apologized for mistreating Muslims and expelling them from Jaffna. Peace negotiations were scheduled for Bangkok.

Another incentive for the *Tigers* to seek peace may be the harsh living conditions

Bodhisattva Avalokiteshvara, 8th–9th century A.D., gilt, bronze and crystal in the National Museum, Colombo

under their rule. Hundreds of thousands are refugees, and mines often litter their abandoned farms. Many buildings suffered greatly in the fighting and have not been repaired; some schools have neither roofs, nor windows, nor many books. Lighting is from kerosene lamps; without electricity, an entire generation is growing up today having never seen a computer or surfed the web. Truly the Tamil people of all political persuasions suffered greatly from the conflict.

Culture: Culturally, modern Sri Lanka looks in two directions for its inspiration. There are extremists who try to exclude one or the other of the two elements, but most people look both to the ancient culture and also to the technical advantages of modern industrial civilization. Examples of this dualism are found among contemporary Sri Lankan artists influenced by European masters but whose works still convey in varying degrees the uniqueness of a native tradition.

The oldest and most famous paintings in Sri Lanka are wall frescoes of maidens at Sigiriya, the palace of a fifth–century king, Kasyapa I. The palace itself lies below a rock summit, and for decades served as a monument to Sinhalese achievements. In the 1990s, archeologists discovered the full extent of the palace gardens, the largest and most complex in Asia. Given the dry climate, the gardens required a complex system of cisterns and irrigation tunnels to maintain fountains, streams and a water garden some 300 feet long.

Much earlier architectural monuments from the past impress the visitor at Anuradhapura, the Buddhist capital in the dry zone for a millennium. Enormous domes known as stupas preserved relics, and temples, and shrines were filled with stone carvings. The city's skillful engineers were masters of designing complexes of buildings complete with large bathing pools. To provide water in the dry zone, the planners laid out a series of reservoirs and aqueducts to supply not only the capital but also villages along the way. In recent years some of these water systems have been restored and put back into service with new irrigation and hydroelectric projects belonging fully to the twentieth century.

Sculpture was another ancient means of artistic expression of beauty and religious feeling, as was also the ancient Sinhala poetry. Literature also took the form of grammatical studies and philosophy. Ancient literary pieces were all written in the Sinhala language, but modern literature appears in Tamil as well, as do newspapers in both languages and English.

The native tradition in culture is prominent in education, where English is being abandoned in primary and secondary education in favor of Sinhala and

Tea pickers on a plantation near Colombo

Tamil. Besides compulsory elementary education, the University of Ceylon, complete with colleges to train both men and women for all essential professions, is another symbol of Sri Lanka's modern face. There are in addition several smaller universities.

The oil industry in the Persian Gulf, though hundreds of miles away, has had a direct impact on Sri Lanka. Traditions in the Gulf, involving Arab restrictions on female work, produced labor shortages and relatively high wages. Sri Lankans found skilled and semi–skilled jobs available. Not only did they send home remittances, they returned with new ideas. The work force in Sri Lanka became healthier, better educated and less male-dominated. A sorely needed drop in the birth rate has been evident.

Economy: During British rule, Ceylon tea became world-famous, and other plantations produced crops like rubber for export. These provided the income and foreign exchange to pay for imports of rice, other foods and manufactured goods. After independence, socialist politicians who distrusted international markets attempted to make the economy less dependent on foreign sales of tea and rubber. Farmers were encouraged to raise food crops for the local market, especially rice, which for some years was distributed free to all.

Today the country remains the world's largest exporter of tea. Hit by competition from East African producers, its share of the market is closer to one–fifth than one–half. Many of the Indian Tamils who formed the industry's workforce were gradually repatriated, and by the late 1990s plantations provided only one–third of the crop. The rest came from 500,000 small farms that sold the green leaves to processors. In the 1990s difficulties in two large export markets, Iraq and Russia, reduced sales and profits. Although the government removed the tea export tax in 1993, it appears that many processors and farmers face serious losses, given low world prices.

Replacing tea as the greatest export are garments and other textiles. Beginning with an investment promotion zone established beside the international airport in 1978, textile manufacturing has spread across the southern part of the country. Low wages and a literate, mostly female workforce have attracted foreign firms and joint ventures to the industry. Other factories now manufacture electronics components for export as well. However, in the mid-1990s workers demanded higher pay and better conditions, and struck a number of firms. Militants even held a manager hostage. This apparently surprised companies, who expected little union activity. In the words of one foreign owner, "We want the government to keep industrial peace and discipline."

Hundreds of thousands of Sri Lankan women also work abroad, chiefly as maids in Kuwait and the United Arab Emirates. When Iraq invaded Kuwait, some 100,000 Sri Lankans, the vast majority of them women, lost their employment and returned home penniless. A decade later, a limited restitution should be reaching these victims of aggression, financed by the Iraqi export of crude oil.

Despite its socialist heritage, the Kumaratunga cabinet announced its intention to privatize a number of its firms in older industries like sugar, paper, and transportation. Sri Lanka's largest single development project consisted of a series of dams on the Mahaweli River in the northeast, the country's largest. Reportely, however, construction flaws have reduced the long-term potential of the project.

With natural beauty, a warm climate and a variety of appealing sights for visitors, tourism developed rapidly in the early 1980s, bringing in about 15% of foreign earnings so badly needed for imports and development. However, because of widespread unemployment and poverty, unless tourists are carefully shepherded around, they face irritating offers and sales pitches by would-be guides and hawkers. In general, tourism is well-managed, and this accounted for much of its success, but the *JVP* attacks on the government included strikes and violence in the tourist centers, wiping out profits in the industry. The return of peace in the south encouraged tourism, with arrivals rising 250% between 1987 and 1994 to 450,000. Tourism continues to grow, despite sharp declines following Tamil suicide attacks or news of fighting at the front. Though tarnished by charges from children's rights groups, tourism plays a major role in the economy.

Before the current ethnic and political violence, Sri Lanka seemed to be showing the way to a relatively advanced quality of life without high incomes or large per–capita use of energy and natural resources. Compared to surrounding countries, the nation is well educated (85% adult literacy, over twice the rate in much richer Saudi Arabia), and its citizens enjoyed average life expectancy rates of over 65 years. They also enjoy 174 non-working days a year, the likely world record. Birth rates and death rates both ranked low, the courts and democracy muddled through, and the potential seemed to exist for a quality of life which, though not rich, allowed the simple pleasures to be enjoyed in relative security.

Ethnic violence threatens to destroy this potential on the narrowly economic as well as the broader human level. Besides its gruesome toll of dead and injured, the war costs 6% of GDP even without expensive arms purchases. Despite modest foreign assistance, the budget deficit may tempt the government to print money to pay its debts. Other economic risks include rising inflation and neglected improvements to roads, electricity and other utilities this is a country without a single expressway. Equally serious, the cumulative psychological effects of almost two decades of strife weaken Sri Lankan society. In his farewell address, President D.B. Wijetunga warned of the moral, social and ethical disintegration of the country.

Expensive arms purchases after the near-loss of Jaffne in 2000 caused substantial economic distress. Higher taxes were imposed to fund purchases of fighter aircraft and artillery, and subsidies were reduced. Some expenses were met by increasing the money supply, fueling inflation and leading to a trade deficit. In 2001 the Central Bank found itself unable to maintain the fixed change rate and simply let the rupee float. It promptly fell in value.

The Future: There is a permanent ceasefire in place, and the *Liberation Tigers of Tamil Eelam* show signs of accepting an autonomous homeland rather than independence. As a result, optimists expect steady progress in the forthcoming peace negotiations. On the other hand, pessimists remember the dictatorial style of the *Tigers'* leader, Velupillai Prabhakaran, and its patterns of terrorist assassinations after terrorist bombings.

Threats to the peace process also exist in Sinhala quarters. The *JVP* expresses a virulent nationalism that twice broke into rebellion, and the party exerts an influence beyond its numerical strength in parliament. Politicians may block concessions for petty or political reasons, and many Buddhist priests strengthen the ranks of those militants unwilling to compromise over national unity. Moreover, the population at large remains suspicious that like the four previous ceasefires, this one two will collapse.

Nevertheless, in a few short months Ranil Wickremesinghe has pulled the country out of the stagnation of a no-win war. No doubt some militants on both sides would prefer him dead to successful. Given a chance, he could bring a very decentralized Sri Lanka the prosperity so long postponed.

A fisherman's catch

WORLD BANK Photo

260

Dependency of Britain

British Indian Ocean Territory

Area: About 22 square miles (57 sq. km.).
Population: No permanent inhabitants, only military personnel.

The British Indian Ocean Territory (BIOT) consists solely of the Chagos Archipelago, which is situated midway between the east coast of Africa and Indonesia on the same underwater ridge as the Maldive Islands and just over 200 miles south of Gan. Until BIOT was organized in 1965, the Chagos Group was a dependency of Mauritius, which was offered some $8.5 million in compensation for the loss. At the same time, three other island groups far to the west with little or no population—Aldabra Islands, Farquhar Group and Iles Desroches—were separated from the administration of the Seychelles (see Dostert, Africa) and put in BIOT, which was created to provide sites for British and American military installations safe from the nationalistic sentiments of independent states.

Britain first considered the use of Aldabra for a military base, but these islands, among the last places on earth almost entirely unaffected by human settlement, contain rare birds and giant tortoises, as well as unique species of invertebrates. A determined "Save Aldabra" campaign led by the Royal Society of Britain, the Smithsonian Institution and the National Academy of Sciences (U.S.), supported by scientists and naturalists everywhere, resulted rather in the leasing of Aldabra to the Royal Society as a wildlife sanctuary. Then control of these three islands groups was returned to the Seychelles when its independence was gained in 1976.

In 1966 the U.S. and Britain signed a 50-year agreement for the use of Diego Garcia, the largest atoll in the Chagos group, as a joint base. The 1,800 inhabitants of this archipelago, the wettest coral isles in the Indian Ocean with some 145 inches of rain a year, were removed by Britain to Mauritius and the Seychelles. In 1971 the U.S. Navy began construction of a jet landing strip and a communications center. Later, the lagoon was dredged for use as an anchorage, fuel storage capacity was increased and the runway was lengthened. By 1988 Diego Garcia had become a major permanent U.S. base, the only one between Italy and the Philippines. Nuclear submarines can be supplied there, while warehouse ships moored in the lagoon stock enough weapons and provisions for an amphibious Marine brigade. Transient Filipino workers have been imported, as Mauritius, which claims sovereignty, withdrew its nationals working there in 1983 in support of the idea of making the Indian Ocean a "zone of peace" and keeping big-power military rivalry out.

After three decades of life in Mauritius and elsewhere, in late 2000 the Chagos islanders won an appeal to the High Court in Britain that restored the islands to them. Arguing that they have not adapted successfully to living in other locations and suffer widespread poverty and distress, the islanders insist on the right of return to Diego Garcia itself. Mauritius likewise demands sovereignty over the islands. However, returning the island to its inhabitants would violate the treaty between the Great Britain and the U.S., and Diego Garcia is the only U.S. base in the Indian Ocean. It proved vital for B-52 bombers during the 1991 Gulf War.

Occupied Territories

Quneitra District "Golan Heights"

Area: About 450 square miles (1,165 sq. km.)
Population: 10,000 Syrians, most of them Druze, plus 12,000 Israeli settlers (estimated).

During the 1967 Arab-Israeli War, Israel seized the southwestern portion of Syria, including its administrative center, Quneitra (or Qunaytra). For two decades the plateau provided tactical military advantages for the Syrian military, who had on occasion shelled Israeli settlements from the heights overlooking the Jordan Valley and Lake Tiberias. As Syrian troops retreated, Israeli forces rapidly occupied Quneitra district, which became known as the Golan Heights, the Hebrew term similar to the Arabic "Jolan" or "Jawlan."

Jolan has good rainfall, especially in the northern part, near the high mountains. Much of it is satisfactory agricultural land, though broken and stony, especially to the north, where the terrain is suitable for little more than pasturage. In addition to the Semitic tribes which had grazed their flocks in Jolan since late Roman Empire times, Shi'a and Druze villagers had established themselves on the flanks of Jabal as-Shaykh (Mount Hermon) by modern times. The main town of Quneitra was largely deserted through the first part of the 19th century, but was revived, beginning in 1873, by Chechen and Cherkes (more commonly known as "Circassian") refugees from the Caucasus Mountains after the Russian Empire imposed its rule on their homeland there.

In the population mosaic of the Golan—typical of many parts of Syria in 1967—there were besides the Druze, Shi'a, Circassian and Arab tribes, also some Turkomans and a sprinkling of Kurds and other scattered minorities. All used Arabic in education and outside their own communities. In the fury of the Israeli invasion, thousands of these peaceful Syrian citizens fled battle scenes, while others were expelled by Israeli troops.

For reasons presumably related to Druze loyalty in Israel, the Israelis permitted only Druze villagers to resume life in the occupied zone; the Circassian, Arab and other inhabitants of the district became displaced persons, mostly around Damascus. During the 1973 October War, Syrian tank and infantry units pushed into the zone, but were eventually thrown back, and Israeli forces advanced close to Damascus. However, the greatest destruction to the town of Quneitra occurred not during warfare, but when the Israel military deliberately ransacked and destroyed buildings, including mosques and a church, before returning them to Syria according to ceasefire agreements.

By 1988 more than a score of Israeli settlements, most of the communal type (kibbutzim) had been founded in Jolan on lands owned by displaced Syrians. Some of these settlements are right on the narrow buffer zone, patrolled by UN observers, separating Israeli and Syrian troops. This is curious, because one of the excuses for invading and holding Jolan was to prevent Syrian artillery from shelling Israeli settlements to the southwest, but shortly after the occupation began, Israeli settlements were built within easy range of Syrian guns.

The Israeli officials who allowed the Druze to remain in Jolan may have been surprised to discover that these Druze were also Syrian Arabs who would not docilely cooperate with Israeli policies. They have protested Israeli economic measures affecting them, including high taxation without corresponding benefits. They have protested restrictions on their freedom of movement from village to village. In an attempt to disrupt them, the Israeli army has at times imposed long curfews to prevent them from carrying out their work; at other times demonstrations were forcefully broken up in confrontations where some were shot to death. When they were told they must have

Israeli identity cards in order to leave their villages for any purpose, as this would have been recognition of the permanency of the occupation, they refused. After long curfews and other measures they succeeded in having the regulation relaxed.

These Druze are in a difficult position. They are obliged to cooperate to some extent with the occupation in order to survive, but not too much, lest if returned to Syrian control they might be considered collaborators.

In 1981 Israeli law was extended over occupied Jolan, and the area was added as a sub–district to the Northern District, one of the six administrative units into which the State of Israel is divided. This act, tantamount to an annexation, was denounced by the UN. Successive attempts to negotiate peace between Israel and Syria have floundered over Syria's demand for a complete Israeli withdrawal and Israel's refusal to do so.

East Jerusalem

Area: 68 square miles (175 sq. km.) form the proposed international zone recommended by the U.N. in 1947.

Population: Nearly 140,000 Muslim and Christian Palestinians, as well as a varying number of foreign residents, mostly associated with church institutions. The number of Israelis living in East Jerusalem is small but growing.

The status of the city of Jerusalem has become a signal part of the strife in the Holy Land. Old Jerusalem, with its numerous shrines, archaic buildings, narrow streets and picturesque walls (last rebuilt in the Ottoman Period), has special significance to Jews, Christians and Muslims. Because of the city's sanctity, observers sometimes overlook the non–religious factors, such as political and economic considerations involved in the present contest for control of the city.

After many generations of relatively little alteration, the 20th century brought massive changes to the city. As the British administrative center of Palestine under a League of Nations Mandate, Jerusalem saw a new city growing up to the west and north of the walled city. The new city, mostly developed for Jewish immigrants, also had modern Arab areas. Then in the plan for partition of Palestine recommended by the General Assembly of the UN in November 1947, Jerusalem was given a separate status. The plan proposed an internationally administered zone of 68 square miles, including all of Jerusalem, the town of Bethlehem to the south, and a number of nearby Arab villages. This plan, however, was not implemented by the UN Security Council and the issue was the subject of an armed contest in 1948.

When an armistice agreement was signed in 1949, the new State of Israel held the western part of the city, from which thousands of Muslim and Christian Palestinians had been forced to flee, while the Kingdom of Jordan held the remainder, including Old Jerusalem, from which several hundred Jews had been safely removed under the auspices of the International Red Cross. The proposed Jerusalem International Zone was ignored in fact— except by foreign governments, as a diplomatic nicety.

Besides forcing both Jews and Arabs from their homes, the armistice divided the city and deprived Jews of all nationalities visiting privileges to their holy places in the Jordanian sector. Two separate cities in fact came into existence, each with its own character and economy, sharing nothing except a name. Jordanian–ruled Jerusalem (Arabic "al-Quds") was conservative and native Arab in character; Israeli Jerusalem was essentially modern European. Psychologically and socially the two cities could have been more than a thousand miles apart.

As a result of the war between Israel and neighboring Arab states in 1967, Israeli military occupation was imposed on Arab Jerusalem. East Jerusalem, as it came to be known, was joined to the municipality of the Israeli city. Israeli authorities then worked systematically to absorb the former Jordanian sector into the large Israeli city, disregarding entirely UN demands that Israel refrain from annexation of East Jerusalem.

Since its conquest of East Jerusalem, Israel has rapidly moved ahead to develop the city as part of its national territory. Homes for Israelis have been built on land seized for development, private buildings have been torn down to make way for public projects and Arab Jerusalemites who fled in 1967 have not been permitted to return to their homes. A number of prominent Arabs accused of resisting the Israeli administration have been deported to Jordan, including the former mayor of Arab Jerusalem.

Israeli spokesmen have declared emphatically that the "reunification" of Jerusalem will never be reversed and that the unified city will remain the capital of

the State of Israel. Against considerable resistance, officials have encouraged the Christian and Muslim Arabs to vote in municipal elections, but have not given them Israeli citizenship (technically, they remain Jordanian citizens). They hope, in general, for deliverance from the present situation, while many Arabs and some Muslims elsewhere are determined that Old Jerusalem will be restored to Arab control.

Palestinian uprisings in the occupied territories which began at the end of 1987 magnified the division between Israeli Jerusalem and East Jerusalem. In spirit they had never been united. There have been separate areas of residence, social life and work, exemplified in the two downtowns. Christian Arabs in Jerusalem, as elsewhere in the occupied territories, have joined their Muslim fellow Palestinians as never before, having learned that the Israelis will not show them preference as the British administration did prior to 1948. Many Arab residents of Jerusalem have torn up their Israeli identity cards, which symbolize their inferior status in the Israeli scheme. Teddy Kollak, defeated after 20 years as mayor, recognized that municipal attempts to unify the two populations failed. "Co–existence in Jerusalem," he said, "is dead."

In 1990 a new furor arose between the communities when Jewish settlers attempted to establish residence at St. Johns Hospice, a Greek Orthodox building and the first attempt to colonize the Christian quarter. Financed secretly by government housing funds, they proved reluctant to leave, despite a loss in the Israeli courts and causing an unprecedented 1–day closure of all Christian shrines in the country.

Disputed Territory

Kashmir

Area: 84,471 square miles (218,670 sq. km.). Of this area, 53,665 square miles (138,992 sq. km.) are controlled by India; 32,358 square miles (83,806 sq. km.) are under the control of Pakistan.

Population: About 4.8 million in the Indian zone; 1.4 million in the Pakistani zone.

The disputed territory of Kashmir, or more properly, Jammu and Kashmir, was ruled by a Hindu Maharaja, Sir Hari Singh, at the time of the partition of British India in 1947 (see India: History). The territory consisted of the districts of Jammu, Kashmir, Ladakh, Gilgit and several smaller areas, all in the northernmost part of British India. The Valley of Kashmir is one of the most pleasant parts of the entire region geographically; Ladakh, the largest district, is in the Himalayas and is mostly ice–bound.

Unrest invaded the region when British India was partitioned and the nation of Pakistan was created. The Maharaja suppressed his Muslim subjects in one area, and soon bands of plundering Muslim tribesmen were streaming toward his capital of Srinagar in Kashmir province. He fled to the city of Jammu and there signed a document on October 26, 1947 incorporating his domains into the Republic of India, although about 75% of the population was Muslim.

Indian troops were flown to Srinagar to save it from the tribesmen and to take control. Troops from Pakistan were drawn into the war which took place in the winter of 1947–48. Under United Nations auspices an agreement to stop shooting was negotiated; it became effective on January 1, 1949. The cease–fire line, which ran through the provinces of Jammu and Kashmir and then into the icy wastes of Ladakh, left India in occupation of about three–fifths of the entire disputed area.

Although the cease-fire halted open warfare, it did not bring peace, and the future of Kashmir remained undecided. Pakistan demanded a plebiscite carried out by the United Nations, but India held local elections and claimed that they served the purpose of a plebiscite—although the future of the territory was not on the ballot, and many Muslims boycotted the elections.

Kashmir remained a subject of great emotion on both sides. But outright violence was not serious until August, 1965, when Pakistan sent armed infiltrators across the Line of Control (LOC) to commit acts of sabotage and terrorism. Indian troops later crossed the LOC in three places, ostensibly to halt infiltration. Since Pakistani public opinion strongly supported fighting, its military launched a conventional invasion of Jammu with tanks and other heavy equipment in September. India's responded by invading West Pakistan, near Lahore, and then farther south with a drive aimed at Karachi. Pakistan struck at India itself with attacks into Punjab and Rajasthan.

After the fighting reached a stalemate, the U.N. Security Council demanded a cease-fire, a decision simplified because both the Soviet Union and the United States opposed the war. The combatants complied, partly because they could not replenish their military supplies from the major powers. However, each side suspected the other of seeking further advantage, and refused to withdraw their forces from positions captured during the fighting.

In early 1966 the Soviet Union invited Pakistani President Ayub Khan and Prime Minister Shastri of India to Tashkent, in the southern Soviet Union. There they were persuaded to sign an agreement for complete withdrawal behind their own borders and the 1949 LOC. Despite the withdrawal, the causes of the dispute remained. In 1999 Pakistani forces and irregulars secretly crossed the LOC and seized several peaks before being dislodged by Indian forces (see India: history). Feelings run strong in both nations, but India shows little desire to seize Pakistani Kashmir, and Pakistan's military recognizes that Indian forces are superior.

A further complication to the Kashmiri problem came when the Communist government of China occupied desolate mountainous regions shown as part of British India. One disputed zone lay in Pakistani Kashmir, but the larger occupied area, the Aksai Chin plateau, borders the Ladakh region of India. Since the 1962 India-China War, it has been occupied by China.

In 1970s, Pakistan and China constructed the Karakoram highway to join their countries across some of the world's highest mountain ranges. The highway is 537 miles long and runs from Kashgar in China's Sinjiang province through Mintaka Pass, at an elevation of 15,000 feet in the Karakoram Range; it then continues south to Gilgit in Kashmir. The highway was a concern not only to India, but also to the United States and the Soviet Union at the time of its construction, but this concern has slowly faded.

After several months of bombings and killings by a small group of Kashmiri secessionists, in early 1990 police fired on a demonstration in Srinagar, killing about 50 people and marking the beginning of a popular uprising. As "freedom fighters" ambushed police, and civilians endured almost continuous curfews, talk of war mounted in New Delhi and Islamabad. Pakistan again demanded a plebiscite to allow Kashmiris to determine their own fate.

India naturally opposes any possible dismemberment, and the minority governments in New Delhi lack the power for concession. Nevertheless, compromise may prove the only remaining alternative to brute force to retain Kashmir. Although the two nations negotiated a cease–fire in the Himalayan heights of Ladakh, where artillery battles had raged at a record 18,000 feet, some observers cautioned that popular feelings, aroused by revolt and repression, could force one weak government or the other into starting a war. The dispute promises to continue.

Regional Organizations

Gulf Cooperation Council

The rulers of Saudi Arabia, Kuwait, Qatar, the United Arab Emirates, Bahrain and Oman agreed in 1981 to form the Gulf Cooperation Council to further their common interests, especially security and defense. Apprehensive of republican sentiments generally, and alarmed by the violent revolution in Iran, the six autocracies sought to protect themselves by cooperation. In 1982, under the leadership of Saudi Arabia, an Arab Consortium of Defense Industries was planned with an initial investment of $10 billion. This faced numerous obstacles, for most member countries lacked any significant manufacturing ability.

The GCC's first practical step was the formation of an Arabian free trade area through elimination of customs barriers between member states. In 1983 they abolished tariffs on agricultural, manufactured and animal products originating in member states. Professional people were also to be allowed freedom to move between member states to work. Other joint projects related to uniformity of educational systems and expansion of educational opportunities such as the Gulf University at Bahrain.

The GCC concerned itself with the escalating war between Iran and Iraq inasmuch as it posed a threat to neighboring nations. In December 1986, Abdulla Bishara, Secretary General of the organization, again expressed concern over the conflict and stressed the GCC's policy of coexistance in the region. He asserted that the war was not the result of cultural animosities, but rather Khomeini's goal of domination of the Persian Gulf, the same goal the deposed Shah had pursued.

By 1990, the GCC showed some signs of achievement and maturity. It shifted its attention from the distant problems of Israel and Lebanon to areas closer to the GCC, including peace between Iran and Iraq. The organization also had formed a brigade–strength joint defense force, stationed in Saudi Arabia.

Although the GCC failed to deter Iraqi aggression against Kuwait, all its members supported the international Coalition in the Second Gulf War. Following the conflict, they formed, with Syria and Egypt, the Arab Mutual Defense Organization, offering those countries substantial assistance in return for a military alliance, but no force was set up.

Significant economic issues remain. The members are divided about relations with the European Community, for some suffer discriminatory tariffs on petrochemical exports. The GCC countries would benefit from a common industrial policy (to avoid duplicating expensive projects), a unified external tariff, and a similarity of subsidies and other benefits to businesses.

The South Asian Association for Regional Co-operation (SAARC)

In 1985, the heads of government from the entire region met in conference in Dhaka and voted to establish the South Asian Association for Regional Co-operation (SAARC). Influenced by the success of alliances like the European Union and ASEAN, the founders hoped to promote economic cooperation (meaning fewer restrictions on trade), and thus reduce poverty and raise standards of living. Other objectives included better relations between countries and the creation of institutions like weather offices that could serve the entire region.

In a series of summits in the early years, SAARC's members agreed to conventions on narcotics and establishing food reserves. They adopted measures to simplify visas and travel between member nations. The Southern Asia Preferential Trading Arrangement adopted at the seventh SAARC Summit in 1993 looked forward to a regional free trade zone by 2001.

Despite these signs of progress, trade remains limited between the seven member nations—Bangladesh, Bhutan, India, the Maldives, Nepal, Pakistan and Sri Lanka. Regulations aimed at member states often mean that many products are smuggled between members or shipped via other nations. The smaller states recognize that disputes between India and Pakistan often immobilize the organization. Indeed it caused the cancellation of the last scheduled summit in 1999. Because the Dhaka Declaration of 1985 forbad official discussions on contentious or bilateral issues, SAARC is unlikely to address the most significant problems of the region.

The League of Arab States

The seven Arab countries which in March 1945 had full or partial independence formed the League of Arab States. All the founding members are in Southwest Asia, except Egypt, located in northeast Africa:

Egypt
Iraq
Lebanon
Saudi Arabia
Syria
Jordan (then TransJordan)
Yemen (Republic of Yemen, 1990)

Later, other nations which considered themselves to possess Arab character joined the League upon attaining political independence or soon thereafter (listed with year of adherence and, for those countries not described in this book, location):

8. Libya (1953), North Africa
9. Sudan (1956), Northeast Africa.
10. Morocco (1958), Northwest Africa.
11. Tunisia (1958), North Africa.
12. Kuwait (1961).
13. Algeria (1962), North Africa.
14. Peoples Democratic Republic of Yemen (1967–1990).
15. Bahrain (1971).
16. Oman (1971).
17. Qatar (1971).
18. United Arab Emirates (1971).
19. Mauritania (1973), Northwest Africa.
20. Somali Republic (1974), East Africa.
21. Palestine (1976).
22. Djibouti (1977), East Africa.

Djibouti, Mauritania and the Somali Republic are the only member nations in which Arabic is not the principal spoken language, though it is the main language used in schools and mosques. Djibouti has indicated its intention of making Arabic the official language and retaining French as a second language.

"Palestine" was admitted to membership by a unanimous vote in September 1976, although the Palestinian Liberation Organization then controlled no territory.

Until March 1979 the League operated out of a headquarters building in Cairo on the east bank of the Nile. When Egypt signed a peace treaty with Israel considered unsatisfactory by other members, Egypt was expelled from the organization and the headquarters was moved to Tunis. Egypt rejoined the League in 1989. The League's majority condemned the invasion of Kuwait, but the sharply divided organization lost its Secretary General and returned its headquarters to Cairo thereafter. An Egyptian diplomat, Ismat Abd al–Majid became Secretary General.

Through efforts of the League, Arabic became the sixth official and working language of the U.N. beginning January 1, 1983. This decision was reached by the Security Council and followed a practice already common in the General Assembly. League members pay the extra expenses of the use of the additional language by the U.N.

Selected Bibliography of Key English Language Sources

Asia—general

Bracken, Paul. *Fire in the East: the Rise of Asian Military Power and the Second Nuclear Age.* New York: HarperCollins Publishers, 1999.

Brown, Michael E. and Sumit Ganguly, eds. *Government Policies and Ethnic Relations in Asia and the Pacific.* Cambridge, MA: MIT Press, 1997.

Diagram Group Staff. *Asian History on File.* New York: Facts on File, 1995.

Embree, Ainslie T. and Carol Gluck, eds. *Asia in Western and World History: a Guide for Teaching.* Armonk, NY: M.E. Sharpe, 1997.

Kleindorfer, Paul, et al., eds. *Energy, Environment, and the Economy: Asian Perspectives.* Northampton, MA: Edward Elgar Publishing, 1996.

Murphey, Rhoads. *A History of Asia.* Reading, MA: Addison-Wesley Educational Publishers, 1996.

Neisbitt, John. *Megatrends in Asia: Eight Asian Megatrends That Are Reshaping Our World.* New York: Simon & Schuster, 1996.

Tan, Gerald. *The Economic Transformation of Asia.* Portland, OR: International Specialized Book Services, 1997.

Tomaselli-Moschovitis, Valerie. *Asia on File.* New York: Facts on File, 1996.

Middle East—general

Abi-Aad, Naji and Michel Grenon. *Instability and Conflict in the Middle East: People, Petroleum, and Security Threats.* New York: Saint Martin's Press, 1997.

Aburish, Said K. *A Brutal Friendship: the West and the Arab Elite.* New York: Saint Martin's Press, 1998.

Andersen, Roy R., et al. *Politics and Change in the Middle East: Sources of Conflict and Accommodation.* Upper Saddle River, NJ: Prentice Hall, 5th ed. 1997.

Anderson, Ewan E., et al. *The Middle East: Geography and Geopolitics.* New York: Routledge, 2000.

Bates, Daniel G., et al. *Peoples and Cultures of the Middle East.* Upper Saddle River, NJ: Prentice Hall, 2001.

Choueiri, Youseff. *Arab Nationalism.* Malden, MA: Blackwell Publishers, 2001.

Cleveland, William L. *A History of the Modern Middle East.* Boulder, CO: Westview Press, 1999.

Dalrymple, William. *From the Holy Mountain: Journey among the Christians of the Middle East.* New York: Henry Holt & Company, 1998.

Deshen, Shlomo and Walter P. Zenner, eds. *Jews among Muslims: Communities in the Precolonial Middle East.* New York: New York University Press, 1996.

Dorraj, Manochehr, ed. *Middle East at the Crossroads: the Changing Political Dynamics and the Foreign Policy.* Lanham, MD: University Press of America, 1999.

Eickelman, Dale F. *Middle East and Central Asia.* Upper Saddle River, NJ: Prentice Hall, 1997.

Feldman, Shai. *Nuclear Weapons and Arms Control in the Middle East.* Cambridge, MA: MIT Press, 1997.

Fernea, Elizabeth W. and Robert A. Fernea. *The Arab World: Forty Years of Change.* New York: Doubleday, rev. ed. 1997.

Fisher, Sydney N. and William L. Ochsenwald. *The Middle East: a History.* New York: McGraw-Hill, 5th. ed. 1996.

Freeman-Grenville, G.S. *Historical Atlas of the Middle East.* New York: Simon & Schuster, 1993.

Gher, Leo A. *Civic Discourse and Digital Age Communications in the Middle East.* Westport, CT: Greenwood Publishing Group, 2000.

Gilbar, Gad G. *The Middle East Oil Decade and Beyond.* Portland, OR: International Specialized Book Services, 1997.

Gilbar, Gad G. *Population Dilemmas in the Middle East.* Portland, OR: International Specialized Book Services, 1997.

Gilsenan, Michael. *Recognizing Islam: Religion and Society in the Modern Middle East.* New York: I.B. Tauris & Company, 2000.

Glasser, Bradley L. *Economic Development and Political Reform: the Impact of External Capital on the Middle East.* Northampton, MA: Edward Elgar Publishing, 2000.

Guazzone, Laura. *Middle East Global Change: the Politics and Economics of Interdependence Versus Fragmentation.* New York: Saint Martin's Press, 1997.

Halliday, Fred. *Nation and Religion in the Middle East.* Boulder, CO: Lynne Rienner Publishers, 2000.

Hansen, Birthe. *Unipolarity and the Middle East.* New York: Saint Martin's Press, 2001.

Herb, Michael. *All in the Family: Absolutism, Revolution, and Democratic Prospects in the Middle Eastern Monarchies.* Albany, NY: State University of New York Press, 1999.

Hess, Andrew C. *Oil and Money: a Global Study of the Middle East in the Oil Era.* Chicago: Firtzroy Dearborn Publishers, 1999.

Hiro, Dilip. *A Dictionary of the Middle East.* New York: Saint Martin's Press, 1996.

Hiro, Dilip. *The Middle East.* Phoenix, AZ: Oryx Press, 1996.

Issawi, Charles P. *The Middle East Economy: Decline and Recovery.* Princeton, NJ: Markus Wiener Publishers, rev. ed. 1996.

Jabar, Faleh A., ed. *Post-Marxism and the Middle East.* Portland, OR: International Specialized Book Services, 1997.

Kamalipour, Yahya R. *The U.S. Media and the Middle East: Image and Perception.* Westport, CT: Greenwood Publishing, 1995.

Kaufman, Burton I. *Arab Middle East and the United States.* Old Tappan, NJ: Macmillan Library Reference, 1996.

Kemp, Geoffrey and Robert E. Harkavy. *Strategic Geography and the Changing Middle East.* Washington, DC: Carnegie Endowment for International Peace, 1997.

Lewis, Bernard. *The Middle East: a Brief History of the Last 2,000 Years.* New York: Simon & Schuster, 1996.

Lewis, Bernard. *Multiple Identities of the Middle East.* New York: Schocken Books, 1999.

Lindholm, Charles. *The Islamic Middle East: an Historical Anthropology.* Malden, MA: Blackwell Publishers, 1996.

Link, P.S., ed. *Middle East Imbroglio: Status and Prospects.* Commack, NY: Nova Science Publishers, 1996.

Maddy-Weitzman, Bruce, ed. *Middle East Contemporary Survey.* Boulder, CO: Westview Press, 2000.

Maoz, Moshe and Ilan Pappe, eds. *Middle Eastern Politics and Ideas: a History from Within.* New York: Saint Martin's Press, 1998.

Maoz, Zeev. *Regional Security in the Middle East: Past, Present, Future.* Portland, OR: International Specialized Book Services, 1997.

McKale, Donald M. *War by Revolution: Germany and Great Britain in the Middle East in the Era of World War I.* Kent, OH: Kent State University Press, 1998.

Norton, Augustus R. *Civil Society in the Middle East.* Boston, MA: Brill Academic Publishers, 1994.

Ovendale, Ritchie. *Britain, the U.S., and the Transfer of Power in the Middle East 1945-1962.* Herndon, VA: Books International, 1996.

Owen, Edward R. *A History of Middle East Economies in the Twentieth Century.* Cambridge, MA: Harvard University Press, 1999.

Owen, Roger. *State Power and Politics in Making of the Modern Middle East.* New York: Routledge, 2000.

Peleg, Ilan, ed. *The Middle East Peace Process: Interdisciplinary Perspectives.* Albany, NY: State University of New York Press, 1997.

Pervin, David J. and Steven L. Spiegel. *Practical Peacemaking in the Middle East, Vol. 1: Arms Control and Regional Security.* New York: Garland Publishing, 1995.

Pervin, David J. and Steven L. Spiegel. *Practical Peacemaking in the Middle East, Vol 2: The Environment, Water, Refugees, and Economic Cooperation and Development.* New York: Garland Publishing, 1995.

Richards, Alan and John Waterbury. *A Political Economy of the Middle East.* Boulder, CO: Westview Press, 1996.

Rubin, Barry, et al., eds. *From War to Peace: Arab-Israeli Relations, 1973-1993.* New York: New York University Press, 1994.

Savir, Uri. *The Process: 1,100 Days That Changed the Middle East.* New York: Random House, 1998.

Soffer, Arnon. Translated by Mory Rosovesky. *Rivers of Fire: the Conflict over Water in the Middle East.* Lanham, MD: Rowman & Littlefield Publishers, 1999.

Tal, David, ed. *The 1956 War: Collusion and Rivalry in the Middle East.* Portland, OR: Frank Cass Publishers, 2000.

Tamini, Sargon. *Islam and Secularism in the Middle East.* New York: New York University Press, 2000.

Vatikiotis, P.J. *Middle East: from the End of Empire to the End of the Cold War.* New York: Routledge, 1997.

Viorst, Milton. *Sandcastles: the Arabs in Search of the Modern World.* New York: Random House, 1994.

Williams, Mary E. *The Middle East: Opposing Viewpoints.* San Diego, CA: Greenhaven Press, 2000.

Islam

Allison, Robert J. *The Crescent Obscured: the United States and Muslim World, 1776-1815.* New York: Oxford University Press, 1995.

Arkoun, Mohammed. *Rethinking Islam: Common Questions, Uncommon Answers.* Boulder, CO: Westview Press, 1994.

Armstrong, Karen. *Islam: a Short History.* New York: Modern Library, 2000.

Braswell, George W. Jr. *Islam: Its Prophet, Peoples, Politics, and Power.* Nashville, TN: Broadman & Holman, 1996.

Brown, L. Carl. *Religion and State: the Muslim Approach to Politics.* New York: Columbia University Press, 2000.

Butterworth, Charles E. and I. William Zartman, eds. *Between the State and Islam.* New York: Cambridge University Press, 2000.

Chebel, Malek. *Symbols of Islam.* New York: Saint Martin's Press, 1997.

Davidson, Lawrence. *Islamic Fundamentalism.* Westport, CT: Greenwood Publishing Group, 1998.

Encyclopedia of Islam. Boston, MA: Brill Academic Publishers, 1997.

Esposito, John L., ed. *The Oxford History of Islam.* New York: Oxford University Press, 2000.

Hathout, Hassan. *Reading the Muslim Mind.* Plainfield, IN: American Trust Publications, 1994.

Hawting, G.R. *The Idea of Idolatry and the Emergence of Islam: from Polemic to History.* New York: Cambridge University Press, 2000.

Huband, Mark. *Warriors of the Prophet: the Struggle for Islam.* Boulder, CO: Westview Press, 1999.

Khan, Muhammad Z., translator. *The Quran.* Northampton, MA: Interlink Publishing Group, 1997.

Kramer, Martin, ed. *The Islamic Debate.* Syracuse, NY: Syracuse University Press, 1997.

Memon, Ali N. *The Islamic Nation: Status and Future of Muslims in the New World Order.* Beltsville, MD: Writer's, Inc., 1995.

Moussalli, Amhad. *Historical Dictionary of Islamic Fundamentalist Movements in the Arab World, Iran and Turkey.* Lanham, MD: Scarecrow Press, 1999.

Nagel, Tilman and Bernard Lewis, eds. *The History of Islamic Theology: from Muhammad to the Present.* Princeton, NJ: Markus Wiever Publishers, 1999.

Noreng, Ystein. *Oil and Islam: Social and Economic Issues.* New York: John Wiley & Sons, 1997.

Renard, John. *Seven Doors to Islam: Spirituality and the Religious Life Of Muslims.* Berkeley, CA: University of California Press, 1996.

Van Donzel, E.J., ed. *Islamic Desk Reference.* Boston, MA: Brill Academic Publishers, 1994.

Viorst, Milton. *In the Shadow of the Prophet: the Struggle for the Soul of Islam.* Boulder, CO: Westview Press, 2001.

Zepp, Ira G., Jr. *A Muslim Primer: Beginner's Guide to Islam.* Fayetteville, AR: University of Arkansas Press, 2000.

Palestinians

Abu-Nimer, Mohammed. *Dialogue, Conflict Resolution, and Change: Arab-Jewish Encounters in Israel.* Albany, NY: State University of New York Press, 1999.

Arnon, Arie and Jimmy Weinblatt. *The Palestinian Economy: between Imposed Integration and Voluntary Separation.* Boston, MA: Brill Academic Publishers, 1997.

Ciment, James. *Palestine Israel: the Long Conflict.* New York: Facts on File, 1997.

Cragg, Kenneth. *Palestine: the Prize and Price of Zion.* Herndon, VA: Cassell Academic, 1997.

Dannreuther, Roland. *Soviet Union and Palestine Resistance.* New York: Saint Martin's Press, 1998.

Diwan, Ishac and Radwan A. Shaban. *Development under Adversity: the Palestinian Economy in Transition.* Washington, DC: The World Bank, 1999.

Farsoun, Samih K. and Christina E. Zacharia. *Palestine and the Palestinians: a Stateless Nation.* Boulder, CO: Westview Press, 1997.

Holliday, Laurel. *Children of Israel, Children of Palestine.* New York: Pocket Books, 1998.

Inbari, Pinhas. *The Palestinians between Terrorism and Statehood.* Portland, OR: International Specialized Book Services, 1998.

Jabar, Hala. *Hezbollah: Born with a Vengeance.* New York: Columbia University Press, 1997.

Kass, Ilana and Bard O'Neill. *The Deadly Embrace: the Impact of Israel and Palestinian Rejectionism on the Peace Process.* Lan-ham, MD: University Press of America, 1996.

Khalidi, Rashid. *Palestinian Identity.* New York: Columbia University Press, 1997.

Kimmerling, Baruch. *Palestinians: the Making of a People.* New York: The Free Press, 1993.

Mattar, Philip. *Encyclopedia of the Palestinians.* New York: Facts on File, 1999.

Nazzal, Nafez and Laila A. Nazzal. *Historical Dictionary of Palestine.* Lanham, MD: Scarecrow Press, 1997.

Peleg, Ilan. *Human Rights in the West Band and Gaza.* Syracuse, NY: Syracuse University Press, 1995.

Robinson, Glenn E. *Building a Palestinian State: the Incomplete Revolution.* Bloomington, IN: Indiana University Press, 1997.

Rouhana, Nadim N. *Palestinians in an Ethnic Jewish State: Identities in Conflict.* New Haven, CT: Yale University Press, 1997.

Shemesh, Moshe. *The Palestinian Entity, 1959-1974: Arab Politics and the PLO.* Portland, OR: International Specialized Book Services, rev. ed. 1996.

Swedenburg, Ted. *Memories of Revolt: the 1936-39 Rebellion and the Palestinian National Past.* Minneapolis, MN: University of Minnesota Press, 1995.

Toubbeh, Jamil I. *Day of the Long Night: a Palestinian Refugee Remembers the "Nabka."* Jefferson, NC: McFarland & Company, 1997.

Persian Gulf

Abdelkarim, Abbas. *Change and Development in the Gulf.* New York: Saint Martin's Press, 1999.

Baldwin, Sherman. *Ironclaw: a Navy Carrier Pilot's Gulf War Experience.* New York: William Morrow & Company, 1996.

Coughlin, Sean T. *Storming the Desert: a Marine Lieutenant's Day-by-Day Chronicle of the Persian Gulf.* Jefferson, NC: McFarland & Company, 1996.

Donnelly, Michael and Denise Donnelly. *Falcon's Cry: a Desert Storm Memoir.* Westport, CT: Greenwood Publishing Group, 1998.

Edington, L. Benjamin and Michael J. Mazarr, eds. *Turning Point: the Gulf War.* Boulder, CO: Westview Press, 1995.

El-Shazly, Nadia El-Sayed. *Gulf Tanker War.* New York: Saint Martin's Press, 1998.

Grossman, Mark, ed. *Encyclopedia of the Persian Gulf War.* Santa Barbara, CA: ABC-CLIO, 1995.

Head, William Jr. and Earl Tilford. *The Eagle in the Desert: Looking Back on the United States Involvement in the Persian Gulf.* Westport, CT: Greenwood Publishing Group, 1996.

Hutchinson, Kevin D. *Operation Desert Shield - Desert Storm: Chronology and Fact Book.* Westport, CT: Greenwood Publishing Group, 1995.

Khadduri, Majid and Edmund Ghareeb. *War in the Gulf, 1990-91: the Iraq-Kuwait Conflict and Its Implications: Views from the Other Side.* New York: Oxford University Press, 1997.

Metz, Helen Chapin, ed. *Persian Gulf State: Country Studies.* Washington, DC: U.S. GPO, 3rd ed. 1994.

Mohamedou, Mohammad-Mahmoud. *Iraq and the Second Gulf War: State Building and Regime Security.* Bethesda, MD: Austin & Winfield Publishers, 1997.

Murray, Williamson and Wayne W. Thompson. *Air War in the Persian Gulf.* Mount Pleasant, SC: Nautical & Aviation Publishing Company, 1995.

Newell, Clayton R. *Historical Dictionary of the Persian Gulf War, 1990-1991.* Lanham, MD: Scarecrow Press, 1998.

Orgill, Andrew. *The 1990-91 Gulf War: Crisis, Conflict, Aftermath: an Annotated Bibliography.* Herndon, VA: Cassell Academic, 1995.

Schwartz, Richard A. *Encyclopedia of the Persian Gulf War.* Jefferson, NC: McFarland & Company, 1998.

Summers, Harry G., Jr. *The Persian Gulf War Almanac.* New York: Facts on File, 1995.

Yetiv, Steve A. *The Persian Gulf Crisis.* Westport, CT: Greenwood Publishing Group, 1997.

Zahlan, Rosemarie Said. *The Making of the Modern Gulf States: Kuwait, Bahrain, Qatar, the United Arab Emirates, and Oman.* Reading, England: Ithaca Press, 1998.

Terrorism

Anderson, Sean and Stephen Sloan. *Historical Dictionary of Terrorism.* Lanham, MD: Scarecrow Press, 1995.

Combs, Cindy C. *Terrorism in the 21st Century.* Upper Saddle River, NJ: Prentice-Hall, 1999.

Crenshaw, Martha and John Pimlott, eds. *Encyclopedia of World Terrorism.* Armonk, NY: M.E. Sharpe, 1996.

Egendorf, Laura K. *Terrorism: Opposing Viewpoints.* San Diego, CA: Greenhaven Press, 2000.

Gearty, Conor. *Terrorism.* Brookfield, VT: Ashgate Publishing Company, 1996.

Grosscup, Beau. *The Newest Explosions of Terrorism: Latest Sites of Terrorism in the 1990's and Beyond.* Far Hills, NJ: New Horizon Press, 1998.

Gurr, Nadine. *The New Face of Terrorism: Threats from Weapons of Mass Destruction.* New York: I.B. Tauris & Company, 2000.

Harmon, Christopher C. *Terrorism Today.* Portland, OR: Frank Cass Publishers, 1999.

Higgins, Rosalyn and Maurice Flory, eds. *Terrorism and International Law.* New York: Routledge, 1997.

Hunter, Thomas B. *The A to Z of International Terrorist and Counterterrorist Organizations.* Lanham, MD Scarecrow Press, 1999.

Kressel, Neil J. *Mass Hate: the Global Rise of Genocide and Terror.* New York: Plenum Publishing, 1996.

Laquer, Walter. *The New Terrorism: Fanaticism and the Arms of Mass Destruction.* New York: Oxford University Press, 1999.

LeMesurier, Charles and Marc Arnold. *Terrorism.* London: Jane's Information Group, 1997.

Mickolus, Edward F. and Susan L. Simmons. *Terrorism, 1992-1995: a Chronology of Events and a Selectively Annotated Bibliography.* Westport, CT: Greenwood Publishing Group, 1997.

Nasr, Kameel B. *Arab and Israeli Terrorism: the Causes and Effects of Political Violence, 1936-1993.* Jefferson, NC: McFarland & Company, 1996.

Netanyahu, Binyamin. *Fighting Terrorism: How Democracies Can Defeat Domestic and International Terrorists.* New York: Farrar, Straus & Giroux, 1995.

O'Ballance, Edgar. *Islamic Fundamentalist Terrorism, 1979-95: the Iranian Connection.* New York: New York University Press, 1996.

Prunckun, Henry W., Jr. *Shadow of Death: an Analytic Bibliography on Political Violence, Terrorism, and Low-Intensity Conflict.* Lanham, MD: Scarecrow Press, 1995.

Stern, Jessica. *The Ultimate Terrorists.* Cambridge, MA: Harvard University Press, 1999.

Tanter, Raymond. *Rogue Regimes: Terrorism and Proliferation.* New York: Saint Martin's Press, 1997.

Taylor, Max and John Horgan, eds. *The Future of Terrorism.* Portland, OR: Frank Cass Publishers, 2000.

Tucker, David. *Skirmishes at the Edge of the Empire: the United States and International Terrorism.* Westport, CT: Greenwood Publishing Group, 1997.

Tucker, Jonathan B., ed. *Toxic Terror.* Cambridge, MA: MIT Press, 2000.

White, Jonathan R. *Terrorism: an Introduction.* Belmont, CA: Wadsworth Publishing Company, 1997.

Wieviorka, Michel. Translated by David G. White. *The Making of Terrorism.* Chicago: University of Chicago Press, 1993.

South Asia—general

Babb, Lawrence A. and Susan S. Wadley, eds. *Media and the Transformation of Religion in South Asia.* Philadelphia, PA: University of Pennsylvania Press, 1995.

Bahri, Deepika and Mary Vasudeva, eds. *Between the Lines: South Asians and Postcoloniality.* Philadelphia, PA: Temple University Press, 1996.

Bose, Sugata and Ayesha Jalal. *Modern South Asia: History, Culture and Political Economy.* New York: Routledge, 1998.

Breton, Roland J. *Atlas of the Languages and Ethnic Communities of South Asia.* Thousand Oaks, CA: Sage Publications, 1997.

Ganguly, Sumit and Ted Greenwood, eds. *Mending Fences: Confidence and Security-Building Measures in South Asia.* Boulder, CO: Westview Press, 1996.

Hewitt, Vernon. *The New International Politics of South Asia.* New York: Saint Martin's Press, 1997.

Hossain, Moazzem. *South Asian Economic Development: Transformation, Opportunities and Challenges.* New York: Routledge, 1999.

Jalel, Ayesha. *Democracy and Authoritarianism in South Asia: a Comparative and Historical Perspective.* New York: Cambridge University Press, 1995.

Krepan, Michael L., ed. *Conflict Prevention, Confidence Building, and Reconciliation in South Asia.* New York: Saint Martin's Press, 1995.

Ludden, David. *An Agrarian History of South Asia.* New York: Cambridge University Press, 1999.

Mitra, Subrata K. And R. Alison Lewis, eds. *Subnational Movements in South Asia.* Boulder, CO: Westview Press, 1996.

Pasha, Mustapha K. *South Asia: Civil Society, State, and Politics.* Boulder, CO: Westview Press, 1999.

Peimani, Hooman. *Nuclear Proliferation in the Indian Subcontinent: the Self-Exhausting "Superpowers" and Emerging Alliances:* Westport, CT: Greenwood Publishing Group, 2000.

Schmidt, Karl J. *An Atlas and Survey of South Asian History.* Armonk, NY: M.E. Sharpe, 1995.

Schwartzberg, Joseph E. *A Historical Atlas of South Asia, 2nd Impression with Additional Material.* New York: Oxford University Press, 1993.

Synnott, Hilary. *The Causes and Consequences of South Asia's Nuclear Tests.* New York: Oxford University Press, 1999.

Tambiah, Stanely J. *Leveling Crowds: Ethno-Nationalist Conflicts and Collective Violence in South Asia.* Berkeley, CA: University of California Press, 1997.

Indian Ocean

Metz, Helen C., ed. *Indian Ocean: Five Island Countries.* Washington, DC: U.S. GPO, 3rd. ed. 1995.

Afghanistan

Adamec, Ludwig W. *Dictionary of Afghan Wars, Revolutions, and Insurgencies.* Lanham, MD: Scarecrow Press, 1996.

Adamec, Ludwig W. *Historical Dictionary of Afghanistan.* Lanham, MD: Scarecrow Press, 1997.

Cordovez, Diego. *Out of Afghanistan: the Inside Story of the Soviet Withdrawal.* New York: Oxford University Press, 1995.

Galeotti, Mark. *Afghanistan: the Soviet Union's Last War.* Portland, OR: Frank Cass & Company, 1995.

Grasselli, Gabriella. *British and American Responses to the Soviet Invasion of Afghan-*

istan. Brookfield, VT: Ashgate Publishing Company, 1996.

Kakar, M. Hassan. *Afghanistan: the Soviet Invasion and the Afghan Response.* Berkeley, CA: University of California Press, 1995.

Magnus, Ralph H. and Eden Naby. *Afghanistan: Marx, Mullah and Mujahid.* Boulder, CO: Westview Press, 1997.

Margolis, Eric. *War at the Top of the World: the Struggle for Afghanistan, Kashmir and Tibet.* New York: Routledge, 2000.

Olesen, Asta. *Islam and Politics in Afghanistan.* Concord, MA: Paul & Company Publishers Consortium, 1995.

Pedersen, Gorm. *Afghan Nomads in Transition.* New York: Thames & Hudson, 1995.

Rubin, Barnett R. *The Fragmentation of Afghanistan: State Formation and Collapse in the International System.* New Haven, CT: Yale University Press, 1994.

Rubin, Barnett, R. *The Search for Peace in Afghanistan: from Buffer State to Failed State.* New Haven, CT: Yale University Press, 1996.

Schuyler, Jones. *Afghanistan.* Santa Barbara, CA: ABC-CLIO, 1992.

Weinbaum, Marvin G. *Pakistan and Afghanistan: Resistance and Reconstruction.* Boulder, CO: Westview Press, 1994.

Bahrain

Khuri, Fuad Ishaq. *Tribe and State in Bahrain: the Transformation of Social and Political Authority in an Arab State.* Chicago: University of Chicago Press, 1980.

Lawson, Fred Haley. *Bahrain: the Modernization of Autocracy.* Boulder, CO: Westview Press, 1989.

Bangladesh

Baxter, Craig. *Historical Dictionary of Bangladesh.* Lanham, MD: Scarecrow Press, 1996.

Choudhury, Dilara. *Constitutional Development in Bangladesh: Stresses and Strains.* New York: Oxford University Press, 1997.

Dayal, Edison. *Food, Nutrition and Hunger in Bangladesh.* Brookfield, VT: Ashgate Publishing Company, 1997.

Heitzman, James and Robert L. Worden, eds. *Bangladesh: a Country Study.* Washington, DC: U.S. GPO, 2nd ed. 1989.

Hossain, Akhtar. *Macroeconomic Issues and Policies: the Case for Bangladesh.* Thousand Oaks, CA: Sage Publications, 1996.

Pokrant, Bob. *Bangladesh.* Santa Barbara, CA: ABC-CLIO, 2000.

Sisson, Richard. *War and Secession: Pakistan, India, and the Creation of Bangladesh.* Berkeley, CA: University of California Press, 1990.

Wahid, Abu N. and Charles E. Weis, eds. *The Economy of Bangladesh: Problems and Prospects.* Westport, CA: Greenwood Publishing Group, 1996.

Warrick, Richard A. and Q. K. Ahmad, eds. *The Implications of Climate and Sea-Level Change for Bangladesh.* Norwell, MA: Kluwer Academic Publishers, 1996.

Wood, Geoffrey D. and Iffath A. Shariff. *Who Needs Credit? Poverty and Finance in Bangladesh.* New York: Saint Martin's Press, 1998.

Bhutan

Apte, Robert Z. *Three Kingdoms on the Roof of the World: Bhutan, Nepal, and Ladakh.* Berkeley, CA: Parallax Press, 1990.

Savada, Andrea Matles, ed. *Nepal and Bhutan: Country Studies.* Washington, DC: U.S. GPO, 1993.

Zeppa, Jamie. *Beyond the Sky and the Earth: a Journey into Bhutan.* New York: Putnam Publishing Group, 1999.

Cyprus

Calotychos, Vangelis, ed. *Cyprus and Its People: Nation, Identity, and the Experience in an Unimaginable Community, 1955-1997.* Boulder, CO: Westview Press, 1998.

Dodd, Clement H. *The Cyprus Imbroglio.* Concord, MA: Paul & Company Publishers Consortium, 1998.

Holland, Robert. *Britain and the Revolt in Cyprus, 1954-1959.* New York: Oxford University Press, 1998.

Joseph, Joseph S. *Cyprus: Ethnic Conflict and International Politics: from Independence to the Threshold of the European Union.* New York: Saint Martin's Press, 1997.

Kitromilides, Paschalis M. *Cyprus.* Santa Barbara, CA: ABC-CLIO, rev. ed 1995.

O'Malley, Brendan. *Cyprus Conspiracy.* New York: I.B. Tauris, 2000.

Panteli, Stavros. *Historical Dictionary of Cyprus.* Lanham, MD: Scarecrow Press, 1995.

Solstein, Eric, ed. *Cyprus: a Country Study.* Washington, DC: U.S. GPO, 4th ed. 1993.

Egypt

Beattie, Kirk J. *Egyptian Politics during Sadat's Presidency.* New York: Saint Martin's Press, 2000.

Boutros-Ghali, Boutros. *Egypt's Road to Jerusalem: a Diplomat's Story of the Strugglefor Peace in the Middle East.* New York: Random House, 1997.

Cromer, Evelyn Baring. *Modern Egypt.* New York: Routledge, 2000.

Elkhafif, Mahmoud A. *The Egyptian Economy: a Modeling Approach.* Westport, CT: Greenwood Publishing Group, 1996.

Gershoni, Israel. *Redefining the Egyptian Nation, 1930-1945.* New York: Cambridge University Press, 1995.

Gorst, Anthony and Lewis Johnman. *The Suez Crisis.* New York: Routledge, 1997.

Harik, Iliya F. *Economic Policy Reform in Egypt.* Gainesville, FL: University Press of Florida, 1997.

Holland, Matthew F. *America and Egypt: from Roosevelt to Eisenhower.* Westport, CT: Greenwood Publishing Group, 1996.

Lucas, Scott. *Britain and the Suez Crisis: the Lion's Last Roar.* New York: Saint Martin's Press, 1996.

Meital, Yoram. *Egypt's Last Struggle for Peace: Continuity and Change, 1967-1971.* Gainesville, FL: University Press of Florida, 1997.

Metz, Helen Chapin, ed. *Egypt: a Country Study.* Washington, DC: U.S. GPO, 5th ed. 1991.

Nagi, Saad Z. *Poverty in Egypt: Human Needs and Institutional Capacities.* Lanham, MD: Lexington Books, 2000.

Sullivan, Denis J. and Sana Abed-Kotob. *Islam in Contemporary Egypt: Civil Society vs. the State.* Boulder, CO: Lynne Rienner Publishers, 1999.

Weaver, Mary Anne. *A Portrait of Egypt: a Journey through the World of Militant Islam.* New York: Farrar, Straus & Giroux, 2000.

Woodward, Peter N. *Nasser.* White Plains, NY: Longman Publishing Group, 1991.

India

Bayly, Susan. *Caste, Society and Politics in India from the 18th Century to the Modern Age.* New York: Cambridge University Press, 2001.

Bouton, Marshall M. and Philip Oldenburg, eds. *India Briefing: a Transformative 50 Years.* Armonk, NY: M.E. Sharpe, 1999.

Burke, Samuel M. and Salim Al-Din Quraishi. *The British Raj in India: an Historical Review.* New York: Oxford University Press, 1995.

Chadda, Maya. *Ethnicity, Security and Separatism in India.* New York: Columbia University Press, 1997.

Chary, M. Srinivas. *The Eagle and the Peacock: U.S. Foreign Policy toward India since Independence.* Westport, CT: Greenwood Publishing Group, 1995.

Chatterjee, Partha, ed. *State and Politics in India.* New York: Oxford University Press, 2000.

Cohn, Bernard S. *Colonialism and Its Forms of Knowledge: the British in India.* Princeton, NJ: Princeton University Press, 1996.

Currie, Bob. *The Politics of Hunger in India: a Study of Democracy, Governance and Kalahandi's Poverty.* New York: Saint Martin's Press, 2000.

Dandekar, Vinayak M. *The Indian Economy, 1947-92: Population, Poverty and Employment.* Thousand Oaks, CA: Sage Publications, 1996.

Dantwala, M.L., et al., eds. *Dilemmas of Growth: the Indian Experience.* Thousand Oaks, CA: Sage Publications, 1996.

Derbyshire, Ian D. *India.* Santa Barbara, CA: ABC-CLIO, rev. ed. 1995.

Edney, Matthew H. *Mapping the Empire: the Geographical Construction of British India.* Chicago: University of Chicago Press, 1997.

Frankel, Francine R., et al., eds. *Transforming India: Social and Political Dynamics of Democracy*. New York: Oxford University Press, 2000.

Ganguly, Sumit, ed. *Understanding Contemporary India*. Boulder, CO: Lynne Rienner Publishers, 2001.

Hansen, Thomas Blom. *Saffron Wave: Democracy and Hindu Nationalism in Modern India*. Princeton, NJ: Princeton University Press, 1999.

Harrison, Selig S., et al., eds. *India and Pakistan: the First Fifty Years*. New York: Cambridge University Press, 1998

Heitzman, James and Robert L. Worden, eds. *India: a Country Study*. Washington, DC: U.S. GPO, 5th ed. 1996.

James, Lawrence. *RAJ: the Making and Unmaking of British India*. New York: Thomas Dunne Books, 1998.

Jayal, Niraja G. *Democracy and the State: Welfare, Secularism, and Development in Contemporary India*. New York: Oxford University Press, 1999.

Jenkins, Rob. *Democratic Politics and Economic Reform in India*. New York: Cambridge University Press, 1999.

Johnson, Gordon. *Cultural Atlas of India*. New York: Facts on File, 1996.

Keay, John. *India: a History*. New York: Grove/Atlantic, 2000.

Kulke, Herman and Dietmar Rothermund. *History of India*. New York: Routledge, 1998.

Maitra, Priyatosh. *The Globalization of Capitalism and Its Impact on Third World Countries: India as a Case Study*. Westport, CT: Greenwood Publishing Group, 1996.

Mansingh, Surjit. *Historical Dictionary of India*. Lanham, MD: Scarecrow Press, 1996.

Mehta, Gita. *Snakes and Ladders: Glimpses of Modern India*. New York: Doubleday, 1997.

Moorhouse, Geoffrey. *India Britannica: a Vivid Introduction to the History of British India*. Chicago: Academy Chicago Publishers, 1999.

Paz, Octavio. *In Light of India: Essays*. San Diego, CA: Harcourt Brace & Company, 1997.

Rao, C. Hanumantha and Hans Linnemann, eds. *Economic Reforms and Poverty Alleviation in India*. Thousand Oaks, CA: Sage Publications, 1996.

Read, Anthony. *The Proudest Day: Indian's Long Road to Independence*. New York: W.W. Norton & Company, 1998.

Royle, Trevor. *The Last Days of the Raj*. North Pomfret, VT: Trafalgar Square, 1998.

Saberwal, Satish. *Roots of Crisis: Interpreting Contemporary Indian Society*. Thousand Oaks, CA: Sage Publications, 1996.

Sachs, Jeffrey D., et al., eds. *India in the Era of Economic Reforms*. New York: Oxford University Press, 2000.

Sekhon, Joti. *Modern India*. New York: McGraw-Hill, 1999.

Sridharan, Kripa. *The ASEAN Region in India's Foreign Policy*. Brookfield, VT: Ashgate Publishing Company, 1996.

Srinivasan, T.N. and Suresh D. Tendulkar. *India in the World Economy*. Washington, DC: Institute for International Economics, 2001.

Sugata, Bose. *Nationalism, Democracy, and Development: State and Politics in India*. New York: Oxford University Press, 1999.

Tharoor, Shashi. *India: from Midnight to the Millennium*. New York: Arcade Publishing, 1997.

Thomas, Raju G. *Democracy, Security, and Development in India*. New York: Saint Martin's Press, 1996.

Tomlinson, B.R. *The Economy of Modern India, 1860-1970*. New York: Cambridge University Press, 1993.

Vanaik, Achin. *The Furies of Indian Communalism: Religion, Modernity and Secularization*. New York: Verso, 1997.

Vohra, Ranbir. *The Making of India: a Historical Survey*. Armonk, NY: M.E. Sharpe, 2000.

Wolpert, Stanley A. *A New History of India*. New York: Oxford University Press, 3rd ed. 1989.

Wolpert, Stanley A. *Nehru: a Tryst with Destiny*. New York: Oxford University Press, 1996.

Iran

Abrahamian, Ervand. *Khomeinism: Essays on the Islamic Republic*. Berkeley, CA: University of California Press, 1993.

Adelkhah, Fariba. *Being Modern in Iran*. New York: Columbia University Press, 2000.

Amuzegar, Jahangir. *Iran's Economy under the Islamic Republic*. New York: Saint Martin's Press, 1994.

Baktiari, Bahman. *Parliamentary Politics in Revolutionary Iran: the Institutionalization of Factional Politics*. Gainesville, FL: University Press of Florida, 1996.

Cordesman, Anthony H. and Ahmed S. Hashim. *Iran: Dilemmas of Dual Containment*. Boulder, CO: Westview Press, 1997.

Cordesman, Anthony H. *Iran's Military Forces in Transition*. Westport, CT: Greenwood Publishing Group, 1999.

Daneshar, Parviz. *Revolution in Iran*. New York: Saint Martin's Press, 1996.

Farmanfarmaian, Manucher and Roxane Farmanfarmaian. *Blood and Oil: Memoirs of a Persian Prince*. New York: Random House, 1997.

Gieling, Saskia M. *Religion and War in Revolutionary Iran*. London: I.B. Tauris, 1999.

Goode, James F. *United States and Iran: in the Shadow of Musaddiq*. New York: Saint Martin's Press, 1997.

Heiss, Mary Ann. *Empire and Nationhood: the United States, Great Britain, and Iranian Oil, 1950-1954*. New York: Columbia University Press, 1997.

Keddie, Nikki R. *Iran and Muslim World: Resistance and Revolution*. New York: New York University Press, 1995.

Mackey, Sandra. *The Iranians*. New York: NAL/Dutton, 1998.

Metz, Helen Chapin, ed. *Iran: a Country Study*. Washington, DC: U.S. GPO, 4th ed. 1989.

Moses, Russell L. *Freeing the Hostages: Reexamining U.S.-Iranian Negotiations and Soviet Policy*. Pittsburgh, PA: University of Pittsburgh Press, 1996.

Peimani, Hooman. *Iran and the United States: the Rise of the West Asian Regional Grouping*. Westport, CT: Greenwood Publishing Group, 1999.

Riesebrodt, Martin. *Pious Passion: the Emergence of Modern Fundamentalism in the United States and Iran*. Berkeley, CA: University of California Press, 1993.

Sciolino, Elaine. *Persian Mirrors: the Elusive Face of Iran*. New York: The Free Press, 2000.

Walsh, Lawrence E. *Firewall: the Iran-Contra Conspiracy and Cover-Up*. New York: W.W. Norton & Company, 1997.

Wright, Robin B. *The Last Great Revolution: Turmoil and Transformation in Iran*. New York: Alfred A. Knopf, 2000.

Iraq

Al-Khalil, Samir. *Republic of Fear: the Inside Story of Saddam's Iraq*. Collingdale, PA: DIANE Publishing Company, 2000.

Arnove, Anthony, ed. *Iraq under Siege: the Deadly Impact of Sanctions and War*. Cambridge, MA: South End Press, 2000.

Baram, Amatzia and Barry Rubin, eds. *Iraq's Road to War*. New York: Saint Martin's Press, 1994.

Bhatia, Shyam and Dan McGrory. *Brighter Than the Baghdad Sun: Saddam Hussein's Nuclear Threat to the United States*. Washington, DC: Regnery Publishing, 2000.

Butler, Richard. *The Greatest Threat: Iraq, Weapons of Mass Destruction and the Crisis of Global Security*. New York: Public Affairs, 2000.

Cockburn, Andrew. *Out of the Ashes: the Resurrection of Saddam Hussein*. New York: HarperCollins, 2000.

Cordesman, Anthony H. and Ahmed S. Hashim. *Iraq: Sanctions and Beyond*. Boulder, CO:Westview Press, 1997.

Danspeckgruber, Wolfgang F. and Charles R. Tripp, eds. *The Iraqi Aggression against Kuwait:Strategic Lessons and Implications for Europe*. Boulder, CO: Westview Press, 1996.

Elliot, Matthew. *Independent Iraq: British Influence from 1941-1958*. New York: Saint Martin's Press, 1996.

Grossman, Mark, ed. *Encyclopedia of the Persian Gulf War*. Santa Barbara, CA: ABC-CLIO, 1995.

Haj, Samira. *The Making of Iraq, 1900-1963: Capital, Power and Ideology*. Albany, NY: State University of New York Press, 1997.

Haselkorn, Avigdor. *The Continuing Storm: Iraq, Poisonous Weapons, and Deterrence*.

New Haven, CT: Yale University Press, 1998.

Lukitz, Liora. *Iraq: the Search for National Identity*. Portland, OR: Frank Cass & Company, 1995.

Metz, Helen Chapin, ed. *Iraq: a Country Study*. Washington, DC: U.S. GPO, 4th ed. 1990.

Mohamedou, Mohammad-Mahmoud. *Iraq and the Second Gulf War: State Building and Regime Security*. Bethesda, MD: Austin & Winfield Publishers, 1997.

Musallam, Musallam A. *Iraqi Invasion of Kuwait: Saddam Hussein, His State and International Power Politics*. New York: Saint Martin's Press, 1996.

Nakash, Yitzhak. *The Shiis of Iraq*. Princeton, NJ: Princeton University Press, 1994.

Rahaee, Farhang, ed. *The Iran-Iraq War: the Politics of Aggression*. Gainesville, FL: University Press of Florida, 1993.

Simons, G.L. *Iraq: from Sumer to Saddam*. New York: Saint Martin's Press, 1994.

Israel

Arain, Asher. *The Second Republic: Politics in Israel*. Chatham, NJ: Chatham House Publishers, 1997.

Avruch, Kevin and Walter P. Zenner, eds. *Critical Essays on Israeli Society, Religion, and Government: Books on Israel*. Albany, NY: State University of New York Press, 1996.

Barkai, Haim. *The Lessons of Israel's Great Inflation*. Westport, CT: Greenwood Publishing Group, 1995.

Barnett, Michael N., ed. *Israel in Comparative Perspective: Challenging the Conventional Wisdom*. Albany, NY: State University of New York Press, 1996.

Bar-On, Mordechai. *In Pursuit of Peace: a History of the Israeli Peace Movement*. Washington, DC: United States Institute of Peace Press, 1996.

Barzilai, Gad. *Wars, Internal Conflicts, and Political Order: a Jewish Democracy in the Middle East*. Albany, NY: State University of New York Press, 1996.

Ben-Ari, Eyal, ed. *Grasping Land: Space and Place in Contemporary Israeli Discourse and Experience*. State University of New York Press, 1997.

Ben Meir, Yehuda. *Civil-Military Relations in Israel*. New York: Columbia University Press, 1995.

Benson, Michael T. *Harry S. Truman and the Founding of Israel*. Westport, CT: Greenwood Publishing Group, 1997.

Bickerton, Ian J. and Carla L. Klausner. *A Concise History of the Arab-Israeli Conflict*. Upper Saddle River, NJ: Prentice Hall, 1997.

Boyarin, Jonathan. *Palestine and Jewish History: Criticism at the Borders of Ethnography*. Minneapolis, MN: University of Minnesota Press, 1996.

Bregman, Ahron. *Israel's Wars, 1947-1993*. New York: Routledge, 2000.

Buchanan, Andrew S. *Peace with Justice: a History of the Israeli-Palestinian Declaration*.

New York: Saint Martin's Press, 2000.

Chesin, Amir S., et al. *Separate but Unequal*. Cambridge, MA: Harvard University Press, 1999.

Cohen, Asher. *Israel and the Politics of Jewish Identity: the Secular-Religious Impasse*. Baltimore, MD: Johns Hopkins University Press, 2000.

Cohen, Avner. *Israel and the Bomb*. New York: Columbia University Press, 1998.

Cohen, Stuart A. *Democratic Societies and Their Armed Forces: Israel in Comparative Context*. Portland, OR: Frank Cass Publishers, 2000.

Cordesman, Anthony H. *Perilous Prospects: the Peace Process and the Arab-Israeli Military Balance*. Portland, OR: Frank Cass & Company, 1996.

Corzine, Phyllis. *The Palestinian-Israeli Accord*. San Diego, CA: Lucent Books, 1996.

Dumper, Michael. *The Politics of Jerusalem since 1967*. New York: Columbia University Press, 1996.

Eban, Abba S. *Diplomacy for the Next Century*. New Haven, CT: Yale University Press, 1998.

Edelheit, Hershel and Abraham J. Edelheit. *Israel and the Jewish World, 1948-1993: a Chronology*. Westport, CT: Greenwood Publishing Group, 1995.

Evron, Boas. *Jewish State or Israeli Nation?* Bloomington, IN: Indiana University Press, 1995.

Ezrahi, Yaron. *Rubber Bullets: Power and Conscience in Modern Israel*. New York: Farrar, Straus & Giroux, 1996.

Freeman, Robert Owen, ed. *Israel's First Fifty Years*. Gainesville, FL: University Press of Florida, 2000.

Garfinkle, Adam. *Politics and Society in Modern Israel: Myths and Realities*. Armonk, NY: M.E. Sharpe, 1997.

Gilbert, Martin. *Israel: a History*. New York: William Morrow & Company, 1998.

Gilbert, Martin. *Jerusalem in the Twentieth Century*. New York: John Wiley & Sons, 1996.

Gordon, Haim. *Quicksand: Israel, the Intifada, and the Rise of Political Evil*. East Lansing, MI: Michigan State University, 1995.

Hartman, David. *Israelis and the Jewish Tradition: an Ancient People Debating Its Future*. New Haven, CT: Yale University Press, 2000.

Hazony, Yoram. *Jewish State*. New York: Basic Books, 2000.

Hohenberg, John. *Israel at 50*. Syracuse, NY: Syracuse University Press, 1998.

Horovitz, David, ed. *Shalom, Friend: the Life and Legacy of Yitzhak Rabin*. New York: Newmarket Press, 1996.

Ilan, Amitzur. *The Origin of the Arab-Israeli Arms Race: Arms, Embargo, Military Power and Decision in the 1948 Palestine War*. Albany, NY: New York University Press, 1996.

Isserlin, Ben. *The Israelites*. New York: Thames & Hudson, 1998.

Karpin, Michael and Ina Friedman. *Murder in the Name of God: the Plot to Kill Yitzhak Rabin*. New York: Henry Holt & Company, 1998.

Karsh, Efraim, ed. *Between War and Peace: Dilemmas of Israeli Security*. Portland, OR: Frank Cass & Company, 1996.

Karsh, Efraim, ed. *From Rabin to Netanyahu: Israel's Troubled Agenda*. Portland, OR: Frank Cass & Company, 1997.

Khatchadourian, Haig. *The Quest for Peace between Israel and the Palestinians*. New York: Peter Lang Publishing, 2000.

Lawless, Richard I. *The Arab-Israeli Conflict: an Encyclopedia*. Santa Barbara, CA: ABC-CLIO, 2001.

Lazin, Frederick A. and Gregory S. Mahler, eds. *Israel in the Nineties: Development and Conflict*. Gainesville, FL: University Press of Florida, 1996.

Levey, Zach. *Israel and the Western Powers, 1952-1960*. Chapel Hill, NC: University Press of North Carolina, 1997.

Levran, Aharon. *Israel after the Storm: Strategic Lessons from the Second Gulf War*. Portland, OR: Frank Cass & Company, 1997.

Levy, Yagil. *Trial and Error: Israel's Route rom War to De-Escalation*. Albany, NY: State University of New York Press, 1997.

Linn, Ruth. *Conscience at War: the Israeli Soldier As a Moral Critic*. Albany, NY: State University of New York Press, 1996.

Litwin, Howard. *Uprooted in Old Age: Russian Jews and Their Social Networks in Israel*. Westport, CT: Greenwood Publishing Group, 1995.

Lomsky-Feder, Edna and Eyal Ben-Ari, eds. *The Military and Militarism in Israeli Society*. Albany, NY: State University of New York Press, 2000.

Makovsky, David. *Making Peace with the PLO: the Rabin Government's Road to the Oslo Accord*. Boulder, CO: Westview Press, 1995.

Metz, Helen Chapin, ed. *Israel: a Country Study*. Washington, DC: U.S. GPO, 3rd ed. 1990.

Netanyahu, Benjamin. *A Place among the Nations: Israel and the World*. New York: Bantam Books, 1993.

Peres, Shimon. *Battling for Peace: a Memoir*. New York: Random House, 1995.

Peres, Shimon. *For the Future of Israel*. Baltimore, MD: Johns Hopkins University Press, 1998.

Peretz, Don. *The Arab-Israeli Dispute*. New York: Facts on File, 1996.

Peri, Yoram, ed. *The Assassination of Yitzhak Rabin*. Stanford, CA: Stanford University Press, 2000.

Plessner, Yakir. *The Political Economy of Israel: from Ideology to Stagnation*. Albany, NY: State University of New York Press, 1993.

Rabin, Leah. *Rabin: Our Life, His Legacy*. New York: The Putnam Publishing Group, 1997.

Rabinovich, Itamar. *The Brink of Peace: the Israeli-Syrian Negotiations.* Princeton, NJ: Princeton University Press, 1998.

Reich, Bernard. *Historical Dictionary of Israel.* Lanham, MD: Scarecrow Press, 1992.

Reich, Bernard and David H. Goldberg. *Political Dictionary of Israel.* Lanham, MD: Scarecrow Press, 2000.

Reich, Bernard. *Securing the Covenant: United States-Israeli Relations after the Cold War.* Westport, CT: Greenwood Publishing Group, 1995.

Reinharz, Jehuda. *Chaim Weizmann: the Making of a Statesman.* New York: Oxford University Press, 1993.

Rouhana, Nadim W. *Palestinian Citizens in an Ethnic Jewish State: Identities in Conflict.* New Haven, CT: Yale University Press, 1997.

Rubin, Barry, et al., eds. *From War to Peace: Arab-Israeli Relations, 1973-1993.* New York: New York University Press, 1994.

Said, Edward W. *The End of the Peace Process; Oslo and After.* New York: Pantheon Books, 2000.

Sela, Avraham. *The Decline of the Arab-Israeli Conflict: Middle East Politics and the Quest for Regional Order.* Albany, NY: State University of New York Press, 1997.

Shafir, Gershon, ed. *New Israel.* New York: HarperCollins, 2000.

Sharkansky, Ira. *Policy Making in Israel: Routines for Simple Problems and Coping with the Complex.* Pittsburgh, PA: University of Pittsburgh Press, 1997.

Sheffer, Gabriel, ed. *U.S.-Israeli Relations at the Crossroads.* Portland, OR: Frank Cass & Company, 1997.

Shindler, Colin. *Israel, Likud, and the Zionist Dream: Power, Politics, and Ideology from Begin to Netanyahu.* New York: Saint Martin's Press, 1995.

Shlain, Avi. *The Iron Wall: Israel and the Arab World.* New York: W.W. Norton & Company, 2000.

Sternhell, Zeev. Translated by David Maisel. *The Founding Myths of Israel: Nationalism, Socialism and the Making of the Jewish State.* Princeton, NJ: Princeton University Press, 1998.

Troen, S. Ilan and Noah Lucas, eds. *Israel: the First Decade of Independence.* Albany, NY: State University of New York Press, 1995.

Van Creveld, Martin. *The Sword and the Olive: a Critical History of the Israeli Defense Force.* New York: PublicAffairs, 1998.

Wheatcroft, Geoffrey. *The Controversy of Zion: Jewish Nationalism, the Jewish State, and the Unresolved Jewish Dilemma.* Reading, MA: Addison Wesley Longman, 1996.

Yiftachel, Oren, ed. *Ethnic Frontiers and Peripheries: Perspectives on Development and Inequality in Israel.* Boulder, CO: Westview Press, 1998.

Jordan

Brand, Laurie A. *Jordan's Inter-Arab Relations: the Political Economy of Alliance Making.* New York: Columbia University Press, 1995.

Fischbach, Michael R. *State, Society and Land in Jordan.* Boston, MA: Brill Academic Publishers, 2000.

Lukacs, Yehuda. *Israel, Jordan, and the Peace Process.* Syracuse, NY: Syracuse University Press, 1996.

Metz, Helen Chapin, ed. *Jordan: a Country Study.* Washington, DC: U.S. GPO, 4th ed. 1991.

Piro, Timothy J. *The Political Economy of Market Reform in Jordan.* Lanham, MD: Rowman & Littlefield, 1998.

Salibi, Kamal. *A Modern History of Jordan.* New York: Saint Martin's Press, 1998.

Satloff, Robert B. *From Abdullah to Hussein: Jordan in Transition.* New York: Oxford University Press, 1994.

Kuwait

Anscombe, Frederick F. *The Ottoman Gulf: the Creation of Kuwait, Saudi Arabia, and Qatar, 1870-1914.* New York: Columbia University Press, 1997.

Clements, Frank A. *Kuwait.* Santa Barbara, CA: ABC-CLIO, rev. ed. 1996.

Cordesman, Anthony H. *Kuwait: Recovery and Security after the Gulf War.* Boulder, CO: Westview Press, 1997.

Crystal, Jill. *Oil and Politics in the Gulf: Rulers and Merchants in Kuwait and Qatar.* New York: Cambridge University Press, 1995.

Longva, Anh Nga. *Walls Built in Sand: Migration, Exclusion and Society in Kuwait.* Boulder, CO: Westview Press, 1997.

Smith, Simon C. *Kuwait, 1950-1965: Britain, the Al-Sabah, and Oil.* New York: Oxford University Press, 1999.

Tetreault, Mary Ann. *Stories of Democracy: Politics and Society in contemporary*

HH Sheikh Rashid Bin Humaid al-Nuaimi, the deceased Ruler of Ajman

Kuwait. New York: Columbia University Press, 1999.

Lebanon

Abraham, A.J. *The Lebanon War.* Westport, CT: Greenwood Publishing Group, 1996.

Abukhalil, Asad. *Historical Dictionary of Lebanon.* Lanham, MD: Scarecrow Press, 1998.

Bleaney, C.H. *Lebanon.* Santa Barbara, CA: ABC-CLIO, 1992.

Colello, Thomas, ed. *Lebanon: a Country Study.* Washington, DC: U.S. GPO, 3rd ed. 1989.

El-Solh, Raghid. *Lebanon and Arabism.* New York: Saint Martin's Press, 1999.

Harris, William. *Faces of Lebanon: Sects, Wars and Global Expansion.* Princeton, NJ: Markus Wiener Publishers, 1997.

Kalawoun, Nasser M. *The Struggle for Lebanon: a Modern History of Lebanese-Egyptian Relations.* New York: I.B. Tauris & Company, 2000.

Malik, Habib C. *Between Damascus and Jerusalem: Lebanon and the Middle East Peace Process.* Washington, DC: The Washington Institute for Near East Policy, 2000.

Phares, Walid. *Lebanese Christian Nationalism: the Rise and Fall of an Ethnic Resistance.* Boulder, CO: Lynne Rienner Publishers, 1994.

Picard, Elizabeth. Translated by Franklin Philip. *Lebanon: a Shattered Country* New York: Holmes & Meier Publishers, 2001.

Ranstorp, Magnus. *Hizb'allah in Lebanon: the Politics of the Western Hostage Crisis.* New York: Saint Martin's Press, 1997.

Schulze, Kirsten E. *Intervention, Israeli Covert Diplomacy and the Maronites.* New York: Saint Martin's Press, 1997.

Shehadi, Nadim and Dana Haffar-Mills, eds. *Lebanon: a History of Conflict and Consensus.* New York: Saint Martin's Press, 1993.

Winslow, Charles. *Lebanon.* New York: Routledge, 1996.

Zamir, Meir. *Lebanon's Quest, 1929-1939.* New York: Saint Martin's Press, 1998.

Zisser, Eyal. *Lebanon: the Challenge of Independence.* New York: I.B. Tauris & Company, 2000.

Maldive Islands

Metz, Helen Chapin, ed. *Indian Ocean: Five Island Countries.* Washington, DC: U.S. GPO, 3rd ed. 1995.

Nepal

Cameron, Mary M. *On the Edge of the Auspicious: Gender and Caste in Nepal.* Champaign, IL: University of Illinois Press, 1998.

Gellner, David, et al., eds. *Nationalism and Ethnicity in a Hindu Kingdom: the Politics and Culture of Contemporary Nepal.* Newark, NJ: Gordon & Breach Publishing Group, 1997.

Savada, Andrea Matles, ed. *Nepal and Bhutan: Country Studies.* Washington, DC: U.S. GPO, 3rd ed. 1993.

Oman

El-Solh, Rahbih, ed. *Oman and the South-Eastern Shore of Arabia.* Milford, CT: LPC/InBook, 1997.

Joyce, Miriam. *The Sultanate of Oman a Twentieth Century History.* Westport, CT: Greenwood Publishing Group, 1995.

Kechichian, Joseph A. *Oman and the World: the Emergence of an Independent Foreign Policy.* Santa Monica, CA: The Rand Corporation, 1995.

Pakistan

Ahmed, Samania and David Cortright, eds. *Pakistan and the Bomb: Public Opinion and Nuclear Options.* Notre Dame, IN: University of Notre Dame Press, 1998.

Blood, Peter R., ed. *Pakistan: a Country Study.* Washington, DC: U.S. GPO, 6th ed. 1995.

Burki, Shahid Javed. *Historical Dictionary of Pakistan.* Lanham, MD: Scarecrow Press, 1999.

Harrison, Selig S., et al., eds. *India and Pakistan: the First Fifty Years.* New York: Cambridge University Press, 1998.

Husain, Ishrat. *Pakistan: the Economy of an Elitist State.* New York: Oxford University Press, 1999.

Hussain, Jane. *A History of the People of Pakistan: toward Independence.* New York: Oxford University Press, 1998.

Looney, Robert E. *The Pakistani Economy: Economic Growth and Structural Reform.* Westport, CT: Greenwood Publishing Group, 1997.

McGrath, Allen. *The Destruction of Pakistan's Democracy.* New York: Oxford University Press, 1999.

Raza, Rafi, ed. *Pakistan in Perspective, 1947-1997.* New York: Oxford University Press, 1998.

Raza, Rafi. *Zulfikar Ali Bhutto and Pakistan 1967-1977.* New York: Oxford University Press, 1997.

Rizvi, Hasan Askari. *Military, State and Society in Pakistan.* New York: Saint Martin's Press, 2000.

Samad, Yunas. *A Nation in Turmoil: Nationalism and Ethnicity in Pakistan, 1937-1958.* Thousand Oaks, CA: Sage Publications, 1995.

Sattar, Babar. *The Non-Proliferation Regime and Pakistan: the Comprehensive Test Ban Treaty as a Case Study.* New York: Oxford University Press, 2000.

Shafqat, Saeed. *Civil-Military Relations in Pakistan: from Zufikar Ali Bhutto to Benazir Bhutto.* Westport, CT: Westview Press, 1997.

Shah, Mehtab A. *The Foreign Policy of Pakistan: Ethnic Impacts on Diplomacy, 1971-1994.* New York: Saint Martin's Press, 1997.

Talbot, Ian. *Pakistan: a Modern History.* New York: Saint Martin's Press, 1999.

Wirsing, Robert G. *India, Pakistan and the Kashmir Dispute: on Regional Conflict and Its Resolution.* New York: Saint Martin's Press, 1994.

Zaidi, S. Akbar. *Issues in Pakistan's Economy.* New York: Oxford University Press, 2000.

Ziring, Lawrence. *Pakistan in the Twentieth Century: a Political History.* New York: Oxford University Press, 1998.

Palestine National Authority

Diwan, Ishac and Radwan A. Shaban. *Development under Adversity: the Palestinian Economy in Transition.* Washington, DC: The World Bank, 1999.

Klieman, Aharon. *Compromising Palestine: a Guide to Final Status Negotiations.* New York: Columbia University Press, 1999.

Mattar, Philip, ed. *Encyclopedia of the Palestinians.* New York: Facts on File, 2000.

Qatar

Anscombe, Frederick F. *The Ottoman Gulf: the Creation of Kuwait, Saudi Arabia, and Qatar, 1870-1914.* New York: Columbia University Press, 1997.

Reich, Bernard and Steven Dorr. *Qatar.* Westport, CT: Westview Press, 1996.

Saudi Arabia

Cordesman, Anthony H. *Saudi Arabia: Guarding the Desert Kingdom.* Westport, CT: Westview Press, 1997.

Fancy, Mamoun. *Saudi Arabia and the Politics of Dissent.* New York: Saint Martin's Press, 1999.

Hart, Parker T. *Saudi Arabia and the United Stated: Birth of a Security Partnership.* Bloomington, IN: Indiana University Press, 1998.

Kostiner, Joseph. *The Making of Saudi Arabia, 1916-1936: from Chieftaincy to Monarchical State.* New York: Oxford University Press, 1993.

Long, David E. *The Kingdom of Saudi Arabia.* Gainesville, FL: University Press of Florida, 1997.

Metz, Helen Chapin, ed. *Saudi Arabia: a Country Study.* Washington, DC: U.S. GPO, 5th ed. 1993.

Pampanini, Andrea H. *Cities from the Arabian Desert: the Building of Jubail and Yanbu in Saudi Arabia.* Westport, CT: Greenwood Publishing Group, 1997.

Peterson, J.E. *Historical Dictionary of Saudi Arabia.* Lanham, MD: Scarecrow Press, 1993.

Vassiliev, Alexei. *The History of Saudi Arabia.* New York: New York University Press, 2000.

Wilson, Peter W. and Douglas F. Graham. *Saudi Arabia: the Coming Storm.* Armonk, NY: M.E. Sharpe, 1994.

Yizraeli, Sarah. *The Remaking of Saudi Arabia: the Struggle between King Sa'ud and Crown Prince Faysal, 1953-1962.* Syracuse, NY: Syracuse University Press, 1998.

Sri Lanka

Athukorala, Prema-Chandra and Sarath Rajapatirana. *Liberalization and Industrial Transformation: Sri Lanka in International Perspective.* New York: Oxford University Press, 2000.

Bartholomeusz, Tessa J. and Chandra R. De Silva, eds. *Buddhist Fundamentalism and Minority Identities in Sri Lanka.* Albany, NY: State University Press of New York Press, 1998.

De Silva, K.M. *Regional Powers and Small State Security: India and Sri Lanka, 1977-1990.* Baltimore, MD: Johns Hopkins University Press, 1995.

Perera, Nihal. *Society and Space: Colonialism, Nationalism and Postcolonial Identity in Sri Lanka.* Boulder, CO: Westview Press, 1998.

Ross, Russell R. and Andrea Matles Savada, eds. *Sri Lanka: a Country Study.* Washington, DC: U.S. GPO, 2nd ed. 1990.

Rotberg, Robert I. *Creating Peace in Sri Lanka: Civil War and Reconciliation.* Washington, DC: Brookings Institution Press, 1999.

Samarasinghe, S.W. and Vidyamali Samarasinghe. *Historical Dictionary of Sri Lanka.* Lanham, MD: Scarecrow Press, 1997.

Wignaraja, Ganeshan. *Trade Liberalization in Sri Lanka: Exports, Technology and Industrial Policy.* New York: Saint Martin's Press, 1998.

Wilson, A. Jeyaratnam. *Sri Lankan Tamil Nationalism: Its Origins and Development in the Nineteenth and Twentieth Centuries.* Vancouver, BC: UBC Press, 1999.

Syria

Agha, Hussein J. and Ahmad S. Khalidi. *Syria and Iran: Rivalry and Co-Operation.* New York: Council on Foreign Relations, 1995.

Commins, David. *Historical Dictionary of Syria.* Lanham, MD: Scarecrow Press, 1996.

Kienle, Eberhard, ed. *Contemporary Syria: Liberalization between Cold War and Peace.* New York: Saint Martin's Press, 1997.

Lawson, Fred H. *Why Syria Goes to War: Thirty Years of Confrontation.* New York: Cornell University Press, 1996.

Perthes, Volker. *Political Economy of Syria under Asad.* New York: Saint Martin's Press, 1997.

Quilliam, Neil. *Syria and the New World Order.* Lowell, MA: Ithaca Press, 1999.

Rabinovich, Itamar. *The Brink of Peace: the Israel-Syrian Negotiations.* Princeton, NJ: Princeton University Press, 1998.

Saunders, Bonnie F. *The United States and Arab Nationalism: the Syrian Case.* Westport, CT: Greenwood Publishing Group, 1996.

Turkey

Ahmad, Feroz. *The Making of Modern Turkey.* New York: Routledge, 1993.

Balim, Cigdem, et al., eds. *Turkey: Political, Social and Economic Challenges in the 1990s.* Boston, MA: Brill Academic Publishers, 1995.

Balkir, Canan and Allan M. Williams, eds. *Turkey and Europe.* New York: Saint Martin's Press, 1993.

Barkey, Henri J. and Graham E. Fuller. *Turkey's Kurdish Question.* Lanham, MD: Rowman & Littlefield, 1997.

Bugra, Ayse. *State and Business in Modern Turkey: a Comparative Study.* Albany, NY: State University of New York Press, 1994.

Dadrian, Vahakn N. *Warrant for Genocide: Key Elements of Turko-Armenian Conflict.* Piscataway, NJ: Transaction Publishers, 1998.

Davison, Andrew. *Secularism and Revivalism in Turkey: a Hermeneutic Reconsideration.* New Haven, CT: Yale University Press, 1998.

Fuller, Graham E. and Ian O. Fuller. *Turkey's New Geopolitics: from the Balkans to Western China.* Boulder, CO: Westview Press, 1993.

Gunter, Michael M. *Kurds and Future of Turkey.* New York: Saint Martin's Press, 1997.

Heper, Metin, et al., eds. *Turkey and the West: Images of a New Political Culture.* New York: New York: Saint Martin's Press, 1993.

Kahveci, Erol, et al., eds. *Work and Occupation in Modern Turkey.* Herndon, VA: Cassell Academic, 1996.

Kasaba, Resat and Sibel Bozdogan, eds. *Rethinking Modernity and National Identity in Turkey.* Seattle, WA: University of Washington Press, 1997.

Kedourie, Sylvia. *Seventy-Five Years of the Turkish Republic.* Portland, OR: Frank Cass & Company, 2000.

Kedourie, Sylvia, ed. *Turkey: Identity, Democracy, Politics.* Portland, OR: Frank Cass & Company, 1998.

Kramer, Heinz. *Changing Turkey: Challenges to Europe and the United States.* Washington, DC: Brookings Institution Press, 1999.

Mango, Andrew. *Turkey: the Challenge of a New Role.* Westport, CT: Greenwood Publishing Group, 1994.

Mastny, Vojtech and Craig Nation, eds. *Turkey between East and West: New Challenges for a Rising Regional Power.* Boulder, CO: Westview Press, 1997.

McDonagh, Bernard. *Turkey.* New York: W.W. Norton & Company, 2000.

Muftuler-Bac, Meltem. *Turkey's Relations with a Changing Europe.* New York: Saint Martin's Press, 1997.

Olsen, Robert, ed. *The Kurdish Nationalist Movement and Its Impact on Turkey in the 1990's.* Lexington, KY: University Press of Kentucky, 1996.

Pitman, Paul M., III, ed. *Turkey: a Country Study.* Washington, DC: U.S. GPO, 4th ed. 1988.

Pope, Hugh and Nicole Pope. *Turkey Unveiled: a History of Modern Turkey.* New York: Overlook Press, 1998.

Rittenberg, Libby, ed. *The Political Economy of Turkey in the Post-Soviet Era: Going West and Looking East?* Westport, CT: Greenwood Publishing Group, 1998.

Togan, S. and V.N. Balasubramanyam, eds. *The Economy of Turkey since Liberalization.* New York: Saint Martin's Press, 1996.

Yilmaz, Bahri. *Challenges to Turkey: the New Role of Turkey in International Politics since the Dissolution of the Soviet Union.* New York: Saint Martin's Press, 1999.

Zürcher, Erik J. *Turkey: a Modern History.* London: I.B. Tauris, 1994.

United Arab Emirates

Al-Fahim, Mohammed. *From Rags to Riches: a Story of Abu Dhabi.* New York: Saint Martin's Press, 1998.

Camarapix Staff. *Spectrum Guide to the United Arab Emirates.* Northampton, MA: Interlink Publishing Group, 1998.

Clements, Frank A. *United Arab Emirates.* Santa Barbara, CA: ABC-CLIO, rev. ed. 1998.

Yemen

Al-Madhaqi, Ahmed Nomen. *Yemen and the U.S.A.: a Super-Power and a Small-State Relationship.* New York: Saint Martin's Press, 1996.

Auchterlonie, Paul. *Yemen.* Santa Barbara, CA: ABC-CLIO, rev. ed, 1998.

Burrowes, Robert D. *Historical Dictionary of Yemen.* Lanham, MD: Scarecrow Press, 1995.

Dresch, Paul. *Tribes, Government, and History in Yemen.* New York: Oxford University Press, 1994.

Portland Community College Libraries

Portland Community College Libraries